GENEALOGICAL PERIODICAL ANNUAL INDEX

KEY TO THE
GENEALOGICAL LITERATURE

Karen T. Ackermann, Compiler
Laird C. Towle, Ph.D., Editor

VOL. 26 1987

Published 1988 By

HERITAGE BOOKS, INC.
1540E Pointer Ridge Place, Bowie, Maryland 20716
301-390-7709

ISBN 1-55613-126-7

A Complete Catalog Listing Hundreds Of Titles On
Genealogy, History, and Americana
Available Free On Request

INTRODUCTION

GPAI is the only comprehensive surname, locality, topical, and book review index to the English-language genealogical periodical literature. The current edition covers 272 genealogical periodicals with over 11,000 index citations.

All the periodicals indexed in GPAI are contributed by their publishers for that purpose. If your periodical was not indexed in this issue of GPAI, you can assure its inclusion in future editions by contributing a file of back issues (to the extent possible) and a current subscription to:

Genealogical Periodical Annual Index
Laird C Towle, Ph.D., Editor
1540E Pointer Ridge Place
Bowie, MD 20716

All current and back issues received will be indexed and included in the next issue of GPAI.

GPAI is protected by copyright law. No part of GPAI may be reproduced by any means without the express permission of the editor, except that brief excerpts may be quoted for book review purposes.

HOW TO USE THE
GENEALOGICAL PERIODICAL ANNUAL INDEX

The Index is based primarily on surname, locality, and topical categories. Look for the desired references under these classifications bearing in mind variant spellings of surnames, and the various names by which a locality may have been known during successive historical periods.

In preparing the index entries, each article is scanned to identify its true content which is often not revealed adequately by its title. Reviews of genealogical, biographical, and historical books published in the 1986-1987 period are cited under the appropriate surname, locality, or topical heading, thus adding greatly to the researcher's ability to locate recently published genealogical material. Heraldry and related subjects are also included. Surname periodicals are noted under the principal spelling of the name, but are not indexed in detail.

Articles dealing with compiled genealogical data, family records, etc., are indexed under the name of the male head of the household or family in most cases. This is followed by his date of birth, marriage, or death when given, or by the approximate date when he flourished. The names of his spouse(s) are also included in the citation followed by the geographic areas where he and/or his descendants are known to have lived as revealed in the article. In those cases where a woman is the principal subject of the article, it is indexed under her name using an analogous format. All spouses are cross-indexed.

Some description of the type and scope of the article is also furnished using abbreviations such as "geneal", "fam rec", and the like. For indexing purposes "geneal" means a compiled genealogical record usually covering three or more generations; "fam rec" means a brief description covering one or two generations; "lineage" usually refers to a multi-generation account of one line of descent.

Articles dealing with source records are indexed under the appropriate geographic heading. For the most part, United States locations are arranged by states, while foreign locations are indexed first by country, then by state or province as appropriate. The citations include a description of the type of records appearing in the article and the time period covered when specified.

Book reviews are indexed under surname, locality, or topic just as are regular articles, except that the citation identifies it as a book review using the abbreviation "bk rev". Author's names and dates of publication have been omitted in the interest of brevity. In a few cases where books by different authors fall into exactly the same index category the authors' names are included in the citation.

GPAI does not index queries, society news, reprinted material, or items of transient interest, but does index all material of archival value. Since many articles could be indexed under several different headings, but normally are not, the reader would be well advised to look for possible alternative headings and spend some time browsing through the Index.

The reference citation to the periodical is given at the end of each index entry using code letters identifying the periodical and the notation - volume:number:beginning page. A table lists the code letters for each periodical indexed along with the address of the publisher and the specific issues indexed.

Extensive use of abbreviations is made in the interest of brevity in the citations. In most cases these are self-evident, but a table of abbreviations is included for reference. The states of the United States are abbreviated by the official two-letter postal designations which are not included in the table.

The periodicals covered by this index will be found in most large genealogical libraries, and in many smaller libraries as well, depending on their areas of interest. If your local library does not have the periodicals you need, try to obtain them by inter-library loan, or purchase the individual back issues needed. If you choose the latter approach, direct a paid-reply postcard to the publisher requesting current information on availability and cost for the specific issues of interest to you.

iv

ABBREVIATIONS

AA	Australia	Col	Colonial
abstr	abstract	collect	collection
AC	Alsace Lorraine	Cong	Congregational
acc	account	corr	correction
add	addition	CZ	Czechoslovakia
admin	administration		
Am	American	d	died
anc ch	ancestor chart	dau	daughter
anniv	anniversary	DE	Denmark
appl	application	desc	descendant
assoc	association	descr	description
AU	Austria	dict	dictionary
auto	autobiography	direct	directory
avail	available		
		emig	emigrant
BA	Bavaria	EN	England, English
bapt	baptised	Epis	Episcopal
b	born	Eur	Europe
BC	British Columbia	Evang	Evangelical
bapt	baptism		
Bapt	Baptist	f	flourished
Bar	Baron, Baroness	fam	family
BE	Belgium	Fed	Federal
bibl	bibliography	FI	Finland
biog	biography	FR	France
bk	book		
BM	Bermuda	GE	Germany
BO	Bohemia	geneal	genealogy
bro	brother	grad	graduate
bus	business	guard	guardianship
c	circa	h	husband
cat	catalog	hist	historical, history
Cath	Catholic	HO	Holland
cem	cemetery	HG	Hungary
cert	certificate		
ch	church	inscr	inscription
child	children	imm	immigrant
CN	Canada	inv	inventory
Co	County	IR	Ireland
		IY	Italy

LDS	Latter Day Saint	QB	Quebec
lib	library		
lic	license	rec	record
Luth	Lutheran	recoll	recollections
		reg	register, regiment
m	married	res	research
marr	marriage	rev	review/Revolutionary
Menn	Mennonite	RU	Russia
Meth	Methodist		
mil	military	sched	schedule
misc	miscellaneous	soc	society
mort	mortality	SN	Sweden
mss	manuscripts	SP	Spain, Spanish
MX	Mexico	ST	Scotland
		supp	supplement
NB	New Brunswick	SW	Switzerland
news	newspaper		
NL	Netherlands	trans	transcription
NS	Nova Scotia	twp	township
NW	Norway		
		Univ	University
ON	Ontario		
obit	obituary	vol	volume
		vr	vital records
pass	passenger	vet	veteran
PE	Prince Edward Island	vol	volunteer
period	periodical		
pet	petition	w	wife
PO	Poland	WE	Wales
Pres	Presbyterian	wid	widow
PU	Prussia	WW	World War
publ	publication		

PERIODICALS INDEXED

AA   Afro-American Historical and Genealogical Society Journal – Afro-American Historical and Genealogical Society, Box 13086 T St. Sta., Washington, DC 20009 7:4 8:1,2

AB   The Appleland Bulletin – The Genealogical Society of North Central Washington, POB 613, Wenatchee, WA 98801 15:2-4 16:1

ACL   Allen County Lines – Allen County Genealogical Society, POB 12003, Ft. Wayne, IN 46862 11:3,4 12:1,2

AFH   Alabama Family History Genealogy News – North Central Alabama Genealogical Society, POB 13, Cullman, AL 35056-0013 8:3

AG   The American Genealogist – Ruth Wilder Sherman, 128 Massasoit Drive, Warwick, RI 02888 62:1-4

AGA   Ancestoring – Augusta Genealogical Society, Inc., POB 3743, Augusta, GA 30904 12:

AGE   Acadian Genealogy Exchange, 863 Wayman Branch Road, Covington, KY 41015 16:1-4

AGS   Austin Genealogical Society Quarterly – Austin Genealogical Society, c/o Texas State Library, Technical Services (SS), Box 12927/Capitol Sta, Austin, TX 78711 28:1-4

AH   Ancestor Hunt – Ashtabula County Genealogical Society, c/o Henderson Library, 54 E. Jefferson St., Jefferson, OH 44047 14:1-4

AIL   American Indian Lines – Am-Toola Publications, E 3308 29th, Spokane, WA 99223 1:1

AL   Alabama Genealogical Exchange, Inc. – POB 2387, Tuscaloosa, AL 35403 3:1-4 4:1

AMG   American Genealogy – POB 1587, Stephenville, TX 76401 2:4

ANC   Ancestry – Palm Beach County Genealogical Society, POB 1746, West Palm Beach, FL 33402 22:1-4

ANE   Aberdeen & North-East Scotland Family History Society Journal – The Family History Centre, 152 King St., Aberdeen, Scotland, UK AB2 3BD 20: 21: 22: 23: 24:

APG   APG Quarterly – Association of Professional Genealogists, POB 11601, Salt Lake City UT 84147 2:1-4

AW   Ancestors West – Santa Barbara County Genealogical Society, POB 1303 Goleta, CA 93116-1303 13:1-4

BAT   Branches & Twigs – Vermont Genealogical Society, Westminster W RFD #3, Putney VT 05346 16:1,2,4

BBQ   The Bermuda Beacon – Alva M Hamilton, 564 Poppy Ln, Santa Maria CA 93455 4:1-4

BC   The Bethel Courier – The Bethel Historical Society, POB 12, Bethel ME 04217 10:3 11:1,4

BCG   The British Columbia Genealogist – The British Columbia Genealogical Society, POB 94371, Vancouver British Columbia, Canada V6Y 2A8 16:1-4
BCN   Newsletter – Bucks County Genealogical Society, POB 1092, Doylestown, PA 18901 6:3,4 7:1
BCS   Barton County Genealogical Society Quarterly – Barton County Genealogical Society, POB 425, Great Bend, KS 67530 7:1-3
BG   The Berkshire Genealogist, Berkshire Family History Society, POB 1437, Pittsfield MA 01202 7:4 8:1-4
BGG   Bulletin – German Genealogical Society of America, POB 29181, Los Angeles, CA 90029 1:7-12
BGS   Boulder Genealogical Society Quarterly – Boulder Genealogical Society, POB 3246, Boulder, CO 80307 19:1-4
BHN   Black Hills Nuggets – Rapid City Society for Genealogical Research, POB 1495, Rapid City SD 57709 20:1-4
BM   The Searcher – Broken Mountains Genealogical Society, Box 261, Chester MT 59522 8:1,2
BWG   Bulletin of the Watauga Assoc of Genealogists – Watauga Assoc of Genealogists, POB 117, Johnson City, TN 37601 16:1,2
CAL   Caldwell County Genealogical Society, Inc. – POB 2476, Lenoir, NC 28645 6:1,2,4
CC   Cracker Crumbs – Manasota Genealogical Society, Inc., 1405 4th Ave. W., Bradenton, FL 34205 10:1-4
CCG   Carrolltonian – Carroll Co Genealogical Society, 50 E Main St, Westminster MD 21157 6:3,4 7:1
CCM   Coweta County Genealogical Society Magazine – Coweta County Genealogical Society, Inc., POB 1014, Newman GA 30264 6:4
CCN   Clark County Genealogical Society & Library, Inc. Newsletter, Library 1511 Main St., POB 2728, Vancouver WA 98668 87:1,2,3,4,6 9-12 86:1-6, 9-12
CCQ   Christian County Genealogical Society Quarterly, POB 174, Taylorville IL 62568 4:1-3
CCS   Champaign County Genealogical Society Quarterly – Urbana Free Library, 201 S Race Street, Urbana, IL 61801 8:4 9:1-3
CDG   Capital District Genealogical Society Newsletter – Box 2175, Empire State Plaza Station, Albany NY 12220 6:1-4
CGS   California Genealogical Society Newsletter, The Flood Bldg Suite 1124, 870 Market St., San Francisco CA 94102 15:5 18:1,3-6
CHG   Chicago Genealogist, Chicago Genealogical Society, POB 1160, Chicago, IL 60690 19:1-4 20:1
CHI   Concordia Historical Institute Quarterly – Concordia Historical Institute, 801 De Mun Avenue, St Louis, MO 63105 59:4 60:1-3
CIC   Searching Illinois Ancestors, Helen Tregillis, Box 392, Shelbyville, IL 62565 3:1-6
CL   The County Line – Genealogical Society of Bay County, POB 662, Panama City FL 32402 5:1-4
CO   Colorado Genealogist – Colorado Genealogical Society, POB 9671, Denver, CO 80209 48:1-4
CPY   The Certified Copy – Greater Cleveland Genealogical Society, POB 9639, Cleveland, OH 44140 15:4 16:1,2
CR   The Circuit Rider – Sangamon Co Genealogical Society, POB 1829, Springfield IL 62705 19:1-4

CRN   Cornsilk, The Geneal Soc of DeKalb Co, POB 295, Sycamore IL 60178 6:1-4

CRT   Crossroad Trails - Effingham County Genealogical Society, POB 1166, Effingham, IL 62401 8:1,2,4

CSB   Copper State Bulletin - Arizona State Genealogical Society, POB 42075, Tucson, AZ 85733 21:1,2

CT   Cumtux, Evelyn Hankel, 1618 Exchange St., Astoria OR 97103 7:2-4

CTA   Connecticut Ancestry - The Stamford Genealogical Society, Inc, c/o Ferguson Library, 96 Broad Street, Stamford, CT 06904 29:3,4 30:1,2

CTN   The Connecticut Nutmegger - Connecticut Society of Genealogists Inc, POB 435, Glastonbury, CT 06033 19:4 20:1-3

DAR   Daughters of American Revolution Magazine - N.S.D.A.R., 1776 D Street, Washington, DC 20006 121:1-9

DCG   The Dakota County Genealogist - Dakota County Genealogical Society, POB 74, South St. Paul, MN 55075 1:3

DE   Downeast Ancestry - Rosemary E Bachelor & Mary H Dormer, POB 398, Machias, ME 04654 10:5,6 11:1-3

DG   Dallas Genealogical Society Quarterly - Dallas Genealogical Society, POB 12648, Dallas, TX 75225 33:1-4

DJ   Delaware Genealogical Society Journal - Delaware Genealogical Society, 505 Market Street Mall, Wilmington, DE 19801 4:1-3

DM   Detroit Society for Genealogical Research Magazine - Detroit Society for Genealogical Research, 5201 Woodward Avenue, Detroit, MI 48202 50:3,4

DS   Deep South Genealogical Quarterly - The Mobile Genealogical Society, POB 6224, Mobile, AL 36660 24:3,4

DWC   De Witt County Genealogical Society Quarterly - De Witt County Genealogical Society, Box 329, Clinton, IL 61727 12:4 13:1-3

EK   The East Kentuckian - Clayton Cox, Box 24202, Lexington KY 40524 22:4 23:1-3

EWA   Eastern Washington Genealogical Society Bulletin - Eastern Washington Genealogical Society, POB 1826, Spokane, WA 99210 24:1-4

FAH   Flemish American Heritage - 18740 13 Mile Rd, Roseville MI 48066 5:1,2

FAM   Families - Ontario Genealogical Society, Box 66 Station Q, Toronto Ontario, Canada M4T 2L7 26:1-4

FC   Forsyth Co Genealogical Society - POB 5715, Winston-Salem NC 27113-5713 5:1-4

FCF   Fulton County Folk Finder - Fulton County Historical Society, 7th & Pontiac Streets, Rochester, IN 46975 87:Spring, Summer, Fall

FCG   The Fayette Connection, Fayette County Genealogical Society, POB 342, Washington Court House, OH 43160 6:3,4 7:1,2

FCT   Freeborn County Tracer - Freeborn County Genealogical Society, POB 403, Albert Lea, MN 56007 :70-74

FF   Fayette Facts - Fayette County Genealogical Society, POB 177, Vandalia, IL 62471 15:3,4

FG   Flint Genealogical Quarterly - Flint Genealogical Society, c/o Mrs R L Richardson,1150 Woodside Dr, Flint, MI 48503 29:1-4

FGS   Federation of Genealogical Societies Newsletter – Federation of Genealogical Societies, 3629 W 147th Pl., Midlothian, IL 60445 11:4

FHC   Family History Capers – Genealogical Society of Washtenaw County MI, POB 7155, Ann Arbor, MI 48107 10:3,4 11:1

FI   Foothills Inquirer – Foothills Genealogical Society of CO, POB 15382, Lakewood, CO 80215 7:1-4

FIR   Fort Industry Reflections, Lucas County Ohio Genealogical Society, 325 N Michigan St, Toledo OH 43624 6:1-4

FLG   The Florida Genealogist – Florida Genealogical Society Inc, POB 10249, Tallahassee, FL 32302 10:2-4 11:1

FP   Footprints – Fort Wayne Genealogical Society, POB 9767, Fort Wayne, TX 76107 30:1-4

FRT   Family Records Today – American Family Records Assoc., 311 E. 12th St., Kansas City, MO 64106 8:1-4

FTH   Family Trails – Historical & Genealogical Assoc. of Mississippi, J. Ratcliff, 618 Avalon Rd, Jackson MS 39206 10:1-4

FTR   The Family Tree – Howard Co Maryalnd Genealogical Society, 7373 Hickory Log Cir, Columbia MD 21045 :97-105

GCB   Grant County Beacon, 24 Herbel Drive, Marion, IN 46952 87:1-4

GCP   Genealogical Computer Pioneer – POB 338, Orem UT 84057 4:12 5:1-4,6 6:1

GD   Genealogy Digest, Genealogy Club of America, Medical Arts Blgd Suite 1007, 54 E South Temple, Salt Lake City UT 84115 17:4 18:1

GEN   Generations – Manitoba Genealogical Society, Box 2066, Winnipeg, Manitoba, Canada R3C 3R4 12:1-4

GF   Gleanings From The West Fields – Pamelyn Ferguson, Westfield Memorial Library, 425 E Broad St, Westfield NJ 07090 8:1-5

GFP   Genealogical Forum of Portland, Oregon, Bulletin – Genealogical Forum of Portland, Oregon, 1410 S W Morrison, Room 812, Portland, OR 97204 36:3,4 37:1,2

GGD   German Genealogical Digest, POB 780, Pleasant Grove UT 84062 3:1-4

GGL   Gaelic Gleanings – Magee Publications, POB 26507, Prescott Valley AZ 86312 6:1-4

GGS   The Georgia Genealogical Society Quarterly – The Georgia Genealogical Society, POB 38066, Atlanta, GA 30334 23:1-4

GH   Genealogical Helper – Everton Publishers Inc, POB 368, Logan, UT 84321 41:1-6

GHS   The Genealogy & History Magazine of the South – Carroll McElligott, Rt 1 Box 103, Harleyville SC 29448 4:1,2

GJ   Genealogical Journal – Utah Genealogical Association, POB 1144, Salt Lake City UT 84110 15:2,3

GJB   Gleanings – Journal of the Beaver Co Genealogical Society, Vivian McLaughlin, Resource & Research Center, Carnegie Free Library, 1301 7th Ave, Beaver Falls PA 15010 11:3,4

GL   Gleanings From the Heart of the Cornbelt – The Bloomington-Normal Genealogical Society, POB B, Normal, IL 61761 21:1-4

GM   Genealogists' Magazine - 14 Charterhouse Bldgs, London EC1M 7BA England 22:6-8
GMN   Genealogical Magazine of New Jersey, Genealogical Society of New Jersey, 132 W Franklin St., Bound Brook NJ 08805 62:1-3
GN   The Nova Scotia Genealogist - The Genealogical Association of Nova Scotia, POB 641 Station M, Halifax, Nova Scotia, Canada B3J 2T3 5:1-3
GP   Georgia Pioneers Genealogical Magazine - Mary Carter, POB 1028, Albany, GA 31702 24:1-4
GQ   German Queries - Bette Topp, W 1304 Cliffwood Ct., Spokane, WA 99218-2917 87:2
GR   The Genealogical Record - The Houston Genealogical Forum, Box 271469, Houston, TX 77277-1469 29:1-4
GRI   GRI News n Notes, Genealogical Research Institute of VA, POB 29178, Richmond VA 23229 6:8,10 7:1,3,6,8-10
GTP   Genealogical Tips - Tip-O-Texas Genealogical Society, Harlingen Public Library, Harlingen, TX 78550 24:4 25:1-3
GWD   Gateway Diggers, Gateway Genealogical Society, c/o Ruth Evans, 618-14th Ave, Commanche IA 52730 6:1-4
GWS   Glasgow & West of Scotland Family History Society Newsletter, 11 Huntly Gardens, Glasgow G12 9AT Scotland :24 :26
HF   Harlan Footprints, Holly Fee, POB 1498, Harlan KY 40831 3:1-3
HH   Hawkeye Heritage - Iowa Genealogical Society, POB 3815, Des Moines, IA 50322 21:4 22:1,2
HJA   Hoosier Journal of Ancestry, POB 33, Little York, IN 47139 11:3 12:1
HL   Heir Lines - Warren County Genealogical Society, 300 E Silver St., Lebanon, OH 45036 1:1-6 2:1-4 3:1-4 4:1-4 5:1-4 6:1
HTR   Heart of Texas Records - Central Texas Genealogical Society Inc, 1717 Austin Avenue, Waco, TX 76701 29:3,4 30:1-3
IAA   Intercom: Afro-Americans Communicating - Preserving Legacies - Rainbow Associates, Martina Brown, POB 13607, Atlanta, GA 30324-0607 1:2-4 2:1,2
IAN   Iowa Genealogical Society Newsletter - Iowa Genealogical Society, POB 7735, Des Moines IA 50322 8:2-5
IFL   Irish Family Links - Irish Genealogical Association, 164 Kingsway, Dunmurry, Belfast, BT 17 9AD Northern Ireland 2:9-10
IG   Illiana Genealogist - Illiana Genealogical and Historical Society, Box 207, Danville, IL 61832 23:1-3
IL   Illinois State Genealogical Society Quarterly - Illinois State Genealogical Society, POB 2225, Springfield, IL 62705 19:2
IMP   Imprints - Genealogical Society of Broward Coounty, Inc, POB 485, Ft Lauderdale FL 33302 6:1,3,4
JC   Johnston Co Genealogical Society Newsletter - Johnston Co Genealogical Soc. 305 Market St, Smithfield NC 27577 13:1-4
JCG   Johnson County Genealogist - Johnson County Genealogical Society & Library Inc, Box 8057, Shawnee Mission, KS 66208 15:1-3
JL   Judaica Librarianship - Assoc of Jewish Libraries, c/o National Foundation of Jewish Culture, 122 E 42nd Street Room #1512, New York City, NY 10168 3:1-2

JMS Je Me Souviens - American-French Genealogical Society, POB 2113, Pawtucket, RI 02861 10:1
KA Kentucky Ancestors - Kentucky Historical Society, POB H, Frankfort, KY 40601 22:4 23:1,2
KFR Kentucky Family Records - POB 1465, Owensboro KY 42301 13:
KIL Knox County Genealogical Society Quarterly - Knox County Genealogical Society, POB 13, Galesburg, IL 61401 14:1,2 15:1-4
KK Kansas Kin - Riley County Genealogical Society, 2005 Claflin Road, Manhattan, KS 66502 25:1-4
KL Kin In Linn, Linn County Genealogical Society, Linn County Historical Library, Box 137, Pleasanton KS 66075 7:1,3,4
KSL Kinfolks, Southwest Louisiana Genealogical Society, POB 5652, Lake Charles LA 70606-5652 11:1-4
LAB Lines And By-Lines, Louisville Genealogical Society, POB 5164, Louisville KY 40205 2:1-4
LC Lake Co Genealogical Society Quarterly, Lake Co Genealogical Society, Cook Memorial Library, 413 N Milwaukee Ave, Libertyville IL 60048 7:1-4
LCC Lancaster Co Connections - Gary T Hawbaker, POB 207, Hershey PA 17033-0207 4:1-4
LCH Lancaster County Heritage - POB 7773, Lancaster, PA 17604-7773 1:1-4 2:1-4 3:1-3
LIC Lost In Canada - Joy Reisinger, 1020 Central Ave., Sparta, WI 54656 13:1-4
LM Laurel Messenger - Somerset County Historical Society, Box 533, Somerset, PA 15501 28:1-4
LOB A Lot of Bunkum - POB 2122, Asheville, NC 28802 8:1-11
LOG Leaves of Greene - Green County Chapter of the OGS, POB 706, Xenia, OH 45385 8:6
LRT Livermore Roots Tracer - Livermore-Amador Genealogical Society, POB 901, Livermore, CA 94550 6:1-4
LWF Lest We Forget - Wyoming County Pioneers, Wyoming County Historical Society, POB 309, Tunkhannock PA 18657 6:1
MA MASSOG - Massachusetts Society of Genealogists, POB 266, Dorchester Center MA 02124 11:1-4
MAD The Maryland & Delaware Genealogist - Box 352, St. Michaels, MD 21663 27:1-4
MCA Marion County Alabama Tracks - Vina Price, Marion County Genealogical Society, POB 607, Hamilton, AL 35570 6:1-3
MCG The Herald - Montgomery County Genealogical & Historical Society Inc., POB 751, Conroe, TX 77305-0751 10:1-3
MCI McHenry Co Illinois Connection Quarterly - McHenry Co IL Genealogical Society, 1011 N Green St, McHenry IL 60050 5:1-4
MCN Madison County Genealogical Society Newsletter - Madison County Genealogical Society, POB 26, Winterset, IA 50273 2:4
MCR Milwaukee County Genealogical Society Reporter - Milwaukee County Genealogical Society, 916 E Lyon Street, Milwaukee, WI 53202 18:1-4
MCS Madison County Genealogical Society Stalker, POB 631, Edwardsville IL 62025 7:1,3
MD Maryland Genealogical Society Bulletin - Maryland Geneal. Society, 201 W Monument Street, Baltimore, MD 21201 28:1-4

MFH   Mennonite Family History, POB 171, Elverson PA 19520-0171
6:1-4
MGR   Midwest Genealogical Register - Midwest Genealogical
Society, Box 1121, Wichita, KS 67201 22:1-3
MH   Menonite Heritage - Illinois Mennonite Historical &
Genealogical Society, POB 819, Matamora, IL 61548 14:1-4
MI   Michigana - Western Michigan Genealogical Society, Library
Plaza N E, Grand Rapids, MI 49502 31:4 32:1-3
MIS   Michiana Searcher - Elkhart County Genealogical Society,
1812 Jeanwood Avenue, Elkhart, IN 46514 19:1-4
MKT   The Marin Kin Tracer - Marin County Genealogical Society,
POB 1511, Novato, CA 94947 10:1-4
MM   Mahoning Meanderings - Mahoning Co Chapter of the OGS,
c/o Mrs Wilms, 3430 Rebecca Dr, Canfield OH 44406 11:1-9
MN   Minnesota Genealogist - The Minnesota Genealogical Society,
Box 16069, St Paul, MN 55116 1817:1-4
MP   The Melting Pot: our ancestral file, DeLoris Lance Dupuis,
1075 Hopemeadow St. POB 562, Simsbury CT 06070 3:1-4
MQ   Mayflower Quarterly - General Society of Mayflower Descen-
dants, POB 297, Plymouth, MA 02361 53:1-4
MSG   Missouri State Genealogical Association Journal - Missouri
State Genealogical Association, c/o Missouri State Library, POB
387 308 E High St, Jefferson City MO 65102 7:1-3
NA   Nebraska Ancestree - Nebraska State Genealogical Society,
POB 5608, Lincoln NE 68505 10:1,2
NAL   Newfoundland & Labrador Genealogical Society Inc. Newslet-
ter - Colonial Building, Military Rd., St. John's, Newfoundland,
Canada A1C 2C9 3:2 4:1
NAS   Northeast Alabama Settlers - Northeast Alabama Genealogical
Society, POB 674, Gadsden, AL 35902 25:4 26:1,2
NC   Family Tree - Northeast Cobb Genealogical Society, POB
1413, Marietta, GA 30061 :89-99 84-88
NCJ   The North Carolina Genealogical Society Journal - North
Carolina Genealogical Soc, POB 1492, Raleigh NC 27602 13:1-4
ND   Nase Dejiny - Box 45, Hallettsville TX 77964 6:1-6
NEH   New England Historical Genealogical Society - NEXUS, 101
Newberry Street, Boston, MA 02116 4:1-4
NER   New England Historical & Genealogical Register - New
England Historic Genealogical Society, 101 Newbury Street, Bos-
ton, MA 02116 141:1-4
NFB   Newsletter - Fellowship of Brethren Genealogists, 1451
Dundee Ave, Elgin IL 60120 19:1,2
NGS   National Genealogical Society Quarterly - National Genealogi-
cal Society, 4527 17th St N, Arlington VA 22207-2363 74:3,4
75:1-3
NPW   The Newsletter of the Prince William County Genealogical
Society, POB 2019, Manassas, VA 22110-0812 5:11,12 6:1-6
NSN   North Suburban Geneal Soc Newsletter, North Suburban
Genealogical Society, Winnetka Public Library, 768 Oak Street,
Winnetka IL 60093 12:1-6
NT   Norwegian Tracks - The Vesterheim Center, The Norwegian
American Museum, Decorah IA 52101 :43,44,45,46

NTT Natchez Trace Traveler - Natchez Trace Genealogical Society, POB 1645, Florence, AL 35631 7:1-4

NW The Wagoner - Northwest Genealogical Society, POB 6, Alliance, NE 69301 9:2 10:1

NWS News From the Northwest, Northwest Suburban Council of Genealogists, POB AC, Mount Prospect IL 60056 7:5 8:1,2

NWT Northwest Trail Tracer - The Northwest Territory Genealogical Society, Lewis Historical Library-LRC, Vincennes University, Vincennes, IN 47591 8:3

NYR New York Genealogical & Biographical Record, 122 East 58th Street, New York, NY 10022 118:1-4

OC Orange County Genealogical Society Quarterly - Orange County Genealogical Society, POB 1587, Orange, CA 92668 24:1-3

OCG Orange County Genealogical Society Quarterly - 101 Main Street, Goshen, NY 10924 17:1-4

OCN Olmsted County Genealogical Society Newsletter, Olmsted County Genealogical Society, Box 6411, Rochester MN 55903 10:1,3-5

OCR Ohio: cross roads of our nation, Ohio records & pioneer families - c/o William Houston, 454 Park Ave. W., Mansfield OH 44906 28:2,3

OG Olympia Genealogical Society Quarterly - Olympia Genealogical Society, c/o Olympia Public Library, 8th & Franklin, Olympia, WA 98501 13:1-3

OH Our Heritage - Louis Dylus, POB 542, Merrifield, VA 22116 2:6

OK Oklahoma Genealogical Society Quarterly - Oklahoma Genealogical Society, POB 12986, Oklahoma City OK 73157 32:1-3

OPC Oklahoma Pontotoc County Quarterly, Pontotoc County History & Genealogy Society, 221 W. 16, Ada OK 74820 18:1-4 19:1

OZ Ozar-Kin - Ozarks Genealogical Society, POB 3494 GS, Springfield, MO 65804 5:1-4 6:1-4 7:1-4 8:1-4 9:1-3

PA Pennsylvania Genealogical Magazine - Genealogical Society of Pennsylvania, 1300 Locust Street, Philadelphia, PA 19107 35:1

PB Pioneer Branches - Northeast Washington Genealogical Society, c/o Colville Public Library, 195 S. Oak, Colville WA 99114 2:3,4 3:1

PCI Poweshiek County, Iowa, Searcher - Poweshiek County Historical & Genealogical Society, 114 S. 3rd St. POB 70, Montezuma IA 50171 9:3,4 10:1

PEL Pellissippian - Pellissippi Genealogical Society, 118 Hicks St., Clinton, TN 37716 8:1-4

PF The Pastfinder - Genealogical Assoc of S W Michigan, POB 573, St Joseph, MI 49085 16:1-4 17:1

PGB Prince George's County Genealogical Society Bulletin - Prince George's County Genealogical Society, POB 819, Bowie, MD 20715 18:8,9 19:1-4

PM Pennsylvania Mennonite Heritage - Lancaster Mennonite Conference Historical Society, 2215 Millstream Road, Lancaster, PA 17602 10:1-4

PN Polish Genealogical Society Newsletter - 984 Milwaukee Ave, Chicago IL 60622 9:2

PP   Pathways & Passages - The Polish Genealogical Society of Connecticut, Inc., 8 Lyle Rd., New Britain, CT 06053 3:2

PS   The Panola Story - The Historical & Genealogical Society of Panola County, Batesville MS 38606 16:2-4

PT   Pioneer Trails - The Birmingham Genealogical Society Inc, POB 2432, Birmingham, AL 35201 29:1-4

PW   The Pioneer Wagon - Jackson County Genealogical Society, POB 471, Independence, MO 64050 7:2-4

QP   Quill Pen - Pittsylvania Historical Society, Rt. 2 Box 419, Axton, VA 24054 :22,23

QY   The Quaker Yeomen - James E Bellarts, 2330 S.E. Brookwood Ave. #108, Hillsboro, OR 97123 14:1-4

RAG   Rota-Gen - Genealogy, 5721 Antietam Drive, Sarasota, FL 33581 8:1-5

RCP   Root Cellar Preserves - Sacramento Genealogical Society, POB 265, Citrus Heights CA 95610 7:1-3 9:4 10:1

RD   Roots Digest - POB 16422, Salt Lake City UT 84116 87:2-6

RDQ   Root Digger Quarterly - Solano County Genealogical Society, POB 2494, Fairfield, CA 94533 5:1

RED   Redwood Researcher - The Redwood Genealogical Society Inc, Box 645, Fortuna, CA 95540 19:3,4 20:1,2

REF   The Reflector - Amarillo Genealogical Society, POB 2171, Amarillo, TX 79105 29:1-4

REG   The Register - Kentucky Historical Society, Old State House, Frankfort, KY 40602 85:1-3

RES   The Researcher - Tacoma Genealogical Society, POB 1952, Tacoma, WA 98401 18:1-4 19:1

RIR   Rhode Island Roots - Rhode Island Genealogical Society, POB 7618, Warwick, RI 02887-7618 13:1-3

RT   Rabbit Tracks - Conejo Valley Genealogical Society, POB 1228, Thousand Oaks CA 91360 4:3,4 5:1,2

SAG   Swedish American Genealogist, POB 2186, Winter Park, FL 32790 7:1-3

SB   The Second Boat - POB 398, Machias ME 04654 8:1-5

SCC   Santa Clara County Historical & Genealogical Society Quarterly - Santa Clara County Historical & Genealogical Society, 2635 Homestead Road, Santa Clara, CA 95051 23:1-4 24:1,2

SCM   The South Carolina Magazine of Ancestral Research - Brent Holcomb, Box 21766, Columbia, SC 29221 15:1-4

SCR   The Genealogical Record of Strafford Co - Strafford Co Chapter NHSOG, POB 322, Dover NH 03820 10:5,6 11:1,2

SCS   The Searcher - Southern California Genealogical Society Inc, POB 4377, Burbank, CA 91503 24:1-12

SD   South Dakota - South Dakota Genealogical Society, POB 873, Pierre SD 57501 6:1,2 2

SGE   The Exchange, Southern Genealogists Exchange Soc, POB 2801, Jacksonville FL 32203 28:122-124

SGI   Southern Genealogical Index - Mountain Press, POB 400, Signal Mountain, TN 37377 4:1

SGS   Seattle Genealogical Society Quarterly Bulletin, POB 549, Seattle WA 98111 36:2-4

SHA   Shallop - Norma Brasier, 36 Comstock Dr., Milford, NH 03055 12:2

SHI Shiawassee Steppin' Stones - Shiawassee Co Genealogical Society, POB 841, Owosso MI 48867 16:3,4 17:1

SIN Southern Indiana Genealogical Society Quarterly - Southern IN Genealogical Society, POB 665, New Albany IN 47150 8:1-3

SIQ Search - International Quarterly for Researchers of Jewish Genealogy, POB 481022, Niles IL 60648 7:1-3

SLB Stagecoach Bulletin for Genealogists, POB 19847, Denver CO 80219 6:106

SLV The SLVGS News - St Lawrence Valley Genealogical Society, Donna Seymour, POB 86, Potsdam NY 13676-0086 5:1-5

SNS Seeking 'N Searching Ancestors - Peggy Smith Hake, Rt 1 Box 52, St. Elizabeth MO 65075 3:1-6

SR Southern Roots & Shoots - Delta Genealogical Society, 70 504 McFarland Ave., Rossville, GA 30741 1:1,2 2:1-4 3:1,3,4

SS The Sonoma Searcher - Sonoma County Genealogical Society, 1019 Kenmore Ln, Santa Rosa CA 95401 14:3,4 15:1

SSO Smoke Signals - Ottawa Co Genealogical Society, Box 1383, Miami OK 74355 4:1

STC St Clair Co Genealogical Society Quarterly - St Clair Co Genealogical Society, POB 431, Belleville IL 62222 10:1-3

STI Stirpes - Texas State Genealogical Society, 2507 Tannehill, Houston, TX 77008 27:1,2

STK Stalkin' Kin - San Angelo Genealogical & Historical Society, POB 3453, San Angelo, TX 76901 14:4 15:1,2

TA Tulsa Annals - Tulsa Genealogical Society, POB 585, Tulsa, OK 74101 22:1-3

TAK The-A-Ki-Ki - Kankakee Valley Genealogical Society, 304 S Indiana Avenue, Kankakee, IL 60901 17:1-3

TB Trail Breakers - Clark County Genealogical Society, 801 S E 119th Avenue, Vancouver, WA 98664 13:2-4 14:1

TCG Troup County Georgia and Her People - Family Tree Publications, 125 Vernon Street, LaGrange, GA 30240 6:4 7:1-3

TE The Eaglet - Polish Genealogical Society of Michican - Burton Historical Collection, 5201 Woodword Ave., Detroit, MI 48202 7:1-3

TEG The Essex Genealogist, The Essex Society of Genealogists, 37 Main St, Saugus MA 01906 7:1-4

TFP The Firelands Pioneer - Firelands Historical Society, 4 Case Ave., Norwalk, OH 44857 2: 7:

TGA The Genealogist - Apache Genealogical Society of Cochise Co, POB 1084, Sierra Vista AZ 85636-1084 12:3,4 13:1

TGC The German Connection - Edna Bentz, 13139 Old West Ave, San Diego CA 92129 11:1-3

TGH The Gazette - Hamilton County Chapter OGS, POB 15851, Cincinnati, OH 45215 1:1

TGO The Genealogist - Australian Institute of Genealogical Studies, POB 68, Oakleigh Victoria, 3166 Australia 5:5,6

THH The Headhunter - TRW Genealogical Society, One Space Park S/1435, Redondo Beach, CA 90278 :97

THT The Thorny Trail - Midland Genealogical Society, POB 1191, Midland TX 79701 15:1,2 16:1

TI The Irish Link - POB 135, South Melbourne, Victoria, Australia 3205 86:11

TLL The Licking Lantern - Licking County Genealogical Society, POB 4037, Newark, OH 43055 12:1-4

TN The Navigator - Norfolk Genealogical Society, Katherine Partridge, 210 Faulk Rd, Norfolk VA 23502 7:1-6

TNB The Notebook - Baltimore County Genealogical Society, POB 10085, Towson, MD 21204 2:1-4 3:3

TOP The Topeka Genealogical Society Quarterly - Topeka Genealogical Society, POB 4048, Topeka, KS 66604 17:1-4

TQ The Quarterly - Historical & Genealogical Society of Indiana Co, Silas M Clark House, S 6th St & Wayne Ave, Indiana PA 15701 7:1-4 (name change to Indiana County Heritage) 11:1

TQR The Quarterly Review - Eastern North Carolina Genealogical Society, POB 395, New Bern NC 28560 13:4 14:1-3

TRC Tri-County Genealogy - Tri-County Genealogical Society, POB 580, Marvell, AR 72366 1:1 2:1,2

TRI Tri-City Genealogical Society Bulletin - Tri-City Genealogical Society, Rt 1 Box 5006, Richland, WA 99352 26:4 27:1 (this should be 27:1-2 throughout text)

TS Treesearcher - Kansas Genealogical Society, Box 103, Dodge City, KS 67801 29:1-3

TST Antique Week (formerly the Tri-State Trader) - Genealogical Department, POB 90, Knightstown, IN 46148 19:47 20:20

TTC The Tree Climber - Aberdeen Area Genealogical Society, POB 493, Aberdeen, SD 57042-0493 11:3

TTH The Tracer - Hamilton County Chapter Ohio Genealogical Society, Ruth Wells, POB 15851, Cincinnati, OH 45215 8:1-4

TTL Timbertown Log - Saginaw Genealogical Society, 505 James Avenue, Saginaw, MI 48607 15:1-4 16:1

TTS The Tombstone - Cochise Genealogical Society, POB 68, Pirtleville AZ 85626 4:1

TTT The Tree Tracers - Southwest Oklahoma Genealogical Society Inc, POB 148, Lawton OK 73502 11:1-4

VA Magazine of Virginia Genealogy - Virginia Genealogical Society, POB 1397, Richmond, VA 23221 25:1-4

VAG The Virginia Genealogist - John Frederick Dorman, Box 4883, Washington, DC 20008 31:1-3

VC Victoria-Crossroads of South Texas - Victoria County Genealogical Society, c/o Victoria County Public Library, 302 N. Main Street, Victoria, TX 77901 8:1,2

VS Virginia Settlers - A. Maxim Coppage, 2225 Hillsborough Ct. #3, Concord, CA 94520 4:1,2

WB Whatcom Genealogical Society Bulletin - Whatcom Genealogical Society, POB 1493, Bellingham, WA 98225 17:1-4

WC Washington - Washington County Chapter of the Ohio Genealogical Society, Catherine J Sams, POB 133, Little Hocking OH 45742 4:1-3

WCG Whitman County Genealogical Society Newsletter - POB 393, Pullman WA 99163 3:3-11 4:1,2

WCK West-Central KY Research Assoc Bulletin - West-Central KY Family Res. Assoc., POB 1465, Owensboro, KY 42301 20:1-4

WI Wisconsin State Genealogical Society Newsletter - Wisconsin State Genealogical Society, Carolyn Habelman, Rt 3 Box 253, Black River Falls WI 54615 33:4 34:1,2

WMG Western Maryland Genealogy - Donna Russell, Catoctin Press, 709 E. Main Street, Middletown, MD 21769 3:1-4

WPG Western Pennsylvania Genealogical Society Quarterly - Western Pennsylvania Genealogical Society, 4338 Bigelow Blvd., Pittsburgh, PA 15213 13:3,4 14:1

WRB Waconda Roots and Branches - North Central Kansas Genealogical Society & Library Inc, POB 251, Cawker City KS 67430 10:1-3

WTC Where The Trails Cross - South Suburban Genealogical & Historical Society, POB 96, South Holland IL 60473 1:1-4 2:1-4 3:1-4 4:1-4 5:1-4 6:1-4 7:1-4 8:1-4 9:1-4 10:1-4 11:1-4 12:1-4 13:1-4 14:1-4 15:1-4 17:1-4

YTD Yesterdays - Nacogdoches Genealogical Society, Box 4634 SFA Station, Nacogdoches, TX 75962 1:1,2 2:1,2 3:1,2 4:1,2 5:1,2 6:1,2 7:1,2

YV Yakima Valley Genealogical Society Bulletin - POB 445, Yakima WA 98907 19:1-3

ABBOTT, John f1655, IR, AA, fam rec TI 86:11:9

Rollin G b1850, w Serilla E Smart, OH, MO, children OZ 7:2:60

Sylvester B b1812, w Alzina Morey, anc ch FF 15:4:134

William Grandison b1839, w Artemsia Nourse, KY, anc ch LAB 2:3:46

ABEL, Adam b1805, Bible rec OCR 28:2:56

Alfred Earl m1913, w Golda Mae Lowhman, Bible rec OCR 28:2:57

John Phenton m1858, w Rhodica J Smail, Bible rec OCR 28:2:56

William Otto b1885, w Mary Effie Chaddock, OH, Bible rec OCR 28:2:55

ABERCROMBIE, Colville f1810, w Mary Lindley, GA, identification of wife GGS 23:4:179

ABLE, Andreas d1851, NJ, geneal, bk rev GH 41:5:189

ABRAMS, Weller see Hattie B PIERSON

ABRAHAM, William d1763, MA, EN anc NGS 74:3:163

ACADIAN GENEALOGY, Cajun/ Creole terms explained AGE 16:3:62

Cem inscr from St Mary's Cem in Charleston SC AGE 16:3:64

Corr to *Hist et Geneal des Acadians* 2nd ed by Arsenault AGE 16:1:8

Exiles in SC AGE 16:1:15 16:2:41

Fam in 1686, bk rev GH 41:2:120

Hist from NS to LA, bk rev BAT 16:2:74

Hist in south LA, bk rev BAT 16:2:74

Pioneers in LA 1765–1803, bk rev AGE 16:4:106

Prisoners at Fort Edward NS 1761–1762 MP 3:4:215

Res guide by Hebert, bk rev KSL 11:4:122

ACADIAN GENEALOGY (cont) Settlers in the Falkland Islands 1763–1767 MP 3:4:222

ACKERMAN, Martha Jane see Joseph MCDOUGALL

ACKLEY, Sarah see William SPENCER

ACREY, Odos E b1876, w Lula Moran, TX, Bible rec YTD 1:1:32

ACUFF, Jeremiah f1840, MO, reminiscence 1874 OZ 7:2:41

ADAIR, Benjamin Joseph b1837, w Nancy Harris, GA, VA, anc ch NAS 26:2:62

ADAMS, Surname period, *Adams Addenda*, 6611 Clayton Rd Rm 104, St Louis MO 63117 – census, cem, marr, v r AL, AR, EN, GA, IL, IN, KY, LA, MA, MO, OH, OR, NY, PA, SC, TN, VT, VA, WV

Christina see George BUTTER-BAUGH

Easter see Miles WEST

Elijah m1813, w Phebe Crosby, NY, Bible rec TFP 2: :43

Fam hist corr to *Adams Fam* by Adams NEH 4:2:76

Henry, MA, geneal, bk rev EWA 24:1:53

Hugh m1845, w Amanda J McCormick, VA, Bible rec NSN 12:2:14

James b1834, WV, IL, anc ch CCS 9:3:101

James f1719, NH, geneal, bk rev EWA 24:1:52

Margaret see John McCRACKEN

Robert b1601, MA, geneal, bk rev GH 41:6:153

Robert C bc1827, MO?, letter OZ 8:1:1

Samuel b1816, w Effie Leonard, KY, IN, Bible rec YV 19:3:106

Sarah f1837, h ___ Bond & Charles Noah Warren, MA, ME, MO, biog NEH 4:2:67

Somerville m1877, w Martha Melvina Odle, Bible rec HTR 30:3:73

1

ADAMS (continued)
W W d1875, OH, IL, obit DWC
13:2:59
William Joseph m1833, w
Deborah Foster Chickering,
MA, Bible rec BG 8:3:69
William Terrel f1885, KS, MO,
geneal, bk rev TS 29:1:28
ADAMSON, John b1705, MD,
Bible rec FG 29:1:24
ADCOCK, Fam hist GA, bk rev
RAG 8:5:13
Fam hist southern US, bk rev
NYR 118:3:187
ADDINGTON, Henry m1799, w
Dorcas Barnard, KY, geneal
KFR 13: :18
ADDKINSON, Revis Jerna b1874,
MS, anc ch PT 29:4:141
ADINGTON, Delilah see Joseph
HUCKABEE
ADKINS, Elizabeth see Richard
GILMAN
Fam marr 1700s VA VS 4:2:96
ADOPTEES, Geneal res aid, or-
phan trains CCS 9:3:82
Geneal res guide by Rillera, bk
rev GH 41:1:122
Geneal res hints, the orphan train
1854-1929 ACL 11:3:87
Records data release OH MM
11:5:31
AELLIN, Margarethe see Hans
Peter HENINGER
AGER, Mary b1788, h John
Forbes, IR, PA, geneal, bk rev
GH 41:5:191
AINSWORTH, Surname period,
The Ainsworth Trading Post,
2101 Mike St, Winnsboro LA
71295
AKINS, William b1756, w
Elizabeth McCorkle, MD, AL,
biog sketch PT 29:4:151
AL(L)BONE(S), Surname period,
The Alborn Enquirer, 1323 12th
Ave #2, San Francisco CA
94122
ALABAMA, Agents for the *Cal-
vinistic Magazine* 1829 roster
AL 3:4:3

ALABAMA (continued)
Baker Co (now Clinton Co), cen-
sus 1870, bk rev FP 30:1:8
Baldwin Co, Bromley-Durant
Cem DS 24:4:180
Bayou La Batre, First Bapt Ch
founding members 1881 roster
SGE 28:121:45
Benton (now Calhoun) Co, census
1850 NAS 25:4:107 26:2:35
Benton Co, census 1840, bk rev
GH 41:1:125
Benton Co, marr 1834-1850, bk
rev AL 4:1:3 GH 41:5:160 NTT
7:3:82
Birmingham, Pratt Mines Bapt
Ch rec misc 1885-1915 PT
29:3:107
Broad Street Meth Ch bapt
1884-1902 DS 24:4:168
Calhoun Co, census 1870 index &
mort sched 1870, bk rev GH
41:2:124 MCG 10:2:91
Calhoun Co, census 1880 index &
mort sched, bk rev GH
41:2:124 MCG 10:2:91
Calhoun Co, Hawkins Fam Cem
NAS 25:4:134
Calhoun Co, marr 1864-1877, bk
rev GH 41:2:124 MCG 10:2:91
Census 1830, bk rev NTT 7:1:2
Census 1860 index, bk rev FLG
10:2:79
Chambers Co, post offices &
postmasters 1833-1983, bk rev
NGS 74:4:305
Chambers Co, residents, bk rev
MCG 10:3:143
Cherokee Co, census 1850 NAS
25:4:115 26:1:1
Cherokee Co, deaths 1850 NAS
26:1:6
Cherokee Co, mort sched 1870
SR 2:3:59
Civil War, Confederate soldiers
& sailors & citizens who died
in Federal prisons & mil
hospitals in the North 1860s
MCA 6:2:59 6:3:104
Civil War, roll of Company C of
19th AL Reg CSA for reunion
held 1904 PT 29:3:97

ALABAMA (continued)

Civil War, sons of Confederate vet 1896-1986, bk rev NTT 7:4:123 (charter 1904) NTT 7:2:78

Clay Co, cem inscr, bk rev GH 41:6:128

Cleburne Co, census 1870 NTT 7:2:42

Cleburne Co, marr 1868-1870 SR 3:3:61 3:4:80

Coffee Co, hist 1841-1970, bk rev FLG 10:2:78

Colbert Co, Cherokee, Elkins & Lindsey ledger 1871-1892 NTT 7:1:4 7:2:54

Colbert Co, Crooked Oak Cem NTT 7:1:12 7:2:50 7:3:90 7:4:127

Colbert Co, Fractional Twp, original survey NTT 7:4:124

Colbert Co, will abstr 1867-1903 NTT 7:1:7 7:2:45 7:3:84

Conecuh Co, Civil War, Confederate soldiers living in co 1907 DS 24:3:128 24:4:209

Coosa Co, deaths 1869-1870 AL 3:1:23

Co formation outline AL 3:3:47 3:4:48

Co rec guide AMG 2:4:20

Cullman Co, ch & cem hist vol 1, bk rev NTT 7:4:122

Cullman Co, deaths 1922 AFH 8:3:79

Dallas Co, Old Cahaba, Confederate & Union Cem DS 24:4:204

Dallas Co, Old Cahaba, New Cem DS 24:3:117

Deaths 1890 abstr from *The Daily Reg* DS 24:3:154 24:4:197

Decatur, Wheeler Reservoir, cem inscr NTT 7:3:83

Dekalb Co, deaths 1860 NAS 25:4:123

Deshler Female Institute, hist & rec 1874-1918, bk rev GH 41:2:125

Franklin Co, Justices of the Peace 1823 roster NTT 7:3:105

ALABAMA (continued)

Franklin Co, Mount Pleasant Cem NTT 7:1:22 7:2:61

Franklin Co, Mount Pleasant United Meth Ch hist sketch & rec misc 1800s NTT 7:1:16 7:2:56

Franklin Co, Taylor Cem NTT 7:3:102

Franklin Co, Tuscumbia, trustee election 1846 NTT 7:1:21

Genery's Gap, geneal collect, bk rev GH 41:3:172 NAS 26:2:68 AFH 8:3:61

Grad & students 1831-1901 of the Univ of AL roster AL 3:3:13

Guntersville, cem inscr, bk rev NTT 7:3:82

Holdings in the U of A Lib AL 3:1:33

Huntsville, delegates of the constitutional convention 1819 AL 4:1:19

Huntsville, depositors in the Huntsville branch Freedmans Savings & Trust Company accounts 1-385 1865-1869, bk rev GHS 4:2:70 FRT 8:2:100 8:3:157 GH 41:2:125 CO 48:3:84 NC :89:3

Huntsville, election of aldermen & constable 1828 AL 3:2:26

Huntsville, geneal misc 1869 abstr from the *Huntsville Advocate* AL 3:2:18

Huntsville, letters left at post office 1828 AL 3:1:46 3:2:23

Jackson Co, census 1840 SR 1:2:16 2:1:7 2:2:32 2:3:56 2:4:78 3:1:8 3:3:59 3:4:82

Jackson Co, marr 1859-1865 SR 1:2:18 2:1:9 2:2:34 2:3:58 2:4:79 3:1:9

Jackson Co, Scottsboro, Old Liberty Cem SR 3:1:11 3:3:60

Jackson Co, track bk 1800s AL 3:3:17

Jackson Co, Woodville, Union Cem AL 3:3:7

Jackson Co, Woodville, Union Primitive Bapt Ch member roster 1840 AL 3:3:18

ALABAMA (continued)

Jefferson Co, census 1900 PT 29:1:19 29:2:58 29:3:89 29:4:129

Jefferson Co, land (public) deposition 1854-1855 PT 29:1:25 29:2:62 29:3:93 29:4:133

Jefferson Co, marr 1872-1874 PT 29:2:50 29:3:84 29:4:125

Jefferson Co, pioneers AFH 8:3:67

Jefferson Co, probate court rec 1844-1851 PT 29:2:54

Lamar Co, index to *A Hist Of Lamar Co AL* by Acee, bk rev NTT 7:3:83

Lauderdale Co, census 1850 agricultural, bk rev NTT 7:2:43

Lauderdale Co, chancery court rec 1827-1830 index, bk rev MCG 10:3:144

Lauderdale Co, co court rec 1829-1839 NTT 7:1:27 7:2:74 7:3:114 7:4:153

Lauderdale Co, Florence, First United Meth Ch rec misc 1870s NTT 7:1:35 7:2:68 7:3:107 7:4:144

Lauderdale Co, inventory rec 1818-1822 AL 3:1:27

Lauderdale Co, marr 1859-1872 NTT 7:1:31 7:2:71 7:3:110 7:4:148

Lauderdale Co, marr lic & cert 1818-1820 AL 3:1:29

Limestone Co, Mooresville Ch of Christ hist sketch AFH 8:3:69

Madison Co, court rec 1842 AL 3:3:3

Madison Co, legislators 1819-1870 roster AL 3:2:16

Madison Co, orphan's court rec 1838 AL 3:2:7

Madison Co, War of 1812, soldiers roster AL 3:2:27

Marengo Co, marr 1818-1836 DS 24:3:122 24:4:182

Marion Co, Civil War, soldiers & sailors & citizens who died in Federal prisons & mil hospitals in the North MCA 6:1:17

ALABAMA (continued)

Marion Co, Hamilton, homestead claims filed 1893-1894 MCA 6:1:3 6:2:44 6:3:88

Marion Co, marr 1896-1898 MCA 6:1:9 6:2:51 6:3:95

Marion Co, mort sched 1860 MCA 6:3:112

Marshall & Jackson Co, Guntersville Reservoir Cem inscr, bk rev GH 41:2:125

Medical Assoc member roster 1870s DS 24:3:149 24:4:200

Mobile, archives (municipal) guide, bk rev GHS 4:2:70

Mobile, geneal misc 1880 & 1888 abstr from news DS 24:3:121

Mobile, land rec 1715-1812 index DS 24:3:138 24:4:187

Mobile, marr 1813-1855, bk rev NGS 74:3:234

Mobile Co, marr 1856-1875, bk rev GH 41:1:125 AL 3:2:11 3:3:45

Mobile Co, orphans court minutes 1813-1837, bk rev GH 41:6:128

Montgomery Co, obit 1821-1840 AL 3:4:4

Morgan Co, letters left at post office 1827 AL 3:1:44

Morgan Co, marr 1829-1830 AFH 8:3:71

Natives mentioned in TX obit AL 3:3:12

Randolph Co, Big Springs, hist of community & ch, bk rev AL 3:3:44

Residents (Anglo-Am) of Spanish AL 1793 roster GHS 4:1:62

Revolutionary War, soldiers who lived in AL & VA AL 4:1:23

Saint Clair Co, census 1820 PT 29:3:101

Saint Paul's Meth Ch new member roster 1886 DS 24:4:178

Sanborn, fire insurance maps 1867-1950 AL 3:4:20

Settlers (early) in northern AL SGE 28:122:15 28:123:45 28:124:17

4

ALABAMA (continued)

Shelby Co, candidates 1818 roster AL 4:1:15

Signers of the constitution of AL PT 29:4:137

Soldiers & wives buried in Biloxi MS AL 3:1:13

Sommerville, letters left at post office 1828 AL 3:2:24

Talladega Co, marr 1833-1846, bk rev GH 41:2:124 MCG 10:2:91

Tallapoosa Co, pioneers, bk rev GH 41:6:128

Talledega Co, election managers 1865 roster SGE 28:121:43

Tuscaloosa Co, hist vol 1 & 2, bk rev GH 41:5:160 (vol 2) KK 25:2:37

Tuskaloosa, geneal misc 1825 & 1829 abstr from the *AL Sentinel* AL 3:1:5

Wilcox Co, marr 1870-1877 DS 24:3:158 24:4:214

ALBERT, Guy E m1893 w Daisy Fairchild, Bible rec IG 23:3:79

Surname period, *Albert Fam News Letter*, Rt 1 Box 41, Houston MO 65483

ALCORN, John bc1740, IR, PA, geneal, bk rev WPG 13:3:52

ALCOTT, Abba Gertrude b1867 h William Neary, NY, lineage SLV 5:1:4

ALEXANDER, Alice b1861, IL, WA, obit TB 13:3:17

Hanah d1822, h William Dinwidely, TN, AL, death notice AL 4:1:17

Jane Cinthelia see John TENBROOK

Mary E b1861, IA, WA, obit TB 13:3:16

Nancy see Abraham WOODY

Peggy see William ROBERTSON

Peter Pine f1853, w Eliza McClure, NY, geneal, bk rev GFP 37:2:69

Sarah see Francis WALLACE

ALFORD, Indiana b1826, IN, KS, anc ch MGR 22:2:90

ALFORD (continued)

James Lodwick b1749, w Susannah Ross, VA, NC, geneal, bk rev GH 41:5:195

ALGATE, Richard Sparehook m1796, w Elizabeth Burrows Outerbridge, BM, fam rec BBQ 4:2:20

ALGER, Fanny f1832, h Joseph Smith Jr, UT, geneal FRT 8:3:142

ALLAMAN, Mena see Ernst KARL

ALLARDICE, David m1841, w Margt Rae, Bible rec MCR 18:4:110

ALLEN, Annanias b1756, NC, KY, TN, AL, geneal, bk rev KA 23:1:36

Charles Merritt b1872, w Ruth Allen, MO, WA, obit TB 13:2:14

David d1824, w Lydia Allen, CT, pension RAG 8:3:16

Dorcas (Wright) see Nathaniel WETMORE

Eliza see John YEAKLEY

Ethan f1775, narrative of captivity, bk rev BAT 16:4:170

Henry b1842, w Alta Verbeck, NY, KS, biog BCS 7:3:2

James m1790, w Hannah ____, Bible rec WTC 13:4:180

James m1885, w Elizabeth Fairchild, IL, Bible rec IG 23:2:58

James Madison b1800, w Jane H Taylor, VA, TN, geneal OZ 6:3:91

Jesse Carter fam rec corr to FLG 9:4:116 FLG 10:2:50

Lavina Pratt see Columbus HAYFORD

Linnie see Samuel DOOLEY

Mary Loretta b1854, h G J Allen, OH, WA, obit TB 13:2:13

Mary see George HEWES

Nathan f1775, narrative of captivity, bk rev GH 41:6:153

Richard bc1560, w Margaret Wyott, EN, CT, geneal CTN 20:1:34

5

ALLEN (continued)
Surname period, POB 28215, Sacramento CA 95828 – bk rev, coat of arms, queries
Surname period, *The Allen Fam Circle & Queries/Newsletter*, 4906 Ridgeway, Kansas City MO 64133
ALLENSWORTH, Ardena (Reynolds) see Charles Fox MONTGOMERY
ALLGOOD, Wyatt bc1788, w Mary Smith, VA, MS, biog sketch FTH 10:3-4:96
ALLISON, Ann see David STUART
Louisa Maria see Vernon Guyon LOCKE
Sarah see Edward MORTON
ALLREDGE, E G d1923, AL, obit AFH 8:3:66
ALLYN, Edward b1663, w Mercy Painter, MA, fam hist LIC 13:2:107
ALSOP, Joseph f1635, New EN, geneal, bk rev GH 41:2:148
Mary see Rufus KING
ALTMAN, Anthony see Marianne Joghs TETOIT
ALWARD, Samantha J see John B WILDER
AMADOR, Pedro f1769, MX, CA, biog sketch LRT 6:1:191
AMADOWNE, Roger f1637, w Joanna Harwood, MA, NY, geneal, bk rev GH 41:2:148
AMBROSE, Barbara see John ZOOK
Cordelia Corilla see John DODSON
Jacob bc 1734, w Margaret Salome, GE, MD, geneal KFR 13: :9
AMERICAN INDIAN, Cherokee (eastern) rec of anc in the US Court of Claims 1906-1910 vol 1, bk rev AIL 1:1:25 FRT 8:4:199 GH 41:5:158 SR 1:2:24
Cherokee (eastern), Hester roll , 1884, bk rev OK 32:1:6 GH 41:2:144
Cherokee, hist, bk rev SGI 4:1:22

AMERICAN INDIAN (continued)
Cheyenne shamanism, ceremonies, & prehistoric origins, bk rev RAG 8:5:26
Constitutions of the Five Tribes FRT 8:3:129
Deed MA 1889 BG 8:3:60
Geneal rec avail in OK HTR 30:2:45
Geneal res guide by Carpenter, bk rev AIL 1:1:26
Geneal res hints VC 8:3:57 AIL 1:1:5 GGS 23:3:120 RES 18:2:70
Geneal res hints OH AA 7:4:147
Geneal res hints, use of the district rec of the Cherokee Nation FRT 8:2:88
Geneal res sources at the GA Department of Archives & Hist guide, bk rev NGS 75:2:155
Hist atlas of Great Lakes, bk rev RAG 8:5:24
Hist by Debo, bk rev SGI 4:1:23
Hist in Clinton Co PA, bk rev WPG 13:3:44
Hist in IA, bk rev RAG 8:3:21
Hist in LA, bk rev RAG 8:1:32
Hist sketch of Indians & Pilgrims MQ 53:4:242
Jena Choctaw, case study in the documentation of Indian tribal identity NGS 75:3:180
Land claims of the Mashpee, Passamaquoddy, & Penobscot Indians of New EN, bk rev NER 141:1:63
Navajo, atlas, bk rev RAG 8:2:25
Osage, rec 1878-1879 in Montgomery Co KS, bk rev OK 32:1:7
Osage tribe member roster OK 1840s-1908 TA 22:1:2 22:2-3:47
Sioux personal property claims, from the original ledger 1876, bk rev GH 41:4:186
Sioux visit Lancaster PA LCH 1:2:54
AMES, Fam rec corr to *V R of Canaan ME* NEH 4:2:76

AMEYE, Guilielmus Drogo bc1738, w Maria Rosa Libeer, Flanders, biog sketch FAH 5:1:19

AMIDON, Elizabeth J see John A WARDLAW
Ralph bc1825, VT, NY, geneal, bk rev DM 50:4:160
Ralph W f1863, NY, geneal, bk rev MI 32:2:75

AMISH, Fam from SW settling in Waldeck & Wittgenstein GE 1750-1850, bk rev GD 18:1:30 GGD 3:2:79 WPG 13:4:38 FRT 8:1:52 SLB 6:2:72 MH 14:1:6 GH 41:2:145
Geneal 1737-1850, bk rev FRT 8:4:197 LM 28:4:291
Geneal collect, bk rev GH 41:2:120 MH 14:1:5 MFH 6:1:34 PM 10:2:44
Hist in modern era PM 10:2:2
Settlement in Butler Co OH, bk rev SGS 36:3:154
Settlements in US that failed 1840-1960, bk rev MFH 6:1:34

AMOS, Hope see John Albert MASHOW

ANDERSDOTTER, Carolina f1897, h Axel Fredrick Svenson, SN, IL, letter CHG 19:2:54

ANDERSON, Ada D see Revilo NEWTON
Andrew d1855, ST, biog GWS :24:2 :26:3
Anna see Anders OLSON
Bailey b1753, w Mary Wyatt, VA, TX, biog YTD 2:1:5
Carl b1868, w Wilhelmina ____, SN, FL, biog sketch IMP 6:1:22
Edwin mc1906, w Charlotte Johnson, FL, biog sketch IMP 6:1:22
Eliza see Nathan UNDERWOOD
Elizabeth J see Thomas J GLASS
Jane L see Joseph T ECCLES
John b182?, w Jennie Carolina Anderson, SN, KS, VA, Bible rec TN 7:5:78

ANDERSON (continued)
Lenora Virginia see Perry Charles BARRINGTON
Rebecca see Richard MacNATT
Sally see Elijah BOWLING

ANDREAN, Alvern f1898, FL, biog sketch IMP 6:1:19

ANDREWS, Alfred see Mary Lee SHIPMAN
David bc1754, NC, MO, geneal, bk rev FRT 8:1:48
Fam hist ME, bk rev BC 11:4:5

ANDRUS, Elisha Shepard b1808, w Lavina Locke, VT, ME, PA, geneal, bk rev WPG 13:4:48 NYR 118:2:116

ANGELL, Ellen see Francis SAGER

ANGST, Gottlieb, w Hannah ____, MN, geneal, bk rev MN 18:3:140

ANIXTER, Fam hist US, bk rev SIQ 7:3:18

ANSLEY, Delia S see Wm RAYL

ANSTOTT, George christened 1718, w Ann Mary ____, BA, MD, geneal, bk rev GH 41:3:170

ANTIS, George Sr f1790, w Margaret ____, NJ, MD, PA, VA, NC, TN, geneal, bk rev WTC 12:4:163

APGAR, Surname period, *The Apgar Fam News*, 416 Runyon Ave, Middlesex NJ 08846

APPLE, Margaret see Albert MAYFIELD

APPLER, Surname period, *Appler Fam Newsletter*, 503 Park Ave, Berkeley Heights NJ 07922

APPLEWHAIT, Arthur see Bridgett NELSON

APPLEWHITE, Dimpsey see George Nikles SPENCER

APRILL, Jacob b1808, w Magdalena Snyder, GE, NY, biog FHC 10:3:53

APT, Anna m1862, h Frank Zivney, WI, fam rec THH :97:15

ARANT, Jacob Mathis b1881, w Sarah Lizzie Culver, AL, anc ch NAS 26:1:21

7

ARCHER, Lodowich b1777, w Mary Mackoy & Martha Harper, SC, GA, geneal, bk rev GH 41:6:153

Surname period, *The Archer Quarterly*, POB 6233, McLean VA 22106 - David of RI & NY, Zachariah of NC, Alexander of SC, fam VA, pensions 1861–1934, census 1820, Isaac of TN, fam OH

ARD, George bc1791, w Abigail Barrow, SC, FL, lineage FLG 10:4:149

ARENDALL, Augusta E b1857, h N B Jones, MO, obit SNS 3:4:3

ARGENTINA, Hist sketch & modern day culture GCP 6:1:29

ARGO, Fam hist EN & US, bk rev GH 41:5:189

ARGOS, John f1680, EN, VA, geneal, bk rev RAG 8:5:23

ARIZONA, Cochise Co, Fish Creek Ch rec 1848–1868 & member roster TGA 12:3:5 12:4:7 13:1:7

Douglas, Calvary Memorial Park cem inscr & sexton's rec TTS 4:1:3

Place names CSB 21:1-2:48

Prescott, Meth Epis Ch rec 1890–1910, bk rev GH 41:5:161

Prescott & Yavapai Co, Bible rec, bk rev GH 41:5:161

Yavapai Co, great reg 1876, bk rev GH 41:5:162

Yavapai Co, Prescott, deeds 1864–1869, bk rev GH 41:5:162

Yavapai Co, Prescott, hospital rec 1890–1910, bk rev GH 41:5:163

Yavapai Co, Prescott, marr 1865–1912 index, bk rev GH 41:5:162

Yavapai Co, Prescott, poll tax 1873–1876, bk rev GH 41:5:160

ARKANSAS, Benton, Ashby Funeral Home rec, bk rev GH 41:5:163

Benton Co, marr 1860–1877, bk rev GH 41:4:187

ARKANSAS (continued)

Cem inscr of southwest AR vol 1, bk rev GH 41:6:128

Chicot Co, census 1860, bk rev GH 41:1:125

Civil War, 27th AR Confederate Inf rec, bk rev GH 41:3:172

Civil War, roster of Dobbins' 1st AR Cavalry TRC 2:1:29 2:2:84

Civil War, soldiers roster TRC 1:1:22

Civil War, Union soldier pension appl index, bk rev GH 41:6:128

Civil War, Union soldiers in AR reg, bk rev GH 41:6:128

Fulton Co, residents 1890–1893, bk rev GH 41:3:172

Geneal res aids in the Dallas Public Lib TS 29:3:85

Geneal res guide by Wagoner, bk rev GH 41:5:163

Geneal soc & lib with addresses CTN 19:4:628

Helena, geneal misc 1898 abstr from *The Helena Weekly Herald* TRC 1:1:27

Helena, Keeshan-Lambert Funeral Home death rec 1917–1920 TRC 1:1:12 2:1:6 2:2:94

Hempstead Co, marr 1875–1900, bk rev GH 41:3:160

Hist sketch TRC 1:1:2

Howard Co, voters 1926, bk rev GH 41:6:129

Izard Co, tax rec 1829–1866, bk rev GH 41:1:125

Legislature hist, bk rev GH 41:2:157

Monroe Co, Hampton Twp, census 1860 TRC 2:1:18 2:2:73

Monroe Co, Surround Hill Twp, census 1860 TRC 1:1:35

Osceola, election ticket 1875 THT 15:1:30

Ozarks, biog stories, bk rev GH 41:6:129

Phillips Co, marr 1821–1875 TRC 2:1:34 2:2:58

Pioneer reminiscences, bk rev FRT 8:4:195

Polk Co, census 1860 OZ 8:3:97

ARKANSAS (continued)

Polk Co, census 1870, bk rev OZ 8:1:25

Prairie Co, census 1890, bk rev GH 41:1:126

Randolph Co, marr, bk rev GH 41:5:163

Reminiscences 1912-1916 abstr from *The AR Pioneers Magazine*, bk rev GH 41:2:126

Saline Co, census 1840, bk rev GH 41:6:129

Searcy Co, census 1880, bk rev GH 41:4:187

Searcy Co, marr 1905-1913, bk rev GH 41:6:130

Sebastian Co, atlas 1887, bk rev GH 41:2:126

Sebastian Co, deeds & mortgages 1861-1866, bk rev GH 41:4:187

Sebastian Co, Fort Smith District, marr 1865-1881, bk rev GH 41:2:126

Sebastian Co, Greenwood District, marr 1873-1880, bk rev GH 41:2:126

Sebastian Co, Lower District, Greenwood Courthouse, marr 1886-1904, bk rev GH 41:2:126

Seminole Nation, census 1860 OK 32:3:94

Sharp Co, index to the *Sharp Co Record* 1877-1883, bk rev GH 41:2:157

Union Co, cem map, bk rev GH 41:2:127

Union Co, census 1900 vol 1, bk rev GH 41:2:127

Washington Co, cem inscr vol 9, bk rev GH 41:4:187

ARMANDO, Adelina see Gaetano BERONIO Sr

ARMITAGE, Edward bc1540, w Elizabeth Bordley, EN, PA, geneal, bk rev WPG 13:3:48

Geo D m1872, w Theoda C Hutchins, WI, Bible rec MCR 18:2:40

George b1718, EN, KS, CO, geneal, bk rev NYR 118:2:120

ARMSTRONG, Angeline see Henry Jacob SANDERSON

ARMSTRONG (continued)

Catherine M see James H MARTIN

James f1855, w Sibella Elliott, ST, IL, geneal, bk rev CSB 21:1-2:41

James Harvey f1862, TX, letters THT 16:1:41

Mary Jane see Joseph SHEPARD

Mary see Alexr Hardy MASSON

William f1762, w Susan ____, IR, children IFL 2:9-10:15

ARNER, Wm G m1863, w Adelle ____, Bible rec WTC 8:3:36

ARNETT, Eliza see Abram BRITTEN

ARNN, Bonde see John Ramsey EARNEST

ARNOLD, Ann see John LISSENDEN

Daisy Bell b1884, KS, NE, anc ch NW 10:1:47

Freelove see Silas GOODRICH

James A b1809, w Anna Pricilla Price, MO, children OZ 5:1:35

John Wesley b1880, w Emma May Cline, MO, Bible rec PW 7:2:62

Jonathan d1799, w Sarah Scott, VA, geneal SGE 28:123:17

Katherine see George Washington GREER

ARRASMITH, Thomas b1733, w Mary (Polly) ____, Bible rec WCG 3:7:54

ARSENAULT, Joachim b1863, w Teresa Gallant, PE, anc ch AGE 16:3:88

ARSENEAULT, Octave m1841, w Sophie Chapdelaine, CN, anc ch AGE 16:2:49

ARTHUR, Hugh m1813, w Margarate Cathcart, Bible rec WPG 13:3:25

ARTINGER, Alois f1898, w Mary Czwiki, AU, PA, geneal, bk rev GH 41:3:175

ARTMAN, Anna Barbara see Nathaniel Butler BANKS

ASHBY, Emily Elizabeth see James Dosy SANDIFER

ASHLEY, Tirzah see Jeremiah SPENCER
ASHTON, Mary see Thomas OLNEY
Thos Lukens m1852, w Martha McGahey, PA, Bible rec BGS 19:3:115
ASKEW, James see Adaline DAVIS
ATHEROLD, Hannah see William BALL
ATHOW, Mary m1877, w Charlie Bottle, Bible rec RES 18:3:133
Richard b1873, EN, Bible rec RES 18:3:134
ATKINSON, Elizabeth see J M C De Les DERNIERE
Noah b1848, w Addie B Caynor, Bible rec OZ 9:2:64
ATTAWAY, A F m1842, w Permelia T Jones, Bible rec YTD 1:1:33
ATWATER, David f1638, CT, geneal, bk rev CTN 19:4:711 GH 41:1:154
ATWOOD, Mary see Lewis WHITE
AUBERY, John Frederick bc1728, w Sarah Hidden, FR, NH, VT, geneal FF 15:3:14
AUCOIN, Michelle see Michel BOUDROT
AUGSPURGER, Catherine see Peter IMHOFF
AUSTIN, Surname period, *Austins of Am*, 23 Allen Farm Ln, Concord MA 01742
AUSTRALIA, Fam hist for beginners by Heradlry & Geneal Soc of Canberra, bk rev GR 29:1:20
Fam hist res guide to sources by Hall, bk rev GJ 15:2:112 NER 141:1:69 GN 5:3:159 TTT 11:4:186
Hist of convicts, bk rev OC 24:1:3
Melbourne, Eureka Stockade, hist IFL 2:9-10:30
Melbourne, patent appl 1857 TGO 5:6:194
Pedlers 1838-1986, bk rev GM 22:7:263

AUSTRALIA (continued)
Prime Ministers 1901-1984 roster OC 24:1:1
Ship wreck of the *Cataraqui*, bk rev TGO 5:5:154
AUSTRIA, Geneal rec avail on microfilm GGD 3:2:95
Geneal res hints RD 87:6:10
AVERY, Phoebe see John MINZEY
AWTREY, John b1780, w Elizabeth Hill, NC, anc ch MCA 6:2:70
AYAULT, Pierre bapt1712, w Marguerite Rousseau, FR, children AGE 16:2:45
AYRES, Dolly Belle see Carl (Charles) MIKSCH
AYRES, Frances b1844, h ___ Boughton, NY, auto TN 7:3:33 7:4:50
John d1675, w Susanna Symonds, MA, geneal, bk rev CCS 8:4:131 NTR 118:1:53
Julia m1789, h Enos Ayres, NY, pension appl OCG 17:3:20
Sarah see Thomas HARTSHORN
BABB, Fam hist New EN, bk rev SB 8:5:185
Phillip b1652, w Mary ___, Isles of Shoals (NH/ME), geneal, bk rev GH 41:5:195
BABCOCK, Irene b1792, MA, NY, anc ch AG 62:3:91
BABCOCK, Stephen m1726, w Anna ___, Bible rec MA 11:2:48
BABCOK, Eleste see Willard MULKINS
BACHELLER, Joseph see Martha Jane WOODMAN
BACHELOR, Lillian Ethel see Jess Edmond WHITE
BACHMAN, John b1729, w Maria Herr, fam rec LCC 4:3:55
BACKMAN, Joseph b1852, w Christine Yoder, FR, MI, biog sketch DM 50:3:106
BACKMANN, William b1815, w Mary Zimmer, GE, IL, biog sketch WTC 4:2:44

BACKUS, William d1664, w Anne Stanton, EN, CT, biog ANC 22:3:113

BADER, Karl Charles b1831, GE, IL, geneal, bk rev GH 41:2:148

BADLAM, William dc1701, w Joane ___ & Mary French, EN, MA, geneal NER 141:1:3 141:2:135

BAER, Surname period, *The Baer Newsletter*, 3–978 SR18–R2, Desher OH 43516

BAFSORE, Kitty see Jonathan MARQUART

BAGGETT, James Robert b1824, TN, anc ch RT 4:4:86

BAGGS, John b1817, w Jane LeGrow, Newfoundland?, anc ch NAL 4:1:7

BAGLEY, Martha Ella see Alva George Henry PAUL

Mason D b1813, w Mary Jane Fowler, CA, biog note SCS 24:4:89

Priscilla Jane see Isaac N RUDDICK

BAHAMAS, Abaco, cem inscr, bk rev GH 41:6:121

BAHAMAS, Settlers in FL, hist sketch FLG 11:1:19

BAHR, John f1849, w Elizabeth Musselman, PA, IL, fam hist MH 14:4:37

BAIL, Elijah f1804, w Susan ___, IL, geneal FF 15:3:63

BAILEY, Augustus Rudolphus b1824, w Lucy Hosmer Smith, VT, geneal, bk rev BAT 16:4:168

Callam Holman b1749, w Judith Ann Gilliam, VA, KY, geneal, bk rev CCS 9:2:60

Grace see Thomas LAWTON

Henry bc1787, w Sarah Elizabeth ___, VA, TX, geneal YTD 1:1:8

Richard, VA, geneal, bk rev SGI 4:1:21

William B b1818, w Mahala Ann Osborn, MA, IL, anc ch ANC 22:1:46

BAIN, Hugh m1715, w Elizabeth Schott, NY, fam hist GD 18:1:9

BAIR, Abraham b1781, w Nancy Erb, anc ch PM 10:4:34

Fam hist 1900s, bk rev GH 41:4:204

BAJKIEWICZ, Bronislaus f1905, PO, OH, MI, fam hist TE 7:3:115

BAKER, Abigal W see David Alfred HALL

Benj Franklin m1873, w Jane Elisabeth Crawford, Bible rec HH 22:1:19

Christine b1716, MA, NH, anc ch AG 62:4:230

Elijah f1835, VT, pension appl RAG 8:1:10

Margaret see Asa SHEPHERD

Martha Elizabeth see Joseph Hamilton HOPKINS

Mathias f1867, letter STK 14:4:195

Philip b1796, w Sarah Bondurant, VA, KY, anc ch ANC 22:4:138

Rebecca see Joel PHELPS

Surname period, *Baker Fam Newsletter*, POB 28215, Sacramento CA 95828 – Wm of TN, Bible rec, census AR & VA, coat of arms, marr, deposition, queries

Susannah (Susan) see Aaron CRISLER

Wm K m1836, w Emma R Phelps, Bible rec YTD 2:1:9

BAKOSKI, William b1877, w Mary Kientz, GE, IL, fam hist sketch WTC 17:4:126

BALAS, Elizabeth Diggs see John HALL

BALCH, Laura see Enoch M WINSLOW

BALDOCK, Mollie Elizabeth bc1825, KY, anc ch JCG 15:3:99

BALDRIDGE, Francis bc1815, w Martha McLendon, TN, anc ch AGS 28:2:68

BALDWIN, Abraham b1827, w Elizabeth Bearden, GA, AR, anc ch NAS 26:2:45

11

BALDWIN (continued)
Alfred b1816, NY, CA, auto SCC 24:2:55
Elizabeth m1716, h Joseph Bond, PA, marr PA 35:1:47
Fam hist VA, bk rev ,NYR 118:2:115
Jesse f1807, NJ, court case GMN 62:2:88
Mary Ann see John (Red) HILL
BALES, Betty Ann see William L LACEFIELD
BALIR, Ann Laird see Alexander MACKLIN
BALL, Edward f1711, w Abigail Blatchley, geneal MI 32:3:112
Mary Ann b1817, h Robert B Bickerdyke, IL, biog sketch WTC 6:2:82
William bc1615, w Hannah Atherold, lineage PGB 19:3:52
BALLARD, Alexander S m1844, w Mary J Hibben, Bible rec FCG 7:1:6
Delphia see Robert CUMMINS
Mary Ann see Leroy Hammond GREEN
William b1603, MA, geneal, microfiche rev GH 41:3:178
William b1795, w Hannah Russell, EN, UT, geneal, bk rev GH 41:6:153
BALLOW, Adeline see Daniel Frederick KANDY
BAMPTON, Sophia M see William WESTERDALE
BANISTER, Clarence Augustus b1900, Bible rec NA 10:1:31
William Franklin b1872, Bible rec NA 10:1:31
BANKS, John f1630, EN, CT, geneal, bk rev CCS 8:4:131
Mary Frances see William Raiford STOREY
Nathaniel Butler b1802, w Anna Barbara Artman, CT, PA, KY, KS, NY, OH, IL, geneal, bk rev NCJ 13:2:119 DM 50:4:174 IG 23:2:63
BANNATYNE, Margaret see William CALDER

BANTINE, William f1639, WE, MA, geneal, bk rev TS 29:1:26
BAPTIST, Death notices 1811-1851 abstr from Freewill Bapt publ, bk rev AG 62:1:62
hist misc vol 1, bk rev NGS 74:3:230
BAR, Hans Heinrich bapt1662, w Anna Hauser, PA, geneal PM 10:1:21
BARBADOS, Hist sketch MP 3:1:47
BARKER, Carrie m1897, w Edgar N Thompson, Bible rec BCG 16:3:84
Soloman W b1816, w Amanda Ocheltree, VA, OH, IL, obit IG 23:2:61
BARKMAN, Jacob m1837, w Rebecca Davis & Mariah Dickson, Bible rec WTC 15:1:33
BARNARD, Dorcas see Henry ADDINGTON
BARNES, Eli d1867, IL, obit CRN 6:4:78
George W bc1794, w Abigail (Abia) Lewis, MD, anc ch GGS 23:1:18
James Terrell b1827, w Mary Jane Lawrence, TN, AL, anc ch AGS 28:2:83
Jane see William FOSHAY
John f1802, NC, anc ch TN 7:6:91
Rachel see Jacob BURGER
BARNET, Eldon Thomas b1877, w Stella Jenkins, OH, WA, biog sketch YV 19:3:86
George b1803, w Quebec Ann Lens, ST, IL, biog sketch WTC 17:4:109
BARNETT, A f1876, TX, letter FP 30:2:74
Clarence L b1858, w Hattie Carter, OR, WA, biog sketch YV 19:1:13
Surname period, *The Barnett Source*, Marsha Bpvey, Rt 1 Box 41, Craigmont ID 83523
BARR, James bc1801, w Susan Ritchie, IR, PA, geneal, bk rev GH 41:3:175

BARR (continued)
Murray G b1862, w Mary Elizabeth Johnston, PA, geneal, bk rev GH 41:3:176
Sinthy b1805, Bible rec FP 30:3:122
BARRAFORD, Fam hist vol 1, bk rev SLV 5:1:12 MQ 53:1:70
BARREN, Fam hist IR, EN, KY, bk rev KA 22:4:242 GH 41:2:148 FRT 8:4:195 CCS 9:2:60
BARRET, Arthur d1828, WV, OH, geneal SGE 28:123:15
BARRETT, Moses f1753, w Mary Dow, EN, CT, geneal CTN 20:2:329
BARRINGER, Katharine see Jonathan ROUTH
BARRINGTON, Perry Charles b1840, w Lenora Virginia Anderson, FL, TX, anc ch MCA 6:2:73
BARRON, David b1805, w Deborah Cowley, Isle of Man, IL, geneal, bk rev NCJ 13:3:183
Hollis A m1901, w Eldora ___, Bible rec HTR 30:2:41
M G see B W RICKERSON
Richard f1833, VA, half-pay claim VAG 31:2:133
Surname period, 374 Perry St, Fostoria OH 44830-2149
Surname period, *The Barron Fam Newsletter*, 607 S Park #18, Salt Lake City UT 84102-333 - Wm of GA, James of VA, Wm births 1700s-1800s, fam MA, Wm of Barbados, Daniel of AR, fam MS
BARRONETT, David b1805, w Deborah Cowley, Isle of Man, NE, IL, geneal, bk rev RES 18:4:189 MSG 7:3:170 IG 23:2:64 RAG 8:4:24
BARROW, Abigail see George ARD
BARROWS, D C m1868, w Mollie J Jones, IL, KS, biog sketch BCS 7:1:9

BARTLE, Charles b1795, IN, cem inscr SIN 8:3:84
BARTLETT, Fam rec misc, bk rev GH 41:6:154
Will Henry see Ollie Lee LANGFORD
BARTLING, Louise see William SEYFARTH
BARTON, E W f1944, WA, reminiscence EWA 24:3:195
Fam hist SN, bk rev CTA 30:1:51
Gideon b1785, ME, obit DE 11:2:60
Thomas Massie b1840, w Sarah Amelia Humphrey, IL, anc ch KIL 15:4:28
BARTRAM, Phebe see Benjamin CUSTIN
BARTRUFF, Fredrika see John BROSEE
BARTSHER, Catharine see Israel ZIMMERMAN
BASCOMBE, Deborah see Thomas BUTTERFIELD
BASHAM, Jerry m1877, w Sarah Ellen Higgs, KY, geneal, bk rev WCK 20:1:14
BASKET, B S d1910, KS, letters testmentary BWG 16:2:149
BASS, Ellen see Daniel R MURPHY Jr
BASSE, Nathaniel b1589, w Mary Jordan, EN, anc ch NAS 26:2:52
William b1654, w Catherine Elizabeth Lanier, VA, anc ch NAS 26:2:50
BAST, Peter m1785, w Catherine Illspach, MD, KY, biog CO 48:1:3
BATCHELDER, Richard Hooker see Jeannette Hussey WOODMAN
Surname period, *The Epistle* POB 398, Machias ME 04654 - Wm of MA, fam ME 1851, Lovisa, fam NH, cem IA, John of ME, Olive of NH, fam IN, soldiers NH, cem ME, births ME, fam VA
BATES, Humphrey b1784, OH, IL, geneal, bk rev CR 19:2:62

BATES (continued)
Martin Van Buren b1837, w Anna Swan, KY, biog EK 23:3:33
BATTIN, John m1830, w Matilda Maxwell, IN, marr cert QY 14:4:7
BAULU, Gabriel Louis bc1772, w Rosalie Brault, FR, anc ch AGE 16:2:48
BAUMAN, Elizabeth see Daniel BENDER
Frederick C d1901, GE, IA, diary abstr 1890–1892 HH 22:2:107
Frederick C d1909, GE, IA, diary abstr 1886–1889 HH 22:1:4
BAUMGARTEN, Geeske see Joseph FIX
BAXTER, G f1873, WA, letter RES 19:1:34
J W m1837, w Vernetta ___, Bible rec YTD 6:2:36
Thomas bc1653, w Temperance (Gorham) Sturgis, ST, MA, geneal NGS 75:1:53
BAYES, Phoebe see Daniel Phillip LEMASTER
BAYLES, Jesse f1770, WV, geneal BWG 16:1:42
BAYNARD, Cecilia Matilda see Thos Henry WILLINGHAM
BAZE, Nettie f19?2, TX, letter STK 14:4:192
BEACH, Hannah b1655, h John Burritt, CT, anc ch EK 23:2:34
BEAKES, Sarah see Francis COX
BEAMAN, Magdalena see David STONER
BEAN, Cinderella Jane see William WILLIAMS
BEANS, Tom A f1905, w Winifred Harlan, NE, biog NW 9:2:22
BEAR, Charlotte see Adam S RYDER
Henry see Virginia LIVINGSTON
BEARD, Aaron w Kizziah Carter, SC, geneal, bk rev RAG 8:2:24
William b1763, w Eleanor Lyons, Northern IR, KY, PA, geneal, bk rev GH 41:2:149 KA 22:4:243 FRT 8:4:196
BEARDEN, Elizabeth see Abraham BALDWIN

BEASMAN, Fam hist MD, bk rev MAD 27:3:118 TNB 2:3:5
Index to A Partial View of the Beasman-Baseman Fam in MD, bk rev GH 41:5:195
Joseph f1705, MD, geneal, bk rev GH 41:1:155
Joseph f1705, w Mary Persias & Sarah ___ & Elizabeth Hawkins, EN, MD, geneal, bk rev GFP 37:2:73 WMG 3:2:92
BEATTY, Susan f1882, h Osborn Monnett, IR, OH, diary abstr TFP 7: :77
BEATY, Sarah E see Andrew Jackson MACE
Sarah J see Joseph STEVENS
BEAUDRY, Hermine see Pierre Evariste LEBLANC
BEAULAURIER, Tony see Louise LaBISSONIERE
BECHTEL, Fam rec misc vol 1, bk rev WTC 5:2-3:101
BECK, Anna Margaretha see Joh Karl Ludwig NOLTE
Anton f1846, w Theresa Schnieper, GE, SW, IL, geneal, bk rev CCS 9:2:59
Catherine see William SANDY
Christian b1798, w Maude Harmon, SW, MI, anc ch MFH 6:1:35
J F b1856, Bible rec YTD 2:2:29
BECKER, Christopher b1869, w Elizabeth Bergen, GE, IL, fam hist WTC 15:4:159
Johann Heinrich b1798, GE, MO, geneal, bk rev GH 41:3:176
Peter f1719, w Anna Dorothy Partmann, GE, PA, biog NFB 19:2:23
BECKLER, Benedict b1839, w Mary Ann Goforth, GE, US, fam hist PEL 8:3:108
BECKLEY, Gordon L d1884, CT, IL, obit MCI 5:3:72
BECKWITH, Lois see John HUNTLEY
Sarah see Penuel FLOYD
BEDARD, Pierre b1705, w M Louise Garneau, FR, anc ch MP 3:1:15

BEDELL, Eliza see George CRITTENDEN

BEDWELL, Robert b1635, EN, DE, geneal, bk rev OZ 6:4:154

BEEBE, Julia Chittenden see William H WITHINGTON
Surname period, *The Beebe Connection*, Rt 1 Box 75, Culbertson NE 69024

BEEK, Joseph bc1775, IR, anc ch AG 62:3:96

BEER, Maria Dorothea see Martinus PALLY

BEERS, Martha see Joseph BIRKETT

BEILER, Anna see Jacob YODER

BELCHER, Elizabeth see John PAINE
Fam rec misc IL FF 15:4:139
Surname period, *Belcher Bulletin*, POB 10, Belcher KY 41513 - Supply biog, prominent Congressmen, patriots

BELEW, J H m1885, w P A Grimes, Bible rec NTT 7:3:117

BELFRAGE, Gustaf Wilhelm d1882, SN, TX, biog SAG 7:1:27

BELGIUM, Settlers in NY & the middle states, hist, bk rev GH 41:4:196 RAG 8:3:24 GGS 23:4:209 CTN 20:2:328 NC :94:2

BELGIUM, Town names, official spelling of Flemish towns FAH 5:1:21

BELL, Charles f1864, MS, auto FTH 10:3-4:71
Daniel f1848, DC, slaves' bid for freedom IAA 1:3:1
David Fawns b1813, w Mary Ann Lyle, ST, WI, geneal, bk rev GH 41:5:190
Donnie Margaret see George Washington CAMPBELL
Fam hist ST, bk rev GH 41:2:149
Grace see Wm Charles WELLS
Jane d1840, h Joshua Bell Sr, IL, cem inscr WTC 2:4:124
John b1789, w Elizabeth Harbison, VA, KY, MO, geneal, bk rev DM 50:3:143 CHG 19:4:155

BELL (continued)
John f1860, w Elizabeth Harbison, KY, MO, geneal, bk rev OZ 9:1:22 IL 19:2:119
Margaret see Juan PERPALL
Silas b1848, MO, obit OZ 5:4:154
Surname period, *Bell Chimes*, Irving Bell, POB 451, Springfield VT 05156
William Jr d1902, OH, obit TLL 12:3:50

BELLAMY, Robert P b1847, Bible rec BWG 16:2:142

BELLEFONTAINE, Jean Baptiste bc1750, fam hist sketch AGE 16:4:112

BELVINS, Elizabeth Hudson see Robert SENSIBAUGH

BENDER, Daniel bc1764, w Magdalena Schlappach & Elizabeth Bauman, PA, geneal, bk rev PM 10:1:48

BENNERS, Judith see Adolf Fredrick HANSEN

BENNETT, Abraham b1764, NY, anc ch OCR 17:1:4
Jefferson b1856, w Caroline Elliott, GA, anc ch GGS 23:2:87
John f1810, NJ, OH, geneal, bk rev NYR 118:4:250
Lydia see Eli RAYNSFORD
Nathaniel b1824, MA, CT, geneal, bk rev CTA 29:4:132
Sarah m1773, h Ebenezer Lewis, MA, parents NEH 4:3:132
Sarah see Samuel TIBBS

BENNITT, Mary see Abel BOTSFORD

BENOIT, Fredrick Lambert b1863, w Octavia Dulude, QB, WA, biog sketch YV 19:3:87

BENSON, Lydia see Joseph DRAPER
Ruth Ann see George F YOUNG

BENTLEY, John bc1759, w Ann Johnson, NC, GA, Rev War rec NC :91:1

BENTZ, Andrew George b1847, w Catherine Hershey, NE, anc ch RED 20:2:16

BERDSELL, Rebecca see Joseph M LEMASTER

15

BERGAN, Martin b1803, w Esther Welsh, IR, IL, fam hist sketch WTC 13:3:107

BERGEN, Elizabeth see Christopher BECKER

BERGHAUS, Johann Philipp II f1797, w Mary Catharina Eisenhauer, CN, geneal GN 5:2:95

BERKEY, Fam hist, bk rev OC 24:1:41

BERKLEY, Martha b1820, OH, anc ch CCS 8:4:136

BERMUDA, geneal res hints BBQ 4:1:2

Old Devonshire Ch rec 1820s BBQ 4:4:41

Pembroke Parish, births & bapt 1645-1673 BBQ 4:1:6

Saint George Parish, v r 1779-1795 as rec by Rev Alexander Richardson BBQ 4:1:6 4:2:21 4:3:32 4:4:42

Saint George Parish, burials 1779 BBG 4:1:7

Will abstr 1700s BBQ 4:1:8 4:2:18

BERNER, Fam hist US, bk rev FRT 8:3:151

John b1844, w Margarette ____, Bible rec WCG 4:2:12

Joseph m1780, w Catharina Borst, NY, geneal, bk rev GH 41:3:177

BERNING, Maria Anna see Frank Joseph SCHELLE

BERONIO, Gaetano Sr b1837, w Adelina Armando, IY, CA, biog sketch SCS 24:1:17

BERRY, Fam rec misc MD & DE MAD 27:3:106

Francis Ellen see Wm B KING

Mary Polly see Hiram RAMSEY

Thomas d1816, Bible rec IG 23:2:61

BERRYHILL, Lillian May see David Williams CASSAT

M W b1815, w K C Broyles, TN, AL, biog OZ 7:3:89

Michael Weeks b1815, w K C (Catherine) Broyles, TN, MO, children OZ 7:3:122

BERRYHILL (continued)

Wm O b1878, w Elva Byrum, NC, FL, biog sketch IMP 6:3:75

BERTHON, Paul see Eleanore LaBISSONIERE

BERTOGLI, Luigi b1863, w Caterina A D M Ori, IY, MA, anc ch AGE 16:3:86

BESELER, Carl Joseph b1814, w Johanna Augusta Strube, GE, TX, geneal, bk rev GH 41:5:190

BETHUNE, Fam rec corr to *The Bethune - Fanueil Genealogy* 1884 NEH 4:4:201

Sarah Catherine see William McLEOD

BETTETT, Vinia see Elisha PADGETT

BEVIN, Deborah see Samuel R GRIFFITH

BEYEN, Hille Harms see Jannes Janssen ZIMMERMAN

BEYSER, Christian mc1762, Luxembourg, anc ch BHN 20:4:172

BIBBER, Hester see Tidence LANE

BIBBINS, Israel b1777, w Mary Robinson, CT, lineage SLV 5:2:8

Louise see Alpheus CONGER

BICKERDYKE, Robert B see Mary Ann BALL

BICKFORD, Lucy see John WATSON

BICKLEY, Mary see Dale CARTER

BIDDLE, Fam rec corr to *Fam Hist Capers* FHC 10:4:93

BIEHN, Johannes bc1700, w Margretha ____, GE, PA, geneal, bk rev GH 41:6:154

BIGGS, Sarah f1880, h ____ Taber, NY, biog AG 62:3:108

BILLIGMEIER, Johanna Serr f1873, ST, NE, letters BHN 20:4:157

BILLINGSLEY, Francis d1684, MD, geneal, bk rev NYR 118:2:116

BILLINGTON, John b1605, EN, MA, anc ch AW 13:1:15

BILLIOU, Isaac b1661, NY, anc ch CR 19:3:130

BINGHAM, Jemima see James Arrington PROPHET

May Lucinda see James Edward SHIPP

BIRD, Augusta f1777, w Annie ___, VT, WI, geneal, bk rev GH 41:5:190

Elizabeth see Andrew HAFFIN

Rachel see James WILSON

BIRDWELL, Addie f1875, PA, reminiscences of school YTD 7:2:13

BIRKETT, Joseph m1816, w Martha Beers, VT, Bible rec BG 8:2:33

BIRKY, Valentine m1887, w Anna Ramseyer, IL, auto MH 14:3:35

BISHOP, David bc1782, w Elizabeth Wolford, VA, KY, biog EK 23:3:15

Elizabeth see William HEGERTY

James C b1836, w Mary Elizabeth Frazier, SC, TX, anc ch AGS 28:2:87

Levi f1842, w Rachel ___, VA, children WTC 14:1:26

Rebecca m1684, h Joseph Whiting, CT, wedding ceremony CTA 30:1:21

BITTINGER, Fam hist MD, bk rev LM 28:3:276

BIVENS, Eliza see John Evans HOLLOWAY

BLACK GENEALOGY, Afro-Am geneal sourcebk, bk rev NCJ 13:3:181

Am Missionary Assoc 1861-1890, bk rev REG 85:1:91

Apprenticeship for Jin f1786 AA 7:4:156

Auto 1760-1865, bk rev CTA 29:3:113

Bibl RD 87:3-4-5:20

Black fam in slavery & freedom 1750-1925, bk rev IAA 2:2:12

BLACK GENEALOGY (continued)

Blacks & Mulattoes in wards 3 & 4 of Chicago in Cook Co IL 1860 AA 8:2:79

Blacks in Allen Co IN who served in WWI AA 8:2:71

Blacks in Cincinnati OH 1880, bk rev GH 41:6:145

Blacks in CT rec 1700s-1800s AA 7:4:157

Blacks in the 1850 census for Seneca Co NY AA 7:4:182

Blacks, Mulattoes, & poor persons in 4 OH co, bk rev NGS 75:1:68

Cem inscr in Lincoln Co MO AA 7:4:162

Civil War & SP-Am War vet buried in Cherry Grove Cem, Xenia OH AA 8:1:39

Civil War, Confederate tax assessments for Rowan Co NC 1863 AA 7:4:177

Civil War, Union vet in 1890 census city & co of St Louis MO including penitentiary at Jefferson City MO AA 7:4:171

District Emancipation Parade, hist sketch IAA 2:2:1

Fam in Manhattan KS 1800s KK 25:1:4 25:2:30

Fam rec avail in the NC Archives AA 8:1:15

Female slaves in the plantation South, bk rev REG 85:1:84

Free Blacks in Westmoreland Co VA 1801 VAG 31:1:40

geneal res hints, use of DC court rec AA 7:4:166

Hist in New Paltz, Ulster Co NY, bk rev NYR 118:1:54

Hist in Nodaway Co MO 1840-1940, bk rev FRT 8:2:103

Hist of slavery, Underground Railroad, & the road to freedom in NY's southern tier, bk rev NYR 118:4:244

Information in publ sources FRT 8:2:78 8:3:121 8:4:183

Marr 1823 & 1827 & roster free Negroes 1847 & 1849, Princess Anne Co VA TN 7:1:12

17

BLACK GENEALOGY (continued)
Marr bonds in Logan Co KY to 1900, bk rev AA 8:2:87
Migration & the role of the ch AA 8:2:51
Migration of the Bass, Tann, & Lewis fam from eastern US to midwest & west US AA 8:1:3
Negroes & mulattoes reg 1857–1863 IN SIN 8:3:88
Pet of residents of Hammonds Plains NS 1862 GN 5:1:40
rec (civilian) in the National Archives, guide, bk rev NGS 74:3:231
Rec misc avail 1860s–1970s US AA 8:1:14
Reg of Negroes, use of IAA 1:4:3
Res guide with case studies by, Streets, bk rev IAA 1:3:10 MSG 7:1:51 TTH 8:3:59 NGS 74:4:312
Res hints for beginners IAA 2:1:4 2:2:4 FRT 8:1:40
Res resources avail AA 8:1:45
Residents 1880 in OH vol 3, bk rev GH 41:1:141 (in Franklin, Fulton, Gallia, & Geauga Co vol 4) GH 41:4:197
Rev War, Black participants 1775–1783, bk rev IAA 2:2:12
Slaves owned by Jonathan Hill Jacocks 1775–1847 NC, roster NCJ 13:4:204
slaves owned by Christopher Melchor 1821–1864 NC, roster NCJ 13:4:199
Slavery in Lancaster Co PA, hist sketch LCC 4:4:4
Sourcebk by Young, bk rev GH 41:4:185 NYR 118:4:245
Tax list 1867 Adair Co KY FRT 8:1:43 8:2:81 8:3:124
Underground railroad 1786–1860 IAA 1:3:3
BLACK, Alexander b1822, w Anne Maria Waggoner, Bible rec TB 13:3:18
Dorothy see William RENKIN
Fam hist 1747– ST, NC, TN, VA, bk rev GH 41:2:159 FRT 8:4:196

BLACK (continued)
John A b1854, w Be Ann Buckhaults, AL, TX, anc ch AGS 28:2:70
John, VA, geneal, bk rev CCS 9:3:99
Robert Johnson b1800, w Mary Black, SC, AR, geneal SGE 28:123:48
Surname period, *Black Fam Res Organization Newsletter*, POB 665, Harrah OK 73045
BLACKADAR, William Hill b1828, NS, mil rec GN 5:3:134
BLACKBURN, Ida L b1867, h M H Huckins, MO, WA, biog sketch TB 13:3:17
Joel b1794, w Anna Fry, NC, AL, children PT 29:2:42
Thornton f1831, w Lucie ____, KY, CN, biog sketch IAA 1:4:1
BLACKWELL, Illinois E see Robert N PADEN
J R b1844, w Hattie Hamilton, IL, biog FF 15:3:28
Mary A see Junius T CAMPBELL
Mary S see Frank H GILMORE
Nathaniel see Joanna HATHAWAY
Robert b1792, w Melinda Stapp & Angelina Eccles & Mary Jane Slusser, KY, IL, biog FF 15:3:25
BLAGDEN, Mabel S see Howard J MARSHALL
BLAIR, Jacob IV b1832, w Sarah Johnson, KY, biog sketch EK 23:2:21
James William see Sarah Jane DeHART
Jane see Lewis TADLOCK
Jasper b1853, w Victoria Angeline Hopkins, KY, biog sketch EK 23:2:21
John f1865, Malinda McKnight, KY, geneal EK 23:1:17
Joseph f1796, w Celia Creech, KY, geneal EK 22:4:17
Mary b1799, h Sevier Tadlock, TN, biog sketch BWG 16:2:128

BLAIR (continued)
Meredith f1878, w Tabitha Ann Cox, KY, geneal EK 23:3:22
Thomas b1825, ST, MN, biog, bk rev MN 18:1:39
William f1835, w Frances Compton, KY, geneal EK 23:2:3
BLAKELY, George Curtis b1874, w Lillie Forster Brown & Celelon Washington (or Warington?) Payne, OH, geneal, bk rev GH 41:2:149 FRT 8:4:197
BLAKEMAN, Curtiss m1799, w Levina Meade, NY, geneal MCS 7:3:141
BLAKESLEE, Herman b1862, w Angie Mallet, PA, fam rec FI 7:4:97
BLAND, Surname period, *Among Cousins*, 154 Delamere Rd, Williamsville KY 14221
Thomas f1769, w Margaret ___ & Rachel Shoulders, WV, geneal, bk rev FRT 8:3:150
Wm C m1844, w Mary Meadow, MS, marr contract CO 48:3:67
BLANDING, Fam hist US, bk rev NYR 118:4:246 OK 32:2:43 MI 31:4:129
Joseph bc1578, WE, geneal, bk rev RES 18:3:139
William b1611, EN, MA, geneal, bk rev CCS 9:2:60
BLANEY, Abigail see Ralph LINDSEY
BLANTINE, William b1611, w Phoebe ___, WE, MA, geneal, bk rev GGS 23:4:210 SLV 5:1:11 NCJ 13:2:119
BLANTON, Gardner b1892, KY, biog sketch EK 23:1:21
BLASS, Maria see Hans ROEH
BLATCHLEY, Abigail see Edward BALL
BLAUVELT, Surname period, *The Blauvelt News*, 522 Saw Mill River Rd, Yonkers NY 10701-4927
BLEDSOE, Ufins see Arter KISSEE

BLEVINS, William Sr bc1735, VA, TN, anc ch EK 23:1:35
BLOODHART, William b1837, w Christina Thomas, OK, anc ch SD 6:1:15
BLOOM, Demeris D see George W MARCHANT
BLOOMFIELD, Ezra f1818, NJ, runaway notice GMN 62:1:11
BLOSSOM, Ann see Henry ROWLEY
BLOUNT, John Gray f1803, NC, papers 1803-1833, bk rev SR 2:2:41
Readding b1791, w Elizabeth Varn, GA, FL, anc ch FLG 10:3:96
BLUMER, Esias b1866, SW, NB, anc ch TB 13:2:39
BLUNK, Hannah see Timothy SHANE
BLUNT, Amanda A see Samuel M HAYNES
Mark L f1860, CO, letter FI 7:2:37
BLYDENBURGH, Augustine dc1685, w Sylvester ___, NY, biog ANC 22:3:110
BLYTHE, James S b1842, w Maggie Redman, Bible rec OC 24:2:73
BOAZ, David b1806, desc, bk rev NYR 118:3:183
Joshua b1810, desc, bk rev NYR 118:3:183
Mary Anthony b1800, h ___ Dallas, desc, bk rev NYR 118:3:183
Nancy Adeline b1833, h ___ Snow, desc, bk rev NYR 118:3:183
Samuel b1809, desc, bk rev NYR 118:3:183
Susan Caroline b1828, h ___ Meacham/Ward, desc, bk rev NYR 118:3:183
Thomas Jr b1815, desc, bk rev NYR 118:3:183
BOCK, Susan b1836, GE, anc ch BHN 20:4:174
BODKIN, Catherine see Tarlton Jones TAYLOR

BOEHM, Henry b1775, w Sarah Hill, PA, biog sketch LCH 1:2:75

BOEHS, Anna see John T NIGHTENGALE

BOEL, Maria see Coenradt TENEYCK

BOEN, Rozalia Theresia see Jan Baptiste SEURYNCK

BOGARDUS, Annetjke bapt1663, NY, anc ch HJA 11:3:236

BOGGS, Surname period, *Boggs Newsletter*, 396 Taylor Rd, Stow MA 01775 - James of IR & DE, fam SC & PA, news MO, Rev War

BOIES, David bc1689, w Anne Huston?, Northern IR, MA, geneal, bk rev WPG 13:3:44

David bc1730, w ____ Forsyth, PA, geneal, bk rev WPG 13:3:44

David f1773, ST, US, geneal, bk rev ANE 23: :20

BOLEN, Henry b1782, VA, KY, OH, geneal, bk rev GH 41:5:190

BOLES, James b1752, w Mary Painter, IR, PA, geneal, bk rev GH 41:3:167

BOLIN, Alfred f1864, MO, biog sketch OZ 9:3:105

BOMAN, Hiram b1781,fam rec HL 1:2:44

BOMBERGER, Christian b1682, w Maria ____, GE, PA, geneal, bk rev PM 10:2:44 MFH 6:2:75

BOND, Joseph see Elizabeth BALDWIN

BONDURANT, Jean b1503, w Gabrielle Brunet, geneal ANC 22:4:142

Surname period, *Bondurant Newsletter*, Mary Beth Lozo, HC 4 Box 233-E, Canyon Lake TX 78133

BONE, Rufus Homer b1855, w Alice Jane Wilson, IA, WA, biog sketch YV 19:3:86

BONHARME, Catherine Catiche b1852 , h Billy Hargrove, LA, biog sketch KSL 11:1:17

BONNET, Peter bc1799, w Elizabeth Liscomb, PA, TN, MO, children OZ 8:2:64

BONVILLAIN, Charlotte see Joseph Benjamin STOUT

BOOGS, James see Margaret SERGENT

BOOKER, Lewis b1754, w Judith Dudley, VA, OH, geneal IG 23:2:50

BOOMGAARDEN, Arend Wiards b1798, w Geeske Poets, Ostfriesland, geneal, bk rev GH 41:1:155

BOOMGARDEN, Jacob Harms b1853, w Harmanna Freerks, GE, IL, geneal, bk rev FRT 8:3:151

BOON, Fam rec misc, bk rev EWA 24:4:265

Thomas d1723, VA, geneal, bk rev CCS 9:2:59

BOONE, Nathan f1853, MO, biog, bk rev OZ 7:2:58

BOOS, Franz Paul m1834, w Anna Barbara Menz & Gertrude Brietling, LA, geneal, bk rev NYR 118:1:52

BOOSEY, Esther Ward see Jehu BURR

BOOTH, Anne see William CHAMBERS

BOOTS, Nancy Jane b1850, h Jordan Johnson, anc ch GJB 11:3:19

BORDLEY, Elizabeth see Edward ARMITAGE

BOREL, Louis Dorcey b1849, w Isora LeBlanc, LA, anc ch KSL 11:3:92

BORN, Daviel D b1813, w Mittie Jane STYLES, GA, anc ch GGS 23:4:201

BORRESEN, Olaf see Anna FREITAG

BORST, Catharina see Joseph BERNER

BORTON, William bc1608, EN, anc ch HJA 11:3:245

BOSTICK, Tristam bc1800, w Ann R ____, SC, FL, lineage FLG 10:4:135

20

BOSTON, Henry f1640, VA, MD, geneal, bk rev MD 28:3:363

BOSWORTH, Edward f1816, MA, OH, geneal, bk rev NYR 118:2:119

BOTSFORD, Abel m1764, w Mary Bennitt, Bible rec CTN 20:3:434

BOTTLE, Charlie see Mary ATHOW

BOUDREAU, Mary Eunice b1841, MA, anc ch TEG 7:4:205

Osite see Hippolyte LEGER

BOUDREAUX, Alida see Auguste HEBERT

Justilia see Oscar MARTIN

BOUDROT, Marguerite m1734, h Germain Theriot, marr AGE 16:4:99

Michel b1601, w Michelle Aucoin, anc ch MP 3:4:270

BOUGHTON, Elizabeth see Andrew MEAD

BOURE, Marie see Vincent BRAULT

BOURG, Antoine f1636, Port Royal, fam rec AGE 16:2:40

Perrine see Jean TERRIOT & Jean THERIAU

BOURGEOIS, Prudent Sr b1842, w Marie Emma Poche, LA, anc ch AGE 16:2:55

BOURNE, Aaron b1695, fam rec AG 62:3:171

Jared bc1612, MA, NH, VT, geneal, bk rev BAT 16:4:169

Richard f1637, MA, geneal suppl 1, bk rev CTN 20:3:517

BOURQUE, Zenon b1800, w Marie Belzire Poirier, LA, anc ch AGE 16:2:56

BOUTON, Fam hist corr to the *Bouton-Boughton Fam* by Boughton SCS 24:5:114

BOUZAGE, Joseph f1762, FR, LA, MS, geneal, bk rev GH 41:4:204

BOVENIGER, Mary see Thomas MULQUIN

BOWEN, Ezra b1783, NH, VT, anc ch AG 62:4:227

BOWEN (continued)

Griffith bc1600, w Margaret Fleming, WE, MA, geneal CTN 19:4:588

Orlander Porter b1818, w Hannah Older, NY, WI, anc ch WB 17:2:71

Robert G b1789, w Mary Wilson, SC, TN, anc ch AGS 28:2:84

Sarah see Robert FULLER

BOWERMAN, Surname period, *Bowerman/Bowman Fam Newsletter*, POB 505, Los Angeles CA 90053

BOWERS, Abner b1812, IN, anc ch CCS 9:3:102

BOWKER, Levi b1783, w Betsy Silby, NH, VT, anc ch NW 9:2:65

BOWLES, John bc1608, w Elizabeth Heath, EN, MA, anc ch TAK 17:3:24

Joseph W f1858, CO, obit CO 48:2:42

BOWLIN, Avalener see George Washington Freeman

BOWLING, Elijah b1785, w Sally Anderson, TN, anc ch BWG 16:1:51

BOWMAN, John bc1764, w Elizabeth Ikenberry, PA, VA, children BWG 16:2:129

Wendell f1709, GE, PA, fam rec BWG 16:2:146

BOWSER, Caroline see George K HALE

BOXELL, Mary see Henry STAUB

BOXLEY, Catherine Spiller see John KIMBROUGH III

BOYD, Anna see William HURST

Greenville see Jane FREEMAN

Hannah Maria see Charles Franklin KLINE

Samuel Newton b1818, w Priscilla Wood, GA, MO, children OZ 8:2:63

BOYES, Sally b1767, NH, anc ch TEG 7:1:39

BOYLE, Surname period, *The Boyle Bulletin*, POB 1149, Richmond, ON, Canada K0A 2Z0

BOZORTH, Jonathan b1761, KY, WA, fam hist sketch TB 13:4:13

BRAASH, Christina Maria Sophia see Friedrich Fritz Christian Johann KRUSE

BRACE, Elizabeth see Jireh ROWLEY

BRADBURY, William bc1821, w Margaret Townsend, EN, US, geneal, bk rev FRT 8:2:104

BRADEN, William b1770, w Euphemia Jackson, IR, PA, KY, IN, geneal, bk rev CCS 9:1:25 NYR 118:1:53

BRADFORD, William d1703-4, MA, cem inscr MQ 53:3:165

BRADHAM, Fam hist SC, NC, GA, FL, TX, IL, IN, bk rev GH 41:2:159 NER 141:3:265 MCG 10:2:89 FRT 8:4:197 GFP 37:2:70 GGS 23:2:103

BRADHAM, James Randolph bc1750, SC, geneal, bk rev CCS 9:3:98

BRADLEY, Fam hist 1643-1746 MA, bk rev GH 41:2:149 SB 8:1:19

BRADNER, John f1730, w Christina Colville, IR, NY, geneal, bk rev NYR 118:4:248

BRADSHAW, Elizabeth see John C COWING

BRADSTREET, Walter P see Charlotte TAYLOR

BRAGG, Edward see Sarah WITT

BRAITHWAIT, Margaret see Robert JOHNSON

BRALLIER, Frank Ellis b1865, w Adella Loomis, CA, OR, auto CT 7:2:35

BRAND, Adam m1599, w? Samuell Goodson, EN, marr rec GM 22:7:257

BRANDAL, Eliza see Elias SMITH

BRANNOCK, Alexander Newton mc1828, w Susan Foster, MD, NC, fam hist OZ 5:3:101

BRANTLEY, William Franklin m1861, w Sarah Louisiana Joiner, Bible rec YTD 1:1:30

BRASCH, Johann f1862, w Maria Wolletsin, Pomerania, IL, fam hist WTC 14:4:137

BRASHER, Sarah Jane see Jim LEMONS

BRAULT, Rosalie see Gabriel Louis BAULU Vincent bc1631, w Marie Boure, LA, geneal AGE 16:1:9

BRAUNER, George Pickens b1896, w Mattie Eldora Davis, Bible rec PW 7:3:117

BRAWNER, William Dudley b1855, w Margaret Elizabeth Madden, GA, anc ch DG 33:1:58

BREAM, Mary see Ebenizer TARBOX

BRECKINRIDGE, Fam hist KY 1760-1981, bk rev REG 85:3:262 John C f1793, VA, KY, biog REG 85:3:197

BREEDEN, Jeremiah b1764, w Elizabeth Hurst, VA, MO, children OZ 8:2:65

BREELER, Abraham f1755, NC, SC, AL, MS, LA, geneal, bk rev NCJ 13:2:119

BREFELD, Christina see Joseph MORITZ

BREIDENBACH, Fam hist US 1757-1978, bk rev CSB 21:1-2:41

BREINER, George Michael mc1756, w Anna Catharina Loy, GE, PA, geneal, bk rev MD 28:4:459

BREITMESITER, Julianna see Georg WESTERMAIER

BRELAND, Jacob f1755, NC, SC, geneal, bk rev GH 41:3:167

BRENGLE, Surname period, *Brengle Branches*, 6619 Pheasant Rd, Baltimore MD 21220

BRETH, Elizabeth see Frederick David SHEPHERD

BRETHREN, Hist in modern era PM 10:2:2

BREWER, Elsie Irene see Hiram Burrows GRIDER

BREWER (continued)
Hannah b1645, h Ephraim Roper, MA, anc ch EK 23:3:34
Henley R m1894, w Minnie L Doyle, Bible rec OZ 5:3:107
William Lawson b1869, w Louisa Landers & Geneva Armetta Graham Collins, MS, TX, children FTH 10:3-4:101
BRICKER, Peter f1837, w Magdalene ___, PA, will LCC 4:2:72
BRIETLING, Gertrude see Franz Paul BOOS
BRIGHT, Eleanor see Thomas ETHERIDGE Elder
Fam hist, bk rev FRT 8:2:102
BRINK, Joshua b1788, w Rebecca Cole, PA, geneal, bk rev GH 41:5:190
BRISTER, Thompson f1770, w Nancy Hockaday, SC, MS, geneal GTP 24:4:74
BRITAIN, Army rec avail, bk rev ANE 23: :21
Geneal dictionary, bk rev BCG 16:2:65
Geneal res guide by Baxter, bk rev MN 18:1:38 ANC 22:1:44 MAD 27:1:36
Geneal res hints CGS 18:3:5
Mercantile claims 1775-1803 VA VAG 31:1:48 31:2:91
Mil rec, use of GH 41:5:5
BRITISH EMPIRE, Dormant, abeyant, forfeited, & extinct peerages, bk rev FAM 26:1:47
BRITISH ISLES, Geneal res hints RES 18:4:164
Mil rec, use of RD 87:1:16
BRITTEN, Abram b1799, w Eliza Arnett, TN, MO, children OZ 9:1:31
BRITTON, William f1799, TN, geneal, bk rev FRT 8:4:198
William, w Sarah M Gates, geneal, bk rev MN 18:3:137
William Sr f1805, TN, geneal, bk rev GH 41:2:149
BROADWAY, A A f1911, NH, ledger 1759-1929, bk rev NCJ 13:1:51

BROADWAY (continued)
Thomas Haywood b1837, w Lavina Catherine Tyler, NC, AR, geneal, bk rev GH 41:6:154 NCJ 13:2:119
BROCK, Sally see Joel PHELPS
BRODHEAD, Daniel b1631, w Ann Salmon, EN, NY, geneal, bk rev GH 41:1:155 GFP 37:2:73
BROMLEY, Ann m1660, h John Knott, EN, NJ, marr rec GMN 62:3:109
BROMWELL, William m1779, w Beulah Hall, PA, MD, geneal, microfiche rev GH 41:6:167
BRONNUM, Severin Christian b1809, w Hannah Pederson, DK, FL, lineage FLG 10:4:138
BROOKS, Anna see Elijah GRAY
Jonathan Addison b1822, w Martha Morrison, MA, anc ch WB 17:4:129
Kennedy b1806, w Elizabeth Hill Butler, IR, OH, anc ch GGL 6:1-2:59
BROSEE, John m1841, w Fredrika Bartruff, PA, Bible rec KA 23:2:101
BROWARD, Napoleon Bonaparte b1857, FL, biog sketch IMP 6:4:95
BROWDER, Mary see Samuel SHELBOURNE
BROWER, Nicholas M C b1835, w Elizabeth Zetter, NY, anc ch ANC 22:2:53
BROWN, Adam f1838, IL, affidavit WTC 6:1:5
Benjamin Franklin b1839, w Jennie Gordon McCornack, NY, geneal, bk rev GH 41:6:154
Caleb b1804, w Cesleeter/Celita ___ & Malinda Osborn & Mary Ann Webb, KY, MO, biog sketch OZ 5:1:34
Charles m1901, w Nelmay VanBuskirk, MO, geneal, bk rev SLB 6:5:221
Charles Marion b1875, w Nelmay Jo Van Buskirk, MO, geneal, bk rev GH 41:3:167

BROWN (continued)

Elizabeth b1787, IL, anc ch CCS 9:2:61

Elizabeth see Abraham THOMPSON

Fam cem Dade Co MO OZ 7:3:114

George A b1826, RI, IL, CO, NE, biog sketch NW 10:1:33

Jennie C see Landon C HAYNES

Joanna see Richard GREEN

John J bc1839, w Fanny Spencer, KY, biog sketch EK 23:1:20

Lemuel b1815, w Catherine Lyman, IL, anc ch WTC 1:4:103

Lillie Forester see George Curtis BLAKELY

Mary Ann see George D SMALLWOOD

Mary b1769, EN, anc ch CR 19:2:96

Mary Louisa b1852, h Alva Walls, OH, IL, obit CRT 8:4:11

Minnie Myrtie see Paul G KING

Nathaniel J f1837, IL, letters WTC 1:4:108

Peter mc1623, w Martha (___) Ford & Mary ___, EN?, MA, biog MQ 53:1:10

Sarah see James C CAMERON

Surname period, *The Brown Fam Newsletter International*, POB 28215, Sacramento CA 95828

Surname period, *The Brown Fam*, 430 Ivy Ave, Crete NE 68333

William b1764,fam rec AG 62:3:88

William bc1725, w Christiana Thompson, ST, PA, geneal, bk rev WPG 14:1:51 CHG 19:4:155 TS 29:1:26 CSB 21:1-2:39

William d1889, w Mary A Tickel, MD, OH, IL, obit CRT 8:4:9

William f1860, w Mary Henninger, NY, IL, biog sketch FF 15:3:30

BROWNE, Chad f1638, MA, RI, children AG 62:4:193

BROWNE (continued)

Judith see Bezaleel RAVENS

BROWNING, James Henry b1855, w Terrisa Jane Clark, AL, TX, anc ch NC :92:9

BROYLES, Catherine see Conrad WILHOIT

K C see M W BERRYHILL

Surname period, *Broyles Fam Newsletter*, Rt 3 Box 178, Clinton TN 37716

BRUBAKER, John f1710, w Anna ___, PA, fam hist LCH 2:2:95

BRUCE, Joseph b1759, w Ruth Lowell, VT, identification of NER 141:3:244

BRUMEL, Elizabeth see Isaac HILL

BRUMLEY,Daniel bc1740, w Elizabeth Oliver, VA, geneal, bk rev GFP 37:2:72

Daniel bc1779, w Patty Wilcoxon & Rachel Patterson & Sarah ___, VA, MO, geneal OZ 9:3:116 (bk rev) KA 23:1:38

Fam hist 1681-1984, bk rev GH 41:4:204

BRUMMER, Bernard b1849, w Mary E Rieman, IL, obit CRT 8:1:26

BRUMMETT, Surname period, *Brummetts All*, POB 9175, Amarillo TX 79105 – births & deaths IN, news, marr & ch rec, will, obit

BRUMMIT, Thomas f1859, NC, letter NCJ 13:4:232

BRUNER, Susannah see Elijah GUM

BRUNET, Gabrielle see Jean BONDURANT

BRUNK, Christopher, IA, geneal, bk rev CSB 21:1-2:43

BRYAN, Margaret Elizabeth b1829, PA, anc ch AA 8:2:93

Philemon Leigh bc1779, w Anne Nancy Hawthorne, NC, FL, lineage FLG 10:4:147

Thomas b1718, VA, anc ch THT 15:1:32

BRYANT, Abijah f1833, ME, pension appl RAG 8:1:10

24

BRYANT (continued)
John Massey b1822, w Miriam S
Osteen, GA, FL, lineage FLG
10:4:137
Rial b1832, w Isabella Catherine
Wornick, TN?, AL, anc ch
NAS 26:1:19
Willialm f1867, IN, IA, Bible rec
HH 21:4:226
BRYDSEN, Alberta see Ernie
DRAKE
BRYSON, William b1779, NC,
cem inscr NCJ 13:3:152
BUCHANAN, Fam rec misc OH
1800s, bk rev GH 41:4:204
James Calloway b1865, w
Florence Morgan Fowler &
Della Slaughter, VA, biog
sketch OPC 18:3:78
John S f1856, w Mary Ann ___,
IL, abstr of title WTC 4:2:55
BUCHEL, Rosa Emilie see Wil-
liams August WESTHOFF
BUCK, Susanna see Thomas
HARTSHORN
BUCKHAULTS, Be Ann see John
A BLACK
BUEHLER, Christian David
b1831, w Margaret Jane
Metsker, GE, IN, IL, MO,
geneal OZ 8:1:29
BUERGER, Anna Amelia see
Louis Carl MILLER
BUFFINGTON, Benjamin see
Hannah SOUTHWICK
BUFORD, Martha McDowell
m1846, h Willis Field Jones,
KY, biog, bk rev REG 85:1:99
BUGG, William Emmanuel
b1848, VA, NC, journal, bk rev
GH 41:2:149
BUHLER, Jacob b1774, w Maria
Wiebe, RA, lineage MFH
6:1:16
BULL, Nathan III bc1775, RI,
anc, bk rev CTN 20:1:136
Nathan III bc1775, RI, PA, anc,
bk rev GH 41:3:167 NYR
118:3:182
Thomas f1635, W Susannah
___, EN, CT, geneal, bk rev
CCS 9:2:59

BULL (continued)
Thomas f1636, w Susannah ___,
CT, geneal, bk rev CTN
19:4:709 (part 4) DM 50:3:144
GH 41:1:156
BULLARD, Frank Dearborn
b1860, w Rose Talbott, ME,
CA, biog sketch SCS 24:7:147
William Bradford b1829, w Lydia
Elizabeth Dearborn, ME, CA,
biog sketch SCS 24:7:147
BULLER, Emmelie see Jessie
YOUNG
BULLOCK, Thomas m1790, w
Lucy ___, Bible rec WTC
8:4:99
William b1764, w Elizabeth
Oliphant, Bible rec YTD 2:1:13
BUMP, Lydia see Bernard N
JUNGLES
BUNDY, William, w Elizabeth
___, RI, NC, geneal, bk rev
NCJ 13:2:120
BUNGALE, Gusta see William
HUBRICH
BUNKER, Benjamin f1851, w
Hannah Judkins, ME, letters &
fam hist DE 10:5:187 11:1:15
Chang-Eng f1839, Siam, NC,
naturalization NCJ 13:2:111
BUNNELL, Surname period, The
Bunnell/Bonnell Newsletter,
POB 62, Laceyville PA 18623
William f1638, w Ann Wilmot,
EN, MA, CT, geneal, bk rev
CTN 20:2:317 RES 18:4:191
BUNSE, Friederike see Gottlieb
Leopold Friedrich GRAU
BUNTON, Martha see John
TUCKER
BURBACH, Philip d1812, w
Elizabeth ___, PA, children
LM 28:4:290
BURBRIDGE, Sally see James
STAPP
BURCH, Eliza see Geo TUCKER
Jacob b1817, w Ann Eliza Lan-
fear & Elizabeth Haynes, fam
hist WTC 17:4:110
BURCHAM, William bc1540, w
Agnes ___, EN, IL, geneal
FF 15:3:87

25

BURCHSTEAD, Anna (Potter) see Ralph LINDSEY

BURCKHARTT, Fam hist GE & MO, bk rev MSG 7:2:111

BURCKLE, Elizabeth see Georg MECKENDORFER

BURDICK, Dorothy see Brownell CORNELL

BURDITT, Sally see Lemuel CHURCHILL

BURGER, Annetje b1800, NY, anc ch BG 8:4:94

Elisabeth Margaretha see Johannes VONDERAU

Jacob bc1825, w Rachel Barnes, TN, KS, children BWG 16:1:37

BURGESS, Olive see Asa LANFEAR

Rebecca Jane see Dandridge Eliphalet KELSEY

BURKE, J H H m1868, w Martha Jane Wright, Bible rec FP 30:2:64

BURKHART, John b1778, w Elizabeth Good, PA, geneal, bk rev PM 10:1:49

Walter f1860, w Emily ____, KY, divorce HF 3:2:70

BURLINGAME, Asa Franklin b1767, RI, MO, anc ch JCG 15:2:63

Lettie Lavella b1859, IL, biog WTC 14:3:92

BURNETT, Jeremiah f1782, w Rosa ____, VA, KY, geneal, bk rev CCS 9:3:98

Surname period, *Burnett Fam Newsletter*, 3891 Commander Dr, Chamblee GA 30341-1854

BURNHAM, Fam hist MA, bk rev NYR 118:4:250

John b1616, MA, geneal, bk rev CTN 20:1:144

John f1635, w Mary ____, MA, geneal, bk rev GH 41:3:167

Rowland f1655, w Alice ____, VA, will BGS 19:3:117

BURNS, James Anderson, KY, biog, bk rev HF 3:2:46

BURR, Jehu f1660, w Esther Ward Boosey & Eliza Prudden, CT, geneal OCG 17:1:3

BURR (continued)

Jehu m1755, w Sarah Griffin, CT, geneal OCG 17:2:11

Sally f1862, h Aaron Burr, PA, pension appl OCG 17:3:22

William F m1862, w Rebecca Lochridge, Bible rec YTD 1:1:25

BURREL, Electa see Russell HARRINGTON

BURRIS, Mary see Van C HALL

BURRITT, John see Hannah BEACH

BURROUGH, Peleg b1748, RI, journal 1778-1798, bk rev NGS 74:4:307

BURROUGHS, Burt E b1862, IL, biog, bk rev GH 41:4:204

BURROW, James b1799, w Martha McGee & Belinda (Shipman) Johnson, NC, MO, children OZ 5:1:35

BURSCHENK, Gertrude see Henry VOGT

BURT, Mary see John MITCHELL

BURTON, George f1660, IR, US, geneal, bk rev GH 41:5:189

BUSBY, Annie Laura see George Washington VARNUM

BUSH, Andrew Jackson b1829, w Emeline Masters, OH, anc ch HL 6:1:23

Anna Belle see Edward Magill WALTERS

Caroline Pearl see Constant STEVENS

Deborah see JohN MACCOONE

BUSHNELL, John L d1853, Bible rec BG 8:3:68

Salome see Henry M MOULD

BUSSER, Jean Jacques bc1725, geneal direct, bk rev NYR 118:3:186

BUTLER, Benjamin Sr f1795, SC, deed SCM 15:1:51

Elizabeth Hill see Kennedy BROOKS

John b1763, w Martha Eels, CT, MA, NY, geneal, bk rev NER 141:1:70

BUTLER (continued)
Simon bc1680, WE, PA, geneal,
bk rev GH 41:1:156
Thomas Clyde b1887, w Ethel
Head & Margie P Davis, TX,
geneal YTD 7:1:9
BUTTERBAUGH, George b1737,
w Christina Adams, PA, anc
ch MFH 6:4:146
BUTTERFIELD, Nathaniel f1694,
w Ann Trimingham, BM, fam
rec BBQ 4:2:20
Thomas f1760, w Deborah Bas-
come, BM, fam rec BBQ
4:2:20
BUTTON, William d1870, MO,
burial OZ 9:3:109
BUTTS, Elizabeth Jane see
James JOHNSON
BUYSE, Johannes b1798, w Bar-
bara DeMuynck, anc ch FAH
5:1:4
BYARS, Henry G d1857,Bible rec
TB 14:1:17
Maria L see Edward LOOMIS
BYERS, Samuel (Sr?) f1773, w
Jane White, PA, VA, geneal,
bk rev GH 41:4:205 GH
41:5:190
BYRD, Adam b1796, Bible rec
RES 18:3:131
James Edward b1817, w Levissa
Mason, MS, anc ch KSL
/11:4:124
John bc1750, VA, geneal, bk rev
GH 41:6:154
Royal George m1905, w Eunice
Shearer, Bible rec RES
18:3:128
William S b1806, OH, letters
1826-1828, bk rev CTA
29:3:112
BYRUM, Elva see Wm O BER-
RYHILL
BYXBY, Walter bc1390, w
Margery ___, EN, MA, geneal
NER 141:3:228
CABALL, Francis m1863, w
Eliza Holmes, EN, TX, anc ch
VC 8:3:71
CADE, Laura see Joseph GREEN

CADWALLADER, Mary Louisa
see Charles A HOUGH
CAIN, Delilah see Phillip WHIT-
TEN
Nicholas bc1705,w Catherine
___, VA, geneal, bk rev GH
41:3:176
CAIRNS, Sarah Jane bc1838, ON,
anc ch BG 8:3:92
CALAHAN, William F b1841, w
Pricilla Trigg, Bible rec FP
30:4:176
CALDER, William b1806, w Mar-
garet Bannatyne, ST, geneal
GWS :24:12
CALDREN, Hedvig f1899, h Karl
Eliason, SN, NJ, FL, biog
sketch IMP 6:1:20
CALDWELL, Andrew f1771, PA,
fam rec LCC 4:1:76
Francis M m1801, w Nancy
Davidson, KY, Bible rec KA
23:2:91
CALIFORNIA, Auburn, district
court rec 1863 RCP 9:3:92
Auburn, geneal misc 1858-1864
abstr from the *Placer Herald*
RCP 9:1:18 9:2:44 9:3:76
Blocksburg, school student roster
1897-98 RED 19:4:12
China Flat voters precinct 1902
index RED 20:1:8
Clark, Booth, & Yardley journal
rec 1850-1869 RCP 9:1:14
9:2:51 9:3:88
Del Norte Co, marr 1860s-1870s
RED 20:1:13
Elk Grove, Elk Grove United
Meth Ch rec 1866-1886 RCP
9:1:11
Ferndale, biog sketches RED
19:3:19
Ferndale, Ferndale Meth Ch
funerals 1932-1940 RED
19:3:16
Fields Landing voters precinct
1902 index RED 19:3:10
Folsom, Trinity Epis Ch rec
1858-1909 RCP 9:2:47
Fortuna, probate rec 1853-1870
RED 20:2:7

CALIFORNIA (continued)
funeral rec of Rev Carl Adolph Nylund 1925-1974 RES 18:1:29
Geneal lib & soc CTN 19:4:628 20:1:17 20:2:219 20:3:521
Geneal rec avail at the CA State Archives RCP 9:2:40
Humboldt Co, biog sketches RED 19:4:19 20:1:19 20:2:19
Humboldt Co, Capetown, direct 1913 RED 20:1:7
Humboldt Co, Carlotta, direct 1913 RED 20:1:7
Humboldt Co, census 1880 RED 19:3:3 19:4:3 20:1:3
Humboldt Co, citizenships granted 1873, 1877, 1892 RED 20:1:11
Humboldt Co, direct 1913 RED 20:2:13
Humboldt Co, District Board of Agri 1895-8 roster RED 19:3:7
Humboldt Co, fatalities 1895 RED 20:1:13
Humboldt Co, Hydesville, hist sketch RED 19:3:10
Humboldt Co, Hydesville Precinct, census 1880 RED 20:2:3
Humboldt Co, notaries public 1895-1897 roster RED 19:3:7
Humboldt Co, post offices & postmasters 1876 roster RED 19:4:15
Humboldt Co, probate rec 1800s-1900s index RED 19:3:11
Humboldt Co, Union District Public School honor roll 1872 student roster RED 20:2:18
Imm from Independence MO 1850 roster OC 24:2:66
Livermore, Asbury Meth Epis Ch hist sketch LRT 6:4:247
Livermore, Saint Michael's Cem LRT 6:4:256
Los Angeles Co, direct 1883-84 for Fountain Valley, Savannah, & Silverado OC 24:3:109
Los Angeles Co, Los Angeles High School grad 1875-1885 roster SCS 24:3:58

CALIFORNIA (continued)
Marin Co, deaths 1873-1892 MKT 10:1:15 10:2:41 10:3:60 10:4:73
Marin Co, hist MKT 10:1:19 10:4:78
Names on the coast & of events 1856-1900 (central CA), bk rev APG 2:3:29
Orange Co, Capistrano, Union High School leaders 1920-1956 roster OC 24:1:18
Orange Co, city incorporations 1888-1962 OC 24:1:2
Orange Co, Fullerton, advertisements 1904 abstr from the *Fullerton Tribune* OC 24:1:17
Orange Co, Long Beach, Polytechnic High School debate teams roster 1914-25 OC 24:3:111
Orange Co, Long Beach, founding fam OC 24:2:63
Orange Co, Los Angeles, settlers 1781 OC 24:1:16
Orange Co, Orange, actors 1887 in play *The Plaza* OC 24:1:21
Orange Co, plat bk 1912 OC 24:1:5 24:2:49 24:3:93
Orange Co, San Francisco, Casino Hispano-Am Club member roster 1879 OC 24:1:24
Orange Co, San Francisco, teachers (10 year) 1876 roster OC 24:1:26
Orange Co, Santa Ana, Dorcas Choral Club member roster 1933 OC 24:3:92
Orange Co, Santa Ana, schools & 1st superintendents 1857-1875 roster OC 24:2:48
Pilgramage for the mothers & widows roster RT 5:2:35
Pioneer biog sketches SCS 24:11:219
Revolutionary War, reg of the CA Soc of the Sons of the Am Rev SCC 23:1-4:34
Riverside Co, Elsinore Precinct, Great Reg 1904 index OC 24:3:113

CALIFORNIA (continued)

Sacramento Co, Sacramento, accidents (fatal) 1879 RCP 9:3:93 9:4:118

Sacramento Co, Sacramento, Clark, Booth, & Yardley journal rec 1860-1869 RCP 9:4:114 10:1:10

Sacramento Co, Sacramento, direct (city & co) 1879-80 RCP 9:1:6 9:2:60 9:3:84 9:4:125 10:1:18

Sacramento Co, Sacramento, pioneer company 18,64 roster RCP 9:4:116

Saint Michael's Cem LRT 6:1:192 6:2:208 6:3:237

San Buenaventura, census 1870 RT 4:3:59 4:4:87 5:1:2 5:2:30

San Diego Co, Mission San Antonio de Pala, Mission Cemetery & Tribal Cemetery of the Pala Nation SCS 24:5:105

Santa Barbara Co, marr 1914-1915 AW 13:1:41 13:2:89 13:3:130 13:4:180

Santa Clara Co, Great Reg 1867 SCC 23:1-4:23

Santa Clara Co, Los Gatos Precinct, Great Reg 1900 SCC 23:1-4:28

Santa Clara Co, San Jose, tax roll 1853 index SCC 23:1-4:17

Santa Clara Co, participants in social event 1877 SCC 23:1-4:16

Santa Clara Co, Gardner, Great Reg 1900 SCC 24:1:24

Santa Clara Co, Guadalupe Precinct, great reg 1900 SCC 24:2:65

Santa Clara Co, Pueblo San Jose census 1778 SCC 24:1:10

Santa Clara Co, San Jose, Franklin School attendance 1917 SCC 24:1:6

Santa Clara Co, San Jose, tax (delinquent) sale 1880/81 SCC 24:2:59

Santa Clara Co, Santa Clara High School grad 1892 SCC 24:2:92

CALIFORNIA (continued)

Santa Clara Co, blue bk (state roster of judicial, executive, & legislative departments of the government & co officers) 1899 SCC 24:1:17

Santa Clara Co, gazetteer (railroad) SCC 24:1:29 24:2:67

Santa Clara Co, great reg 1867 SCC 24:2:47

Santa Clara Co, homestead declarations 1880s-1890s SCC 24:1:12

Santa Clara Co, marr lic 1850s-1914 SCC 24:1:34

Santa Clara Co, marr lic 1863-1906 with surname beginning with "E" SCC 24:2:61

Santa Clara Co, news indexes 1860 & 1868 to the *Santa Clara Union* & the *San Jose Telegraph* SCC 24:2:51

Santa Clara Co, tax sale 1876/77 delinquent SCC 24:1:5

Santa Rosa, earthquake victims 1906 roster SS 15:1:8

Scotia, school students 1903 roster RED 19:4:16

Shasta Co, McArthur-Burney Falls Memorial State Park cem SCC 23:1-4:22

Solano Co, Rockville Cem RDQ 5:1:2

Solano Co, Vallejo, hist sketch RDQ 5:1:12

Sonoma Co, divorces 1859-1902 SS 14:3:39

Sonoma Co, geneal misc 1887 abstr from *The Sonoma Democrat* SS 14:3:45 14:4:58

Sonoma Co, Santa Rosa, cem inscr 1852-1980, bk rev GH 41:3:172

Spruce Grove voters precinct 1902 index RED 19:4:12

Sutter Co, Aburn School District student roster 1902 RCP 9:2:53

Trinity Co, Civil War, First Company Vol roster 1861 RED 20:2:11

Weitchpec voters precinct 1902 index RED 19:3:10

CALIFORNIA (continued)
World War I, pilgrimage for the mothers & widows of soldiers, sailors, & marines of the Am Forces now interred in the cemeteries of Eur RT 5:1:7

CALKINS, Marcia Averill m1840, h Daniel Gifford, Bible rec IG 23:2:59

CALL, Mary C see Asa MORRIS

Rebecca see Nathaniel GORHAM

Silas B b1838, w Julia Lamberg & Nancy Emmaline Lunceford Snall, NH, CA, biog sketch SCS 24:4:89

CALLAWAY, Benjamin m1825, w Mary Melton, Bible rec RT 5:2:48

CALSON, Fam hist, bk rev GEN 12:4:23

CAMBRON, Mary Theresa b1821, BE, KS, anc ch JCG 15:1:28

CAMERON, Eliza J f1884, h ___ Gleason, CA, letter NW 10:1:15

James C b1764, w Sarah Brown, IR, SC, GA, geneal TCG 6:4:1

Lewis b1824, w Martha Ellen ___, IN, IL, fam hist sketch CRT 8:3:16

CAMP, Benjamin Washington b1846, w Nancy Maria May, MS, AK, TX, anc ch AGS 28:2:100

CAMPBELL, Alexander b1799, w Nancy McSwain, NC, lineage FLG 10:3:101

Angus m1803, w Ann Langwill, ST, QB, anc ch GGL 6:1-2:59

Charity see Thomas CLARK

Duncan d1867, ST, CN, geneal, bk rev GN 5:3:161

Fam hist add AR & MO to Ozar'kin vol 8 Fall 1986 page 94 OZ 9:3:123

Flora Jane see Alan Dougal MCKINNON

Frances Maria see Andrew McCLURE

George Washington b1869 w Donnie Margaret Bell, AR, CO, children BWG 16:1:37

CAMPBELL (continued)
Isaac b1843 w Isabelle Cook, OH, geneal, bk rev GH 41:1:156

James b1808, TN, TX, biog AGS 28:4:160

Jamy m1783 w Isabel Campbell, Bible rec NA 10:1:12

John f1838 w Mary Lunny, ST, WI, geneal, bk rev SGS 36:4:207 MN 18:2:91 CO 48:3:85

Junius T m1832?, w Mary A Blackwell, Bible rec OZ 7:1:26

Letitia see Thomas ENGLISH

Mary Ellen see William J MCKELVEY

Mrs C M f1900, KS, letter BCS 7:1:1

Tunis f1863, GA, biog, bk rev REG 85:3:272

CANADA, Alberta, v r address CTN 19:4:715

Ancient Order of United Workmen assessment notices 1882-1884 FAM 26:4:234

Births, marr, & deaths 1871-1910 abstr from the *Renfrew Mercury*, bk rev FAM 26:4:243

British Columbia, geneal holdings (card file index) of BCGS sources BCG 16:4:127

British Columbia, geneal res sources FAM 26:2:67

British Columbia, high schcool students 1901-1902 roster BCG 16:3:74

British Columbia, lighthouse keepers, bk rev BCG 16:1:29

British Columbia, Merritt, hist, bk rev BCG 16:3:100

British Columbia, pet of Nanaimo & Comox constituencies 1884 BCG 16:1:2

British Columbia, revenue collectors 1901-1902 BCG 16:2:58

British Columbia, Royal Engineers roster addenda BCG 16:4:123

British Columbia, Skeena Valley, pioneer memories, bk rev BCG 16:3:103

CANADA (continued)
British Columbia, v r address CTN 19:4:715

British Columbia, Victoria, Ross Bay, residents 1800s MP 3:2:91

British Columbia, Victoria, hist of automobiles 1864-1914, bk rev BCG 16:4:143

British Columbia, Victoria, liquor lic 1868 roster BCG 16:1:6

British Columbia, Victoria, women arriving 1862 on board the *Tynemouth* to marry local men BCG 16:4:125

Cape Breton County, Boisdale, hist, bk rev GN 5:1:25

Census 1871, use of PF 16:2:47

Census 1891, use of GH 41:2:5

Convicts roster at peniteniary 1847 LIC 13:3:133

Departments of Public Works, payments made 1851 LIC 13:1:38

Geneal rec avail at the Public Archives of CN GN 5:1:28

Geneal res guide by Baxter, bk rev RAG 8:1:26 KA 23:1:33 WPG 13:3:40 CTN 20:2:327 IL 19:2:113 SGS 36:4:205 DM 50:4:161

Geneal res hints AIL 1:1:23

Geneal res hints, searching for anc in the army GN 5:2:104

Geneal works annotated biblio, bk rev GN 5:2:95 FAM 26:3:175

Grand Bank, hist, bk rev NAL 4:1:24

Halifax, ship pass lists 1881-1921 avail SLV 5:4:12

Hist of the prairies 1600- , bk rev BCG 16:4:144

Imm to Neche ND prior to 1920 FAM 26:1:33

Labrador, Hopedale, Moravian Mission, adults received into ch membership 1856-1882 NAL 3:2:6

London District, surrogate court reg 1800-39 FAM 26:4:213

CANADA (continued)
Manitoba, Argyle, hist of medical profession 1880-1985, bk rev GEN 12:4:21

Manitoba, Baldure, Argyle, hist, bk rev GEN 12:4:19

Manitoba, Binscarth, hist, bk rev GEN 12:4:23

Manitoba, Blumenfeld, hist, bk rev GEN 12:4:24

Manitoba, census 1881, bk rev FAM 26:4:239

Manitoba, census 1891, use of GEN 12:3:9

Manitoba, Clandeboye, hist, bk rev GEN 12:4:24

Manitoba, Cypress River, hist 1885-1985, bk rev GEN 12:4:24

Manitoba, Darlingford, hist 1870-1970, bk rev GEN 12:4:20

Manitoba, Dominion City, hist, bk rev GEN 12:4:21

Manitoba, Dufferin, hist 1880-1980, bk rev GEN 12:4:27

Manitoba, Ellice, hist 1883-1983, bk rev GEN 12:4:21

Manitoba, Flin Flon, hist 1933-1983 (pictorial), bk rev GEN 12:4:22

Manitoba, Garsona dn Tyndall, Brokenhead, Beausejour, hist 1875-1981, bk rev GEN 12:4:19

Manitoba, geneal res aid, Fort LaReine Museum GEN 12:4:28

Manitoba, geneal res aid, maps GEN 12:3:18

Manitoba, Geysir District, hist 1880s-1980s, bk rev GEN 12:4:21

Manitoba, Gimli, hist 1887-1987, bk rev GEN 12:4:22

Manitoba, Gladstone, Anglican Ch hist, bk rev GEN 12:4:23

Manitoba, Glenboro, hist 1880-1980 (pictorial), bk rev GEN 12:4:21

Manitoba, Killarney, hist 1882-1982, bk rev GEN 12:4:21

Manitoba, Kinosota-Alonsa District, hist 1923-1983, bk rev GEN 12:4:23

CANADA (continued)

Manitoba, Lauder, hist, bk rev GEN 12:4:26

Manitoba, marr & death notices 1859-1881 abstr from news index, bk rev FAM 26:4:239

Manitoba, Morden, hist, bk rev GEN 12:2:31

Manitoba, Mossgiel, hist, bk rev GEN 12:4:20

Manitoba, North Cypress, hist, bk rev GEN 12:4:25

Manitoba, Oak Bluff District, hist, bk rev GEN 12:4:27

Manitoba, Oak Lake, hist, bk rev GEN 12:4:21

Manitoba, Pembina, hist, bk rev GEN 12:4:22

Manitoba, Rathwell, hist, bk rev GEN 12:4:20

Manitoba, Rhineland, hist 1884-1984, bk rev GEN 12:4:19

Manitoba, Sandy Lake, hist, bk rev GEN 12:4:22

Manitoba, Teulon, hist, bk rev GEN 12:4:19

Manitoba, v r address CTN 19:4:715

Manitoba, Waldof, Vermilion Bay, Eagle River area, hist, bk rev GEN 12:4:25

Manitoba, Wallace, hist 1882-1982, bk rev GEN 12:4:24

Manitoba, Westbourne, hist, bk rev GEN 12:4:23

Manitoba, Whitehead, hist 1883-1983, bk rev GEN 12:2:31

Natives in Jackson Co WI 1862-1865 LIC 13:4:188

New Brunswick, marr to 1839, bk rev BCG 16:3:102

New Brunswick, NS, & PE, residents in the Am Civil War GN 5:3:149

New Brunswick, Queens Co, marr 1812-1861, bk rev GJ 15:3:181

New Brunswick, Saint John Co, Saint John City, marr from the British Conquest to 1839, bk rev CTN 19:4:714 GH 41:1:124 RAG 8:5:22 NYR 118:2:114

CANADA (continued)

New Brunswick, v r 1847-1850 abstr from news, bk rev GH 41:3:158 (1854-56) GN 5:2:102

New Brunswick, v r address CTN 19:4:695

Newfoundland, Bonne Bay, fam of the south-arm of the Bay 1800s-1930s, bk rev NAL 4:1:26

Newfoundland, Brigus, contributors to repeal fund 1844 roster NAL 3:2:18

Newfoundland, v r address CTN 19:4:695

Northwest Territories, v r address CTN 19:4:695

Notaries 1621-1759 roster, bk rev LIC 13:4:223

Nova Scotia, assessments, tax grantees, tenants, etc 1765-1789, bk rev IL 19:2:117

Nova Scotia, Baie Saint Marie Parish reg 1799-1801, bk rev BAT 16:1:22

Nova Scotia, fishermen 1830-1873 deaths GN 5:3:153

Nova Scotia, geneal rec avail RED 19:3:8

Nova Scotia, geneal res guide by Punch, bk rev SLB 6:4:168 MA 11:3:82

Nova Scotia, Halifax, provisions 1783 abstr GN 5:2:108

Nova Scotia, letters from travellers 1700s-1800s, bk rev GN 5:1:24

Nova Scotia, marr & bapt 1865-1900 performed by Rev George Wethers GN 5:3:164

Nova Scotia, natives buried in General Protestant Cem, St John's, Newfoundland GN 5:1:41

Nova Scotia, natives in Prince Edward Island marr lic 1871-1888 GN 5:2:106

Nova Scotia, Rawdon, Rawdon Anglican Ch marr 1866-1900 GN 5:3:166

Nova Scotia, v r 1769-1812 abstr from news GN 5:1:31

CANADA (continued)

Nova Scotia, v r address CTN 19:4:695

Ontario & Northwest Territories, census 1881, bk rev FAM 26:4:239

Ontario, births, marr, & deaths 1844-1847 abstr from *The Globe*, bk rev FAM 26:4:239

Ontario, births, marr, & deaths 1871-1900 abstr from the *Renfrew Mercury*, bk rev GH 41:3:159

Ontario, Clinton Twp, Clinton & Grimsby, Pres Ch rec 1819-1870 FAM 26:1:26

Ontario, direct 1857, bk rev LIC 13:4:223

Ontario, Frontenac, Lennox, & Addington Co, geneal res guide by Aitken & Broughton, bk rev FAM 26:4:236

Ontario, geneal res address guide, bk rev NGS 75:3:232

Ontario, geneal res hint, problems with pinpointing birth dates in 19th century sources FAM 26:2:95

Ontario, Goderich, victims of the *Merida* which sank in the Great Lakes 1916 FAM 26:2:88

Ontario, Huron Co, Halton-Peel, census 1871, bk rev FAM 26:1:53

Ontario, Lennox & Addington Co, Richmond Twp, census 1851 FAM 26:1:49

Ontario, marr bonds 1803-1834, bk rev GH 41:5:153

Ontario, marr notices, bk rev GH 41:2:119

Ontario, marr rec avail OC 24:2:72

Ontario, marr rec of the RLDS Ch 1900 FAM 26:3:131

Ontario, Middlesex Co, Mosa Twp, Mosa, hist 1804-1841 FAM 26:3:160

Ontario, Newmarket, Industrial Home, inmates unclaimed at death 1800s-1900s FAM 26:4:225

CANADA (continued)

Ontario, place names for fam res, bk rev FAM 26:4:240

Ontario, Renfrew Co, Brudenell & Lyndoch Twp, census 1881, bk rev FAM 26:1:49

Ontario, settlers in Invermay, Saskatchewan FAM 26:3:170

Ontario, v r address CTN 19:4:596

Ontario, Waterloo & Wellington Co, fam res guide by Taylor, bk rev FAM 26:1:49

Ottawa, Saint Andrew's Pres Ch marr 1829-1881 & bapt 1829-1873 LIC 13:2:79 13:3:150 13:4:207

Oxford Co, election (contested) 1844 LIC 13:1:14

Parish reg held at the Public Archives of CN, list, bk rev FAM 26:1:53

Prince Edward Island, geneal rec & repositories FAM 26:1:2

Prince Edward Island, v r address CTN 19:4:596

Prince Edward Island, geneal res hints CC 10:4:3

Quebec & Montreal, ship pass lists 1900-1919 avail SLV 5:4:9

Quebec, fam 1600s-1700s, bk rev RT 5:2:47

Quebec, geneal bibl LIC 13:2:71

Quebec, geneal res hints FAM 26:3:148

Quebec, Grosse Isle, cem inscr FAM 26:4:201

Quebec, Parish St-Romain-de-Hemmingford, extracts from parish reg pertaining to fam resident in the US 1850-1876 LIC 13:3:124

Quebec, Quebec City, census 1815-1816 LIC 13:4:189

Quebec, ship pass lists 1865-1900 avail SLV 5:4:8

Quebec, Stanstead, Parish Sacre Coeur de Jesus, extracts from rec pertaining to fam resident in US 1826-1834, 1848-1860 LIC 13:1:28 13:2:74

33

CANADA (continued)
Queens Co, roads 1829–1830 GN 5:1:36
Return of convicts at the penitentiary 1847 roster LIC 13:4:182
Richmond Co, hist outline 1521–1835 GN 5:1:35
Saskatchewan, v r address CTN 19:4:596
Toronto, Saint George Soc of Toronto hist & member roster 1834–1967, bk rev GM 22:8:304 V r avail MCS 7:3:115 OCN 10:1:6
Women in fur-trade soc in western CN 1670–1870, bk rev FAM 26:4:238
CANFIELD, Jared b1789, VT, OH, geneal, bk rev GH 41:5:190
Surname period, *Canfield Fam Assoc Publ*, 1144 N Gordon, Wichita KS 67203 – Sarah Elizabeth diary, cem NY, land IN, cem PA & VA & NY & CT, census 1900 CA
CANNADY, Wagstaff bc1740, VA, NC, geneal, bk rev NCJ 13:1:53
CANTRALL, Eli b1824, w Zerilda ____, IL, relationship with other Cantralls in IL CR 19:2:49
Zurilda b1826, h William R Ross & Peter Lanterman Jr & Eli Cantrall, IL, obit CR 19:1:32
CANTRELL, Deliliah see William NOLEN Sr
CANTWELL, Surname period, *The Cantwell-Conteville Fam Assoc Newsletter*, 3402 Fairlawn Dr, Glenview IL 60025–4520
CAPELL, William T m1854, w Cecily Jane Martin, Bible rec EK 23:2:32
CAPLES, John F b1831, w Sarah J Morrison, OH, WA, biog TB 14:1:13
CAPPS, Ebenezer b1798, EN, IL, geneal FF 15:4:115

CAPPS (continued)
Henry B m1867, w Elizabeth Whitehurst, Bible rec TN 7:6:94
CARAHER, Fam rec IR, bk rev RAG 8:1:32
Surname period, *Journal of the Caraher Fam Hist Soc*, 71 King St, Crieff, Perthshire, Scotland UK PH7 3HB
CARATHERS, Fam cem TN BWG 16:2:134
CARD, Nellie E see William J NELSON
CARDON, Philippe b1801, w Marthe Marie Tourn, IY, geneal, bk rev GH 41:3:167
CAREY, Winget bc1766, w Mary Reynolds, DE, geneal, bk rev GH 41:1:157
CARGILLE, Charles E f1903, TN, partnership agreement PEL 8:3:113
CARLAW, Isabella see George LAW
CARLEY, William bc1830, w Emily Harman, NY, PA, MN, geneal, bk rev WPG 14:1:49
CARLILE, Joseph f1688, ME, geneal, bk rev CTN 20:1:141
CARMACK, Surname period, *Carmack Cousins Newsletter*, 221 Frawley Rd, Chattanooga TN 37412
CARMAN, Finette see Isaac Mills GILLETT
CARPENTER, Charles Henry f1841, ME, indenture DE 11:1:14
Martha m1738, h Reese Meredith, PA, biog SB 8:5:170
Mary see Alexander SPURLOCK
CARR, Benjamin m1613, w Margaret/Martha Hardington, EN, anc ch BHN 20:2:61
Matilda b1807, KY, IL, anc ch CCS 9:2:64
Robert Dale b1846, w Sarah Mariah Ray, Bible rec HJA 11:3:182
CARRIER, Martha d1692, MA, death TGA 13:1:6

CARRINGTON, George f1791, VA, deposition concerning land NCJ 13:2:71
CARSON, James W see Sarah Jane DeHART
CARTER, Dale b1744, w Mary Bickley, VA, geneal, bk rev BWG 16:1:65
Eliza see David Richard PINSON
Fam cem inscr Greene Co TN BWG 16:2:117
Fam hist 1713-1900s, bk rev IG 23:2:63
Fam hist EN, NJ, MS, bk rev NYR 118:1:56
Fam rec misc southern US, bk rev GH 41:1:157
Fam rec misc, bk rev GH 41:3:167 GH 41:5:190
Haley M b1837, w Louisiana T Carter, LA, geneal, bk rev KSL 11:3:75
Hattie see Clarence L BARNETT
Joel Anderson b1850, w Millie Hassell, anc ch GGS 23:1:17
Loucinda see William S GRAVES
Louisiana T see Haley M CARTER
Mary see William HUNTER
Philip Ray, KS, auto, bk rev TS 29:1:26 TOP 17:2:35
Rachel see Benjamin JACKSON
Rebecca see Samuel KELLER
Samuel Crawford b1880, w Irene Isabelle McClendon, GA, FL, lineage FLG 10:4:139
William b1770, EN, NJ, MS, geneal, bk rev CCS 9:1:24
CARTWRIGHT, Peter b1758, w Frances Gaines, VA, IL, biog sketch CR 19:4:167
CARVER, Susanna see Thomas GREER
CARY, Hannah see John TAYLOR
CASE, A I f1836, OH, biog sketch AH 14:2:55
Zopher b1816, OH, biog sketch AH 14:2:55
CASEY, Hetty see James EL-LISON

CASSADAY, Richard see Mary WALKER
CASSAT, David Williams b1844, w Lillian May Berryhill, PA, IA, geneal, bk rev SB 8:5:184
CASSIDY, Mary see Patrick McCAFFREY
CASTLE, Christopher Columbus b1858, w Elizabeth Lemaster, KY, biog sketch EK 23:1:21
Eperson b1843, w Sarah Daniel, KY, biog sketch EK 23:2:20
CASTLEMAN, Benjamin A see Virginia LIVINGSTON
CASTLEY, John M m1854, w Fannie H Washington, TX, Bible rec YTD 6:2:34
CASTO, Andrew b1761, NJ, fam rec FI 7:3:62
CATES, John f1782, TN, geneal, bk rev GH 41:6:155
Mary see Charles Harrison OWEN
CATHCART, Margarate see Hugh ARTHUR
CATHEY, James b1790, NC, MO, anc ch CCS 8:4:137
CATHOLIC, Hist in Rich Twp IL WTC 15:4:147
Roman Cath ch rec, use of NGS 74:4:272
Sacramental rec of the Roman Cath Ch of the Archdiocese of New Orleans 1718-1750 vol 1, bk rev KSL 11:3:75
CATLETT, John f1650, VA, IL, geneal, bk rev CCS 9:3:97
CAVE, John Jr bc1794, w Jane Tolbert, VA, MO, children OZ 5:2:78
CAYNOR, Addie B see Noah AT-KINSON
CESLER, Charles D m1899, w Ella Lowe, OH, Bible rec FCG 6:3:42
CHACON, Rafael b1833, NM, CO, biog, bk rev RAG 8:1:24
CHACY, Sarah see James A VIN-CENT
CHADDOCK, Mary Effie see William Otto ABEL

CHADWICK, Lydia see Alexander CRAVER

Sue Elizabeth see Henry Clay JACKSON

CHAMBERLAIN, Fam rec misc vol 1, bk rev IL 19:2:110

CHAMBERS, Stephen d1789, PA, duel LCH 2:1:4

William f1761, w Anne Booth, VA, geneal, bk rev GH 41:5:190

William m1831, w Maria ____, Bible rec HH 21:4:217

CHANCE, Ann bc1802, LA, TX, anc ch STK 15:1:38

CHANDLER, Albert Benjamin b1898, w Mildred ____, KY, biog REG 85:2:138

Ioa Jerusha b1855, MA, IA, anc ch BHN 20:4:175

Joseph Sr d1805, NC, geneal, bk rev GH 41:6:155

Michael H bc1797, w Frances F Ludlow, IR, US, geneal GJ 15:3:128

Tobias b1551, w Johane Momford, EN, anc ch SB 8:3:90

CHANNEL ISLANDS, Fam in North Am, bk rev MN 18:4:186

News 1750-1920 avail, bk rev ANE 23: :20

CHAPDELAINE, Sophie see Octave ARSENEAULT

CHAPIN, John b1804, w Eliza Clark, MA, OH, anc ch OG 13:3:68

Moses B see Irenia DEMARANVILLE

CHAPLIN, Thomas B b1822, SC, diary 1845-1858, bk rev CTA 29:3:112

CHAPMAN, Fanny see David HATCH

Jane see Henry MERCER

CHARBONEAU, Louis b1812, w Adelaide Harriette Delcour, MO, biog FAM 26:1:12

CHARTER, Elizabeth see Kintchen Dudley DOSSEY

CHASE, Eugene b1836, w Lydia Spencer, PA, anc ch TRC 2:1:47

CHASE (continued)
James Wiser b1831, w Esther Amanda Weston, MA, CA, biog sketch SCS 24:6:129

CHAUVIN, Marie Rose see Louis TRUDEAU

CHENETTE, Joseph Isaie b1820, w Felicite Marie Gagnon & Louisa Virginia Bullock McLin, CA, biog sketch SCS 24:5:113

CHEROKEE NATION, Vinitia, subscribers to *The Vinitia Leader* 1906 OK 32:1:23

CHESTEEN, Amanda Roselee see David Samuel WARE

CHEVALIER, Joseph O d1904, w Odeil Goulet, QB, MN, geneal, bk rev SLV 5:1:11

CHICKERING, Deborah Foster see William Joseph ADAMS

Fam crest & shield TEG 7:4:181

Mary see John KNIGHT

CHILD, Ephraim bc1593, w Eizabeth ____, MA, marr AG 62:1:28

CHILDRESS, Sarah see James K POLK

CHILSON, Arthur James d1929, w Della Zelma Smith, IA, CA, anc ch BGS 19:4:188

CHIRINO, Jose Antonio bc1755, w Maria Antonia de Mora, LA, anc ch YTD 7:1:17

Maria Faustina see Andre Jean Baptiste VASCOCU

CHISM, Martha A see William Washington WEBB

CHOWNING, Theophilus bc1796, w Mary Sherman, VA, IN, geneal, bk rev GH 41:3:167 FRT 8:4:201

CHRISOPE, Martha J see John N MOORE

CHRISTENSEN, Inga Marie Larsen see Christen OTTESEN

CHRISTLIEB, Surname period, *Jacob's Ladder*, Box 57 Ridge Rd, Glens Falls NY 12801

CHRISTMAS, Surname period, *Christmas Tree*, Heritage, 263 S 23 Ave, Cornelius OR 97113

CHRISTNER, Hans b1732, SW, PA, ON, OH, geneal MFH 6:3:100

CHRISTOPHERSDTR, Sidsel see Lars MATRAND

CHRISTULE, John b1857, w Agnes Jecszko, Lithuania, anc ch AGE 16:2:52

CHRISTY, John d1781, w Agnes Drennon, PA, geneal, bk rev GH 41:3:177

CHRITTON, Christopher Santford b1793, w Eura Eaton Drake, VA, geneal, bk rev GH 41:5:191

CHRONEMILLER, Thomas b1783, w Elizabeth Gartman, PA, geneal LCH 1:2:68

CHURCH, Jerry f1845, NY, diary, bk rev WPWG 13:3:45

CHURCHILL, Lemuel m1833, w Sally Burditt, Bible rec WTC 2:3:98

CHURCHMAN, Ann see John ROGERS

CISLOR, Catherine b1816, MD, anc ch OG 13:2:40

CISSEL, Mariel Rebecca b1837, MD, anc ch MD 28:3:331

CIVIL WAR, Claims of the Mixed Commission of British & Am Claims 1871-1873 NGS 75:2:141

Confederate geneal res guide to archive collect by Neagles, bk rev APG 2:3:27 WPG 14:1:47 AW 13:2:70 WMG 3:3:140 GH 41:4:186 NTT 7:2:43 CTN 20:2:320 RAG 8:3:25 RCP 9:4:129 NCJ 13:3:181 OZ 9:3:121 STI 27:2:36 PGB 19:1:11 VAG 31:3:231 GGS 23:3:159 NYR 118:4:243 RAG 8:5:25 RES 19:1:23 GFP 36:4:178

Confederate index to The Confederate Vet, bk rev APG 2:3:30 NCJ 13:3:182

Confederate Navy reg of officers 1861-1865, microfiche rev GH 41:2:162

CIVIL WAR (continued)

Confederate prisoners who died in Rock Island (IL) Prison, bk rev WTC 3:4:169

Encyclopedia, bk rev REG 85:3:270

Geneal res aid, The Confederate Magazine SCS 24:12:231

Geneal res hints SS 14:4:61

Geneal res hints for beginners HTR 30:3:81

Hist of occupation in Nashville TN 1862-1863, bk rev REG 85:1:88

Hist of the Battle of New Market, bk rev SGI 4:1:22

Index to the Atlas to Accompany the Official Records of the Union & Confederate Armies SCM 15:4:222

Maps, bk rev DS 24:4:218

Medicine at Chickamauga Battlefield, bk rev SR 2:2:42 3:4:89

Pardons by President Andrew Johnson for soldiers who lived in AL, VA, WV, GA, bk rev GH 41:4:186 FTH 10:3-4:95 CAL 6:4:90 SGI 4:1:21 DS 24:3:164

Prisons list for North & South RD 87:6:28

Soldiers stationed near Edinburg in Hidalgo Co TX 1860 GTP 25:3:75

Union geneal rec search hints CCG 7:1:7

CLAPP, Elijah b1801, w Harriet Ford, MA, geneal, bk rev GH 41:6:155

CLAPPER, Mary see John Calvin KAGARICE

CLARK, Bethuel b1766, w Ann Nancy _____, Bible rec RAG 8:2:12

Costa see William Stewart ROSS

Daniel b1622, w Mary Newberry, EN, CT, geneal, bk rev GH 41:2:162

Elihu b1727, CT, anc ch BG 8:2:39

Eliza see John CHAPIN

37

CLARK (continued)
Fam hist TN, bk rev GD 17:4:14
Fam muster roll abstr for Con-
federate service GTP 25:2:34
Frances see Mathias
RICHARDSON
Hannah d1805, h ___Sherman,
CT, anc CTN 20:2:314
John m1767, w Mary Moore,
Bible rec OZ 8:3:109
John m1856, w Samantha O Rus-
sel, Bible rec HH 21:4:215
Joseph Addison b1815, TN, TX,
biog YTD 5:2:42
Mariah see Uriah SIPPLE
Martha Ann see Elbridge Gerry
HALL
Mary see Issac Wilsey
WINEGORD
Robert bc1745, VA, anc ch EK
22:4:35
Terrisa Jane see James Henry
BROWNING
Thomas f1739, PA, geneal, bk
rev FRT 8:1:48
Thomas m1797, w Charity
Campbell, SC, marr rec SCM
15:2:102
William b1771, IN, anc ch CCS
9:3:101
William bc1700, NC, geneal, bk
rev FRT 8:2:105
CLARKE, Mary see Edward GIL-
MAN
Nathaniel m1663, w Elizabeth
Somerby, MA, geneal,
microfiche rev GH 41:2:163
CLAWSON, Rodolphus see Sarah
Anna JEWEL
CLAY, Henry f1823, w Lucretia
Hart, KY, political career REG
85:1:1
CLAYPOOLE, Fam hist 641 BC –
1900 AD, bk rev IG 23:2:63
CLAYTON, George b1796, NC,
cem inscr NCJ 13:3:152
Joseph Alvey b1817, w Amanda
Poole, TN, TX, biog sketch
DG 33:4:237
Zebulon bc1672, w Mary
Hartshorne, NJ, anc ch BHN
20:2:66

CLEARY, Surname period, *The
Cleary News*, 2983 Bayside Ct,
Wantagh NY 11793
CLEMENS, James b1734, PA,
geneal, bk rev WPG 13:3:51
CLEMMENS, Elizabeth Jane
b1850, MO, anc ch TB 13:4:36
CLEMONS, Sarah see John Allen
SALMON
CLEPPE, Jacobus b1722, w
Maria Anna (Van) Wielant,
Flanders, biog sketch FAH
5:1:20
CLEVELAND, Ursula see James
SIMMONS
CLEVINGER, George Washington
Sr m1841, w Rebecca
Robertson Langham, Bible rec
YTD 4:2:2
CLIBORN, Fam rec misc EN &
VA, bk rev NGS 74:4:304 GH
41:1:158
John Sr b1760, TN, VA, geneal,
bk rev FRT 8:3:153
CLIFFORD, Mary Livena see
Francis Marion THOMAS
CLIFTON, Mary A see Thomas
COATES
Nathan mc1794, w Elizabeth
Wilson & Elizabeth Davis,
NC, TN, MO, biog OZ 6:4:141
CLINE, Addam m1849, w Mary A
Jackson, Bible rec RT 4:4:106
Emma May see John Wesley
ARNOLD
CLINGMAN, Alexander B b1806,
w Ann M ___, NC, TN, AR,
biog KSL 11:4:107
CLOE, Poly Ann see James A
DAVIS
CLOSSON, Lydia see Simeon
GUILD
CLOTHIER, Lois see Uriah
MALLERY
CLOUD, Henry f1836, IL,
preemption affidavit WTC
3:4:165
CLOVER, Surname period, *Clover
Fam Exchange*, 1861 Cameo
Ct, Redding CA 96002 – Bible
rec, fam NY, census 1860 PA,
cem inscr

CLUTTER, Catherine d1892, IL, obit CRT 8:4:16

CLUXTON, Michael bc1640, CT, geneal FF 15:3:65

COALTER, Jack f1861, GA, biog sketch TI 86:11:30

James f1823, AL, collect bond NTT 7:1:37

COATES, Thomas m1858, w Mary A Clifton, DE, Bible rec MAD 27:1:20

COATNEY, Surname period, *Coatney/Courtney Exchange*, 25956 S Rhoten Rd, Aurora OR 97002-9306

COBB, Elizabeth f1839, GA, letter GGS 23:1:11

Isaac Eames b1789, MA, cem inscr MQ 53:3:165

COBBS, Henry D b1813, Bible rec AB 16:1:13

COBERLEY, Fam hist suppl 1986, bk rev VAG 31:3:228

COBERLY, James Stell b1723, NJ, VA, geneal, bk rev DWC 12:4:116

James Stell b1723, NJ, VA, geneal, bk rev PA 35:1:49 OK 32:1:6 NCJ 13:1:54 NGS 75:2:155 GGS 23:1:44 EWA 24:1:52

COBLYE, Martha see William THROOP

COCHRAN, Gertrude Clarice see Charles Hebert PADGHAM

John F b1811, w Sarah Millican, Bible rec OZ 8:3:112

Martha Melvina see James Terry LOMAX

COCHRON, Margaret see John YEAKLEY

COCKE, Martha Patsy see John McKENZIE

COCKERHAM, Fam hist SC & MS, bk rev FTH 10:3-4:95

John bc1735, MS, geneal, bk rev GH 41:5:191

CODY, Surname period, *Geneal & Hist Rev of the International Cody Fam Assoc*, 215 S Vernon Ave, Kissimmee FL 32741

COE, Clarissa see David HUDSPETH

Fam rec MD 1651-1900 MD 28:1:51

COFFEY, Leland b1805, Bible rec CAL 6:4:82

COFFIN, Nicholas b1550, w Joan ___, EN, lineage SB 8:4:128

COFFMAN, Mary d1907, h John Pritchard, OH, obit TLL 12:3:54

COHEE, Benjamin Jr b1788, w Nancy Ann Holland, DE, IN, anc ch MAD 27:2:77

COLCORD, Elizabeth see Robert EVANS

COLDWELL, Binoni Franklin b1809, w Susannah F Roberts, TN, geneal OZ 6:3:123

COLE, Edward see Grace RAVENS

Surname period, *The Cole Courier*, 1521 Sunset Dr, North Platte NE 69101 - census, bk rev, data base

COLEMAN, Hannah see Asa MARTIN

John bc1740, PA, geneal, bk rev GH 41:6:155

COLES, Edward b1786, VA, IL, auto MCS 7:3:131

COLLIER, Isaac d1868, w Mary Lockey, EN, VA, anc ch AGS 28:2:98

John Lendsey Monroe b1867, w Chloe Etta Hales, AL, anc ch NAS 26:2:44

COLLINGS, Reuben m1832, w Mary Johnson, Bible rec KA 23:2:86

COLLINS, Caroline see William LIGHTFOOT

Eleanor see William DeLOACH

Elizabeth A b1834, h R S Reed, CT, IL, obit MCS 7:1:41

Geneva Armetta Graham see William Lawson BREWER

Gladys Key f1953, WA, biog sketch PB 3:1:9

John b1819, w ___ Willis & Mary Cowden, TN, TX, MO, geneal OZ 7:2:71

COLLINS (continued)
Jonathan f1738, w Ann Collins, PA, geneal, bk rev WPG 13:4:48
Shubael m1857, w Mary Anne Talboys, WI, marr rec WI 34:2:132
COLORADO, Boulder Co, estate files 1880s-1904 BGS 19:1:3 19:2:47 19:3:93 19:4:145
Boulder, Nederland, Co Cem BGS 19:2:55
Boulder, Women's Christian Temperance Union member roster BGS 19:4:155
Clear Creek Co, Central, Masonic monument inscr FI 7:3:69
Clear Creek Co, Georgetown, deaths 1892-1921 FI 7:1:13 7:2:52
Denver, council rec 1860-1861 name index CO 48:4:108
Direct (business) 1897-8 FI 7:2:42
Florrisant, hist, bk rev GH 41:3:160
Geneal misc 1859-1899 abstr from the *Silver State Rec* FI 7:3:83
Geneal resource rec BGS 19:3:112
Gilpin Co, biog sketches index to *Hist of Clear Creek & Boulder Valley CO* 1880 FI 7:2:47
Gilpin Co, Central, Gregory monument inscr FI 7:3:70
Gilpin Co, geneal holings at the State Archives FI 7:3:71
Golden, Boston Company hist sketch FI 7:2:36
Golden, businesses 1902 FI 7:2:32
Golden, presidents/mayors, city clerks, & treasurers 1871-1910 roster FI 7:3:74
Jamestown, cem inscr BGS 19:4:158
Jefferson Co, biog sketches index to *Hist of Clear Creek & Boulder Valley CO* 1880 FI 7:2:46

COLORADO (continued)
Jefferson Co, births 1873-1914 FI 7:3:77 7:4:104
Jefferson Co, geneal rec avail at the CO State Archives FI 7:2:44
Jefferson Co, hist of Sheriff's department 1859-1984, bk rev FI 7:3:73
Jefferson Co, marr 1881-1895 FI 7:1:24 7:2:50 7:3:75
Lincoln Co, Kanza Cem CO 48:1:8
Marr 1859-1862 abstr from the *Am Monthly Magazine* FI 7:1:6
Mesa Co, Fruita, Elmwood Cem inscr, bk rev GH 41:2:127
Montrose Co, marr 1883-1900, bk rev GH 41:2:128
Our Lady of Guadalupe Ch marr 1860-1881 CO 48:1:12 48:2:48 48:3:72 48:4:98
Park Co, Buckskin Cem FI 7:1:19
Photographers 1859-1901 of Clear Creek, Gilpin, Jefferson, & Park Co FI 7:4:102
Rio Blanco Co, Thornburg Massacre victims CO 48:3:69
Routt Co, Gardner Cem CO 48:3:70
Wedding anniversaries 1943 CO 48:2:39
Weld Co, Pleasant View Cem BGS 19:3:101
COLORADO TERRITORY, District #3, Mount Vernon Precinct, poll bk 1861 & 1869 FI 7:3:68
COLSON, Mary m1904, h John Wagner, Bible rec PGB 18:9:150
COLT, John bc1625, w Mary Fitch & Ann Skinner, CT, lineage SB 8:4:133
Lyman f1862, IA, letter AB 15:3:70
COLTER, Edward Francis b1830, w Margie Dial & Rebecca McNerlyn Osborn, MO, fam rec MSG 7:2:95

COLVER, Edward f1635, New EN, NY, PA, OH, MI, geneal, bk rev GRI 7:1:4

COLVILLE, Christina see John BRADNER

COLVIN, Hannah Francis see John H SMITH

COMBS, Fam hist & letters, bk rev CO 48:3:84

Fam hist EN & VA, bk rev GH 41:1:158

Thomas Hicks bc1780, w Kezziah Hayes (Mayes?), NC, IN, geneal & letters, bk rev GGS 23:3:156 NYR 118:2:121 MA 11:3:77 OK 32:1:6 BAT 16:1:24 CSB 21:1-2:42

COMEAU, Honore b1715, w Marguerite Poirier, Acadia, anc ch AGE 16:4:118

Jonathan b1812, w Elizabeth Brinker, Bible rec OCR 28:2:58

COMPUTER, Anc software rev for Tandy computer GCP 5:3:14

Apple II updates GCP 4:12-5:1:27

Bulletin board systems (privately owned) with geneal sections in US GCP 6:1:44

Buying hints GH 41:1:172 SCS 24:7:143 WRB 10:1:9 SLB 6:6:256

Company interested in geneal GCP 5:6:7

Database managers rev CCS 9:3:94 FRT 8:3:116 WRB 10:2:5

Electronic LDS anc file prototype, use of GCP 5:4:21

Fam Heritage File, software rev GCP 5:4:31

Fam hist writ guide for WordStar, bk rev GH 41:5:152

Fam Reunion III latest release 3.1 for IBM PC computers GCP 4:12-5:1:25

Fam Roots, program rev FRT 8:2:103

Geneal database preparations for on-line res (VA) GCP 4:12-5:1:17 5:2:35

COMPUTER (continued)

Geneal res guide by Andereck & Pence, bk rev NGS 74:4:309

Geneal software avail for the Macintosh GCP 5:3:18

Geneal use guide by Cosgriff, bk rev GH 41:5:152

Geneal, use of NEH 4:1:30

GEnie, use of GCP 5:5:6

Glossary for bulletin board users GCP 4:12-5:1:13

Glossary MIS 19:4:97

Hints for beginners OK 32:1:9

Indexing software guide, bk rev CTA 30:1:52 APG 2:3:29

Kaypro 2000 computer rev GCP 5:6:23

Laser printers, use of GCP 5:2:7

LDS electronic card catalog, use of GCP 5:3:3

Manuscript (for Lotus), rev CGS 18:5:5

Pathway utilities bridge for PAF 2.0 to Roots II GCP 5:5:18

Programs for geneal CTN 20:2:226

Roots II 2.0, use of GCP 4:12-5:1:34

Software rev of Fam Move NPW 6:6:51

Software rev of GEnie GCP 5:6:24 6:1:6

Software rev of Roots II SB 8:2:50

Software rev of WordPerfect GCP 6:1:21

Software selection hints FRT 8:1:6

Software, use of OK 32:2:47

Surge protection GCP 5:5:21

Tafel matching system, use of GCP 5:4:10

Telecommunications, use of GCP 5:2:23 CTN 20:3:406

Use guide by Andereck & Pence, bk rev IAA 1:3:10

Use hints CCS 9:1:28 CTN 19:4:597 MIS 19:1:3

Use hints, computer files FCG 6:4:61

Use hints, database managers FCG 6:3:41

COMPUTER (continued)
Use of BGS 19:2:61 19:3:111
FRT 8:4:164 GR 29:4:137 HF
3:3:105 OK 32:3:86 CC 10:4:6
PN 9:2:27
Word processing FRT 8:2:87
Word processor buying hints CCS
9:2:56
COMSTOCK, Amasa d1789, CT,
cem inscr CTN 19:4:617
CONE, Frances see William
PUGH
CONGER, Alpheus b1802, w
Louise Bibbins, VT, Bible rec
SLV 5:4:7
Emma see Hugh Templeton
THOMSON
CONKLIN, Benjamin b1743, w
Bethia Conkling, Bible rec
DAR 121:3:174
Jacob b1790, Bible rec DAR
121:3:174
James O m1849, w Rebecca
Purdy, Bible rec DAR
121:3:180
Joseph b1764, NJ, Bible rec DAR
121:3:180
Joseph f1779, w Mary ___, NJ,
will abstr DAR 121:3:180
Joshua m1800, w Deborah ___,
Bible rec DAR 121:3:180
Mary d1805, NJ, will abstr DAR
121:3:190
CONKLING, Mary E b1840, Bible
rec DAR 121:3:180
CONKLYN, Jacob b1724, Bible
rec DAR 121:3:174
CONNECTICUT, Apprentices
1637-1900, bk rev,CTA
29:4:132 AW 13:2:71 GFP
36:4:177 GH 41:4:188 PGB
19:1:11 APG 2:3:27 WPG
14:1:47 GGS 23:3:158 NYR
118:4:243 RES 19:1:21 CTN
20:2:321 NTT 7:2:43 RAG
8:3:25 RCP 9:4:130 OZ 9:3:121
STI 27:2:36 NCJ 13:3:178
Ashford, deaths before 1850 CTN
19:4:750 20:1:174 20:2:365
Ashford, marr 1750-1850 CTN
19:4:762 20:1:186 20:2:377
20:3:568

CONNECTICUT (continued)
Avon, deaths before 1850 CTN
20:2:367
Barkhamsted, Cong Ch prayer
list 1838 CTN 20:1:54
Barkhamsted, deaths before 1850
CTN 20:2:369 20:3:556
Bozrah, Gardner Cem CTN
19:4:616
Bozrah, Johnson Cem CTN
19:4:615
Bozrah, Old Leffingwell Cem
CTN 19:4:616
Bozrah, Parker Cem CTN
19:4:616
Brookfield, cem inscr 1745-1985,
bk rev FRT 8:4:200
Clinton, deaths 1809-1878 CTN
20:1:2 20:2:196
Colchester, geneal rec extracts,
bk rev MQ 53:3:224 GH
41:4:188
Colchester, geneal rec 1700s NC
:94:3
Corr & add to *Hist of New
Mild,ford & Bridgewater CT* by
Orcutt CTN 20:3:399
Geneal & fam hist sources, bk
rev CTN 19:4:710
Geneal data from the resolves &
private acts 1837-1838 CTA
30:2:55
Geneal references from the
proceedings of the CT Medical
Soc 1800s-1900s CTA 30:2:73
Granby, town rec vol 1 & 2, bk
rev GH 41:5:164
Hartford District, probate rec
1729-1750, microfiche rev GH
41:4:213
Marr rec avail 1700s-1800s CTN
19:4:578
Middletown, births 1730-1850
CTN 19:4:756 20:1:180
20:2:371 20:3:562
Middletown, centennial address,
bk rev GH 41:6:130
Mort sched 1850-1860-1870, bk
rev CTA 29:4:131
Naugatuck, Cong Ch rec 1781-
1901, bk rev TTH 8:4:96 CTN
20:3:519 GH 41:5:194

CONNECTICUT (continued)
New London Co, Colchester, Second Soc Ch bapt 1741-1796 DM 50:3:133 50:4:181
New London Co, marr before 1850 CTN 19:4:603 20:1:28 20:2:220 20:3:414
New Milford, Center Cem inscr before 1800 CTN 20 :2:233 20:3:422
New Milford, Gallows Hill Cem CTN 20:3:423
New Milford, Gaylordsville Cem CTN 20:3:424
New Milford, Long Mountain Cem CTN 20:3:426
New Milford, Northville Cem CTN 20:3:424
New Milford, Prickett District Cem CTN 20:3:425
Newington, census 1776, bk rev NGS 75:1:67
North Haven, Cong Ch catechisms 1783-1793 CTN 20:1:147
North Haven, hist, bk rev BAT 16:2:75
North Haven, roster of men who served under the King in the pre-Rev period CTN 20:1:134
North Stonington, Civil War, bk rev CTN 20:1:139
Norwich, house lots (original) CTN 20:3:437
Ridgebury, Cong Ch death rec 1840s-1890s CTA 29:4:115
Simsbury, Simsbury Town Meeting hist 1670-1986, bk rev RAG 8:3:26
South Windsor, Old Burying Ground inscr, bk rev NYR 118:3:180
Stamford, Farms School reg 1851 CTA 29:3:71 (1856-1860, 1886) CTA 29:4:121
Suffield, elementary & high school student roster 1906 CTN 20:3:408
Thompson, Bates Cem CTN 19:4:617
Thompson, Old East Thompson Cem CTN 19:4:617

CONNECTICUT (continued)
Thompson, West Thompson Cem CTN 19:4:618 20:1:44
Thompson, Wilsonville Cem CTN 20:1:48
Tolland, hist to 1861, bk rev CTN 19:4:709 GH 41:2:128
Union, hist 1900s, bk rev NYR 118:3:181
V r avail MN 18:1:17
Warren, Old Cem CTN 20:3:427
Wethersfield, births before 1850 CTN 19:4:582 20:1:18 20:2:209 20:3:400
Wethersfield, geneal & biog, bk rev GH 41:6:127
Windsor, geneal rec misc 1635-1703, bk rev CTN 19:4:709 GH 41:1:126 NYR 118:2:113
Woodbridge, East Side Burying Ground cem inscr before 1800 CTN 20:1:48 20:2:231
Woodbridge, Milford Side Cem inscr before 1800 CTN 20:2:232
Woodbridge, North West Cem inscrip before 1800 CTN 20:2:233
Woodstock, estates found in Pomfret probate court rec 1752-1831, bk rev AG 62:3:191
CONNER, James K m1846, w Rebecca Mercer, Bible rec FCG 6:3:50
Martha see James Mattison PENNINGTON
CONNOLLY, Charles Huntley b1854, w Statira Goff, WV, FL, lineage FLG 10:3:98
CONOVER, Thomas d1836, IL, cem inscr IG 23:2:47
CONREY, Surname period, *Clan Conrey*, 3724 Sudbury Ave, Jacksonville FL 32210
CONROE, Lois f1911, h ___ Woodridge, TX, auto MCG 10:2:94
CONROY, Barnard bc1824, w Mary Flannigan, IR, CA, biog sketch SCS 24:6:129
Fam papers EN, bk rev GM 22:8:305

CONROY (continued)
Stephen Bernard b1856, w Jennie Isabelle Fowler, CA, biog sketch SCS 24:6:129
CONVERSE, James H b1842, w Margaret C Romine, MD, biog IG 23:3:82
CONWAY, Edwin bc1610, w Martha Eltonhead, lineage PGB 19:3:52
COOK, Abraham b1731, w Phebe Mills, will QY 14:3:6
Allen b1798, w Lethe Cook, NC, will QY 14:3:6
Daniel b1739, w Rebecca Owen, NJ, geneal AG 62:4:207
Isaac b1763, w Rachel Cook, NC, will QY 14:3:8
Isabelle see Isaac CAMPBELL
John Franklin b1819, w Martha Elizabeth Parks, GA, anc ch GGS 23:2:86
Mary see John McCUBBIN
Paul m1898, w Catherine Vannatta, AR, DC, marr notice TRC 2:1:38
Robert d1919, IA, WY, obit HH 22:1:15
Thomas d1805, w Mary Cook, NC, will QY 14:3:7
William m1826, w Ruth Small, NC, IN, biog GCB 87:2:7
COOKE, F J b1816, NC, TN, TX, auto MCG 10:1:25
Thomas bapt1600, EN, MA, RI, geneal, bk rev NER 141:3:263 AG 62:3:187
William m1832, w Sarah Smith, Bible rec OCR 28:3:113
COOKSON, Thomas bapt1709, PA, in-law dispute LCC 4:4:27
COOPER, Elizabeth b1793, Bible rec DM 50:4:159
Pete C b1850, NE, biog NW 9:2:23
Susan see James McDORMAN
Thomas b1821, w Ellenor Hewson, EN, IL, fam hist sketch WTC 2:2:39
COPELAND, Leander b1836, w K A Putman, NC, TX, geneal NAS 26:1:9

COPELAND (continued)
Roscoe Pulaski m1862, w Frances Jane Holmes, Bible rec FHC 10:4:86
William b1758, w Mary (Polly) (Earle?) IR, SC, anc ch NAS 26:1:13
William d1797, SC, geneal NAS 26:2:39
CORBIN, George R b1836, KY, MO, biog sketch OZ 9:3:108
John b1803, w Caroline Clarissa Dunham, PA, CA, biog sketch SCS 24:6:129
CORMIER, Marie see Charles GAUDET
CORNELL, Brownell b1800, w Dorothy Burdick & Rachel Ellis, NY, geneal, bk rev GH 41:6:155
Smith b1799, w Lucy Ann Wait, NY, geneal, bk rev GH 41:6:156
CORSER, Prudence B see David WHALEY
CORSONS, Surname period, Corsons, 21 Snughaven Rd, Richmond VA 23228
COSBY, Maria bc1797, VA, geneal NGS 75:1:5
Sophronia see James Andrew KIGHT
COSSEY, Kiturra see Ben G W JONES
COTTEN, Ann Mariah see William Washington HARRISON
COTTON, Elizabeth see Thomas KING
COUCH, Charles Fredrick b1841, w Allic Montville, diary BG 8:4:95
Jacob f1775, SC, deed SCM 15:2:91
Laurena see Thomas J CURL
COULTER, Catherine Ann see William F McALLISTER
COUNTRYMAN, Margaret see Henry HORNING
COUPE, Thomas m1840, w Maria White, Bible rec WB 17:3:100
COVEN, Phebe see Abial LANDERS

COVENHOVEN, John m1752, w Lydia Predmore, NJ, PA, geneal, bk rev WPG 13:3:45

COVER, Isabella see James Cornelius WELCH

COVINGTON, Larkin A bc1796, w Ann Minefee, VA, TN, anc ch GGS 23:1:13

William H b1865, w Lola Roebuck, KY, FL, biog sketch IMP 6:3:76

COWANS, Fam members in Civil War IL IG 23:3:83

COWCHE, Agnes see John HANSCOMBE

COWDEN, Lucy A b1840, h Asa M Dowell & John A Wright, IL, MT, obit BGS 19:1:23

Mary see John COLLINS

COWGER, Adam bc1788, w Keziah Davis, KY?, VA?, TN, geneal, bk rev GH 41:2:150

COWING, John C m1854, w Elizabeth Bradshaw, WI, IL, biog WTC 9:4:131

COWLEY, Deborah see David BARRONETT

Deborah see David BARRON or BARRONETT

COX, Amy b1758, h Thomas Cox & Levi Lane, NC, IN, geneal QY 14:1:5

Fam hist VA & KY, bk rev GH 41:1:159

Francis m1694, w Sarah Beakes, geneal QY 14:2:6

James Ray b1870, MO, KS, anc ch MGR 22:3:136

James W b1826, w Hannah Hale, TN, geneal BWG 16:2:141

John f1677, w Joan ___, BM, will abstr BBQ 4:3:31

Mark P f1848, KY, VA, geneal, bk rev KA 22:4:241

Mira E f1869, AR, letter GTP 24:4:77

Surname period, *Cox Heritage*, Janet Damm, SE 310 Camino, Pullman WA 99163

Tabitha Ann see Meredith BLAIR

CPYLE, Flora see Tocie NELISSE

CRABTREE, Priscilla see Richard PRICE

CRAFT, Fam hist US, bk rev NGS 74:3:224

CRAFTON, Martha see Henry HAWKINS

CRAIG, Edward f1717, DE, geneal MAD 27:1:26

John dc1892, w Sally Page, KY, heirs KA 23:1:2

Surname period, *Craig-Links*, POB 645, Twain Harte CA 95383

William m1900, w Maude L Roush, KS, Bible rec TOP 17:3:86

CRAIN, Caroline b1836, Bible rec OZ 5:2:68

CRAMER, Danial b1854, PA, IL, obit CRT 8:4:36

CRANDALL, Herman f1838, IL, preemption affidavit WTC 3:4:162

Samantha Ann see Andrew McCLURE

CRANE, Fam letters 1900s YTD 5:2:37

Surname period, *Crane Flock Newsletter*, POB 965, Lehigh Acres FL 33970-0965

CRARY, Joseph Smith b1795, w Mehitable Stewart, NY, IL, geneal WTC 4:2:65

CRAVEN, Peter f1744, VA, NC, geneal, bk rev NCJ 13:2:120

CRAVER, Alexander b1819, w Lydia Chadwick, NC, IL, obit CRT 8:2:20

CRAWFORD, Alexander b1715, w Mary McPheeters, IR, VA, anc ch GGL 6:4:147

Fam hist suppl ST & MO 1977-1985, bk rev MSG 7:1:49

Jane Elisabeth see Benj Franklin BAKER

Jesse b1784, Bible rec YTD 7:1:5

Jesse f1812, TX, declaration YTD 3:1:2

Surname periodical, *The Crawford Exchange*, 121 S 168, Seattle WA 98148-1611

45

CRAWFORD (continued)
William d1805, GA, anc ch THT 15:1:27
CRAWLEY, Margaret C see John Ardis Bradley WARD
CRAYNE, Nong Emma see Perry Maxwell WOODALL
CREAMER, James b1817, w Ann Twiford, VA, fam rec TN 7:6:82
CREE, Robert Sr bc1735, w Janet Hamilton, North IR, anc ch HL 5:3:87
CREECH, Celia see Joseph BLAIR
Sarah see Peley (Sturgeon) SHORT
CREED, Fam marr NC, bk rev NCJ 13:2:120
CREEGAR, Wilhelmina b1825, OH, anc ch PF 16:1:30
CREEK, Killean bc1750, w Margaret ___, GE, IN, anc ch WB 17:1:32
CRESAP, Thomas b1694, w Hannah Johnson, EN, MD, geneal, bk rev GH 41:5:191 VAG 31:3:227
CRESSON, Cristina b1650, BE, anc ch CR 19:3:130
CRESWICK, Minnie M see Albert H ELLIS
CREWS, Hannah see Isaac H HOLLINGSWORTH
CRICE, John C Breckenridge b1863, w Caroline Rich, KY, IL, anc ch MIS 19:3:69
CRIDER, Frederick bc1805, w Mary ___, NC, children BWG 16:2:147
CRILL, Jerry b1858, w Sarah Gilbert, IN, ID, geneal, bk rev GH 41:4:205
William, w Mary Catherine Frantz, IN, geneal, bk rev GFP 37:2:73
CRISLER, Aaron b1775, w Susannah (Susan) Baker, VA, OH, geneal, bk rev GH 41:2:150
CRISPE, Benjamin f1636, w Bridget ___, MA, children AG 62:1:25

CRITTENDEN, George f1890, w Eliza Bedell, MO, geneal OZ 5:1:1
CROCKETT, Samuel f1715, VA, geneal, bk rev GH 41:6:156
CRONER, Susanna see Tobias MUSSER
CROOM, Mary E A Hare see Daniel HICKS
CROSBY, Fam direct, bk rev RAG 8:3:23
Phebe see Elijah ADAMS
William Chase b1806, w Mary Wilson & Susan W Dinsmore, NH, MA, CA, TX, biog GR 29:4:161
CROSS, Janett b1872, Bible rec BGS 19:3:115
CROSSLAND, Fam hist 1775–1986 US, bk rev OK 32:2:44
Lemuel Pinckney bc1775, w Rodicia Leek, EN, NC, geneal, bk rev GH 41:1:159
CROSSLEY, Lemuel Pickney bc1775, EN, CN, geneal, bk rev FRT 8:3:153
CROSSMAN, John bc1588, EN, MA, geneal, bk rev GH 41:4:205
CROSSWHITE, G H f1866, TN, letter BWG 16:1:50
CROUCH, William Albert mc1822, w Laurena Garrett, MO, AR, geneal YTD 4:1:4
CROWDER, William bc1730, w Hannah Rous, NY, biog, bk rev FRT 8:1:50
CROWTHER, Alfred b1835, w Agnes Rushworth, EN, IL, obit CRT 8:4:37
CRUMBAKER, Samuel William b1854, w Martha Elizabeth Lawrence, OH, WA, fam rec EWA 24:2:118
CRUMBLEY, Myrtle d1915, AL, death AFH 8:3:81
CULBERTSON, Henry W b1777, w Mary Taylor, fam rec BGS 19:2:63
William bc1789, w Sarah Elizabeth ___, NC, MO, children OZ 5:3:125

CULBREATH, Augustus Edward b1832, w Lucy Elizabeth Richardson, GA, AR, anc ch TRC 2:2:103

CULLABY, Mr f1845, OR, visit with CT 7:2:15

CULLEN, John b1811, IR, NY, WI, geneal, bk rev NYR 118:3:182

John b1811, w Olive Wilkie, IR, NY, WI, geneal, bk rev PGB 18:9:156 GH 41:2:150

CULLUMBER, George H b1827, Bible rec LOG 8:6:64

CULVER, Henry d1730, w Rebecca Finch, MD, geneal MD 28:4:416

Sarah Lizzie see Jacob Mathis ARANT

CULVERWELL, Richard J A b1802, w Mary Ann Tuell, MD, CA, biog sketch SCS 24:9:181

CUMMINGS, Elizabeth see John HARMON

William J b1830, w Nancy Caroline Rebecca O'Pry, LA, AR, anc ch YTD 7:1:15

CUMMINS, Robert bc1770, w Delphia Ballard, VA, biog EWA 24:1:71

CUNDIFF, Eleanor A d1886, h ____ Cundiff, OH, IL, obit DWC 13:3:92

CUNNINGHAM, Fam rec corr to *The Ancient & Honorable Artillery Company* by Roberts NEH 4:4:200

CURL, Thomas J m1833, w Laurena Couch, Bible rec YTD 4:1:17

William H m1828, w Annie ____, Bible rec OZ 7:2:75

CURRY, Agnes Belle see Jeremiah Michael KENNEDY

Ora Mae f1927, TX, letter STK 14:4:190

Thomas, w Sarah McCarthy, geneal, bk rev GH 41:2:150

CURTIN, John Joseph b1885, w Elsie Needham, AA, biog sketch TI 86:11:12

CURTIS, Rhoda see Thomas TRUESDELL

CUSHING, Fam hist 1905-1969 with suppl, bk rev CTN 20:1:138

William d1493, EN, anc ch AW 13:1:22

CUSHMAN, Martha see Nathaniel HOLMES

CUST, Annaritta d1797, geneal, bk rev BCG 16:4:142

CUSTER, Arnoldus d1739, w Rebecca Nuzam, GE, PA, anc ch STK 14:4:185

CUSTIN, Benjamin b1780, w Rosannah Lamont & Phebe Bartram, NY, OH, geneal CTN 20:3:522

CUTHBERT, John bc1804, w Ellen ____, IR, anc ch GGL 6:1-2:60

CZECHOSLOVAKIA, Geneal rec avail in CO ND 6:4:6

Geneal res aid, the Embassy of the Czechoslovak Socialist Republic ND 6:4:15

Geneal res collect ND 6:3:9

Geneal res hints RD 87:2:10

Geneal words in EN OCN 10:1:11

Hist sketch & modern day culture GCP 5:6:29

Imm pass lists to New Orleans 1879-1899 & Galveston 1896-1906 vol 2, bk rev FRT 8:1:50

Legislators (US) with CZ anc, col times to present, bk rev MD 28:4:466

Lib (US) with geneal holdings ND 6:2:19

Months of the year with EN translation CR 19:3:111

Moravia, glass industry, hist sketch ND 6:2:10

Natives in Louisville, Boulder, Co CO ND 6:4:4

Ship pass list 1852 on board the *Maria* ND 6:3:2

Ship pass list 1879 from Bremen to NY on board the *S S Donau* ND 6:5:12

Ship pass lists 1879 ND 6:3:10 6:4:8

CZECHOSLOVAKIA (continued)
Ship pass list to Galveston 1880 on board the *America* ND 6:2:12

Superstitious beliefs in TX ND 6:5:2

Surnames, common ND 6:4:2

Surnames & village of origin ND 6:4:10

Villages of origin, names abstr from Bohemian tombstones ND 6:5:8

CZWIKI, Mary see Alois ARTINGER

D'AUGE, James b1660, VA, geneal, bk rev NCJ 13:1:54

D'WOLFE, Eliza see Wm VERNON

DACHSTATTER, Georg f1709, GE, NY, geneal, bk rev NYR 118:4:248

DAHLBERG, Mary E b1876, CO, obit FI 7:4:101

DAILEY, William H m1853, w Vesta Hadley, Bible rec HJA 11:3:182

DAKOTA TERRITORY, Pennington Co, Rochford, census 1880 BHN 20:3:103

DALE, Catherine see Nicholas STRAW

John f1683, w Katherine Fletcher, EN, MD, geneal, bk rev GH 41:2:160 41:4:205

DALEY, James m1810, w Katharine R Groat, Bible rec TFP 2: :87

DALLEY, Hannah see Robert McCOOL

DALRYMPLE, Fam rec corr to *The Hist Of Bethel ME* by Lapham NEH 4:3:164

Nathaniel m1836, w Electa Haskins, Bible rec BG 8:2:35

DALTON, Edwin b1849, w Ida Jeanette Lee, IL, anc ch KIL 15:3:32

Henry f1884, CA, will SCS 24:9:176

Jane Elizabeth see John William FOOTE

DALTON (continued)
Surname period, *The Journal of the Dalton Geneal Soc*, 2 Harewood Close, Reigate, Surrey RH 2 0HE England – births, marr, obit, Witney Daltons, Am Yorkshire Daltons

DALY, Arthur f1881, Kilchleagh, geneal GGL 6:1-2:24

DAMERON, Surname period, *The Dameron-Damron Fam Newsletter*, Kathleen Near, 1754 Darrah Ave, Simi Valley CA 93063

DANCER, S P b1843, Bible rec FP 30:2:66

DANDRIDGE, John d1804, w Elizabeth ____, VA, pension appl RAG 8:2:32

DANIEL, Rebecca see William WHITAKER

Sarah see Eperson CASTLE

Solomon dc1863, MO, estate OZ 8:3:122

DANIELS, Brittain bc1814, w Mary Hibbard, KY, geneal HF 3:3:132

Enoch Jr bc1800, w Delilah ____, GA, FL, lineage FLG 10:4:144

DARBY, Fam hist MD, TN, AL, bk rev NTT 7:1:3

DARE, Elizabeth J see James M ROBINSON

Mary see Peter FLICKINGER

DARWIN, Sally H see Henry P NETTLES

DAUB, Mathias b1759, w Margaretha Laux, GE, anc ch MCI 5:1:25

DAUGHERTY, Allethea see John H SHEPARD

Fam hist US, bk rev GRI 7:8:59

Surname period, *Daughtery Fam Assoc Newsletter*, POB 41213, Plymouth MN 55441

DAVENPORT, Surname period, *The Davenport Newsletter*, 3510 McMillan, Tyler TX 75701

DAVIDSON, Brackett b1796, w Delilah Hardison, VA, MO, children OZ 5:2:78

DAVIDSON (continued)
Louisa Catherine see John Newton EARNEST
Mary Anne see James Alexander STRODE
Nancy see Francis M CALDWELL
Thompson E f1832, KY, deed TA 22:1:25
DAVIES, Charles f1725, w Hannah Matson, PA, NC, geneal, bk rev NGS 74:3:224
Charles f1725, w Hannah Matson, PA, NC, geneal, bk rev AG 62:3:185
DAVIS, Adaline m1878, h James Askew, TX, Bible rec YTD 7:2:25
Amos see Almira HARVEY
Andrew Jackson b1832, w Catherine Zachary, IN, WA, biog sketch YV 19:2:51
Benjamin Jr b1903, GA, NY, biog AA 8:1:27
Edward bc1734, WV, KY, geneal, bk rev NYR 118:4:246
Elizabeth Hiester see Moore Lee PORTEUS
Elizabeth see Nathan CLIFTON
Esther see William LAMPTON
Fam births & marr MD 1600s MAD 27:4:130
Fam hist NC, bk rev NYR 118:2:122
George Washington m1861, w Sarah E Ezell, Bible rec WTC 15:1:34
J J C m1874, w Sophronia Ann Edwards, KY, Bible rec KA 23:2:107
James A m1841, w Poly Ann Cloe, Bible rec YTD 7:2:25
Jefferson f1863, biog of Civil War days, bk rev REG 85:3:271
John f1714, w Anne Purefoy, EN, MA, geneal, bk rev NYR 118:1:58
John W m1859, w Armazinda Lack, Bible rec OZ 8:1:35
Katherine see John GODFREY
Keziah see Adam COWGER

DAVIS (continued)
Leslie E b1892, ME, memoirs BC 11:1:3
Leslie E f1910, ME, reflections BC 11:4:1
Louis bc1858, MS, auto FTH 10:1-2:121
Margie P see Thomas Clyde BUTLER
Mark P b1769, SC, Bible rec YTD 4:1:1
Martha see James D FOWLER
Mary Elizabeth see Henry Baker GARNHAM
Mattie Eldora see George Pickens BRAUNER
May Florence see Fred Almyr DODGE
Nancy Jane see William Calvin DENNIS
Patty Blackburn, geneal, bk rev NCJ 13:3:184
Rebecca Ann b1840, Bible rec NTT 7:3:118
Rebecca see Jacob BARKMAN
Robert b1752, w Nancy Agnes Caldwell, VA, MO, fam rec MSG 7:3:156
Sarah see Ignatius HARDIN
Surname period, *Davis Fam Newsletter*, POB 28215, Sacramento CA 95828 – bk rev, coat of arms
Thomas b1711, EN, VT, NH, MA, geneal, bk rev CCS 9:1:25
William Dunbar m1828, w Maria Morse, Bible rec NCJ 13:4:198
William Franklin b1848, w Mary Eliza Vincent, ME, geneal TEG 7:3:140
William Peck b1809, w Angelina J Pratt, PA, CA, biog sketch SCS 24:1:17
DAVITT, Michael b1846, IR, biog TI 86:11:36
DAWES, Henry L m1844, w Electa A Sanderson, Bible rec BG 8:3:70
Surname period, *Dawes Fam Newsletter*, 1535 Macken Ave, Crescent City CA 95531 – births, marr, memorials

DAWLEY, Catherine Lenora see Alfred FELLER or FELLOWS
DAWSON, Elizabeth d1799, IR, TN, anc ch TB 13:3:38
Elizabeth see Lorenzo Dow VAWTER
Emma see Cornelius Britiffe TULLY
Ezekiel m1808, w Hannah McFadden, AL, TN, geneal YTD 2:1:1
Jennie E see David HARMON
Mary Patience see Arch S DOB-BINS
DAY, Surname period, *Day Researcher*, 319 Houston Lake Blvd, Centerville GA 31028 - marr NC, fam NJ & AL & VA & KY, cem, deaths, ch reg, Bible rec, imm, wills, census 1860 TN, obit
DEAN, Catherine see John SAGAR
DEAR, Elizabeth see Daniel MORSE
DEARBORN, Lydia Elizabeth see William Bradford BULLARD
Sylvanus b1809, ME, Bible rec DE 11:2:52
DEARDORFF, Benjamin Franklin f1908, w Frances Tombaugh, WA, fam hist AB 15:4:99
DEAYARMAN, Anna see Joseph B FRIEDT
DEBURGH, William Fitzadelm f1175, IR, fam hist notes, microfiche rev GH 41:6:167
DECHAZEAU, Jean bc1670, FR, VA, geneal SGE 28:122:49
DECRENAY, Anne Henrietta Catherine see Gabriel Louis LeGRAND
DEETER, Isaac b1787, w Elizabeth Kaylor, MD?, PA, geneal NFB 19:2:32
DEFORE, William J b1839, w Mary O Pence, GA, anc ch NC :93:8
DEHART, Sarah Jane b1853,h James W Carson & James William Blair, KY, biog sketch EK 22:4:21

DELANEY, Catherine T see Edward M ROSS
DELARAUE, Jacques b1623, w Anne Fosse, FR, QB, geneal, bk rev RIR 13:1:3 SGS 36:4:205 NYR 118:3:181 GH 41:1:162 CO 48:4:104 FRT 8:3:153
DELAWARE, Chester Bethel burials before 1900 DJ 4:1:5 4:2:31
Church rec misc, bk rev MAD 27:4:149
Coffen Run Cem DJ 4:3:58
Divorces 1897 MAD 27:1:16 27:2:49
Holy Rinity (Old Swedes) Ch bapt rec 1713-1762 DJ 4:1:11 4:2:37 4:3:65
Kent & Sussex Co, v r 1686-1800, bk rev NGS 74:4:310 GH 41:2:128 MAD 27:4:148 WPG 13:4:41 MD 28:4:462
Kent Co, census 1684 MAD 27:1:14
Kent Co, Hollandsville, marr & deaths 1867-1870 abstr from the copybk of Georgina Marie Cooper DJ 4:3:62
Kent Co, land rec gleanings 1600s MAD 27:4:136
Kent Co, tax list 1726 MAD 27:4:132
Kent Co, wills & admin 1680-1800 index, bk rev MAD 27:1:38
Marr 1884 MAD 27:3:108
Mil rec, muster roll of officers, non-commissioned officers, & privates detached from the 2nd Reg 1st Brigade of DE Mil commanded by Lt Col David Nevin 1814 MAD 27:4:134
Mil rec, names from a return of Capt Benjamin Noxon's Company in the pay of the 3 lower co 1758 DJ 4:1:23
Milford, hist, bk rev MAD 27:2:64
New Castle Co, Brandywine Hundred, marr 1842-1867 MAD 27:1:18 27:2:50 27:3:96 27:4:142

DELAWARE (continued)
New Castle Co, tax assessment 1816-1817, bk rev MAD 27:4:150 GH 41:2:128 MD 28:4:463
Revolutionary War, soldiers (pensioners) residing in KY MAD 27:2:52
Sussex Co, census 1860, bk rev MAD 27:2:72
Sussex Co, orphans court 1760-1764 index DJ 4:1:21 4:2:44 4:3:72
Sussex Co, wills & admin 1680-1800 index, bk rev MAD 27:1:38
War of 1812, muster roll of 2nd Company of artillery attached to 1st brigade DE mil 1814 MAD 27:2:94
War of 1812, muster roll of Major C P Comegys reg 1813 MAD 27:3:95
Wilmington, direct 1814, bk rev MAD 27:3:117
Wilmington, hist of original settlements, bk rev GH 41:6:131
DELCOUR, Adelaide Harriette see Louis CHARBONEAU
Nicholas B f1780, FR, BE, CN, NY, MO, geneal, bk rev MSG 7:3:169
DELOACH, Riley f1850, GA, bounty land appl SGE 28:121:24
William f1745, w Eleanor Collins, VA, will abstr SGE 28:123:44
DELONG, George m1903, TX, 50th anniversary STK 15:1:16
DELOZIER, Perrin L see Juliana PAGE
DEMAR, John Erskine b1694, w Catherine Surplus, EN, NH, geneal, bk rev WPG 13:3:43
DEMARANVILLE, Irenia b1808, h Moses B Chapin, NH, IL, obit AH 14:1:21
DEMARIS, Fam corr to *The Demaris Tree*, bk rev SGS 36:4:207

DEMORA, Maria Antonia see Jose Antonio CHIRINO
DEMOSS, Surname period, *DeMoss Information Exchange*, RR 3 Box 222, Carthage IL 62321-9803 - taxes VA & PA, census 1860 OH, Thomas of MD, cem MD, Civil War, marr KY, census 1860 AL
DEMTER, Anton Barthold bapt1695, w Ilse Catharine Siepken, GE, anc ch AGS 28:2:69
DEMUYNCK, Barbara see Johannes BUYSE
DENMARK, Aalborg, Aistrup, marr 1832 MN 18:2:69
Geneal terms in EN WRB 10:2:15 OCN 10:1:11
Hist of imm to Am, bk rev OC 24:3:127
Hist sketch MP 3:2:72
DENNEY, Charles Wesley see Adelaide HOTHERSALL
DENNIS, Robert see Sarah HOWLAND
William Calvin b1830, w Nancy Jane Davis, KY, geneal, bk rev NGS 75:2:156
DENNISON, Sarah see Abel S HINCKLEY
DENT, Fam cem St Francois MO MSG 7:3:157
DERBY, Sylvester b1780, w Mary Richardson VT, NY, anc ch WTC 1:4:107
DERNIERE, J M C De Les d1843, w Elizabeth Atkinson, NS, cem inscr GN 5:3:141
DERR, Philip b1750, w Barbara Koogle, MD, geneal, bk rev WMG 3:3:139 GH 41:5:191
DERRAR, John b1815, w Rosa ___, GE, OH, anc ch CPY 16:1:17
DERTHICK, Fam hist EN & US, bk rev TOP 17:1:3
Fam hist, bk rev CSB 21:1-2:40
John f1683, w Susanna Ransom, EN, MA, geneal, bk rev RES 18:2:81

DESHAZO, Louis f1829, w Mary Littlejohn, SW, MS, AL, geneal SGE 28:121:47

DETAMORE, Jacob b1831, NE, anc ch CCS 8:4:138

DETAR, William f1841, w Sarah Jane ____, IA, fam rec HH 22:1:20

DETHICK, John b1674, CT, geneal, bk rev CCS 8:4:132

DETTY, Jesse David b1819, w Mary Gedney, OH, KS, obit KL 7:4:14

DEUTRICH, Katharina see William HEMANN

DEUTSCHE, William Sr b1825, w Dorothea Hinze, GE, IL, biog WTC 8:4:89

DEVOUR/DEVORE, Alfred see Elizabeth HAWKINS

DEWEESE, William bc1732, VA, anc ch FF 15:4:133

DEWEY, Experience see John GILLETT

DEWITT, George Washington b1800, w Minerva Pope? & Malinda Stow, VA, MO, children OZ 6:2:76

DEWOLF, John b1751, w Susanna ____, fam rec BCG 16:1:25

Rachel see Peter STRONG

DEYN, Jane see William PRESTON

DIAL, Margie see Edward Francis COLTER

DICK, Harmon f1786, w Margaret ____, PA, OH, geneal, bk rev OCR 28:3:151

DICKERSON, James b1790, KY, geneal, bk rev GH 41:4:205

DICKEY, John Jay b1842, w Sara Ida Phillips, KY, diary index, bk rev GH 41:2:150

DICKINS, Fam hist VA, TN 7:5:67 7:6:84

DICKINSON, Benjamin f1789, w Mary ____, BM, will abstr BBQ 4:3:31

Enos C m1846, w Sarah A Gibbs, WI, Bible rec GFP 37:2:68

Martha see J R ERVIN

DICKINSON (continued)
Richard b1827, w Mary S Whitley, AL, MS, anc ch MCA 6:1:34

DICKIRSON, James bc1790, KY, geneal, bk rev GFP 37:2:72

DICKSON, Mariah see Jacob BARKMAN

Mary see Daniel Hayes MAHONEY

William M b1795, w Lavinia Steele, SC?, anc ch TRC 2:2:102

DIEDERICH, Barbara d1892, h Michael Diederich, IL, obit CRT 8:4:32

DIEHL, George Sr d1918, w Louise Goebel, GE, IL, obit CRT 8:4:30

DIEKMAN, Wilhelmina d1935, IL, obit WTC 4:2:48

DIERKS, Catherine see Joseph YELKIN

DIETZMAN, Fam cem Iowa Co WI WI 34:1:36

DIGREGORIO, Fam hist IY, bk rev MA 11:3:77

DIKE, James d1792, w Mary Narramore, CT, cem inscr CTN 19:4:617

DILDINE, Fam rec misc 1709-1850 US, bk rev WPG 14:1:52

DILL, James bc1766, w Helena Kimble, PA, TX, fam rec YTD 3:2:10

DILLARD, Elizabeth see Charles DUNCAN

DILTEY, Hans Johann Jacob b1679, GE, NY, geneal, bk rev GH 41:4:205

DIMICK, Cordelia see George W THISLER

DIMON, Thomas f1650, CT, geneal, bk rev MI 32:3:96

DINSMORE, Susan W see William Chase CROSBY

DINWIDELY, William see Hanah ALEXANDER

DIRKE, Cornelius Eberadus b1824, w Antje Oetten Ulderke, GE, IL, geneal, bk rev FRT 8:2:106

DISBROW, Hannah see Jabez SHERWOOD

DISHEROON, John Timothy Crenshaw b1844, w Cornelia Ran Sitz, GA, AL, anc ch PT 29:2:49

DIX, Andrew N m1848, w Susan Waite, MA, Bible rec CO 48:4:95

DIXON, Mary see Ezekiel GULLETT

Polley see John B JESSE

Sally f1862, MS, auto FTH 10:3-4:69

Sarah see Joseph WISBY

DOAN, Rachel see Isaac HINES

DOANE, Ezra f1835, MA, IL, rec abstr GTP 24:4:70

Fam reunion report 1986, bk rev GH 41:5:191

DOBBINS, Arch f1867, AR, biog TRC 2:2:80

Arch S b1827, w Mary Patience Dawson, TN, AR, biog TRC 2:1:27

Surname period, *The Dobbins Files*, Rt 1 Box 48 B1, Farmersville TX 75031

DOCKRAY, William bc1804, w Zilpha Scott, NC, AL, fam rec AGS 28:2:85

DOCKSTADER, Fam hist GE & NY, bk rev TS 29:2:69

Georg f1709, w Anna Elisabeth ___, GE, NY, geneal, bk rev GH 41:3:168

DODD, Catherine see Alexander Ayers LAWSON

DODGE, Frank b1846, w Anna Hills, IL, CA, biog note SCS 24:3:61

Fred Almyr b1859, w May Florence Davis, IL, CA, biog sketch SCS 24:3:61

George Asa b1844, w Louisa Wait, IL, CA, biog note SCS 24:3:61

DODGEN, Fam hist EN & US, bk rev AGS 28:2:56

DODSON, John b1831, w Cordelia Corilla Ambrose, Bible rec KFR 13: :10

DOEPP, William b1831, w Pauline Stoltze, GE, IL, biog WTC 6:1:21 (fam hist) WTC 8:3:13

DOHNER, Surname period, *Dohner Fam Newsletter*, 4071 Ranch de la Vista B1 #68, Palmdale CA 93551 - reunions, queries, obit, cem

DOLBEER, Cutter m1831, w Abba Terry, Bible rec GF 8:4:31

DOLLARHIDE, Jesse bc1785, w Nancy Pierson, NC, OH, IN, anc ch GCP 5:3:31

DOMINY, Fam hist 1795-1985 US, bk rev KK 25:2:37

DONALDSON, Thomas b1816, w Mahalia Huggins, anc ch FF 15:4:134

DONNIG, Friedrich Wilhelm b1811, w Christine Marie Ilsabein Schnake, anc ch FF 15:4:133

DOOLEY, Moses d1822, KY, OH, geneal, bk rev VAG 31:1:67

Samuel b1799, w Linnie Allen & Polly Stevens, OH, MN, biog sketch MN 18:4:170

DOPP, Surname period, *Dopp Fam Newsletter*, 503 Welty St, Greensburg PA 15601

DORMAN, Stephen m1785, w Roxana Grover, Bible rec BG 8:3:72

DOSSEY, Kintchen Dudley bc1798, w Elizabeth Charter, anc ch LAB 2:3:49

DOTY, Anna see James PARKER

DOUCETTE, Fam hist FR & CN, bk rev GEN 12:2:31

DOUD, Harriet E b1841, OH, biog TFP 2: :92

DOUGHERTY, Cornelius d1887, IR, IL, anc ch CCS 8:4:137

Isaac bc1793, w Rachel Slimp, VA, MS, anc ch TRC 1:1:44

DOUGHTY, Surname period, *The Doughty Tree*, POB 203, Mays Landing NJ 08330 - fam tradition, fam ME, John C & desc

DOUGLAS, Susan J see Thomas R PASSONS

DOUGLASS, Sarah see Nathaniel SMITH Jr
DOWDELL, Sarah Martha see James Hill FULLILOVE
DOWDY, Grover Garfield Sr b1896, w Lee Ella Gautney, AL, anc ch NAS 26:1:17
DOWELL, Asa A see Lucy A COWDEN
DOWNS, Elizabeth see John WALTRIP
DOWSETT, Thomasine, h Thomas Hale, MA, EN anc NER 141:2:128
DOYLE, Minnie L see Henley R BREWER
DOZIER, Fam hist Norfolk Co VA, bk rev GH 41:6:156
Mary Frances see Enoch WHITEHURST
DRAGUNAS, Anthony A m1938, w Ruth Richter, marr lic CPY 15:4:87
DRAKE, Dorothy L see David P PARADIS
Ernie b1887, w Alberta Brydsen, WI, WA, biog sketch YV 19:1:12
Eura Eaton see Christopher Santford CHRITTON
Fam rec corr to *Fam Hist & Geneal* by Salisbury NEH 4:4:201
Lewis m1791, w Mary ___, Bible rec HL 1:3:74
Samuel f1646, CT, NY, biog AG 62:3:143
DRALLE, August b1851, w Catherine Mohnman, GE, IL, biog sketch WTC 8:4:90
DRAPER, Joseph m1779, w Lydia Benson, Bible rec TFP 7: :69
DRENNON, Agnes see John CHRISTY
DREW, Nathaniel f1790, SC, deed SCM 15:3:162
DREWS, Sophia see Henry Martin John KRABBE
DRIMAN, Martha Ann see Columbus WHITMIRE
DRIVER, Gideon b1799, MD, PA, anc ch CCS 8:4:137

DRUM, Andrew f1886, w Mary Drum, MI, will abstr FG 29:2:49
DRUMMOND, Margaret (Campbell) see Alexander MAGRUDER
DRURY, Hugh b1616, MA, geneal, bk rev SB 8:4:138 BAT 16:4:169
DRYSDALE, Fam hist 1788-1985 CN, bk rev GEN 12:4:25
DUDGEON, Richard f1790, w Sarah Grant, IR, PA, OH, geneal, bk rev FRT 8:4:200 GH 41:3:168
DUDLEY, Edward f1637, EN, VA, geneal, bk rev GH 41:5:191
Edward f1637, EN, VA, geneal, bk rev FRT 8:4:201
Elizabeth b1727, CT, anc ch CIC 3:4:95
Fam hist EN & southern US, bk rev RAG 8:4:23 FCF Summer-Fall 1987
Judith see Lewis BOOKER
Thomas b1576, EN, MA, geneal, microfiche rev GH 41:2:163
DUGAN, George William b1810, geneal, bk rev OZ 6:2:81
DUGGAN, Frances see David FUTCH
Johanna see Patrick DUNN
DUHRING, Fredericke see Julius Frederick VIEDT
DULUDE, Octavia see Fredrick Lambert BENOIT
DUMAS, Pierre b1756, w Mary Huntley, FR, NY, geneal, bk rev GH 41:5:191
DUNBAR, Anstice b1786, RI, anc ch BG 8:1:9
DUNCAN, Alexander m1820, w Helen Herd, ST, AA, fam hist ANE 20: :10
Charles b1751, w Elizabeth Dillard, VA, geneal OPC 18:2:34
Effie Lenora see William Right HOPKINS
James Russell b1839, w Sara E Scott, KY, MO, biog sketch SNS 3:6:5
Matilda see David MORRISON

DUNCAN (continued)
Peter E bc1808, w Edith Reid, SC, GA, anc ch NAS 25:4:129
Rush Floyd b1846, w Leila Fuquay, MO, CA, anc ch NW 10:1:49
DUNDASS, Samuel Rutherford f1849, MO, CA, diary of trip to CA 1849-1850, bk rev BCG 16:4:149
DUNGEY, John Wesley b1833, w Hannah Ann Scoggins, ST, anc ch GGL 6:3:107
DUNHAM, Caroline Clarissa see John CORBIN
Nathaniel bc1662, w Mary ___, MA, rec misc AG 62:1:5
DUNKER, Hist sketch in Newton Co MO OZ 5:2:47
DUNLAP, Thomas b1842, EN, TX, anc ch CR 19:1:5
DUNLOP, John f1682, ST, US, biog NGS 74:3:171
DUNN, James bc1780, w Dicy Martin, EN, VA, geneal, bk rev GH 41:4:205
Patrick b1825, w Johanna Duggan, IR, MO, CA, biog sketch WTC 17:4:112
Thomas Jefferson b1845, KY, IL, diary abstr 1900, 1908-1911, 1915-1916 CRT 8:2:5
DUNSON, William Henry b1833, w Delila Evaline Paty, GA, AL, anc ch NAS 26:2:66
DUPUIS, Zoe see Jean Pierre LABORDE
DUPY, Surname period, *Dupy Fam Newsletter*, 1715 Enclave Pkwy #307, Houston TX 77077
DURHAM, Allen f1888, TN, letter BWG 16:2:151
DURIER, Jean bapt1654, NJ, geneal, bk rev NYR 118:1:55
DURKEE, Surname period, *Durkee Fam Newsletter*, 3753 E 15th St, Long Beach CA 90804
DURLAND, Mary M see William Henry GOBLE
DURNBAUGH, Samuel b1791, w Margaret Holverstot, OH, anc ch LOG 8:6:60

DURRANCE, William Hutto b1815, w Sarah Harriet Robertson, GA, FL, lineage FLG 10:4:150
DURST, John M b1797, w Harriet M Jamison, anc ch PT 29:3:114
DUTCH GENEALOGY, Households in US population censuses 1850-1860-1870, bk rev GH 41:4:185 NYR 118:4:242
DUTTON, Phebe A (Howard) see Samuel GOODRICH
DYE, George d1909, IL, obit CRT 8:4:38
EAGLE, Sophia see Jesse HODGE
EAGLESON, William Hugh b1818, w Josephine Louise Godard, IR, LA, anc ch KSL 11:4:125
EAGLESTON, Benjamin f1792, MD, geneal TNB 2:4:2
EAGLESTONE, John bc1673, MD, geneal TNB 2:3:3
EAKIN, Maria see Andrew McCORNACK
EARLEY, Simeon R f1847, w Almira E Earley, GA, will TCG 6:4:26
EARLY, Annie see Thomas A MCCLONE
Thomas f1810, KY, geneal HF 3:1:23
EARNEST, H B f1876, TX, biog STK 15:1:10
John Newton b1831, w Louisa Catherine Davidson, AL, anc ch NAS 26:2:43
John Ramsey b1823, w Sarah Hazel McClure & Bonde Arnn, TN, KS, MO, children OZ 8:2:63
EATON, Fam hist NS 1760-1975, bk rev RAG 8:3:26
John f1640, w Anne ___, NS, MA, geneal, bk rev CTN 19:4:713
EBAUGH, Emma Guinn see Benjamin Wilson HANNAH

ECCLES, Angelina see Robert BLACKWELL
Joseph T b1807, w Jane L Anderson, KY, IL, biog sketch FF 15:3:29
EDDOWES, Ralph b1751, w Sarah Kenrick, EN, PA, Bible rec NER 141:4:309
EDDY, Mercy Stafford f1861, VT, diary abstr 1861-1883 BAT 16:2:52 16:4:159
Oscar see Mercy STAFFORD
EDGAR, Alexander f1835, w Elizabeth Rogers, CT, TX, fam hist sketch KSL 11:3:70
EDGE, Fam hist KY, MD, PA, EN, bk rev WCK 20:2:31
EDGMON, Rebecca Pierce f1884, TN, letter BWG 16:2:151
EDMONDS, Amanda Virginia f1859, VA, journals 1859-1867, bk rev MAD 27:3:115
EDSON, Surname period, *The Edsonian*, 138 S Main St, Brewer ME 04412
EDWARDS, Benjamin f1825, MS, TX, biog YTD 6:2:27
Ethelinda see Edward LEWIS
Henry bc1800, KY, geneal, bk rev CR 19:2:62
James Johnson see Juliana PAGE
Mary (Stanborough) see John HORSINGTON
Millie see Lazarus EDWARDS
Sophronia Ann see J J C DAVIS
William f1770, SC, GA, geneal, bk rev GGS 23:1:45
Wm S m1837, w Sarh P Patrick, KY, Bible rec KA 23:2:103
EDY, Cyna see Richard HAGADORN
EENIGENBURG, Harry b1859, w Louisa Phillips, IL, biog WTC 4:2:47
EGGEN, Rosa see John S HOERNER
EGLE, Jacob f1878, w Barbara Roth & Mary Elizabeth Mosier, PU, NE, geneal, bk rev WPG 13:4:45

EISENHAUER, Mary Catharina see Johann Philipp BERGHAUS II
ELAM, Joel d1797, w Phebe Hill, VA, anc ch FF 15:4:131
Mary see Francis P LEMASTER
ELDER, David f1835, PA, diary TQ 11:1:8
Fam hist Phillips Co AR TRC 2:2:89
Louisine Waldron see Henry Osborne HAVEMEYER
ELDRIDGE, Clyde Mulford, geneal, bk rev OC 24:1:43
Jesse f1853, w Isabela ___, TN, will GR 29:2:70
ELIASON, Karl see Hedvig CALDREN
ELIS, Anna Margaret see Fridrich KERCH
ELKINS, Fam hist WV, bk rev GH 41:2:160
ELLARD, Jonathan b1795, w Rutha McAdams, SC, AL, anc ch NAS 26:2:47
ELLER, Surname period, *The Eller Chronicles*, Rt 2 Box 145-D, Whittier NC 28789
ELLINGSWORTH, James P m1869, w Aliace A Robbins, Bible rec DJ 4:3:70
ELLIOTT, Benjamin m1804, w Elizabeth ___, Bible rec OZ 8:3:111
Caroline see Jefferson BENNETT
Eliza see William HOBSON
Elizabeth see Thomas H THOMSON
John C bc1849, w Missouri A ___, GA, OK, TX, geneal OPC 19:1:2
Sibella see James ARMSTRONG
Surname period, *Elliott Fam Quarterly*, 10 Quiet Hills Cr, Pomona CA 91766 – marr KY & IL, ch rec NJ & PA, census VA & MI & VT, probate VA & MA & ME & OH, land WV & PA, lineages
Thomas bc1750, w Mary ___, NC, GA, geneal OPC 18:4:92

ELLIS, Albert H b1862, w Minnie M Creswick, IL, MO, anc ch FF 15:4:138

Benjamin I bc1739, w Rachel Pressmill, TN, geneal OZ 8:2:61

Deborah Macomber see Harvey FARRINGTON

Elizabeth see Thomas OUTERBRIDGE

Fam hist MD, bk rev FRT 8:4:198

James f1730, w Mary Veatch, MD, PA, WV, OH, VA, geneal, bk rev BAT 16:4:167 NER 141:1:71 CTN 19:4:712 WPG 13:4:39 RAG 8:3:23

Rachel see Brownell CORNELL

ELLISON, James b1806, w Hetty Casey, TN, MO, geneal OZ 9:3:117

ELMORE, David b1786, SC, IN, anc ch TOP 17:3:91

William Monroe b1838, w Catherine Lindley, NC, GA, anc ch NWT 8:3:29

ELSBREE, Charles Clarke see Edna Lorena REDING

ELSBURY, Agnes see Robert REDMON

ELTONHEAD, Martha see Edwin CONWAY

EMERICH, Katherine see Frederic MAURER

EMERICK, Johannes bc1717, GE, PA, desc, bk rev KK 25:1:18

EMERSON, Fam hist EN & MA, bk rev TS 29:1:25 NYR 118:1:57 CCS 9:1:24 AG 62:3:186 SGS 36:4:205 MD 28:2:239 CSB 21:1-2:40

EMMERT, Fam hist TN & IL, bk rev BWG 16:1:66

Valentine D b1826, w Alzira ___, TN, IL, geneal, bk rev IL 19:2:117 GH 41:4:206

ENDEBROCK, Myrtle see Adolph LUERSSON

ENGEL, John Louis d1918, w Ida Rath, IL, obit CRT 8:4:30

Katherina see Heinrich HUBACH

ENGLAND, Adventurers & emig, bk rev FAM 26:3:176

Army rec location guide, bk rev BCG 16:4:146

Banbury, gaol rec 1829-1838, bk rev GM 22:7:263

Bedfordshire or Buckinghamshire, deserters, discharges, & prisoners of war from the British 16th Reg of foot during the Am Rev NGS 74:4:280

Birth & bapt rec, use of APG 2:4:23

Board of Guard rec, use of FRT 8:4:166

Burials & births 1768-1770 on the Gulf Coast of West FL, Ch of EN rec, bk rev SCS 24:3:62 STI 27:1:27 CHG 19:1:20 NYR 118:3:179 RAG 8:3:22

Cambridge University, armorial, bk rev GH 41:1:122

Census reg districts index, bk rev BCG 16:3:105

Censuses & census-taking 1800s GM 22:7:258 22:8:282

Ch (medieval) hist, bk rev BCG 16:4:142

Charles II's noble desc GM 22:7:244

Convict experience in Am bibl TNB 2:2:1

Domesday Bk, bk rev SCS 24:4:90 ANC 22:1:43 EWA 24:1:53 NGS 74:3:231

Domesday Bk, hist background of EWA 24:2:140

Emig 1607-1660 roster, bk rev WCK 20:4:60 SCM 15:4:221

Extinct & dormant baronetcies, bk rev FAM 26:1:47

Falaise Roll 1066, bk rev EWA 24:2:138

Fam hist res guide for beginners by Pelling, bk rev RAG 8:3:25

geneal rec avail on microfilm in the US, bk rev CTN 19:4:712

Geneal repositories GGL 6:1-2:4

Geneal repositories in London NEH 4:2:57

Geneal res aid, Bodleian Lib (Oxford) GM 22:8:277

ENGLAND (continued)

Geneal res guide by Mellen, bk rev NGS 75:2:153

Geneal res guide by Cole, bk rev ANE 21: :26

Geneal res guide for beginners by Pelling, bk rev ANE 23: :22

Geneal res guide to Rec Offices, bk rev AG 62:3:185

Geneal res hints CC 10:1:2 CR 19:1:8 WTC 7:4:159 FRT 8:1:35

Geneal res hints, a guided tour through an EN pedigree GH 41:1:23

Geneal res sources in the mss collect of the Geneal Soc of UT, bk rev RES 18:3:137

grad of Oxford University who settled in New EN 1600s CTA 29:3:73

Handwriting reading guide, bk rev ANE 23: :22

Heralds' visitations 1533 BCG 16:1:8

Hist sketch & modern day culture GCP 5:6:33

Imm to US mid-1800s, hist, bk rev KA 23:2:112

Land grants in west FL 1766-1776, bk rev GH 41:4:188

Land tax rec, use of CO 48:2:45 TTT 11:3:123 FRT 8:2:61

London, Christchurch bapt reg 1724-1812 GM 22:7:251

London, geneal repositories NEH 4:2:57

London, hist (pictorial), bk rev BCG 16:1:30

London, transportees to southern col & West Indies 1703 NGS 74:4:290

Loretto Reg 1867-1873 GGL 6:1-2:39

Magna Charta barons & their desc, bk rev EWA 24:2:139

Maps for geneal & local hist GM 22:6:197

Marr patterns 1700s GM 22:8:289

Marr, census, & other indexes for fam hist by Gibson, bk rev BCG 16:3:104

ENGLAND (continued)

Mil rec, location of Army rec, bk rev RAG 8:4:26

Mss collect of the Geneal Soc (UT), bk rev TTT 11:1:27

Names collect by Dunkling, bk rev NYR 118:3:179

Natives buried or born on the Gulf Coast (US), rec of the Ch of EN in West FL 1768-1770, bk rev GH 41:2:157

News (local) 1750-1920 avail, bk rev GM 22:7:264 RAG 8:4:23 BCG 16:3:105 ANE 23: :20

Origins of the pass onboard the *Mary & John* 1630, bk rev CCS 9:1:25

Parish reg res guide by McLaughlin, bk rev BCG 16:3:103

Parish reg, uses & limitations GM 22:8:298

Pedigrees contained in co & local hist, the heralds' visitations, & in the more important geneal collect, index, microfiche rev GH 41:3:177

Poor rec res guide by McLaughlin, bk rev BCG 16:3:103

Public Rec Office, use of, bk rev FAM 26:2:113

Rec of the board of guard, use of CO 48:3:87

Record offices guide, bk rev NGS 74:3:235

Senlac, Battle Abbey, muster roll, bk rev EWA 24:2:139

Settlement papers, use of CO 48:1:6 TTT 11:2:58

Settlements in the US, bibl THH :97:14

Ship pass list 1630 to MA on board the *Mary & John*, bk rev EWA 24:2:138 (vol 1 & 2) CCS 8:4:130 DM 50:3:144 (vol 3 & 4) CTN 20:2:318

Suffolk Co, wills 1629-1640, bk rev GH 41:2:157

Surname inheritance statistical probabilities, bk rev GM 22:8:305 ANE 23: :21

ENGLAND (continued)

Surname origins CC 10:3:6

Surrey, probate inventories 1500s–1800s index, bk rev GM 22:8:304

Thorney, communal solidarity in a migrant community GM 22:6:210

Tithe surveys, use of, bk rev CTA 29:3:112

V r (Am) 1731–1868 abstr from the *Gentleman's Magazine*, bk rev NCJ 13:2:118

Victorian era illus, bk rev BCG 16:2:66

Waltham Forest, bread & baking memories c1913–1950, bk rev GM 22:8:304

Worcestershire, Bengeworth, St Peter's cem inscr BCG 16:1:12

WWI, Army resources guide, bk rev BCG 16:4:146

ENGLEDOW, John m1808, w Elizabeth Simpson, VA, TN, TX, geneal YTD 7:2:7

ENGLISH, Andrew d1749, PA, geneal, bk rev NYR 118:2:121

James b1838, w Helen Jane Pickett, IR, CO, NE, anc ch NW 9:2:62

Joshua f1755, IR, SC, geneal, bk rev NCJ 13:1:54

Thomas b1788, w Letitia Campbell, VA?, TN?, MO, children OZ 5:1:36

ENKE, Johanna b1836, h August Schorman & Louis Wente & John Wohltman, GE, IL, obit CRT 8:1:16

EPPERSON, Richard m1798, w Rebeckah Haden, Bible rec OZ 9:1:26

ERB, Esther see Samuel Y SHANTZ

Nancy see Abraham BAIR

ERICKSON, Elvira b1897, WI, birthday bk WI 34:1:54

ERICSSON, Carl Charles August b1864, w Adele Theresia ____, SN, FL, biog sketch IMP 6:1:21

ERIKSEN, Marthe see Even PEDERSEN

ERISMAN, Henry M f1863, PA, letters LCC 4:1:83 4:2:64 4:3:70 4:4:88

ERNST, Ferdinand d1824, w Mary Ann ____, IL, biog sketch FF 15:4:122

ERVIN, J R m1832, w Martha Dickinson, Bible rec TTT 11:1:21

ESKER, Frank d1917, w Mary Goeckner, IL, obit CRT 8:4:41

ESKEW, David Bryant b1851, SC, GA, geneal, bk rev GGS 23:3:155

ESPY, Josiah bc1672, w Priscilla Mitchell, Northern IR, US, geneal, bk rev WPG 14:1:54 GH 41:5:195

ESSEX, Mary Jane see Bushrod TAPP

ESTES, Fam rec GA PT 29:1:14

Surname period, *Estes Trails*, Rt 1 Box 373, Philadelphia MS 39350–9762

ETCHISON, James m1791, w Christina Miller, IN, geneal, bk rev NCJ 13:3:184

ETHEREDGE, Thomas f1671, w Christian ____, VA, will abstr GR 29:3:91

ETHERIDGE, Aaron f1739, w Sarah Hanbury, VA, will abstr GR 29:3:92

Fam cem Virginia Beach VA TN 7:1:12

Thomas Elder f1719, w Eleanor Bright, VA, will abstr GR 29:3:91

ETHIOPIA, Hist sketch & modern day culture GCP 5:6:37

EUBANKS, Frances see Jefferson Y JONES

EUROPE, Col emig, human background of GM 22:6:216

Geneal res guide by Baxter, bk rev FGS 11:4:16 GM 22:7:262

Geneal res guide by Law, bk rev GGD 3:4:191

Marr bargain, women & dowries in hist, bk rev CTA 29:3:111

EVANGELICAL, Obit of ch members 1836-1974, bk rev MI 32:3:91

EVANS, Isaac b1800, PA, biog sketch HL 1:2:54

Jesse d before 1829, AL, affidavit concerning estate NTT 7:1:33

John bc1630, w Elinor ___, WE, NH, geneal SCR 10:6:55

John f1884, EN, KS, geneal, bk rev TOP 17:2:36

Nancy Jane b1850, h William Fox, OH, IL, anc ch CCS 9:3:100

Nathan d1764, PA, trust papers LCH 2:1:24

Robert bc1630, w Elizabeth Colcord & Ann Thompson, WE, NH, geneal SCR 10:5:44

Sarah see Barney S SUTLIFF

Thomas f1767, NJ, indenture AG 62:4:219

EVELYN, Fam coat of arms MD & DE MAD 27:3:110

EVERS, Margaret f1936, ST, New Zealand, biog sketch GWS :26:11

EVERSON, Margaret see William M MUSSELMAN

EWING, Jane b1799, TN, anc ch MGR 22:3:136

Thomas f1726, Bible rec PA 35:1:48

EZELL, Sarah E see George Washington DAVIS

Thomas f1858, w Nancy Ezell, TN, will NTT 7:1:38

FAGAN, J A m1873, w Elenora J Grant, Bible rec YTD 2:1:14

FAIRBANKS, Henry m1823, w Harriet F Williams, Bible rec BG 8:3:71

FAIRCHILD, Daisy see Guy E ALBERT

Elizabeth see James ALLEN

FAITH, Jane (Wall) see John WALTRIP

FARLEY, Elizabeth see Patrick O'LEARY

John Sr bc1485, EN, geneal, bk rev GH 41:3:168

FARLEY (continued)

William b1837, w Elizabeth Tennessee Johnson & Manerva Johnson & Rosa Johnson, KY, pension HF 3:3:142

FARNHAM, Peter f1687, w Hannah Wilcoxson, CT, geneal, bk rev AG 62:1:33

FARQUHAR, Grace see Alexander Edward PHILLIPS

FARRINGTON, Harvey b1797, w Deborah Macomber Ellis & Rachel ___, MA, NY, fam rec MQ 53:2:84

Lydia see Eleazer LINDSEY

FARSON, Johannie d1902, GE, anc ch NW 10:1:47

FAUCETT, Richard f1790, w Nancy Whitlock, SC, children PT 29:3:117

FAULKNER, Christian see John Jack MITCHELL

FEASTER, Levi b1786, w Elizabeth Reed, MD, MO, children OZ 5:1:37

FEE, John Gregg f1864, KY, work at Cap Nelson 1864-1865 REG 85:1:29 (bk rev) REG 85:2:163

FELICIAN, Fam hist in the shaping of Am Polonia TE 7:2:61

FELKER, Jacob d1819, SC, anc ch AGS 28:2:102

FELKER, Stephen b1825, w Widow Daugherty, TN, MO, biog sketch OZ 9:1:23

FELLER, Alfred b1828, w Catherine Lenora Dawley, NY, geneal, bk rev GH 41:4:213

Niclaus f1709, GE, NY, geneal, bk rev NYR 118:4:250

FELLOWS, Alfred b1828, w Catherine Dawley, NY, OH, geneal, bk rev GFP 37:2:72 CTN 20:2:317

Obil f1802, NY, geneal, bk rev NYR 118:1:51

FENNER, Thomas m1792, w Rosanna McDonald, RI, Bible rec RIR 13:3:53

FENTRESS, Mary b1874, Bible rec TN 7:2:28

FERGUSON, Charles William m1900, w Emma Kate Mason, Bible rec WCG 3:9:84

FERO, Mary Anne see George SENEY

FERRAR, Nicholas d1620, EN, VA, geneal GJ 15:2:37

FERRIER, Thomas b1705, w Hester Lucky, IR, NY, geneal, microfiche rev GH 41:2:163

FICK, Fam hist CHI 59:4:165

FIELD, Christina b1807, NC, IL, anc ch CCS 9:3:102

Henrietta see William MOSS

Nelson d1917, w Sarah Layton, IL, obit CRT 8:4:45

Samuel b1834, w Matilda Layten, IL, obit CRT 8:4:40

Thomas f1859, ME, CA, letters DE 11:3:100

FIELDS, Surname period, *Fields Fam Findings*, 4740 Roosevelt Ave, Sacramento CA 95820 – census 1850 OR, marr PA, fam OH & IN, census IA & RI & KY, marr MS, census 1900 KS, census 1870 WV

FIJI, Hist sketch & modern day culture GCP 5:6:41

FINCH, Alethea see Uriah HILL Jr

Rebecca see Henry CULVER

FINLEY, Caroline see James MONTGOMERY

David b1871, w Nancy ____, Bible rec IG 23:2:58

John see Sarah MOORE

FINN, Colman b1823, KY, IL, geneal, bk rev CR 19:4:174

FINNELL, Diantha Taylor see Grant Burge HURT

FINNEY, Ann see Thomas THOMPSON

Fam hist MD, AL, TX, bk rev GH 41:3:168

FIRESTONE, M William b1799, w Elizabeth ____, VA, AL, anc ch PT 29:3:111

FIRMAN, John f1630, w Mary ____, GA, geneal, bk rev FRT 8:2:103

FISCHBACH, Elisabeth see John Jacob RICHTER

FISH, Fam rec misc vol 1, bk rev CTN 20:1:138 NYR 118:3:187

FISHER, Adam d1757, GE?, US, geneal, bk rev CTN 19:4:714 KK 25:3:56 WPG 13:4:44 MN 18:4:186

Anthony Wayne b1819, w Catharine Elizabeth Schetroupf, PA, fam hist LCH 3:1:32

Christina see Wendell MILLER

Conrad f1857, w Frances ____, Bible rec YV 19:1:21

Rebecca see William WELBON

Rose Rosa b1836, GE, anc ch SD 5:4:120

FISK, John m1842, w Phebe Sloan, NY, fam rec DM 50:3:132

FITCH, Mary see John COLT

FITCHPATRICK, Martha see Thomas P MAYNARD

FITZHERBERT, Rebecca b1827, ME, anc ch TEG 7:4:206

FIX, Joseph b1834, w Geeske Baumgarten, IA, anc ch WB 17:2:70

FLAGG, Fam letters 1816-1854, bk rev RAG 8:4:24

FLAGLER, Henry M b1830, NY, FL, biog sketch IMP 6:4:95

FLANAGAN, Terrance d1822, KY, anc ch SIN 8:3:85

FLANNIGAN, Margaret see John TRAYNOR

Mary see Barnard CONROY

FLEMING, Margaret see Griffith BOWEN

Mary b1788, SC, AL, anc ch PT 29:2:47

FLEMISH GENEALOGY, Death rec avail at the Geneal Soc of Flemish-Am FAH 5:2:26

FLESHMAN, Mary Ann see Mose SHUCK

FLETCHER, Katherine see John DALE

FLICKINGER, Peter b1730, w Mary Dare, GE, anc ch MFH 6:2:75

FLICKNER, Nancy b1810, h James EVans Miller, KY, CA, biog sketch SCS 24:7:147

FLINNER, Johannes bc1720, GE, MD, anc ch TB 13:2:36

FLINT, Thomas R b1858, fam rec WTC 14:3:118

William b1802, w Elisabeth Pitcher, Bible rec HJA 11:3:179

FLOOD, Thomas L d1898, VT, MN, obit RAT 16:1:19

FLORIDA, Alachua Co, Fort Harlee Precinct, voter roster 1848 FLG 10:3:93

Alachua Co, voter roster 1830 for upper district FLG 10:2:80

Alligator/Lake City, postmasters 1830-1948 roster SGE 28:121:18

Apalachicola, hist, bk rev CCM 6:4:81

Bay Co, direct (educational) 1915-1916 CL 5:1:4 5:2:8 5:3:12 5:4:16

Bay Co, Panama City, geneal misc 1914 abstr from the *Panama City Pilot* CL 5:4:15

Benton (now Hernando) Co, voter roster 1845 FLG 10:3:88

Bradford Co, electors 1876 FLG 11:1:4

Broward Co, cem list IMP 6:4:107

Broward Co, ch hist sketches IMP 6:4:101

Broward Co, Dania, Woodlawn Cem IMP 6:3:81 6:4:108

Broward Co, geneal misc 1897 IMP 6:3:77 (1912) IMP 6:1:18

Broward Co, geneal misc 1912 abstr from news IMP 6:4:113

Broward Co, geneal rec sources public & private IMP 6:4:105

Broward Co, hist sketch IMP 6:4:97

Broward Co, lib roster IMP 6:4:106

Census 1870 index, bk rev FLG 10:3:120

Co pioneer desc cert through 1986 FLG 10:2:67

FLORIDA (continued)

Duval Co, census 1850 index SGE 28:124:33

Duval Co, voter roster 1845 FLG 10:2:47

Emig to US 1780s NGS 75:3:226

Escambia Co, cem inscr, bk rev GH 41:4:188

Fam in 1850 who had someone b in AL AL 4:1:4

Field officers of the FL Mil 1830 roster FLG 11:1:12

Franklin Co, Apalachicola, hist, bk rev NC :92:2

Franklin Co, marr lic 1874-1884 SGE 28:123:33 28:124:53

Geneal res sources ANC 22:2:56

Hillsborough Co, cem inscr 1840-1985 vol 2 & 3, bk rev FLG 11:1:31 GH 41:5:164

Hypoluxo, hist sketch ANC 22:4:132

Jackson Co, voter roster 1845 FLG 10:4:125

Jacksonville, Morocco Temple charter members 1888 roster SGE 28:122:22

Jacksonville, Riverside Memorial Park Cem SGE 28:121:1 28:123:1 28:124:6

Jefferson Co, voters 1845 roster FLG 11:1:25

Madison Co, third precinct, voter roster 1838 FLG 10:3:116

Manatee Co, marr 1889-1899 CC 10:1:6 CC 10:2:9 10:3:9 10:4:9

Marr & death notices 1837-1860 abstr from the *Southern Christian Advocate* SGE 28:121:11

Nassau Co, census 1850 index SGE 28:122:19

Palm Beach Co, hist, bk rev ANC 22:4:157

Panama City, visitors 1914 CL 5:3:11

Pasco Co, West Pasco, hist, bk rev GH 41:2:157

Pensacola, burials & christenings reg 1770-1771 GHS 4:2:4

Pioneer desc cert through 1986 FLG 10:2:51

FLORIDA (continued)
Saint Johns Co, census 1850 index SGE 28:123:55
South Dade Co, hist, bk rev FLG 11:1:32
Suwannee Co, Live Oak, Pine Grove Meth Ch cem & hist ANC 22:1:8 22:3:88
Volusia Co, vet reg (deceased), bk rev CC 10:4:4
Wakulla Co, voter roster 1845 FLG 10:3:89
FLOURNOY, Jean Jacques b1686, w Elizabeth Williams, VA, geneal, microfiche rev GH 41:4:213
FLOYD, Penuel d1815,w Sarah Beckwith, NC, geneal, bk rev GH 41:1:160
FLYNN, Charles E, fam rec corr to FLG 10:1:cover FLG 10:2:50
FLYNT, Surname period, *News & Echoes for Flynt/Flint & Assoc Fam*, 2270 Overton Rd, Augusta GA 30904
FONDAH, Rebecca see Henry GROESBECK
FONTAINE, Jean de la f1099, geneal, bk rev GH 41:6:156
John de la f1563, VA, geneal, bk rev DS 24:4:218
FOOTE, William bc1797, w Jane Elizabeth Dalton, EN, Newfoundland, geneal, bk rev GH 41:2:151
FORBES, Charles bc1720, w Ann Ward, NC, anc ch NAS 26:2:63
Charles L b1847, w Adelaide Weir, MI, WA, biog sketch TB 13:2:12
David b1752, w Margaret Sterling, ST, VA, biog NPW 6:6:53
John see Mary AGER
FORD, Ana b1815, TN, anc ch BWG 16:1:50
Benjamin F dc1873, KS, estate KL 7:4:11
Harriet see Elijah CLAPP
John A b1848, w Malinda C Sherrill, IN, IL, obit BGS 19:1:22

FORD (continued)
John A b1856, AL, anc ch THT 15:2:12
Martha (___) see Peter BROWN
FOREMAN, David b1755, w Elizabeth Horine, KY, geneal, bk rev CCS 9:2:60
FOREST, James b1782, w ___ Gordon & Freelove (Dutchard?) Snow, VA, IL, AR, MO, geneal OZ 7:1:31
FORGEY, Eizabeth see William ROLLER
FORKNER, Surname period, *The Forkner Clan Newsletter*, POB 165, Gallatin Gateway MT 59730
FORNEY, Mary Magdalene see Charles TIMMONS
FORRESTER, Louisa see Andrew C SKIDMORE
William Sr f1749, w Mary ___, IR, PA, VA, NC, geneal LOB 8:6:79
FORSTER, Thomas b1774, w Orra Sams, NC, geneal LOB 8:7:100
FORSYTH, Elizabeth Rogers see James Alfred GRIFFITH
FOSDICK, Martha see Richard HOLDEN
FOSHAY, Matthew b1748, w Elizabeth Gravenstein, NY, geneal NYR 118:3:156
William bapt1721, w Jane Barnes, NY, geneal NYR 118:4:222
FOSSE, Anne see Jacques DeLaRUE or DeLaRAUE
FOSTER, Benjamin Franklin b1817, w E Caroline Wolfe & Mary Ann Carter Holder, NC, geneal LOB 8:8;116
Daniel b1726, w Anne Ingalls, MA, ME, biog sketch DE 10:5:171
Susan see Alexander Newton BRANNOCK
FOUCAULT, Jean Francois dit b1641, w Elisabeth Provost, lineage AIL 1:1:22
FOUCH, Hugh b1699, w Mary Parkins, VA, anc ch HL 5:2:57

FOULKES, Surname period, *Kin Foulkes*, POB 2040, Pinetop AZ 85935

FOUNTAIN, Bazzle Manley b1845, w Lavinia Miles, SC, GA, anc ch GGS 23:1:19

FOUST, Jonathan b1802, Bible rec OCR 28:3:115

FOWLER, Florence Morgan see James Calloway BUCHANAN

Henry L, w Emma L Minkler, fam hist, bk rev GH 41:6:156

James D bc1794, w Martha Davis, VA, CA, biog sketch SCS 24:4:89

Jennie Isabelle see Stephen Bernard CONROY

Mary Jane see Madon D BAGLEY

FOX, Eliza see George William SUITER

Elkanah bapt1730, CT, biog CTN 20:3:428

John Lewis see Lydia Jane TWOMBLEY

John S b1804, w Mary ___, OH, anc ch BGS 19:1:39

Lydia see Abraham WELTY

William see Nancy Jane EVANS

FRANCE, Geneal terms in EN WRB 10:2:15 CTN 20:1:50 MP 3:1:60 OCN 10:1:11

Troops in the MS Valley & on the Gulf Coast 1745, bk rev CHG 19:2:108 DM 50:3:144 GH 41:2:121

FRANDSEN, Michael b1851, w Emilea B Preston, DK, IL, MN, anc ch FCT :74:28

FRANK, Fam hist, bk rev TNB 2:3:5

FRANKS, Peter m1808, w Rachal Hitt, Bible rec HTR 30:1:9

S R see Francis Marion SCOTT

FRANTZ, Adam f1795, w Barbara ___, GE, MD, VA, geneal, bk rev GH 41:3:168

Mary Catherine see Wm CRILL

Michael Sr b1687, SW, PA, biog NFB 19:2:24

FRARY, Fam hist, bk rev AG 62:3:192

FRARY (continued)

John f1637, w Prudence Townsend, EN, MA, geneal, bk rev CTN 19:4:708 GH 41:1:160

Surname period, *Frary Fam Journal*, Harmony Rd, RFD 1 #162, Northwood NH 03261

FRASER/DEFOY, Elizabeth see Leon E PROVOST

FRAZER, David d1902, w Sara ___, IR, cem inscr GGL 6:3:103

James D m1857, w Mary Frances Lane, NY, IL, fam hist WTC 17:4:120

FRAZIER, Francis II b1842,ST, NC, IN, geneal, bk rev NYR 118:2:115

John F m1809, w Mary Scot, TN, IN, geneal, bk rev GH 41:5:192

Mary Elizabeth see James C BISHOP

FREDERICK, Jacob b1791, w Catherine Stevens, NY, Bible rec OCG 17:3:23

Surname period, *Frederick Forerunners*, 3803 MacNicholas Ave, Cincinnati OH 45236 – marr IN, v r OH, census indexes, marr PA, land TX, marr WV & OH, chancery rec, cem OH

FREEMAN, Fam rec misc NS, bk rev NER 141:3:263

George Washington m1851, w Avalener Bowlin, KY, Bible rec KA 23:2:99

Jane b1840, h Greenville Boyd, MO, obit SNS 3:2:5

FREERKS, Harmanna see Jacob Harms BOOMGARDEN

FREITAG, Anna m1919,h Olaf Borresen, IL, FL, biog sketch IMP 6:1:20

Oscar bc1862, w Christina Lawrence, NW, FL, biog sketch IMP 6:1:20

FRENCH, Hains bc1760, w Irene Learnard, VT, biog BAT 16:1:16

Mary see William BADLAM

FRENCH (continued)
Nancy Whitney b1825, NY, IL, biog, bk rev GH 41:4:211
FRENCH-CANADIAN GENEAL-OGY, Biog sketches vol 4, bk rev GH 41:1:154 GD 17:4:14 CTN 20:1:146 (vol 5) LIC 13:3:168
hist in New EN, bk rev NER 141:1:61 RAG 8:4:22
Hist sketch of area in CN GCP 5:5:29
Res hints for beginners BCG 16:2:46
Settlement in Champlain Islands, Grand Isle Co VT before 1880, bk rev NYR 118:2:114
FREY, Magdalena see Jacob MOSEMAN
FREYERMOUTH, Sarah S see Gottlieb SHEAROUSE
FRICK, Barbara see Henry E MYERS
FRICKER, Anthony f1814, PA, ledger, bk rev WPG 13:3:47
FRIEDT, Joseph B m1856, w Anna Deayarman, Bible rec AB 15:3:65
FRIEND, Surname period, *The Friendship News of the Friend Fam Assoc of Am*, POB 613, Park Ridge IL 60068
FRIESS, Anna Ursla m1699, NY, anc ch PF 16:1:23
FRIGGENS, Ann see William MURLY
FRISBIE, Edward bc1621, CT, geneal, bk rev GH 41:6:157
John Francis m1851, w Epifania Vallejo, NY, CA, marr rec SS 14:3:40
Walter M m1917, w Mary Emma Hogan, TX, Bible rec YTD 2:1:9
FRITZ, Gertrude see John HOH-MANN
FROBEL, Anne S b1816, VA, diary, bk rev VAG 31:1:68 REG 85:2:184
FROGG, John f1747, VA, deed NPW 6:1:6

FROHMAN, Juliana bc1819, GE, anc ch BHN 20:4:173
FROSHAUER, John d1801, TN, anc ch TN 7:5:71
FROST, Fam cem OH with connections in MD & PA WPG 13:3:56
Fam hist, bk rev MI 32:3:96
Surname period, *Frost on the Vine*, 4050 Burleson Retta Rd, Burleson TX 76028
FRY, Anna see Joel BLACK-BURN
John f1775, PA, OH, geneal, bk rev WPG 13:4:38
Kate A f1859, PA, autograph bk LCC 4:1:63 4:2:51 4:3:40 4:4:92
FUCHS, Eva see Peter WAGNER
FULFORD, Jordan bc1778, w Margaret ___, US, geneal, bk rev GH 41:5:192
Perlina see Stephen HOL-LINGSWORTH
FULHAM, Tabitha see George PARKHURST
FULL, Elura b1887, h James Lane, SD, geneal, bk rev FRT 8:3:151
FULLBRIGHT, Arthur Lloyd b1891, w Pearl H Swope, MO, WA, biog YV 19:1:9
FULLER, Earl Reuben see Adella Alcesta SCOTT
H C Sr b1827, AL, Bible rec YTD 5:2:41
Henry C Sr b1837, w Fannie Hall, AL, TX, obit YTD 5:2:24
Robert, w Sarah Bowen, MA, geneal, bk rev GH 41:5:192
FULLERTON, Catherine Edith b1893, h ___ Oyler, memories, bk rev GH 41:6:162
FULLILOVE, James Hill b1848, w Sarah Martha Dowdell, LA, AL, anc ch KSL 11:1:29
FULTON, Anna Elizabeth b1873, h Oscar Robertson, IL, obit CRT 8:4:36
Fam group sheets, bk rev GH 41:4:191

FULTON (continued)

Hugh f1829, w Margaret Fulton, OH?, will OPC 19:1:25

Robert f1751, IR, MA, NH, ON, geneal, bk rev GH 41:3:176

FUNFROCK, Johannes bc1530, FR?, GE?, MD, PA, geneal, bk rev FRT 8:2:107 DWC 13:2:57 CR 19:4:174 CRT 8:4:6

FUNK, George b1813, w Mary A Mayer, GE, KS, geneal KK 25:2:31

Henry b1760, w Anne Meyer, PA, anc ch MFH 6:1:35

FUNKHOUSER, Ann see Christopher SHOWALTER

John f1857, w Elizabeth ____, IL, will CRT 8:1:30

FUQUAY, Leila see Rush Floyd DUNCAN

FUSTING, Fam hist GE & US, bk rev CRT 8:4:6

GABBERT, John b1774, w Judith Tuley, VA, KY, geneal, bk rev WCK 20:1:14

GACHNOUWER, Jacob m1624, w Margaretha Peter, SW, GE, fam hist MFH 6:2:69

GAGER, William, EN, MA, CT, geneal, bk rev NYR 118:1:56

GAGNON, Felicite Marie see Joseph Isaie CHENETTE

GAINES, Frances see Peter CARTWRIGHT

Mildred b1802, KY, anc ch CR 19:3:135

GALE, George b1670, EN, MD, geneal MD 28:3:279

GALEENER, Fam hist, bk rev OC 24:1:44 QY 14:1:7 SCC 24:1:7 TOP 17:2:35

GALLANT, Teresa see Joachim ARSENAULT

GALLEGOS, Elena see Santiago GURULE

GALLOWAY, George b1700, w Rebecca Junkin, ST, OH, anc ch KIL 15:3:31

Jane see Columbus WHITMIRE

GALVEZ, Bernardo de b1746, SP, MX, TX, biog sketch DAR 121:2:68

GANTVOORT, Fam hist US, bk rev MI 32:3:95

GANTZ, Louisa see Christoph SCHOENSTEDT

GARD, Surname period, *Guardian*, POB 790, Benton City WA 99320

GARDEN, George b1813, w Janet Barnet, QB, IL, fam hist sketch WTC 17:4:125

GARDNER, Elizabeth b1817, TX, anc ch THT 16:1:12

Eveline S b1831, NY, IA, anc ch TB 14:1:37

George b1807, w Elizabeth Whitehead, NC, fam hist TQR 14:1:45

Henry Wood m1846, w Mary Brown Rathbone, RI, geneal, bk rev NYR 118:1:57 FLG 11:1:30

John b1834, w Mary J Scofield, NY?, MI, biog sketch DM 50:3:106

John f1804, ST, NY, biog sketch NGS 74:3:173

John M b1857, w Mary Helton, MO, obit SNS 3:4:3

Julia see John TYLER

Rachel Ann (Patterson) see Jacob Archibald MONTGOMERY

GARLAW, Thomas see Robina Strachan MURRAY

GARMON, Surname period, *Garmon Newsletter*, 28111 Mtn Meadow Rd, Escondido CA 92026

GARNEAU, M Louise see Pierre BEDARD

GARNER, Easther f1845, NC, letter NCJ 13:4:234

Hiarm f1909, MO, letter OZ 6:2:57

Margaret see Ephraim MCCULLOUGH

GARNHAM, Henry Baker b1823, w Mary Elizabeth Davis, ST, CA, biog sketch SCS 24:1:17

GAROUTTE, Michael f1775, FR, NJ, geneal, bk rev NYR 118:2:123

GARRARD, James f1790, KY, deed GRI 7:1:6

GARRETT, Charles b1815, TN, anc ch PT 29:1:8 TB 13:2:39

Laurena see William Albert CROUCH

Neriva see Charles W NEW-BERRY

GARRETTSON, Fam hist corr & add MD MD 28:4:447

Ruthen d1664, w Mary Utie, MD, geneal MD 28:3:304

GARRISON, James C b1792, w Diana Kyle, VA, MO, children OZ 5:1:37

Surname period, *The Garrison Gazette*, 23 Lee St, Winchester KY 40391

GATES, Sarah M see William BRITTON

Surname period, *Gates Researcher*, 319 Houston Lake Blvd, Centerville GA 31028

GATEWOOD, John f1663, VA, geneal, bk rev GH 41:4:206

Lucy see William HAYES Sr

GATTON, Surname period, *Gatton Newsletter*, POB 365, Beech Bottom WV 26030

GAUDET, Alexis b1809, w Marie Richard, QB, anc ch MP 3:1:66

Charles bc1714, w Marie Cormier, NS, anc ch MP 3:1:67

Francoise m1644, h Daniel LeBlanc, lineage AGE 16:3:77

GAULA, Claude f1560, SW, anc ch HJA 11:3:241

GAUTNEY, Bloom Fite b1873, w Mary Della Mayes, AL, anc ch NAS 26:1:18

Lee Ella, see Grover Garfield DOWDY Sr

GAY, Martin Baker b1803, w Johann Evans Stewart, VA, OR, geneal OZ 7:1:1

GEDNEY, Mary see Jesse David DETTY

GEE, Isaac bc1761, NY, MI, geneal, bk rev NYR 118:3:186

GEER, Fam rec corr to *Geer Geneal* by Geer NEH 4:3:164

GEER (continued)

Surname period, *Geer Fam Assoc Newsletter*, 1480 Byrd Dr, Berwyn PA 19312

GEIER, Maria Josepha see Michael Anton REPP

GEIGER, Margaret Elizabeth see Daniel HOGAN

GEISLER, Samuel b1793, w Catherine Bowman, PA, TN, children BWG 16:2:147

GEORGE, Fam crest & shield TEG 7:1:11

GEORGIA, Andersonville, hist sketch of prison, cem, & town MCI 5:3:74

Atlanta, residents 1878 roster GGS 23:3:142

Augusta, Cath Mission (1700s) FR refugees & IR imm, hist sketch AGA 12: :17

Augusta, Cedar Grove Cem AGA 12: :47

Augusta, First Pres Ch rec 1856–1894 AGA 12: :38

Augusta, Magnolia Cem AGA 12: :71

Augusta, Roman Cath Ch of the Most Holy Trinity rec 1810–1824 AGA 12: :8

Augusta, St Matthew's Evangelical Luth Ch rec 1800s–1900s AGA 12: :61

Augusta, Summerville Cem AGA 12: :19

Baker, Dougherty, & Randolph Co, census 1860, bk rev CCM 6:4:81

Baldwin Co, geneal rec misc 1800s GP 24:1:45

Bibb Co, firemen roster 1831 GGS 23:2:93

Biog sketches of legislators 1871–1872 index GGS 23:1:7

Bulloch Co, census 1850 index SGE 28:121:19

Camden Co, census 1860, bk rev TCG 6:4:71

Carroll Co, census 1870, bk rev GH 41:1:126

Carroll Co, marr lic 1827–1980 index, bk rev SB 8:3:103

GEORGIA (continued)

Carroll Co, medical practitioners reg, bk rev SB 8:3:103

Catoosa & Walker Co, Civil War, muster roll of 2nd Company D 1st Confederate Reg Inf Army of TN SR 3:3:52 3:4:76

Catoosa Co, sheriffs 181-1986 & treasurers 1881-1922 roster SR 3:4:78

Cem direct & bibl of GA cem reference sources, bk rev CC 10:2:3 OZ 7:4:148

Census 1840 (vets), bk rev NTT 7:2:44

Census 1860 index, bk rev GH 41:3:172

Chandler Co, Bapt ch rec avail GGS 23:2:105

Chatham Co, census 1860, bk rev GH 41:1:126

Chatham Co, Savannah, deaths 1803-1806, bk rev GH 41:1:127 (1807-1811) GH 41:1:127

Chatooga Co, census 1870, bk rev SR 2:1:16

Civil War, Confederate soldiers buried in Mt Olivet Cem, Frederick Co MD GGS 23:1:29

Civil War, Confederate soldiers buried in Macon cem GGS 23:3:127

Civil War, Confederate vet at Old Soldiers Home 1901-1930 GGS 23:1:1

Civil War, hospitals in Walker, Catoosa, & Dade Co, bk rev GH 41:4:188

Civil War, unreported losses GGS 23:4:188

Clayton Co, cem inscr, bk rev NTT 7:1:3

Co formation outline PT 29:2:66

Cobb Co, Civil War, Confederate pensions 1880-1920 NC :89:7

Cobb Co, gravestones found at co police department NC :99:2

Cobb Co, marr 1865-1938 index NC :89:4 :90:5 :91:3 :92:4 :93:3 :94:5 :96:3 :97:3 :98:6 :99:5

GEORGIA (continued)

Cobb Co, marr 1865-1966 index NC :89:5 :90:7 :91:6 :92:7 :93:6 :94:7 :95:4 :96:4 :97:5

Cobb Co, mort sched 1850 NC :93:2

Cobb Co, mort sched 1860 NC :97:7 :98:3

Col rec 1700s-1800s GP 24:1:7 24:2:51 24:3:99

Confederate soldiers vol 1, bk rev WPG 14:1:49

Coweta Co, cem inscr, bk rev GGS 23:2:101 GH 41:2:158 AL 3:1:38 3:3:45

Dade Co, birth cert 1879-1906 SR 2:4:74

DeKalb Co, mil roster 1836 GGS 23:2:91

Doughtery Co, marr 1853-1903, bk rev GH 41:6:132

Elbert Co, geneal rec misc 1800s GP 24:1:23 24:2:57 24:3:111 24:4:174

Fannin Co, Allen Cem SR 3:1:21

Fannin Co, cem inscr vol 2, bk rev GH 41:6:132

Fannin Co, census 1860, bk rev GH 41:2:129 GGS 23:3:158

Fannin Co, census 1870, bk rev GH 41:2:129 GGS 23:3:158

Fannin Co, census 1880, bk rev GH 41:6:132

Fannin Co, Friendship Bapt Ch cem SR 2:4:76

Fannin Co, Greenway Cem SR 3:1:4

Fannin Co, Hickory Flats Cem SR 3:1:7

Fannin Co, Kirby Cem SR 3:3:56

Fannin Co, marr 1854-1894, bk rev SR 2:2:42 SR 3:4:89

Fannin Co, marr 1854-1901, bk rev GGS 23:3:157 GH 41:6:132

Fannin Co, marr 1854-64 SR 1:2:12 2:1:4 2:2:28 2:3:55

Fannin Co, Tilley Cem SR 3:1:5 (corr & add) SR 3:4:79

Fannin Co, will & misc estate rec 1854-1865 & 1868-1929 index GGS 23:2:62

68

GEORGIA (continued)

Floyd Co, geneal misc vol 3, bk rev GGS 23:2:102

Franklin Co, geneal rec misc 1700s-1800s GP 24:1:31 24:2:68 24:3:130 24:4:153

Freedman's Bureau rec & letters 1865-1866, bk rev NC :89:3 FRT 8:2:100

Geneal rec 1770s-1780s GP 24:4:147

Geneal res guide by Schweitzer, bk rev SCM 15:3:180 SCS 24:9:183 VAG 31:3:234 WPG 14:1:55 GGS 23:4:210 GH 41:5:164 SCS 24:10:202 SLB 6:5:222 KA 23:2:110

Geneal res sources at the GA Archives GGS 23:4:175

Geneal workbk by Brooke & Davis, bk rev SCS 24:11:221

Georgia Asylum inmates roster 1842-1853 GGS 23:1:31

Glynn Co, Saint Simons Island, hist, bk rev GH 41:2:158

Greensboro Bapt Ch member roster 1821-1834 GGS 23:4:181

Gwinnett Co, geneal misc 1827-1840 abstr from Athens GA news GGS 23:1:45 SCM 15:1:59

Gwinnett Co, Suwanee Bapt Ch member roster 1828-1875 GGS 23:2:56 23:3:122

Hancock Co, census 1850, bk rev GH 41:6:132

Hancock Co, geneal rec misc 1800s GP 24:1:11 24:2:72 24:4:179

Hist, geneal, & rec sources guide by Davis, bk rev SCM 15:4:222

Imm from Great Britain, bk rev SB 8:3:103

Intestate rec before 1832, bk rev NGS 74:3:236

Irwin Co, Frank Primitive Bapt Ch Cem GGS 23:4:192

Jasper Co, hist, bk rev GGS 23:2:102

Jefferson Co, geneal rec misc 1800s GP 24:1:43

Jefferson Co, marr 1805-1828 GGS 23:1:10

GEORGIA (continued)

Jefferson Co, naturalizations 1803-1857 GGS 23:1:30

Jones Co, census 1850 GP 24:1:35 24:2:84 24:3:100 24:4:186

Jones Co, will 1780s-1889 abstr GP 24:1:39 24:2:88 24:3:136

Land grants, lost surveys 1755-1775 GGS 23:3:117

Lincoln Co, geneal & hist, bk rev GH 41:4:188

Lone Oak, Allen-Lee Memorial United Meth Ch hist 1844-1985, bk rev GH 41:6:132

Macon Co, census 1860, bk rev CCM 6:4:81

Macon, geneal misc 1837-1838 abstr from *The Southern Post* GGS 23:4:170

Marr bk 4, bk rev AL 3:4:17

Marron Co, estate rec 1839-1849 GGS 23:2:70

McIntosh Co, estates & homesteads c1872-c1900 rec avail GGS 23:1:36

McIntosh Co, McIntosh Co Academy, minutes of the commissioners 1820-1875 & acct bk of students 1821-1834, bk rev GH 41:2:158

Newton Co, marr 1820s-1860s GP 24:1:4 24:2:80 24:3:128 24:4:172

Peach & Crawford Co, cem inscr, bk rev NTT 7:1:2

Pensioners, bk rev GH 41:2:129

Pickens Co, map 1903, bk rev GGS 23:1:45

Pike Co, cem inscr, bk rev NTT 7:1:2

Pioneer geneal rec misc GGS 23:4:166

Pioneers geneal, bk rev FAM 26:2:114

Putnam Co, geneal rec misc 1800s GP 24:2:92 24:3:134 24:4:183

Putnam Co, marr 1808-1913 GP 24:1:27

Rabun Co, geneal misc 1800s, bk rev TCG 7:4:60

GEORGIA (continued)

Residents b in SC SCM 15:3:140

Rev War, soldiers' deaths, bk rev SB 8:3:103

Rev War, soldiers biog sketches GP 24:1:19 24:2:63 24:3:117 24:4:167

Richmond Co, geneal rec misc 1790s-1840s GP 24:1:15 24:2:76 24:3:105 24:4:159

Richmond Co, jurors roster of Superior & Infrior courts 1782-1783 & 1790 AGA 12: :35

Savannah to Augusta, map 1779, bk rev GGS 23:1:45

Settlers (col), bk rev SB 8:3:103

Spaulding Co, marr & deaths 1882-1896 abstr from the *Griffin Weekly* & the *Griffin Weekly News & Sun*, bk rev GH 41:5:164

Tattnall Co, geneal rec avail GGS 23:2:61

Tax digests 1789-1817 index, bk rev GGS 23:2:101 NER 141:2:164 NCJ 13:1:52 GH 41:2:158 STI 27:1:27

Troup Co, Bethel Meth Ch rec 1888-1893 TCG 6:4:47 7:1:49 7:2:31 7:3:41 7:4:43

Troup Co, census 1850 TCG 6:4:39 7:1:44 7:2:23 7:3:33 7:4:27

Troup Co, Civil War, Confederate Vet lic exemption affidavits 1887-1915 TCG 7:2:39

Troup Co, Civil War, muster roll of Company B 60th Reg GA Vol Inf, Evans' Brigade, Gordon's Division, Army of Northern VA CSA TCG 7:4:35

Troup Co, Civil War, muster roll of Company E 41st Reg GA Vol Inf Army of TN CSA TCG 6:4:43 7:1:36 7:2:27 7:3:37

Troup Co, deed abstr 1827-1829 TCG 6:4:30 7:1:27 7:2:15 7:3:29 7:4:31

Troup Co, marr 1845-1849 TCG 6:4:35 7:1:23 7:2:19 7:3:25 7:4:19

GEORGIA (continued)

Troup Co, obit index 1800s-1900s TCG 6:4:56

Troup Co, pony homestead exemptions 1873 TCG 6:4:52 7:1:32 7:2:35 7:3:47 7:4:39

Troup Co, Rev War, patriots biog sketches TCG 7:3:51

Walker Co, Bible rec, bk rev GH 41:4:188 GH 41:3:160 SR 3:1:20

Walker Co, Villanow, Fowler's Chapel Ch school roster 1800s-1900s SR 1:2:14 2:2:30 2:3:53

War of 1812, index to service rec, bk rev CC 10:2:3 CHG 19:2:108 GH 41:4:188 SCM 15:4:223 FLG 11:1:30

War of 1812, pensioners vol 1 & 2, bk rev GGS 23:2:103

Warren Co, census 1860, bk rev GH 41:1:127

Whites among the Cherokees 1828-1838, bk rev GH 41:6:131

Wiregrass, pioneers roster SGE 28:122:53

GERARDY, Pierre f1854, FR, LA, geneal, bk rev KK 25:3:56

GERIN-LAJOIE, Jean b1728, PQ, anc ch FTR :102:7

GERLITZ, Elizabeth see Joseph Christopher LEINWEBER

GERMANN, Daniel IV b1756, SW, anc ch TB 13:3:39

GERMANY, Alphabet TGC 11:3:59

Anc searchers, bk rev GH 41:2:119

Archives with addresses TGC 11:2:46 AB 15:4:91

Asburgh, ship pass list to Baltimore MD 1852 on board the *A Chesebrough* MD 28:2:214

Atlas 1986, bk rev GGD 3:1:17

Baden-Wurttemberg, hist TGC 11:1:16

Bavaria, hist sketch GGD 3:1:

Bavaria, Narburger testements 1659-1757 GGD 3:3:144

Bayern, geneal rec on microfilm GGD 3:2:96

GERMANY (continued)

Bayern, Rosenheim, birth reg 1607-1665 GGD 3:2:88

Berlin, hist BGG 1:7:61 1:8:73

Berlin, parish reg 1583- , use of BGG 1:9:81 1:10:91 1:11:107

Brandenburg, hist sketch & map GGD 3:1:

Bremen, pass bound to NY 1855-1862 with places of origins vol 2, bk rev DM 50:3:141 NGS 74:4:315

Casualties of the 7 Weeks' War (1866) & the Franco-PU War (1870-1871), bk rev MCR 18:2:52

Census rec 1835, 1840 when under Danish rule TGC 11:1:26

Culture in eastern OH, bk rev PM 10:3:40

East Friesen, imm to US, bk rev IL 19:2:120

East Friesen, settlers in IL, IA, SD, & MN 1847-1916, bk rev FRT 8:1:48

Emig to North Am 1700s, bk rev AG 62:3:125

Fam hist res in the GE Democratic Republic by Wellauer, bk rev GGD 3:3:133

Fam res guide for beginners by Konrad, bk rev WTC 5:2-3:106

Geneal rec avail at the Wilson Lib (MN) OCN 10:1:12

Geneal rec avail on microfilm GGD 3:3:153 3:4:212

Geneal rec deciphering guide, bk rev NCJ 13:3:182

Geneal res aid, Der Christliche Botschafter PF 17:1:11

Geneal res aid, locating GE entries in the Fam Hist Lib Catalog & the International Geneal Index GGD 3:3:122

Geneal res aid, news GGD 3:3:107

Geneal res aid, testament rec & their use GGD 3:3:118

Geneal res aid, using Meyer's Orts U Verkers lexikon TGC 11:1:6

GERMANY (continued)

Geneal res aids, bk, period, & organizations TGC 11:3:79

Geneal res guide by Baxter, bk rev BAT 16:4:167 WCK 20:3:47 GGD 3:3:133 GH 41:6:123

Geneal res guide by Smith, bk rev MFH 6:4:131

Geneal res guide to GE Democratic Republic, bk rev GH 41:4:185

Geneal res guide to East GE by Wellauer, bk rev MCR 18:3:79

Geneal res guide to GE in RA, bk rev GGD 3:3:132 BCG 16:4:147 GH 41:6:124

Geneal res guide to GE anc in PO & the Prussian east, bk rev GGD 3:4:193

Geneal res hints CC 10:2:4 NW 10:1:22

Geneal res hints & addresses RD 87:1:10

Geneal res hints for fam with Turkish or Moorish blood BGG 1:12:111

Geneal res hints, imm CHG 20:1:19

Geneal res hints, using mil rec GGD 3:2:47

Geneal res hints, using ship pass lists BGS 19:3:105

Geneal terms in EN WRB 10:2:15 CTN 20:1:50 PCI 9:3:4 OCN 10:1:11

Hamburg, gold & silver wirepullers roster 1713 GGD 3:2:88

Hamburg, index 1855 GGD 3:1:31 3:2:91 3:3:148 3:4:207

Hamburg, ship pass list 1866 on board the *Allemanria* MN 18:3:128

Hamburg, testements housed at the St Johannis Monastery 1700s-1800s GGD 3:3:146

Handwriting & type smaples HL 5:3:72

Hannover, testements housed in the Hannover City Archive 1400s-1700s GGD 3:3:146

GERMANY (continued)

Hanover, natives settling in Benton Co MO TGC 11:3:73

Hesse, hist sketch TGC 11:2:51

Hessen, ch bk & civil reg avail, bk rev GGD 3:4:192

Hessen, geneal rec avail on microfilm GGD 3:2:96

Hessen-Darmstadt, Brandau, emig 1800s BGG 1:8:77 1:9:84

Hist 1942–1945, bk rev REG 85:1:96

Hist in col GA, bk rev NGS 74:4:316

Hist in col US, bk rev RAG 8:1:22 WPG 13:4:44

Hist of Royal houses, bk rev GM 22:6:225

Hist sketch of the GE Empire & its political divisions GJ 15:3:123

Imm from Bremen to NY 1855–1862, bk rev SGS 36:2:102 PA 35:1:52 FAM 26:3:175 NYR 118:1:50

Imm to Am 1800s, geneal guide by Wellauer, bk rev CHI 59:4:190

Imm to GA 1733–1783, bk rev PA 35:1:50

Imm to US 1865–1866 MI 31:4:125

Index of GE surnames in the *Geneal Res Direct* (GRD) BGG 1:12:117

Index to *Familienkundliche Nachrichten* (FANA) BGG 1:7:64 1:10:96 1:11:104 1:12:116

Index to *Praktische Forschungshilfe* (PRAFO) BGG 1:9:86

Lauban District, Schlesien, geneal res aids GGD 3:4:176

Maps avail & use of GGD 3:1:6

Mecklenburgs, geneal sources guide, bk rev GGD 3:4:193

Mercenaries in CN 1700s NGS 75:3:228

Months of the year with EN translation CR 19:3:111

Names Anglicized RD 87:6:30

GERMANY (continued)

Natives in col Am, bk rev SB 8:1:19

News, use of GGD 3:4:167

Niedersachsen, hist TGC 11:3:66

Oldenburg, testaments (short & unprinted) 1483–1600 avail GGD 3:4:203

Palatinate (western), emig to North Am 1700s vol 2, bk rev NGS 74:3:232 PA 35:1:49 FAM 26:2:112

Palatine imm decennial index 1975–1985 vol 1–10, bk rev GH 41:3:171

Palatine, Frankweiler, Calvinist Parish v r 1683–1800 GGD 3:2:89

Pommern, ch & civil rec avail GGD 3:1:27 3:2:93 3:3:151 3:4:210

Preussen, Hessen–Nassau, geneal rec avail on microfilm GGD 3:2:96

Preussen, Rheinland, geneal rec avail on microfilm GGD 3:2:97

Preussen, Schlesien, geneal rec avail on microfilm GGD 3:2:97

Preussen, Westpreussen, geneal rec avail on microfilm GGD 3:2:97

Revolutionaries of 1848 & imm to Am, bk rev NGS 75:2:153

Rhine Province, ch reg inventory, bk rev GGD 3:4:192

Rhineland, geneal rec sources GGD 3:3:114

Rhineland, geneal rec sources GGD 3:4:173

Rhineland, hist GGD 3:1:2

Rhineland, Wiesbaden, testaments 1575–1779 avail GGD 3:4:204

Sachsen (Prussia), Osterburg, mil muster rolls 1572 GGD 3:2:89

Saxony, testaments (old, unreg) 1554–1699 avail at the Oschatz Council Archive GGD 3:4:204

Schleswig-Holstein, hist sketch & map GGD 3:1:

GERMANY (continued)

Schleswig-Holstein, Sande Parish Kreis Stormarn, census 1845 GGD 3:4:205

Settlers in col Am, bk rev GQ 87:2:21

Settlers in GA 1733-1783, bk rev GH 41:1:126 ev SGS 36:2:103

Settlers in PA 1743-1800, bk rev BCG 16:1:32

Settlers in Renfrew Co ON, bk rev FAM 26:3:176

Seven Weeks War & Franco-PU Wa,r, casualties 1866 & 1870-1871, bk rev GGD 3:1:18 TS 29:2:69 TGC 11:1:25 GH 41:3:159

Silesia, civil reg avail, bk rev GGD 3:4:193

Soundex coding for GE names TGC 11:3:64

Trier, hist GGD 3:2:64

Troops in the North Am War of Independence 1776-1783, bk rev TGC 11:3:78 GH 41:6:122

University of Tuebingen, biog sketches 1830-1980, bk rev GJ 15:3:180

Westfalen, hist sketch & map GGD 3:1:

Wuerttemberg, ch reg inventory, bk rev GGD 3:4:192

Wuerttemberg, emig index vol 1, bk rev AG 62:1:57 MD 28:1:111 GHS 4:2:69 RES 18:1:18 GJ 15:2:107 (vol 2) NTT 7:1:3

GERRITSE, Mary f1887, NY, OR, journal CT 7:3:22 7:4:25

GETTY, Fam hist 1631-1865 ST, IR, US, bk rev MGR 22:2:85 WPG 13:4:46

Joseph bc1745, w Jane ____, IR, PA, OH, IN, IA, IL, KS, geneal, bk rev TS 29:3:107 WPG 14:1:55 NYR 118:4:251

GETTYS, Fam hist IR, PA, OH, IN, IL, IA, KS, bk rev MD 28:2:239 SCS 24:4:91

GEUTHER, John George b1805, w Kunigunde Pfitzemeier, GE, US, fam hist WTC 17:1:37

GFELL, William A b1890, OH, reflections TFP 7: :51

GIBBENS, John S bc1825, w Emily Permelia Pettis, EN, IA, fam rec SLB 6:6:280

GIBBS, Emeline see Charles HAWLEY

Peter f1745,w Ann ____, BM, fam rec BBQ 4:1:10

Sarah A see Enos C DICKINSON

Thomas f1701, w Mary ____, BM fam rec BBQ 4:1:10

GIBSON, Ruben see Mary Elizabeth WILES

Sarah Ann see David RANDALL

Thomas f1829, SC, TN, MS, suit SCM 15:2:70

William Green Lee b1821, w Mary Elizabeth Majors, AL, anc ch NAS 26:1:14

GIDDINGS, Absolem F b1853, h Eliza E Million, OH, obit AH 14:1:22

GIFFORD, Daniel see Marcia Averill CALKINS

GILBERT, Abigail see Daniel SHAYS

Fam estate divisions Harford Co MD 1807-1894 MD 28:2:144

Fam rec Harford Co MD 1700s-1800s, bk rev TNB 2:2:5

Gulbrand Hansen b1842, w Hedda Syversen Matterand, NW, WA, anc ch WB 17:4:131

Isaac f1781, w Elizabeth ____, Bible rec YV 19:3:104

Lemuel f1830, MA, testimonial BG 8:4:88

Sarah see Jerry CRILL & Thomas ROBERDS

Thomas b1582, desc, bk rev OC 24:1:37

GILCHRIST, Alexander b1721, ST, NY, geneal, bk rev GH 41:2:151

GILES, Fam crest & shield TEG 7:1:11

William f1673, w Dorcas ____, MD, geneal MD 28:2:226

GILL(E)(I)LAND, Surname period, *Gill(e)(i)land, Res Aide*, 11863 207th St, Lakewood CA 90715

GILL, Mary see Reuben Clarke SHORTER

GILLESPIE, Edwin D d1929, w Bessie Gillespie, IL, obit MCS 7:1:16

GILLET, Surname period, *Gillet Pride n Joy*, 1103 W 1st, McCook NE 69001

Catharine b1788, NY, anc ch OCG 17:2:13

GILLETT, Isaac Mills b1814, w Finette Carman, NY, IL, fam hist WTC 17:4:122

John b1671, w Experience Dewey & Eunice ____, CT, biog AG 62:3:78

GILLIAM, Judith Ann see Callam Holman BAILEY

GILLILAND, Louisa Jane see John B B MARTIN

GILMAN, Edward b1587, w Mary Clarke, EN, MA, lineage SB 8:1:15

Richard f1672, w Elizabeth Adkins, CT, geneal, bk rev FRT 8:3:148

GILMORE, Frank H b1833, w Mary S Blackwell, IL, biog sketch FF 15:3:27

Hugh Miles f1857, diary of trip through TX 1857 HTR 30:3:75

Margaret b1855, h Jake Kelso, MO, memories of Civil War OZ 8:4:156

GILPATRICK, Hannah b1787, NH, anc ch TEG 7:3:158

GITTINGS, Susannah see John Wilson

GIVENS, Samuel Echols bc1855, w Hannah Hilton, PA, OK, anc ch KL 7:4:13

GLANCY, James b1765, w Elizabeth Lighthill, PA, OH, geneal, bk rev GH 41:3:168

GLASS, John Peter b1734, GE, PA, geneal, bk rev GH 41:4:206

Thomas J b1778, w Elizabeth J Anderson, VA?, KY, IN, geneal, bk rev CCS 8:4:130

GLENDINNING, Fam hist IR, bk rev CTN 20:3:518

GLOVER, Betsey Ann see Stephen MERWIN

John I m1786, w Sarah ____, NY, Bible rec CTA 29:3:98

GOBLE, Fam hist MA, bk rev FLG 10:3:120

Samuel b1807, w Sarah ____, OH, IA, anc ch MGR 22:2:88 CCS 9:2:62

William Henry b1813, w Mary M Durland, NY, biog sketch OCG 17:2:15

GOBLISS, Mary see John D SMITH

GOCHENAUER, Samuel f1892, GE, IN, will & estate rec MIS 19:3:53

GODARD, Josephine Louise see William Hugh EAGLESON

GODDARD, Daniel f1646, CT, geneal, bk rev DM 50:4:162

Fam rec misc, bk rev NER 141:1:71

GODFREY, Caleb d1803, w Mary Maxfield, RI, geneal RIR 13:2:35

John m1722, w Katherine Davis, RI, biog sketch RIR 13:2:34

Phylow Frances see Jacob Jake ROBERTS

GODWIN, Alexander b1795, w Margaret M McLaughlin, AL, fam rec PT 29:4:150

Alexander M b1795, w Margaret M McLaughlin & Missouri T Lavett Windser, SC, AL, children PT 29:2:43

Mary Reid f1826, GA, FL, fam hist FLG 10:3:94

Mary see Arthur WHITEHEAD

GOEBEL, Louise see George DIEHL

GOECKNER, Mary see Frank ESKER

GOETSCHIUS, Mauritius d1735, SW, NY, geneal, bk rev NYR 118:4:249

GOFF, John b1717, VA, geneal, bk rev GH 41:6:157

Statira see Charles Huntley CONNOLLY

GOFORTH, Mary Ann see Benedict BECKLER
GOLD, Fam cem Palo Pinto Co TX FP 30:4:177
GOLDEN, Louis F d1886, TX, death notice DG 33:3:169
GOLNIK, Friedrich W b1857, w Carolina Henriette Kothke, PO, MN, anc ch FCT :73:19
GOMER, Amanda F see Vincent SHILLING
GONCE, Fam hist, bk rev NTT 7:1:3
Rudolph bc1745, w Polly McDade, GE?, PA?, geneal, bk rev NCJ 13:2:120
GONN, John b1790, w Mary Norman, KY, TX, fam rec AGS 28:2:96
GOOCH, Mary see James TERRY
GOOD, Elizabeth see John BURKHART
GOODE, Martha see Hiram PARSONS
GOODENOUGH, Surname period, Goodenoughs' Ghosts, 3756 Knox St, St Joseph MI 49085 - marr VT, cem NY, v r MA, Edmund & desc, Arnold will 1882, Orson J 1836-1895
GOODFELLOW, Timothy f1745, NY, NJ, geneal, bk rev NYR 118:4:249
GOODMAN, Freda see Henry George MUNRO
William b1833, w Jennie Rea, WI, Bible rec MCR 18:4:111
GOODNER, Matilda see Calvin P MILLER
GOODRICH, Maggie M see Evan E JONES
Moses m1831, w Alma Harris, NY, Bible rec FG 29:4:112
Samuel b1816, w Charlotte Perry & Phebe A (Howard) Dutton, NY, lineage SLV 5:3:13
Silas b1775, w Freelove Arnold, CT, lineage SLV 5:5:2
GOODRIDGE, Mary see Arthur THRESHER
GOODSON, Fam cem MO GTP 25:1:28

GOODSON (continued)
Samuell see Adam BRAND
GOODWIN, Hannah see John WATSON
John see Hannah JACKSON
Surname period, The Goodwin News, 13430 Mirella St, Pensacola FL 32507
William C b1837, NY, KS, obit SLV 5:5:3
GORDON, James d1889, w Mary Gordon, IR, cem inscr GGL 6:3:102
James f1860, NY, census rec MI 31:4:121
GORHAM, Nathaniel b1738, w Rebecca Call, MA, biog DAR 121:8:684
GORMAN, John f1853, w Anna ___, IR, NY, IL, biog sketch WTC 8:4:90
GOSLING, Agnes d1639, EN, MA, anc ch AW 13:1:21
GOSS, Alice see L R SELLERS
Banjamin Franklin m1851, w Louisa Perry, Bible rec GGS 23:1:25
Jonathan Carver Sr d1882, lineage FI 7:2:49
GOSSELIN, Lucien-Hippolyte b1883, biog JMS 10:1:76
GOSSMAN, Henry m1909, w Josie Stroud, IL, wedding CRT 8:4:35
GOTT, Catherine see Abraham SMOCK
GOTTGE, Ludwig f1754, PA, geneal, bk rev WPG 13:4:45
GOUGH, John Baptist f1833, MD, MO, pension appl MD 28:3:325
GOULD, Anna Maud f1887, ME, diary of trip to San Francisco, bk rev GH 41:4:206 CTN 20:3:519 DE 11:2:71
GOULET, Odeil see Joseph O CHEVALIER
GOUMAZ, Peter b1800, w Marie Josephine Lambert, SW, IL, biog FF 15:4:142
GRACY, Fam hist NY & TX, bk rev AGS 28:1:15

GRAHAM, Walter f1833, VA, half pay claim VAG 31:2:133

GRALERS, Anna Maria see Johann SUHRE

GRAMM, Henry f1864, IN, letters RT 5:1:23

GRANDSTAFF, Adam bc1786, w Martha ___, VA, OH, anc ch RED 19:3:14

GRANT, Elenora J see J A FAGAN

Mary Frances see Joseph C MARTIN

Sarah see Richard DUDGEON

Ulysses Simpson f1869, US, hist of homestead in IR IFL 2:9-10:21

GRASSHOFF, Frederick d1918, w Wilhelmina Will, NY, IL, obit CRT 8:4:31

GRASTY, Fam census 1880 Pittsylvania Co VA FRT 8:1:41

GRAU, Gottlieb Leopold Friedrich f1854 w Friederike Bunse, GE, IL, fam hist WTC 14:4:145

GRAVENSTEIN, Elizabeth see Matthew FOSHAY

GRAVES, Fleming R bc1810, w Mary Ann Hiatt, KY, biog MSG 7:3:133

James William b1843, w Margaret Sageser, KY, MO, biog MSG 7:3:134

Surname period, *The Graves Fam Newsletter*, 261 South St, Wrentham MA 02093 - Hiram of New EN & CN, Ira of VA, Walter of TN & KY, George of CN, Samuel of MA, John Samuel of SC

William S b1818, w Loucinda Carter, anc ch NWT 8:3:28

GRAWERT, Elsie Sophie Johann see Johann Christian Frederick MOLLER

GRAY, Elijah b1799, w Anna Brooks, VA, TN, MO, geneal OZ 7:2:73

John f1820, MA, pension appl RAG 8:1:10

GRAYSON, John dc1734, VA, TX, geneal, bk rev NYR 118:2:118

GREAR, James m1687, w Ann Taylor, ST, MD, geneal, bk rev GH 41:3:168

GREAT BRITAIN, Hist of Celts 5 B.C.-664 A.D., bk rev WPG 13:3:48

marr, census, & other indexes guide, bk rev NGS 74:3:235 AG 62:3:185

Probate jurisdictions guide, bk rev NGS 74:3:235 AG 62:3:185

Rec Offices use guide by Church & Cole, bk rev BCG 16:4:145 GM 22:7:262

GREECE, Hist sketch MP 3:2:76

GREEN, Ann see Eijah MELTON

Benjamin d1902, OH, obit TLL 12:3:50

David b1766, MA, biog AG 62:3:151

John William m1878, w Louisa Johnson, Bible rec HH 21:4:225

Joseph b1855, w Laura Cade, EN, WA, biog AB 16:1:12

Leroy Hammond b1840, w Mary Ann Ballard, GA, anc ch NAS 26:1:22

Richard bc1795, w Frances (Fanny) ___ & Joanna Brown, NC, MO, children OZ 9:1:27

William m1864, w Georgiana McDaniel, NC, Bible rec TQR 14:1:40

William D see Idress HOWARD

William Dancy b1852, w Elizabeth Francis Tolbert, AL, anc ch NAS 26:1:15

GREENE, Alta see William Theodore SCOTT

Nathaniel f1779, papers 1779, bk rev REG 85:3:267

GREENFIELD, Sallyan see Alexander Hamilton HOCHSTRASSER

GREENLEAF, Israel f1781, MA, pension appl RAG 8:1:10

GREENWELL, Fam hist EN & KY, bk rev RAG 8:5:22

Fam hist VA, MD, KY, 1700s- , bk rev IL 19:2:119 TS 29:2:70 CO 48:4:104

GREENWELL (continued)

James bc1770, w Anastatia ___, MD?, KY, CA, geneal, bk rev PGB 19:1:10

Richard f1653, VA, geneal, bk rev NCJ 13:3:184

GREER, Fam rec misc GA, NC, TN, geneal, bk rev GH 41:5:192

George Washington b1833, w Nancy Redford & Katherine Arnold, TN, geneal, bk rev GH 41:2:151

James f1674, IR, MD, GA, geneal, bk rev NTT 7:2:44

James f1674, w Ann Taylor, MD, GA, geneal, bk rev NTT 7:3:82

Jason Martin Sr b1804, w Sarah Ann Sanders, SC, NC, VA, geneal, bk rev GHS 4:1:73 SCM 15:1:59

Thomas b1760, VA, GA, obit GGS 23:4:191

Thomas bc1710, w Susanna Carver, IR, NC, geneal, bk rev VAG 31:1:65 GH 41:4:206 YCG 7:3:59 NCJ 13:3:184

GREGG, Carrie Morton see Galen Luther STONE

Craven b1829, w Catharine Stewart, PA, geneal, bk rev GH 41:6:157

GREGORY, Isaac bc1730, w Alse ___, SC, geneal, bk rev GH 41:3:176

GRESHAM, Surname period, *Gresham - Any Way You Spell It*, POB 834194, Richardson TX 75083

GRIDER, Hiram Burrows b1899, w Elsie Irene Brewer, TX, children FTH 10:3-4:100

GRIER, Agnes b1787, NC, SC, anc ch THT 16:1:13

GRIFFIN, John bc1804, w Mary Chapman, EN, IL, geneal, bk rev GH 41:5:196

Mary f1833, h ___ Sheldon, NY, OH, auto TFP 2: :75 7: :59

Samuel b1753, w Sarah Scarf, WE, MD, geneal, bk rev GH 41:6:157

GRIFFIN (continued)

Sarah see Jehu BURR

Susannah M see William Curtis LEDFORD

William m1843, w Elizabeth Harvey, Bible rec OZ 7:2:77

GRIFFITH, Isaac f1831, w Elizabeth ___, DE, will abstr MAD 27:3:98

James Alfred b1801, w Elizabeth Rogers Forsyth, NC, CA, biog sketch SCS 24:10:201

John f1788, DE, will abstr MAD 27:2:53

Joseph f1810, DE, will abstr MAD 27:2:53

Martha f1777, DE, will abstr MAD 27:3:98

Samuel f1786, DE, will abstr MAD 27:2:53

Samuel R f1799, w Deborah Bevin, PA, OH, geneal, bk rev GH 41:5:192

GRIFFITHS, Eleanor b1778, WE?, Bible rec MCR 18:1:8

John b1842, w Jenette Williams, WE, NA, obit NA 10:1:5

P L f1868, WE, IL, letter CHG 19:2:111

GRIFFITHS, Philip f1870, WE, IL, letter CHG 19:3:130

GRIGG, William Pitt b1765, w Joanna Jane ___, Cornwall, MD, anc ch MAD 27:3:119

GRILLS, Matilda see JohN YEAKLEY

GRIMES, P A see J H BELEW

GRIMM, Adam b1822, w Elizabeth Mains, GE, PA, biog sketch LM 28:4:291

GRISHAM, Thompson b1817, w Polly Wheeler, TN, IL, MO, children OZ 7:2:73

GRISSOM, Marin Elizabeth see James Monroe NEIGHBORS

GRISWOLD, John E m1821, w Lucia Ann Meacham, Bible rec CTN 20:2:243

GROCE, Surname period, *Groce Fam Newsletter*, POB 28215, Sacramento CA 95828 - census PA, GA, TN, TX, VA

GROESBECK, Henry m1830, w Rebecca Fondah, NY, Bible rec DM 50:3:105

GROETHAUSEN, Herman f1709, GE, PA, fam hist LCC 4:3:15

GROFF, Fam rec misc Eur & PA, bk rev GH 41:1:161 NYR 118:2:117

GROOME, Amy see George JEWELL

GROSS, Edmond f1853, w Hetty ____, VA, pension HF 3:3:141

GROVE, Michael bc1757, PA, biog sketch RES 18:1:41

GROVER, Roxana see Stephen DORMAN

GROVES, Nicholas b1788, w Roxanna Stearns, VT, MI, biog FHC 11:1:5

GRUBB, Eugene Housel b1850, w Isadore E White, PA, CA, anc ch RED 20:2:15

GRUBBS, Cynthia see Stephen SERGEANT

GRUENENWALD, Christian f1853, SW, CA, fam hist sketch OC 24:1:27

GRUNERT, Maximilian Eugen f1850, NC, Moravian birthday bk 1700s-1800s FC 5:3:4

Maximilian Eugen f1850, birthday bk FC 5:4:4

GRUWELL, Timothy m1803, w Alice ____, Bible rec HH 21:4:216

GRYNIER, Phillippe bc1548, w Mary ____, EN, CN, geneal, bk rev GH 41:2:151

GUEST, Moses b1750, VA, NC, SC, GA, MS, TX, geneal, bk rev GHS 4:2:71

GUILD, Simeon m1786, w Lydia Closson, Bible rec RT 4:3:70

GUILLET, Marie-Charlotte see Joseph-Philippe OUABARD

GULLEDGE, Margaret Alice f1905, TX, letter FP 30:3:124

GULLETT, Ezekiel bc1776, w Mary Dixon, MD?, NC?, OH?, geneal, bk rev GH 41:4:206

GUM, Elijah b1786, w Susannah Bruner, KY, MO OZ 9:2:67

GUMP, William m1820, w Margaret Whitlach, PA, service rec RAG 8:1:19

GUPTILL, Thomas f1670, w Mary ____, NH, geneal, bk rev FRT 8:3:149

GURULE, Santiago m1699, w Elena Gallegos, NM, geneal NGS 75:1:37

GUSTIN, A L b1834, w Eliza J McMullen, IL, KS, biog sketch BCS 7:1:10

Susana see J C WILCONS

GUTHALS, Johann b1835, w Anke Margaretha Guthal, GE, NE, anc ch BGS 19:1:41

GUTHRIE, Fam hist IR & US, bk rev WPG 13:3:46

GUTTERY, John Scott b1864, w Anna Nixon, OH, autograph bk HL 2:2:38

GUYTON, John f1719, EN, MD, OH, OR, geneal, bk rev NYR 118:1:55 CCS 9:1:25

HAAKSMA, John Jacob b1851, w Jetske Sytzes (Wieringa), HO?, IL, geneal AB 15:3:73

HABERLE, John Ludwig b1793, w Christiana C Miller, GE, PA, geneal, bk rev GH 41:6:157

HACKEROTT, August Heinrich George m1822, w Marie Dorothea Elizabeth Kruger, GE, US, geneal, bk rev GH 41:5:192

HACKLER, Conrad bc1775, w Nancy ____, VA, fam rec AGS 28:2:80

HACKNEY, Wilson b1816, w Mary Barclay Kimbrough, KY, MO, geneal OZ 7:2:71

HADDAN, Harold Lee b1906, OR, auto CT 7:4:3

John M b1842, w Jennie E Johnston, PA, IL, biog sketch CCS 8:4:115

HADDIX, Mary M b1836, VA, WV, anc ch FTR :101:8

HADDOCK, Fam legends EN, ST, NC, bk rev KK 25:3:56 CTA 30:1:53 17:3:68 TS 29:2:70 DS 24:3:165

HADDOCK (continued)
John Sr bc1720, NC, MO, geneal, bk rev PGB 19:1:10 GH 41:5:192
HADEN, Rebeckah see Richard EPPERSON
HADLEY, George f1628, MA, NY, geneal, bk rev NYR 118:1:50
George C f1858, EN, MA, MO, geneal, bk rev MSG 7:3:171
Leo G b1863, EN, MA, MO, geneal, bk rev CTA 29:3:112
Paul b1880, IN, biog, bk rev GH 41:2:130
Vesta see William H DAILEY
HAFFIN, Andrew m1851, w Elizabeth Bird, IA, marr rec PCI 9:4:4
HAG, Hans Jorg f1748, PA, codicile PA 35:1:1
HAGADORN, Richard f1819, w Cyna Eddy, Bible rec CTN 20:3:436
HAGAN, Surname period, *The Hagan Hist Soc Newsletter*, Box 12346, N Kansas City MO 64116
Thomas Clarke b1793, w Tabitha Wedding, VA, KY, geneal, bk rev WCK 20:2:31
HAGBERG, Karl J b1873, SN, Bible rec GFP 36:4:167
HAGER, August b1843,w Mary Barbara Reiter, GE, NY, MO, geneal, bk rev GH 41:2:151 FRT 8:4:198
HAGERTY, Catherine see John M TARPEY
HAGOOD, Sarah see William SIMMONS
HALDORSEN, Johan f1867, w Beret Olsdatter Svinaas, NW, QB, MN, geneal, bk rev GH 41:4:206
HALE, Andrew f1847, GA, will TCG 6:4:26
George K bc1826, w Caroline Bowser, TN, children BWG 16:2:121
Hannah see James W COX
Thomas see Thomasine DOWSETT

HALES, Chloe Etta see John Lendsey Monroe COLLIER
HALEY, John b1822, w Elizabeth Kunzen, GE, NY, CN, IL, geneal WTC 17:4:112
HALL, Bartlett Marymond bc1811, w Harriet L McClure, TN, TX, geneal YTD 6:2:1
Beulah see William BROMWELL
Caleb Mastin b1821, Bible rec KA 23:2:87
David Alfred b1804, w Abigal W Baker, NY, anc ch BHN 20:3:124
Elbridge Gerry m1849, w Martha Ann Clark, MA, geneal, bk rev GH 41:1:161
Eliakim see Eunice MOSS
Fannie see Henry C FULLER Sr
Jesse b1815, w Margaret S Taylor & Frances A Wisecarver, TN, MO, children OZ 8:2:64
John m1881, w Elizabeth Diggs Balas, VA, Bible rec TN 7:1:11
John W f1857, TN, IL, death in Alton (IL) prison MCS 7:3:105
Jonathan m1785, w Mercy ____, VT, Bible rec DAR 121:4:335
Thomas Randolph m1860, w Clarinda Beecher Phillips, MD, Bible rec DAR 121:5:335
Van C b1800, w Mary Burris, SC, anc ch NAS 25:4:130
HALLMARK, George b1805, w Sarah Tipton, AL, fam hist MCA 6:1:25
HAM, Martha Mary Ann,see William Henry LAWRENCE
HAMBRICK, A L f1861, w Rebecca ____, VA, letters KSL 11:1:14
HAMBROOK, Surname period, *The Hambrook Herald*, 37 Walden Cr, Regina, Sask, S4N 1L1 Canada - Annie Catherine of BC, fam in EN, marr EN 1703-1833 & 1865-1870, parish reg EN 1563-1703

HAMERSK(I)Y, Surname period, *Hamersky & Allied Fam Newsletter*, POB 3939, Chula Vista CA 92011

HAMILTON, Alexander f1804, w Elizabeth ____, biog LAB 2:2:22

Fam crest & shield TEG 7:2:63

Harvey William b1813, w Mary Susan Kitchens, anc ch PT 29:3:113

Hattie see J R BLACKWELL

Janet see Robert CREE Sr

Mary see Benjamin WREATH

Robert dc1834, NC, AR, WA, fam hist sketch & lineage EWA 24:4:257

Surname period, *The Connector*, 14326 Blackmon Dr, Rockville MD 20853

HAMLIN, Orah m1912, h Robert McClung, OK, Bible rec MGR 22:2:87

HAMM, Maria Barbara see Georg Friedrich SCHINDEL

HAMMER, Charles dc1893, WI, burial rec WI 33:4:256

HAMMOCK, C C f1862, letter THT 15:1:25

HAMMOND, Surname period, *Hammond Fam Assoc Quarterly*, 6619 Pleasant Rd, Baltimore MD 21220 – census 1850 AL, cem SC, John & John Johnson Hammond fam

HAMP, Hans f1520, GE, geneal, bk rev OK 32:2:44

Johann Jakob f1817, w Euphrosina Kittelberger, GE, PA, OH, geneal, bk rev GH 41:6:158

HANCHETT, Lyman L b1822, CT, NY, IL, geneal, bk rev NYR 118:2:115

Thomas b1620, w Deliverance Langton, EN, CT, VT, MI, geneal, bk rev NER 141:1:70 NYR 118:1:54

HANCOCK, Anthony f1630, w Sarah (Sary) Wilson & Ruth MacCane, EN, MA, geneal, bk rev GH 41:2:151 WPG 13:3:51

HANCOCK (continued)

Frederick M m1858, w Mary Elizabeth ____, Bible rec GN 5:2:70

William f1651, VA, geneal, bk rev VAG 31:1:66

HAND, Phebe see John ROCKWELL

HANDLEY, James Ella see Isaac Patrick HOPKINS

HANGESBERG, Anna Maria b1782, anc ch AG 62:3:90

HANNA, Katherine see William Worder PARDICK

HANNAH, Benjamin Wilson b1860, w Emma Guinn Ebaugh, AL, anc ch BGS 19:3:135

HANRAHAN, Roger f1860, w Ellen ____, IL, census rec MCS 7:3:114

HANSCOMBE, John bc1550, w Joan ____ & Agnes Cowche, ME, geneal TEG 7:2:85

HANSEN, Adolf Fredrik b1755, w Judith Benners, SN, St Barthelemy, obit SAG 7:1:32

HAPPES, Fam hist SW & US, bk rev FRT 8:3:151

HARAPIAK, Fam hist 1858–1986 Ukraine & CN, bk rev GEN 12:4:25

HARBERT, Mary C see John Wesley ROBERTS

HARBISON, Elizabeth see John BELL

HARDEMAN, Fam hist TX, bk rev FP 30:1:9

HARDESTY, Surname period, *Bits O' Hist Newsletter*, 1546 W Farwell, Chicago IL 60626

HARDIN, Ignatius m1781, w Sarah Davis, MD, geneal MAD 27:2:56 27:3:102

J Alvin, geneal, bk rev QY 14:1:7

HARDISON, Delilah see Brackett DAVIDSON

HARDMAN, Maria Louise see Turlington Walker HARVEY

HARDWICK, Surname period, *Hardwick Hunting*, Shirley Hornbeck, POB 1019, Temple City CA 91780–1019

HARDY, Richard b1775, w Ann Williams, SC, geneal TCG 7:4:1

HARGRETT, Thomas f1854, w Barbara S Slappey, GE, NC, geneal, bk rev GGS 23:1:45

HARGROVE, Billy see Catherine Catiche BONHARME

HARKER, Edward Bermont b1848, PA, geneal, bk rev WPG 14:1:51

HARKINS, William b1829, w Emaline Amanda Rowe, Bible rec OCR 28:2:60

HARLAN, Winifred see Tom A BEANS

HARLOW, Benjamin d1816, MA, cem inscr MQ 53:3:165

HARMAN, Mary Frances f1800s, h ____ Smith, geneal rec collect OZ 6:3:119

HARMON, David b1834, w Jennie E Dawson, Bible rec OZ 9:2:63

John b1617, w Elizabeth Cummings, EN, MA, lineage SB 8:5:177

Maude see Christian BECK

HARNISH, Samuel b1704, w Anna Elizabeth ____, PA, anc ch RAG 8:1:14

HARP, William Henry f1870, w Mary Wilson, children BWG 16:1:55

HARPER, Elizabeth see Isaac REED

Martha see Lodowich ARCHER

Peter b1810, PA, service rec AGS 28:2:31

Susanna b1817, KY?, VA?, IL, KS, anc ch CR 19:2:98

HARRELL, Barbara Ellen see Adam ROYDER

James William b1826, w Elisabeth ____, AR, AL, geneal, bk rev GH 41:4:206

James William b1826, w Elisabeth ____ & Sarah A E Wallingsford, AR, geneal, bk rev GFP 37:2:73

Newton b1832, w Mary Ellender Harris, GA, anc ch NC :98:9

HARRINGTON, Antipas m1804, w Esther Smith, NH, VT, children RED 20:1:10

Chas Wesley b1860, w Mary E Sutton, MI, CN, anc ch KIL 15:2:32

Fam rec corr to *Harrington Fam Geneal Gazetteer* by Harrington NEH 4:3:164

Harvey d1858, AL, obit SGE 28:121:44

Joseph b1792, w Rachel Weaver, NY, IL, geneal WTC 14:4:146

Oramel Warren b1829, w Martha C Heath, VT, MN, geneal, bk rev NYR 118:2:121

Russell b1821, w Electa Burrel, Bible rec BG 8:3:68

HARRIS, Alma see Moses GOODRICH

Daniel b1831, w Lydia Harris & Rachel Thornton & Hannah Thornton, IN, UT, MX, biog CSB 21:1-2:11

Elizabeth Helen see William Albert KING

Elizabeth T see Thos P WASHINGTON

Fam hist IL, bk rev GGS 23:4:210 CCS 9:2:60

Mary Ellender see Newton HARRELL

Nancy see Benjamin Joseph ADAIR

Susan see Acker RULAND

HARRISON, Andrew d1718, VA, biog, bk rev IL 19:2:109

Andrew f1671, EN, VA, geneal, bk rev MD 28:1:113 RAG 8:5:21

Frances see Thomas SHANDS

Patience see Austin ODELL

Surname period, *Harrison Heritage*, 2816 Sloat Rd, Pebble Beach CA 93953

William Washington b1813, w Ann Mariah Cotten, VA, FL, lineage FLG 10:4:134

HARSTAD, Bjug m1877, w Guro Omlid, NW, MN, biog sketch CHI 60:3:112

HART, Aaron b1854, w Ellen
Patty, GA, TX, anc ch NAS
26:1:12
Christopher b1753,w Elizabeth
Richards, PA, geneal, bk rev
WPG 13:3:48
Henry f1600, EN, IR, US, geneal,
microfiche rev GH 41:2:163
John b1784, PA, geneal, bk rev
GH 41:1:161
Lucretia see Henry CLAY
Nehemiah d1796, NY, geneal, bk
rev FRT 8:3:150
Surname period, *The Hart Forum*,
POB 161, N Webster IN 46555
– naturalizations TX, Thomas
of NC, anc ch, marr SC, cem
TN, Bible rec
HARTER, Barbara see Maxmilian
OKENFUSS
Fam hist NY, bk rev NYR
118:2:116
HARTMANN, Heinz f1939, GE,
NY, auto, bk rev NYR
118:3:179
HARTSFIELD, Andrew I bc1700,
w Sarah Lynn ____, children
THT 15:1:28
HARTSHORN, Mary see Zebulon
CLAYTON
Thomas bc1614, w Susannah
Buck & Sarah (Ayres) Lamson,
MA, lineage SB 8:3:87
Thomas f1635, w Susanna Buck
& Sarah Ayres, EN, MA,
geneal, bk rev SB 8:1:18 FRT
8:2:101
HARTZLER, C A f1912, IL, biog
MH 14:4:39
HARVEY, Almira b1828, h Amos
Davis, PA, IA, NE, obit NA
10:2:53
Blassingame W b1792, w
Elizabeth Stone & Nancy Scog-
gins & Eliza Mary Ann
Prather, SC, LA, TX, geneal,
bk rev GH 41:5:192
Casimir b1818, w Edelire (Luce)
Poirier, QB, anc ch AGE
16:2:54
Elizabeth Jane see Thomas Red-
man LAWLESS

HARVEY (continued)
Elizabeth see William GRIFFIN
Thomas b1634, NC, biog sketch
NCJ 13:4:204
Turlington Walker b1835, w
Maria Louise Hardman, NY,
IL, biog WTC 3:4:147
William Henry b1877, CO, bapt
cert FI 7:2:47
HARWOOD, Joanna see Roger
AMADOWNE
Thomas Moore b1827, w Cordelia
Brown, VA, TX, letters 1879–
1881 AGS 28:3:132
HASKINS, Electa see Nathaniel
DALRYMPLE
HASSELL, Millie see Joel Ander-
son CARTER
HATCH, David m1827, w Fanny
Chapman, anniversary notice
AH 14:3:96
Joseph R m1850, w Ann E Wil-
liams, Bible rec RT 4:3:68
Lewis b1757, MA, NY, geneal,
bk rev NYR 118:2:119
Rufus m1800, w Hepzibah
McNeil, Bible rec MCR
18:3:80
Thomas bc1598, w Grace ____,
EN, MA, geneal, bk rev GH
41:2:160
HATFIELD, Sarah E b1841, IL,
funeral card SR 1:1:3
HATHAWAY, Heil Bronson
m1892, w Anna Mabel Skeels,
WA, biog sketch TB 13:4:15
Joanna b1685, h Nathaniel
Blackwell, MA, fam rec AG
62:1:30
HATHCOCK, Benjamin bc7142,
VA, geneal, bk rev GH
41:2:152
HAUK, Michael bc1778, SC, anc
ch CR 19:1:6
HAUSAUER, Elizabeth see Jacob
MARZOLF
HAUSER, Anna see Hans Heinrich
BAR PM 10:1:21
HAVEMEYER, Henry Osborne
m1883, w Louisine Waldron
Elder, NY, geneal, bk rev NYR
118:3:183

HAVENS, Rhoda see Daniel SHAYS

HAVERSTICK, Ann see Adam KENDIG

HAWAII, V r avail LRT 6:2:211

HAWES, Experience see Ebenezer SPROAT

HAWES, Richard f1810 VA, KY, geneal, bk rev KA 22:4:245

Samuel f1704, w Anne Walker, VA, geneal, bk rev GH 41:2:160

HAWKES, Surname period, *Hawkes Talks*, POB 362, Boynton Beach FL 33425

HAWKINS, Elizabeth b1824, h Alfred Devour/DeVore, VA, KY, MO, obit SNS 3:4:3

ELizabeth see Joseph BEASMAN

Fam rec misc, bk rev GH 41:1:161

Giles m1840, w Martha Jesse, KY, Bible rec KA 23:2:81

Henry b1837, w Anna Eliza Shanks, AL, anc ch NAS 26:2:67

Henry f1845, w Martha Crafton, IA, OR, fam hist GFP 37:2:63

HAWLEY, Charles b1813, w Emeline Gibbs, NY, IL?, anc ch CCS 9:1:31

Styles W f1846, NH, letter GTP 24:4:67

HAWORTH, Rutha May see Fred Lester McCREA

HAWTHORNE, Anne Nancy see Philemon Leigh BRYAN

HAYDEL, Perinne see Christophe ROUSSEL

HAYDEN, Fam group sheets 1630-1900, bk rev GH 41:4:207 WPG 14:1:52

Harriet May see George Wycliff WATKINS

Josiah b1733, MA, geneal, bk rev CTN 20:1:142

HAYES, Kizziah see Thomas Hicks COMBS

William Sr b1766, w Lucy Gatewood, EN?, KY, geneal, bk rev WTC 10:3-4:128

HAYFORD, Columbus m1866, w Lavina Pratt Allen, ME, obit DE 11:3:89

HAYMAN, Henry bc1632, w Elinor ___, EN, VA, geneal, bk rev GH 41:2:152

James bc1800, w Delilah Martin, GA, FL, lineage FLG 10:4:143

HAYMORE, Surname period, *The Haymore Fam of North Am*, 4518 Clearwater Dr, Corpus Christi TX 78413

HAYNES, Elizabeth see Jacob BURCH

Landon C m1882, w Jennie C Brown, biog sketch BWG 16:2:117

Samuel M b1849, w Amanda A Blunt, IN, IL, obit CRT 8:4:44

HAYS, Samuel m1819, w Susanna Smith, Bible rec AG 62:4:223

HAYWOOD, Margaret see Richard PARROTT Sr

HAZEN, Daniel f1775, NJ, NB, geneal, bk rev NYR 118:4:249

HEAD, Ethel see Thomas Clyde BUTLER

HEADEN, B F f1852, diary abstr SCC 24:1:1

HEADMAN, Mary Sevier Hoss f1950, TN, letter BWG 16:1:32

HEARN, Eliza see Wiley SMITH

HEATH, Elizabeth see John BOWLES

Martha C see Oramel Warren HARRINGTON

HEATHERLEY, Fam hist TN, bk rev PEL 8:4:158

HEAVEL, Polly E see James T THOMPSON

HEBB, Christopher b1724, EN, US, geneal, bk rev BAT 16:1:24

HEBERLING, Elizabeth see Peter MARTIN

John bc1777, w Mary Crumley, MD, VA, OH, fam rec AGS 28:2:76

Rebecca see Thomas LEWIS II

HEBERT, Auguste b1864, w Alida Boudreaux, LA, anc ch AGE 16:2:50

HEGERTY, William m1878, w Elizabeth Bishop, WI, Bible rec MCR 18:2:36

HEGETSWEILER, Lidia Louisa see Armstead Pride TAYLOR

HEIDEMANN, Mathilda L see Frank E KRUEGER

HEILIGER, Margaretha see Johannes LOWRANCE

HEISEY, M Luther b1881, PA, biog LCH 3:3:144

HELTON, Mary see John M GARDNER

HEMANN, William, w Katharina Deutrich, GE, geneal, bk rev GH 41:4:209

HEMENWAY, Ralph b1585, w Elizabeth Hewes, EN, MA, geneal, bk rev SLV 5:1:11

HEMMION, Eleanor see Heinrich MERKER

HENDERSON, Jane b1798, TN, IA, anc ch RED 19:4:9

Leon Lucius b1887, w Sallie Octavia Hendry, FL, lineage FLG 10:4:154

Robert b1835, w Sarah Mildred Thompson, KY, AR, anc ch TRC 2:1:45

HENDRICKSZ, Hendrick f1673, PA, geneal, bk rev WPG 13:4:38

HENDRIX, N J E m1850, w Sarah Ann White, TN, Bible rec OZ 6:1:20

HENDRY, Sallie Octavia see Leon Lucius HENDERSON

HENINGER, Hans Peter f1625, w Margarethe Aellin, GE, US, geneal, bk rev GH 41:1:161

HENNEN, James f1786, w Ann Waters, IR, US, geneal SIQ 7:3:43

HENNINGSEN, Inga see Nels J RASMUSSEN

HENRY, Francis bc1768, w Margaret _____, SC, geneal SCM 15:1:3

James b1774, w Esther Patterson & Arabella Henry, SC, geneal SCM 15:2:73

HENRY, Patrick f1789, VA, biog, bk rev VAG 31:1:70

Surname period, *Henry Chronicles*, 6420 Highway 2, Sandpoint ID 83864 – marr PA, fam OH, fam KY, census MO

HERALD, Adam Bernard b1831, w Elizabeth Stinson, GE, IL, anc ch GGS 23:4:200

HERALDRY, Am & British 1982–1985 suppl, bk rev GHS 4:2:69 GN 5:3:156 CTN 20:2:321 GH 41:4:186

Terms, basic MAD 27:1:30 27:3:99

HERBACH, Peter b1674, NL, anc ch CR 19:3:132

HERBERT, Augustus b1829, w Margaretha Sahr, GE, IL, biog sketch WTC 8:4:91

HERD, Helen see Alexander DUNCAN

HERMANN, Augusta see Johann Friederich REIMER

HERNDON, David m1816, w Mary Moreman, Bible rec YTD 1:1:27

Mary Charlotte see Jessie PERKINS

HERON, James Gordon b1749, ST, NJ, biog WTC 7:1:29

HERR, Maria see John BACHMAN

HERREN, Johannah b1841, GE, SD, anc ch BHN 20:4:171

HERRICK, Henry b1604, EN, MA, geneal, bk rev CCS 9:1:24 NYR 118:1:57

Henry Jr b1640, MA, anc ch TEG 7:3:160

HERRINGTON, Hannah see Leonard WILTSE

HERSCHE, Christian d1729, SW, anc ch MFH 6:1:35

Fam marr rec at Appenzell SW 1621–1725 MFH 6:1:15

HERSCHY, Heinrich see Anna SCHALLENBERGER

HERSHBERGEE, Lydia see John LEHMAN

HERSHEY, Catherine see Andrew George BENTZ

HERSHEY (continued)
Elizabeth see Peter RISSER
HESS, Fam hist 1755-1982, bk rev NYR 118:1:55
John R b1828, PA, geneal, bk rev MFH 6:1:34
HESSON, Elinor b1820, FR, PA, anc ch BG 8:4:91
HESTER, Wiley Robertson d1929, AL, obit NTT 7:4:143
HEWES, Elizabeth see Ralph HEMENWAY
George f1682, w Mary Allen, MA, IL, geneal WTC 6:2:60
William b1761, w Abigail Woodcock, MA, IL, fam hist WTC 6:1:39
HEWSON, Ellenor see Thomas COOPER
HEYEN, Heba see Siebrand Algers OLTMANNS
HIATT, Fam res notes QY 14:3:1
HIBBARD, Joseph Butts b1822, w Olive H Pratt, anc ch FF 15:4:139
Mary see Brittain DANIELS
HIBBEN, Mary J see Alexander S BALLARD
HICKEY, Joshua Middleton d1886, w Nancy Liggett, anc ch NWT 8:3:27
Mary Augusta see Patrick Joseph KENNEDY
HICKLE, Devault bc1730, w Eve ___, FR, geneal, bk rev GH 41:4:207
HICKMAN, Fam group sheets, bk rev GH 41:4:191
Robert b1865, MO, autograph bk OZ 8:4:143
HICKOX, Almira Helen see Orestes Seymour REED
HICKS, Ann 1783, MD, will MD 28:2:224
Daniel b1754, w Mary E A Hare Croom, NC, AR, fam rec TRC 2:1:2
Jenny see Ellis W JONES
Nancy b1801, VA, IA, anc ch TN 7:4:54
Thomas m1801,w Kizziah Hayes, NC, Bible rec TS 29:1:25

HICKS (continued)
William Robert m1880, w Cordelia Jane Scaife, SC, fam rec TRC 2:2:68
HIDDEN, Sarah see John Frederick AUBREY
HIGGINS, David f1789, CT, letter TFP 2: :38
Deborah see William WOODMAN
HIGGINSON, Robert f1645, EN, VA, rec misc TN 7:6:88
HIGGS, Sarah Ellen see Jerry BASHAM
HILBORN, Surname period, *Hilborn Fam Journal*, 42 Sources Blvd #8, Pointe Claire, QB, Canada H9S SH9
HILDEBRANDT, Henry f1862, IL, biog WTC 8:3:23
HILL, Elisabeth see William WILLIAMS
Elizabeth see John AWTREY
Georgia Alice see Daviid D PRUITT
Henry bc1660, VA, geneal, bk rev GH 41:4:207
Isaac b1772, w Elizabeth Brumel, CT, OH, fam hist TFP 7: :92
James W m1838, w Margaret Jane Williamson, fam rec KA 22:4:225
John (Red) b1835, w Mary Ann Baldwin, NB, CA, biog sketch RED 19:3:11
John f1848, w Sarah Hill, GA, will TCG 7:2:13
Lon C b1862, TX, biog GTP 25:1:1
Margaret see James Cross Van Houten
Mary C see Robert Jabez POWELL
Naomi see Adam THOMPSON
Oliver Lee b1886, w Naoma Estella Martin, GA, anc ch NC :91:9
Phebe see Joel ELAM
Sarah d1792, h Silas Hill, CT, cem inscr CTN 20:3:425
Sarah see Henry BOEHM

HILL (continued)

Uriah Jr, w Alethea Finch, geneal, microfiche rev GH 41:5:197

HILLIARD, Elizabeth see William WHITE

Fam hist, bk rev FRT 8:3:150

Surname period, *Hilliard Hist* 3111 Pyramid Dr, Ceres CA 95307

HILLS, Anna see Frank DODGE

HILTON, Hannah see Samuel Echols GIVENS

HINCKLEY, Abel S b1803, w Sarah Dennison, CT, OH, biog sketch CPY 16:2:38

HINDE, Estella Anne b1879, OH, biog sketch TFP 2: :85

HINDMAN, Mildred Stanfield b1829, h ____ Doxey, TN, AL, memoirs AW 13:2:60

HINES, Isaac b1802, w Rachel Doan, NC, OH, Bible rec PGB 19:4:62

Martin bc1832, w Margaret Kennedy, IR, KY, geneal LAB 2:1:1

HINMAN, Surname period, *Hinman Heritage*, 81 Richard Rd, Hanson MA 02341

HINSON, Fam hist, bk rev NCJ 13:2:121 GH 41:2:160

John Sr d1845, SC, geneal, bk rev GH 41:6:159

HINZE, Dorothea see William DEUTSCHE Sr

HISAW, Surname period, *Hisaw Fam Newsletter*, 6411 S Quay St, Littleton CO 80123

HISLE, Surname period, *Hisle-Hysell Newsletter*, 2649 Briarwood Dr, San Jose CA 95125

HISPANIC GENEALOGY, Biog sketches of 10 best Chicans 1932 AH 14:2:62

Hist development of geneal organizations in Span Am GJ 15:3:162

Missions of TX 1659-1792 STI 27:2:30

Res guide by Ryskamp, bk rev STI 27:2:36 FAM 26:4:237

HITCHCOCK, Eunice see John HOWARD

HITE, Joseph Sr b1731, lineage VS 4:1:85

HITER, William bc1810, anc ch RT 4:4:107

HITT, Rachal see Peter FRANKS

HIX, Fam heads 1790-1850 NY, bk rev BAT 16:2:76

Fam heads 1790-1850 VT, NH, MA, bk rev BAT 16:2:76 MA 11:3:76

Mary P see Joseph M WICKHAM

HOBART, Edmund b1574, EN, US, geneal, microfiche rev GH 41:2:163

Lizzie Harvey b1851, VT, KS, fam hist sketch WRB 10:3:9

HOBB, Leroy d1953, KY, biog LAB 2:4:56

HOBSON, William b1793, w Eliza Elliott, IR, New Zealand, biog sketch TI 86:11:31

HOCHSTEDLER, Barbara see Christian STUTZMAN

HOCHSTETLER, Catherine see John C SHROCK

HOCHSTRASSER, Alexander Hamilton b1808, w Sallyan Greenfield, NY, Bible rec MSG 7:1:33

HOCKADAY, Nancy see Thompson BRISTER

HODGE, Jesse b1820, w Sophia Eagle, NC, MO, children OZ 9:2:68

Robert f1672, MD, geneal MAD 27:2:60

William d1764, w Elizabeth ____, MD, geneal MAD 27:3:104

HODGEN, Robert b1742, w Sarah LaRue, PA?, EN?, KY, VA, biog EWA 24:3:217

HODGES, Anna Elizabeth see George Robert LANGFORD

HOERNER, John S b1846, w Rosa Eggen, GE, IL, biog sketch MCS 7:1:16

HOFFER, Matthias b1718, w Anna Maria Wohlweider, SW, PA, geneal, bk rev GH 41:1:162

HOFFMAN, Anna Maria see Bernhard KUTER

Benjamin b1827, w Elizabeth Rhoads, PA, fam hist LCH 2:3:114

Elizabeth M see Henry SPRAU

HOGAN, Daniel b1819, w Margaret Elizabeth Geiger, FL, lineage FLG 10:4:145

Margaret E see Charles H KEITH

Mary Emma see Walter M FRISBIE

HOGLAND, Elizabeth see William T HOLT

HOHMANN, John bc1805, w Gertrude Fritz, GE, PA, geneal, bk rev WPG 13:4:45

HOLCOMB, L B b1810, MI, letter MI 32:1:31

Louisa see Orson STOCKWELL

HOLDEN, Jeanne see Peter McBride

Richard b1609, w Martha Fosdick, EN, MA, geneal WTC 2:1:24

Roseanna b1849, h Thomas McConnell, IR, AA, biog IFL 2:9-10:2

Sophia see Johannes C HOOVEL

HOLDER, Mary Ann Carter see Benjamin Franklin FOSTER

HOLL, Andrew f1855, IL, biog WTC 8:4:92

HOLLAND, E A see Wm TURLEY

Geneal words in EN OCN 10:1:11

Hist sketch MP 3:2:98

James d1852, Bible rec YV 19:1:21

Nancy Ann see Benjamin COHEE Jr

Surnames WPG 14:1:37

HOLLEY, Claira b1860, IN, IL, anc ch CCS 9:3:100

HOLLINGSWORTH, Isaac H bc1771, w Hannah Crews, OH, children HL 3:1:10

Nesbit Gurley b1884, AL, cem inscr NAS 25:4:134

Surname periodical, *Hollingsworth Reg*, 3250 W 108th St, Inglewood CA 90303

HOLLINGSWORTH (continued)

Valentine b1632, w Ann Ree, OH, geneal HL 2:2:51

Stephen b1797, w Perlina Fulford, NC, FL, lineage FLG 10:4:133

HOLLISTER, Helen M see Loss PARSONS

HOLLOWAY, Allen f1848, w Susan Holloway, GA, will TCG 7:2:11

John Evans b1839, w Eliza Bivens, IL, anc ch KIL 15:2:30

HOLLSTEIN, George Johan b1800, w Ana Kunegund Wagner, GE, IL, fam hist sketch WTC 2:2:41

HOLLY, Barbara see Hans NAFZIGER

Fam letter collect 1842-1845 NY & CT CTA 29:3:76

John b1618, w Mary ____, EN, MA, CT, lineage CTA 29:3:100

HOLM, Henry J b1857, w Louise Sahs, IL, biog sketch WTC 17:4:134

HOLMES, Alex f1920, IL, hist & reminiscences 1920-1933, bk rev GH 41:6:159

Eliza see Francis CABALL & George Washington OTIS

Frances Jane see Roscoe Pulaski COPELAND

Mary see Benjamin KING

Nathaniel b1692, w Martha Cushman, MA, geneal NGS 74:3:204

HOLMSTEDT, Ernst Wilhelm b1828, SN?, geneal corr SAG 7:3:136

HOLOWAY, Robert f1854, NC, letter CAL 6:2:35

HOLT, Elizabeth see Elijah HOTHERSALL

Mary see Aaron STARK

William T b1785, w Elizabeth Hogland, NC, AL, fam rec PT 29:1:15

HOLTON, George dc1821, w Phebe ____, VA, children RAG 8:1:12

Louise see Matthew Ramey LEMASTER

HOLVERSTOT, Margaret see Samuel DURNBAUGH

HOLWAT, Lemuel m1809, w Betsey Lovell, fam rec MQ 53:3:160

HONSSINGER, Susan Q see George R JAMES

HOOD, Fam hist, bk rev BWG 16:1:64

William Pickett m1831, w Matilda Howe, Bible rec BGS 19:3:116

HOOK, Mathias bc1747, w Catherine ___, MD?, PA, geneal, bk rev WPG 13:3:52

Mathias f1780s, MD, PA, geneal, bk rev NYR 118:2:122 NGS 74:4:304

HOOKER, Thomas bc1586, w Susanna ___, EN, HO, New EN, NM, geneal, bk rev GH 41:5:196 GH 41:5:196

HOOPER, John Marion b1850, w Mary Wilson, TN, MO, fam hist sketch KSL 11:4:118

HOOPES, Fam rec collect vol I & II & III, bk rev CHG 19:2:108

HOOTMAN, Catherine see Edward RAILSBACK

HOOVEL, Johannes C b1836, w Sophia Holden, NW, IA, MN, WI, geneal, bk rev TS 29:1:27 BAT 16:4:170 CTN 20:3:517 MA 11:3:76 MD 28:4:459

HOOVER, Christian f1855, w Mary Hoover, MS, will FTH 10:3-4:76

John b1756, w Elizabeth Keefer, anc ch MFH 6:4:146

HOPKINS, Elizabeth see Benjamin LAKE

Fam coat of arms MD & DE MAD 27:3:110

Isaac Patrick, w James Ella Handley, MO, fam hist, bk rev TOP 17:3:69

Joseph Hamilton b1822, w Martha Elizabeth Baker, IN, MO, biog MSG 7:2:108

Salina see James PARRISH

Solomon f1934, MO, anniversary OZ 7:4:146

HOPKINS (continued)

Tabitha b1745, CT, anc ch BG 8:1:11

Victoria Angeline see Jasper BLAIR

William Right b1878, w Effie Lenora Duncan, GA, anc ch NC :95:9

Willis b1821, w Margaret Jackson, GA, TX, fam rec AGS 28:2:90

HOPPER, Fam deaths 1829-1854 MO OZ 5:2:66

HOPPING, Pamelia see Chester MARSHALL

HORE, Thomas bc1477, w Margery ___, EN, MA, geneal NER 141:1:22

HORINE, Elizabeth see David FOREMAN

HORNBECK, Surname period, *Hornbeck Hunting*, Shirley Hornbeck, POB 1019, Temple City CA 91780-1019

HORNE, Harriet Caroline see Daniel Webster TRASK

HORNING, Henry b1791, w Margaret Countryman, NY, anc ch FCT :71:59

HORSINGTON, John bc1640, w Mary (Stanborough) Edwards, EN, New EN, geneal NER 141:1:38

HORSLEY, James f1721, EN, MD, geneal, bk rev GH 41:6:159

HORTON, Thomas bc1640, WE?, geneal, bk rev GH 41:4:207

HORTT, M A b1880, w Lenore ___, UT, FL, biog sketch IMP 6:3:76

HOSKINS, Elmira C see Benton Cylvester THRASHER

HOSMER, Thomas b1603, w Frances ___, EN, MA, CT, geneal, bk rev CCS 8:4:131

HOSS, Elijah Embree b1839, TN, auto BWG 16:2:120

HOSTETTER, Jacob f1712, w Anna ___, PA, geneal, bk rev GH 41:1:162

HOTHERSALL, Adelaide b1867, h Charles Wesley Denney, CA, biog sketch SCS 24:9:181

Elijah b1825, w Elizabeth Holt, EN, CA, biog sketch SCS 24:9:181

HOUGH, Charles A b1853, w Mary Louisa Cadwallader, OH, biog sketch HL 1:2:53

HOUGHTON, Sarah J b1819, anc ch MGR 22:2:88

HOUP, Surname period, *The Houp, Houpe, Houpt, Haupt Fam Hist Quarterly*, POB 608, Alma AR 72921 - letters 1927, deaths IN, obit KY

HOUSE, Frances Marion b1841, w Mary Elizabeth Phillips, TN, TX, anc ch AGS 28:2:86

T W dc1880, TX, memorial & funeral GR 29:3:115

HOUSTON, Burnetty f1841, AL, letter YTD 6:2:43

John Carroll b1813, w Mary Virginia ____, FL, lineage FLG 10:4:142

HOVEY, Clarissa see John F PARSONS

HOWARD, Anna see Medina PRESTON

Charles b1842, IL, obit IG 23:3:91

Ebenezer f1768, MA, biog NER 141:4:291

Fam crest & shield TEG 7:2:63

Fred Shepherd, KS, diary of trip to Yellowstone National Park, bk rev TS 29:3:108

Idress f1848, h William D Green, KY, inheritance dispute HF 3:1:7

John bc1767, w Eunice Hitchcock, MA, VT, geneal, bk rev GH 41:6:160

John C f1853, w Matilda ____, KY, divorce HF 3:1:7

Thomas bc1769, w Nancy Hughes, MD, biog MD 28:1:48

HOWE, Bridget Mary see Timothy O'KEEFE

Matilda see William Pickett HOOD

HOWELL, Emily see John Buckner SUMNER

Wm John Henry d1940, w Minnie Rose Moore, WE,, anc ch NAS 26:2:65

HOWLAND, Albert b1826, w Eliza Jane Niles, NE, NE, anc ch NW 9:2:64

Charles W m1875, w Jessie E Mitchell, Bible rec MCR 18:4:113

Henry bc1613, w Mary ____, EN, MA, geneal NGS 75:2:106

John f1620, w Elizabeth Tilley, EN, MA, biog sketch SB 8:5:173

Sarah bc1645, h Robert Dennis, RI, MA, geneal NGS 75:3:216

HOXIE, Eliza M see Edward B SHOVE

HOXSEY, James C b1857, w Elizabeth Purcell, IL, obit MCS 7:3:127

HOYLE, Armada (Wilson) see Samuel Joseph SIMMONS

HOYT, Fam rec addenda CTN 20:3:574

Maria see Hosea Huston SAWYER

Surname period, *Hoyt's Issue*, Rt 9 Box 453, Watson Rd, Paducah KY 42001

HUBACH, Heinrich m1835, w Katherina Weyersmuller & Katherina Engel, GE, fam rec BGS 19:2:65

HUBBARD, Gurdon Saltonstall b1802, w Watseka (Indian), VT, IL, biog WTC 1:12

Sophia W d1796, Bible rec BG 8:4:101

HUBER, Magdeline see Hans Georg SCHAPPLEY

HUBRICH, William b1823, w Gusta Bungale, PU, NY, IL, biog sketch CRT 8:2:19

William d1910, w Gusta Bungale, PU, IL, obit CRT 8:4:8

HUCKABEE, Joseph m1822, w Delilah Adington, Bible rec MCI 5:4:92

HUCKINS, M H see Ida L BLACKBURN

HUDGINS, Humphrey Deggs b1735, EN, NC, geneal, bk rev GH 41:6:160

HUDSON, Mary Ellen b1854, OK, anc ch MGR 22:3:137

HUDSPETH, Almery see Mathias Stephen SPEER

Benjamin bc1815, w Sarah May, NC, MO, children OZ 7:3:120

David b1777, w Clarissa Coe, NC, KY, MO, geneal OZ 7:3:119

Giles b1784, w Discretion ____, NC, KY, MO, children OZ 7:3:121

HUFFMAN, Emma (Potts) see William VANDERIPE

HUGGINS, Mahalia see Thomas DONALDSON

HUGHES, A W f1854, journal 1854-1860 DJ 4:2:35

Alexander Willoughby f1849, DE, journal abstr 1849-1853 DJ 4:1:16

Barnabas f1749, w Elizabeth ____, PA, land rec LCC 4:3:27

Elias f1827, OH, biog sketch TLL 12:3:55

Eliza b1837, h Charles Saul Hughes, Bible rec HH 21:4:223

William bc1730, VA, geneal, bk rev GH 41:1:162

William Ellsworth b1867, w Huldah Jane Place, Bible rec HH 21:4:223

HUGHLITT, Maude Delle see Silas Walter SEARLE

HUGUENOT GENEALOGY, Hist in CN, bk rev GN 5:3:161

Hist of FR Huguenots FLG 10:3:83

Hist sketch SLV 5:1:10 CTN 20:3:397

Hist sketch in western PA WPG 13:3:31

Refugees settling in col Am, bk rev NYR 118:2:114

HUGULEY, John Walter b1882, w Rosa Angelyn Moore, AL, anc ch MCA 6:1:36

HUIRAS, Andrew f1850, w Anna Maria Lautenschlager, BA, WI, geneal, bk rev GH 41:3:169

HULET, Jane see Adam MOTT

HULL, Milton B f1862, IL, mil rec BGS 19:1:12

Peter, w Barbara Ann Keith, geneal, bk rev GH 41:5:193

Surname period, *Hull Fam Newsletter*, 19259 Harleigh Dr, Saratoga CA 95070

HUMBLE, Squire b1856 w Laura Jones, KY, KS, biog sketch TTT 11:4:159

HUMPHREY, Sarah Amelia see Thomas Massie BARTON

HUMPHREYS, William f1825, IR, TN, geneal BWG 16:1:46

HUMPHRIES, Bennett d1836, w Elizabeth ____, SC, will abstr SIQ 7:3:4

Charles f1837, w Elizabeth ____ & Mary Smith, SC, will abstr SGE 28:122:14

HUMRICH, George f1847, w Carrie ____, IL, KS, auto MP 3:2:121 3:3:177 3:4:233

HUNGARY, Map showing HG & Romanian principalities during the Hussite period ND 6:5:7

HUNNICUTT, John f1676, EN, VA, geneal, bk rev SCS 24:8:165

HUNSICKER, Sarah see Abraham KOLB

HUNT, Levicy see Squire SIMMONS

Louisa Benjamin see John Orange TAPLIN

Sarah see Samuel SMITH

HUNTER, Henry b1676, w Nancy Kennedy, ST, IR, ME, biog DE 10:5:180

Henry b1768, w Ruth Robinson, ME, fam rec DE 11:1:23

John Mercer Garnett b1805, w Elizabeth Woodbury, GA, lineage FLG 10:4:151

Mary Ann see Joseph MCCRACKIN

Nancy see John POWERS

HUNTER (continued)
William m1657, w Cicely ____ &
Mary Carter, MA, NC, geneal
TQR 14:3:127
HUNTLEY, John b1730,w Lois
Beckwith, CT, anc ch ANC
22:3:105
Mary see Pierre DUMAS
HURLBURT, Anna bc1787, h
Samuel Root, CT, anc AG
62:3:129
John W m1883, w Carrie Belle
Nichols, Bible rec BG 8:4:103
Zella E see Ira Henry SLATER
HURSEY, John Calhoun b1840, w
Lula Wilson, SC, anc ch ANC
22:2:68
HURST, Elizabeth see Jeremiah
BREEDEN
William b1640, w Anna Boyd,
VA, TN, geneal, bk rev WPG
13:3:42
HURT, Grant Burge b1853, w
Diantha Taylor Finnell, MO,
AL, Bible rec YTD 3:2:4
HUSBAND, William f1773, w
Elizabeth ____, MD, will MD
28:2:223
HUSTED, Henry P b1794, w Mary
____, NY, IL, children KL
7:3:19
Lyman S b1823, w Keziah Jane
McGowan, OH, IL, KS,
children KL 7:3:20
HUSTON, Chambers m1830, w
Margarett Pritz, Bible rec LM
28:4:291
Henry m1889, w Alma Sewell,
Bible rec HH 22:1:16
HUTCHINS, Theoda C see Geo D
ARMITAGE
HUTCHINSON, Amos d1827, NY,
anc ch BG 8:3:62
HUTCHISON, Phebe see Isaac
OAKS
HUTHMAN, Johann Henrich
b1722, w Charlotta Maria
Johann Witten, GE, anc ch
BHN 20:2:63
HYLER, Susannah Evelyn see
Isham B ROBERTS

IDAHO, Federal land appl
rejected vol 5, bk rev GH
41:5:165
Kootenai Co, marr 1881-1900, bk
rev EWA 24:3:210
News avail 1893-1963 EWA
24:4:266
IKENBERRY, Elizabeth see John
BOWMAN
ILIFF, Fam rec misc, bk rev GH
41:1:162
ILLINOIS, Alexander Co, taxes
1847 unpaid CIC 3:4:83
Allerton, hist 1887-1987, bk rev
GH 41:6:136
Arlington Heights, births &
deaths 1935 (Palatines) NWS
7:5:46
Arlington Heights, geneal misc
1936 abstr from the *Arlington
Heights Herald* NWS 8:2:18
Bachelors Grove Cem WTC
7:1:19
Biog sketches abstr from the
Hist Encyclopedia of IL 1910
CIC 3:6:125
Bloomingdale Twp, births &
deaths 1936 NWS 8:1:8
Bond Co, births 1866-1915 index,
bk rev GH 41:5:166
Boone Co, census 1840, bk rev
GH 41:6:134
Boone Co, census 1860, bk rev
GH 41:6:134
Boone Co, geneal sources CIC
3:1:2
Boone Co, marr 1851 CIC 3:1:2
Bourbonnais, Ch of the Maternity
of the Blessed Virgin Mary
death rec 1847-1985, bk rev
GH 41:6:165
Bremen Twp, hist sketch WTC
7:1:1
Bremen Twp, Trinity Evangelical
Luth Ch hist sketch & rec
misc 1860s WTC 7:1:3
Burials performed by Rev Bur-
rows WTC 2:4:134 3:2:70
3:3:102
Carlinville, obit 1856-1861 index
to the *Free Democrat*, bk rev
GH 41:3:172

ILLINOIS (continued)

Cass Co, geneal sources CIC 3:1:3

Census (agricultural), use of CIC 3:1:19

Central IL heads of fam b prior to 1850 who d or whose wives d during 1910 GL 21:1:24 21:2:55

Champaign Co, births 1881-1882 CCS 8:4:124 9:1:6 9:2:52 9:3:83

Champaign Co, bounties paid to wolf hunters 1842-1845 CCS 9:1:20

Champaign Co, census (agricultural) 1850 CCS 8:4:115 9:1:10 9:2:45

Champaign Co, census 1850, bk rev CRT 8:4:7

Champaign Co, citizenship papers 1929-1930 CCS 9:3:75

Champaign Co, geneal misc 1864-1866 abstr from *The Central IL Gazette* CCS 8:4:128 9:1:20 9:2:96 9:3:96

Champaign Co, geneal sources CIC 3:1:3

Champaign Co, geneal rec 1850, bk rev IL 19:2:111

Champaign Co, Glover, hist sketch of shootout 1913 CCS 9:3:93

Champaign Co, Mahomet Twp, Bethel/Harris Cem CCS 9:1:3

Champaign Co, marr 1879-1880 CCS 9:3:88

Champaign Co, naturalizations (loose papers) 1800s CCS 8:4:132 9:1:16

Champaign Co, Sadorus Twp, Rice Cem CCS 9:2:40

Champaign Co, Saint Joseph Ch Immaculate Conception Cem CCS 8:4:111

Champaign Co, Sidney Twp, Bliss Cem CCS 9:3:80

Champaign Co, Sidney Twp, school hist sketch CCS 9:1:5

Chicago, geneal res hints for southern communities WTC 13:2:51

ILLINOIS (continued)

Chicago, Gethesame United Ch of Christ bapt 1900s CHG 19:1:8 19:2:73

Chicago, McCormick Optical College student roster 1899 CHG 19:1:22

Chicago, naturalizations 1868 CHG 19:2:39

Chicago, Saint Ansgarius Protestant Epis Ch marr 1867-1879 SAG 7:3:113

Chrisman, Chrisman United Meth Ch hist, bk rev IG 23:2:64

Christian Co, deaths pre-1900 index CCQ 4:2:22 4:3:26

Christian Co, geneal sources CIC 3:1:4

Christian Co, marr 1839-1866 CIC 3:1:5 3:2:30 3:3:57 3:5:105 3:6:121

Christian Co, May Twp, hist & landowners 1872 roster CCQ 4:3:2

Christian Co, naturalizations 1860-1891 CCQ 4:2:20

Christian Co, Pana Twp, hist & landowners 1872 roster CCQ 4:2:1

Christian Co, Prairieton Twp, hist & landowners 1872 roster CCQ 4:1:1

Civil War, 37th Inf Fremont Rifles roster 1861 WTC 9:1:5

Civil War, roster of IL 2nd Cavalry Company C 1861 BGS 19:4:179

Clark Co, geneal sources CIC 3:1:6

Clark Co, taxes 1841 & 1843 unpaid CIC 3:4:85

Clay Co, Black Hawk War, muster roll for Capt John Onslott's Company 1832 CIC 3:2:31

Clay Co, geneal sources CIC 3:2:31

Clay Co, taxes 1844 delinquent CIC 3:6:122

Clinton Co, Civil War, muster roll for 22nd Inf Reg Company A CIC 3:2:32

ILLINOIS (continued)

Clinton Co, geneal sources CIC 3:2:32

Clinton Co, taxes 1837 delinquent CIC 3:6:122

Coles Co, Civil War, muster roll for 25th IL Inf Company E CIC 3:2:33

Coles Co, geneal sources CIC 3:2:33

Coles Co, land rec 1830s–1840s abstr CIC 3:6:123

Coles Co, letters left at post office 1841 CIC 3:4:85

Cook Co, Black Hawk War, muster roll for odd battalions 1832 CIC 3:2:34

Cook Co, Bloom Twp, Chicago Heights, Bloom Pres Ch hist sketch & cem inscr surname index WTC 6:1:24

Cook Co, Bloom Twp, Glenwood, hist WTC 11:4:143

Cook Co, Bloom Twp, Sauk Village, St James Ch hist sketch & cem inscr surname index WTC 6:1:25 (hist sketch of St James Parish) WTC 11:4:157

Cook Co, Bloom Twp, Steger, hist WTC 11:4:125

Cook Co, Bloom Twp, WWI, soldiers roll of honor roster WTC 1:1:18

Cook Co, Bloom Twp, census 1850 WTC 1:1:7

Cook Co, Bloom Twp, census 1860 index WTC 6:1:14

Cook Co, Bloom Twp, hist WTC 6:1:1

Cook Co, Bloom Twp, land owners (15 of the earliest) WTC 6:1:6

Cook Co, Bremen Twp, Blue Island, Civil War, vet roster WTC 12:2:81

Cook Co, Bremen Twp, Bremen, Civil War, vet roster WTC 12:2:78

Cook Co, Bremen Twp, Bremen, census 1870 WTC 12:2:93

Cook Co, Bremen Twp, Midlothian ch hist WTC 12:2:53

ILLINOIS (continued)

Cook Co, Bremen Twp, Orland, Civil War, vet roster WTC 12:2:85

Cook Co, Bremen Twp, Palos, Civil War, vet roster WTC 12:2:87

Cook Co, Bremen Twp, Tinley Park, nameless cem WTC 12:2:56

Cook Co, Bremen Twp, United Meth Ch Cem WTC 12:2:57

Cook Co, Bremen Twp, Worth, Civil War, vet roster WTC 12:2:83

Cook Co, Bremen Twp, census 1860 index WTC 7:1:25

Cook Co, Bremen Twp, hist sketch & census 1850 WTC 1:2:37

Cook Co, Bremen Twp, land rec 1830s–1850s WTC 7:1:13

Cook Co, Bridgeport, hist sketch 1800s CHG 20:1:10

Cook Co, Calumet & Hyde Park Twp area, ch hist WTC 13:2:64

Cook Co, Calumet & Hyde Park Twp area, land rec 1839–1850 WTC 8:1:24

Cook Co, Calumet City, hist sketch WTC 6:3:109

Cook Co, Calumet region, Lansing, obit 1972 WTC 6:3:118

Cook Co, Calumet region, hist sketch WTC 6:3:89

Cook Co, Calumet Twp, census 1870 WTC 13:2:83

Cook Co, Calumet Twp, hist sketch WTC 8:1:1

Cook Co, Calumet, Civil War vet roster WTC 13:2:80

Cook Co, Chicago & Alton Railroad direct 1869 names & occupations WTC 17:3:103

Cook Co, Chicago, Ancient Free & Accepted Masons 1912–1913 roster CHG 20:1:21

Cook Co, Chicago, Calumet Club member roster WTC 1:2:44 1:3:88 1:4:114 2:1:29 2:2:61 10:3–4:129

Cook Co, Chicago, direct (business) 1871 CHG 20:1:13

Cook Co, Chicago, geneal & hist sources guide by Szucs, bk rev CTA 29:4:132 AW 13:2:73 GH 41:4:189 NCJ 13:3:178 PGB 19:1:10 APG 2:3:27 WPG 14:1:47 GFB 37:1:24 GGS 23:3:159 NYR 118:4:243 RES 19:1:22 CTN 20:2:322 NTT 7:2:42 SIQ 7:1:19 STI 27:2:36 RAG 8:3:22 RCP 9:4:129 OZ 9:3:121

Cook Co, Chicago, hist, bk rev WTC 4:4:161

Cook Co, Chicago, lawyers 1857 WTC 1:1:13

Cook Co, Chicago, memories 1834 WTC 7:2:71

Cook Co, Chicago, natives marrying in ON 1857–1869 CHG 19:4:152

Cook Co, Chicago, Old St Mary's Ch rec index 1833–1844, bk rev GH 41:6:136

Cook Co, Chicago, pensioners 1883 roster, bk rev AG 62:1:59 IL 19:2:115

Cook Co, Chicago, war memorials &/or hist markers CHG 19:4:162

Cook Co, Chicago, ward maps 1837–1970, bk rev GH 41:6:165

Cook Co, Chicago, Wunders Cem inscr, bk rev AG 62:1:58

Cook Co, Country Club Hills, St John's Luth Ch parishioner roster & bapt 1830s–1850s WTC 13:4:182

Cook Co, Crete, biog sketches, WTC 15:3:130

Cook Co, Crete, organizations & business houses 1922 WTC 15:3:112

Cook Co, Crete Twp, farmers & breeders 1918 WTC 15:3:105

Cook Co, Crete United Meth Ch hist & rec 1800s WTC 15:3:98

Cook Co, DesPlaines, Saint Mary's Cem CHG 19:2:65

Cook Co, direct (farmers') for southern part of co 1918 WTC 9:3:119 10:2:56 10:3–4:157 11:1:15

Cook Co, geneal sources CIC 3:2:34

Cook Co, Hazel Crest, hist sketch WTC 13:4:149

Cook Co, Hyde Park Twp, hist sketch WTC 8:1:14

Cook Co, Hyde Park, Civil War vet WTC 13:2:81

Cook Co, Lansing, settlement & biog sketches WTC 6:3:99

Cook Co, Lemont, geneal misc 1897 abstr from *The Observer* WTC 17:3:98

Cook Co, Lemont, vol fire department roster WTC 17:3:99

Cook Co, Lemont Twp, Crete, Civil War, vet roster WTC 12:4:167

Cook Co, Lemont Twp, Keepatau/Palmyra/Lemont, postmasters roster 1840–1928 WTC 17:3:80

Cook Co, Lemont Twp, Lemont, Civil War, vet roster WTC 12:4:142

Cook Co, Lemont Twp, Lemont, census 1870 WTC 12:4:168

Cook Co, Lemont Twp, Lemont, quarry strike 1885 WTC 1:4:100 12:4:148

Cook Co, Lemont Twp, St James of the Sag Cem WTC 1:4:116

Cook Co, Lemont Twp, St Patrick's Ch hist & cem WTC 7:3:105 (Christmas offering roster 1897) WTC 17:3:100

Cook Co, Lemont Twp, WWI & WWII, casualties roster WTC 17:3:105

Cook Co, Lemont Twp, biog sketches WTC 1:4:109

Cook Co, Lemont Twp, census 1850 WTC 1:4:131 (1860 index) WTC 7:3:117

Cook Co, Lemont Twp, ch hist sketch WTC 12:4:139

Cook Co, Lemont Twp, geneal resources in the South Suburban Geneal & Hist Soc Lib (IL) WTC 17:3:97

Cook Co, Lemont Twp, hist WTC 7:3:85

Cook Co, Lemont Twp, land rec 1830s-1840s WTC 7:3:114

Cook Co, Lemont Twp, land sales reserved for the IL-MI Canal 1850s-1860s WTC 7:3:111

Cook Co, Lemont Twp, taxes 1852 WTC 17:3:82

Cook Co, Maine Twp, Maine, Maine Cem WTC 6:3:126

Cook Co, Manhattan Twp, ch hist sketch WTC 13:3:103

Cook Co, marr 1887 CHG 19:1:5

Cook Co, Matteson, Elliott Cem WTC 10:2:51

Cook Co, names once in common use WTC 4:4:170

Cook Co, Orland Twp, Christ Luth Ch member roster 1898-1913 WTC 14:2:55

Cook Co, Orland Twp, Old GE Meth Cem WTC 14:2:65

Cook Co, Orland Twp, Orland Memorial Park cem inscr WTC 9:1:26

Cook Co, Orland Twp, Orland Park, Christ Luth Cem WTC 2:2:45

Cook Co, Orland Twp, Orland, hist sketch WTC 2:2:35

Cook Co, Orland Twp, Tinley Park, GE Meth Ch marr 1880-1897 WTC 14:2:62

Cook Co, Orland Twp, biog sketches WTC 2:2:43

Cook Co, Orland Twp, census 1850 WTC 2:2:50

Cook Co, Orland Twp, census 1860 index WTC 9:1:12

Cook Co, census 1870 WTC 14:2:67

Cook Co, Orland Twp, geneal sources WTC 14:2:46

Cook Co, Orland Twp, hist WTC 14:2:50

Cook Co, Orland Twp, landowners (original) 1830s-1850s WTC 9:3:111

Cook Co, Orland Twp, officers (principal) 1851-1884 roster WTC 9:1:3, 33

Cook Co, Palatine, Sayles Cem WTC 1:1:28

Cook Co, Palos Twp, hist sketch & biog sketches WTC 2:4:109

Cook Co, Palos Twp, Oak Hill Cem WTC 2:4:119

Cook Co, Palos Twp, Sacred Heart Cem WTC 14:4:156

Cook Co, Palos Twp, census 1850 WTC 2:4:125

Cook Co, Palos Twp, census 1860 WTC 9:3:90

Cook Co, Palos Twp, census 1870 WTC 14:4:169

Cook Co, Palos Twp, ch hist sketch WTC 14:4:154

Cook Co, Palos Twp, geneal res sources WTC 14:4:163

Cook Co, Palos Twp, hist sketch WTC 9:3:85

Cook Co, place names of long ago WTC 17:3:90

Cook Co, Pullman, hist sketch WTC 13:2:71

Cook Co, Rich Twp, St John's Ch hist sketch & fam memberships 1849-1934 WTC 3:2:75

Cook Co, Rich Twp, St Paul Evangelical Luth Ch hist sketch & cem inscr WTC 15:4:152

Cook Co, Rich Twp, biennial report of the co spuerintendent of schools 1910 WTC 3:2:67

Cook Co, Rich Twp, census 1850 WTC 3:2:50

Cook Co, Rich Twp, census 1870 WTC 15:4:168

Cook Co, Rich Twp, hist sketch & biog sketches WTC 3:2:47

Cook Co, Richton, St Paul's Ch funerals 1868-1968 WTC 3:2:59

Cook Co, Richton, St Paul's Ch marr 1870-1900 WTC 3:2:56

Cook Co, Thornton, Civil War vet roster WTC 13:4:170

Cook Co, Thornton Twp, Mount Forest Cem WTC 14:3:121

Cook Co, Thornton Twp, Harvey, Ascension Ch bapt & marr 1899-1909 WTC 13:4:156

Cook Co, Thornton Twp, Harvey, Academy Meth Ch bapt, marr, & probationers 1892-1910 WTC 13:4:164

Cook Co, Thornton Twp, Harvey, Ingalls Memorial Hospital staff member roster 1931 WTC 8:3:16

Cook Co, Thornton Twp, Hazel Crest Community Ch hist WTC 13:4:141

Cook Co, Thornton Twp, South Holland, hist sketch WTC 3:4:155

Cook Co, Thornton Twp, Thornton, hist sketch WTC 3:4:159

Cook Co, Thornton Twp, census 1860 WTC 4:2:70

Cook Co, Thornton Twp, census 1870 index WTC 8:3:28

Cook Co, Thornton Twp, hist WTC 8:3:1

Cook Co, Thornton Twp, hist sketch & census 1850 WTC 3:4:123

Cook Co, Thornton Twp, land rec 1872-1957 WTC 13:4:151

Cook Co, Thornton Twp, land-owners (original) WTC 6:3:97 8:3:7

Cook Co, Washington Heights, hist WTC 8:1:3

Cook Co, Worth, poll bk 1892 WTC 5:2-3:107

Cook Co, Worth Twp, Blue Island, biog sketches WTC 5:2-3:108

Cook Co, Worth Twp, Blue Island, First Evangelical Luth Ch rec misc 1860s-1880s WTC 4:4:165

Cook Co, Worth Twp, Chicago Ridge, hist WTC 11:2:50

Cook Co, Worth Twp, Oak Lawn, hist WTC 11:2:41

Cook Co, Worth Twp, Soldier's Home residents 1870 roster WTC 4:4:154

Cook Co, Worth Twp, cem hist WTC 4:4:157

Cook Co, Worth Twp, census 1850 WTC 4:4:144

Cook Co, Worth Twp, census 1860 WTC 5:2-3:63

Cook Co, Worth Twp, hist sketch WTC 4:4:135

Counties & co seats MP 3:1:62

Crawford & Clark Co, surnames abstr from the *Hist of Crawford & Clark Co IL* 1883 CIC 3:1:7

Crawford Co, Black Hawk War, Capt Highsmith's detachment roster 1832 CIC 3:3:58

Crawford Co, geneal sources CIC 3:1:6 3:3:58

Cumberland Co, census 1870, bk rev GH 41:1:127

Cumberland Co, Civil War, 21st IL Inf roster CIC 3:3:59

Cumberland Co, geneal sources CIC 3:3:59

Cumberland Co, geneal misc 1870 abstr from news CIC 3:5:106

Cumberland Co, taxes 1843 unpaid CIC 3:4:86

DeKalb Co, census 1880, bk rev NGS 74:3:228

DeKalb Co, Civil War, 13th IL Inf Company E roster CIC 3:3:61

DeKalb Co, death notices 1870s-1880s CRN 6:3:53

DeKalb Co, DeKalb Twp, hist CRN 6:2:25

DeKalb Co, DeKalb Twp, land-owners roster & map 1868 CRN 6:2:40

DeKalb Co, geneal misc 1870s-1880s abstr from the *Sycamore True Republican* CRN 6:4:80

DeKalb Co, geneal sources CIC 3:3:60

ILLINOIS (continued)

Fayette Co, geneal sources CIC 3:1:9

Fayette Co, taxes 1838 delinquent CIC 3:6:128

Fayette Co, Vandalia, geneal misc 1820-1821 abstr from the *IL Intelligencer* CIC 3:2:36

Ford Co, geneal sources CIC 3:4:89

Franklin Co, biog contained in the *Hist of Gallatin, Saline, Hamilton, Franklin, & Williamson Co IL* CIC 3:3:65

Franklin Co, Eastern Twp, cem inscr, bk rev GH 41:3:172

Franklin Co, geneal sources CIC 3:4:89

Franklin Co, taxes 1846 & 1848 unpaid CIC 3:4:90

Fulton Co, Canton, geneal rec 1885-1917, bk rev GH 41:4:189

Fulton Co, Canton, Murphy-Sedgewick Funeral Home rec 1885-1917, bk rev GH 41:5:166

Fulton Co, geneal sources CIC 3:5:108

Gallatin Co, geneal sources CIC 3:1:13 3:5:108

Gallatin Co, marr indexes, bk rev GH 41:6:134

Gallatin Co, surnames abstr from the *Hist of Gallatin, Saline, Hamilton, Franklin, & Williamson Co IL* 1887 CIC 3:1:14

Gallatin Co, taxes 1847 delinquent CIC 3:6:127

Green Garden Twp, hist sketch WTC 7:1:45

Greene Co, Carrollton Twp, cem inscr, bk rev GH 41:6:134

Greene Co, census 1840, bk rev GH 41:6:134

Greene Co, census 1850, bk rev GH 41:6:134

Greene Co, geneal sources CIC 3:6:124

Greene Co, marr 1870-1891, bk rev GH 41:6:135

Greene Co, public domain land tract sales to patentees index, bk rev GH 41:6:135

ILLINOIS (continued)

Greene Co, White Hall Twp, cem inscr, bk rev IL 19:2:110

Hamilton Co, Black Hawk War, muster roll for Capt James Hall's Company 1832 CIC 3:1:15

Hamilton Co, geneal sources CIC 3:1:14

Hamilton Co, marr lic 1884 abstr from the *Hamilton Co Herald* CIC 3:2:37

Hamilton Co, McLeansboro, geneal misc 1885 abstr from the *Hamilton Co Herald* CIC 3:1:14

Hamilton Co, McLeansboro, geneal misc 1890-1891 abstr from the *Leader* CIC 3:3:66

Hamilton Co, will abstr 1821-1915, bk rev GH 41:3:160

Hancock Co, geneal sources CIC 3:2:39

Harvey, biog sketches WTC 3:4:154

Harvey, Harvey Meth ch hist sketch & marr 1892-1908 & funerals 1917-1921 WTC 3:4:135

Hazel Crest, hist sketch WTC 4:2:63

Highland Park, Grace Cem NSN 12:1:3 12:2:17 12:3:27

Hist, bk rev WTC 3:3:100

Index to *Hist of Marion & Clinton Co*, bk rev IL 19:2:113

Iroquois Co, hist, bk rev GH 41:2:158 IL 19:2:114

Jackson & Randolph Co, Black Hawk War, roster of Capt Alex M Jenkins Company 1832 CIC 3:5:111

Jackson Co, taxes 1846 unpaid CIC 3:4:90

Jefferson Co, taxes 1848 unpaid CIC 3:4:91

Jersey Co, Jerseyville, geneal misc 1913-1915, 1919 abstr from the *Jerseyville Republican* MCS 7:3:128

Johnson Co, taxes 1845-48 delinquent CIC 3:6:127

Macoupin & Madison Co, birth & marr rec, bk rev GH 41:4:189

Macoupin Co, Carlinville, obit 1858–1861 index to the *Carlinville Free Democrat*, bk rev IL 19:2:117

Macoupin Co, marr 1846–1851 index, bk rev GH 41:2:130

Macoupin Co, marr 1851–1854 index, bk rev GH 41:3:172 IL 19:2:115

Macoupin Co, obit index to the *Bunker Hill Gazette* 1898–1899, bk rev GH 41:1:128

Macoupin Co, Staunton Twp, cem inscr, bk rev GH 41:1:128

Macoupin Co, Staunton, obit index 1898, 1906–1907 to the *Staunton Times* & the *Staunton Star*, bk rev GH 41:1:128

Macoupin Co, Staunton Twp, cem inscr, bk rev IL 19:2:116

Madison Co, births 1846–1861 MCS 7:1:14

Madison Co, cem inscr vol 3, bk rev IL 19:2:115

Madison Co, centennial celebration 1912 MCS 7:3:99

Madison Co, deaths 1878 MCS 7:1:39

Madison Co, Edwardsville, St Boniface Cath Ch deaths 1870–1872 MCS 7:1:12

Madison Co, Edwardsville, geneal misc 1850 abstr from the *Madison Rec* MCS 7:3:117

Madison Co, Edwardsville, marr lic 1905 MCS 7:1:31 7:3:121

Madison Co, Edwardsville, probate proceedings 1905 abstr MCS 7:3:120

Madison Co, Edwardsville, social doings 1905 abstr from the *Intelligencer* MCS 7:1:30

Madison Co, geneal misc 1912, 1913, 1917, 1924, 1929 abstr from news MCS 7:1:33

Madison Co, Hurican Fork, Regular Bapt Ch in Christ minutes 1818–1819 MCS 7:1:25

Madison Co, Pleasant Ridge, St John's Luth Ch bapt 1853–1856 MCS 7:3:134

Madison Co, Rev War, biog sketches of heroes MCS 7:1:17

Madison Co, vet admitted to IL Soldiers' & Sailors' Home 1887–1910 MCS 7:1:2

Marion Co, geneal rec misc 1822–1906, bk rev IL 19:2:116

Marion Co, landowners index 1892, bk rev IL 19:2:116

Marion, recollect of life during the Great Depression, bk rev CCS 8:4:130

Marshall Co, census 1860, bk rev GH 41:5:166

Marshall Co, census 1870, bk rev GH 41:5:167 IL 19:2:112

Mason Co, atlas map 1874 index, bk rev GH 41:3:160 GH 41:3:160

Mason Co, Bath, mortician rec 1882–1921, bk rev GH 41:3:160

Mason Co, cem inscr, bk rev GH 41:2:130 GH 41:3:161

Mason Co, farm ownership plat bk 1936, bk rev GH 41:4:189

Mason Co, map 1900s, bk rev GH 41:5:167

Mason Co, marr 1867–1877 index, bk rev GH 41:5:167

McDonough Co, Emmet Twp, pioneers, bk rev GH 41:4:189 KA 23:2:109

McDonough Co, geneal sources CIC 3:2:41

McDonough Co, letters at post office 1835 CIC 3:2:41

McDonough Co, marr 1881–1889, bk rev GH 41:6:135

McHenry Co, admin, executors, & guard 1849–1855 MCI 5:1:8 5:2:37 5:3:69 5:4:98

McHenry Co, Antioch (Lake), Strang Funeral Home, residents/burials 1930s–196s MCI 5:1:19

McHenry Co, atlas 1872, bk rev, GH 41:5:168

ILLINOIS (continued)

McHenry Co, census 1840, bk rev GH 41:5:168

McHenry Co, census 1860, bk rev GH 41:5:167

McHenry Co, Civil War, mil draft list 1863 MCI 5:3:59 5:4:105

McHenry Co, early settler cert MCI 5:1:3

McHenry Co, employees of the WI Division Chicago & Northwestern Railway 1912–1942 MCI 5:2:45

McHenry Co, Greenwood Twp, ledger bk of William Allen 1860-1881 MCI 5:3:63

McHenry Co, Greenwood, index to the Greenwood Centennial bklet 1940 MCI 5:4:101

McHenry Co, mort sched 1850 MCI 5:3:65

McHenry Co, mort sched 1860 MCI 5:4:87

McHenry Co, Old Settlers' Assoc member roster 1876 MCI 5:1:7

McHenry Co, public domain listing 1787- MCI 5:1:14 5:2:31

McHenry Co, Riley Twp, hist sketch MCI 5:1:23

McHenry Co, Seneca Twp, hist sketch MCI 5:3:64

McHenry Co, settler (early) cert MCI 5:4:91

McHenry Co, v r 1850s-1940s MCI 5:2:44

McHenry Co, Walkup's Add 1925-1920s-1940s abstr MCI 5:4:95

McHenry Co, Walkup's Addition abstr MCI 5:3:77

McHenry Co, Waukegan, Peterson Funeral Home rec 1871-1901 MCI 5:4:98

McHenry Co, Woodstock, automobile owners 1905 MCI 5:4:100

McLean Co, Anchor, Anchor Cem MH 14:1:3

McLean Co, Bloomington, direct, (business) 1855-6 GL 21:1:11 21:2:45 21:3:70 21:4:99

ILLINOIS (continued)

McLean Co, geneal rec misc 1858-1957 GL 21:1:7 21:2:41 21:3:73 21:4:105

McLean Co, Lytleville, hist sketch GL 21:1:8

McLean Co, Saybrook, obit & marr 1880s-1949 GL 21:3:66 21:4:109

Menard & Mason Co, index to the *Hist Of Menard & Mason Co* 1879, bk rev GH 41:3:160

Menard Co, census 1860, bk rev WTC 8:3:37

Menard Co, marr 1901-1931, bk rev GH 41:4:189

Migrations outline 1684-1920 RT 4:3:74

Momence, geneal misc 1871, 1874 abstr from the *Kankakee Gazette* TAK 17:1:9 17:2:17

Monroe Co, geneal sources CIC 3:1:16

Monroe Co, taxes (delinquent) 1833 CIC 3:1:17

Mort sched 1850 for co of Peoria through Woodford vol 3, bk rev WTC 3:4:170

Moultrie Co, taxes 1843 unpaid CIC 3:4:91 (1846 delinquent) CIC 3:5:110 (1849 delinquent) CIC 3:5:109

Natives dying in NV & CA 1960s CHG 19:1:3

Nauvoo, geneal misc 1842-1843 abstr from news CIC 3:2:39

New Lenox Twp, farmers & breeders 1918 WTC 14:3:101

New Lenox Twp, Marley Community Ch member roster 1833-1983 WTC 14:3:108

News holdings of the IL State Hist Lib CRT 8:2:28

Normal, Soldiers' Orphans' Home, hist sketch & residents roster 1860s-1870s IL 19:2:69

Pekin, Black Hawk War, Capt John G Adams' Company roster 1832 CIC 3:3:74

Peoria Co, Black Hawk War, roster of Capt Abner Ead's Company 1832 CIC 3:5:109

ILLINOIS (continued)

Perry Co, taxes 1838 delinquent CIC 3:6:128

Perry Co, taxes 1850 unpaid CIC 3:4:92

Pet to the IL General Assembly 1823 IL 19:2:102

Pgrry Co, census 1860, bk rev GH 41:1:129

Pioneer roster 1800s IL 19:2:65

Platt Co, marr 1874-1910, bk rev GH 41:6:135

Pope Co, census 1870 & mort sched, bk rev GH 41:3:161

Pope Co, geneal sources CIC 3:1:17

Pope Co, Shawneetown, geneal misc 1820 abstr from the *IL Gazette* CIC 3:1:18

Probate rec 1874 abstr from the *Kankakee Gazette* TAK 17:1:10

Putnam & Marshall Co, hist to 1860, bk rev GH 41:5:169

Putnam Co, geneal sources CIC 3:5:110

Randolph Co, geneal sources CIC 3:5:111

Richland Co, Bonpas Twp, Walnut Grove Cem inscr, bk rev IL 19:2:120

Richland Co, geneal sources CIC 3:1:19 3:5:112

Rock Island Co, geneal sources CIC 3:5:113

Rock River Meth Conference, parishes & dates served by Rev Joseph Burrows including burials performed 1913-1953 WTC 2:2:65

Saint Clair Co, Belleville Co, Hospital & Poorhouse residents 1870 roster STC 10:2:97

Saint Clair Co, Black Hawk War, Capt John Thomas Company roster 1832 CIC 3:3:73

Saint Clair Co, Centreville Cem Assoc extracts STC 10:2:84

Saint Clair Co, coroners' inquests 1870 STC 10:2:90

Saint Clair Co, court rec 1809-1811 index STC 10:1:36

ILLINOIS (continued)

Saint Clair Co, East Dutch Hill Cem STC 10:1:41

Saint Clair Co, Floraville, St Paul's United Ch of Christ marr 1859-1985 STC 10:3:116

Saint Clair Co, geneal sources CIC 3:3:72

Saint Clair Co, Millstadt, St James Cath Ch hist sketch STC 10:3:148

Saint Clair Co, Millstadt, Zion United Ch of Christ fam reg STC 10:1:1

Saint Clair Co, Millstadt, hist 1837-1987 STC 10:3:150

Saint Clair Co, Millstadt Twp, St James Cath Cem STC 10:3:132

Saint Clair Co, Millstadt Twp, Old Cath Cem STC 10:3:147

Saint Clair Co, Millstadt Twp, Old Millstadt City Cem STC 10:2:65

Saint Clair Co, Millstadt Twp, White Cem STC 10:2:89

Saint Clair Co, New Athens Twp, Meng Cem STC 10:1:40

Saint Clair Co, Sawtown cem rec bk early 1900s STC 10:1:33

Saint Clair Co, St Liborius Cem inscr, bk rev STC 10:1:39

Saint Clair Co, Stookey Twp, Peter's Cem STC 10:2:98

Saint Clair Co, vet admitted to IL Soldiers' & Sailors' Home 1887-1910 STC 10:2:53

Saint Clair Co, West Casey Twp, Bauer Cem STC 10:1:44

Saline Co, census 1865, bk rev IL 19:2:118

Saline Co, marr 1879-1910, bk rev IL 19:2:118

Saline Co, surnames abstr from the *Hist of Gallatin, Saline, Hamilton, Franklin, & Williamson Co IL* 1887 CIC 3:2:42

Sangamon Co, city, twp, & co hist avail at the Lincoln Libr (IL) CR 19:3:108

Sangamon Co, co court jurors 1858 roster CR 19:3:114

ILLINOIS (continued)

Sangamon Co, Cotton Hill Twp, Horse Creek Cem corr CR 19:3:113

Sangamon Co, Cotton Hill Twp, cem inscr, bk rev GH 41:1:129

Sangamon Co, grad (8th grade) roster 1915 CR 19:3:115

Sangamon Co, hist sketches of twp CR 19:4:175

Sangamon Co, index vol 2 part 2, bk rev GH 41:5:169

Sangamon Co, letters & wills 1850-1874 avail CR 19:2:58 19:3:140 19:4:183

Sangamon Co, marr lic appl 1879-1880 CR 19:2:63

Sangamon Co, marr 1871-1877, bk rev GH 41:6:135

Sangamon Co, Mechanicsburg Twp, Mechanicsburg Cem corr CR 19:1:39 19:3:113

Sangamon Co, naturalization papers (minors) final oath 1892-1906, bk rev GH 41:2:130

Sangamon Co, naturalization rec, index to minor children 1892-1906 CR 19:2:88

Sangamon Co, naturalizations & declarations of intent 1859-1906, bk rev GH 41:1:129

Sangamon Co, Pecan Bottom, celebration 1834 CR 19:3:125

Sangamon Co, pioneer doctors CR 19:1:23

Sangamon Co, Rev War, heroes of Valley Forge buried in co CR 19:2:56

Sauganash, World War II, honor roll memorial 1941-1945 CHG 19:1:27

Schuyler Co, hist, vol 2, bk rev IL 19:2:113

Scott Co, hist, bk rev WTC 7:3:123

Settlement of central IL CRT 8:1:17

Shawneetown, hist, bk rev FRT 8:2:105

Shelby Co, cholera victims 185 5 roster CIC 3:6:131

ILLINOIS (continued)

Shelby Co, divorces 1843-1850 CIC 3:1:20

Shelby Co, geneal misc 1800s abstr from news CIC 3:3:69 3:4:93 3:5:114

Shelby Co, obit 1870s-1880s abstr from news CIC 3:2:42 3:6:129

Shelby Co, geneal sources CIC 3:1:20

Shelby Co, surnames beginning with M 1800s abstr from misc rec CIC 3:1:21 3:2:44

Ship pass lists 1852-1853 IL 19:2:107

Stark Co, Company B 33rd IL Inf roster CIC 3:3:72

Stark Co, geneal sources CIC 3:3:71

Stephenson Co, atlas & plat bk 1871-1894-1913, bk rev GH 41:1:130

Stephenson Co, cem with known mil burials CIC 3:3:74

Stephenson Co, geneal sources CIC 3:3:73

Streator, hist, bk rev GH 41:5:170

Swansea, hist 1886-1986, bk rev STC 10:1:39

Tazewell & Mason Co, portrait & biog rec, bk rev MCG 10:2:89

Tazewell Co, cem inscr (7 vol), bk rev MCG 10:2:90

Tazewell Co, census 1860 & index, bk rev MCG 10:2:90

Tazewell Co, geneal sources CIC 3:3:74

Tazewell Co, map 1864, bk rev MCG 10:2:91

Tazewell Co, marr 1827-1877, bk rev MCG 10:2:90

Teutopolis, geneal misc 1908 abstr from the *Teutopolis Press* CRT 8:3:18

Thornton Twp, Berger's Cem WTC 4:2:51

Thornton Twp, land grants 1841-1850 WTC 7:1:42

Thornton Twp, Thornton, direct (village) 1907 WTC 4:2:64

ILLINOIS (continued)

Undertakers roster pre-1900 WTC 17:2:48

Union Co, Black Hawk War, muster roll for Capt B B Craig's Company 1832 CIC 3:2:45

Union Co, geneal sources CIC 3:2:45

Union Co, pioneer sketches, bk rev GH 41:4:189

Union Co, taxes 1847 & 1848 unpaid CIC 3:4:92

University of IL Baccalaureate class roster 1894-1900 IL 19:2:85

Vandalia, geneal misc 1821-1822 abstr from the *IL Intelligencer* CIC 3:3:64

Vandalia, geneal misc 1833, 1893, 1872 abstr from the *IL Advocate & State Reg* CIC 3:1:9

Vermilion Co, Blount Twp, Fairchild Cem IG 23:2:42

Vermilion Co, Boy Scout Troop (1st) member roster IG 23:2:53

Vermilion Co, Catlin Grammar School student roster c1918 IG 23:3:80

Vermilion Co, Catlin, settlers reg 1885 IG 23:3:72

Vermilion Co, Civil War, muster roll for 25 IL Inf Company A CIC 3:2:46

Vermilion Co, Civil War, soldier biog sketches IG 23:3:84

Vermilion Co, geneal sources CIC 3:2:45

Vermilion Co, Indianola, geneal misc 1905 & 1915 abstr from the *Indianola Weekly Gazette* IG 23:1:13

Vermilion Co, Indianola, soldiers' graves decorated 1908 IG 23:3:71

Wabash Co, Black Hawk War, detachment for Capt Elias Jordan's Company 1832 CIC 3:2:47 (Capt John Arnold's Company 1832) CIC 3:2:46

ILLINOIS (continued)

Wabash Co, geneal sources CIC 3:2:46

War of 1812, Daniel G Moore's Company roster CIC 3:3:68

War of 1812, muster roll for Capt William Jones' Company 1813 CIC 3:2:40

Warren Co, births 1876-1915, bk rev GH 41:3:161 GH 41:5:169

Warren Co, deaths & obit 1902-1906 abstr from Moffitt bk vol 8, bk rev GH 41:5:169

Warren Co, geneal sources CIC 3:2:47

Warren Co, marr 1829-1915 female index, bk rev GH 41:5:170

Warren Co, Monmouth Twp, Monmouth Cem inscr, bk rev GH 41:3:161 (including Glendale) GH 41:5:194

Warren Co, Monmouth, 1953-1959 abstr from cem rec, bk rev GH 41:5:168

Warren Co, Monmouth, obit 1960-1965 abstr from cem rec, bk rev GH 41:5:169

Warren Co, War of 1812, soldiers buried in co CIC 3:2:47

Washington Co, geneal sources CIC 3:1:22

Washington Co, taxes (unpaid) 1833 CIC 3:1:23

Wayne Co, Black Hawk War, muster roll of Capt James N Clark's Company 1832 CIC 3:1:23

Wayne Co, geneal sources CIC 3:1:23

Wayne Co, Wayne City, Long Prairie Bapt Ch rec 1852-1951, bk rev GH 41:3:161

White Co, Black Hawk War, muster roll for Capt John McCann's Company CIC 3:1:24

White Co, geneal sources CIC 3:1:24

Will Co (now Kankakee Co), Yellowhead Twp, title to property abstr 1838-1924 WTC 5:4:126

ILLINOIS (continued)

Will Co, Beecher, St Luke United Ch of Christ Cem WTC 10:1:19

Will Co, Country Club Hills, St John's Luth Ch bapt 1852-1855 WTC 14:1:28

Will Co, Crete Twp, Civil War, Union soldiers roster WTC 6:2:53

Will Co, Crete Twp, Crete Meth Ch hist sketch & founders roster WTC 6:2:71

Will Co, Crete Twp, Crete, hist sketch & biog sketches WTC 1:3:65

Will Co, Crete Twp, Trinity & Zion Luth Cem WTC 11:3:96

Will Co, Crete Twp, census 1860 index WTC 6:2:73

Will Co, Crete Twp, mil rec, hist of the 9th IL Cavalry Reg WTC 6:2:51

Will Co, Crete Twp, mil rec, hist of the 100th IL Inf Reg WTC 6:2:49

Will Co, Crete Twp, mil rec, vet buried in twp 1700s-1900s WTC 6:2:70

Will Co, Crete, census 1850 WTC 1:3:73

Will Co, direct 1859-1860 WTC 2:3:99

Will Co, Florence Twp, Starr Grove Cem WTC 12:3:130

Will Co, formation WTC 2:3:107

Will Co, Frankfort Twp, Frankfort, hist WTC 12:1:1

Will Co, Frankfort Twp, Chelsea, hist sketch WTC 6:4:139

Will Co, Frankfort Twp, Frankfort, Civil War, vet roster WTC 12:1:13

Will Co, Frankfort Twp, Frankfort/Scheer/Osgood Cem WTC 6:4:151

Will Co, Frankfort Twp, Hickory Creek, settlement WTC 6:4:135

Will Co, Frankfort Twp, Mokenas, Civil War, vet roster WTC 12:1:17

ILLINOIS (continued)

Will Co, Frankfort Twp, New Lenox, Civil War, vet roster WTC 12:1:18

Will Co, Frankfort Twp, biog sketches WTC 2:1:20

Will Co, Frankfort Twp, hist sketch & 1850 census WTC 2:1:1

Will Co, Frankfort, Immanuel Ev Luth Ch bapt 1853-1923 WTC 17:1:13

Will Co, Frankfurt Twp, census 1870 WTC 12:1:29

Will Co, geneal printed res sources WTC 14:3:89

Will Co, Grant Park, Zion Luth Ch (Sollitt) marr 1873-1894 & deaths 1872-1894 WTC 5:4:129

Will Co, Green Garden Twp, Crete, Civil War, vet roster WTC 12:3:114

Will Co, Green Garden Twp, GE Meth Ch hist & cem WTC 7:1:49

Will Co, Green Garden Twp, Green Garden, Civil War, vet roster WTC 12:3:112

Will Co, Green Garden Twp, St Peter's Cem WTC 5:1:19

Will Co, Green Garden Twp, Union Cem WTC 2:3:91

Will Co, Green Garden Twp, census 1860 index WTC 7:2:61 (1870) WTC 17:1:1

Will Co, Green Garden Twp, ch & cem hist sketch WTC 12:3:109

Will Co, Green Garden Twp, formation WTC 2:3:108

Will Co, Green Garden Twp, hist sketch & biog sketches WTC 2:3:80

Will Co, Green Garden Twp, land rec 1840s-1850s WTC 7:1:58

Will Co, Green Garden Twp, settlers (1st) WTC 7:2:70

Will Co, Green Garden Twp, voter rolls 1853-1856 WTC 2:3:104

ILLINOIS (continued)

Will Co, Monee Twp, property owners 1842 WTC 4:1:20

Will Co, Monee Twp, real estate owners 1878 WTC 4:1:27

Will Co, Monee, St Paul's Ch bapt 1859-1861 WTC 14:1:20

Will Co, New Lenox Twp, biog sketches WTC 4:3:122

Will Co, New Lenox Twp, census, 1850 WTC 4:3:107 (1860 index) WTC 9:2:47 (1870) WTC 14:3:122

Will Co, New Lenox Twp, direct (business) 1873 WTC 9:2:70

Will Co, New Lenox Twp, land owners (rural) 1873 roster WTC 9:2:67

Will Co, New Lenox Twp, residents 1830s-1860s WTC 9:2:63

Will Co, New Lonox Twp, hist WTC 4:3:95

Will Co, Peotone & Will Twp, life in early 1900s WTC 15:1:36

Will Co, Peotone Twp, ch hist WTC 15:1:25

Will Co, Peotone Twp, direct (business) 1873 WTC 9:4:143

Will Co, Peotone Twp, farmers & breeders 1918 WTC 15:1:6

Will Co, Peotone Twp, hist sketch WTC 9:4:125

Will Co, Peotone Twp, landowners roster 1873 WTC 9:4:138

Will Co, Peotone Twp, postmasters 1857-1963 roster WTC 9:4:136

Will Co, Peotone Twp, St John's North Peotone Cem WTC 9:4:144

Will Co, Peotone Twp, settlers 1830s-1870s roster WTC 9:4:130

Will Co, Peotone Twp, supervisors 1866-1873 roster WTC 9:4:129

Will Co, Peotone Twp, West Peotone, West Peotone Pres Cem WTC 9:4:155

ILLINOIS (continued)

Will Co, place names of long ago WTC 17:3:95

Will Co, settlers pre-1835 roster WTC 10:3-4:103

Will Co, Sherbourne Twp, census 1850 WTC 5:4:115

Will Co, Sherbourne & Momence Twp, settlers WTC 5:4:147

Will Co, Spencer, hist sketch WTC 9:2:43

Will Co, Trenton Twp, census 1850 WTC 2:3:84

Will Co, Washington Twp, census 1860 WTC 10:1:10

Will Co, Washington Twp, direct (business) 1873 WTC 10:1:1

Will Co, Will Twp, census 1860 WTC 10:1:41

Will Co, Will Twp, farmers & breeders 1918 WTC 15:1:17

Will Co, Will Twp, hist sketch WTC 10:1:39

Will Co, Will Twp, land owners 1873 roster WTC 10:1:45

Will Co, Will Twp, officials 1859-1880 WTC 10:1:47

Will Co, Will Twp, real estate owners 1878 WTC 4:1:25

Will Co, Wilton Center Cem WTC 10:3-4:108

Will Co, Wilton Twp, Civil War, mil roll WTC 5:1:3

Will Co, Wilton Twp, Twelve Mile Grove, hist sketch WTC 10:3-4:95

Will Co, Wilton Twp, biog sketches WTC 5:1:7

Will Co, Wilton Twp, census 1850 WTC 5:1:8

Will Co, Wilton Twp, hist sketch WTC 5:1:1

Will Co, Wilton Twp, postmasters roster 1847-1901 WTC 10:3-4:102

Will Co, Worth Twp, Blue Island, deaths 1900- WTC 5:2-3:43

Williamson Co, index to *Hist of Gallatin, Saline, Hamilton, Franklin, & Williamson Co IL* 1887 CIC 3:6:132

ILLINOIS (continued)

Winnebago Co, direct of farmers & breeders 1917, bk rev GH 41:4:190

World War I, roll of honor WTC 1:2:49

World War I, soldiers from Fort Sheridan who d in war, roster WTC 2:1:27

ILLSPACH, Catherine see Peter BAST

IMHOFF, Peter b1819, w Catherine Augspurger, GE, IL, geneal MH 14:1:1

IMMING, Mary d1909, IL, obit CRT 8:4:39

INDEX, Biog & geneal master index 1986, bk rev BG 8:2:42

Michigan Surname Index, bk rev NGS 75:2:154

Pass & imm lists index 1986 suppl, bk rev GJ 15:2:110

To articles in the *St Louis Geneal Soc Quarterly* 1968–1986, bk rev GH 41:6:143

To geneal & pedigrees in the *New EN Hist & Geneal Reg* vol 1–50, bk rev GH 41:1:124

To imm & naturalization rec held by Chicago Heights Free Public Lib WTC 10:2:66 10:3–4:168

To Saint Louis Geneal Soc surnames 1987, bk rev RAG 8:4:26

To Sonoma Co (CA) Geneal Soc surnames being res, bk rev GH 41:5:194

To surnames of the Contra Costa Co (CA) Geneal Soc, bk rev FRT 8:3:152 OC 24:2:85

To surnames of the Root Cellar Sacramento Geneal Soc, bk rev GH 41:6:130

to *The Am Geneal* (subjects) vol 1–60, bk rev DM 50:3:144 AG 62:1:63

To the *Dallas* (TX) *Morning News* Fam Tree 1986 columns by Thetford, bk rev SLB 6:4:168 DG 33:2:116

INDEX (continued)

To the Geneal Soc of Southern IL, surnames, bk rev GH 41:5:165

To the *Journal of the Assoc for the Preservation of the Memorials of the Dead* (IR) surnames & placenames vol 1–7 1888–1909, microfiche rev GH 41:5:197

To the *Loyalist Gazette*, bk rev FAM 26:3:177

To the *MN Geneal* 1980–1986, bk, rev SCS 24:1:18 GH 41:2:138

To the spouses of the DAR patriots, bk rev NYR 118:1:54

To the Whittier Area (CA) Geneal Soc surnames 1985–1986, bk rev WPG 13:3:43

To topographic & other map coverage & catalog of publ maps, bk rev CC 10:2:3

To unpubl personal names in rec offices & lib EN, bk rev RAG 8:5:24

INDIAN TERRITORY, Census 1860 OK 32:1:18 32:2:49

Marr rec avail 1890–1907 TA 22:1:17

Muskogee, marr 1890–1893, bk rev GH 41:4:198

Pontotoc Co, Chickasaw rolls OPC 18:3:62

INDIANA, Allen Co, Civil War, substitutes & bounty lists ACL 11:3:80 11:4:107 12:1:19 12:2:42

Allen Co, Fort Wayne, geneal misc 1890 abstr from the *Fort Wayne Morning Journal* ACL 11:3:83 11:4:111 12:1:16 12:2:58

Allen Co, Fort Wayne, public school teachers roster 1890 ACL 12:1:12

Allen Co, inheritance tax rec 1914–1928 ACL 12:2:51

Allen Co, physicians & accouchers 1881–1889 roster ACL 12:1:23 12:2:47

INDIANA (continued)

Benton Co, Ambia, hist, bk rev GH 41:2:131

Brown Co, biog sketches HJA 11:3:183

Brown Co, hist sketch GCB 87:1:9

Carroll Co, hist sketch GCB 87:2:4

Cass Co, hist sketch GCB 87:7:6

Civil War, 73rd IN Vol field & staff officers TB 14:1:32

Civil War, hist of 13th IN Cav Reg 1863-1865, bk rev GH 41:6:136

Clay Co, hist, bk rev GH 41:6:136

Crawford Co, estray bk A 1818-1895 HJA 12:1:8

Crawford Co, land rec 1818-1820 HJA 12:1:6

Crawford Co, marr 1828-1830 HJA 12:1:9

Dearborn Co, Civil War, rec of the 16th Reg of IN Company E HJA 12:1:85

Elkhart, New Parish High School grad roster 1931 MIS 19:4:91

Elkhart Co, declarations of intent 1906-1912 MIS 19:4:98

Elkhart Co, Locke Twp, Mayville School student roster 1877-1878 MIS 19:1:4

Elkhart Co, Washington Twp, Trout Creek Chapel hist sketch MIS 19:2:44

Floyd Co, Georgetown, Ch of the United Brethren in Christ member roster 1885 SIN 8:3:80

Fulton Co, marr 1835-1850 FCF 87:Spring Summer-Fall 1987

Geneal res hints LAB 2:4:60

Grant Co, Civil War, expired soldiers roster GCB 87:1:4

Grant Co, Landess, hist sketch GCB 87:2:5

Grant Co, Marion, geneal misc 1869-1870 abstr from the *Marion Weekly Chronicle* GCB 87:2:9

Grant Co, octagenarians roster 1907 GCB 87:2:8

INDIANA (continued)

Grant Co, Soldiers Home, geneal rec 1897 GCB 87:1:7 87:2:11

Grant Co, St Joe Reformed Ch hist sketch GCB 87:7:8

Grant Co, twp formations GCB 87:1:8

Grant Co, Van Buren Twp, biog sketches GCB 87:7:7

Grant Co, Van Buren Twp, land owners roster 1835-1841 GCB 87:2:6

Grant Co, Van Buren, Central Ch of Christ hist sketch & rec misc GCB 87:7:9

Grant Co, Van Buren, land tract rec (original) 1836-1840 GCB 87:7:4

Grant Co, Van Buren Twp, East Ch of Christ hist sketch GCB 87:4:10

Grant Co, Van Buren Twp, Far-rville, geneal misc 1800s GCB 87:4:3

Grant Co, Van Buren Twp, land tract rec 1830s GCB 87:4:4

Grant Co, Van Buren Twp, schools hist sketch & student roster 1905-1918 GCB 87:4:6

Grant Co, will abstr 1865-1874 GCB 87:1:6 87:2:10

Greene Co, hist sketch HJA 11:3:188

Hamilton Co, Greenwood Friends Cem QY 14:3:8

Harrison Co, Lanesville, business hist sketch SIN 8:3:75

Hist by Madison, bk rev REG 85:2:173

Howard Co, census 1850, bk rev GH 41:2:130

Jackson Co, mort sched 1850 HJA 11:3:190

Jefferson Co, discharge rec 1864-1865 HJA 11:3:192 12:1:13

Jennings Co, Vernon Twp, census 1840 HJA 11:3:195 12:1:17

Johnson Co, Ninevah Twp, census 1860 HJA 11:3:198 12:1:22

Knox Co, marr 1807-1820 NWT 8:3:21

INDIANA (continued)

Lake Co, census 1840 WTC 6:3:93

Land entries 1820–1831 vol 3, bk rev GH 41:4:190

Land rec accessible by computer GCP 5:6:11

Lawrence Co, Civil War, rec of the 16th Reg of IN Company D HJA 11:3:233

Madison, architecture (early), bk rev RAG 8:1:25 REG 85:3:268

Marion Co, geneal rec misc 1800s, bk rev RES 18:2:80

Martin Co, marr 1820–1846 HJA 12:1:27

Martin Co, probate rec 1821–1838 HJA 12:1:34

Migrations outline 1684–1920 RT 4:3:74

Monroe Co, marr 1818–1840 HJA 12:1:36

Morgan Co, land rec HJA 12:1:49

Morgan Co, probate rec 1822–1836 HJA 12:1:45

Naturalization rec, use of MIS 19:1:14

Noble Co, cem inscr from Allen, Green, Jefferson, & Swan Twp vol 4, bk rev GH 41:5:171

Noble Co, Orange & Wayne Twp, cem inscr, bk rev GH 41:4:190

Orange Co, land rec HJA 11:3:203

Religion, guide to hist resources, bk rev MIS 19:3:75

Rush Co, marr 1833–1837 HJA 11:3:208

Rush Co, naturalizations 1857–1890 HJA 11:3:219 12:1:55

Rush Co, probate rec 1822–1834 HJA 11:3:214

Rush Co, Walker Twp, census 1860 HJA 12:1:57

Saint Joseph Co, South Bend, Cedar Grove Cem inscr, bk rev PP 3:2:20 GH 41:4:190 TE 7:2:92 TE 7:2:92 TTH 8:4:94 PN 9:2:34

Scott Co, marr 1840–1848 HJA 11:3:222

INDIANA (continued)

Scott Co, Scottsville, fam hist in the Public Lib (IN) SIN 8:3:93

Shelby Co, deeds 1822–1829 HJA 12:1:65

Shelby Co, Liberty Twp, hist 1914–1986, bk rev GH 41:5:171

Shelby Co, marr 1843 HJA 12:1:68

Shelby Co, probate rec 1822–1836 HJA 12:1:60

Sullivan Co, census 1870, bk rev GH 41:5:194

Switzerland Co, deeds 1815–1819 HJA 11:3:231

Warren Co, cem inscr, bk rev GH 41:2:131

Warren Co, marr 1828–1853, bk rev GH 41:2:131

Warren Co, Williamsport, developement plans 1981, bk rev GH 41:2:132

Washington Co, Covenanter (Rice) Cem SIN 8:3:84

Washington Co, wills 1821–1830 HJA 11:3:229

INGALLS, Anne see Daniel FOSTER

Benjamin b1728, w Mary White, MA, ME, biog sketch DE 10:5:171

Edmund bc1598, EN, MA, geneal, bk rev FRT 8:2:102

Eleazer Stillman f1850, IL, CA, diary of trip to CA 1850–51, bk rev BCG 16:4:149

Fam rec corr to *The Geneal & Hist Of The Ingalls Fam In Am* by Burleigh NEH 4:3:165

Surname period, *The Ingalls Inquirer*, 5640 W Chadwick Rd, DeWitt MI 48820

INGERSOLL, Chester f1828, w Pheobe Weaver, VT, IL, fam hist WTC 17:4:121

Fam hist 1620–1986, bk rev FRT 8:2:102

INGRAHAM, Joseph m1806, w Nancy Potter, Bible rec BG 8:4:102

INNES, Robert f1872, IL, abstr of title WTC 4:2:58

INSLEE, Surname period, *Inslee Index*, 601 West 17th, Ada OK 74820

IOWA, Appanoose Co, Brazil, hist, bk rev TOP 17:2:36

Bible rec vol 5, bk rev GH 41:4:190

Biog index, bk rev APG 2:1:31

Black Hawk Co, Waterloo, geneal misc 1869-1865 abstr from *The Waterloo Courier*, bk rev GH 41:2:132

Cerro Gordo Co, index to *Hist of Franklin & Cerro Gordo Co IA* 1883, bk rev GH 41:5:172

Cerro Gordo Co, mort sched 1860-1870-1880, bk rev GH 41:5:171

Civil War, soldiers in KS roster TOP 17:3:73 17:4:106

Clayton Co, Grand Meadow Cem HH 22:1:45

Clinton Co, Clinton, student grad (8th grade) 1893 roster GWD 6:3:

Clinton Co, declaration of intentions 1867-1874 GWD 6:1:

Clinton Co, Lyons High School grad 1879-1885 roster GWD 6:4:

Council Bluffs, deaths, serious injuries, & illnesses 1894 abstr from the *Nonpareil*, bk rev GH 41:1:130

First Evangelical Luth Ch, Swede Ridge Cem HH 22:1:48

Geneal rec misc vol 3, bk rev GH 41:4:190

Grundy Center, First Pres Ch hist 1869-1983, bk rev FRT 8:2:106

Hamilton Co, Cass Twp, Cass Cem HH 22:1:22

Henry Co, Cedar Creek Friends Cem QY 14:3:9

Hist, bk rev RAG 8:3:24 8:5:26

Jones Co, Madison Twp, Madison Center Cem inscr, bk rev GH 41:5:172

Madison Co, Civil War, hist sketch of the IA Graybeards MCN 2:4:2

IOWA (continued)
Madison Co, deaths 1941 MCN 2:4:5

Monroe Co, wills 1845-1904 index HH 21:4:189

Muscatine Co, census 1910, bk rev GH 41:6:137

Natives in the Benton Co OR 1910 census HH 22:2:65

Pensioners 1887 HH 22:1:14

Poweshiek Co, marr 1861-1865 PCI 9:3:15 9:4:13 10:1:10

Ship pass list 1883-1884 HH 21:4:196

Spanish-Am War, muster-in roll for Capt P O Refsell's Company K 52nd Reg of Inf IA Vol HH 21:4:227

V r avail 1800s-1900s PCI 9:3:11 IAN 8:3:12

IRELAND, Aghadowey Pres Ch rec 1845-1890 IFL 2:9-10:35

Ballykilcline, emig 1847-1848 MP 3:1:8

Bapt 1885-1887 performed by Rev Francis Carolan GGL 6:4:122

Cem inscr GGL 6:4:134

Co Armagh, ch reg avail IFL 2:9-10:9

Co Armagh, freeholders roster 1813-1819 GGL 6:1-2:18 6:3:79 6:4:139

Co Louth, Collon Parish, geneal extracts from the notebk of Rev Carolan 1796-1921 GGL 6:3:97

Co Louth, Monasterboice, cem inscr GGL 6:3:103

Co Meath, Slane Parish, geneal extracts from the notebk of Rev Carolan 1550-1924 GGL 6:3:99

Co Tipperary, hist & soc, bk rev FAM 26:1:50

Co Tyrone, Third Pres Ch rec 1800s GGL 6:4:127

Cork, 3rd battalion royal Munster fuslilers reg rec 1793-1906, microfiche rev GH 41:5:197

Cork, ship pass list 1826 to CT GGL 6:3:111

ITALY, Geneal res guide by Reed, bk rev BCG 16:1:30

Geneal res hints CPY 16:1:11 GD 18:1:25

Geneal terms with EN translations CTN 20:1:51

Hist sketch GCP 5:5:33

Imm to Lake Charles LA, bk rev KSL 11:4:123

Imm to Tangipahoa Parish LA found in 1910 census, bk rev GH 41:4:192

Imm to WA 1853-1924, bk rev SGS 36:2:101

Ship pass list to US 1894 on board the *La Bretagne* MP 3:2:104

Surname origins by Fucilla, bk rev WCK 20:3:47 NYR 118:4:240 NCJ 13:3:183 BG 8:2:42 GH 41:5:155 GHS 4:2:73 OC 24:3:126

JACK, Jane A see Albert Nathaniel REYNOLDS

JACKSON, Benjamin b1835, w Rachel Carter, NS, biog GN 5:1:10

Caleb m1800, w Zernah Keith, MA, Bible rec RED 19:4:13

Daniel bc1797, w Nancy Woodruff, SC, GA, geneal, bk rev GGS 23:4:208

Euphemia see William BRADEN

Fam cem Jackson Co TN SGE 28:122:18

Fam crest & shield TEG 7:3:121

Fam hist lower VA, bk rev VAG 31:2:101

Fam hist lower VA VAG 31:1:11 31:2:101

Fam hist TX, bk rev AGS 28:2:55

Fam hist WV & VA, bk rev NYR 118:2:123

Hannah d1777, h John Goodwin, MA, cem inscr MQ 53:3:165

Henry Clay b1839, w Sue Elizabeth Chadwick, MO, obit SNS 3:5:3

Jesse Dewey b1903, w Emma Parthena Lynn, AL, IL, anc ch MCA 6:2:72

JACKSON (continued)

Low dc1851, w Margaret Wood, IL, estate MCS 7:1:37

Margaret see Willis HOPKINS

Margaret _____ see William WILLIAMS

Mark bc1740, w Martha Warren, VA, geneal VAG 31:3:195

Mary A see Addam CLINE

Robert G f1842, w Elizabeth P Tucker, children PT 29:2:43

William d1710, VA, lineage VA 25:1:3

JACOBS, James b1805, VA, TX, obit YTD 5:2:24

JAHN, Friedrich Ludwig b1778, GE, biog sketch BGG 1:12:115

JAMES, Evan d1917, IL, obit CRT 8:4:46

Frank f1907, OK, biog sketch TTT 11:4:189

George R m1861, w Susan Q Honssinger, Bible rec OZ 5:2:67

Jesse Edwards Jr m1900, w Stella McGown, MO, marr OZ 9:2:51

JAMESON, Fam hist, bk rev NGS 75:1:61

JAMISON, Harriet M see John M DURST

JANES, Surname period, *Janes Fam Newsletter*, 401 E Daugherty, Bardstown KY 40004 – fam hist, Abel lineage

JANNEY, Nancy C see Zachariah LOWNES

Surname period, *The Janney Journal*, Box 344, Monticello UT 84535

JANSEN, Cornelius b1822, PU, RA, NE, geneal, bk rev WTC 5:2-3:101

JAPP, William A see Frieda LANGER

JAQUITH, Abraham mc1643, w Ann Jordan, MA, geneal, bk rev GFP 37:2:71

JARED, John b1837, w Hannah Whitacre & Rachel Palmer, TN, geneal, bk rev GH 41:3:176

JAREK, Regina see Antoni SZAREK

JARVIS, Hiram b1823, w Mary J Shaver, Bible rec NGS 74:4:254

John Henry b1888, Bible rec KFR 13: :3

JECSZKO, Agnes see John CHRISTULE

JEFFERSON, Thomas f1806, VA, hist sketch of his home Poplar Forest DAR 121:1:5

JEFFERY, John b1728, w Elizabeth Irons, NJ, OH, fam hist HL 2:1:10

JENKINS, Edith see Frank H LEWIS

Eliza Lee see Thomas Silas KIRBY

Stella see Eldon Thomas BARNET

Verlinda (Lamar) see Matthew RUSSELL

JENNINGS, Huldah Hill see James TOMPKINS

Tyree m1792, w Hannah McKinney, ST?, VA, anc ch BHN 20:2:65

JESSE, John B m1804, w Polley Dixon, VA, Bible rec KA 23:2:78

Martha see Giles HAWKINS

JESSUP, John f1637, MA, CT, geneal, bk rev FRT 8:1:51

JESUIT, Hist in OR, bk rev EWA 24:3:211

JEWEL, Sarah Anna b1863, h Rodolphus Clawson, OH, geneal, bk rev GH 41:1:162

JEWELL, George bc1710, w Amy Groome, MD, geneal, bk rev GH 41:6:160

JEWETT, Dorothy see Benjamin Franklin NEWHALL

Fam hist Old Pittston ME DE 11:2:44

JEWISH GENEALOGY, Atlas of the Jewish World, bk rev JL 3:1-2:108

Folklore, bk rev JL 3:1-2:109

Geneal res hints & interview questions FRT 8:1:13

JEWISH GENEALOGY (cont)

Guide to mss sources in the Lib of Congress JL 3:1-2:112

Guide to Richmond VA sources SIQ 7:2:24

Hebrew names dictionary, bk rev JL 3:1-2:110

Hebrew word processing JL 3:1-2:17

Hist by Alpher, bk rev JL 3:1-2:110

Hist of Jews in Augusta GA AGA 12: :29

Hist sketch of settlement in Lancaster PA LCC 4:3:74

Holocaust-era geneal res sources SIQ 7:1:5 7:2:5

Mordy collect of EN-Jewish geneal SIQ 7:2:20

Res guide by Rottenberg, bk rev NGS 74:4:317 AG 62:1:57 MSG 7:1:49 OK 32:1:5 SGS 36:3:156 36:4:208

Res guide to Israel by Sack, bk rev GGD 3:2:79 CTN 20:2:323 GHS 4:2:73 NCJ 13:3:182 KA 23:2:114 WCK 20:3:47 GH 41:5:154

Res guide to Savannah GA sources SIQ 7:3:20

Res hints FRT 8:2:70 8:3:135 MP 3:1:9 ANC 22:4:160 FRT 8:4:178

Res sources guide to Seattle WA SIQ 7:1:16

Resources in NY area, bk rev JL 3:1-2:110

Soc with addresses US, CN, EN, FR, Israel, & SW SIQ 7:1:30

Soundex GCP 5:5:23

Sources for GE-speaking Jewry SIQ 7:1:20

Yizkor (memorial) bk avail SIQ 7:1:11 7:2:6

JINNETTE, William b1849, w Miss Marsden, IR, AA, biog sketch TI 86:11:31

JOHANNISSON, Johan, w Cathrina ____, SN, US, geneal, bk rev KK 25:1:17

JOHNSON, Amelia see Mason STREETER

JOHNSON (continued)

Ann see John BENTLEY

Belinda (Shipman) see James BURROW

C W f1867, settling in MN MN 18:1:3

Elizabeth Tennessee see William FARLEY

F M m1852, w Delaina Medley, Bible rec OZ 9:1:24

Fam hist NW, ST, CN, LA, bk rev GH 41:6:160

Fam hist suppl, bk rev GH 41:1:162

Gertrude see William H PIERCE

Hannah see Thomas CRESAP

Isaac m1741, w Susanna Thayer, MA, geneal, bk rev GH 41:6:161

James bc1607, w Margaret ___ & Abigail Oliver, EN, MA, geneal TEG 7:4:187

James bc1815, w Elizabeth Jane Butts, KY, CA, fam rec SLB 6:4:174

James Sr d1909, w Harriet Morton, KY, IL, obit CRT 8:4:37

Jordan see Nancy Jane BOOTS

Leonia E b1872, MO, cem inscr OZ 7:3:114

Louisa see John William GREEN

Manerva see William FARLEY

Mary Elizabeth see John Bailey KNIGHT

Mary see Reuben COLLINGS

Nancy Ann see Thomas A MILLS

Rebekah see Rufus PERKINS

Robert bc1643, VA, geneal, bk rev WTC 12:1:26

Robert, w Margaret Braithwait, WE, PA, OH, geneal, bk rev GH 41:2:153

Rosa see William FARLEY

Samuel b1776, NJ, anc ch BG 8:1:12

Sarah see Jacob BLAIR IV

Surname period, *Johnson Journal*, 5048 J Parkway, Sacramento CA 95823 – marr 1877–1900 AR, index 1866 CA, cem RI, settlers CO, Rev soldiers KY

JOHNSON (continued)

William Baker m1822, w Charlotte Hook Pankey, Bible rec SIN 8:3:81

JOHNSTON, Humphrey bc1776, w Margaret Whitcroft & Catherine Palmer, IR, ON, geneal FAM 26:1:35

Jennie E see John M HADDEN

John f1837, w Ellen ___, ST, ON, geneal, bk rev GH 41:3:176

Mary Elizabeth see Murray G BARR

Nancy Graston see Julius WOODWARD

Thomas b1777, w Nancy B (Bryant?), NC?, GA?, anc ch NAS 26:2:49

JOINER, Sarah Louisiana see William Franklin BRANTLEY

JONES, Ann see George WATKINS

Ben G W b1823, w Kiturra Cossey, TN, MO, geneal OZ 9:2:49

Charles dc1900, w Sarah ___, TX, anc ch AGS 28:2:94

Ellis W m1887, w Jenny Hicks, PA, Bible rec WPG 13:4:36

Evan E m1886, w Maggie M Goodrich, OH, Bible rec MM 11:9:48

Fam rec misc vol 1, bk rev GH 41:1:162

Green R m1834, w Margaret E ___, anc ch FF 15:4:135

James b1779, w Elizabeth White, Bible rec OZ 9:3:107

James bc1782, w Mary ___, anc ch FF 15:4:135

James C m1851, w Sarah McGlasson, IL, Bible rec WTC 9:1:16

Jefferson Y bc1811, w Frances Eubanks, TN, TX, biog YTD 5:2:31

John Dudley f1867, TX, auto STK 15:2:52

Jonathan B bc1802, w ___ Brooks & Nancy (Doty) Ireland, NC, MO, geneal OZ 6:4:137

JONES (continued)

Laura see Squire HUMBLE

Mary Ann see Silas Engle SEYBERT

Mollie J see D C BARROWS

N B see Augusta E ARENDALL

Permelia T see A F ATTAWAY

Richard H b1804, NC, GA, geneal TCG 7:2:1

Richard R m1895, w Mary J Hubbel, Bible rec BGS 19:4:163

Sarah see William RODNEY

Surname period, *Jones Fam Newsletter*, POB 28215, Sacramento CA 95828 – bk rev, coat of arms

Surname period, *The Jones of Am*, 1661 Lauranceae Way, Riverdale GA 30296

Thomas dc1740, w Amey ____, VA, geneal, bk rev GH 41:6:161

William f1876, KS, criminal court case KL 7:1:3

Willis Field see Martha McDowell BUFORD

JORDAN, Elizabeth see William LEETE & David WALLER

Mary see Nathaniel BASSE

William see Julia MCCORKELL

JORIS, Hillegonda see Jan Cornellissen VANHOORN

JOSLIN, Keziah see Samuel LINDSEY

JOYNER, Fam hist VA, bk rev GH 41:6:161

Thomas d1694, EN, VA, geneal, bk rev GH 41:4:207

JUDD, Sarah bc1695, CT, anc ch AB 15:3:67

JUDKINS, Charles f1752, VA, bond GRI 7:10:78

Hannah see Benjamin BUNKER

Silas b1833, CA, cem inscr RDQ 5:1:10

Surname period, *The Judkins Journal*, 1538 NW 60th, Seattle WA 98107

JUDSON, Noadiah b1763, w Clarinda Kirtland, CT, NY, Bible rec NYR 118:2:96

JUDY, Nancy see Moses WHITESIDE

JUNGLES, Bernard N b1856, w Lydia Bump, IL, biog WTC 17:4:127

JUNKIN, Rebecca see George GALLOWAY

KAGARICE, John Calvin b1850, w Mary Clapper, PA, KS, geneal, bk rev FRT 8:2:105 CHG 19:1:21

KAGG, Elin Mattsdotter f1598, anc ch SAG 7:1:38

KAISER, George Edward b1875, w Caroline Moritz, OH, anc ch DG 33:1:56

Johann Christian b1806, w Johanne Karoline Kaiser, GE, fam rec AGS 28:2:66

KALAHER, Patrick f1850, IR, IL, fam hist GL 21:3:75

KALKBRENNER, Gabriel b1797, GE, IL, geneal, bk rev STC 10:1:39

KAMPMEIER, Minna F see Wilhelm SCHAPERKOTTER

KANABELL, Anna see Chris ZUG

KANDY, Chuck F see Mary A STEWART

Daniel Frederick m1846, w Adeline Ballow, NY, BIble rec WTC 14:2:80

KANNEWURF, Charles f1857, GE, IL, geneal, bk rev GH 41:3:169

KANSAS, Andale, hist 1885-1985, bk rev TS 29:1:27

Atchison Co, cem inscr, bk rev GH 41:5:194 GH 41:6:137 MGR 22:3:134

Barton Co, Galatia, biog sketches BCS 7:2:8 7:3:11

Barton Co, marr 1872-1885 BCS 7:1:3 7:2:6 7:3:3

Barton Co, plat bk 1902 BCS 7:1:6

Beloit, Zion Evangelical Luth Ch rec 1886-1986, bk rev GH 41:3:161

Brown Co, cem inscr. bk rev GH 41:4:190

KANSAS (continued)

Bucklin, hist 1887-1987, bk rev TS 29:1:27

Butler Co, cem inscr vol 1, bk rev GH 41:4:190 GH 41:6:137

Butler Co, geneal res guide by Afton, bk rev GH 41:6:138

Cawker City, Dutch settlers reunion 1911 WRB 10:3:13

Cawker City, Sts Peter & Paul Ch bapt 1880s WRB 10:2:12

Cem abandoned & semi-active vol 2, bk rev FRT 8:2:105

Centenarians 1899 biog sketches TOP 17:2:57 17:3:83

Cherokee Co, Baxter Springs, Lowell Cem inscr, bk rev TOP 17:4:100

Civil War, problems of travel KK 25:4:67

Clay Co, Hayes Cem KK 25:3:54

Co formation KL 7:3:17

Comanche Co, naturalization rec 1901-1926 TS 29:2:75

Cowley Co, cem inscr, bk rev GRI 7:8:59 GH 41:6:138

Decatur Co, Altory Twp, Kanona Cem TS 29:3:93

Decatur Co, Kanoma, Big Timber Community settlers roster TS 29:3:101

Doniphan Co, Iowa Point, letters remaining at post office TOP 17:1:19

Edwards Co, Kinsley, World War I, men reg for draft 1917 TOP 17:1:15 17:2:52

Finney Co, naturalizations 1885-1979, bk rev GH 41:2:132

Geneal misc 1883 abstr from the *Reveille* TS 29:1:22

Geneal rec misc vol 1, 2, & 3, bk rev TOP 17:4:100

Geneal res centers in westen KS TS 29:1:5 29:2:55

Gray Co, postmasters roster 1874-1986 TS 29:1:13

Harvey Co, geneal res guide by Crozier, bk rev GH 41:1:130

Holyrood, hist 1886-1986, bk rev TS 29:1:27

KANSAS (continued)

Jackson Co, Douglas Twp, Point Pleasant Public School souvenir 1915 TOP 17:1:14

Jefferson Co, cem inscr 1854-1986, bk rev GH 41:2:133

Jewell & Mitchell Co, pioneer hist sketch WRB 10:1:10

Jewell Co, Esbon, Esbon High School alumni 1907-1983 roster WRB 10:1:12 10:2:8

Johnson Co, biog sketches of early settlers JCG 15:1:7 15:2:43 15:3:77

Johnson Co, land abstr 1858-1859 JCG 15:1:19 15:2:54

Johnson Co, Lenexa, Salem Evangelical Luth Ch bapt 1848-1910 JCG 15:1:15 15:3:8415:2:50

Johnson Co, McCamish Twp, residents 1874 JCG 15:2:47

Johnson Co, Monticello Twp, landowners 1874 JCG 15:3:81

Johnson Co, patrons abstr from the *Standard Atlas of Johnson Co KS* 1902 JCG 15:1:22 15:2:56

Johnson Co, Spring Hill Twp, landowners 1874 JCG 15:1:13

Kearny Co, geneal misc 1893 abstr from the *Kearny Co Advocate* TS 29:2:65 29:3:109

Linn Co, Centerville Twp, Kohlsburg School student roster 1910 & 1918 KL 7:4:9

Linn Co, drought of 1860 KL 7:3:13

Linn Co, geneal misc 1887-1891 KL 7:1:4

Linn Co, geneal misc 1887 abstr from the *Pleasanton Observer* KL 7:3:1

Linn Co, hist sketch 1893, 1901, 1907, 1908 KL 7:3:16

Linn Co, LaCygne, geneal misc 1891-1892 abstr from the *LaCygne Journal* KL 7:1:11 7:4:1

Linn Co, LaCygne, marr 1880s-1890s KL 7:3:11

Linn Co, obit & marr 1986–1987 KL 7:1:18

Linn Co, Pleasanton, geneal misc 1886 abstr from *The Pleasanton Observer* KL 7:1:6

Maiza, hist, bk rev FRT 8:4:200

Maps & direct index to the Walsworth reprint (1982) of the 1887 official state atlas of KS, bk rev GH 41:6:137

Marion Co, census 1870 MGR 22:1:28 22:2:67 22:3:114

Marion Co, Hillsboro, hist, bk rev MGR 22:3:135

Miami Co, cem inscr vol 1, bk rev FRT 8:4:199

Miami Co, ch hist, bk rev FRT 8:4:199

Miami Co, fam hist & stories 1861–1986, bk rev GH 41:6:138

Miami Co, Independence School student roster 1909 TOP 17:4:110

Miami Co, marr 1855–1867, bk rev TOP 17:3:68

Miltonvale, Miltonvale Wesleyan College grad 1914 NW 9:2:17

Mitchell Co, Grellet Academy, hist sketch WRB 10:2:14

Natives dying in OR 1984–1985 TOP 17:2:58 17:3:81

Natives in CA obit 1982 TOP 17:4:111

Nemaha Co, geneal misc 1885–1886 abstr from the *Oneida Monitor* TOP 17:3:80

Nemaha Co, index to *Hist* 1916, bk rev GH 41:1:130

Nemaha Co, marr lic 1892 TOP 17:4:117

Ness Co, Ransom High School, hist, bk rev TS 29:1:28

News holdings direct, bk rev MN 18:4:187

Osborne Co, Jackson Twp, Grantham School Dist #63 student roster TOP 17:4:109

Pawnee Co, Burdett, Brown's Grove Cem vet burials TS 29:2:71

Pioneers, use of Federal rec left behind MGR 22:3:110

Pottawatomie Co, postmasters & postoffices 1870–1927 KK 25:2:32 25:3:49

Reno Co, cem inscr, bk rev BAT 16:1:25

Reno Co, geneal res guide by Crozier, bk rev GH 41:1:131

Reno Co, Plevna, hist 1886–1986, bk rev TS 29:1:27

Riley Co, ch hist sketches KK 25:2:35

Riley Co, commissioners 1855–1986 KK 25:1:9

Riley Co, funeral cards 1800s–1900s KK 25:1:7

Riley Co, Hayes Meth Ch hist sketch KK 25:3:53

Riley Co, hist sketch of northern area KK 25:4:64

Riley Co, Manhattan, deaths 1871–1877 reported in *The Nationalist* KK 25:2:24 25:3:47 25:4:68

Riley Co, obit 1901–1930 abstr from the *Enterprise*, bk rev KK 25:2:37

Riley Co, Ogden, ch hist sketch KK 25:1:13

Riley Co, WWII, honor roll KK 25:2:25

Russell Co, Centre Twp, Dubuque Luth Cem BCS 7:2:2

Sedgewick Co, naturalizations 1870–1906 MGR 22:3:126

Sedgwick Co, geneal res guide by Crozier, bk rev GH 41:1:131

Sedgwick Co, Maize, hist, bk rev GH 41:2:133

Sedgwick Co, marr 1890–1891 MGR 22:1:11 22:2:57 22:3:105

Sedgwick Co, naturalizations 1870–1906 MGR 22:1:16 22:2:76

Settlers forgotten, bk rev GH 41:5:172

Shawnee Co, geneal misc 1884 abstr from the *North Topeka Mail* TOP 17:2:55

KANSAS (continued)

Shawnee Co, Mission & Soldier Twp, cem inscr vol 3, bk rev GH 41:4:190

Sheridan Co, Saline Twp, Bethel Christian Cem TS 29:2:73

Stafford Co, Lincoln Co, Pleasant Ridge Cem BCS 7:3:6

Sterling, cem inscr, bk rev GH 41:2:133

Sumner Co, marr 1876-1878 MGR 22:1:25 22:3:123

Sumner Co, Union School student roster 1882-1883 MGR 22:2:56

Topeka, bapt 18902-1920s performed by Rev J W Reed TOP 17:1:9

Topeka, centenarian biog sketches TOP 17:4:114

V r & geneal sources publ in KS geneal soc period, direct TOP 17:2:39

Woodson Co, marr 1860-1985, bk rev GH 41:6:166

KARL, Ernst b1832, w Mena Allaman, GE, PA, geneal, bk rev FRT 8:2:104

KARN, Charles f1886, MI, will abstr FG 29:2:49

KAST, Fam hist NY, bk rev NYR 118:2:116

KAUFFMAN, Ellen Virginia b1842, h Isaac Newton Rickard, VA, KS, geneal, bk rev FRT 8:2:103

KAUZLARICH, William b1868, w Helena Kovacevich, Yugoslavia, WA, biog sketch YV 19:2:48

KAYLOR, Elizabeth see Isaac DEETER

KEANE, Henry H P b1829, w Margaret Ryan, IR, anc ch GGL 6:3:108

KEAR, John Cears bc1763, VA?, MD, OH, geneal, bk rev MD 28:3:363

KEARY, Charles m1896, w Nellie R Loyd, OH, marr rec CPY 16:1:16

KECK, Conrad b1755, PA, NC, TN, geneal, bk rev TS 29:1:25

KECK (continued)

Diana Lovest b1861, IN, MI, WI, anc ch BWG 16:1:38

Fam hist TN, bk rev BWG 16:1:64 VAG 31:1:68

KEEFER, Eliz see John HOOVER

KEHLER, John H Jr b1828, VA?, MD?, CO, biog sketch FI 7:1:5

KEISTER, Frances Elizabeth b1866, h James L Lambert, VA, NE, obit NA 10:1:3

KEITH, Barbara Ann see Peter HULL

Charles H m1834, w Margaret E Hogan, Bible rec KK 25:2:34

J H m1848, w Jane O'Neal, Bible rec HTR 30:2:44

James Sr bc1720, EN, VA, geneal, bk rev WTC 10:3-4:156

Zernah see Caleb JACKSON

KELLAMS, Jacob b1804, w Rebecca Roberts, IN, Bible rec HJA 12:1:5

KELLER, Elizabeth see Jacob REISINGER

Fam hist PA, bk rev RAG 8:5:26

Mary see John MOORE

Samuel f1826, w Rebecca Carter, TN, fam rec BWG 16:2:135

KELLEY, Addison b1812, OH, Bible rec TFP 7: :70

Elizabeth see Wm J OWENS

Jane see Daniel O ROBINSON

KELLIS, Dudley bc1800, VA, SC, TX?, anc ch STK 14:4:205

KELLY, Allison Woodward b1844, Bible rec STK 14:4:204

Daniel d1834, w Elizabeth ___, PA, NY, MI, IL, geneal NYR 114:3:137 114:4:225

Henry Joseph b1832, w Catherine Quinlevan, IR, AA, biog sketch TI 86:11:6

Hugh, w Jane Meehan, IR, anc ch FF 15:4:132

Mary b1641, MA, NJ, anc ch HJA 11:3:244

Nathan b1760, w Hannah Miller, DE, OH, anc ch HL 5:2:53

Patrick d1823, IR, ME, death notice AG 62:1:27

KELSEY, Benjamin d1877, IL, cem inscr WTC 2:4:124

Dandridge Eliphalet b1818, w Mercy Lacock & Elizabeth Boatman Wilson & Rebecca Jane Burgess, diary abstr 1867-1903 TOP 17:1:21

KELSO, Jake see Margaret GIL-MORE

Surname period, *Kelso Correspondence*, 287 Clark Dr, Cedar Falls IA 50613

KEMP, Fam rec misc, bk rev GH 41:1:163 NYR 118:1:54

KEMPF, Joseph Sr bc1809, w Theresa Wolf, TX, anc ch AGS 28:2:79

KENDIG, Adam m1817, w Ann Haverstick, PA, Bible rec LCH 2:2:97

KENEDY, Albert R d1919, ON, NE, biog sketch NW 9:2:25

KENNEDY, George Henry m1857, w Nancy Jane Rodgers, Bible rec WPG 13:3:28

George L Jack b1876, w? Josephine Margaret ___, OK, cem inscr OPC 18:1:10

Jeremiah Michael b1886, w Agnes Belle Curry, IL, anc ch KIL 15:3:35

Margaret see Martin HINES

Mary see John STEVENS

Nancy see Henry HUNTER

Patrick Joseph b1858, w Mary Augusta Hickey, MA, anc ch GCP 4:12-5:1:

Robert Cobb f1864, LA, attempt to burn NY, bk rev NYR 118:3:178

KENNY, Neil b1831, w Mary Bond, IR, EN, WI, Bible rec MCR 18:2:39

KENRICK, Sarah see Ralph ED-DOWES

KENTUCKY, Adair Co, cem inscr vol 6, bk rev KA 23:2:119

Adair Co, census 1810-1840, bk rev NGS 75:1:67 GJ 15:3:180

Adair Co, marr 1867-1869, bk rev KA 22:4:244

KENTUCKY (continued)

Allen Co, cem inscr vol 2, bk rev NCJ 13:3:178 GH 41:3:173 KA 23:1:37

Allen Co, census 1820-1840, bk rev GEK 23:1:5 GH 41:4:191 WCK 20:2:28 VS 4:1:84

Archival & mss repositories guide, bk rev REG 85:3:282 GH 41:4:191

Barren Co, census 1820, bk rev GHG 41:4:191

Barren Co, census 1810-1840, bk rev GH 41:1:132

Barren Co, geneal rec direct, bk rev SCS 24:9:183

Bath Co, censuses 1820-1840, bk rev NGS 75:2:157

Bath Co, marr bonds (loose) 1812-1825 EK 22:4:32 23:1:22 23:2:11 23:3:18

Bath Co, Sharpsburg, Gossett Hill Cem EK 22:4:10

Berea, abolitionism 1854-1864, bk rev REG 85:1:72

Big Sandy Valley, hist, bk rev EK 23:2:10 KA 23:2:118

Biog sketches in state, regional, & co hist, index, bk rev TTH 8:2:35

Boone Co, census 1850, bk rev MN 18:1:37

Boone Co, census 1810-1840, bk rev GJ 15:3:180 NGS 75:1:67

Boone Co, census 1850, bk rev NGS 75:1:67 GJ 15:3:180

Bourbon Co, censuses 1810-1840, bk rev NGS 75:2:157 GJ 15:3:180

Bourbon Co, census 1850, bk rev KA 22:4:242 GH 41:1:132

Boyle Co, marr bonds 1842-1879, bk rev KA 23:2:113

Caldwell Co, tax lists 1808-1811, bk rev KA 23:1:36 GH 41:3:161

Calloway Co, plat bk, bk rev GH 41:6:138

Cem inscr vol 5, bk rev KA 22:4:245

Census 1830 index to 14 co vol 1, bk rev WTC 3:4:169

121

KENTUCKY (continued)

Trigg Co, hist 1885-1985, bk rev KA 23:1:35

Trigg Co, hist misc vol 1, bk rev GH 41:1:134

Trigg Co, marr 1852-1859 & 1861, bk rev KA 23:1:34 GH 41:3:162

Trimble Co, deaths 1852-1859, bk rev KA 23:1:39

Trimble Co, marr 1852-1859, bk rev KA 23:1:39

Warren Co, census 1810-1840, bk rev KA 23:1:38 WCK 20:2:27 GH 41:3:173 TTH 8:4:96

Warren Co, deed abstr 1797-1812 vol 1, bk rev OK 32:1:7 (1812-1821) OK 32:1:8

Washington Co, census 1810-1840, bk rev KA 23:1:35 WCK 20:2:27 GH 41:3:173

Washington Co, wills 1792-1853, bk rev GH 41:5:173 KA 23:2:117

Whitesville, St Mary of the Woods death reg 1885-1979, bk rev WCK 20:2:27

Whitley Co, census 1850 (annotated), bk rev GH 41:2:134 CTN 20:1:138 KA 23:1:36 (index) KA 22:4:248

Whitley Co, marr 1860-1864 EK 23:2:17

Women reformers 1900s REG 85:3:237

Woodford Co, census 1810-1840, bk rev WCK 20:4:59

KERCH, Fridrich bc1752, w Anna Margaret Elis, PA, geneal, bk rev WPG 13:3:45

KERN, Emma M see Edward S OLAH

George Jacob b1805, w Mary Ann Long, GE, PA, MI, biog sketch FHC 11:1:3

KERR, John bc1759, w Eleanor Warden, PA, geneal, bk rev GH 41:2:152

KERSHNER, Surname period, *Kershner Kinfolk*, 1449 Fox Run Dr, Charlotte NC 28212

KESLER, Johannes b1728, w Eva Dorthea Leman, GE?, SW?, PA, VA, geneal, bk rev FRT 8:2:107

KETCHAM, Surname period, *Ketcham Kables*, 2133 Hermitage Dr, Davison MI 48423

KETTLE, Barbara E d1906, h George Edward Kettle, CO, obit CO 48:2:42

KEYES, Solomon f1653, MA, VT, WI, geneal, bk rev NYR 118:3:184

KEYSER, Fam hist VA, first Keyser fam in Page Co VAG 31:1:27

KIDDOO, James f1780, PA, geneal, bk rev SB 8:4:138

KIEHLE, Abraham Jr see Elizabeth SHAY

KIENTZ, Mary see William BAKOSKI

KIGHT, James Andrew d1859, w Sophronia Cosby, GA, anc ch NAS 26:2:48

KILBOURN, Benjamin b1799, CT, Bible rec CTN 20:2:244

KILLINGSWORTH, James f1667, EN, VA, geneal, bk rev GH 41:1:163

KILLOUGH, Fam hist sketch IR & US PT 29:4:151

Robert b1838, w Margaret Jane McCaughan, IR, anc ch GGL 6:3:107

KILMER, Fam hist OH, MI, IN, KS, NE, OK, WA, OR, bk rev FRT 8:2:104

Fam hist US vol 1, bk rev RES 18:1:19 (vol 2) RES 19:4:190

KILT, Conrad f1743, NY, geneal, bk rev NGS 75:1:62

KIMBLE, Helena see James DILL

KIMBROUGH, John III b1794, w Catherine Spiller Boxley, VA, MO, geneal OZ 7:2:72

Mary Barclay see Wilson HACKNEY

KINCHELOE, Cornelius f1693, w ___ Williams?, VA, geneal BWG 16:2:138

124

KINCHELOE (continued)
Elizabeth see Grandison WEBB
KING, Anna see James RAMBIN
Augustus bc1814, w Margaret Sonne, GE, KY, geneal KFR 13: :5
Benjamin m1854, w Mary Holmes, OH, marr rec CPY 16:1:16
Elizabeth see George TUCKER
Hazel Iola see Alexander A KOPPES
Heyden m1852, w Phebe ____, Bible rec MGR 22:2:87
John m1856, w Melinda J Love, WA, biog TB 13:3:15
Paul G m1897, w Minnie Myrtie Brown, Bible rec OC 24:1:25
Peter b1780, w Bettie Payne, IR, KY, geneal KFR 13: :4
Robert b1763, w Mary ____, children RAG 8:2:12
Rufus b1755, w Mary Alsop, MA, lineage SB 8:5:172
Samuel A b1820, w Frances A Mercer, SC, GA, anc ch GGS 23:2:90
Thomas b1760, w Elizabeth Cotton, VA, KY, desc KFR 13: :8
Thomas f1836, w Elizabeth King, TN, will YTD 5:2:21
William Albert b1836, w Elizabeth Helen Harris, NC, geneal, bk rev NCJ 13:1:54
William B m1859, w Francis Ellen Berry, Bible rec KFR 13: :1
William R m1844, w Elizabeth Ann Leggitt, Bible rec HTR 29:3:84
KINNEY, Paul Palmer b1875, w Susan Whipple, MI, MN, geneal DM 50:4:169
Spencer Eugene b1848, w Adelia Ann Palmer, MI, geneal DM 50:3:123
KINSER, Joseph b1800, w Anna McLaughlin/McGlothan, VA, MO, biog sketch OZ 5:2:77
KINSLAND, Surname period, *Kinsland Newsletter*, POB 533, Candler NC 28715

KINZIE, John b1763, ON, IL, biog WTC 1:2:31
Juliette A m1830, h John H Kinzie, WI, hist of life in Northwest Territory, bk rev CIC 3:5:104
KIRBY, Joshua b1823, OH, IA, anc ch CCS 8:4:138
Thomas Silas b1861, w Eliza Lee Jenkins, AL, geneal AL 3:3:47
KIRCHNER, Charles C b1834, MD, biog, bk rev WPG 13:3:51
KIRKMAN, George Sr f1712, w Elizabeth ____, MD, IL, geneal FF 15:3:71
KIRKPATRICK, John Robert b1743, w Agnes Patterson, PA, geneal, bk rev GH 41:3:169
Margaret/Mary b1800, KY, IL, anc ch CR 19:3:134
KIRTLAND, Clarinda see Noadiah JUDSON
KISINGER, Ann f1893, IA, letter STK 14:4:188
KISSEE, A C dc1902, MO, illness OZ 7:4:140
Arter b1810, w Ufins Bledsoe, KY, O, children OZ 5:2:77
KISTLER, Elizabeth see Elias SMITH
KITCH, Eliz see Adam STICKEL
KITCHEL, Catherine see John LEONARD
KITCHENS, Mary Susan see Harvey William HAMILTON
KITLEY, Thomas f1738, EN, MD, fam hist TNB 2:1:3
KITTLEBERGER, Euphrosina see Johann Jakob HAMP
KITZEROW, Georg Frederich Helmuth b1801, GE, WI, geneal, bk rev CTN 20:1:138
KJELSSON, Olof b1801, w Elin Nilsdotter, SN, SD, geneal SAG 7:2:51
KLEISS, Marie Anna b1875, anc ch BHN 20:4:142
KLEMGARD, Edwin Neal b1901, WA, biog sketch WCG 3:4:28
KLEMM, Anna Luise see William SITZ

KLEPPER, Fam hist, bk rev MCG 10:2:89

Jacob b1741, GE, US, geneal, bk rev GH 41:6:161

KLINE, Charles Franklin m1865, w Hannah Maria Boyd, PA, Bible rec TOP 17:2:49

KLIPPENSTEIN, Johann b1847, w Helena Kroeker, PU, RA, geneal MFH 6:2:54

KLOSS, George, w Rosa Scheidt, IL, fam hist WTC 6:1:22

KNECHT, Elsbeth see Jacob WOLFENSBERGER

KNEISLEY, George C m1895, w Ottie Dell Lee, Bible rec MCG 10:1:17

KNICKERBOCKER, Edwin L f1886, w Ellen H Knickerbocker, MI, will abstr FG 29:2:49

KNIEF, Maria see Friedrich WILLE

KNIGHT, Fam hist, bk rev AGE 16:4:107

Henry f1797, w Mary/Marie Magdelaine Liqueur, PA, LA, geneal, bk rev GH 41:6:166 KSL 11:3:75

John Bailey b1838, w Mary Elizabeth Johnson, VA, geneal, bk rev FRT 8:1:50

John bc1598, w Mary Chickering, EN?, MA, anc ch TAK 17:2:24

Richard bc1711, VA, geneal, bk rev GH 41:3:169

Surname period, *Knight Letter*, 2108 Grace St, Ft Worth TX 76111

KNIGHTON, Richard R dc1817, SC, will THT 16:1:48

KNISELEY, John b1748, Bible rec MFH 6:2:65

KNOCH, Emma b1878, IL, biog GD 17:4:15

KNOTT, John see Ann BROMLEY

KNOWLTON, Sarah bc1715, MA, anc ch YV 19:2:47

KNOX, Archie d1902, OH, obit TLL 12:3:50

John b1777, w Margaret McKay, IR, PA, fam rec CTN 20:3:520

KOLAR, John b1833, w Mary Kuesh, Bohemia, IL, fam hist WTC 17:4:131

KOLB, Abraham b1771, w Sarah Hunsicker, Bible rec MFH 6:3:104

Johannes H b1809, w Catharine Schwartley, Bible rec MFH 6:3:104

KOLP, Jacob b1845, w Elizabeth Kolp, Bible rec MFH 6:3:104

KONOW, Herman f1880, w Dorothea Tappert, GE, IL, fam hist sketch WTC 17:4:126

KOOGLE, Barb see Philip DERR

KOPPES, Alexander A b1898, w Hazel Iola King, IA, Bible rec PW 7:3:117

KORTWRIGHT, Eliza see James MONROE

KOTHKE, Carolina Henriette see Friedrich W GOLNICK

KOUNS, Miram see Archer WOMACK

KOVACEVICH, Helena see William KAUZLARICH

KRABBE, Henry Martin John b1838, w Sophia Drews, GE, IL, obit CRT 8:1:15

KRAETZ, Cecilia see August RITTEL

KREFELD, Surname period, *Krefeld Imm & Their Desc*, 7677 Abaline Way, Sacramento CA 95823

KREHBIEL, Michael d1752, w Anna Weyl, GE, anc ch MFH 6:2:75

KROEGER, Mary Elizabeth see Jacob VANDERHORST

KROEKER, Helena see Johann KLIPPENSTEIN

KROON, Frank d1897, w Charlotta ____, SN, MN, anc ch WB 17:4:132

KROPF, Christian f1711, SW, FR, HO, PA, geneal MFH 6:1:4

KRUEGER, Frank E b1871, w Mathilda L Heidemann, Pomerania, MN, anc ch FCT :74:29

KRUEGER (continued)

Friedrich C b1850, w Caroline Sager, GE, TX, anc ch VC 8:1:21

KRUEGER, Ludwig f1851, GE, IL, fam hist WTC 4:4:141

Marie Dorothea Elizabeth see August Heinrich George HACKEROTT

KRUMM, Henry b1826, w Sophia ____, GE, anc ch WTC 8:3:35

KRUSE, Friedrich Fritz Christian Johann b1836 w Christina Maria Sophie Braash, IL, biog sketch WTC 8:1:11

KUCH, Christian b1815, w Anna Barbara Saul, GE, IL, fam hist sketch WTC 2:2:37

KUESH, Mary see John KOLAR

KUNDERS, Margaret see Reyner TYSON

KUNTZI, Christian d1774, SW, US, geneal, bk rev NFB 19:1:8

KUNZEN, Elizabeth see John HALEY

KURTZIN, Anna see David PLANK

KUSTER, Mary see Frederick Christian Propper

KUTER, Bernhard f1748, w Anna Maria Hoffman, GE, PA, geneal, bk rev BWG 16:2:155

KYLE, Diana see James C GARRISON

LABISSONIERE, Anna b1892, h Joseph A Slavin, MN, WA, geneal YV 19:1:29

Eleanore b1873, h Paul Berthon, ON, WA, geneal YV 19:3:92

Louise b1899, h Tony Beaulaurier, ID, WA, geneal YV 19:2:68

LABORDE, Jean Pierre b1814, w Zoe Dupuis, LA, anc ch AGE 16:2:53

LACEFIELD, William L bc1817, w Betty Ann Bales, TN, AL, AR, anc ch TRC 1:1:43

LACEY, Sallie M see Frank H LAWLER

LACK, Armazinda see John W DAVIS

LACOCK, Joseph d1760, PA, geneal, bk rev WPG 13:4:41

Mercy see Dandridge Eliphalet KELSEY

LACY, Moses f1790, w Henrietta Pratt, KY, MO, geneal OZ 9:1:29

LADY, Jacob f1805, w Mary Lady, PA, geneal CCS 9:1:26

LAEXANDER, David f1761, w Elizabeth ____, ST, IR, US, geneal, bk rev GFP 37:2:69

LAFFERTY, S C f1841, w Martha A L ____, KY, Bible rec KA 23:2:105

LAGARCE, Catherine see Edmond SAINT PIERRE

LAKE, Benjamin b1765, w Elizabeth Hopkins, RI, children RIR 13:2:23

Eleazer bc1767, w Mercy Dill, ME, biog sketch DE 11:3:98

Fam hist TX THT 15:2:16

Mary see Josiah MOORE

LAMAR, Fam hist, bk rev OC 24:3:127

John S b1794, w Elizabeth Woollen, NC, IN, anc ch BGS 19:1:40

LAMB, John Sr f1840, w Cloey ____, AL, biog sketch NTT 7:4:143

Sarah Jane see Franklin STEIGELMAN

Surname period, *Lamb's Pastures*, 2983 Bayside Ct, Wantagh NY 11793

LAMBERG, Julia see Silas B CALL

LAMBERT, Elizabeth see John MEEKER Sr

James L see Frances Elizabeth KEISTER

Marie Josephine see Peter GOUMAZ

Mary A see William A SARTIN

Surname period, *Newsletter of the Lambert/Lambarth Fam Assoc*, 1000 W 5th St, Tempe AZ 85281

LAMMERS, Caroline Camilla see John J MOORE

127

LAMONT, Rosannah see Benjamin CUSTIN

LAMP, Jacob b1794, w Susanna Snyder, OH, anc ch HL 5:2:59

LAMPTON, Mark bc1648, w Elizabeth Piggott?, MD, geneal ANC 22:4:144

William b1682, w Francis Martin White & Esther Davis, MD, VA, anc ch ANC 22:4:140

LAMSON, Sarah (Ayres) see Thomas HARTSHORN

LAND, William b1836, NY, PA, CA, obit RCP 9:4:111

LANDERS, Abial m1825, w Phebe Covel, Bible rec CTN 20:1:56

Louisa see William Lawson BREWER

LANDIS, Louisa L see William Wesley WYLAND

Surname period, *Lander's Landings*, 3110 Z St, Vancouver WA 98661

LANE, James see Elura FULL

Levi see Amy COX

Mary Frances see James D FRAZER

Samuel f1858, w Mary Wilson, IR, ON, geneal, bk rev FRT 8:3:151 GH 41:4:207

Tidence b1724, w Hester Bibber, MD, geneal, bk rev GH 41:2:152

LANFEAR, Ann Eliza see Jacob BURCH

Asa b1793, w Olive Burgess, NY, IL, fam hist WTC 17:4:129

LANGDON, Elizabeth Edwards see Norris PECK

LANGER, Frieda b1890, h William A Japp, GE, IL, obit NWS 7:5:48

LANGFORD, George Robert b1839, w Anna Elizabeth Hodges, FL, lineage FLG 10:4:129

Ollie Lee b1886, h Will Henry Bartlett Sr, GA, TX, fam rec YTD 4:2:4

LANGHAM, Rebecca Robertson see George Washington CLEVINGER Sr

LANGLEY, Abigail f1748, VA, journal abstr VA 25:3:53

LANGREHR, Henry see Emma VOGT

LANGSTON, Emily m1859, h Andrew Washburn, Bible rec BCG 16:3:86

LANGTON, Deliverance see Thomas HANCHETT

LANGWILL, Ann see Angus CAMPBELL

LANIER, Catherine Elizabeth see Williams BASSE

LANTERMAN, Peter Jr see Zurilda CANTRALL

LANTZ, William Andrew b1865, w Dora Elizabeth Tomilson, IN, anc ch MIS 19:2:42

LAREAU, Fam hist FR & QB, bk rev CHG 19:4:154

LARSON, John L b1867, w Olive Nelson, SN, FL, biog sketch IMP 6:1:19

LARUE, Sarah see Rob HODGEN

LATIMER, Robert f1635, EN, MA, CT, TN, TX, geneal, bk rev FRT 8:1:48

LAUDERMAN, William bc1801, w Cynthia Ann ____, KY, IN, anc ch BGS 19:3:133

LAUGHLIN, John f1740, w Jane Mathias, PA, NC, TN, IL, IA, geneal, bk rev GH 41:2:160

LAUTENSCHLAGER, Anna Maria see Andrew HUIRAS

LAUX, Margaretha see Mathias DAUB

LAVENDER, Surname period, *Lavender Line*, Lavender Agency, Dess Lavender, POB 884, Bay Minette AL 36507

LAW, George b1812, w Isabella Carlaw, ST, MN, geneal, bk rev GH 41:2:152

LAWLER, Frank H m1878, w Sallie M Lacey, TN, TX, Bible rec YTD 5:1:22

LAWLESS, Thomas Redman b1828, w Elizabeth Jane Harvey, MO, anc ch BGS 19:1:42

LAWRENCE, Christina see Oscar FREITAG

LAWRENCE (continued)
Deborah see Jacob MOTT
Joseph m1830, w Elizabeth
(Pitts) Reese, GA, marr notice
GGS 23:4:174
Martha Elizabeth see Samuel
William CRUMBAKER
Mary Jane see James Terrell
BARNES
William Henry b1850, w Martha
Mary Ann Ham, geneal, bk rev
GH 41:6:161
LAWSON, Alexander Ayers
b1827, w Catherine Dodd, biog
sketch OZ 5:3:124
Surname period, *Lawson Letters*,
728 N Lucia, Redondo Beach
CA 90277
LAWTON, Thomas f1638, w
Elizabeth ___ & Grace
Bailey, EN, RI, biog sketch
RIR 13:1:2
LAXTON, Jim d1878, NC, hang-
ing CAL 6:4:75
LAYMAN, Fam rec vol 1 & 2, bk
rev CCS 9:2:60
Fam rec misc vol 2, bk rev DG
33:2:120 GH 41:4:207
LAYTON, Francis f1774, w
Elizabeth West, EN, NS,
geneal, bk rev GH 41:2:152
Sarah see Nelson FIELD
LEACH, John Miller f1863, Civil
War notebk STK 14:4:197
LEACHMAN, Thomas f1640, VA,
geneal, bk rev GH 41:5:193
Thomas f1840, VA, geneal, bk
rev GH 41:4:207
LEADEN, Bridget see Patrick
MCGEE
LEARNARD, Irene see Hains
FRENCH
LEBLANC, Daniel see Francoise
GAUDET
Isora see Louis Dorcey BOREL
Pierre Evariste b1853, w Her-
mine Beaudry, CN, biog sketch
AGE 16:1:13
Taddeus Nicolas b1819, w Hen-
riette Richard, NB, anc ch
AGE 16:3:84

LEBLEU, Bartholome f1781, LA,
biog KSL 11:4:101
LECRONE, Elizabeth b1815, h
John LeCrone, VA, IL, obit
CRT 8:4:43
Hugh d1892, IL, obit CRT 8:4:42
LEDBETTER, Susan T see Ed-
mond L PAYNE
LEDFORD, Curtis Burnam b1876,
w Addie King Ledford, KY,
recollections, bk rev SCS
24:6:130
William Curtis b1859, w Susan-
nah M Griffin, GA, AL, anc ch
SR 3:4:86
LEE, Ann see Samuel STUR-
TEVANT
Catherine see Matthew WILDER
Sr
Eunice Jerusia see Ira RUSSELL
Fam reunion NC 1912 JC 13:3:54
Henry f1772, VA, lease GRI
7:9:69
Ida Jeanette see Edwin DALTON
James J b1840, EN, WI, IA, anc
ch BG 8:3:64
Lemuel f1819, NY, IL, geneal
FF 15:3:5
Nathaniel f1748, VA, geneal, bk
rev NYR 118:2:115
Ottie Dell see George C KNEIS-
LEY
LEEK, Rodicia see Lemuel
Pinckney CROSSLAND
LEEPER, Margaret see George B
YOUNG
LEETE, William f1639, w
Elizabeth Jordan, VT, biog
sketch BAT 16:2:74
LEFAUCHEUR, Jean bc1674, w
Eva Matthyse, FR, NY, geneal
NYR 118:2:76
LEFTWICH, Martha Ann see
Harvey Sylvester WAKEFIELD
LEGER, Hippolyte b1819, w Osite
Boudreau, NB, anc ch AGE
16:3:83
LEGGETT, Henry G b1868, Bible
rec KA 22:4:236
LEGGITT, Elizabeth Ann see
William R KING

LEGRAND, Gabriel Louis bc1700, w Anne Henrietta Catherine deCrenay, FR, MO, geneal MSG 7:2:87

LEGROW, Jane see John BAGGS

LEHMAN, John b1818, w Lydia Hershberger, PA, anc ch MFH 6:4:146

LEICHLEITER, Surname period, *Leichleiter & Variants*, 4201 Wildflower Cir, Wichita KS 67210

LEIDIG, Fam rec misc IL FF 15:4:143

George f1828, w Sophia Remann, IL, geneal FF 15:3:33

LEINWEBER, Joseph Christopher b1879, w Elizabeth Gerlitz, Bible rec WCG 4:2:12

LEMAN, Eva Dorthea see Johannes KESLER

LEMASTER, Daniel Phillip f1854, w Phoebe Bayes, KY, geneal EK 23:2:29

Elizabeth f1853, h Joseph Williams, geneal EK 22:4:27

Elizabeth see Christopher C CASTLE

Francis P f1858, w Mary Elam, KY, geneal EK 23:1:11

Joseph M b1800, w Elizabeth Sophronia Miller & Rebecca Berdsell, GA, TN, MO, children OZ 9:1:29

Matthew Ramey b1853, w Louise Holton, KY, fam rec EK 23:3:20

Rachel f1847, h John Ramey Wheeler, KY, geneal EK 23:3:27

Sarah see Francis M WHEELER

LEMEN, George B b1809, w Charity Swisher, OH, IL, obit DWC 13:3:89

LEMMON, Jacob f1807, w Mary Smith, MO, biog OZ 5:4:143

LEMONS, Jim d1917, w Sarah Jane Brasher, OK, anc ch NAS 25:4:131

LENDRUM, Mary see Samuel OSBOURNE

LENOIR, Fam letters 1838-1899 TN, bk rev CAL 6:4:90

LENOX, H C d1865, w Sally Wilson, VA, OH, obit NW 10:1:12

LENS, Quebec Ann see George BARNET

LEONARD, Effie see Samuel ADAMS

John b1783, w Catherine Kitchel, NY, NJ, VT, OH, geneal, bk rev BAT 16:1:25 GH 41:1:162

LESTER, James Sr b1660s, VA, SC, geneal TCG 7:1:1

LETSON, Robert b1794, w Irene Thaxton, SC, geneal, bk rev GH 41:6:161

LEVERICH, Kate b1858, fam rec IG 23:3:89

LEVISON, Sam bc1854, NY, geneal SIQ 7:3:5

LEWIS, Abigail (Abia) see George W BARNES

Ebenezer see Sarah BENNETT

Edward m1815, w Ethelinda Edwards, CT, Bible rec CTN 20:3:432

Etta May see Marion Edward MCIRVIN

Frank H b1872, w Edith Jenkins, RI, FL, lineage FLG 10:4:152

Henry b1793, Bible rec GFP 36:4:164

Martha see Samuel LINCOLN

Nicholas f1847, w Harriett W Lewis, GA, will TCG 6:4:27 7:1:40

Sarah see John C LONG

Thomas II b1815, w Rebecca Heberling, OH, IA, fam rec AGS 28:2:77

William W b1784, TX, anc ch THT 16:1:14

LIBBY, Surname period, *The John Libby Fam Assoc & Libby Homestead Corp Newsletter*, POB 265, Scarborough ME 04074

LIBEER, Maria Rosa see Guilielmus Drogo AMEYE

LICHTI, Catherine see Hans MEYER

LIGGETT, Nancy see Joshua Middleton HICKEY

LIGHT, John R b1804, Bible rec HTR 30:3:72

Lucinda Ellen see Thomas ROGERS

LIGHTFOOT, William bc1830, w Caroline Collins, NC, anc ch GGS 23:4:199

LIGHTHILL, Elizabeth see James GLANCY

LILE, Richard W b1799, w Susan Jane McColster, Bible rec WTC 14:4:166

LINCOLN, Abraham f1861, IL, PA anc FCT :72:5 (see also Mary TODD)

Joseph b1640, MA, anc ch PF 17:1:6

Samuel b1619, w Martha Lewis, geneal HL 1:3:70

LIND, Olof f1893, w Anna Olofsdotter, SN, US, geneal, bk rev GH 41:2:153

LINDHOLM, Lydia Laurentia b1878, h Simon Chester Ashley Ring, MN, SD, anc ch SAG 7:2:88

LINDLEY, Catherine see William Monroe ELMORE

Israel b1833, Bible rec WCG 3:4:29

Mary see Colville ABERCROMBIE

LINDSEY, Christopher f1640, w Margaret ____, MA, geneal TEG 7:1:17

Eleazer bc1716, w Lydia Farrington, MA, geneal TEG 7:4:194

Elizabeth see Jesse TERRY

James Monroe b1828, w Mary Jane Newport, TN, MO, children OZ 9:2:69

Ralph b1712, w Abigail Blaney & Anna (Potter) Burchstead, MA, geneal TEG 7:3:123

Samuel b1697, w Keziah Joslin, MA, geneal TEG 7:2:71

LINN, Philip Edmond b1811, w Mahala McDannald, PA, geneal, bk rev WPG 13:4:38

LINNELL, Clara see George H LITTLEFIELD

LINSE, Mathilde Friederike Henriette see Adolf PFUND

Sadie Evangeline b1908, h Aubrey C Shelton, WA, biog sketch YV 19:1:8

LINTON, Mary Ann see John Franklin STARK

LIPPARD, John d1804, w Catherine ____ & Elizabeth Sassaman, anc ch FF 15:4:132

LIQUEUR, Marie Magdelaine see Henry KNIGHT

LISCOMB, Elizabeth see Peter BONNET

LISSENDEN, John m1851, w Ann Arnold, OH, marr rec CPY 16:1:16

LIST, Hans f1470, GE, US, geneal, bk rev CHG 19:2:109

Johann Georg f1719, GE, PA, OH, KY, geneal, bk rev TOP 17:3:68 FRT 8:4:199

LITCHFIELD, Remember see Henry LUCE

LITHUANIA, Fam in Luzerne Co PA, bk rev CGS 18:1:16

Hist outline 1219-1944 OH 2:6:

Hist sketch of Lithuanians in GE OH 2:6:

LITTLE, Elizabeth see William McGEORGE

Emily see James L WARD

Fam crest & shield TEG 7:3:121

Henry f1882, MI, letter MI 32:3:83

James W bc1787, w Elizabeth May, AL, KY, anc ch PT 29:4:145

LITTLEFIELD, George H b1842, w Clara Linnell, ME, biog sketch DE 11:1:22

Mary see Mast TREADWELL

LITTLEJOHN, Mary see Louis DeSHAZO

LITWILLER, Jacob bc1759, w Anna Maria Maurer, Alsace, ON, lineage MFH 6:2:53

LIVESAY, Surname period, *Livesay Bulletin*, 104 Linden Ave, Mercersburg PA 17236

LIVINGSTON, Gilbert f1785, w Joy Livingston, BM, will abstr BBQ 4:3:31

James b1834, w Nancy Taylor, ST, anc ch GGL 6:3:108

Virginia b1848, h Benjamin A Castleman & Henry Bear, KY, MO, biog sketch SNS 3:6:5

LOCHRIDGE, Rebecca see William F BURR

LOCKE, Julia see Robert E RISING

Lavina see Elisha S ANDRUS

Sarah Ellen see Joseph MORROW

Surname period, *Locke Fam Assoc Newsletter*, 102 Crookes Spring Rd, Chelmsford MA 01863

Surname period, *Lookin' for Lockes*, 7765 Fairview Rd, Tillamook OR 97141 – deed TN, census 1850 MI, Wm of NM, tax list NC, Bible rec NC, fam OH, marr TN

Vernon Guyon b1827, w Louisa Maria Allison, CN, MA, biog sketch GN 5:1:29

LOCKEY, Mary see Isaac COLLIER

LOCKWOOD, Joseph f1777, VT, rec misc APG 2:3:1

Lucretia m1787, w Nathanial Wood, VT, geneal res APG 2:1:1

LOFTON, Prudence see Daniel PLUMMER

LOMAX, James Terry m1873, w Martha Melvina Cochran, MS, Bible rec HTR 30:3:73

LOMBARD, Henry Huntington b1865, w Aimee Porter, WA, biog sketch YV 19:3:115

LONG, Alexr m1817, w Catherine Zane, OH, Bible rec MSG 7:3:153

John C b1821, w Sarah Lewis, NS, PA, IN, anc ch MIS 19:1:7

Mary Ann see George Jacob KERN

Samuel see Elizabeth Almira Collins REED

LONGACRE, Daniel b1778, OH, geneal, bk rev GH 41:2:153

LOOK, Surname period, *Look...ing*, 2816 Sloat Rd, Pebble Beach CA 93953

LOOMIS, Edward m1877, w Maria L Byars, Bible rec TB 14:1:19

Joseph f1638, w Mary White, MA, geneal, bk rev GH 41:4:209

Phebe see Martin H TRAVER

LORENTZ, Johannes f1710, GE, NY, NJ, NC, geneal, bk rev NYR 118:3:187

LOSS, Sarah A see Hiram PARSONS

LOTHROP, John b1584, EN, MA, biog CTN 19:4:716

LOTT, Letitia see William LOVE

LOUGHRIDGE, Elizabeth Jane b1817, h Henry M Walters, WV, OH, IN, fam hist FCF 87:Spring

LOUISIANA, Acadia Parish, successions 1883–1899 KSL 11:1:7 11:2:45 11:3:82

Biog sketches of naturalized citizens 1921 KSL 11:3:87

Bonavia, imm 1809 biog sketches YTD 3:1:12

Calcasieu Parish, Dutch Cove Cem KSL 11:4:103

Calcasieu Parish, hist vol 1, bk rev KSL 11:4:123

Calcasieu Parish, marr 1910–1915 KSL 11:1:23 11:2:40 11:3:72

Calcasieu Parish, Niblett's Bluff Cem KSL 11:1:21 11:2:50 11:3:68

Calcasieu Parish, Toomey Cem SGE 28:121:42

Cem inscr of northwest vol 1, bk rev FRT 8:3:150 GH 41:3:163

Civil War, index to membership appl in the United Dau of the Confederacy LA Division 1898-1907, bk rev NYR 118:1:53

East Feliciana Parish, marr 1834–70 THT 15:2:27

LOUISIANA (continued)

East Feliciana Parish, notarial rec 1838 & 1841 THT 15:2:14

Geneal column 1966-1970 by Winston DeVille, bk rev GH 41:4:192

Geneal res guide by Ryan, bk rev DS 24:3:165 GH 41:3:163

Imm & naturalization papers 1921-1923 KSL 11:4:119

Imm 1900s abstr from the 15th District Court rec KSL 11:1:11

Index of membership appl to the LA Soc of the Sons of the Am Rev, bk rev KSL 11:4:122

Lake Charles, geneal misc 1869-1878 abstr from *The Echo* KSL 11:2:54 11:3:77 11:4:111

Land grants & decisions 1800s SGE 28:121:37 28:122:23 28:123:12 28:124:29

Mourning customs KSL 11:2:36

Natchitoches Parish, biog & hist memoris, bk rev NGS 74:4:305 NTT 7:4:122

Natchitoches, hist 1729-1803, bk rev NTT 7:4:122

Natchitoches, land claims 1779-, bk rev KSL 11:2:49

Natives attending Mount St Mary's in Emmitsburg MD 1809-1865 AGE 16:3:79

New Orleans, ship pass list 1842 on board the *Southern* SGE 28:121:44

Opelousas Post, census 1771, bk rev GH 41:2:134

Pearl River, Crawford Cem SGE 28:122:40

Rapides Parish, geneal guide to fam after the Civil War, bk rev GH 41:2:134

Saint Tammany Parish, Carpenter Cem SGE 28:122:40

Saint Tammany Parish, Sun, Sun Bapt Ch Cem SGE 28:123:37

Saint Tammany Parish, cem inscr for Eldridge Magee Cem, Singletary Cem, Old Cooper Cem, Evans Creek Cem, & Valentine Cem SGE 28:124:12

LOUISIANA (continued)

Settlers as taken from land claims in the Eastern District of the Orleans Territory, bk rev GH 41:1:134

Vermilion Parish, hist, bk rev GH 41:6:139

War of 1812, soldiers, bk rev GH 41:5:174

LOVE, Melinda J see John KING

Surname period, *Love Letters*, POB 2040, Pinetop AZ 85935

William b1799, w Letitia Lott, PA, anc ch MP 3:2:132

LOVEALL, Elizabeth see William Washington SPICER

LOVELESS, John b1755, w Rachel VanHook, KY, anc ch CCS 9:2:63

LOWE, Aaron Harvey b1809, w Minney _____, NC, MO, children OZ 9:3:118

Ella see Charles D CESLER

Surname period, *Lowe News Is Good News*, 1887 Yallup Rd, St Johns MI 48879

LOWELL, Percival f1639, EN, MA, geneal TEG 7:1:3

Ruth see Joseph BRUCE

LOWENGUTH, Margaretha see Johann Jacob RUNNINGER

LOWHMAN, Golda Mae see Alfred Earl ABEL

LOWNES, Zachariah m1835, w Nancy C Janney, OH, marr rec HL 1:3:80

LOWRANCE, Johannes b1666, w Margaretha Heiliger, GE?, NJ, geneal, bk rev GH 41:2:153

LOWREY, Lazarus b1688, w Millie Edwards, IR, PA, geneal, bk rev WPG 13:3:42

Lazarus f1729, IR, PA, VA, TN, TX, geneal, bk rev SLB 6:2:72

LOWTHER, Fam hist EN & US, bk rev GH 41:2:153 FRT 8:4:197

LOY, Anna Catharina see George Michael BREINER

Elizabeth see Martin WYRICK

fam reunion 1897 CRT 8:1:23

Mary b1799, IL, obit CRT 8:4:16

LOYALIST GENEALOGY, Names & fam from the Haldimand Papers, bk rev WPG 13:3:47

Vignettes & sketches, bk rev NYR 118:4:249

LOYD, Fam cem Greene Co MO OZ 7:3:114

Nellie R see Charles KEARY

LOZANO, Santos f1915, TX, biog GTP 25:1:7

LUCAS, James b1818, EN, WI, Bible rec WTC 15:3:141

Martin Luthar b1861, w Mary Eliz Maness, MO, anc ch BGS 19:2:89

LUCE, Fam hist 1640–1985 vol 4, bk rev GH 41:6:161

Henry mc1666, w Remember Litchfield, EN?, MA, geneal, bk rev GH 41:1:163

LUCKEN, Jan f1684, w Mary Tyson, Bible rec BGS 19:4:164

LUCKY, Hester see Thomas FERRIER

LUDE, Emma see Harmon MILLER

LUDEMAN, Heye Hindrichs Janshen see Agthe Alken WESTERMANN

LUDLOW, Frances F see Michael H CHANDLER

LUDWIG, Eva see Peter WIES

John f1861, w Appollonia ____, IL, fam hist WTC 13:1:16

LUEBBEKER, Anna Margaretha see Joan Henrich REKER

LUERSSEN, Vernon b1906, IL, obit NWS 7:5:48

LUESSON, Adolph d1917, w Myrtle Endebrock, IL, obit CRT 8:4:24

LUKEN, Margaret b1727, Bible rec BGS 19:4:165

LUM, John b1776, w Rebekah Sheriden, TX, Bible rec YTD 4:2:1

LUNDRIGAN, Michael d1883, death rec NAL 3:2:19

LUNDY, Samuel b1800, w Ann Qua, ST, IR, ON, fam rec BCG 16:4:139

LUNNY, Mary see John CAMPBELL

LUPTON, Mary J m1873, h Council Bryan Midyett, Bible rec TQR 14:1:18

LUTHER, Martin b1483, GE, geneal, bk rev CHI 60:3:141

Martin Delphos b1845, w Matilda Ann Swain, NC, anc ch MIS 19:1:6

Martin f1513, GE, biog, bk rev CHI 60:1:43

Rebecca see John MCCONNELL

Surname period, *The Luther News*, 235 Hollow Ridge Dr, Atens GA 30607

William f1830, IL, biog sketch FF 15:3:69

LUTHERAN, Ch rec, use of BCN 6:4:43

Education (higher) in North Am, hist, bk rev CHI 60:1:42

Hist in Brazil during WWII CHI 59:4:147

Hist in US 1623–1988 TGC 11:1:20

Hist of Saxons in MO 1839– CHI 60:1:2

Hist of the Saxon Luth imm to East Perry Co MO 1839, bk rev CHI 59:4:190

Hist sketch of 12 fam from Frederick Co MD going to New Harmony IN 1827 MD 28:4:413

Orthodoxy in col NY & William Christopher Berkenmeyer CHI 60:1:19

settlement in PA 1682–1982, bk rev CTN 19:4:706

Theological effects on the issues of the small catechism prepared in or for Am prior to 1850, bk rev CHI 60:1:46

LUTTON, James bc1760, w Ellen Taylor, MD, geneal, bk rev WPG 13:3:51

LUXEMBOURG, Emig to US vol 1 & 2, bk rev GH 41:6:123

LUXEMBURG, Hist sketch in Will Co IL WTC 13:1:6

LYBOLT, Abraham bc1795, NY, anc ch OCG 17:4:27

LYDON, Surname period, *A Look At The Lydons*, 1312 Devanport Dr #7, Lexington KY 45504

LYGON, ELizabeth see William NORWOOD

LYLE, Julia Margaret see Benjamin C PALMORE

Mary Ann see David Fawns BELL

LYMAN, Catherine see Lemuel BROWN

LYNCH, Annie f1930, CA, letter MSG 7:3:140

LYNN, Emma Parthena see Jesse Dewey JACKSON

LYON(S), Surname period, *The Lyon's Tale*, 34960 N Lincoln Ave, Lake Villa IL 60046

LYONS, Eleanor see William BEARD

Elizabeth b1815, NY, IL, anc ch CCS 9:2:63

MABIE, Fam rec misc NY, bk rev NYR 118:4:246

MACBEAN, Surname period, *Clan MacBean in North Am*, POB 657, Alamosa CO 81101

MACCANE, Ruth see Anthony HANCOCK

MACCOONE, John m1656, w Deborah Bush, MA, biog RIR 13:1:7

MACDONALD, Andrew mc1796, w Jean Moodie, ST, fam rec, bk rev SCS 24:10:203

John f1823, CN, diary abstr 1823-1837, bk rev FAM 26:1:52

Mary see Samauel THOMSON

MACE, Andrew Jackson m1867, w Sarah E Beaty, TN, biog sketch PEL 8:2:2

MACFIE, Fam rec misc 1600s-1700s IR GGL 6:4:119

MACGILLIVRAY, William f1771, w Joanna Mackensie, Dunmaglass, geneal GGL 6:1-2:11

MACIORA, Feliks Faustyn b1878, w Wiktoria Zysk, PO, CT, geneal, bk rev GH 41:6:161

MACKENSIE, Joanna see William MacGILLIVRAY

MACKINLAY, Wm E W f906, TX, letter EK 23:3:3

MACKLENDEN, Dennis d1906, ST, NC, geneal, bk rev GH 41:6:162

MACKLIN, Alexander d1819, w Ann Laird Blair, TN, geneal BWG 16:1:45

MACKOY, Mary see Lodowich ARCHER

MACNATT, Richard b1706, w Rebecca Anderson, ST, PA, DE, geneal, bk rev GH 41:4:208

MACNEILL, Jane d1897, IR, anc ch CCS 8:4:136

MACY, Thomas f1635, EN, MA, geneal, bk rev FRT 8:1:49

MADDEN, Henry d1867, IL, obit CRN 6:4:78

Margaret Elizabeth see William Dudley BRAWNER

MADDOX, Claud Allen b1916, w Frances Helen Meeks, TX, fam rec BWG 16:1:54

MADDY, William f1738, EN, VA, geneal, bk rev GH 41:6:161

MADEIRA, Mary Ely b1836, h James Schwartz Madeira, PA, fam origin & Eur geneal TTT 11:3:107

MADISON, Ambrose f1723, w Frances Taylor, VA, hist sketch of home Montpelier DAR 121:3:156

Mary D see James D McNEIL

MAHAN, John m1857, w Jane Mahan, Bible rec OZ 5:3:105

MAHNESMITH, George b1816, w IL, anc ch JCG 15:3:100

MAHONEY, Daniel Hayes f1869, w Mary Dickson, IL, biog sketch IG 23:2:48

MAINE, Belfast, hist to 1825, bk rev GH 41:4:192

Bethel, Northwest Bethel Road, reflections on by Elwin L Wilson BC 10:3:1

MAINE (continued)

Boothbay, Southport, & Boothbay Harbor, hist, bk rev GH 41:6:139

Brownville, Brownville Village Cem DE 11:3:103

Cape Elizabeth, hist, bk rev DE 11:1:30 GH 41:5:174 RAG 8:3:24

East Poland Meth Campground, hist, bk rev CTN 20:1:143

Exeter, deaths 1841–1854 DE 11:2:53

Gardiner & Pittston, soldiers War of 1812 DE 11:2:46

Gardiner, steamboating on the Kennebec 1819–1874 DE 11:3:90

Marr 1833–1852 abstr from the *ME Farmer* DE 11:3:95

Natives living in Minneapolis MN area 1800s DE 10:5:166

Natives settling in MN 1800s DE 11:1:19 11:2:56

Norway, hist 1786–1886, bk rev CTN 19:4:705

Oxford Co, hist architecture, bk rev BC 11:1:2

Oxford, annals, bk rev CTN 20:2:322

Pawlnalborough, marr & intention to marr 1760–1802, bk rev GH 41:4:192

Penobscot Co, Hampden, ministers who filed marr 1840–1854 DE 10:5:168

Pioneers 1623–1660, bk rev GH 41:1:134

Piscataquis Co, hist, microfiche rev GH 41:4:213

Portland, Eastern Cem inscr, bk rev GH 41:6:139

Portland, Western Cem inscr, bk rev GH 41:6:140

Sea captains working out of Boston, hist NEH 4:2:65

Ship pass list 1852 to San Francisco on board the *J W Paige* DE 11:1:25

Turner, hist to 1886, bk rev NGS 75:3:230

Union, hist, bk rev CTN 20:2:320

MAINE (continued)

Waldeboro, geneal rec 1800s RAG 8:3:7

Waldo Co, Frankfort, deaths 1800s–1900s DE 10:5:172

Waldo Co, Frankfort, marr 1800s DE 11:1:10 11:2:61

Waldobor, War of 1812, soldiers with GE names DE 11:2:48

Wells & Kennebunk, hist, bk rev TST 20:20:32

World War I, men who died in CN service 1917–1919 DE 11:1:9

MAINS, Elizabeth see Adam GRIMM

MAJORS, Mary Elizabeth see William Green Lee GIBSON

MALCOM, Minerva T see Williams MURTY

MALECHA, Charles b1856, w Maria Theresa Picha, BO, MN, anc ch FCT :70:49

MALLERY, Uriah m1808, w Lois Clothier, Bible rec BG 8:4:100

MALLET, Angie see Herman BLAKESLEE

MALLICOAT, Daniel Love b1818, w Mary Malinda Whittenberg, TN, MO, biog sketch OZ 5:3:126

S A J f1862, TN, letter OZ 7:2:44

MANESS, Mary Eliz see Martin Luthar LUCAS

MANLEY, Surname period, *Manley Fam Newsletter*, 171 Nathan Dr, Bohemia NY 11716 – homes, reunions, Bible rec

MANNING, Cynthia see Isaiah THOMAS

Joseph b1793, w Margaret Phariss, TN, MO, children OZ 9:3:115

MANSFIELD, Alexander b1837, w Elizabeth Raines, Bible rec SR 1:2:21

Lydia b1774, MA, anc ch TEG 7:1:41

MANY, Surname period, *Magny Fam Assoc Newsletter*, 62 Glendale Ave, Middletown CT 06457

MAPLES, Annia L see Charles King WAUGH

MARCHANT, George W m1849, w Demeris D Bloom, Bible rec HH 21:4:220

MARCO, Fam hist IY, bk rev MA 11:3:77

MARIE, Jacques m1728, w Laetitia Maria Anna Staige, EN, VA, geneal, bk rev EWA 24:1:53

MARIS, George b1632, EN, PA, anc ch HJA 11:3:239

MARQUART, Jonathan b1792, w Kitty Bafsore, IN, biog ACL 12:1:13

MARRINER, John f1771, NC, will TQR 13:4:151

MARRIOTT, Joseph b1832, w Ann Radcliff, EN, CA, AA, biog note SCS 24:4:89

Joseph Jr b1865, w Anna Catherine Yelkin, CA, biog note SCS 24:4:89

MARS, Surname period, *Mars Exchange*, POB 31, Napa CA 94559

MARSDEN, William b1838, EN, WI, biog BGS 19:2:66

MARSH, Benjamin f1833, MA, pension appl RAG 8:1:10

Ebenezer b1735, MA, anc ch BG 8:4:93

MARSHALL, Aaron Sr bc1750, VA, OH, geneal SB 8:3:102

Chester b1780, w Pamelia Hopping, IL, fam hist WTC 9:2:52

Howard J m1883, w Mabel S Blagden, WA, Bible rec YV 19:3:103

John b1621, EN, MA, geneal, microfiche rev GH 41:3:178

John f1558, EN, VA, geneal, bk rev GH 41:1:163

John f1650, EN, VA, geneal, bk rev FRT 8:3:152 SB 8:4:138

MARTIN, Asa b1822, w Hannah Coleman, OH, anc ch HL 5:2:52

Calvin b1834, OH, MI, TN, anc ch PF 16:1:30

MARTIN (continued)

Cecily Jane see William T CAPELL

Charles Caffery bc1765, w Susannah A Richardson, VA, TN, geneal, bk rev GHG 41:5:193

Christian b1669, w Ells/Elizabeth ____, SW, PA, geneal PM 10:3:13

Delilah see James HAYMAN

Eula Palestine see Emmett MEEKS

Fam crest & shield TEG 7:4:181

Henry f1840, OH, IN, IL, fam hist sketch CCS 8:4:122

James f1847, w Elizabeth ____, AL, will PT 29:2:44

James H d1921, w Catherine M Armstrong, IL, obit CRT 8:4:33

John B B b1817, w Louisa Jane Gilliland, AL, TX, geneal BWG 16:1:52

Joseph C m1870, w Mary Frances Grant, Bible rec KA 23:2:84

Josiah m1805, w Alice Virden, Bible rec DJ 4:3:68

Mahala b1822, OH, fam hist HL 2:1:18

Miliver b1811, w Jane Thomas, GA, anc ch GGS 23:1:14

Moses T b1860, w Zylpha Winfrey, KY, MO, obit SNS 3:2:5

Naoma Estella see Oliver Lee HILL

Nicholas f1751, w Susannah ____, MD, rec misc NFB 19:1:9

Oscar b1850, w Justilia Boudreaux, LA, anc ch KSL 11:3:91

Peter b1764, w Elizabeth Heberling, VA, OH, children SGE 28:123:16

Sarah see Samuel NEILL

Surname period, *Martin Fam News*, RR1 Box 26, Union IA 50258

MARTIN (continued)

Surname period, *Martin Fam Quarterly*, POB 140880, Dallas TX 75214 – res bk & services, population estimates, Adam Martin

Thomas Sr f1776, NC, geneal, bk rev SB 8:3:103

William m1833, w Susan M Hawthorn, Bible rec PS 16:3:43

MARVIN, Sarah Ann see David RANDOL

MARYE, James f1714, w Laetitia Maria Anna Staige, FR, VA, geneal, bk rev NGS 74:3:225

MARYLAND, Allegany Co, marr 1791– MAD 27:1:10

Allegany Co, marr 1791–1847 WMG 3:1:30 3:2:82 3:4:155

Anne Arundel Co, officials 1651–1682 MAD 27:1:4 27:2:48

Anne Arundel Co, wills 1777–1918 index, bk rev GH 41:2:135

Anne Arundel, Prince George's, & Howard Co, geneal res hints PGB 19:2:23 19:3:46

Baltimore & Carroll Co, particular assessment lists 1798, bk rev NGS 74:4:310 GH 41:2:135 WPG 13:4:40 TNB 2:4:4 MD 28:4:461

Baltimore & Harford Co, St John's & St George's Parish reg 1696–1851, bk rev GH 41:5:174

Baltimore, Cath ch rec 1783–1800, bk rev AGE 16:4:105

Baltimore, coroner inquest reports index 1827, 1835–1860, 1864, & 1867, bk rev NGS 74:4:309

Baltimore, death notices 1851–18603 abstr from the *Baltimore Sun*, bk rev MAD 27:3:116 GH 41:2:136 MAD 27:4:150 NYR 118:4:244 TNB 2:4:4

Baltimore, deaths 1800s (suspicious), bk rev TNB 2:4:3

Baltimore, fire 1857 MD 28:2:201

Baltimore, foreign born people buried in area cem TNB 2:2:3

MARYLAND (continued)

Baltimore, pass arrivals 1820–1834, bk rev MAD 27:4:146

Baltimore, ward changes 1797–1918 MD 28:4:467

Baltimore, wards 1797–1978 guide, bk rev WPG 13:4:45

Baltimore City, Archives guide, bk rev WPG 13:4:45

Baltimore City, city council presidents roster 1800s–1900s MD 28:3:300

Baltimore City, coroner inquest 1800s index, bk rev MAD 28:4:460

Baltimore City, longevity roster 1880–1889 (persons over 70), bk rev GH 41:2:136 NGS 74:4:310 MD 28:4:460 TNB 2:4:3

Baltimore City, tax rec 1798–1808 index, bk rev WPG 13:4:45

Baltimore Co, cem inscr vol 2, bk rev MAD 27:3:116

Baltimore Co, cem inscr in western part of co vol 3, bk rev TNB 2:2:4

Baltimore Co, cem inscr vol 4, bk rev MAD 27:4:150 WPG 13:4:40 TNB 2:4:3 GH 41:2:135

Baltimore Co, Civil War, Union soldiers roster MD 28:3:323

Baltimore Co, court cases 1809–1811 abstr TNB 2:1:1

Baltimore Co, inhabitants 1692–1763, bk rev TNB 3:3:5 GH 41:5:175 WPG 14:1:48

Baltimore Co, land rec 1687–1699 MD 28:4:372

Baltimore Co, manufacturing villages hist, bk rev MD 28:1:115 TNB 2:2:4

Baltimore Co, Old Middletown Cem burials of War of 1812 & Civil War vet MD 28:3:322

Baltimore Co, Saint John's & St George's Parish reg 1696–1851, bk rev TNB 3:3:5 WPG 14:1:48

Baltimore Co, St Peters Cem MD 28:2:128

MARYLAND (continued)

Baltimore Co, tax list 1783, bk rev WPG 13:4:40

Bibl of the MD-PA border controversy, & the Mason-Dixon Line, bk rev GH 41:1:144

Calvert Co, land rec 1785-1867, bk rev MAD 27:3:117

Caroline Co, cem inscr vol 2, bk rev MAD 27:2:74

Caroline Co, cem inscr vol 3, bk rev MAD 27:3:118

Caroline Co, Preston, Bethesda United Meth Ch minister roster 1785-1958 MAD 27:1:8

Carroll Co, Civil War, draft roster CCG 6:4:55

Carroll Co, geneal holdings of the Carroll Co Government & Court CCG 6:3:47

Carroll Co, geneal misc 1833 abstr from the *Carrolltonian* CCG 7:1:6

Carroll Co, guard 1837-52 WMG 3:1:18 3:2:63 3:3:115 3:4:172

Carroll Co, Keysville, Evangelical Luth Ch bapt 1872-1900 MAD 27:1:22 27:2:59

Carroll Co, marr lic 1837-1899, bk rev PGB 19:3:42 GH 41:6:166

Catactin Furnace, Harriet Chapel, hist, bk rev WMG 3:3:141

Cecil Co, geneal res guide by McCall & Alexander, bk rev TNB 3:3:5

Cecil Co, land patents, bk rev WPG 13:4:41

Census 1820 index, bk rev NGS 74:4:316 MAD 27:2:73

Civil War, Confederate soldiers, bk rev GH 41:3:163 WPG 13:4:40

Cumberland, marr & deaths 1864-1867 abstr from the *Cumberland Alleganian*, bk rev WPG 13:3:49 WMG 3:1:42

Dorchester Co, fact bk, bk rev MAD 27:3:117

Eastern Shore, citizens 1659-1750, bk rev WPG 13:3:49

MARYLAND (continued)

Eastern Shore, citizens 1695-1750, bk rev MAD 27:4:148

Eastern Shore, mort sched 1870 & 1880, bk rev MAD 27:3:117

Eastern Shore, v r 1760-1800 of the Jesuit missions, bk rev GH 41:2:135 WPG 13:4:41

Elopements & other fam problems 1729-1789 LCC 4:1:73

Fam in western co, bk rev MAD 27:4:149 WMG 3:3:140

Frederick & Carroll Co, pioneers 1725-1985, bk rev STI 27:2:37 WPG 14:1:51

Frederick, Evangelical Reformed Ch rec 1746-1800, bk rev WMG 3:3:139 WPG 13:4:40 GH 41:3:173

Frederick Co, court minutes 1771 WMG 3:3:104

Frederick Co, Frederick, Monacacy Luth Cong & Evangelical Ch bapt 1742-1779 vol 3, bk rev APG 2:2:30 GH 41:4:193

Frederick Co, geneal res guide by Russell, bk rev GH 41:4:193 TNB 3:3:5 MD 28:4:461 MN 18:3:138

Frederick Co, geneal roster collect 1765-1775, bk rev GH 41:2:136 WMG 3:2:91

Frederick Co, hist 1721-1743, bk rev WMG 3:3:138 MFH 6:4:131

Frederick Co, marr lic 1778-1810, bk rev WMG 3:3:138 WPG 13:4:40 GH 41:3:173 MD 28:3:365

Frederick Co, Middletown, Christ Reformed Ch rec 1770-1840 vol 1, bk rev WMG 3:1:43 GH 41:1:135

Frederick Co, Middletown, Zion Luth Ch rec 1781-1826 vol 2, bk rev GH 41:4:193

Frederick Co, pioneers 1721-1743, bk rev GH 41:4:193 WCK 20:2:29 VAG 31:3:229 WPG 14:1:45 MN 18:4:188 KA 23:2:114 MD 28:3:364

MARYLAND (continued)

Frederick Co, Urbana District, Bells Chapel Cem WMG 3:2:89

Frederick Co, will bk 1 WMG 3:1:36 3:2:70 WMG 3:3:107

Frederick Co, wills 1770s WMG 3:4:147

Garrett Co, cem inscr, bk rev PGB 19:3:42 WMG 3:4:191

Garrett Co, place names MAD 27:3:84 27:4:124

Geneal misc 1786-1789 abstr from western news, bk rev NGS 74:4:311 (1799-1805) NGS 74:4:311 (1806-1810 vol 3) WPG 14:1:48 TNB 3:3:6 MD 28:4:464 (1806-1810 vol 9) GH 41:5:174

Geneal, biog, & hist source rec index, bk rev MFH 6:1:34 WPG 13:3:40

Georgetown, geneal misc 1789-1799 abstr from news, bk rev GH 41:2:128

Harford Co, index to *Hist Sketches of Harford Co MD* by Mason Jr MAD 27:1:24 27:2:58

Harford Co, Rev War, company list MAD 27:4:126

Harford Co, Susquehanna Hundred, Association of Freemen roster 1775 MAD 27:3:88

Harford Co, War of 1812, muster roll of the 42nd Reg MAD 27:4:127

Hist of the Chesapeake & Ohio Canal, bk rev DM 50:4:161

Kent Co, cem inscr, bk rev MAD 27:1:37

Kent Co, hist 1900-1980, bk rev MD 28:3:364

Kent Co, hist graves, private burial grounds, & cem inscr, bk rev MD 28:1:114

Kent Co, mil & oaths of allegiance 1775, bk rev MAD 27:1:37

Kent Island, Stevensville, Christ Ch Parish, marr, funerals, & bapt 1846-1908 MD 28:3:254

MARYLAND (continued)

Marr 1884 MAD 27:3:108

Middletown Valley, births, marr, & deaths recorded by Rev John C Bucher 1828-43 WMG 3:1:10 3:2:57 3:3:131 3:4:163

Middletown, Christ Reformed Ch rec vol 1, bk rev APG 2:2:30

Middletown, Zion Luth Ch rec 1781-1826 vol 2, bk rev APG 2:2:30 WMG 3:4:190

Monocacy, Potomac, & Rock Creek Hundreds, taxables 1733 WMG 3:3:99

Montgomery Co, geneal misc 1855-1899 abstr from the *Montgomery Co Sentinel*, bk rev GH 41:4:193 WMG 3:3:140

Montgomery Co, War of 1812, soldier roster, bk rev NGS 74:4:311 (vol 7) WPG 13:3:49 WMG 3:1:43 GH 41:2:158

Montgomery Co, will abstr 1826-1875, bk rev GH 41:5:175 WPG 14:1:48

Myersville, Luth bapt 1832-1849 & 1861-1897, bk rev NGS 74:3:228 MD 28:4:462

Natives in OH 1798-1818 PGB 19:3:44

Natives living in Adams Co PA CCG 6:3:36

Naturalizations in col MD, bk rev WMG 3:2:93

News abstr (western) 1786-1805 (vol 1 & 2), bk rev MAD 27:3:116

Prince George's Co, coroner inquests 1719-1883 MD 28:3:284

Prince George's Co, inventories 1712-1714 MAD 27:1:6 27:2:44

Prince George's Co, Rev War, soldiers roster PGB 19:2:31

Prince George's Co, War of 1812, soldier roster, bk rev NGS 74:4:311 MAD 27:2:72

Prince George's Co, will abstr 1698-1770 PGB 18:9:152 18:10:168 PGB 19:3:48 19:4:68

Queen Anne's Co, Rev War, endeavours & exertions 1775-1783, bk rev MAD 27:1:37

MARYLAND (continued)

Residents who found themselves in PA because of border changes MAD 27:3:92

Saint Mary's Co, 1st election district, cem (private) list MAD 27:3:86

Saint Mary's Co, lower house roster 1600s-1700s MAD 27:2:46

Saint Mary's Co, manors of MAD 27:1:12

Saint Mary's Co, residents in executive & legislative branches of MD provincial government 1600s-1700s MAD 27:1:13

Saint Peters Cem MD 28:3:270

Settlers 1633-1680, bk rev SGS 36:2:103 KA 22:4:278 WPG 13:3:39 OK 32:1:5 WMG 3:1:44

Settlers from the Palatinate, bk rev CRT 8:4:6

Somerset Co, marr 1796-1871, bk rev NCJ 13:1:52 GH 41:2:136

Sparrows Point, hist reg of the police department 1901-1986, bk rev TNB 2:2:5

Subscr to *Poems on Several Occasions* by Barry 1807 MD 28:4:452

Surnames in vertical file at the Baltimore Co Geneal Soc TNB 2:4:1

Talbot Co, geneal rec vol 1 & 2, bk rev GH 41:6:140

Talbot Co, marr lic 1850-1875, bk rev GH 41:1:135 MAD 27:3:115

Talbot Co, Royal Oak, hist, bk rev MAD 27:3:115

Talbot Co, will abstr 1669-1675 MAD 27:3:90 27:4:128

Talbot Co, Wittman, Lancashire Fam Graveyard MD 28:1:27

Towson, Towson Pres Ch hist sketch & rec misc 1880-1926 MD 28:1:85

War of 1812, invasion by EN 1812-1815, bk rev WPG 13:3:40

Washington Co, land rec abstr liber C WMG 3:2:76 3:3:123

MARYLAND (continued)

Washington Co, land rec 1780s WMG 3:4:180

Washington Co, letters left at post offices 1833 WMG 3:4:186

Washington Co, St Mark's Epis Ch hist, bk rev GH 41:5:175

Wills 1634-1777 index, bk rev WCK 20:1:12 OK 32:1:5

Worcester Co, wills 1742-1758, bk rev GH 41:2:137 (1759-1769) WPG 14:1:48 GH 41:5:175

MARZOLF, Jacob b1780, w Elizabeth Hausauer, FR, US, geneal MFH 6:3:106

MASHOW, John Albert b1805, w Hope Amos, SC, biog AA 8:2:57

MASON, Edward b1757, Bible rec SCR 11:1:8

Emma Kate see Charles William FERGUSON

Levisson see James Edward BYRD

Surname period, *Mason Fam Newsletter*, 363 S Park Victoria Dr, Milpitas CA 95035

MASSACHUSETTS, Allston-Brighton, hist 1630-1980s, bk rev NER 141:1:67

Amherst, hist, bk rev NER 141:4:362

Ashland, v r 1895-1898 MA 11:1:13 11:2:40 11:3:70 11:4:104

Berkshire Co, Cheshire, census 1855 BG 8:1:5 8:2:43 8:3:78

Berkshire Co, Cheshire, geneal sources at Cheshire Lib BG 8:4:87

Berkshire Co, geneal rec avail at the Alford Lib BG 7:4:87

Berkshire Co, geneal resources in Sandisfield Piblic Lib BG 8:1:3

Berkshire Co, Hancock, town rec 1700s index BG 8:3:73

Berkshire Co, Richmond & Lenox, Justice of the Peace rec 1825-1865 BG 7:4:89

MASSACHUSETTS (continued)

Boston, births, marr, & deaths 1633-1683, bk rev GH 41:4:193

Boston, sea captains from ME NEH 4:2:65

Braintree, hist, bk rev NER 141:2:161

Braintree, hist sketch 1790 NEH 4:3:128

Bristol Co, guard rec 1751-1755 NGS 74:4:299

Bristol Co, probate rec 1687-1745 abstr, bk rev GH 41:4:193 NCJ 13:3:179 KA 23:2:112 MN 18:4:188 WCK 20:3:49 WPG 14:1:46

Bristol Co, Swansea, hist 1600s, bk rev GH 41:5:176

Cambridge, hist 1630-1877 & index, bk rev GH 41:3:163

Censuses 1855 & 1865 (state), bk rev NER 141:2:163

Charlton, births 1894 MA 11:3:74

Colrain, settlers (early), bk rev NGS 75:3:237

Dedham, births 1686-1700 CTN 19:4:609

Dedham, cem inscr, bk rev NGS 75:1:68

Dedham, deaths 1637-1720 CTN 20:3:388

Dedham, hist, bk rev NER 141:1:67

Dukes Co, sailors 1850 NGS 74:4:287

Duxbury, master mariners 1867 NEH 4:1:21

Enfield, hist sketch 1865 NEH 4:4:190

Essex Co, geneal res hints TEG 7:3:113

Essex Co, probate index 1638-1840, bk rev APG 2:2:29 GH 41:6:140

Fairhaven, v r vol 4, bk rev GH 41:2:137

Framingham, Ch of Christ rec 1701-1870 MA 11:3:65 11:4:115

Franklin Co, geneal rec avail MA 11:1:7 11:2:34

MASSACHUSETTS (continued)

French & Indian Wars, officers & soldiers 1755-1756, bk rev AG 62:3:124

Geneal rec avail in the MA Archives MA 11:2:54

Geneal rec avail by city & town MA 11:3:87 11:4:106

Geneal res aid, court rec of the Supreme Judicial Court 1600s-1700s TEG 7:2:97

Greenfield, Federal Street Cem MA 11:1:4

Halifax & Hull, census (state) 1855 & 1865, bk rev GH 41:2:137 AG 62:3:128

Hanson, census (state) 1855 & 1865, bk rev CTN 20:1:139

Hist (3 episodes), bk rev WCG 3:6:46

Hist of col MA, bk rev WCG 3:6:46

Marshfield, warnings-out 1600s-1700s AG 62:1:49

Mayflower compact signers, biog sketches RAG 8:4:12

Mayflower source rec concerning southeastern MA, Cape Cod, & the island of Nantucket & Martha's Vineyard, bk rev NGS 74:3:236

Middleborough, v r vol 1, bk rev AG 62:1:63 APG 2:2:29

Middlesex Co, Newton, hist 1639-1800, bk rev GH 41:6:140 CTN 20:3:516

Narragansett, land grants & col wars hist TEG 7:4:171

Newburyport, Female Charitable Soc birth rec 1793-1827 TEG 7:1:15

North Middleborough, Third Cong Ch hist 1748-1980, bk rev MN 18:3:138

Old Bridgewater, cem inscr, bk rev NGS 75:3:237

Pepperell, v r to 1850, bk rev AG 62:1:63

Pet 1757 index SLB 6:4:157

Pioneers 1620-1650, bk rev TCG 6:4:72

MASSACHUSETTS (continued)
Place names current & obsolete
direct, bk rev CTN 20:1:141
MQ 53:3:222 BG 8:1:4 RIR
13:2:21 GH 41:4:193 NER
141:3:262 APG 2:3:30 NYR
118:4:245
Plymouth Col, hist 1620-1691,
bk rev NYR 118:4:242 RAG
8:2:26 AW 13:2:70 GFP
36:4:178 GH 41:4:187 PGB
19:1:11 VAG 31:3:231 WPG
14:1:47 GGS 23:3:158 RES
19:1:21 NER 141:4:360 STI
27:2:36 MQ 53:3:222 NCJ
13:3:179 NTT 7:2:43 OZ
9:3:122 CTN 20:2:320 RCP
9:4:130
Plymouth Rock, hist MQ
53:3:166
Salem, witchcraft trials, bk rev
BCG 16:2:66
Sandwich, hist, bk rev AG
62:1:61
Sherborn, census (state) 1855 &
1865, bk rev CTN 20:1:139
Ship pass list 1630 on board the
Mary & John, vol 2, bk rev
FRT 8:2:107 (vol 3) GH
41:4:187
Ship pass list from EN 1620 on
board the *Mayflower* MP
3:3:187
Source rec for the *Mayflower*, bk
rev EWA 24:2:138
Southwick, residents of foreign
birth 1850-1880 MA 11:2:42
Stow, census (state) 1855 &
1865, bk rev GH 41:2:137 AG
62:2:128
Suffolk Co, court rec avail
1629-1799 RD 87:1:14
V r bibl, microfiche rev MN
18:3:140 GFP 37:2:69 DM
50:3:142 GH 41:1:166 NER
141:2:163 OK 32:1:7 GH
41:3:177
Wellesley, cem inscr, bk rev
CTN 20:2:327 GH 41:3:173
Westborough, deaths & marr
1873-1876 MA 11:1:16 11:2:36
11:3:83 11:4:112

MASSACHUSETTS (continued)
Worcester, Hoganas Soc member
roster 1904-1921 SAG 7:3:97
Wrentham, notifications & warn-
ings out 1732-1789 NER
141:3:179 141:4:330
MASSEY, Veda E m1869, h John
H Onstott, Bible rec OZ 7:1:24
MASSON, Alexander Hardy b1804,
w Mary Armstrong, ST, QB,
geneal, bk rev GH 41:2:153
Jane see Henry George MUNRO
MASTERS, Emeline see Andrew
Jackson BUSH
MASTON, Carrie see Burr Peyton
MCCONNAHA
MATHEWS, Henry Allen b1842, w
Isabelle Lavinia Phelps, FL,
lineage FLG 10:3:100
MATHIAS, Elizabeth see John A
THOMAS
Jane see John LAUGHLIN
MATRAND, Lars b1720, w Sidsel
Christophersdtr, NW, anc ch
WB 17:4:133
MATSON, Hannah see Charles
DAVIES
MATTER, Valtin f1751, w
Catherine ____, MD, biog
WMG 3:1:3
MATTERAND, Hedda Syversen
see Gulbrand Hansen GIL-
BERT
MATTHEWS, Charlotte Mary see
John SEE
Phineas b1770, w Mary Russel,
MA, OH, biog sketch RAG
8:5:16
Susannah b1756, MA, OH, anc ch
OCG 17:3:19
Tabitha McKnight see Robert F
MITCHELL
William Riley b1797, w Nancy
____, VA, MO, fam rec BWG
16:2:148
MATTHYSE, Eva see Jean
LEFAUCHEUR
MATTOCKS, Surname period,
Mattocks Newsletter, 9345 S
Citrusin, Sun Lakes AZ 85248
MATTSDOTTER, Britta see Peter
Gunnerson RAMBO

MAUCK, Daniel bc1742, w Miss Harnsberger & Rebecca Baker?, GE, VA, children BWG 16:2:153

MAURA, Joseph Bruno bc1787, w Ana Josephine Wilkins, FL, lineage FLG 10:4:155

MAURER, Anna Maria see Jacob LITWILLER

Baltas bc1720, w Elizabeth ___ & Eva Rupertin, SW, PA, lineage LCC 4:2:44

Frederic b1831, w Katherine Emerich, GE, KY, anc ch LAB 2:3:55

MAXFIELD, Mary see Caleb GODFREY

MAXSON, Elizabeth b1754, RI, NY, anc ch OCG 17:3:19

Rebecca see Hugh MOSHER

MAXWELL, John Joseph bc1814, w Margaret Victoria O'Donovan, ST, anc ch GGL 6:4:148

Matilda see John BATTIN

MAY, Elizabeth see James W LITTLE

Nancy Maria see Benjamin Washington CAMP

Sarah see Benjamin HUDSPETH

MAYBEE, James William m1915, w Pearle Newlee, CA, Bible rec BGS 19:4:166

MAYER, Mary A see George FUNK

MAYES, James b1827, w Mary A Mitchell, NC, AL, anc ch NAS 26:1:20

Kizziah see Thomas Hicks COMBS

Mary Della see Bloom Fite GAUTNEY

MAYFIELD, Albert b1822, w Margaret Apple, IN, anc ch CCS 9:1:30

Lutecia see Allen McELROY

MAYNARD, Thomas P b1846, w Martha Fitchpatrick, KY, biog sketch EK 23:2:20

MAYS, Nancy Day f1892, NC, letter CAL 6:4:92

MAYSE, Clara see Alexander Brabson TADLOCK

George f1873, VA, travels DG 33:3:170

MAYWALT, Mary Ann see John William SHEETS

MAZIQUE, Laura Graig d1907, h Alex Mazique, fam hist sketch IAA 1:2:1

MCADAMS, Rutha see Jonathan ELLARD

MCALLISTER, William F m1853, w Catherine Ann Coulter, fam rec WPG 13:3:24

MCANULTY, Elizibeth see William Burke RAMSAY

MCBRIDE, Millie see William H SIMMONS

Peter bc1851, w Jeanne Holden, IR, IN, anc ch FCT :72:8

MCCABE, James f1750, w Ann Pettigrew, IR, US, geneal, bk rev GN 5:2:97

James, w Ann Pettigrew, geneal, bk rev GH 41:2:154

MCCAFFREY, Patrick b1823, w Mary Cassidy, IR, VT, children BAT 16:4:158

MCCAIN, Sarah Ann see Andrew Jackson WORLEY

MCCALLISTER, James f1917, IL, letter CRT 8:4:23

MCCALLUM, Martha (Osborne) see Philip TURPIN

MCCARRAN, Catherine see Lawrence MULLEN

MCCARTHA, Mamie Warren see William Malone NEWELL

MCCARTHY, George Buchanan b1803, w Margaret ___, PA, OH, fam hist MM 11:6:35

Sarah see Thomas CURRY

MCCARTY, Joseph b1817, w Mary Surface, OH, biog NFB 19:2:37

MCCAUGHAN, Margaret Jane see Robert KILLOUGH

MCCAULEY, Nancy d1858, NC, AL, burial permit SGE 28:124:55

MCCHESNEY, Lucinda see John Protheroe STEWART

MCCLAGHRY, William d1713, w Katherine Reed, IR, NY, geneal, bk rev NGS 75:3:235

MCCLAUGHRY, Matthew bc1665, w Margaret Parks, IR, NY, IL, fam hist WTC 2:4:113

Thomas f1765, IR, NY, geneal, bk rev NYR 118:1:59

MCCLELLAN, Edward Wheldon, w Grace Trafford, MA, geneal, bk rev IMP 6:1:27

Michael f1749, ST, MA, geneal, bk rev GH 41:4:207

MCCLENDON, Irene Isabelle see Samuel Crawford CARTER

Mary A B b1820, GA, anc ch PT 29:2:46

MCCLONE, Thomas A m1889, w Annie Early, SD, commemorative plaque SS 15:1:10

MCCLUGEN, Fam rec misc IL FF 15:4:141

MCCLUNG, Robert see Orah HAMLIN

MCCLURE, Andrew m1835, w Samantha Ann Crandall & Frances Maria Campbell & Mary Warren, Bible rec AB 15:4:98

Eliza see Peter Pine ALEXANDER

Harriet L see Bartlett Marymond HALL

Sarah Hazel see John Ramsey EARNEST

MCCOLL, Hugh R d1847, w Catherine ____, NC, cem inscr NCJ 13:3:143

MCCOLLEY, Trusten P b1793, DE, biog MAD 27:1:21

MCCOLLUM, Fam hist AR 1860-1986, bk rev CCS 9:1:24

MCCOLSTER, Susan Jane see Richard W LILE

MCCONNAHA, Burr Peyton b1826, w Carrie Maston, VA, CA, biog sketch RED 19:3:18

MCCONNELL, John d1911, w Rebecca Luther, IR, CA, anc ch RED 19:3:15

Myron m1899, w Bessie ____, IN, bk rev NYR 118:3:186

MCCONNELL (continued)
Thomas see Roseanna HOLDEN

MCCOOL, Robert b1817, w Hannah Dalley, PA, anc ch MIS 19:1:5

MCCORKELL, Julia d1905, h William Jordan, IL, obit MCS 7:1:29

MCCORKLE, Elizabeth see Williams AKINS

MCCORMICK, Amanda J see Hugh ADAMS

MCCORNACK, Andrew b1817, w Maria Eakin, ST, IL, geneal, bk rev GH 41:6:166

Jennie Gordon see Benamin Franklin BROWN

John b1810, w Martha Melinda McMillan, ST, US, geneal, bk rev GH 41:3:169

Robert Pascal b1844, w Mary Milroy, IL, geneal, bk rev GH 41:1:163

MCCOY, Nannie m1893, h William R Templeton, Bible rec FCG 7:1:8

MCCRACKEN, John bc1750, w Margaret Adams, TN, geneal BWG 16:1:40

MCCRACKIN, Joseph b1819, w Mary Ann Hunter, Northern IR, PA, geneal, bk rev GH 41:2:154

MCCRAY, Louise see John YEAKLEY

MCCREA, Fred Lester m1890, w Rutha May Haworth, OR, Bible rec GFP 36:4:165

MCCREARY, Sallie b1855, h E McCreary, TX, cem inscr STI 27:1:18

MCCUBBIN, James P f1785, w Mary Cook, NC, KY, MO, geneal OZ 9:2:65

MCCUISTION, Thomas b1809, TN, TX, fam hist YTD 6:1:17

MCCULLOCH, Robert f1778, IR, SC, GA, EN, biog sketch & letter abstr NGS 74:3:196

MCCULLOUGH, Alexander m1797, w Susan Nance, VA, geneal, bk rev GH 41:2:161

MCCULLOUGH (continued)
Ephraim b1824, w Margaret Garner, IR, MI, biog sketch DM 50:4:192
MCDADE, Polly see Rudolph GONCE
MCDANIEL, Fam pedigrees, bk rev GH 41:5:196
Fam rec misc IR, ST, EN, US, bk rev GH 41:1:163
Georgiana see William GREEN
Mary E see Joseph STEVENS
Surname period, *McDaniel Fam Newsletter*, 1550 California St, San Francisco CA 94109
William b1794, w Sarah ____, SC, TX, geneal YTD 7:2:1
MCDANNALD, Mahala see Philip Edmond LINN
MCDONALD, Asa f1836, NY, IL, fam hist sketch WTC 4:3:132
Permilia see Lawrence RANKSTON
MCDORMAN, James b1800, w Susan Cooper, NC, OH, obit FCG 6:4:71
MCDOUGAL, Thomas bc1837, KY, biog GJ 15:3:116
MCDOUGALL, Joseph b1822, w Martha Jane Ackerman, Bible rec OCR 28:3:116
Marietta m1867, h David Swart, OH, Bible rec DM 50:4:163
MCELROY, Allen bc1828, w Lutecia Mayfield, TN, TX, fam rec AGS 28:2:91
James d1817, IR, cem inscr GGL 6:3:103
Vincent Roy b1894, Bible rec MCI 5:2:43
MCFADDEN, Fam cem inscr SC 1800s DAR 121:3:192
Isaac f1818, w Mary ____, will abstr DAR 121:3:212
Sarah Caroline m1830, h William Wylie, Bible rec DAR 121:3:192
Thomas f1823, SC, will abstr DAR 121:3:212
Thomas m1780, w Sarah Witherspoon, Bible rec DAR 121:3:192

MCFADDIN, Elizabeth see Joseph MONTGOMERY
MCFALLS, William b1805, VA, anc ch CR 19:1:4
MCFARLAND, Issabella see Robert STITT
MCGAHEY, Martha see Thos Lukens ASHTON
MCGEE, E M b1818, w Sarah Moss, KY, MO, obit PW 7:3:114
Martha see James BURROW
Patrick m1898, w Bridget Leaden, IL, marr appl MCS 7:3:106
Thomas b1844, w Mary J Saddler & Nancy J Plymate, PA, IL, biog sketch KL 7:3:4
MCGEORGE, William bc1785, w Elizabeth Little, ST, NB, geneal RED 20:2:17
MCGLASSON, Sarah see James C JONES
MCGLYNN, Annie see Wiliam TOLE
MCGOVERN, Fam hist DE & NJ DJ 4:2:25 4:3:49
MCGOWAN, Keziah Jane see Lyman S HUSTED
MCGOWN, Stella see Jesse Edwards JAMES Jr
MCGRATH, Mary Agnes see Charles NICHOLSON
MCINTERFEER, Johannes f1729, w Phronik ____, Rotterdam, GE, US, geneal, bk rev GH 41:4:207
MCINTIRE, Jane see Matthew RUSSELL
MCIRVIN, Marion Edward b1869, w Etta May Lewis, MO, WA, biog sketch TB 13:2:12
MCJUNKIN, J Neville f1913, w Jessie Pitts, FL, biog sketch IMP 6:3:75
MCKAMIE, Philip f1847, w Sarah McKamie, GA, will TCG 7:1:40 7:2:11
MCKAY, Margaret see John KNOX
MCKEAN, Eliza Adair see James RITCHEY

MCKELVEY, William J b1852, w Mary Ellen Campbell, ON, MI, biog sketch DM 50:4:192

MCKENZIE, John bc1780, w Martha Patsy Cocke, VA, geneal EK 22:4:11

Lafayette f1860, w Mary Ann Sparks, KY, geneal EK 23:3:13

Mary Jane b1829, h Phillip Stambaugh, VA, KY, geneal EK 23:2:22

Oliver f1852, w Matilda Strong, KY, geneal EK 23:1:26

MCKINLEY, Charles f1776, w Janet ____, NC, geneal, bk rev NCH 13:3:185

MCKINNEY, Hannah see Tyree JENNINGS

Mary Etta see Thomas Wesley RICHARDSON

Surname period, *McKinney Maze*, 2750 W 232 St, Torrance CA 90505 – Samuel of IA, fam PA, Calvert of WV, notes OH & NC, res NJ, land & census rec IL, census IN, cem NC, land VA

Surname period, *McKinneys & Kin Fam Newsletter*, David McKinney, 817 Curtis Dr, Nashville TN 37207-1301

MCKINNON, Alan Dougal b1814, w Flora Jane Campbell, NC, FL, anc ch PT 29:3:111

MCKINSEY, George b1762, fam rec HL 1:2:44

MCKISIC, Jane bc1815, PA, anc ch FTR :101:9

MCKNIGHT, Malinda see JOhn BLAIR

Margaret C see John C NELSON

William f1856, TN, will YTD 7:1:1

William mc1738, w Jane Morton, ST, PA, fam hist YTD 3:2:12

MCKOWN, Herbert I see Lucille M MENARD

John b1721, ST, NY, anc ch OG 13:1:8

MCLAUGHLIN, Margaret M see Alexander M GODWIN

Matilda see Thomas MOOR

MCLAUGHLIN/MCGLOTHAN, Anna see Joseph KINSER

MCLEAN, Nathaniel f1807, w Hester Nutt, OH, biog sketch HL 3:2:60

MCLENDON, Martha see Francis BALDRIDGE

MCLEOD, William bc1788, w Sarah Catherine Bethune, ST, FL, lineage FLG 10:4:146

William Sr f1776, ST, biog ANE 23: :8

MCLIN, Louisa Virginia Bullock see Joseph Isaie CHENETTE

MCMAHAN, Fam hist & biog sketches, bk rev GH 41:2:163

MCMILLAN, Martha Melinda see John McCORNACK

MCMULLEN, Eliza J see A L GUSTIN

MCNEAL, Fam letters MI FG 29:4:118

MCNEIL, Hepzibah see Rufus HATCH

James D b1846, w Mary D Magruder, ST, KY, anc ch LAB 2:3:47

MCNEILL, James m1879, w Katie Ella Wingo, Bible rec FP 30:3:115

MCPHEETERS, Mary see Alexander CRAWFORD

MCPHERSON, Daniel bc1682, w Ruth Shires, ST, DE, PA, geneal, bk rev GH 41:2:154

MCQUISTON, William b1763, PA, anc ch RT 4:3:82

MCSWAIN, Nancy see Alexander CAMPBELL

MCVAY, Surname period, *McVay-McVeigh-McVey Fam Archives*, 2114 Martingale Dr, Norman OK 73069

MCVEY, Henry m1848, w Abbie Moon, IA, marr rec PCI 9:4:4

MEACHAM, Lucia Ann see John E GRISWOLD

MEAD, Andrew m1780, w Elizabeth Boughton, Bible rec TFP 7: :71

Silas F b1812, w Harriett Risdon, CT, MI, letter FHC 10:4:79

MEADE, Levina see Curtiss BLAKEMAN

MEADOW, Mary see Wm C BLAND

MEALLS, Mary An see Jefse SUMMERS

MEANS, Eleanor see James MONTGOMERY

MECKENDORFER, Georg b1655, w Elizabeth Burckle & Ottilia Schaffer & Veronica Meier, GE, PA, geneal, bk rev GFP 37:2:71

MEDLEY, Delaina see F M JOHNSON

MEDLIN, Amelia see Rezin SMITH

MEEHAN, Jane see Hugh KELLY

MEEK, Thomas M m1869, w Amanda Roper, Bible rec HTR 29:3:82

MEEKER, John Sr bc1760, w Elizabeth Lambert, OH, fam rec HL 4:3:73

MEEKS, Emmett b1882, w Eula Palestine Martin, TX, children BWG 16:1:53

Frances Helen see Claud Allen MADDOX

MEGGS, Vincent b1583, w Miss Churchill, CT, geneal, bk rev GH 41:4:208

MEIER, Hans d1721, OH, geneal, bk rev GH 41:6:162

MEISNER, Casper d1879, Europe, IA, anc ch OG 13:3:68

MEIXEL, Andreas f1728, w Anna Maria Schwab, GE, PA, geneal, bk rev FRT 8:1:51

MELSON, Emery d1918, IL, obit CRT 8:4:46

MELTON, Elijah m1817, w Ann Green, SC, AL, biog YTD 2:2:1 3:1:5 3:2:24 4:1:27

Mary see Benjamin CALLAWAY

Surname period, *Milton/Melton Pot*, 6809 Thunderhead Cir, Orangevale CA 95662

MELVILLE, David dc1730, w Mary Willard & Mary (Mills) Willard, ST, MA, RI, geneal NGS 74:4:257

MENARD, Lucille M m1907, h Herbert I McKown, WA, biog sketch YV 19:1:49

MENKE, Elizabeth Dedich see Peter PIEPER

MENNONITE, Emig from Gaasterland, Friesland 1853–1854 MFH 6:3:93

Geneal holdings of the Mennonite Hist Lib & Archives of eastern PA MFH 6:3:96

Geneal res aid, the Mennonite Lib & Archives TS 29:1:19

Hist in Dauphin Co PA PM 10:2:12

Hist in modern era PM 10:2:2

Hist in ON 1786–1986, bk rev PM 10:1:49

Hist of Hierschau RA, bk rev BCG 16:4:143

Hist of ministers in ON, bk rev BCG 16:1:33

Hist of Reformed Mennonites in Mitchell Co KS MFH 6:3:110

Hist of Willow Springs cong in Bureau Co IL MH 14:2:13 14:3:27

Hist sketch of Mennonite Ch of Normal IL MH 14:3:25

Index to imm on US pass lists 1872–1904, bk rev GH 41:2:121

Names in Reformed Ch rec 1826–1829 in Chambersburg PA MFH 6:3:94

Palatine census 1664–1793, bk rev FRT 8:4:199 GGD 3:3:134 GH 41:5:159 WPG 14:1:55

Rural life at Hans Herr House Museum PM 10:4:2

Stories of women, bk rev PM 10:3:39

MENSCH, Jacob B b1835, PA, letter collect MH 14:2:22

MENZ, Anna Barbara see Franz Paul BOOS

MERCER, Edward d1763, VA, anc ch OPC 18:1:6

Frances A see Samuel A KING

Henry m1821, w Jane Chapman, IR, children IFL 2:9–10:14

Rebecca see James K CONNER

148

MERCER (continued)

Surname period, *Mercer Memories*, Rt 2 Box 690, Metaline Falls WA 99153

MERCHANT, Berry f1878, TN, TX, auto YTD 6:2:38

MEREDITH, Mathias b1866, w Margaret Stone, MO, obit SNS 3:3:3

Reese see Martha CARPENTER

MERIWEATHER, Martha see Benjamin TALIAFERRO

MERKER, Heinrich b1807, w Eleanor Hemmion & Christina Schilling, GE, OH, IL, geneal WTC 3:2:64

MERRIAM, Fam rec corr to *The Hist & Geneal of the Lexington MA Munroes* by Munroe NEH 4:2:76

MERRILL, Emily see John UDELL

MERRIMON, Fam hist, bk rev BWG 16:1:65

MERSHON, Henry m1728, w Mary Yard, NY?, NJ, anc ch NAS 26:2:57

Nancy see John MOREN

MERTENS, Charlotte Wilhelmine b1835, GE, CA, anc ch OG 13:3:69

MERVYN, Roger bc1430, EN, anc ch AW 13:2:65

MERWIN, Stephen m1809, w Betsey Ann Glover, Bible rec CTN 20:3:435

Surname period, *Milestones*, 4113 49th St NW, Washington DC 20016

MESHER, Margaret see James WILSON

MESNARD, Margaret see O A MITCHELL

METHODIST, Biog sketches of ministers 1784-1984, bk rev FRT 8:4:197

Death notices 1851-1860 abstr from the *Christian Guardian*, bk rev GH 41:2:119

Fourth quarterly conference minutes 1853 BWG 16:1:29

METHODIST (continued)

Hist sketch of Primitive Meth in Pig Patch WI WI 33:4:245

Yellowstone conference, bk rev GH 41:4:195

METHODOLOGY, Abbreviations for US & foreign countries AMG 2:4:16

Am & Brit geneal & heraldry 1982-1985 suppl, bk rev FAM 26:4:241 NYR 118:4:240

Am Digest System, use of FLG 10:3:92

Am reference geneal, bk rev NYR 118:2:113

Anc of the Collins Co (TX) Geneal Soc members, bk rev MCG 10:3:144

Archival & mss repositories in NC, bk rev FGS 11:4:17

Archives (state) address list HTR 30:1:7

Audio & video recording preservation hints NSN 12:5:45

Auto writing guide by Kanin, bk rev SGS 36:4:210 FAM 26:4:242 MA 11:3:79 TCG 6:4:73

Bibl almanac, bk rev VAG 31:1:69

Bible rec publ in the PGCGS Bulletin, index PGB 19:4:64

Biog & geneal master index 1987, bk rev RAG 8:1:32 CTN 20:1:140 GH 41:3:171 GN 5:2:99 NYR 118:2:112 VAG 31:1:70 (1986) MAD 27:2:74

Biog almanac 3rd edition, bk rev GN 5:2:100 GH 41:3:171 NYR 118:3:179

Biog dictionaries & related works 2nd ed, bk rev CTN 19:4:708 MAD 27:4:147 CTA 29:4:131 NYR 118:1:50

Biog writing outline WTC 7:4:158

Birth cert ordering addresses IAN 8:5:7

Birth date calculations from death date GFP 36:4:175

Birth date computing table WTC 7:1:24 RDQ 5:1:11

METHODOLOGY (continued)

Birth date computation from gravestones RES 18:4:172 FCF 87:Spring

Birth rec, use of NSN 12:3:26

Business (small) structuring hints APG 2:4:3

Calendar changes KSL 11:2:43

Calendar conversion from FR Republican to Gregorian MCS 7:3:107

Calendar, Julian & Gregorian AL 3:4:32

Calendar variations & uses of GGD 3:2:72

Calendars 1776–2000 FCT :72:6

Cem art meanings HTR 29:3:85

Cem reading hints WTC 8:2:73

Cem rec, use of SCS 24:1:8 CC 10:3:5

Cem res hints HL 5:4:94

Census 1790 hist sketch NPW 6:5:46

Census 1790–1860 transparent overlay maps set #1, bk rev GGS 23:2:102

Census 1790–1910 data avail TTH 8:3:60

Census 1790–1920 map guide, bk rev WCK 20:3:46 EK 23:2:10 GH 41:5:156 OC 24:3:126 KA 23:2:119

Census 1850, 1860, 1870 key, bk rev GH 41:5:157

Census 1880 key, bk rev NGS 74:4:313

Census items 1790–1980 HTR 29:4:116

Census rec avail by state & year CCQ 4:3:24

Census rec, use of Fed MIS 19:1:17

Census rec, use of agricultural census NCJ 13:2:80

Census rec, use of US, bk rev NYR 118:3:180 DCG 1:3:2

Ch & pastoral rec in the archives of the United Ch of Christ & the Evangelical & Reformed Hist Soc (PA), bk rev WPG 13:4:47

METHODOLOGY (continued)

Ch archives & repositories with addresses THT 15:2:24 AB 16:1:14 BHN 20:4:136 CSB 21:1–2:29

Ch hist preservation & writing, bk rev NTT 7:2:44

Ch rec, use of THT 15:2:23

classification system of the LDS Geneal Soc Lib CPY 15:4:86

Co rec direct guide 1987 SLB 6:2:47

Coat of arms explained SAG 7:1:1

Courthouse rec guide vol 1, bk rev NYR 118:3:178

Cousin chart SS 14:3:56 CC 10:1:10 KFR 13: :20

Death memorial cards at the Geneal Soc of Flemish Am FAH 5:1:16

Death terms FCF 87:Spring

Direct (city), use of FP 30:1:27 PF 16:2:57

Direct city & co, use of CR 19:2:54

Document editing guide by Kline, bk rev APG 2:2:27

Document handling hints SIN 8:3:94

Emig, imm, & naturalization explained RT 5:1:19

Fam & community hist sources, bk rev WTC 7:3:124

Fam & local hist sources in the National Archives, bk rev GH 41:6:121

Fam hist & geneal writing guide by Barnes, bk rev CGS 18:5:11

Fam hist bk avail SLB 6:3:105

Fam hist document facsimilies, bk rev BCG 16:3:99

Fam hist hints for beginners FP 30:4:211

Fam hist holdings at the Topeka (KS) Geneal Soc Lib TOP 17:4:104

Fam hist printing & publ guide, bk rev GH 41:5:152

Fam hist publ hints GM 22:6:203

Fam hist questionnaire FI 7:4:93

METHODOLOGY (continued)

Fam hist res guide by Cole, bk rev BCG 16:4:141

Fam hist writing & publ hints GJ 15:2:50 GEN 12:1:26 HF 3:1:20 BCG 16:1:22

Fam hist writing guide by Alessi & Miller, bk rev OC 24:3:125

Fam hist writing guide by Seeber, bk rev ANC 22:1:43

Fam hist writing guide by Templeton, bk rev ANE 21: :27

Fam newsletter, use of MCR 18:4:102

Fam one-name period, bk rev GH 41:1:123

Fam reunion planning hints GH 41:1:5

Fam reunion planning hints SLV 5:5:13

Fam tales & treasures guide, by Alessi & Miller, bk rev KA 23:2:118

Fam tradition, evaluating hints LCH 1:4:176

Funeral home rec, use of MCR 18:3:72 OC 24:2:72

Geneal & heraldry 1982–1985, Am & British, bk rev VAG 31:2:147

Geneal & hist soc world-wide 1986-87, list, bk rev FRT 8:2:102 GH 41:1:123

Geneal & rec agents association, bk rev RAG 8:2:21

Geneal 15-generation 1-fam line chart, rev GH 41:3:158

Geneal as pastime & profession by Jacobus, bk rev SLB 6:3:123 PA 35:1:51

Geneal bibl, bk rev NGS 74:3:234 FAM 26:1:48

Geneal bk & articles in print compendium, bk rev TS 29:3:107 FRT 8:4:196

Geneal by mail, letter writing hints AW 13:4:148

Geneal Column Direct 2nd ed, bk rev RAG 8:1:21

Geneal crossword puzzles, bk rev GH 41:3:158

METHODOLOGY (continued)

Geneal dictionary, bk rev GH 41:2:157 SGS 36:4:206

Geneal document organizing hints WB 17:1:1

Geneal filing system TB 13:2:3

Geneal filing system guide by Carlberg, bk rev GH 41:4:212

Geneal for librarians, bk rev BCG 16:4:148

Geneal game, rev GH 41:5:194

Geneal holdings at the NARA (Denver CO), microfilm CO 48:2:43

Geneal holdings of the Federal, Way LDS Geneal Lib CCN 87:3:3

Geneal holdings of the Mid-Columbia Reg Lib (WA) CCN 87:3:3

Geneal holdings of the Waltham (MA) Public Lib MP 3:4:255

Geneal humor by Baselt, bk rev NYR 118:1:51

Geneal humor by Galeener-Moore, bk rev HF 3:1:3 NCJ 13:2:118

Geneal in the Lib of Congress 2nd suppl 1976-1986, bk rev GH 41:4:187

Geneal letter-writing hints MKT 10:4:71

Geneal Period Annual Index vol 22 1983 & 23 1984, bk rev NGS 75:1:66 (vol 24 1985) GH 41:1:123 NER 141:2:164 CAL 6:4:90 TNB 3:3:5 BCG 16:4:147 AG 62:3:191 GN 5:2:98

Geneal perspectives in soc his,t by Crandall & Taylor, bk rev TTH 8:2:35 FRT 8:2:103 GN 5:2:101 NEH 4:2:55 REG 85:1:74

Geneal pitfalls guide by Rubincam, bk rev GH 41:4:185

Geneal problem-solving hints HL 4:3:71

Geneal publ (current), bk rev MN 18:2:92 IL 19:2:111

Geneal rec avail at the LDS Long Beach East branch THH :97:24

METHODOLOGY (continued)

Geneal rec checklist MCG 10:3:158

Geneal rec organizing hints MFH 6:2:46

Geneal res & organization guide by Heisey, bk rev AGS 28:4:152

Geneal res aid, Hudson's Bay Company Archives FAM 26:1:17

Geneal res aid, Cornell University SCS 24:12:239

Geneal res aid, National Archives KS City Branch, use of MGR 22:3:131

Geneal res aid, National Archives field branches addresses CAL 6:4:96

Geneal res aid, tape recorders CR 19:4:194

Geneal res aid, the Draper Mss, bk rev CC 10:4:7

Geneal res aid, the OK Hist Soc MIS 19:4:88

Geneal res aid, the Regenos Collect KIL 15:3:1

Geneal res aid, the US Serial Set & Indexes MCR 18:4:109

Geneal res aid, the Wilson Collect KIL 15:4:1

Geneal res aids for free & useful addresses, bk rev GH 41:6:120

Geneal res at an LDS branch lib, use of SLB 6:3:117

Geneal res by a profession, what to expect APG 2:3:14

Geneal res charts, bk rev WTC 7:1:35

Geneal res dictionary national & international 1986 & guide to geneal soc, bk rev MD 28:2:238 FLG 10:2:79 AG 62:3:122 PA 35:1:55 (1987) TOP 17:3:69 TS 29:2:69 ANE 23: :21 GN 5:3:158 GR 29:2:63 NCJ 13:3:182 WPG 14:1:52 GGS 23:3:157 BM 8:2:64 OK 32:2:44

Geneal res facilities in Washington DC AB 16:1:6

METHODOLOGY (continued)

Geneal res for beginners by Curtis & Fagg, bk rev TTT 11:3:132

Geneal res for beginners by National Geneal Soc, bk rev MSG 7:1:52

Geneal res guide against pitfalls by Rubincam, bk rev NCJ 13:3:183

Geneal res guide by Alessi & Miller, bk rev RCP 10:1:24

Geneal res guide by Cosgriff, ,bk rev AG 62:3:188 LRT 6:1:191

Geneal res guide by Crandall, bk rev LIC 13:1:53 SLB 6:3:124

Geneal res guide by Curtis & Fagg, bk rev AMG 2:4:8

Geneal res guide by Galeener-Moore (humorous), bk rev TTH 8:1:12 FTR :105:4 SGS 36:4:210 TTT 11:4:187 WCK 20:3:49 WPG 14:1:46 FAM 26:4:242 BCG 16:4:148 SLB 6:5:221 KA 22:4:242 FRT 8:1:52 VAG 31:2:148 SCM 15:2:120 MN 18:1:37 GH 41:4:184 CGS 18:4:16 DG 33:2:117 LIC 13:3:168 OC 24:2:84 OK 32:2:43

Geneal res guide by Hall 8th ed, bk rev GH 41:2:118

Geneal res guide by Linder, bk rev WTC 11:2:61

Geneal res guide by Rogers, bk rev MN 18:1:38

Geneal res guide by Rubincam, bk rev GFP 36:4:177 OZ 9:3:122

Geneal res guide for beginners & intermediate geneal by Carlberg, bk rev GH 41:4:212

Geneal res guide for beginners by Crandall, bk rev DM 50:3:142 AG 62:1:57 NYR 118:1:59

Geneal res guide for beginners by Lacy GH 41:4:184

Geneal res guide starter kit by Clark, bk rev WPG 13:3:45

Geneal res guide to ethnic geneal by Smith, bk rev BCG 16:4:142

METHODOLOGY (continued)

Homestead rec, use of MA 11:1:10

Immigration & naturalization rec held at Chicago Heights Free Public Lib, index WTC 11:1:24 11:2:63

Immigration rec, use of SCS 24:3:55

Indenture & apprenticeship rec, use of CTN 19:4:621

Index & abstr of col documents in the Eugene P Watson Memorial Lib (LA), bk rev GH 41:2:134

Indexes, fallibility of APG 2:2:1

Indices, use of GR 29:4:149

International Geneal Index, microfiche rev CTA 29:4:131

Interviewing hints LCH 1:3:137

Land divisions MCI 5:2:49

Land grant rec, use of CC 10:3:8

Land grants & homestead rec, use of SLB 6:6:259

Land measurements THT 15:1:9

Land rec terms CRN 6:1:3 LC 7:3:67

Land rec, use of FCT :73:15

Land tract finding hints WMG 3:1:26

Land twp maps, reading hints TRC 2:1:32

Latin for fam hist by McLaughlin, bk rev BCG 16:3:102 ANE 21: :26

Latin terms PF 17:1:17

Letter writing hints RDQ 5:1:6 AW 13:1:50

Lib & reference facilities in the District of Columbia area, bk rev NGS 75:3:233

Lib res hints, use of the National Archives Atlanta Branch WCK 20:2:24

Lib res hints WCK 20:2:20

Libraries in southern CA area RT 4:4:89

Library, use of GH 41:4:7

Lineage paper preparations hints SCS 24:12:237

Maiden name res hints KIL 14:2:29 RES 19:1:18

METHODOLOGY (continued)

Marks & brands, use of FP 30:2:69

Marr cert avail, where to write WTC 7:2:65

Marr lic avail at the San Jose (CA) Hist Museum SCC 23:1-4:11

Marr lic returns, use of TST 19:47:13B

Marr rec search hints CCS 9:3:87

Marr rec, proof of SLV 5:3:13

Marr-related definitions CL 5:2:7

Medical terms 1700s & 1900s FCG 6:3:45 SS 14:4:49 CCQ 4:3:23

Medical terms, hard to understand MFH 6:1:28 6:2:64

Memory writing guide, bk rev GH 41:5:153

Microfiching service of the Am Geneal Lending Lib GCP 5:2:20

Migration in hist contexts, bk rev AG 62:3:121

Mil personnel rec search hints TTT 11:2:69

Mil rec avail at the NY State Archives CDG 6:2:6

Mil rec avail at the San Bruno (CA) Archives LRT 6:1:197

Mil rec, use of RES 18:3:109 WCG 4:2:18

Name (given) abbreviations AL 4:1:18

Names (fam), bk rev AW 13:2:72

Names, Guinness Bk of, bk rev NCJ 13:1:53 GH 41:2:118

Naming patterns, use of TST 19:47:12B

Naming patterns for Dutch, GE, SW, & ST names TRC 2:2:66

National res direct, national & internation 1987, & guide to geneal soc, bk rev DG 33:2:119

Naturalization rec, use of WTC 15:3:115

Naturalization & citizenship rec, use of IMP 6:3:67

Naturalization rec, types of data recorded FCT :73:25

METHODOLOGY (continued)

News geneal & query columns with addresses REF 29:1:6

News geneal column direct, bk rev TTT 11:3:130 SLB 6:1:5 (3rd ed) GH 41:6:121

News geneal column direct update SLB 6:3:125

News holdings of the Contra Costa Co (CA) Lib CGS 18:3:14

News on file at Eastern Washington Univ – JFK Lib Archives EWA 24:3:200

News preservation hints PCI 9:4:8 SCR 11:2:16

News res guide by Hosman, bk rev NYR 118:1:52

News, use of in fam hist, bk rev GM 22:8:306

News, use of LCH 2:2:93 MN 18:4:181 CC 10:2:5 SHI 16:3:15 YV 19:2:66

Newsletter, use of SIQ 7:2:14

Nicknames for men and women SCR 11:1:5 GH 41:2:11 ACL 11:3:78 (women only) PW 7:3:99

Obituary, use of HL 1:4:116

Occupations list CRT 8:3:44

Occupations of pioneers AB 15:4:103

One-name studies reg 5th ed, bk rev RAG 8:4:23

Oral hist compilation guide by Arthur, bk rev WCK 20:4:60 BAT 16:4:171 GH 41:6:120

Oral hist interview hints FCT :70:41 TTH 8:1:15

Oral hist preservation guide by Fletcher, bk rev GH 41:3:158

Oral hist rec guide for video & audio tapes by Davis & Black & MacLean, bk rev GD 18:1:30 GGD 3:3:134 GH 41:4:184 BCG 16:3:100

Oral hist transcribing & editing guide by Baum, bk rev MAD 27:2:75

Paper preservation hints GD 18:1:21 TTC 11:3:63

METHODOLOGY (continued)

Pass & imm lists index 1985 suppl, bk rev MAD 27:1:38 (1986 suppl) CTN 19:4:706 MAD 27:3:114 GH 41:5:158 (1987 suppl) APG 2:2:28 GH 41:5:158 GN 5:3:160 VAG 31:3:234 CTN 20:3:519

Pass & imm lists index guide to publ arrival rec US & CN 1600s–1800s 1984 suppl, bk rev AG 62:3:188

Pass & imm lists index, bk rev RAG 8:4:22

Passport rec, use of SCS 24:7:146

Period source index 1986 annual vol, bk rev GH 41:3:159 KA 23:2:117 CTN 20:3:518 WPG 14:1:54

Photograph & news preservation hints RES 18:2:67

Photograph dating hints TB 13:2:17 MGR 22:1:24

Photograph dating based on women's clothing VC 8:3:66

Photograph identification guide, bk rev GGS 23:1:46

Photographs collect, use, & care guide by Weinstein & Booth, bk rev BCG 16:2:65

Photographs, use of LCH 3:2:88

Postal guides, use of SLV 5:4:5

Preservation hints AA 8:1:34 NPW 5:12:3 TGA 13:1:3 GD 17:4:23

Preservation of documents, lamination AH 14:2:53

Private claims, use of OCR 28:2:49

Publ (self) guide by Poynter, bk rev BCG 16:2:67

Publ short-run bk guide by Poynter, bk rev BCG 16:4:145

Query writing hints AIL 1:1:17 SLB 6:5:207

Relationship chart FCT :70:47 GJB 11:4:20 TRC 2:1:39 CC 10:4:11

Relationship terms – cousin & nephew FTR :99:7

METHODOLOGY (continued)

Religious denominational archives TS 29:2:63

Secondary evidence, how to convert to primary evidence GJ 15:2:31

Secret soc with addresses SLV 5:1:3

Secret soc, names & worldwide distributions RD 87:2:18

Ship pass & imm lists 1987, bk rev BM 8:2:64

Ship pass list 1630 on board the *Mary & John*, bk rev NYR 118:4:245

Ship pass list 1894 from Southampton to NY on board the *SS New York* MP 3:4:228

Ship pass list, use of PP 3:2:17

Ship pass lists (new) availa at the National Archives MKT 10:1:6

Ship pass lists, arrivals at Galveston rec avail MKT 10:1:7

Ship pass lists, obscure ports US MIS 19:1:8

ship pass lists, use of FTR :97:5

Ship pass lists direct 1890-1930 to ports of NY, Philadelphia, Boston, & Baltimore, bk rev WCK 20:3:48

Ship pass lists of vessels arriving at NY City 1820-1897, use of rec DG 33:1:22

Social security numbers, use of TE 7:1:40 RES 19:1:15

Southern Claims Commission rec, use of CL 5:1:3

State abbreviations AB 16:1:2

Surname bklets publ guide, bk rev GH 41:4:184

Surname meanings NPW 5:12:4

Surname origins from EN, IR, ST, & WE by Stein, bk rev CTN 20:1:143 LOB 8:6:65 GH 41:3:171

Surname origins NEH 4:3:127

Surname reg of the Southwest NE Geneal Soc, bk rev GH 41:2:140

Surnames & given names origins bk rev CTN 19:4:714

METHODOLOGY (continued)

Tax rec, use of HTR 30:2:56

Texile preservation hints GL 21:4:115

Tombstone rubbing hints FIR 6:4:42

Township rec, use of FRT 8:1:7

Transcripts & abstr, use of GD 17:4:28

V r bureaus US NW 9:2:70

V r costs US SCC 23:1-4:27 SHI 16:4:19 SCS 24:11:216

V r, birth & death rec fees by state with addresses EWA 24:2:110 WCG 3:4:31

V r, use of RES 18:2:71

V r, where to write IAA 1:4:5

Video & audio taping guide, bk rev CTA 30:1:53

Wife's name locating hints RT 4:3:78

will & estate rec avail at the VA State Lib, bk rev AW 13:1:39 FRT 8:3:149

World hist outline 501 BC to 30 BC FTH 10:1-2:72

METZ, Johann Adam b1791, Bavaria, anc ch OCR 17:1:4

MEXICAN WAR, Index to pension appl, bk rev EWA 24:1:53

Pension files 1886-1926 index, bk rev GH 41:3:159 GH 41:6:124

MEXICO, Geneal res guide by Konrad, bk rev GH 41:6:124

Hist sketch MP 3:4:213

MEYER, Anne see Henry FUNK

Catherine see Samuel RUEGGER

Hans bc1739, w Catherine Lichti, FR, CN, lineage MFH 6:1:14

Philipp Louis f1870, TX, letter AGS 28:3:129

MEYERS, Gotleib m1901, w Clara Belle Pangborn, OH, marr TFP 2: :27

MICHEL, Philip m1898, w Mary Stender, IL, marr appl MCS 7:3:106

MICHIGAN, Adrian, marr bk 1875-1890 of Rev Alfred G Dunston DM 50:3:103

MICHIGAN (continued)

Albion, banks & bankers, bk rev FRT 8:3:148

Albion, hist (ethnic), bk rev FRT 8:3:148 FRT 8:3:148

Allegan Co, Casco Twp, atlas 1895 index MI 31:4:136

Allegan Co, Clyde Twp, atlas 1895 index MI 32:1:27

Allegan Co, Dorr Twp, atlas 1895 index MI 32:2:47

Allegan Co, Fillmore Twp, East Saugatuck Cem inscr, bk rev GH 41:4:194

Allegan Co, Fillmore Twp, atlas 1895 index MI 32:3:85

Berrien Co, Berrien Twp, Long Lake Cem PF 16:3:78

Berrien Co, marr 1831–1856 PF 16:1:11 16:2:37 16:3:65

Berrien Co, Niles, Silverbrook Cem mausoleum PF 16:3:85

Berrien Twp, Franklin Cem PF 16:2:50

Calhoun Co, Albion, biog sketches, bk rev GH 41:1:135

Cass Co, deaths 1895 PF 16:4:109

Cem inscr publ in *The Pastfinder* PF 16:2:49

Census, co hist, & v r sourcebk, bk rev GH 41:3:163

Civil War, Grand Army of the Republic 1861 roster MI 31:4:141

Detroit, ledger 1779–1785 kept by Ann Brown DM 50:3:107

Direct (lib), bk rev DM 50:4:160

Eaton Co, Civil War, vet 1888 roster MI 31:4:134 32:1:25 32:2:45 32:3:115

Geneal misc 1830s & 1850s abstr from news DM 50:3:127

Geneal res guide to northwest by Wilson, bk rev DM 50:3:143

Geneal sourcebk of census, co hist, & v r, bk rev DM 50:4:160

Geneal sources & resources by McGinnis, bk rev MN 18:2:91 GH 41:4:193 WPG 14:1:45 SGS 36:4:208 AG 62:3:190 CTN 20:2:325 OC 24:2:81

MICHIGAN (continued)

Genesee Co, babies delivered by Dr Orill N Reichard 1906–1951 FG 29:1:28 29:2:58 29:4:116

Genesee Co, Civil War, men who served from, enlisted in, resided in, or otherwise assoc with co 1861–1865 FG 29:1:22 29:2:54 29:4:110

Genesee Co, deaths 1875–1877 FG 29:1:20 29:2:52 29:3:81 29:4:108

Genesee Co, Fenton Twp, geneal res handbk FG 29:3:62

Genesee Co, geneal res sources FG 29:1:2 29:2:33

Genesee Co, geneal res handbk FG 29:4:92

Genesee Co, marr 1860s FG 29:1:18 29:2:50 29:3:79 29:4:106

Genesee Co, will abstr 1886 FG 29:3:83

Grand Traverse Co, Paradise Twp, Barnum Memorial Cem inscr, bk rev GH 41:3:173

Ionia Co, geneal misc 1870s–1890s MI 32:1:17

Kent Co, Grattan Twp, Parnell, St Patrick's Cath Ch rec 1854–1875 MI 31:4:145

Kent Co, papers (first) index MI 32:3:97

Kent Co, Parnell, St Patrick's Cath Ch rec MI 32:1:4 32:2:57 32:3:107

Kent Co, residents MI 32:2:51

Lenawee Co, Macon Twp, GE Evangelical Luth Ch rec 1860s–1880s DM 50:3:112 50:4:175

Lenawee Co, scrapbk memoirs 1879–1922, bk rev GH 41:6:140

Manchester, geneal misc 1887–1890 abstr from the *Manchester Enterprise* FHC 11:1:9

Marquette, St John the Bapt marr 1872–1899 JMS 10:1:38

Mecosta Co, Aetna Twp, Aetna Twp Cem DM 50:3:137 50:4:185

MICHIGAN (continued)

Mecosta Co, direct (official) 1871 MI 32:3:110

Mecosta Co, geneal rec 1880–1910 MI 32:2:63

Mil rec, Farragut Post #32 GAR officers & members 1913 roster MI 32:2:72

Mount Carmel, WWII, roster of soldiers TE 7:3:125

Natives in Macoupin Co IL 1860 PF 16:1:21

Northeastern, geneal res guide, bk rev GH 41:5:176

Oakland Co, direct (surnames of Soc) vol II 1986, bk rev CTN 19:4:705

Oceana Co, taxable inhabitants 1873 roster MI 32:1:30

Osceola Co, Normal, student roster 1908 MI 32:3:90

Saginaw Co, Civil War, census 1894 soldiers, sailors, & marines TTL 15:1:15 15:2:44 15:3:76 15:4:108 16:1:12

Saginaw Co, deaths 1867–1868 TTL 15:1:16 15:2:42 15:3:74 15:4:106 16:1:10

Saginaw Co, declarations of intention 1852–1859 TTL 15:1:8 15:2:40 15:3:72 15:4:104 16:1:8

Saginaw Co, East Saginaw Twp, East Saginaw, census 1860 TTL 15:1:2 15:2:34 15:3:66 TTL 15:4:98 16:1:2

Saginaw Co, East Saginaw, Pioneer Fire Company #1 roster 1858 TTL 15:1:24 15:2:54 15:3:86 TTL 15:4:115 16:1:29

Saginaw Co, Frankenmuth Twp, St Lorenz Luth Cem TTL 15:1:18 15:2:50 15:3:82 15:4:119 16:1:18

Saginaw Co, marr 1866–1867 TTL 15:1:10 15:2:47 15:3:81 15:4:111 16:1:13

Saginaw Co, Saginaw, geneal misc 1856–1857 abstr from the *Saginaw Enterprise* TTL 15:2:61 15:4:124 16:1:31

MICHIGAN (continued)

Saginaw Co, Saginaw, Oakwood Cem inscr of soldiers, sailors, & marines TTL 15:1:11 15:2:45 15:3:79 15:4:109 16:1:14

Saginaw Co, Tittabawassee Twp, Freeland, Pinegrove Cem TTL 15:1:13 15:2:48 15:3:77 15:4:113 16:1:16

Saint Joseph High School roster 1917–1933 PF 16:1:15 16:2:41 16:3:72 16:4:103 17:1:12

Shiawassee Co, Bancroft, high school grad 1888–1940 roster SHI 16:3:1 16:4:3

Shiawassee Co, Bennington Twp, tax payers 1880 roster SHI 17:1:9

Shiawassee Co, civil office holders 1800s–1904 roster SHI 16:3:20

Shiawassee Co, gazetteer 1880 SHI 16:3:7

Shiawassee Co, marr 1837–1847 SHI 17:1:1

Shiawassee Co, marr 1867–1887, bk rev GH 41:1:136

Shiawassee Co, Ovid High School grad 1914 SHI 16:4:18

Shiawassee Co, owners of Maytag washers 1927 SHI 17:1:17

Shiawassee Co, Perry Twp, tax-payers 1880 roster SHI 17:1:12

Shiawassee Co, WWI, draft lottery 1917 SHI 16:4:13

Upper Peninsula, geneal res guide, bk rev GH 41:5:176

V r, use of MIS 19:1:12

Washtenaw Co, Dexter, Dexter High School grad roster 1877–1903 FHC 10:3:72

Washtenaw Co, Manchester Twp, census 1845 FHC 11:1:7

Washtenaw Co, Manchester Twp, landowners 1895 index FHC 11:1:11

Washtenaw Co, Manchester Twp, mort sched 1850 FHC 11:1:6

Washtenaw Co, Manchester Twp, poll list 1844 FHC 11:1:22

MICHIGAN (continued)

Washtenaw Co, Manchester Twp, teachers 1893 roster FHC 11:1:14

Washtenaw Co, Manchester Village, landowners 1895 index FHC 11:1:14

Washtenaw Co, naturalizations 1833–1836 FHC 10:4:87

Washtenaw Co, obit 1847–1899 abstr from *Der Christliche Botschafter* FHC 11:1:15

Washtenaw Co, probate rec 1828–1831 FHC 10:3:65

Washtenaw Co, Roman Cath Religious Soc of Freedom trustees 1851 roster FHC 11:1:19

Washtenaw Co, Saline, First Pres Ch member roster 1831–1846 FHC 10:3:74 10:4:89

Washtenaw Co, Saline Twp, mort sched 1850 FHC 10:4:85

Washtenaw Co, Saline Twp, Saline Village, Civil War, vet of the Union Army & widows of deceased vet 1890 FHC 10:4:83

Washtenaw Co, Scio & Webster Twp, Dexter Village, landowners roster & map 1895 FHC 10:3:63

Washtenaw Co, Scio Twp, Delhi & Scio, landowners roster & map 1895 FHC 10:3:64

Washtenaw Co, Scio Twp, Dexter Village, census 1845 FHC 10:3:55

Washtenaw Co, Scio Twp, landowners roster & map 1895 FHC 10:3:60

Washtenaw Co, Scio Twp, mort sched 1870 FHC 10:3:68

Washtenaw Co, Scio Twp, voter reg 1859–1860 FHC 10:3:69

Washtenaw Co, Webster, Meth Epis Ch trustees roster 1863 FHC 10:3:59

Watervliet Twp, residents (aged) roster 1906 PF 16:4:115

Wayne Co, Huron Twp, census 1884 DM 50:3:128 50:4:189

MICHIGAN (continued)

Wyandotte, biog sketches of Poles TE 7:3:110

Wyandotte, cem locations TE 7:3:118

Wyandotte, Polish businesses TE 7:3:106

Wyandotte, WWI, draft list TE 7:3:120

MICK, Surname period, *Mick Fam Newsletter*, 6555 Manson Dr, Waterford MI 48095

MICKLE, Charity f1923, IL, will MP 3:2:118

MIDDAUGH, Joseph f1807, NY, geneal, bk rev NYR 118:3:182

MIDDLEMAS, John bc1828, w Paradine Frances Wilson, EN, IL, geneal IG 23:2:48

MIDYETT, Council Bryan see Mary J LUPTON

MIILROY, Mary see Robert MCCORNACK

MIKSCH, Carl (Charles) b1868, w Dolly Belle Ayres, Bohemia, PA, CA, anc ch GJB 11:3:24

MILES, John b1795, w Elmira ____, GA, annual return of estate NC :93:1

Lavinia see Bazzle Manley FOUNTAIN

MILLER, Alma see Satterwaite ROWDEN

Boyd f1809, IR, VA, KY, MO, biog sketch SNS 3:2:3

Calvin P b1847, w Matilda Goodner, VA, IL, biog IG 23:2:51

Catharine see Henry WHITAKER Jr

Christiana C see John Ludwig HABERLE

Christina see James ETCHISON

Daniel b1756, w Barbara ____, VA, geneal, bk rev GH 41:2:154

Daniel D b1847, w Lydia B Troyer, OH, geneal, bk rev WTC 5:2-3:104

Elizabeth Sophronia see JosephA M LEMASTER

Elizabeth see John REID

159

MILLER (continued)

Fam members in Lancaster Co PA, census 1850 LCH 1:2:78

Frances see Thomas NELSON

George L b1855, NY, anc ch CCS 8:4:136

Hannah see Nathan KELLY

Harmon m1909, w Emma Lude, IL, marr notice CRT 8:2:41

Henry L see Marinda SCHECTER

Isaac m1841, w Mary Ann Rofs, Bible rec RED 19:4:15

James Evans see Nancy FLICKNER

John O b1832, w Barbara Reihl, MD, anc ch MFH 6:4:146

Joseph b1780, PA, anc ch LCH 1:1:27

Joseph f1765, IR, MD, KY, geneal KFR 13: :11

Maria see John RAUB

Mary Jane b1836, h Joseph P Talbott, IN, CA, biog sketch SCS 24:7:147

Samuel W f1864, letters WTC 12:3:117

Sarah A see Thomas S STREETER

Schmidt Christian d1847, w Magdalena ____, biog LM 28:3:273

Sherrills Carl b1859, w Anna Amelia Buerger, IA, geneal, bk rev GH 41:1:163

Surname period, *Miller Fam Newsletter*, POB 28215, Sacramento CA 95828 - bk rev, cem, census 1880 VA, coat of arms, marr, queries

Susan Jane see Nehemiah Johnson TEMPLETON

Tabitha b1829, h Alva Walls & Uriah Miller, OH, IL, obit CRT 8:4:11

Wendel f1754, w Christina Fisher, NC, geneal, bk rev NCJ 13:3:185

MILLICAN, Sarah see John F COCHRAN

MILLS, Elizabeth see Morgan Young

Phebe see Abraham COOK

MILLS (continued)

Simon f1639, CT, geneal, vol 2, bk rev MCG 10:2:89

Thomas A b1815, w Nanch Ann Johnson, TN, MO, geneal OZ 5:3:122

MILNER, Catharine b1810, OH, IL, anc ch CR 19:4:173

MILTENBERGER, Surname period, *Miltenberger Fam Assoc Quarterly*, 3617 Abrams Rd, Dallas TX 75214

MILTON, Surname period, *Milton/Melton Pot*, 6809 Thunderhead Cr, Orangevale CA 95662 - rec from AL, AR, GA, IL, IN, KY, MD, MT, MO, NC, OH, SC, TN, TX, VA

MINEFEE, Ann see Larkin A COVINGTON

MINKLER, Emma L see Henry L FOWLER

MINNESOTA, Austin, marr & death notices 1871-1872 abstr from the *Reg* MN 18:2:77

Cem transcr list MN 18:3:114 18:4:171

Crow Wing Co, Brainerd, Evergreen Cem inscr, bk rev MN 18:4:188

Dakota Co, Inver Grove Heights, Union Cem DCG 1:3:3

Eden Prairie, Eden Prairie Cem & Chanhassen Cath Cem inscr, bk rev GH 41:4:194

Farm hist, bk rev GH 41:4:194

Freeborn Co, Freeman Twp, map c1920 FCT :74:27

Freeborn Co, Hayward Twp, map c1920 FCT :70:48

Freeborn Co, Mansfield Twp, map c1920 FCT :72:7

Freeborn Co, Nunda Twp, map c1920 FCT :73:17

Freeborn Co, Oakland Twp, map c1920 FCT :71:58

Freeborn Co, post offices 1800s-1908 FCT :72:3

Geneal res guide by Porter, bk rev MSG 7:1:52 MN 18:3:137 TTC 11:3:61

MINNESOTA (continued)

Geneal sources (unique & unusual) at the MN Hist Soc MN 18:4:155

Natives obit in Modesto CA 1980s MN 18:2:60

Olmsted Co, Eyota, Holy Redeemer Cem OCN 10:3:5 10:4:10 10:5:7

Olmsted Co, pensioners 1883 roster OCN 10:4:8

Renville Co, index to names in *Hist* 1916, bk rev GH 41:1:136

Saint Charles, Civil War, soldier roster MN 18:1:29

Scott Co, Montgomery, St John's Luth Cem burials 1872-1985, bk rev MN 18:3:139

Sherburne Co, hist, bk rev GH 41:5:176

Ship pass list 1883 from DK on board the *Australia* MN 18:1:43 from Hamburg on board the *Westphalia* MN 18:1:44 from Liverpool & Queenstown on board the *Cephalonia* MN 18:1:44 SW on board the *Labrador* MN 18:1:43

Ship pass list 1884 from Antwerp, Hamburg, & Liverpool MN 18:4:177 from Liverpool & Queenstown on board the *City of Chester* MN 18:3:145 from Liverpool & Queenstown on board the *City of Chicago* MN 18:2:87 from Antwerp on board the *Rhynland* MN 18:3:145 Antwerp on board the *Belgenland* MN 18:1:45 from Hamburg on board the *Westphalia* & the *California* MN 18:2:84 18:3:145 from Bremen on board the *Weser* MN 18:2:85 from GE on board the *Neckar* & the *Rhynland* MN 18:2:83 from Liverpool 1884 on board the *City of Montreal* MN 18:2:86

Steele Co, cem that have been transcr MN 18:1:46

Washington Co, St John the Bapt Ch Cem MN 18:2:65

MINNESOTA (continued)

Washington Co, St Matthew's Luth Ch Cem MN 18:1:32

Washington Co, Woodbury, St John's Luth Ch Cem MN 18:3:119

Winona Co, geneal res sources at the Winona Co Hist Soc Lib MN 18:3:136

Winona Co, Rollingstone, hist, bk rev GH 41:5:177

Wright Co, geneal sources MN 18:3:130

MINNESOTA TERRITORY, Saint Peter, marr & death notices 1855-1858 abstr from the *St Peter Courier* MN 18:1:13

MINOR, Manasseh b1647, w Lydia Moore & Frances West, CT, diary abstr MP 3:4:261

MINTER, Elizabeth see William RIDDLE

MINZEY, John m1820, w Phoebe Avery, ST, MI, biog sketch FHC 11:1:4

MISSISSIPPI, Adams Co, Jersey settlement, hist of the desc, bk rev RAG 8:1:24

Amite Co, Richard Bates Cem FTH 10:3-4:47

Cem & Bible rec, bk rev GH 41:5:177

Civil War, census 1890 index to vet &/or widows, bk rev ANC 22:1:43

Civil War, Confederate rec of Covington, Jones, & Wayne Co, bk rev DS 24:4:217

Civil War, soldiers buried out-of-state FTH 10:3-4:104

Clinton, Mississippi College student roster 1854-73 FTH 10:1-2:76 10:3-4:49

Covington Co, census 1820-1840, bk rev GH 41:4:194

DeSoto Co, hist (photo) 1836-1986, bk rev GH 41:1:136

Geneal misc 1827, 1839, 1843, 1845, 1859 abstr from news FTH 10:1-2:1 10:3-4:1

Geneal misc 1863 abstr from *The Daily Citizen* STK 15:1:18

MISSISSIPPI (continued)

Grenada Co, cem inscr vol 1, bk rev GH 41:5:177

Hancock Co, cem inscr from unnamed cem SGE 28:122:41

Index to *Biog & Hist Memoirs of MS* vol 2 (chapters 1, 2, & 3) SLB 6:6:267

Indianola, Indianola City Cem inscr, bk rev FRT 8:2:100

Jasper Co, census 1840 & 1850 & state census 1866, bk rev GH 41:2:138

Jones Co, marr 1827-1880, bk rev GH 41:2:138

Land grants & decisions 1800s SGE 28:122:37 28:123:29

Lauderdale Co, marr 1839-1864, bk rev GH 41:5:177

Lincoln Co, Little Bahala Cem FTH 10:1-2:110

Lincoln Co, New Hope Meth Ch Cem FTH 10:3-4:60

Lineage charts vol 3, bk rev CCM 6:4:81

Louisville, First Bapt Ch rec misc 1835-1853 FTH 10:1-2:100

Madison Co, Pearl River Meth Ch Cem FTH 10:1-2:66

Map of co 1836 FTH 10:3-4:108

Marr & deaths 1837-1863 abstr from news vol 1, bk rev GH 41:6:141 FTH 10:3-4:95

Mil commissions reg 1837-1846 GHS 4:1:65

Mil commissions 1837-1846 GGS 4:2:48

Panola Co, Batesville, centennial PS 16:3:46

Panola Co, education eneumeration 1877 by district & school area PS 16:2:1

Pike Co, Holmesville, burials SGE 28:124:48

Scott Co, Harperville Memorial Park cem inscr FTH 10:3-4:80

Scott Co, Hillsboro Bapt Ch Cem FTH 10:1-2:88

Scott Co, marr 1872-1900, bk rev GH 41:5:177 KA 23:2:117 FTH 10:3-4:95

MISSISSIPPI (continued)

Settlers as taken from land claims in the MS Territory, bk rev GH 41:1:136

Stone Co, McHenry, Bond Cem SGE 28:121:25

War of 1812, soldiers index DS 24:3:143 24:4:192

Wayne Co, cem inscr, bk rev DS 24:3:164 GH 41:5:177

MISSOURI, Adair Co, atlas 1875 & 1898, bk rev GH 41:2:139

Adair Co, atlas 1911, bk rev GH 41:4:194

Adair Co, cem inscr, bk rev MSG 7:1:51

Adair Co, settlers (old) reg 1889, bk rev MSG 7:1:51

Andrew Co, geneal misc 1876-1900 abstr from news, bk rev GH 41:4:194

Barry Co, deaths 1883-1885 OZ 6:3:105

Barry Co, obit 1890-1909 OZ 7:3:91

Barton Co, wills 1898-1909 index OZ 6:1:27

Benton Co, geneal res sources OZ 7:4:136

Bolivar, student rosters 1907-1908 OZ 7:2:45

Butler Co, cem (hist) vol 1, bk rev GH 41:4:194

Butler Co, census 1850, bk rev GH 41:4:194

Camden Co, Armstrong Cem OZ 5:2:61

Camden Co, Hillhouse Cem OZ 8:3:103

Camp meetings, hist sketch OZ 5:2:45

Carter Co, Snider Graveyard OZ 6:1:18

Cedar Co, deaths 1883-1889 OZ 9:1:12 9:2:74

Cedar Co, geneal res sources OZ 9:1:10

Cedar Co, marr 1865-1874 OZ 5:2:70 5:3:111 5:4:150

Cedar Co, voters 1868 roster OZ 9:1:18

MISSOURI (continued)

Charlton Co, Keytesville, hist 1833–1983, bk rev GH 41:2:140

Christian Co, Benton Twp, Ragsdale or Sunrise Cem OZ 9:3:109

Christian Co, births 1883–1887 OZ 8:2:69 8:3:119

Christian Co, Hyde Cem OZ 7:3:113

Christian Co, post offices & postmasters roster 1870s–1920s OZ 5:2:55

Civil War, Farragut-Thomas Post #8 Grand Army of the Republic roster 1897 PW 7:3:101

Civil War, killed & wounded of 72nd Reg enrolled military mil in the Battle of Springfield 1863 OZ 9:3:129

Clark Co, marr 1879 (unrecorded) MSG 7:3:152

Clay Co, marr 1822–1852, bk rev SR 3:4:88

Co rec avail on microfilm guide, bk rev FRT 8:1:51

Cole Co, cem inscr, bk rev GH 41:3:163

Cole Co, General Assembly members 1800s–1900s roster SNS 3:5:2

County rec avail on microfilm guide, bk rev MSG 7:1:50

Crawford Co, geneal misc 1896 abstr from the *Crawford Co Telephone* OZ 9:3:103

Crawford Co, geneal misc 1902 abstr from the *Crawford Co Democrat* OZ 6:3:127

Crawford Co, geneal res sources OZ 9:3:99

Crawford Co, natives in OK Territory 1902 OZ 7:1:4

Crawford Co, Teacher's Institute roster 1896 OZ 9:3:101

Dade Co, Greenfield, Henry School student roster 1879 OZ 8:2:50

Dade Co, Mt Pisgah Bapt Ch hist sketch 1840–1897 OZ 5:1:9

MISSOURI (continued)

Dade Co, postmasters 1832–1925 roster OZ 6:1:7

Dale Co, Rock Prairie Bapt Assoc hist sketch OZ 6:4:144

Dallas Co, death notices 1886–1891 abstr from the *Buffalo Reflex*, bk rev GH 41:4:195

Dallas Co, geneal misc 1899 abstr from *The Record* OZ 6:2:53

Dallas Co, geneal misc 1887 abstr from *The Buffalo Reflex* OZ 9:3:125

Dallas Co, public school fund 1869–1870 OZ 8:4:138

Deaths 1808–1854 abstr from news, bk rev WPG 14:1:49

Dent Co, deaths 1883–1885 OZ 5:3:117

Dent Co, ex-Confederate 7th Annual encampment 1903 roster OZ 6:1:5

Dent Co, geneal res sources OZ 6:1:16

Douglas Co, Arden Cem OZ 8:1:31

Douglas Co, Eden School student roster 1902, 1903, 1907 OZ 6:1:30

Douglas Co, Maggard Cem OZ 9:1:32

Douglas Co, marr 1890 OZ 7:1:15

Douglas Co, Ongo, Hall Cem OZ 6:4:143

Douglas Co, school rec 1872–1887 OZ 7:3:112

Douglas Co, Wright Cem OZ 9:1:32

G A R Post #219 Republic member roster OZ 7:3:116

Gasconade Co, General Assembly members SNS 3:6:3

Geneal misc 1860–1870 abstr from southwest MO news, bk rev GH 41:4:194

Geneal misc 1867 abstr from the *Tri-Weekly Patriot* OZ 9:2:70 9:3:110

General Assembly members 1812–1937 roster (territorial government) SNS 3:4:3 3:5:2

163

MISSOURI (continued)

Jefferson City, hist sketch SNS 3:5:4

Jefferson Co, hist of Gravois Road in northwest section of co, bk rev MSG 7:1:50

Kansas City, Union Cem inscr, bk rev FRT 8:2:106 TS 29:1:26

Knox Co, atlas 1876, bk rev GH 41:2:139

Laclede Co, geneal misc 1889 abstr from the *Laclede Co Republican* OZ 7:4:142

Laclede Co, geneal misc 1908 abstr from *The Lebanon Republican* OZ 8:4:150

Lafayette Co, marr 1888-1901, bk rev GH 41:2:139

Land (school) sales 1832-1930, bk rev GH 41:6:141

Lawrence Co, deaths 1883-1893 OZ 7:1:19 7:2:61 7:3:109

Lawrence Co, Stahl Cem OZ 6:3:93

Lawrence Co, Sycamore Bapt Ch hist sketch & member roster 1856-1895 OZ 5:2:49

Legislators (state) 1812-1937 roster SNS 3:1:3 3:3:6

Macon Co, atlas 1875, bk rev GH 41:2:139

Macon Co, atlas maps 1918, bk rev GH 41:4:195

Macon Co, Fletcher Cem GTP 25:2:47

Macon Co, Humphreys-Phipps Cem GTP 25:2:47

Macon Co, obit 1889-1903 part 1, bk rev GH 41:5:178

Marble Creek, Red School, hist sketch & student roster 1873-1874 MSG 7:1:42

Maries Co, Campground Cem OZ 9:1:3

Maries Co, deaths 1883-1884 OZ 7:1:34

Maries Co, geneal res sources OZ 6:4:150

Maries Co, Mt Etna Christian Ch hist sketch & member roster 1890 OZ 9:1:1

MISSOURI (continued)

Marion Co, census 1830, bk rev GH 41:6:141

Marr before 1840, bk rev WCK 20:1:13 TCG 6:4:67 OC 24:1:41

McDonald Co, deed abstr (early) OZ 7:1:9 OZ 7:2:65

McDonald Co, deeds index 1853-1869 MSG 7:2:96 7:3:141

McDonald Co, geneal misc 1883 abstr from news OZ 9:3:95

McDonald Co, public officials, witnesses, & deceased residents 1850s-1890s OZ 7:2:68

Miller Co, Brumley, Brumley Ch 50th anniversary celebration 1933 SNS 3:6:7

Miller Co, geneal misc 1875 abstr from news OZ 9:2:59

Miller Co, geneal misc 1881 abstr from the *Miller Co Vindicator* SNS 3:1:2

Miller Co, geneal res sources OZ 9:2:52

Miller Co, letters of admin 1860-1862 SNS 3:1:6 3:2:2

Miller Co, marr 1840-1843 SNS 3:1:6 3:2:6 3:3:6 3:4:6 3:6:3

Miller Co, probate rec 1837-1863 index SNS 3:3:2 3:4:2 3:5:2

Miller Co, wills before 1870 OZ 9:2:54 9:3:130

Mississippi Co, census 1870, bk rev GH 41:4:195

Mississippi Co, taxable lands 1845, bk rev GH 41:3:174

Moniteau Co, hist, bk rev FRT 8:1:51

Monroe Co, wills & admin 1850-1870, bk rev GH 41:2:140

Newton Co, postmasters 1832-1925 OZ 7:3:123 7:4:143

Newton Co, Six Bulls, pioneers vol 2, bk rev GH 41:1:138 (vol 3) GH 41:6:141 (vol 4) GH 41:1:137

Newton Co, Six Bulls, pioneers divorce & naturalization rec 2nd series, bk rev GH 41:6:141

Newton Co, Six Bulls, pioneers cem & Bible rec vol 14, bk rev GH 41:6:142

165

MISSOURI (continued)

Nodaway Co, census 1890 special, bk rev GH 41:5:178 GH 41:6:142

Nodaway Co, Maryville, Price Funeral Home rec 1902-1914, bk rev GH 41:6:142

Oregon, Bowers Mill, hist, bk rev GH 41:5:179

Organization bk 2(3) of the MO State DAR Lib MSG 7:3:160

Osage Co, geneal res sources OZ 8:2:66

Osage Twp, Red School hist sketch SNS 3:5:5

Ozark Co, deaths 1887-1889 OZ 5:3:110

Ozark Co, geneal misc 1881 & 1883 abstr from the *Weekly Ozark Co News* OZ 5:2:76 8:1:33

Ozark Co, geneal res sources OZ 5:3:108

Ozark Co, Jackson Twp, Upton Cem OZ 8:4:144

Patentees index 1819 NSG 7:1:1

Pensioners 1903 roster OZ 8:3:108

Pike Co, Calumet Twp, cem inscr vol 2, bk rev MSG 7:1:51

Pike Co, Hartford Twp, cem inscr vol 3, bk rev MSG 7:1:51

Pioneers vol 2, bk rev GH 41:5:178

Polk Co, geneal misc 1905-1907 abstr from the *Bolivar Free Press* OZ 6:4:148

Polk Co, geneal res sources OZ 7:2:52

Polk Co, land sales, bk rev OZ 5:2:65

Polk Co, letters of admin 1856-1861 OZ 7:2:49

Polk Co, postmasters roster 1832-1925 OZ 6:2:71 6:3:111

Pulaski Co, geneal res sources OZ 7:1:22

Pulaski Co, land patents 1845-1901 OZ 9:1:5

Pulaski Co, wills 1833-1875 index OZ 7:1:12

MISSOURI (continued)

Rec of the Ancient Free & Accepted Masons MSG 7:2:61

Reynolds Co, hist, bk rev GH 41:5:178 OZ 9:3:123

Reynolds Co, hist, bk rev MSG 7:3:170

Saint Charles Co, cem inscr (Cath), bk rev GH 41:6:142

Saint Charles Co, census 1860, bk rev GH 41:6:143

Saint Clair Co, deaths 1870-1872 OZ 6:4:155

Saint Clair Co, geneal res sources OZ 8:3:98

Saint Clair Co, letter list 1867 OZ 7:4:138

Saint Louis Co, cem inscr vol 4, bk rev RAG 8:4:26 GH 41:6:142

Saint Louis Co, St Louis, census 1860 index, microfiche rev GH 41:5:197

Saint Louis, intentions 1860-1864 MSG 7:3:121

Saline, cem inscr, bk rev GH 41:2:140

Saline Co, marr 1820-1874, bk rev GH 41:2:140

Settlers as taken from land claims in the MO Territory, bk rev GH 41:1:137

Settlers from Rhine River Valley in FR, GE, & SW, bk rev MSG 7:3:170

Shannon Co, geneal misc 1884 abstr from *The Eminence Current Wave* OZ 6:1:31

Shannon Co, geneal res sources OZ 8:4:145

Shelby Co, maps 1915, bk rev GH 41:6:142

Shelby Co, old settlers 1889-1901, bk rev GH 41:6:142

Slicker War, hist, bk rev OZ 6:4:154

Springfield, births, anniversaries, & obit for people b1850-1870 abstr from scrapbk OZ 8:1:5 8:2:51 8:3:101 8:4:147

Springfield, geneal misc 1866-1867 abstr from the *Tri-Weekly Patriot* OZ 9:1:38

MISSOURI (continued)

Springfield, geneal misc 1930s–1940s OZ 9:1:35 9:2:81 9:3:119

Springfield, Springfield National Cem OZ 8:1:14

Taney Co, Blair Cem OZ 7:3:115

Taney Co, Bradleyville Cem OZ 6:2:63

Taney Co, Jasper Twp, Meadows Cem OZ 5:2:59

Taney Co, Merriman Cem OZ 7:2:57

Texas Co, geneal misc 1889–1893 abstr from news OZ 7:4:147

Texas Co, geneal res sources OZ 6:2:60

Texas Co, probate rec 1871–1943 index OZ 8:1:7 8:2:73 8:3:123 8:4:151

Union Co, cem inscr, bk rev GD 18:1:30

v r avail AW 13:1:48

Vernon Co, geneal res sources OZ 5:2:62

Verona, Sacred Heart Cath Ch rec 1874-1981, bk rev OZ 6:2:80

Wayne Co, Gunther-Hay Cem MSG 7:3:137

Wayne Co, Hinkle Cem MSG 7:3:137

Wayne Co, Patterson, Warren-Daffron Cem MSG 7:1:36

Wayne Co, Williams-Russell Cem MSG 7:3:138

Webster Co, Henderson Lodge hist sketch & past masters 1874-1974 OZ 7:3:95

Webster Co, Marlin School hist sketch & student roster 1871–1900 OZ 8:2:55

Wright Co, Gasconade Twp, Binkley-Coday Cem OZ 7:3:114

Wright Co, geneal misc 1899 abstr from *The Mansfield Mail* OZ 5:4:142

Wright Co, geneal res sources OZ 7:3:100

Wright Co, Macedonia Lodge, member roster OZ 9:2:84

MISSOURI (continued)

Wright Co, marr 1850s–1890s OZ 6:3:114

Wright Co, New Home Cem OZ 6:1:13

Wright Co, New Home Freewill Bapt Ch hist sketch & member roster OZ 6:1:11

MISSOURI RIVER VALLEY, Geneal res guide by Ostertag, bk rev RAG 8:4:25 TTT 11:4:186 MSG 7:3:169

MITCHEL, Calvin b1816, Bible rec WTC 13:4:181

Ensign b1787, Bible rec WTC 13:4:181

MITCHELL, Alexander C b1840, PA, IL, Bible rec WTC 12:3:136 13:4:179

David bc1768, IR, PA, geneal, bk rev FRT 8:4:201

David f1786, w Elizabeth Steere, IR, PA, VA, geneal, bk rev GH 41:5:196

Harrison b1843, TN, MS, anc ch AA 7:4:187

Jessie E see Charles W HOWLAND

John b1784, w Mary Burt, Bible rec WTC 12:3:135

John Jack b1784, w Mary Burt & Christian Faulkner, NJ, PA, Bible rec WTC 13:4:178

Mary A see James MAYES

Morris dc1860, MO, letter OZ 5:4:141

O A d1892, w Margaret Mesnard, IN, IL, obit CRT 8:4:32

Priscilla see Josiah ESPY

Robert F b1801, w Tabitha McKnight Matthews, OH, TX, biog YTD 5:1:31

Sarah see Amos MORRIS

MIX, Cynthia b1821, CT, anc ch BG 8:1:10

MIZE, Isaac d1809, VA, KY, geneal, bk rev NYR 118:2:122

MOBLEY, William b1807, w Sarah ____, SC, anc ch PT 29:4:138

MOCOLA, Rosina see Martin OKRUHLIK

MOHLAR, Jacob f1773, w Elizabeth ____, MD, will MD 28:2:222

MOHNMAN, Catherine see August DRALLE

MOLLER, Johann Christian Frederick b1822 w Elsie Sophie Johann Grawert, GE, anc ch NW 9:2:63

MOLLESTON, Fam hist DE MAD 27:4:144

MOMFORD, Johane see Tobias CHANDLER

MONFORT, Henry b1789, Bible rec TB 13:4:16

MONK, Felix G f1848, TN, gift THT 16:1:10

MONNETT, Mildred b1890, OH, biog TFP 2: :9

Osborn see Susan BEATTY

MONROE, James b1758, w Eliza Kortwright, VA, NY, anc RDQ 5:1:7

MONTANA, Chouteau Co, Fort Benton, naturalization rec 1800s-1900s BM 8:1:25 8:2:71

Crow Rock, Co, hist, bk rev FRT 8:4:195

Flathead Co, Kalispell, Conrad Memorial Cem index, bk rev GH 41:1:138

Hill Co, direct (homesteaders) 1915 BM 8:1:15 8:2:52

News avail FGS 11:4:11

Yellowstone Co, marr 1881-1899, bk rev GH 41:1:138

MONTANEY, James b1799, FR, NY, geneal, bk rev OZ 5:2:65

MONTGOMERY, Charles Fox f1820, w Ardena (Reynolds) Allensworth, KY, MO, biog sketch OZ 7:3:103

Fam cem TX STI 27:2:11

Jacob Archibald m1811, w Rachel Ann Gardner, TN, biog sketch OZ 7:3:103

James b1820, w Caroline Finley, PA, geneal, bk rev WPG 13:3:50

James m1771, w Eleanor Means, PA, geneal, bk rev GH 41:4:208

MONTGOMERY (continued)

Jefferson Davis f1838, TN, MO, biog OZ 7:3:102

Joseph m1817, w Elizabeth McFaddin, Bible rec SCM 15:4:187

Margaret see Owen SHANNON

Mary Elizabeth m1871, w E J Painter, MO, fam rec OZ 6:1:24

William Rhadamanthus b1839, w Emma Jane Northcutt & Anna Towers, GA, fam rec NC :90:3

MOODIE, Jean see Andrew MAC-DONALD

MOODY, Francis b1769, VA, geneal, bk rev FLG 10:2:78 RAG 8:2:22 OC 24:1:37

Lenora Belle see John Wilson WALWORTH

MOOG, Herrmann m1856, w Wilhelmina Emma Zimmerman, MD, Bible rec MD 28:2:233

MOON, Abbie see Henry MCVEY

Anna b1822, TN, anc ch PT 29:1:9

Sarah Telulah see William T WALDEN

MOOR, Thomas b1815, w Matilda McLaughlin, TN, anc ch NAS 26:2:46

MOORE, David b1796, w Nancy M Thompson, VA, KY, geneal OZ 6:3:122

Elizha b1819, w Emily Langevan, EN, IL, anc ch FF 15:4:137

Elve see Jno Stewart SLACK

Fam hist 1732-1891 MD, bk rev IL 19:2:118

John m1781, w Mary Keller, NC, GA, fam rec PT 29:4:148

John J b1822, w Caroline Camilla Lammers, KY, CA, biog sketch SCS 24:5:113

John N m1878, w Martha J Chrisope, Bible rec OZ 8:4:139

Joseph G f1881, ME?, biog DE 11:3:84

Josiah b1749, w Mary Lake, NJ, geneal, bk rev FRT 8:4:200

MOORE (continued)

Lucinda see Lafayette WAR-NOCK

Lydia see Manasseh MINOR

Martha b1704 MA, anc ch BG 7:4:94

Mary b1782, Bible rec HTR 30:3:71

Mary see John CLARK

Minnie Rose see Wm John Henry HOWELL

Rosa Angelyn see John Walter HUGULEY

Sarah b1765, h John Finley, PA, VA, geneal IG 23:3:76

Sarah Susan d1873, IL, cem inscr STC 10:2:96

Shildes f1732, WE, MD, geneal, bk rev NCJ 13:1:54 MAD 27:2:72

Vincent b1775, DE, Bible rec DJ 4:1:18

MOOSBERG, Frank Olof b1871, w Anna Cristina Trofast, SN, TX, geneal, bk rev GH 41:3:170 FRT 8:4:200

MORAN, Lula see Odos E ACREY

MORDECAI, Moses b1707, w Esther Whitlock, GE, EN, PA, Bible rec NCJ 13:4:200

MORELAND, Nancy see Thomas SIMPSON

Surname period, *The Moreland Muster*, Mona Williams, POB 1654, Soquel CA 95073

MOREMAN, Mary see David HERNDON

MOREN, John b1794, w Nancy Mershon, IR?, KY, anc ch NAS 26:2:55

MOREY, Alzina see Sylvester B ABBOTT

MORFORD, Surname period, *Morford Historian*, Rt 1 Box 43-C, Shelley ID 83274

MORGAN, Florene S see Justus P WILBER

John Hunt f1862, biog, bk rev REG 85:2:162

Richard f1658, NH, geneal, bk rev BAT 16:1:22

MORGAN (continued)

Surname period, *Morgan Migrations*, 3690 Country Ln, Charlottesville VA 22901

MORIARTY, Surname period, *The Moriarty Clan Newsletter*, 1410 2nd Ave, Newport MN 55055

MORITZ, Caroline see George Edward KAISER

MORITZ, Joseph b1833, w Christina Brefeld, GE, IL, obit MCI 5:1:22

MORLEY, John James f1898, w Nella Ina Soule, IL, fam hist LC 7:1:11

John W m1855, w Hannah (Proctor) Roy, Bible rec DM 50:3:132

MORMON, Maritine encyclopedia of migration 1830-1890, bk rev RAG 8:5:24

MORRELL, Surname period, *Morrell, Morrill Fam Assoc Newsletter*, 3312 E Costilla Ave, Littleton CO 80122 – court rec NH, census 1850 NJ, James of AR, fam EN

MORREY, James bc1762, w Mary Whareham, EN?, geneal, bk rev GH 41:2:154

MORRIS, Aaron Taylor m1886, w Mabel Edwina Hutchinson, TX, Bible rec YTD 2:1:21

Ahijah W b1770, Bible rec YTD 2:1:16

Amos d1813, w Sarah Mitchell, KY, geneal, bk rev GH 41:5:193

Asa b1879, w Mary C Call, PA, CA, biog RCP 10:1:14

Elizabeth Allison see Hiram PIPES

Fam deaths TX 1903-1940, bk rev GH 41:6:162

J P m1856, w Sarah M Morris, Bible rec YTD 2:1:19

Jhony M b1824, w Jane Elizabeth Onions, AL, TX, fam rec STK 15:1:41

Joseph d1849, SC, obit THT 15:2:21

Philip f1760, VA, fam GRI 7:3:22

MORRIS (continued)

Robert b1734, EN, MD, PA, biog YV 19:3:107

Sylvester b1797, w Susanna Weston, CT, biog, microfiche rev GH 41:2:163

Thomas f1637, w Elizabeth ___, CT, geneal, microfiche rev GH 41:2:163

MORRISON, David b1831, w Matilda Duncan, IR, IL, biog WTC 15:1:13

Martha see Jonathan Addison BROOKS

Sarah J see John F CAPLES

MORRISS, Lyonell f1691, VA, deed VAG 31:3:193

MORROW, Jane see Richard PROCTOR

Joseph b1809, w Sarah Ellen Locke, MO, geneal, bk rev GH 41:2:154

MORSE, Daniel m1837, w Elizabeth Dear, Bible rec FP 30:1:11

Dinah b1729, MA, anc ch BG 8:2:37

Maria see William Dunbar DAVIS

MORTON, Edward b1764, w Sarah Allison, VA, geneal, bk rev FRT 8:2:107

Edward b1764, w Sarah Allison, PA, VA, WV, geneal & suppl 1, bk rev NGS 75:1:62

Harriet see James JOHNSON Sr

Jane see William MCKNIGHT

MORY, Mariah see Petrus WEBSTER

MOSEMAN, Fam rec corr to *The Bemis Hist & Geneal* by Draper NEH 4:2:76

Jacob b1795, w Magdalena Frey, PA, desc direct, bk rev MFH 6:4:131

MOSER, Johann Christian f1734, w Anna Maria ___, PA, desc AG 62:3:82

MOSES, William m1783, w Sarah Tinkler, Bible rec GN 5:1:2

MOSHER, Asa b1771, w Bethiah, MA, OH, anc ch RED 20:1:15

MOSHER (continued)

Augustus m1833, w Maria ___, Bible rec DAR 121:3:190

Fam cem inscr, deed abstr, marr, & will abstr MA, ME, & NY 1700s–1800s DAR 121:3:190

Hugh bc1633, w Rebecca Maxson, geneal, bk rev GH 41:6:162

Nicholas bc1666, RI, fam rec RIR 13:3:60

MOSIER, Mary Elizabeth see Jacob EGLE

MOSLEY, Ann see Lewis Griffin WESTMORELAND

MOSS, Eunice b1726, h Eliakim Hall, CT, biog note CTN 19:4:626

MOSS, Sarah see E M MCGEE

William b1824, w Henrietta Field, AR, CA, biog sketch SCS 24:5:113

MOTHERSHED, Martha see John WILKINSON

MOTT, Adam f1635, w Jane Hulet, EN, NY, geneal, bk rev GH 41:3:169

Jacob f1790, w Deborah Lawrence, NY, geneal, bk rev NYR 118:4:248

MOTTER, Henry bc1767, w Catharine Schmid, MD, geneal WMG 3:2:51

MOULD, Henry M m1867, w Salome Bushnell, NY, Bible rec BG 8:2:32

MOULDIN, Betty see Christopher Columbus WHITMIRE Sr

MOULTON, John bc1415, EN, NH, geneal NER 141:4:313

MUCKLEROY, Elijah m1816, w Catharine ___, Bible rec YTD 1:1:31

MUIR, Fam index to *The Muri Fam*, bk rev GH 41:6:162

MULKEY, John f1720, VA, fam hist, bk rev GFP 37:2:71

MULKINS, Willard m1834, w Eleste Babcok, Bible rec HH 21:4:214

MULLANEY, Matthew b1785, w Elleanor ___, IR, MI, biog sketch DM 50:3:106

MULLEN, Lawrence b1845, w Catherine McCarran, EN, MI, biog sketch DM 50:3:106

MULLER, Jacob f1752, GE, PA, biog NWT 8:3:16

MULQUIN, Thomas b1831, w Mary Boveniger, IR, IL, obit CRT 8:4:41

MULVAHILL, Catherine b1830, IR, IL, obit GL 21:1:20

MULVEHILL, Michael d1886, IL, death notice GL 21:1:10

MUMFORD, William R m1868, w Frances A Olin, Bible rec WTC 9:3:117

MUNRO, Henry George b1869, w Jane Masson & Freda Goodman, ST, WA, biog sketch YV 19:1:11

MUNSON, Clara b1861, OR, biog CT 7:3:20

MURBACH, Jakob b1780, w Verena Ruedi, geneal, bk rev GH 41:6:162

MURLEY, John f1849, w Rebecca ___, EN, IL, fam hist NSN 12:1:6

MURLY, William b1796, w Ann Friggens, EN, geneal NSN 12:6:55

MURPHY, Andrew Daniel m1879, w Mary Matilda Triplet, Bible rec OZ 6:2:68

Andrew J f1864, w Unity ___, IN, biog note SIN 8:3:87

Daniel R m1859, w Ellen Bass, Bible rec OZ 6:1:19

Sidney see William WOOTEN

Surname periodical, *Murphy Fam Newsletter*, POB 28215, Sacramento CA 95828 - bk rev, coat of arms

MURRAY, Robina Strachan m1889, h Thomas Garlaw, ST, fam rec GWS :26:15

MURTY, William m1864, w Minerva T Malcom, Bible rec HH 21:4:188

MUSSELMAN, Christina see Christian A OVEREHOLTZER

Elizabeth see John BAHR

William M b1805, w Margaret Everson, PA, KY, anc ch LAB 2:3:48

MUSSER, Fannie see Abram L SHENK

Tobias b1776, w Susanna Croner, PA, fam rec LM 28:1:256

MUSSON, James f1758, BM, fam rec BBQ 4:2:20

James f1792, w Mary Paynter, BM, fam rec BBQ 4:2:20

MUSTION, Aalfred b1819, Bible rec OZ 6:2:70

MYERS, Christian Hoover b1833, w Fannie Matilda Winkler, OH, IN, TX, geneal, bk rev PM 10:4:44

Henry E b1813, w Barbara Frick, PA, geneal PM 10:4:12

Jacob b1803, PA, anc ch JCG 15:1:29

NAFZIGER, Hans bc1712, w Barbara Holly, GE, biog MFH 6:4:129

Ulrich f1715, w Magdalena ___, GE, US, geneal MFH 6:3:84

NAFZINGER, Peter f1898, w Lydia Yoder, US, biog MFH 6:4:137

NAGLE, Fred f1865, BC, diary abstr BCG 16:4:114

NANCE, Susannah see Alexander McCULLOUGH

NARRAMORE, Mary see James DIKE

NATION, James Anderson b1901, w Myrtle Della Sands, TN, geneal, bk rev GH 41:1:163

NEAL, Amos b1810, w Sarah Weaver, KY, IL, geneal, bk rev DWC 13:2:57

Silas b1841, IL, pension claim GL 21:4:114

NEARY, William see Abba Gertrude ALCOTT

NEBRASKA, Alliance, Alliance High School grad 1915 NW 9:2:16

NEBRASKA (continued)

Alliance, Saint Agnes Academy grad 1915-1926 NW 9:2:16

Box Butte Co, Alliance, naturalizations 1907-1908 NW 9:2:67

Box Butte Co, Box Butte Precinct, voter roster 1908 NW 10:1:11

Box Butte Co, marr 1887-1914 NW 9:2:37 10:1:34

Burt Co, Tekamah, First Pres Ch hist sketch & minsiters roster 1873-1922 NA 10:2:47

Chadron, Chadron State Normal School yearbk 1920 NW 9:2:33

Crawford, Arch Cullers Post #138 Am Legion member roster 19?? NW 10:1:21

Dawes Co, marr 1892 NW 9:2:27 10:1:24

Dawes Co, vet roster 1923 NW 9:2:45

Dawes Co, Whitney Cem NW 9:2:57 10:1:19

Dawson Co, poll tax list (partial) 1882-1884 NA 10:1:32

Dodge Co, school grad 1898 NA 10:1:25

Frontier Co, Mount Zion Cem NA 10:2:57

Furnas Co, Hendley, geneal misc 1912 abstr from *The Hendley Delphic* NA 10:2:52

Garden Co, Ash Hollow Cem NA 10:2:70

Geneal misc 1900 abstr from the *Aurora Sun* NA 10:1:22

Geneal misc 1908 abstr from the *Shickley Herald* NA 10:1:13

Geneal misc 1917 abstr from the *Falls City Journal* NA 10:1:4

Geneal res sources TS 29:2:49

Geneal res sources at the NE State Hist Soc NW 10:1:43

Hemingford, cem inscr NW 9:2:11

Hemingford, Hemingford High School student roster 1931 NW 10:1:16

Hemingford, teacher's institute participants 1895 NW 9:2:18

NEBRASKA (continued)

Hist sketch of car manufacturing 1895-1930s NA 10:1:19

Hist sketch of domestic life 1850s NA 10:2:67

Hitchcock Co, Culbertson, v r 1883-1884 abstr from *The Sun* NA 10:2:81

Immanuel Cem & Ch 1880-1980 NA 10:2:59

Jefferson Co, cem list NA 10:1:6

Knox Co, index to *An Hist Sketch Of Knox Co NE* by Draper NA 10:2:73

Lakeview Cem interments NA 10:2:78

Local hist & geneal reference guide, bk rev GH 41:3:174

Natives who died in WA 1984-1986 NW 9:2:19 10:1:33

Nemaha Co, census 1910, bk rev GH 41:3:164

Omaha, marr lic 1937,NW 9:2:69

Platte Co, Walker Twp, Looking Glass Cem NA 10:2:48

Richardson Co, Salem, geneal misc 1923 abstr from the *Salem Standard* NA 10:1:4

Sarpy Co, residents 1885,NA 10:2:66

Sheridan Co, Rushville, businesses 1913 NW 9:2:35

Sheridan Co, vet roster 1923 NW 9:2:45

Spalding, St Michael's Parish, centennial, bk rev GH 41:3:164

Tobias High School alumni roster 1891-1900 NA 10:1:23

Willow Co, voter reg 1917 NA 10:2:54

NEBRASKA TERRITORY, Census 1854-1857 avail NW 10:1:45

NEEDHAM, Elsie see John Joseph CURTIN

NEELY, Fam hist, bk rev GGS 23:3:155

NEGLEY, Fam hist US vol 1, bk rev CSB 21:1-2:41

NEIGHBORS, James Monroe b1827, w Marin Elizabeth Grissom, SC, AL, geneal, bk rev NTT 7:2:42

NEILL, Mary Margaret b1856, Bible rec GFP 36:4:168

Samuel f1857, w Sarah Martin, IR, geneal IFL 2:9-10:51

NEILSON, Louise Maria see Charles C SMITH

NELISSE, Tocie f1896, w Flora Coyle, OH, marr lic appl CPY 16:1:16

NELMS, Lemuel H b1826, w Nancy Camp, GA, AL, fam rec PT 29:4:148

NELSON, Alice see Neil SHEHERD

Bridgett d1737, h Arthur Applewhait, EN, cem inscr BCG 16:1:7

Charlotte Adeli b1838, IN, OR, anc ch OG 13:1:8

Harold C f1937, OR, auto CT 7:4:10

John C b1866, w Margaret C McKnight, IL, anc ch KIL 15:4:27

Marren b1834, NW, WI, anc ch TB 13:4:38

Nels b1867, w Ella ___, DK, MI, MT, biog & letters TRI 26:4:56 27:1:4

Olive see John L LARSON

Thomas B b1767, w Martha Williams, NC, anc ch THT 15:1:33

Thomas m1859, w Frances Miller, IN, geneal, bk rev GH 41:1:164

William J b1857, w Nellie E Card, WA, biog sketch YV 19:1:11

NESBIT, Elizabeth see John TAYLOR

NETTLES, Henry P b1814, w Sally H Darwin, TN, Bible rec OZ 9:2:61

NEVADA, Biog & geneal sketch index, bk rev FRT 8:2:106 GH 41:3:164

Cem inscr for southern NV, microfiche rev GH 41:3:177

Cem inscr vol 1, bk rev GH 41:4:195

NEVE, Thomas Pleasant b1857, Bible rec STK 14:4:208

NEVILL, Anne see Bryan WHITFIELD

NEW ENGLAND, Captives carried to CN during the old French & Indian wars, bk rev NGS 74:3:229

Direct of anc heads 1620-1700, bk rev LRT 6:4:253 FAM 26:3:177

Fam (tycoons) of royal desc NEH 4:2:69 4:3:159 4:4:192

Fam hist, bk rev CCM 6:4:80

Geneal of Ellis, Pemberton, Willard, Prescott, Titcomb, Sewall, & Longfellow, & allied fam by Titcomb, bk rev GH 41:4:205 CTN 20:1:143

Geneal res address guide, bk rev NGS 75:3:232

Geneal res guide by Crandall, bk rev FAM 26:3:173

Geneal res hints FRT 8:1:34 8:2:86

Geneal, bk rev RIR 13:3:48

Hist 1610-1763, bk rev BCG 16:3:104

Imm for whom royal desc has been proved, virtually proved, improved, or disproved since c1960, a bibl survey NER 141:2:92

Louisburg victory 1745, bk rev VAG 31:2:151

Marr prior to 1700, bk rev GJ 15:2:109

Pioneers of CT & MA, bk rev AGE 16:4:107

NEW HAMPSHIRE, Architecture, guide, bk rev CTA 29:3:111

Census 1800 heads of fam, bk rev GH 41:6:143 SB 8:4:138

Coos country & vicinity, hist sketches collect, bk rev MQ 53:3:223 GH 41:4:195

Geneal digest 1623-1900 vol 1, bk rev NER 141:1:72 CTN 20:1:137 GH 41:1:139

Geneal notices 1765-1800 abstr from the NH Gazette, bk rev GH 41:2:140

NEW HAMPSHIRE (continued)

Hampton, settlers from Ormesby, St Margaret, Norfolk NER 141:2:114

Hist sketch of Somersworth, Great Falls, & Rollinsford SCR 11:2:17

Hist sketches, bk rev CTN 20:1:145 GH 41:4:195

Isles of Shoals, hist, bk rev BAT 16:1:23 GH 41:2:141

Mount Washington, experiences of a scientific expedition 1870-1, bk rev BAT 16:2:78 GH 41:3:159

Names changed 1679-1883 GJ 15:2:67

Newington, hist 1630- , bk rev RAG 8:2:24

Pioneers 1623-1660, bk rev see MAINE, Pioneers 1623-1660

Portsmouth & Dover, hist, bk rev GH 41:4:195

Portsmouth, hist (maritime), bk rev CTN 20:2:328 DE 11:2:71

Portsmouth, hist of medicine 1623-1983, bk rev NER 141:4:362

Strafford Co, holdings at the Dover (NH) Public Lib SCR 10:5:47 10:6:54 11:1:3

Strafford Co, inferior court rec 1773-1783 abstr, bk rev GH 41:3:164

Strafford Co, origin SCR 11:1:7

White Mountains, chronicles, bk rev GH 41:5:179 BAT 16:4:169

NEW JERSEY, Atlantic Co, Great Egg Harbour Twp, overseers of the poor rec 1777-1832 GMN 62:1:21

Cape May Co, overseers of the poor rec 1804-1881 GMN 62:1:39 62:2:69 62:3:107

Connecticut Farms, CT Farms Pres Ch member roster 1800-1859 GF 8:1:4 8:2:14

Court (Supreme) cases 1727-1760 GMN 62:2:63 62:3:110

Cumberland Co, hist, bk rev GH 41:3:174

NEW JERSEY (continued)

Essex Co, mort sched 1850 GMN 62:1:43 62:2:54

French & Indian Wars, muster rolls 1757-1758 GMN 62:1:12

Geographic dictionary, microfiche rev GH 41:2:162

Hist collect index, bk rev NTT 7:1:2

Hist of southern co, bk rev BCG 16:2:67

Hunterdon Co, Pattenburg Meth Chyard Cem GMN 62:3:117

Mercer Co, Harbourton Bapt Chyard Cem GMN 62:2:71 62:3:140

Mexican War, Company E 1847-1848 GMN 62:2:49

Middlesex Co, court rec to 1721 SB 8:3:102

Middlesex Co, hist of court system, bk rev GH 41:2:141

Monmouth Co, atlas 1873, bk rev FRT 8:2:101

Monmouth Co, atlas 1889, bk rev FRT 8:2:101

Monmouth Co, freeholders list 1790, bk rev NGS 74:4:306

Monmouth Co, marr 1795-1843 GMN 62:1:33 62:2:89 62:3:120

Morris Co, geneal, bk rev MN 18:1:40

Natives listed in the 1850 mort sched for CA, IA, & PA GMN 62:3:101

New Providence, marr 1806-1824 performed by Rev Elias Riggs GF 8:5:37

Passaic Co, Paterson, deaths 1832-1833 GMN 62:1:9

Queries, bk rev IL 19:2:117

Revolutionary War, roster of the Continental Line who were eligible to membership in the Soc of the Cincinnati, bk rev GH 41:4:196 WPG 14:1:49 GGS 23:4:209

Revolutionary War, census index, bk rev GH 41:5:180

Scotch Plains Bapt Ch death rec 1747-1835 GF 8:1:8

NEW JERSEY (continued)

Somerset & Hunterdon Co, heirs to estates 1809-1904, bk rev DM 50:3:142

Sussex Co, map, bk rev IL 19:2:116

Warren Co, atlas, bk rev IL 19:2:116

Warren Co, Finesville Cem GMN 62:3:97

West Fields, Connecticut Farms, Pres Ch member roster 1800-1859 GF 8:3:22

Westfield Pres Ch minutes of session 1815-1828 GMN 62:1:27 62:2:77 62:3:135

Wills 1689-1890 index to testators, bk rev ANC 22:4:157

NEW MEXICO, San Juan Co, cem inscr addendum, bk rev GH 41:3:164

San Juan Co, cem inscr vol 1 addendum, bk rev FRT 8:4:201

San Juan Co, marr 1887-1912, bk rev FRT 8:4:201 GH 41:3:164

Sheep trade 1700-1860 hist, bk rev RAG 8:4:21

NEW YORK, Albany District, Clarksville & New Salem, subscriber roster 1888 CDG 6:4:5

Brooklyn, Park Cong Ch tourists to Richmond & Norfolk 1885 AW 13:1:49

Broome Co, hist (pictorial), bk rev NYR 118:3:176

Buffalo, geneal res hints MA 11:3:68

Buffalo, Polish businesses list TE 7:2:75

Buffalo, Polish ch list TE 7:2:70

Buffalo, Polish soldiers WWI serving in Polish Army & in Am Army roster TE 7:2:54

Buffalo, St Stanislaus Parish firsts TE 7:2:80

Chancery court rec NYR 114:3:137

Civil War, hist & rec of the 8th NY Vol Cavalry, microfiche rev GH 41:3:177

Clarksville, hist 1835-1985 GH 41:4:196 NYR 118:3:178

NEW YORK (continued)

Columbia Co, Canaan Twp, proprietors 1754-1758 roster RAG 8:4:10

Cornell & Ithaca, hist (pictorial), bk rev NYR 118:3:176

Council minutes 1668-1783, bk rev GH 41:6:143

Court of Appeals, hist 1847-1932, bk rev CTA 29:3:111

Ellis Island, hist & geneal res guide, bk rev CHG 19:1:21

Erie Co, depositories of local rec, bk rev CTN 19:4:711

Gazetteer of the 1860 census, bk rev RES 19:1:24

Geneal rec avail MI 31:4:130

Geneal res sources at the Heritage Center Lib (NY) MP 3:4:239

Harlem, Reformed Dutch Ch rec 1800s NYR 118:1:31 118:2:95 118:3:161 118:4:217

Hist of Dutch NY (economic & social), bk rev NYR 118:1:50

Huntington, overseers of the poor rec 1752-1861, bk rev AA 8:2:87 NYR 118:2:112

Index to *Gazetteer of the State of NY* by French, bk rev RAG 8:5:22

Kings Co, census 1865 OCG 17:1:7 17:2:15 17:3:20

Law bk patrons 1792 roster NYR 118:2:85 118:3:150 118:4:213

Lewis Co, Osceola, hist (pictorial), bk rev NYR 118:3:178

Long Island, geneal abstr from, the NY Geneal & Biog Rec, bk rev APG 2:1:29

Long Island, geneal rec sources, bk rev GH 41:4:196 NYR 118:4:240

Long Island, geneal, bk rev WPG 13:4:37 PA 35:1:53 GH 41:3:164 NGS 75:3:230 NYR 118:3:175

Long Island, geneal abstr from the *NY Geneal & Biog Rec*, bk rev CTN 20:2:326

Long Island, hist of mil 1653–1868, bk rev BAT 16:1:24

Long Island City, hist 1630–1930, bk rev NYC 118:4:241

Marr & deaths 1835–1855 index to *NY Herald*, bk rev GH 41:4:196 CTN 20:2:325 NYR 118:3:176 OC 24:2:84

Natives who were members of the Soc of MI & living in MI 1886, roster DM 50:3:99

New Lebanon, marr 1832–1852 performed by Ira Hard RAG 8:4:16

New Netherland documents collect 1640–1665, bk rev NYR 118:4:241

New Netherland, Curaco papers 1640–1665, bk rev GH 41:5:159

New York City, apprentices 1800s, bk rev GH 41:1:139 MQ 53:1:71

New York City, apprentices 1800s, bk rev NGS 75:1:65 NYR 118:2:112

New York City, birth rec, use of NYR 118:1:27

New York City, marr & deaths 1835–1855 index to the *NY Herald*, bk rev APG 2:3:26 WPG 14:1:45 CR 19:4:192

New York City, pass list manifest 1820–1824 index, bk rev GH 41:4:196

Niagara Co, hist to 1902, bk rev GH 41:4:196

Ontario Co, cem rec index, bk rev GH 41:5:180

Orange Co, geneal depositories of local rec guide, bk rev GH 41:5:181

Orange Co, Goshen, Pres Ch bapt 1796–1815 OCG 17:1:7 17:2:16 17:3:23 17:4:31

Orange Co, Goshen, geneal misc 1844 abstr from the *Independent Republican* OCG 17:3:23 17:4:31

Orange Co, New Windsor, Pres Ch marr 1774–1775 OCG 17:4:31

Orange Co, Newburgh, Meth Epis Ch circuit rec 1790–1808 OCG 17:1:5 17:2:14 17:3:23 17:4:30

Orange Co, Walden, First Reformed Ch member roster 1891–1903 OCG 17:1:6 17:2:14 17:3:21 17:4:29

Orange Co, will abstr 1800–1804 OCG 17:1:5 17:2:14 17:3:21 17:4:28

Potsdam, First Pres Ch memorial stained glass windows SLV 5:4:7

Potsdam, St Mary's New Cem SLV 5:1:13 5:2:9 5:3:10

Queensbury, boundary line AG 62:3:101

Reidsville, Meth Ch reg 1903–1932 CDG 6:1:3

Rensselaer Co, direct of geneal rec, bk rev CSB 21:1–2:42

Ridgebury, Pres Ch elders roster 1792–1954 OCG 17:3:21

Rockland Co, hist, bk rev CTA 30:1:53

Saint Andrew's Soc biog reg, bk rev DG 33:2:116

Saint Lawrence Co, Hermon, M E Ch marr 1883–1905 SLV 5:5:7

Saint Lawrence Co, marr 1870–1882 performed by Erastus W White SLV 5:1:5

Schenectady Co, depositories list, bk rev LWF 6:1:7

Schenectady, maps (col), bk rev FRT 8:2:101

Schoharie District, tax list 1780 NGS 74:4:295

Ship pass list from Havre de Grace 1837 on board the *Burgandy* CTN 20:2:215

Soc of MI vet roster 1886 DM 50:4:165

Staten Island, hist to 1877, bk rev NYR 118:1:53

Ticonderoga, land owners 1811–1813 roster NYR 118:1:30

Turloch, Turloch Mil roster 1775–84 FAM 26:2:81

Ulster & Orange Co, name changes 1891–1894 OCG 17:1:7

NEW YORK (continued)

Ulster Co, Shawangunk, Reformed Protestant Dutch Ch rec 1750-1920, bk rev CTN 19:4:707 DM 50:3:143 NYR 118:1:51

V r 1777-1834 (eastern), bk rev APG 2:1:30 WPG 13:4:37 NYR 118:3:176 CTN 20:2:324 KA 23:1:38 TST 20:20:32 GH 41:3:164 IL 19:2:119 NGS 75:3:231

V r 1813-1850 (central), bk rev NGS 74:3:236 MAD 27:2:73 EWA 24:3:210 FAM 26:1:51

V r 1835-1850 (northeastern) NYR 118:3:135 118:4:203

Washtenaw Co, Manchester, Carr ledger bk 1833-1834 FHC 11:1:1

West Clarksville, hist 1835-1985, bk rev RAG 8:5:25

West Point, U S Mil Academy, official reg of officers & cadets 1843 SLB 6:2:70 6:3:115 6:4:165 6:5:223 6:6:263

NEW ZEALAND, Freeholders 1882, microfiche rev GH 41:5:197

NEWBERRY, Charles W b1865, w Neriva Garrett, GA, anc ch NC :94:9

Jonathan b1740, Bible rec SS 15:1:9

Mary see Daniel CLARK

NEWBOLD, John f1816, BM, will abstr BBQ 4:3:31

NEWBOULD, John f1799, BM, will abstr BBQ 4:3:31

NEWBOUND, Sarah see Samuel TINLEY

NEWCOMB, Lois b1772, NB, anc ch TEG 7:3:157

NEWCOMER, Emma Catherine see Merritt H TATMAN

NEWELL, William Malone b1856, w Mamie Warren McCartha, AL, anc ch MCA 6:1:32

NEWFOUNDLAND, Hearts Content, pet for dog act 1888 NAL 4:1:4

NEWFOUNDLAND (continued)

Village Belle, roster of crew & fam aboard the *Brigus* 1872, presumed lost at sea NAL 4:1:14

NEWHALL, Benjamin Franklin b1802, w Dorothy Jewett, MA, biog TEG 7:4:182

NEWLEE, Pearle see James William MAYBEE

NEWPORT, Mary Jane see James Monroe LINDSEY

NEWTON, Revilo m1866, w Ada D Anderson, IL, Bible rec MGR 22:2:86

NICHOLS, Carrie Belle see John W HURLBURT

Charles Elika see Martha Atwood TAYLOR

Surname period, *Nichols Nostalgia*, POB 2040, Pinetop AZ 85935 – fam group sheets, fam VA & EN & IA & OH, origins, Mexican War pension appl, marr IL, Thomas of NY, fam of RI

NICHOLSON, Anna f1860, KS, geneal, bk rev IL 19:2:112

Charles f1860, w Mary Agnes McGrath, IR, KS, geneal, bk rev CHG 19:4:154

NICKERSON, Jeptha b1804, w Sophere Rider & Sally Smith, MA?, fam rec MQ 53:4:238

NIEMERG, Tony d1918, IL, obit CRT 8:4:31

NIGHTENGALE, John T f1874, w Anna Boehs, RA, KS, geneal, bk rev TS 29:1:25

NILES, Eliza Jane see Albert HOWLAND

NILSDOTTER, Anna see Ander Jansson YELM

Elin see Olof KJELSSON

NIXON, Anna see John Scott GUTTERY

NOAH, Alfred b1873, OK, cem inscr OPC 18:1:11

NOBLES, Elizabeth see Charles ROACH Sr

NOE, Nathan f1861, w Sirena ____, KY, divorce HF 3:1:6

NOLEN, William Sr b1760, w
Deliliah Cantrell, VA, TN, anc
ch GGS 23:2:85
NOLTE, John Karl Ludwig b1820,
w Anna Margaretha Beck, GE,
MD, Bible rec WMG 3:3:141
NOON, Anna b1822, TN, anc ch
TB 13:2:38
NORFLEET, Sarah see John
YOUNG
NORMAN, John f1776, DE, mil
rec MAD 27:4:143
Mary see John GONN
NORRIS, Allevenia see Edward
Magill WALTERS
Jane see Isaac PATTEN Sr
Mercy b1773, h Asa Raymond,
MA, biog AG 62:3:120
Sarah Ann see David WOMACK
Jr
NORTH CAROLINA, Alexander
Co, census 1850, bk rev GH
41:6:143
Apprentice indentures to 1850
NCJ 13:1:13 13:3:164
Archival & mss repositories
direct, bk rev APG 2:3:29
Bakersville, hist sketch BWG
16:2:124
Beaufort Co, mil rec, affective
men roster 1781 TQR 14:2:65
Bertie Co, estates vol 1, bk rev
NCJ 13:2:114
Bladen Co, census 1860, bk rev
NCJ 13:1:51
Bladen Co, descriptive list 1782
TQR 14:2:64
Brunswick Co, census 1850, bk
rev NCJ 13:3:174
Brunswick Co, tax list 1772 TQR
14:1:35
Buncombe Co, Asheville, hist
tidbits LOB 8:10:154
Buncombe Co, census 1810 LOB
8:1:12 8:2:26 8:4:56 8:5:70
8:6:90 8:9:142 8:10:158
Buncombe Co, deaths 1887–1904
index LOB 8:1:6 8:2:20 8:3:34
8:4:50 8:5:66 8:6:86 8:8:125
8:9:139
Buncombe Co, geneal rec in
courthouse LOB 8:9:140

NORTH CAROLINA (cont)
Buncombe Co, holdings of Pack
Lib LOB 8:7:108
Buncombe Co, land grant entries
1794 LOB 8:7:106 8:8:120
Buncombe Co, marr bonds
1741–1868 index LOB 8:2:24
8:3:42 8:4:58
Buncombe Co, officials prior to
1872 roster LOB 8:11:167
Buncombe Co, Rev War, pensions LOB 8:2:18 8:3:32 8:4:48
8:5:64 8:6:84 8:7:96 8:8:117
Buncombe Co, wills & estate
admin (lost) 1792–1825 LOB
8:8:113 8:9:136
Buncombe Co, wills 1834–1844
LOB 8:4:54 8:5:72 8:6:82
8:7:98 8:8:122 8:9:130 8:10:150
Caldwell Co, birth cert (delayed)
1800s–1900s CAL 6:1:11
Caldwell Co, court of pleas &
quarter sessions 1847–1852 vol
2, bk rev GH 41:1:140 NCJ
13:3:174
Caldwell Co, death cert 1800s–
1900s CAL 6:1:6
Caldwell Co, fam articales
1876–1878 abstr from the
Lenoir Topic, bk rev GH
41:6:143
Caldwell Co, geneal misc 1875–
1876 abstr from the Caldwell
Messenger, bk rev GH 41:4:212
NCJ 13:3:174
Caldwell Co, geneal misc abstr
from news vol 1, bk rev GH
41:1:140 NCJ 13:3:174
Caldwell Co, geneal misc 1878
abstr from The Lenoir Topic
CAL 6:1:14 6:2:27
Caldwell Co, marr 1870s–1880s
CAL 6:1:3
Caldwell Co, tax list 1842 CAL
6:2:36 6:4:83
Cape Fear, hist of Scots settle-
ment, bk rev NCJ 13:2:116
Caswell Co, natives in Webster
Co MO census 1860 OZ 9:2:83
Catawba Co, census 1850, bk rev
GH 41:4:197 NCJ 13:3:175

NORTH CAROLINA (continued)

Chatham Co, marr 1772-1868, bk rev SCM 15:3:180 GH 41:6:144

Children of settlers of GE desc 1783-1792 NCJ 13:3:142

Chowan Co, tax lists 1784-1799 NCJ 13:4:206

Civil War, hist of the last Tarheel Mil 1861-1865, bk rev FLG 11:1:32

Columbus Co, census 1850, bk rev NCJ 13:3:175

County formations outline PT 29:1:32

Craven Co, court minutes 1749-1756, bk rev NCJ 13:3:175

Craven Co, gazetteer 1880-1881 TQR 14:2:85

Craven Co, marr bonds 1780s-1860 TQR 13:4:176 14:2:69 14:3:117

Craven Co, marr & death notices 1828-1831 TQR 14:3:110

Craven Co, New Bern, court minutes 1801 TQR 14:2:78

Craven Co, New Bern, direct (city) 1880-1881 TQR 14:2:83

Craven Co, postmasters roster 1800s-1900 TQR 14:1:41

Cumberland Co, Dunn's Creek Monthly Meeting QY 14:2:1

Cumberland, census 1770-1790, bk rev KA 23:2:115

Cumberland Co, tax list 1755 NCJ 13:3:134

Davidson Co, census 1850, bk rev FRT 8:2:101

Davidson Co, census 1860, bk rev FRT 8:2:101

Duplin Co, guide & gazetteer, bk rev FRT 8:1:50

Duplin Co, hist, bk rev SGI 4:1:22

Edgecombe Co, census 1830, bk rev GH 41:5:195

Estate papers 1754-1756 list TQR 14:1:22

Fam searchers & geneal direct, bk rev SCM 15:2:119

Federal court rec catalogue, bk rev SCM 15:4:223

NORTH CAROLINA (continued)

Forsyth Co, Belews Creek District, census 1860 FC 5:1:32

Forsyth Co, Civil War, mil roster 1861-1865 FC 5:1:48

Forsyth Co, court rec 1852 FC 5:3:23

Forsyth Co, minutes 1851-1852 of the court of pleas & quarter sessions FC 5:1:4 5:4:21

Forsyth Co, Mt Tabor Meth Ch cem inscr FC 5:3:49 5:4:60

Forsyth Co, Salem, Wayside Hospital, patients roster (1860s?) FC 5:3:44

Forsyth Co, will abstr 1870-1901 FC 5:2:15 5:3:31 5:4:38

Franklin Co, census 1830, bk rev GH 41:5:181

Gates Co, deaths 1915-1929 abstr from the files of Truitt Bonney TN 7:3:37 7:4:52

Gates Co, deed abstr 1776-1803, bk rev NCJ 13:2:114 GH 41:4:197

Gates Co, minutes of co court of pleas & quarter sessions 1812-1817, bk rev NCJ 13:1:51

Geneal holdings of the Asheville-Buncombe Technical Institute LOB 8:10:156

Geneal res hints NGS 75:1:15

Granville Co, taxables 1762 NCJ 13:1:22 13:2:100

Granville District, land grant abstr 1748-1863, bk rev CGS 18:1:16 NGS 74:4:307 STI 27:1:27

Greene Co, cem inscr 1750-1970, bk rev NCJ 13:3:175

Guard bonds & civil actions 1686-1789 (broken series) (includes VA) NCJ 13:2:90

Guildford Co, Brick Ch rec misc 1770s- , bk rev GH 41:2:141

Halifax Co, census 1830, bk rev GH 41:5:181

Halifax Co, estate rec 1835-1855 vol 3, bk rev NCJ 13:2:115

Harnett Co, census 1860, bk rev NCJ 13:1:51

NORTH CAROLINA (continued)

Harnett Co, census 1870, bk rev NCJ 13:1:52

Henderson Co, Rickman Cem NCJ 13:3:171

Hertford Co, index to *The Col & State Hist of Hertford Co NC*, bk rev GH 41:6:144

Iredell Co, estate papers 1788–1915 inventory, bk rev GH 41:6:144 NCJ 13:3:175

Iredell Co, marr 1905–1912 NCJ 13:4:227

Johnston Co, marr 1862–1899, bk rev NCJ 13:2:116

Johnston Co, marr reg 1867–1880 vol 1, bk rev NCJ 13:2:115

Johnston Co, Bentonville, cem marker & monument inscr JC 13:1:17

Johnston Co, Civil War, Confederate soldiers roster JC 13:1:3 13:2:20 13:3:40 13:4:61

Johnston Co, estate divisions 1790s–1840s JC 13:1:10 13:3:47

Johnston Co, land red 1813–1817 JC 13:4:66

Johnston Co, Rev War, anc of Smith-Bryan dau JC 13:3:45 13:4:71

Kinston, marr & death notices 1855–1859 abstr from *The Am Advocate* NCJ 13:1:2

Land grants in SC, bk rev GH 41:1:147 NCJ 13:1:53 WCK 20:1:12 NGS 75:3:231

Land grants in Gibson Co TN 1788–1796, bk rev GH 41:5:185

Lawyers 1859 roster SGE 28:123:51 28:124:13

Lincoln Co, hist (architectural), bk rev GH 41:4:197

Lincoln Co, hist, bk rev GD 18:1:30

Lincoln Co, land entries 1783–1795 abstr, bk rev NCJ 13:3:176

Lincoln Co, land entries 1798–1825 abstr, bk rev NCJ 13:3:176

NORTH CAROLINA (continued)

Magistrates' glossary of technical terms & phrases post-Civil War NCJ 13:1:45 13:2:112

Martin Co, mil? men after 1754 NCJ 13:2:113

Mil rec, militiamen paroled 1780 at Charleston SC NCJ 13:3:140

Mills River, Meth Ch Cem NCJ 13:3:145

Moore Co, Bible rec vol 1, bk rev NCJ 13:3:176

New Bern, geneal misc 1800s abstr from the *New Bern Mirror* TQR 13:4:156 14:3:107

New Bern, hist of the Sturdy Beggar Lounge TQR 14:3:103

New Bern, letters at post office 1777 TQR 14:3:116

Old Dobbs Co, geneal rec misc, bk rev NCJ 13:2:114

Onslow Co, bastardy bonds 1764–1850 NCJ 13:2:72

Orange Co, Granville, proprietary land office abstr of loose papers 1751–1763 vol 1, bk rev SCM 15:3:179

Orange Co, land purchasers vol 1, bk rev NCJ 13:3:176

Pasquotank Co, headrights 1680 NCJ 13:2:89

Pasquotank Co, taxables 1694 NCJ 13:2:91

Perquimans Co, must roll TQR 14:2:61

Pitt Co, Rev War, muster roll 1775 TQR 14:1:32

Religious groups other than Moravians in back country FC 5:2:4

Rev War pension appl NCJ 13:1:32 13:3:153

Rev War, invalid pensioners, widows & orphans c1795 roster NCJ 13:4:240

Rev War, service rec & settlements NCJ 13:2:92 13:4:235

Rev War, soldiers roster, bk rev SGS 36:3:157

Roanoke, backgrounds & preparations for voyages 1584–1590, bk rev NCJ 13:2:116

NORTH CAROLINA (continued)

Rockingham Co, census 1800, bk rev GH 41:2:142

Rowan (later Davie) Co, Cooleemee Plantation hist, bk rev NCJ 13:3:185

Rutherford Co, marr 1779–1868, bk rev NGS 74:3:236

Sampson Co, deaths 1894 abstr from news NCJ 13:2:83

Sampson Co, marr 1893–1894 abstr from news NCJ 13:3:163

Southport (Smithville) & surrounding area, cem inscr, bk rev GH 41:4:197 SCM 15:3:180 AGS 28:2:59

Stanly Co, marr 1851–1904, bk rev NCJ 13:3:177

State rec 1700s–1800s TQR 14:1:2

Surry Co, cem inscr #14, bk rev NCJ 13:1:52

Surry Co, cem inscr #15, bk rev NCJ 13:1:52

Surry Co, cem inscr & obit, bk rev NCJ 13:3:177

Surry Co, census 1800, bk rev GH 41:4:197

Surry Co, land entries 1778–1781, bk rev NCJ 13:3:177

Taxpayers 1679–1790 vol 2, bk rev WCK 20:4:60 SCM 15:4:221 NTT 7:4:123

Taxpayers 1701–1786, bk rev TCG 6:4:72 NTT 7:4:123

Transylvania Co, election rec 1902–1908, bk rev NCJ 13:2:115

Tryon & Lincoln Co, land entries abstr 1788–1780, bk rev NCJ 13:3:176

Warren Co, Warren Plains Bapt Ch hist 1785–1985, bk rev NCJ 13:3:177

Wayne Co, census 1850, bk rev NCJ 13:2:116 GH 41:4:197

Wayne Co, minutes of co court 1833 NCJ 13:2:66

Wayne Co, wills 1780–1868 vol 1, bk rev NCJ 13:2:115

Wills & admin 1753–90 abstr NCJ 13:4:218

NORTH CAROLINA (continued)

Wills & testaments guidelines NCJ 13:2:84

Wills 1665–1900 testator index, bk rev GH 41:4:196 VAG 31:3:230 SCM 15:2:119 AGS 28:3:123 NCJ 13:2:123

Wilmington, geneal misc 1807–1816 abstr from news vol 5, bk rev NCJ 13:3:176

Yadkin Co, marr 1867–1872 FC 5:1:51 5:2:47

Yancey Co, census 1850, bk rev GH 41:1:140

Yancey Co, census 1880 index, bk rev GH 41:2:142

Yancey Co, Indian removal 1838 LOB 8:7:104

Yancey Co, interviews 1981–1985, bk rev LOB 8:3:30

NORTH DAKOTA, Emmons Co, census 1900, bk rev, OC 24:1:41

Minotward Co, hist, bk rev GH 41:1:140

Renville Co, cem inscr, bk rev GH 41:6:144

Ward Co, Minot, hist, bk rev FRT 8:3:148

Williams Co, declarations of intention & naturalizations 1892–1955 index, bk rev GH 41:4:197 RAG 8:5:25

NORTH, Fam hist EN & BM BBQ 4:4:36

NORTHCUTT, Emma Jane see William Rhadamanthus MONTGOMERY

NORTHERN IRELAND, Census material of geneal value in the Public Rec Office FAM 26:2:73

Geneal repositories GGL 6:1–2:5

Geneal res guide by Neill, bk rev GH 41:1:122

Taxation & mil rec of geneal importance avail in the Public Rec Office FAM 26:1:8

NORTHERN, James Edward b1848, w Henrietta Eliz Northern VA, anc ch MAD 27:2:78

NORTON, Oliver W see Henrietta WILLCOX

Thomas b1582, w Grace ____, EN, MA, CT, geneal SB 8:5:178

NORWAY, Census indexes avail 1865, 1875, 1900 NT :44:180 :46:188

Ch rec avail 1700s–1800s NT :43:176 :46:188

Geneal words in EN OCN 10:1:11

Months of the year with EN translation CR 19:3:111

NORWOOD, Elizabeth see Arthur A SEALE

William b1545, w Elizabeth Lygon, EN, MA, geneal, bk rev GH 41:5:196

NOURSE, Artemsia see William Grandison ABBOTT

NOWLAN, Patrick d1882, death rec NAL 3:2:19

NOWLIN, P R m1882, w Mollie L Valliant, TX, marr rec DG 33:1:52

NOYES, Fam in New EN direct, bk rev LRT 6:4:253

NUNES, Sarah see Thomas POSTLES

NUNN, Fam hist VA 1700s, bk rev FRT 8:4:198

NUTT, Hester see Nathaniel McLEAN

NUZAM, Rebecca see Arnoldus CUSTER

NYE, Surname period, *The Nye Fam Assoc Inc Newsletter*, Box 134, E Sandwich MA 02537

NYSTROM, Ernest d1858, death SAG 7:2:49

O'CONNOR, Mary see Ramey ROBERTS

O'DELL, Surname period, *The O'Dell Diggin's*, POB 2040, Pinetop AZ 85935 – pensioners OH & IL, Rachel b1806 NC, fam OH & MD & NY & CO, census 1835 NY, cem NY, Georgia Irene of KS, wills NJ

O'DONOVAN, Margaret Victoria see John Joseph MAXWELL

O'KEEFE, Timothy m1863, w Bridget Mary Howe, IR, IA, geneal RT 5:2:50

O'LEARY, Patrick b1808, w Elizabeth Farley, IR, US, lineage SLV 5:4:2

O'NEAL, Augustus b1857, w Lucinda Sturdivant, desc TCG 7:4:48

James f1848, w Mary Frances ____, GA, will TCG 7:4:23

Jane see J H KEITH

O'PRY, Nancy Caroline Rebecca see William J CUMMINGS

OAHL, Dora see William SCHREIBER

OAKS, Isaac b1777, w Phebe Hutchison, NC, TN, geneal, bk rev SGS 36:3:155

OCHELTREE, Amanda see Soloman W BARKER

ODELL, Austin m1817, w Patience Harrison, Bible rec DM 50:4:163

Sylvia m1840, h Charles Thayer, OH, Bible rec OCR 28:3:116

ODLE, Martha Melvina see Somerville ADAMS

ODOM, Eldridge b1808, w Mary Walker, TN, children BWG 16:2:133

ODUM, Fam res notes NC & SC, bk rev GH 41:2:161

OGBURN, James Eldridge m1791, w Edith Youngblood, NC, fam hist JC 13:4:74

OGLETREE, John Sr b1740, geneal, bk rev GH 41:2:154

OHIO, Ashland Co, Lake Twp, geneal res guide by Ashland Co, bk rev GH 41:1:141

Ashtabula Co, Ashtabula High School grad roster 1913 AH 14:1:22

Ashtabula Co, Ashtabula, Children's Home hist sketch & resident roster 1880s–1890s AH 14:1:33

Ashtabula Co, Ashtabula, geneal misc 1849 abstr from the *Sentinel* AH 14:2:45

OHIO (continued)

Ashtabula Co, Ashtabula, lawyers roster 1816-1850 AH 14:2:66

Ashtabula Co, Colebrook, deaths 1884 AH 14:2:72

Ashtabula Co, Conneaut, geneal misc 1884, 1888 abstr from *The Conneaut Reporter* AH 14:1:16 14:4:114

Ashtabula Co, court house hist sketch AH 14:1:31

Ashtabula Co, emig 1800s AH 14:4:118

Ashtabula Co, Farnham, Durkee Cem inscr & hist sketch AH 14:4:119

Ashtabula Co, geneal misc 1850 abstr from the *Astabula Senteniel* AH 14:4:139

Ashtabula Co, geneal misc 1890 abstr from the *Geneva Times* AH 14:4:140

Ashtabula Co, Geneva, Normal Business College grad roster AH 14:1:8

Ashtabula Co, Jefferson, deaths 1905 AH 14:3:96

Ashtabula Co, Jefferson Twp, deaths 1933 AH 14:2:72

Ashtabula Co, Maple Grove Cem AH 14:4:121

Ashtabula Co, voter roster 1813 & 1843 AH 14:2:70 14:3:105

Ashtabula Co, Williamsfield, hist sketch AH 14:1:28

Belmont Co, probate court rec avail CPY 15:4:89

Birth & death rec, use of OCR 28:3:97

Census 1850 index, bk rev CRT 8:4:7

Cincinnati, geneal resources, bk rev BAT 16:2:77

Cincinnati, Pioneer Assoc 1885 member roster TTH 8:1:22 8:2:51 8:4:101

City & co direct avail, bk rev GH 41:3:165

Clark Co, geneal resources HL 1:4:129

OHIO (continued)

Clermont Co, wills, estates, & guard 1800-1851, bk rev GH 41:3:174

Clinton Co, death notices & obit 1838-1867 abstr from news, bk rev WTC 6:2:87

Columbiana Co, census 1820, bk rev GH 41:3:164 WPG 13:4:49

Columbiana Co, geneal misc 1800s abstr from news vol 1, bk rev WPG 13:4:49

Counties list HL 1:2:60

Erie Co, postal hist TFP 2: :19

Fayette Co, Cecilians Music Club member roster 1936-1937 FCG 7:2:29

Fayette Co, Jefferson Twp, Black Oak School student roster 1876-1877 FCG 6:4:62

Fayette Co, Jefferson Twp, Edgefield School student roster 1879 FCG 6:4:62

Fayette Co, post offices 1833 list FCG 7:2:24

Fayette Co, Spring Grove Ch hist sketch & pastors roster 1885-1930 FCG 6:4:63

Fayette Co, Washington Cem FCG 6:3:46 6:4:64 7:1:11 7:2:25

Firelands, railroads TFP 2: :52

Geneal & local hist sources index, bk rev GH 41:1:141

Geneal rec direct, bk rev GH 41:2:159 WPG 13:3:52 PA 35:1:54

Geneal res guide by Fenley, bk rev NYR 118:2:113

Geneal res hints IMP 6:3:70 NGS 75:2:81

Government (local) rec avail AH 14:1:35

Greene Co, lands (Congress) LOG 8:6:63

Greene Co, tax duplicate 1812 LOG 8:6:62

Hamilton Co, Cleves Pres Ch bapt 1830-1857 TTH 8:1:17 8:2:36 8:3:73 (church roll 1847-1869) TTH 8:4:109

OHIO (continued)

Hamilton Co, declaration of intention & naturalization rec avail at the co courthouse TTH 8:4:98

Hamilton Co, estate rec 1870s–1880s index TTH 8:3:78

Hamilton Co, First GE Protestant Ch deaths 1862 TTH 8:3:76

Hamilton Co, geneal res hints HL 1:2:62

Hamilton Co, geneal res addresses, bk rev GH 41:5:182

Hamilton Co, marr 1820-1826 TTH 8:1:13 8:3:75 8:4:97

Hamilton Co, pioneer cem inscr TTH 8:2:37

Henry Co, McClure, hist (oral), bk rev GH 41:5:182

Huron Co, Berlin Heights, hist TFP 7: :27

Huron Co, Chappelle Creek, legends & stories TFP 7: :41

Huron Co, Firelands, grantees (original) TFP 7: :73

Huron Co, Florence Twp, voters 1837 TFP 7: :95

Huron Co, marr 1804-1886 performed by Rev John Murphy Judson TFP 7: :36

Huron Co, New London, Day Cem add TFP 7: :56

Huron Co, Sandusky, multischools building project hist 1800s TFP 7: :1

Huron Co, True Romance Club members marr more than 40 years as of 1929 TFP 7: :13

Huron Co, Wakeman High School, 50th anniversary class of 1885 TFP 7: :87

Lake Co, Rev War, soldiers & widows, bk rev GH 41:4:198

Land purchasers 1800-1840 (southeast), bk rev PA 35:1:53 WCK 20:1:12 DM 50:3:141

Land purchasers 1800-1840 (southwest), bk rev NGS 74:4:316 APG 2:3:27 SGS 36:2:102 PA 35:1:53 CRT 8:4:7 DM 50:3:141

OHIO (continued)

Lawrence Co, census 1880 index, bk rev FRT 8:1:52

Letters 1793-1810, bk rev GD 17:4:14

Licking Co, Fallsbury Twp, hist TLL 12:4:77

Licking Co, geneal misc 1902 abstr from the *Newark Am Daily Tribune* TLL 12:3:56

Licking Co, Hanover Twp, hist TLL 12:1:9

Licking Co, Hopewell Twp, hist sketch TLL 12:3:61

Licking Co, Madison Twp, hist TLL 12:2:33

Licking Co, marr 1858-1888 abstr from obit 1904 TLL 12:4:74

Licking Co, marr 1877 & 1880 TLL 12:3:56

Licking Co, Newark, marr 1830-1896 abstr from news obit TLL 12:1:17

Licking Co, Newark, marr 1800s abstr from obit TLL 12:4:82

Licking Co, Newark, obit 1879-1880 abstr from *The Newark Am Tribune* TLL 12:1:19

Lucas Co, births, marr, & legal notices 1839 abstr from the *Maumee Express* FIR 6:1:3 6:2:17 6:3:31 6:4:43

Lucas Co, chancery rec 1843-1846 FIR 6:1:5 6:2:15 6:3:33 6:4:45

Lucas Co, navigators on the Maumee 1829-1835 FIR 6:4:42

Lucas Co, Port Lawrence Twp, tax list 1837 FIR 6:1:7 6:2:19 6:3:29 6:4:47

Mahoning (Trumbull) Co, poll lists 1807 & 1811 MM 11:8:43

Mahoning Co, Beaver Twp, Good Hope Ch rec 1815-1895, bk rev GH 41:4:198

Mahoning Co, Civil War, soldier discharges MM 11:1:SD25 11:2:SD27 11:3:SD29 11:4:SD31 11:5:SD33 11:6:SD35 11:7:SD37 11:8:SD39 11:9:SD41

OHIO (continued)

Mahoning Co, coroner's inquests 1890s–1905 MM 11:5:CI5 11:6:CI7 11:7:CI9 11:8:CI9 11:9:CI13

Mahoning Co, geneal res hints MM 11:4:

Mahoning Co, guard 1846–1860, bk rev GH 41:4:198

Mahoning Co, guard docket 1860–1865 MM 11:2:GD2-1 11:3:GD2-3 11:4:GD2-5 11:5:GD2-7 11:6:GD2-9 11:7:GD2-11 11:8:GD2-13 11:9:GD2

Mahoning Co, obit 1912–1919 MM 11:5:27

Mahoning Co, Rayen alumni direct 1907–1914 MM 11:1:3 11:2:11 11:3:17

Marietta, First Cong Ch rec vol 1, bk rev GH 41:6:145

Marietta, Harmar Cong Ch rec 1840–1855, bk rev GH 41:6:145

Marr rec abstr from *The Old Northwest Geneal Quarterly*, bk rev PA 35:1:54

Monroe Co, commissioners' journal 1815–1835, bk rev GH 41:2:159

Morgan Co, census 1900 index, bk rev GH 41:2:142

Morgan Co, marr 1869–1878, bk rev GH 41:4:198

Morgan Co, mort sched 1850 OCR 28:2:77

Muskingum Co, geneal misc 1814–1879 vol 6, bk rev GH 41:2:142

Muskingum Co, index to *Hist* 1882 by Everhart, bk rev GH 41:1:142

Muskingum Co, Union Twp, New Concord, rec misc 1833–1902, bk rev NYR 118:3:180

New Washington, St John's Evangelical Luth Ch hist, bk rev FRT 8:2:100

News 1793–1810, bk rev CR 19:1:22

Noble Co, atlas 1876 index, bk rev GH 41:4:198

OHIO (continued)

Noble Co, census 1860 index, bk rev NGS 75:1:67

Noble Co, census 1870 & 1880 index, bk rev GH 41:2:143

Noble Co, fraternal & patriotic soc 1859–1909, bk rev GH 41:2:143

Northwest Ordinance, significance of AH 14:1:4

Obit 1838–1870 abstr from news in Defiance, Fulton, Henry, Paulding, Putnam, Williams, & Wood Co, bk rev GH 41:3:165

Ohio Valley, pioneers, bk rev GH 41:4:197

Olena School hist TFP 2: :107

Pensioners 1883 index, bk rev FCG 7:2:23 GH 41:5:181 LOB 8:6:65

Pioneers roster HL 1:3:90

Portage Co, Randolph Twp. Randolph Hillside Cem OCR 28:2:62

Preble Co, Jackson Twp, Campbellstown School District #5 student roster 1892–1894 HL 2:1:22

Purchasers of land in southwestern OH 1800–1840, bk rev GH 41:1:141 AG 62:3:121

Putnam Co, Columbus Grove, Bogart Cem inscr, bk rev WPG 13:3:48

Putnam Co, Kalida, death, admin, marr, & misc notices 1845–1854 abstr from the *Kalida Venture*, bk rev GH 41:5:183

Putnam Co, Kalida, letters at post office 1845–1854, bk rev GH 41:5:183

Putnam Co, Monroe Twp, cem inscr, bk rev GH 41:3:174

Putnam Co, Pleasant Twp, Columbus Grove, Bogart Cem inscr, bk rev GH 41:1:142

Rev War & War of 1812, patriots bibl annotated, bk rev NGS 74:4:312 OCR 28:3:151

Rev War, pensions OCR 28:2:85

OHIO (continued)

Rev War, pensions rejected FCG 7:2:32

Richland Co, Sandusky Twp, criminal docket 1844-1895 OCR 28:3:106

Rocky River, hist CPY 16:2:39

Ross Co, geneal direct of rec, bk rev GH 41:6:166

Rural Dale, Rural Lodge #157 IOOF, hist BHN 20:3:103

Scioto Co, marr 1803-1860, bk rev NGS 75:2:156 WPG 13:4:37 SGS 36:4:209 APG 2:3:26 GH 41:3:165

Settlements & frontier defenses in southwest OH 1788-1795, bk rev TTH 8:2:35

Settlers purchasing land 1800-1840 in southeast, bk rev WMG 3:1:44

Settlers purching land 1800-1840 in southwest, bk rev WMG 3:1:44

Source rec abstr from the *OH Geneal Quarterly*, bk rev GJ 15:2:112

State fair 1853 HL 1:5:143

Tax rec 1800-1825, bk rev NGS 74:3:234

Tax rec c1800-c1830, bk rev GJ 15:2:111

Van Wert Co, marr 1852-1864, bk rev GH 41:4:198

Virginia Mil District, land patents vol 4 part 2, bk rev NGS 75:1:66

Warren Co, Agricultural Soc officers roster 1850-1872 HL 1:5:144

Warren Co, apprenticeship & indenture 1824-1832 & 1864-1867, bk rev GH 41:4:198 TTH 8:4:94

Warren Co, census 1840 pensioners HL 2:3:88

Warren Co, citizenship papers 1850s-1890s HL 3:3:75 3:4:101

Warren Co, Civil War, Wilson Guard Company roster HL 1:4:120

OHIO (continued)

Warren Co, Civil War, soldiers discharged HL 1:3:87 1:4:106 1:5:149 2:1:8 2:2:33 2:3:86 3:1:12 3:2:36 3:3:66 3:4:95 4:1:8 4:2:33 4:3:68 4:4:105 5:1:18 5:2:44 5:3:69 6:1:8

Warren Co, Clearcreek Twp, settlers (early) roster HL 1:1:19

Warren Co, Clearcreek Twp, Springboro, Friends Cem HL 1:3:82

Warren Co, Clearcreek Twp, Springboro, United Brethren Ch pastor assignments 1837-1910 HL 2:3:72

Warren Co, clerk of court bk avail 1800s HL 3:3:71

Warren Co, co fair 1853 HL 1:5:138

Warren Co, cook bk c1900 participants roster HL 5:2:40

Warren Co, court officers roster 1803-1875 HL 4:3:84

Warren Co, deed abstr vol 1 & 2 HL 2:2:32

Warren Co, deed res hints HL 1:5:157

Warren Co, deeds 1799-1830 index HL 3:1:7 3:2:38 3:3:68 3:4:98 4:1:11 4:2:36 4:3:87 4:4:96 5:1:10 5:2:35 5:3:66 5:4:95 6:1:16

Warren Co, Deerfield Twp, Mason, hist HL 1:1:8

Warren Co, Deerfield Twp, Unity Cem HL 1:2:50

Warren Co, Franklin Bapt Ch hist sketch HL 4:3:75

Warren Co, Franklin Meth Ch marr 1859-1875 HL 1:1:20 1:2:48

Warren Co, Franklin Twp, Tapscott Cem HL 1:4:103

Warren Co, guard 1818-1823 HL 2:1:26 4:1:6 4:2:39 4:3:65

Warren Co, Harlan Twp, Osborn Cem HL 2:1:21

Warren Co, hist outline 1803-1860 HL 1:1:5

Warren Co, imm to IN HL 3:1:11

OHIO (continued)

Warren Co, jurors 1866 roster HL 1:4:131

Warren Co, jury (grand) 1808–1811 roster HL 1:3:91

Warren Co, Lebanon, letters at post office 1866 HL 3:2:43

Warren Co, Lebanon, student roster 1798 HL 1:1:5

Warren Co, marr 1803–1815 HL 1:4:108

Warren Co, marr 1822–1823 abstr from the *Warren Co News* HL 4:3:79

Warren Co, Mason, Muddy Creek (Keltner) Cem HL 1:1:32

Warren Co, Massie Twp, Harveysburg, hist sketch HL 2:3:66

Warren Co, Massie Twp, Oregon Mill ledger 1863 HL 2:2:43

Warren Co, McClure Funeral Home rec 1898–1899 HL 1:3:76

Warren Co, mil officers roster 1804 HL 4:3:74

Warren Co, Muddy Creek Cem HL 4:3:80

Warren Co, muster roll of the Union Guards HL 4:3:78

Warren Co, obit 1825 abstr from the *Star & Gazette* HL 4:1:15

Warren Co, obit 1866, 1876 abstr from the *Western Star* HL 1:3:78 1:4:118

Warren Co, obit 1919–1923 index HL 5:1:15 5:2:46 5:3:74 6:1:13

Warren Co, persons attending the golden wedding of Josiah & Clarissa Warwick 1879 HL 1:2:38

Warren Co, pet 1834 HL 3:1:22 3:2:42

Warren Co, pioneer fam roster HL 5:2:49 5:3:80 5:4:97

Warren Co, Rev War, soldiers roster HL 1:1:24 (corr & add) HL 1:2:47

Warren Co, Springboro, High School commencement exercises 1898 HL 3:2:46

Warren Co, Springboro, reminiscence 1850s HL 2:3:80

OHIO (continued)

Warren Co, tavern lic 1852 HL 3:1:21

Warren Co, tax list 1810 HL 1:1:14

Warren Co, Turtlecreek election 1854 HL 1:4:123

Warren Co, Turtlecreek Twp, settlers (early) roster HL 1:1:4

Warren Co, Unity Cem HL 4:3:81

Warren Co, War of 1812, soldier roster HL 4:1:27

Warren Co, Washington School hist sketch HL 6:1:20

Warren Co, Washington Twp, directors roster 1866–1905 HL 4:3:90 4:4:101

Warren Co, Washington Twp, Ft Ancient School student roster 1881–1888 HL 3:1:14

Warren Co, Washington Twp, hist sketch HL 1:4:124

Warren Co, Washington Twp, School District #5 1895–1896 student roster HL 2:1:25

Warren Co, Waynesville, High School grad roster 1872–1906 HL 2:3:76

Warren Co, WWII, vet, bk rev GH 41:2:142

Warren Co,, Springboro, Miami Valley College HL 1:4:115

Washington Co, Aurelius Twp, census 1890 special sched of surviving soldiers, sailors, marines, & widows of the Civil War WC 4:1:5

Washington Co, Barlow Twp, census 1890 special sched of surviving soldiers, sailors, marines, & widows of the Civil War WC 4:1:6 4:2:9

Washington Co, births 1869 WC 4:1:7

Washington Co, deaths 1868–1870 WC 4:1:8 4:3:11

Washington Co, hist sketch of Unitarian Universalists WC 4:3:8

Washington Co, imm & naturalization abstr 1808–1840, bk rev GH 41:6:144

187

OHIO (continued)

Wellsville, Iris Lodge rec 1848–1920 OCR 28:3:118

Williams Co, Jefferson Twp, cem inscr, bk rev GH 41:3:165

Wills & estates to 1850, index, bk rev CR 19:1:22

Wood Co, atlas 1875–1912, bk rev GH 41:6:144

Wood Co, Bloom Twp, cem inscr, bk rev GH 41:2:143

Wood Co, Henry & Jackson Co, Faylor, Hough, Sherman, & Bethel Cem inscr, bk rev GH 41:5:182

Wood Co, Henry & Jackson Twp, New & Old Maplewood Cem inscr, bk rev GH 41:5:182

Wood Co, Milton Twp, Milton Twp Cem & St Louis Cath Ch Cem inscr, bk rev GH 41:5:182

Wood Co, wills, estates, guard 1851–1900, bk rev GH 41:2:143

World War I, roster of the 112th Engineers of the 37th Div OH Hq Det which arrived in FR 1818–1819 CPY 16:1:4 16:2:33

Youngstown, Swedish Mission Ch, hist & ch reg rec & ministerial acct 1886–1930, bk rev GH 41:2:144

OKENFUSS, Maxmilian m1850, w Barbara Harter, geneal, bk rev MSG 7:3:171

OKLAHOMA, Anadarko, Mary Gregory Memorial Mission School rec 1898–1907 TTT 11:1:7

Beckham Co, Erick, Garrett Cem OK 32:3:107

Beckham Co, Erick, Vannerson Cem OK 32:3:108

Beckham Co, obit & inscr from Buffalo-Poarch, Old Sayre, Old Doxey, & Mulberry Cem, bk rev GH 41:1:142

Centerville, District 107, hist 1902–1942, bk rev OK 32:1:6

Choctaw Academy student roster 1826 OK 32:3:89

Coal Co, Boiling Springs Indian Cem OPC 18:1:12

OKLAHOMA (continued)

Coal Co, Boiling Springs, Salt Creek Cem OPC 18:1:12

Coal Co, Calvary Cem OPC 18:1:9

Coal Co, Jackson Twp, Globe Cem OPC 18:1:7

Coal Co, Keel Fam Cem OPC 18:1:9

Coal Co, Legal Cem OPC 18:1:9

Coal Co, Lehigh, Finley Cem OPC 18:1:10

Coal Co, Lone Star Cem OPC 18:1:11

Coal Co, map OPC 18:1:14

Coal Co, Okely or Oconee Cem OPC 18:1:11

Coal Co, Old Davis Cem OPC 18:1:10

Comanche Co, news avail on microfilm TTT 11:4:170

Craig Co, Bluejacket, Bluejacket Cem OK 32:3:96

Geneal rec misc by Bivins, Murphy, & Tankersley, bk rev CAL 6:4:91 CCN 87:6: TTC 11:3:61

Geneal res hints SCS 24:4:75

Green Co, Broken Arrow & Coweta, cem inscr vol 1, bk rev GH 41:2:159

Haskell Co, marr vol 1, bk rev GH 41:4:199

Hobart, direct (business) 1905 TTT 11:1:23

Index to appl for reg for homestead entry within the Kiowa, Comanche, & Apache ceded lands TTT 11:2:86 11:3:141

Indian Territory, Muskogee, geneal misc 1893–1897 abstr from the *Muskogee Weekly Phoenix*, bk rev GH 41:1:143

Ireton, hist, bk rev GH 41:2:144

Jefferson Co, marr 1907–1920 TTT 11:2:93 11:3:117

Latimer Co, Red Oak City Cem inscr, bk rev GH 41:4:199

Lawton Land District, index to appl for reg for homestead entry within the Kiowa, Comanche, & Apache ceded lands 1901 TTT 11:4:161

OKLAHOMA (continued)
Lawton, automobiles (Ford) sold & delivered 1913 TTT 11:4:190
Lawton, hist sketch TTT 11:4:160
Lawton, Lawton Monument Company rec 1800s-1900s TTT 11:1:14 11:2:76 11:3:112 11:4:166
LeFlore Co, lic of 13 dentists & 73 doctors 1905-1918, bk rev GH 41:1:142
Mayes Co, hist, bk rev GH 41:5:183
McAlester, Chaney's Funeral Home rec vol 1, bk rev GH 41:4:199
McClain Co, hist bk 1, bk rev OK 32:1:7 GH 41:3:165
McClain Co, hist bk 2, bk rev GH 41:6:145
Miami, First United Meth Ch rec 1891-1984, bk rev OK 32:2:44
Muldrow, hist 1887-1987, bk rev GH 41:6:146
Ottawa Co, Bluejecket, Bluejacket Cem inscr of Am service men SSO 4:1:10
Ottawa Co, Century, direct 1917-1918 business SSO 4:1:16
Ottawa Co, Sixkiller Cem inscr, bk rev GH 41:4:199
Ottawa Co, Tar River direct SSO 4:1:14
Place names, bk rev RAG 8:2:25 SGI 4:1:21
Pontotoc Co, Ada Garden Club member roster 1934-1935 OPC 19:1:18
Pontotoc Co, Ada Jr High School grad 1940 OPC 18:1:28
Pontotoc Co, Allen, marr 1919-1921 OPC 19:1:26
Pontotoc Co, executor's inventory & affidavits bk A OPC 18:2:44 18:3:71
Pontotoc Co, marr 1910-1925 OPC 18:1:16 18:2:53 18:3:79
Pontotoc Co, Stratford, geneal misc 1926-1931 abstr from the *Stratford Star* OPC 18:1:21 18:3:75 19:1:19

OKLAHOMA (continued)
Roger Mills Co, Kiowa, Kiowa Cem inscr, bk rev OZ 6:3:115
Sequoyah Co, births vol 1, 2, & 3, bk rev GH 41:6:145
Sequoyah Co, cem inscr vol 6 & 7, bk rev GH 41:2:144
Stephens Co, census 1910 for Brown, King, & Hope Twp, bk rev TTT 11:4:188
Tulsa Co, cem inscr vol 1, bk rev GH 41:6:145 (vol 1 & 2) SB 8:3:103
War of 1812, index to vol soldiers TTT 11:2:98
Washita Co, Corinth Cem OK 32:2:45
World War I, Field Hospital Co 359 90th Division 1918-1919 OK 32:1:11
OKLAHOMA TERRITORY, Caddo Co, St Patrick's Mission 1898-1907 student roster TTT 11:4:175
Census 1890 TA 22:1:18 22:2-3:34
Comanche Co, Commissioner's proceedings 1901-1905 TTT 11:1:36 11:2:81 11:3:146 11:4:181
Fort Sill, Cache Creek Mission School rec 1881-1887 TTT 11:2:73
OKRUHLIK, Martin f1870, w Rosina Mocola, Moravia, TX, photograph ND 6:1:12
OLAH, Edward S m1940, w Emma M Kern, marr rec CPY 15:4:87
OLDER, Hannah see Orlander Porter BOWEN
OLDFIELD, Jonathan bc1789, NY, OH, IL, anc ch OCG 17:4:28
OLIN, Frances A see William R MUMFORD
OLIPHANT, Elizabeth see William BULLOCK
OLIVER, Abigail see James JOHNSON
Elizabeth see Daniel BRUMLEY
Fam census rec 1726-1966, bk rev BWG 16:2:156

189

OLIVER (continued)

George b1726, VA, NC, geneal, bk rev GH 41:6:162

Jonathan f1769, NJ, accusation GMN 62:3:134

OLMSTEAD, Lucy Ann b1837, ON, anc ch TB 13:4:35

OLMSTED, Louisa Mary b1848, NY, VT, anc ch AG 62:4:228

OLNEY, Thomas bc1600, w Mary Ashton, EN, RI, biog sketch RIR 13:2:22

OLOFSDOTTER, Anna see Olof LIND

OLOMON, Jim d1844, w Sylvia Mary Tisinger, EN, anc ch FF 15:4:138

OLSON, Anders b1793, w Anna Anderson, SN, anc ch KIL 15:2:27

OLTMANNS, Siebrand Algers m1805, w Heba Heyen, GE, IL, geneal, bk rev FRT 8:2:107

OMLID, Guro see Bjug HARSTAD

ONIONS, Jane Elizabeth see Jhony M MORRIS

ONSTOTT, John H see Veda E MASSEY

OPWA, Fort Madison, voter reg rec 1928 HH 22:2:77

ORCHARD, Ruth M see Philip W PARKER

OREGON, Board of Directors of the OR Pioneer Assoc 1876 roster TB 14:1:26

Clatsop Co, Columbia River, life on CT 7:3:14

Clatsop Co, geology of south coast CT 7:2:3

Clatsop Co, Point Adams Packing Company, hist CT 7:3:3

Clatsop Cp, Seaside Resort, hist sketch CT 7:2:32

Columbia Co, Veronia, Clear Creek Cem YV 19:2:76

Douglas Co, Hermann Precinct, voters list & poll bk 1920, bk rev GH 41:1:143

Hist of the Sisters of St Mary 1886-1986, bk rev EWA 24:3:211

OREGON (continued)

Jackson Co, births 1863-1910, bk rev GH 41:4:199

Jackson Co, divorce index, bk rev GH 41:3:174

Jackson Co, funeral notices, bk rev GH 41:5:183

Jackson Co, Medford, Eastwood IOOF Cem inscr, bk rev GH 41:4:199

Jackson Co, naturalizations, declaration of intention, & cert of citizenship 1833-1905, bk rev GH 41:3:174

Jackson Co, poll tax list 1894-1895, bk rev GH 41:3:174

Jackson Co, Rogue River, Woodville Cem inscr, bk rev GH 41:4:199

Josephine Co, Williams, cem inscr, bk rev GH 41:4:199

Lane Co, Junction City, cem inscr (Danish) GFP 36:4:171

Lorane, hist, bk rev GH 41:5:184

Mayflower anc, bk rev GH 41:1:143

Mort sched 1880 index GFP 36:3:116

Multnomah Co, cem locations GFP 36:3:119

Name index to the *Illustrated Hist of Central OR*, bk rev FRT 8:2:104

Polk Co, Dallas Cem inscr, bk rev GH 41:2:144

South County, Indian trails CT 7:2:27

Spencer Butte, pionners, bk rev OZ 5:3:104

Yamhill Co, pioneer fam roster GFP 36:3:137 36:4:187 37:1:37 37:2:87

Clatsop Co, census 1850, bk rev GH 41:3:174

ORELL, Q L m1881, w N C Shilling, Bible rec FP 30:4:174

ORI, Caterina A D M see Luigi BERTOGLI

ORRELL, Surname period, *The Orrell Fam Geneal Assoc Newsletter*, 145 Sanford Ave, Catonsville MD 21228-5140

OSBORN, Jane f1838, IL, will abstr IG 23:1:11

Mahala Ann see William B BAILEY

Malinda see Caleb BROWN

Rebecca McNerlyn see Edward Francis COLTER

William b1764, w Elizabeth Osborn, NC, biog sketch BGS 19:1:19

OSBOURNE, Samuel b1827, w Mary Lendrum & Mary Ann Slack, PA, geneal, bk rev GH 41:5:193

OSTEEN, Miriam S see John Massey BRYANT

OTIS, George Washington m1827, w Eliza Holmes, Bible rec RT 4:3:69

OTTERSON, Sarah d1807, NC, estate TQR 13:4:154

OTTESEN, Christen b1847, w Inga Marie Larsen Christensen, DK, MN, anc ch FCT :72:9

Jacob Aal f1852, NW, WI, biog, bk rev CHI 60:3:141

OUABARD, Joseph-Philippe m1725, w Marie-Charlotte Guillet, fam hist JMS 10:1:3

OUTERBRIDGE, Daniel Woolridge f1789, w Sarah Seon, BM, fam rec BBQ 4:2:20

ELizabeth Burrows see Richard Sparehook ALGATE

Thomas b1573, w Elizabeth Ellis & Ann ____, BM, geneal BBQ 4:2:13

Thomas f1688, w Martha Stowe, BM, geneal BBQ 4:3:24

OUTMAN, Stephen S b1849, w Hattie Roberts, KS, MO, biog sketch KL 7:3:12

OVERALL, Surname period, *Overalls All Over*, 133 Kingwood Dr, Chattanooga TN 37412 - fam KY & VA & MO, John of KY, preachers,

OVERBECK, Elizabeth f1908, IL, birthday CRT 8:4:35

OVERFELT, John dc1842, TN, will BWG 16:1:35

OVERHOLSER, Surname period, *Overholser Fam Assoc Bulletin*, 413 Appletree Rd, Cap Hill PA 17011

OVERHOLTZER, Christian A b1740, w Christina Musselman, PA, geneal, bk rev GH 41:6:162

OWEN, Charles Harrison, w Mary Cates, NC, geneal, bk rev GH 41:6:162

David d1790, w Sarah Schmeitzler, PA, fam rec add BWG 16:2:140

Gideon f1833, w Nancy Owen, NY, pension appl NGS 74:3:174

OWENS, Gideon b1765, w Nancy ____, NY, identity of wife NYR 118:3:143

Wm J m1900, w Elizabeth Kelley, NE, marr rec NW 9:2:15

OWINGS, Fam hist 1685-1985, bk rev RAG 8:3:23

Richard f1685, MD, geneal, bk rev NYR 118:2:118 TNB 2:2:5

PACE, Eliza Jane d1914, NC, MO, anc ch CCS 9:2:63

John K b1825, w Jane Wallis, TN, MO, children OZ 8:1:26

PADDOCK, Jonathan f1833, w Mercy Weaver, NY, IL, fam hist WTC 17:4:116

PADEN, John Thomas b1859, w Isabelle Reeder, GA, anc ch NC :93:9

Robert N b1830, w Illinois E Blackwell, KY, IL, biog sketch FF 15:3:26

PADGETT, Elisha bc1795, w Vinia Bettett, SC, FL, lineage FLG 10:4:153

PADGHAM, Charles Hebert b1877, w Gertrude Clarice Cochran, NY, WA, biog sketch YV 19:2:50

PAGE, Ebenezer f1810, MA, NY, OH, geneal, bk rev NYR 118:3:184

Juliana b1816, h James Johnson Edwards & Perrin L Delozier, TN, IL, MO, geneal, bk rev NYR 118:2:123

PAGE (continued)

Sally see John CRAIG

Sarah Elizabeth see James Madison SMALL

PAIGE, John b1685, NC, geneal, bk rev GH 41:6:163

PAINE, John b1658, w Elizabeth Belcher & Martha ____, MA, RI, geneal RIR 13:3:49

PAINTER, E J see Mary Elizabeth MONTGOMERY

Mary see James BOLES

Mercy see Edward ALLYN

PALATINE GENEALOGY, Settlers in NY, bk rev EWA 24:1:53

PALERMO, Fam hist IY, bk rev MA 11:3:77

PALLY, Marinus m1737, w Maria Dorothea Beer, SW, IL, geneal, bk rev GH 41:6:163

PALMER, Adelia Ann see Spencer Eugene KINNEY

Catherine see Humphrey JOHNSTON

Fam hist NY, bk rev NYR 118:4:250

Rachel see John JARED

Sarah see Henry ROWLEY

Walter bc1585, EN, MA, CT, geneal, bk rev NGS 75:3:235

Walter bc1585, MA, CT, geneal, bk rev CTN 19:4:707

PALMORE, Benjamin C b1853, w Julia Margaret Lyle, VA, TX, anc ch AGS 28:2:67

PALMS, Jan Jr b1700, w Joanna Truyts, MI, geneal FAH 5:1:7

PAMPLIN, Sally see Samuel SHELBOURNE

PANGBORN, Clara Belle see Gotleib MEYERS

PANKEY, Charlotte Hook see William Baker JOHNSON

PARADIS, David P b1908, w Dorothy L Drake, WA, biog sketch YV 19:1:12

Peter George b1860, QB, WA, biog sketch YV 19:1:12

PARCHER, Elias f1690, NH, VT, MA, OH, geneal, bk rev BAT 16:4:171

PARDICK, William Worder b1853, w Katherine Hanna, IN, CA, biog sketch SCS 24:1:17

PARIS, Fam cem Grayson Co KY KA 22:4:237

PARK/E/S, Surname period, *The Newsletter of the Parke Soc Inc*, 805 Evergreen Dr, Reading PA 19610

PARKE, Surname period, *Newsletter of the Parke Soc*, POB 590, Milwaukee WI 53201
– Richard of SC, Jacob of MA, Timothy & desc, fam in EN, John of VT

PARKER, Elizabeth A see John H SHORT

James bc1752, w Anna Doty, KY, OH, IL, geneal, bk rev NYR 118:3:182

Mary Whitefield see Nehemiah Draper WELCH

Philip W f1860, w Ruth M Orchard, EN, IL, CA, biog sketch SCS 24:3:61

Surname period, *Parker Papers*, S 4204 Conklin, Spokane WA 99203

PARKHURST, George m1725, w Tabitha Fulham, MA, fam rec NEH 4:2:73

PARKINS, Mary see Hugh FOUCH

PARKINSON, Mary Ann Nutucase b1836, EN, OR, Bible rec GFP 37:2:66

PARKMAN, Ebenezer d1782, MA, diary abstr 1765–1767 MA 11:1:20

PARKS, Margaret see Matthew MCCLAUGHRY

Martha Elizabeth see John Franklin COOK

Otis Henry b1821, NY, anc ch BG 8:3:63

PARRISH, James m1877, w Salina Hopkins, Bible rec NTT 7:2:67

PARROTT, Richard Sr d1686, w Margaret Haywood, VA, anc ch WB 17:1:33

PARSONS, Bridget (Knight) see William VARNEY

PARSONS (continued)
Fam hist, bk rev IG 23:2:63
Hiram b1826, w Martha Goode, AL, MO, fam hist sketch OZ 6:2:78
Hiram m1828, w Sarah A Loss, NY, Bible rec DAR 121:5:333
John F m1804, w Clarissa Hovey, Bible rec DAR 121:5:334
Johnathan b1797, w Lydia Patterson, NC, MO, children OZ 6:2:75
Loss m1858, w Helen M Hollister, Bible rec DAR 121:4:334
Nancy see Thomas STOKES
Timothy b1769, NY, CT, Bible rec DAR 121:4:333
William f1776, VA, heirs TN 7:1:13
PARTMANN, Anna Dorothy see Peter BECKER
PASSONS, Thomas R b1828, w Susan J Douglas, TN, CA, biog sketch SCS 24:5:113
PATE, Susannah bc1820, NC, anc ch CR 19:4:168
PATENAUDE, Surname period, *Our Fathers - Paternoster-Patenotre-Patenaude-Patenode*, 639 Pontiac Rd, Oxford MI 48051
PATRICK, Sarh P see Wm S EDWARDS
PATTEN, Isaac Sr, w Jane Norris, IN, geneal, bk rev NYR 118:2:120
PATTERSON, Agnes see John Robert KIRKPATRICK
Esther see James HENRY
Lydia see Johnathan PARSONS
Matthew f1762, NC, GA, MS, geneal LOB 8:10:149
Rachel see Daniel BRUMLEY
S T see Mahala A WELCH
PATTON, Mary Ann see John Kilman STORIE
Surname period, *Patton Exchange Letter*, 305 Shoshone Ct, Toms River NJ 08753
PATTY, Ellen see Aaron HART

PATY, Delila Evaline see William Henry DUNSON
PAUL, Agnes b1852, ON, anc ch CR 19:4:172
Alva George Henry b1856, w Martha Ella Bagley, NH, CA, biog sketch SCS 24:4:89
PAYNE, Bettie see Peter KING
Celelon Washington see George Curtis BLAKELY
Clelon Warington see George Curtis BLAKELY
Edmond L m1874, w Susan T Ledbetter, AL, Bible rec VC 8:2:46
John Calvin b1855, w Emily Sneed, AL, anc ch NAS 25:4:127
PAYNTER, Mary see James MUSSON
PAYTON, Yelverton b1755, VA, KY, geneal, bk rev NYR 118:2:122
PEABODY, Francis b1614, EN, anc ch FTR :97:7
PEACE, Pleasant Marion bc1790, w Mary J ___, NC, AL, MO, geneal OZ 7:1:33
PEARCE, Fam hist EN & US, bk rev THT 15:1:29
PEARRE, William b1791, MD, cem inscr WMG 3:4:189
PEARSON, Martha see Henry STEDDOM
William B b1861, TN, Bible rec YTD 3:2:1
PEASLEE, Mark b1777, NH, anc ch BG 8:3:65
PECK, Norris m1822, w Elizabeth Edwards Langdon, Bible rec CTN 20:1:57
PEDEN, John f1772, w Mary Smith, PA, SC, geneal, bk rev GH 41:3:170
PEDERSEN, Even m1885, w Marthe Eriksen, Bible rec RT 5:2:49
PEDERSON, Hannah see Severin Christian BRONNUM
PEEPLES, Henry Madison mc1719, w Martha ___, Bible rec MCG 10:3:147

193

PEET, John b1597, CT, geneal, bk rev SGS 36:3:154 GH 41:3:170

PELS, Evert Everts m1641, w Jannetje Sijmons, HO?, marr rec NYR 118:2:75

PENCE, Abraham f1807, SC, geneal, bk rev GH 41:3:177

Mary O see William J DeFORE

PENINGTON, J G f1849, AR, CA, letters SCS 24:1:15

James m1844, w Eliza Lowe?, Bible rec BCG 16:2:63

PENNINGTON, James Mattison b1820, w Martha Conner, SC, AL, anc ch MCA 6:2:71

William bc1764, NC, anc ch EK 23:1:36

PENNOYER, Robert f1635, New EN, NY, CN, geneal, bk rev NYR 118:1:56

PENNSYLVANIA, Allegheny (now Pittsburgh), Union Dale Cem inscr, bk rev GH 41:1:146 GH 41:2:146 (vol 6, 7, & 8) GH 41:4:199

Allegheny Co, cem inscr vol 1, bk rev GH 41:1:146

Allegheny Co, McCandless Twp, Herr's/Norr's Chapel Cem WPG 13:3:9

Allegheny Co, Pittsburg, architecture, bk rev WPG 13:3:42

Allegheny Co, Pittsburgh, geneal misc 1797-1803 abstr from the *Pittsburgh Gazette*, bk rev GH 41:2:146

Allegheny Co, Pittsburgh, Smithfield Street Meth Ch bapt 1832-1879, bk rev GH 41:5:184 WPG 14:1:53

Allegheny Co, wills 1789-1844 abstr, bk rev VAG 31:3:233

Armstrong Co, Boggs Twp, Calhoun Cem WPG 14:1:38

Armstrong Co, Bradys Bend & Perry Twp, cem inscr, bk rev WPG 14:1:50

Armstrong Co, Civil War, donations roster 1861 WPG 13:4:31

PENNSYLVANIA (continued)

Armstrong Co, Freeport, hist 1876-1886, bk rev GH 41:4:200

Armstrong Co, Madison Twp, Kellersburg, hist, bk rev WPG 13:4:47

Armstrong Co, Sugar Creek Twp, Sugar Creek, St Patrick's Roman Cath Ch bapt 1803, 1805, 1812, 1837-1980, bk rev WPG 13:3:41

Beaver Co, Beaver, geneal misc 1830-58 abstr from the *Argus*, bk rev GH 41:2:145

Beaver Co, Civil War, draftees 1862 roster GJB 11:3:13

Beaver Co, Darlington Twp, Darlington, Greersburg Academy student roster 1802-1902 WPG 13:3:53

Beaver Co, deaths 1800s WPG 14:1:42

Beaver Co, debate roster 1848 WPG 13:4:63

Beaver Co, Frankfort Springs, Male & Female Academy & Normal School student roster 1873 GJB 11:4:15

Beaver Co, Hanover Twp, Harsha, School student roster 1901 GJB 11:4:18

Beaver Co, Hopewell Twp, New Sheffield School student roster 1908 GJB 11:4:19

Beaver Co, Hopewell Twp, tax list 1813 GJB 11:4:2

Beaver Co, Hopewell Twp, White Oak Flats Pres Ch member roster 1810 GJB 11:4:17

Beaver Co, marr prior to 1830 implied by Will Bk A GJB 11:3:1

Beaver Co, North Beaver Twp, tax list 1803 GJB 11:4:11

Beaver Co, Ohioville Borough, Highland Cem GJB 11:3:9

Beaver Co, pet 1838 WPG 14:1:41

Beaver Co, warrantee & patent maps index, bk rev GH 41:1:146

PENNSYLVANIA (continued)

Bedford Co, Bible rec (unrecorded), bk rev GH 41:6:146

Bedford Co, marr 1791-1798, bk rev WPG 13:3:55

Bedford Co, tax lists 1772 WPG 14:1:31

Berks Co, Rev War, soldiers, bk rev NYR 118:3:180

Berks Co, Rockland Twp, Dryville, Mertz/Dryville/Rockland/Christ Evangelical Luth Ch rec misc 1750-1900, bk rev WPG 13:4:43

Berks Co, Rockland Twp, Mertz Ch pastoral rec of Rev B E Kramlich 1860-1900, bk rev WPG 13:4:43

Bibl of PA-CT controversy, bk rev GH 41:1:144

Bibl of western PA rivers, bk rev GH 41:1:144

Blair Co, deaths 1849-1852 abstr from the *Blair Co Whig* WPG 13:3:10

Bucks Co, ch cong 1887 list BCN 7:1:7

Bucks Co, death rec sources BCN 7:1:3

Bucks Co, declarations & naturalizations 1802-1906, bk rev MN 18:1:40

Bucks Co, declarations & naturalizations 1802-1906, bk rev NGS 75:3:237

Bucks Co, geneal res aid, Bk of Arrivals to 1687 BCN 6:3:33

Bucks Co, hist (development) sketch BCN 7:1:1

Bucks Co, marr notices 1835-1860 vol 3, bk rev RAG 8:2:26 (vol 2 & 3) GH 41:4:200

Bucks Co, marr notices 1804-1860 abstr from the *Bucks Co Intelligencer*, bk rev PM 10:3:41

Bucks Co, marr notices 1804-1834 abstr from the *Intelligencer*, bk rev NYR 118:4:244

Bucks Co, road pet & rec, use of BCN 6:4:49

PENNSYLVANIA (continued)

Bucks Co, Southwest Rockhill Twp, early settlers MFH 6:1:26

Bucks Co, twp data to help with geneal res BCN 7:1:4

Butler Co, declarations of intention to naturalize filed by members of the Harmony Soc 1810-1811 WPG 13:4:17

Butler Co, Middlesex Twp, census 1840 unmicrofilmed page WTC 12:3:137

Butler Co, Rev War vet settling in co, bk rev GH 41:6:166

Cambria Co, Loretto, St Michael's Roman Cath Ch bapt & burials 1797-1899, bk rev WPG 13:3:41

Centre Co, emig to KS 1878-1879 roster TS 29:3:92

Chester Co, Conestoga Twp, Conestoga, tax list 1718 LCH 1:1:9

Chester Co, elopements & other fam problems 1729-1789 LCC 4:2:67 4:3:46 4:4:83

Chester Co, Great Valley Pres Ch Cem PA 35:1:17

Clearfield Co, geneal misc 1854-1855 abstr from the *Raftman's Journal* WPG 14:1:25

Dauphin Co, cem inscr vol 2, bk rev GH 41:4:200

Dauphin Co, Harrisburg, Zion Luth Ch pastoral acts 1795-1827, bk rev GH 41:4:200

Dauphin Co, marr 1785-1810, bk rev GH 41:4:200

Easton, hist, bk rev AG 62:3:124

Erie Co, Summit Twp, abandoned cem WPG 13:4:64

Fam hist & geneal, bk rev MAD 27:1:38

Fayette & Greene Co, marr performed by Rev Job Rossell 1845-1884, bk rev WPG 13:3:42

Fayette Co, Sheets School reunion 1912 WPG 13:3:34

PENNSYLVANIA (continued)

Fayette Co, War of 1812, hist on OH frontier & soldier roster WPG 13:4:3

Forest Co, cem inscr, bk rev GH 41:5:184 WPG 14:1:48 FCG 7:1:5 TTH 8:4:95

Fort Pitt, hist outline to 1976 WPG 13:3:3

French & Indian Wars, hist, bk rev WPG 13:3:42

Fulton Co, census 1850, bk rev GH 41:2:146

Fulton Co, tax (US direct), bk rev NGS 74:3:230

Fulton Co, wills 1850-1900 index, bk rev GH 41:4:200

Geneal & hist rec collect, bk rev SCS 24:2:34

Geneal mss to collect of the Geneal Soc of PA, bk rev PA 35:1:54 CC 10:4:5

Geneal mss user's guide, bk rev BAT 16:2:77

Geneal rec avail at the Geneal Soc of PA PA 35:1:29

Geneal res aid, PA Archives LCC 4:3:31

Geneal res guide by Schweitzer, bk rev AG 62:3:123 NGS 75:1:59 PA 35:1:54

Geneal res in the State Lib of PA & the PA State Archives MKT 10:2:28

Germantown, settlers index to *The Settlement of Germantown & the Causes Which Led To It* ANC 22:2:81

Greene Co, Cumberland District, Huston's School souvenir bklet 1903 WPG 13:3:57

Hist, bk rev WTC 5:2-3:102

Hist (chronology) of western PA & District of West Augusta VA, bk rev GH 41:1:144

Hist 1786-1797 western PA, bk rev LRT 6:1:204

Hist of col PA, bk rev GGD 3:2:79

Hist outline 1860-1898 for Pittsburgh & western PA WPG 14:1:9

PENNSYLVANIA (continued)

Hist sketch of the GE 7th Day Bapt Ch 1728-1987 SLB 6:6:265

Index to *Notes & Queries* by Egles, bk rev GH 41:2:145

Indiana Co, atlas 1871 abstr TQ 7:4:5

Indiana Co, Banks Twp, Bear Run Reformed Pres Cem WPG 13:3:19

Indiana Co, Bethel Pres Cem TQ 7:1:4 7:2:2

Indiana Co, biog sketches TQ 7:1:6 7:2:6 7:3:5

Indiana Co, Conemaugh Twp, Clarksburg Reformed Pres Cem WPG 13:3:29

Indiana Co, hist sketch TQ 7:4:2

Indiana Co, house type of the 1920s TQ 11:1:12

Indiana Co, place names TQ 11:1:19

Indiana Co, Saltsburg, hist, bk rev TQ 11:1:23

Johnstown, marr & deaths 1881-1885 abstr from the *Cambria Tribune*, bk rev GH 41:3:165

Lancaster Co, Bart Twp, hist sketch LCC 4:3:52

Lancaster Co, Bart Twp, warran,tee map 1800s roster LCC 4:4:60

Lancaster Co, biog annals index LCC 4:2:61 4:3:35 4:4:69

Lancaster Co, births 1852-1855 LCH 3:1:35 3:2:90 3:3:141

Lancaster Co, Brecknock & Caernarvon Twp, hist sketch LCC 4:4:57

Lancaster Co, Civil War, muster rolls abstr from news LCH 2:3:120

Lancaster Co, Clay Twp, hist sketch LCC 4:4:58

Lancaster Co, Cocalico Twp, hist sketch LCC 4:4:58

Lancaster Co, Colemanville Meth Cem LCH 2:4:154

Lancaster Co, Conestoga Twp, tax (direct) 1798 & census 1800, bk rev APG 2:2:30

PENNSYLVANIA (continued)

Lancaster Co, Conestoga, Donegal, Tulpehocken, & Pequea, tax lists 1725 LCH 1:1:12

Lancaster Co, Conoy Twp, Wickersham School, hist, bk rev PM 10:2:45

Lancaster Co, death reg 1852–1855 LCH 1:1:20 1:2:58 1:3:139 2:1:9 2:2:75 2:3:136 2:4:162

Lancaster Co, Donegal Pres Ch & cem inscr LCH 1:3:104 (marr 1807–1821) LCH 1:3:132 (member roster 1776) LCH 1:4:154

Lancaster Co, East Donegal Twp, map 1875 LCH 1:3:130

Lancaster Co, First Reformed Chyard Cem LCC 4:1:70

Lancaster Co, geneal misc 1799–1800 abstr from the *Lancaster Journal* LCH 2:1:44

Lancaster Co, government beginnings LCH 1:1:3

Lancaster Co, hist LCC 4:1:4 4:2:4 4:3:4 4:4:7

Lancaster Co, hist of Amish, Mennonites, & Brethren 1880 PM 10:1:2

Lancaster Co, hist sketch & geneal PM 10:1:13

Lancaster Co, Lancaster, Concord/Shreiner's Cem LCC 4:3:57 4:4:74

Lancaster Co, Lancaster, recollections 1830 LCC 4:3:21

Lancaster Co, letters of attorney bk 1 LCH 1:2:88

Lancaster Co, Manor Twp, Salem, Evangelical Assoc Cem LCC 4:2:57

Lancaster Co, marr 1752–1786 performed by Rev John Waldschmidt LCH 3:3:104

Lancaster Co, marr reg 1852–1855 LCH 2:4:171 3:1:16 3:2:58 3:3:146

Lancaster Co, Marticville United Meth Ch & cem inscr LCH 1:1:32

PENNSYLVANIA (continued)

Lancaster Co, midwife rec 1791–1815 of Susanna Muller LCH 3:2:65

Lancaster Co, Pequea Twp, map 1875 LCH 1:2:76

Lancaster Co, Pequea Twp, Pequea, tax list 1721 LCH 1:1:11

Lancaster Co, pet to create co LCH 1:1:16

Lancaster Co, War of 1812, vet markers placed 1937 LCH 2:3:104

Lancaster Co, warrants 1734–1742 extracted from the Taylor Papers LCH 3:1:4

Lancaster Co, White Oak Dunker cong member roster 1770 NFB 19:1:20

Leigh Co, Lynn Twp, Jacksonville, Jacob's Union Ch/Rosenthal/DeEcker Kirche rec misc 1807–1980, bk rev WPG 13:4:43

Lehigh Co, Salisbury Twp, Jerusalem Union Ch rec misc 1741–1911, bk rev WPG 13:4:43

Lehigh Co, Upper Saucon Twp, Friendensville, Frieden's Ch rec misc 1700s–1800s WPG 13:4:42

Lehigh Co, Weissenberg Twp, Seiberlingsville, St Paul's Luth Cong bapt 1874–1934, bk rev WPG 13:4:42

Leola, Forest Hills Mennonite Ch hist 1946–1986 PM 10:3:2

Lib res guide by Morris, bk rev GH 41:1:144

Luzerne Co, Braintrim Twp, census 1830 LWF 6:1:13

Luzerne Co, Braintrim Twp, census 1842–1843 LWF 6:1:18

Luzerne Co, geneal rec direct, bk rev LWF 6:1:7 PA 35:1:54

Maps, use of connected warrantee maps MFH 6:1:20

Marr & deaths 1831–1832 abstr from western PA news WPG 13:4:50

PENNSYLVANIA (continued)

Marr & deaths 1832 abstr from *The Westmoreland Intelligencer* WPG 14:1:43

Marr prior to 1810, bk rev CTN 20:2:327

Mifflin Co, fam & rec before 1800, bk rev GH 41:6:146

Monroe Co, census 1850, bk rev WPG 13:3:43

Montgomery Co, Upper Hanover Twp, Goshenhoppen, Red Hill, St Paul's/6 Cornered Ch/New Luth Ch rec misc 1739–1868, bk rev WPG 13:4:43

Montgomery Co, West Norriton Twp, cem inscr, bk rev GH 41:3:165

Naturalization pet indexes to the US Circuit & Districts Courts for eastern PA 1795–1951, use of ANC 22:1:3

Obit 1837–1862 abstr from the *Reformed Pres Magazine* (western PA), bk rev GJB 11:4:6

Pennsylvania Land Co shareholders c1762 NGS 74:4:290

Philadelphia, St Joseph's Roman Cath Ch bapt 1791, 1796–1799, bk rev WPG 13:4:45

Philadelphia, geneal misc 1828 abstr from *The Souvenir* BGS 19:1:25 19:2:76 19:3:122

Philadelphia, GE Reformed Ch bapt 1762–1763 performed by Rev Friedrich S Rothenbueler PA 35:1:9

Philadelphia, pass arrivals 1800–1819, bk rev MAD 27:1:36

Philadelphia Co, tax list 1693 ANC 22:2:72

Pittsburgh, direct (merchants) 1813 WPG 13:3:21

Pittsburgh, geneal misc 1797–1803 abstr from the *Pittsburgh Gazette*, bk rev WPG 13:3:52

Pittsburgh, High School applicants 1881 WPG 13:4:32

PENNSYLVANIA (continued)

Pittsburgh, hist outline to 1976 WPG 13:4:21

Pittsburgh, police 1841 roster WPG 14:1:42

Pittsburgh, Trinity Chyard cem inscr, bk rev VAG 31:3:232

Reading, cigar manufacturers 1898 roster OC 24:1:28

Red Hill, St Paul's Luth Ch, pastoral rec of Rev Vrederick Waage 1830–1890, bk rev WPG 13:4:43

Rev War, soldiers who settled in OH OCR 28:2:83

Rev War, soldiers living in states other than PA, bk rev GH 41:4:199

Somerset Co, commissioners rec, use of LM 28:1:253

Somerset Co, estates 1846–1848 LM 28:1:255 28:2:266 28:3:277 28:4:288

Somerset Co, hist in wood, stone, & brick LM 28:1:252 28:2:257 28:4:281

Somerset Co, Johnsburg, hist sketch & cem inscr LM 28:3:269

Somerset Co, Johnsburg, St John's Luth Ch marr 1800s LM 28:4:286

Somerset Co, Paint Twp, hist sketch LM 28:2:262

Somerset Co, Shanksville, craftsmen LM 28:2:267

Somerset Co, Summit Twp, craftsmen LM 28:1:245

Venango Co, French Creek Twp, Polk (Waterloo), hist, bk rev WPG 13:4:46

Visits by Rev John Cuthbertson 1779 WPG 13:4:30

Washington Co, index to the *Commemorative Biog Rec of WA Co PA*, bk rev GH 41:4:200

Washington Co, Union Twp, Mingo Pres Ch rec 1782–1982 WPG 14:1:15

Washington Co, tax (direct) 1798 index, bk rev VAG 31:3:233

PENNSYLVANIA (continued)

Westmoreland Co, Derry Twp, Old Salem Ch hist 1786-1986, bk rev WPG 13:4:47

Westmoreland Co, geneal sources guide, bk rev GH 41:6:146

Westmoreland Co, hist sketch WPG 13:3:20

Westmoreland Co, Rostraver Twp, letters left at post offices 1899 WPG 14:1:14

Westmoreland Co, Upper Burrell Twp, hist 1879-1979, bk rev WPG 13:4:47

Wyoming Co, marr & deaths 1843-1845 LWF 6:1:21

Wyoming Co, Monroe Twp, hist sketch LWF 6:1:19

Wyoming Co, news publ 1841-1931 LWF 6:1:45

Wyoming Co, post offices 1851-1865 LWF 6:1:20

Wyoming Co, Tunkhannock Boro, Harrison Street School hist sketch LWF 6:1:8

Wyoming Co, will abstr 1869-1879 LWF 6:1:28

York Co, births 1852-1855, bk rev LRT 6:4:253

PENNSYLVANIA DUTCH, Hist (pictorial), bk rev PM 10:4:42

PENNSYLVANIA GERMAN, Farming life in pictures, bk rev PM 10:4:45

PENROSE, Osborn m1855, w Susan A Wood, OH, Bible rec WB 17:3:98

PENSON, L Jane see William PIERSON

PENTICOST, John m1632, w Joane Smyth, MA, EN origins AG 62:3:118

PEPPER, Fam hist corr to *Pepper Geneal* by Landon NEH 4:1:32

PERKINS, Jacob f1812, w Elizabeth ___, PA, geneal, bk rev WPG 13:3:47

Jessie b1799, w Mary Charlotte Herndon, IA, anc ch SD 6:1:10

PERKINS (continued)

Rufus m1797, w Rebekah Johnson, Bible rec BG 8:2:36

Surname period, *Perkins Fam Newsletter*, 363 S Park Victoria Dr, Milpitas CA 95035

PERPALL, Juan bc1762, w Margaret Bell, Minorca, Bahamas, lineage FLG 10:4:130

PERRIN, David bc1795, w Elizabeth ___, NS, OH, anc ch FIR 6:2:23

PERRY, Charlotte see Samuel GOODRICH

Louisa see Benjamin Franklin GOSS

Lucy f1852, SC, power of attorney SCM 15:4:209

PERSHING, John J d1948, biog, bk rev REG 85:1:93

PERSIAS, Mary see Joseph BEASMAN

PERSON, Alfred T f1862, letter THT 15:1:26

PETER, Margaretha see Jacob GACHNOUWER

PETERS, Christopher C bc1824, IN?, VA?, MO, geneal, bk rev GH 41:5:192

Fam cem St Clair Co IL STC 10:2:94

Henry Jr 1763, w Mary Waite, VA, geneal, bk rev GH 41:4:208

PETERSON, Garrett f1775, w Nancy Smock, NY, geneal, bk rev GH 41:6:163

PETREE, William Henry b1815, w Elizabeth J Turbyville, AL, anc ch AGS 28:2:82

PETRIKIN, Jennie d1906, h J M B Petrikin, CO, obit CO 48:2:42

PETTIGREW, Ann see James McCABE

PETTIS, Emily Permelia see John S GIBBENS

PETTIT, John B b1789, w Altha Irish, VT?, NY?, MN, anc ch FCT :73:18

Sarah E see Joseph W ROBERTSON

PETTIT (continued)
Surname period, *The Pettit Correspondent*, Michael Cooley, 263 Water St, Santa Cruz CA 95060
PFITZEMEIER, Kunigunde see John George GEUTHER
PFUND, Adolf b1839, w Mathilde Friederike Henriette Linse, SW, WI, biog CHI 60:3:125
PHARISS, Margaret see Joseph MANNING
PHELPS, Angeline see James H SMITH
Emma R see Wm K BAKER
Fam hist EN, New EN, VA, KY, bk rev KA 23:2:113
Isabelle Lavinia see Henry Allen MATHEWS
Joel b1755, PA, NJ, geneal DM 50:4:155
Joel b1798, w Rebecca Baker & Sally Brock, MA, MI, geneal DM 50:3:116
Richard T f1832, KY, geneal, bk rev GH 41:4:208
Samuel bc1750, w Elizabeth ___, IR, VA, geneal, bk rev GH 41:2:155
Surname period, *Phelps Fam News*, Dallas L Phelps, 1002 Queen St, Camden SC 29020
PHILIPS, William b1766, w Elizabeth Iser, PA, geneal, bk rev GH 41:4:208
PHILLIMORE, Reginald Phillimore b1855, EN, biog sketch NEH 4:4:196
William Phillimore Watts b1853, EN, biog sketch NEH 4:4:197
PHILLIPS, Alexander Edward b1889, w Grace Farquhar, EN, geneal, bk rev GH 41:6:163
Ann see Frederick SMITH
Clarinda Beecher see Thomas Randolph HALL
Louisa see Harry EENIGENBURG
Margaret see Charles REED
Mary Elizabeth see Frances Marion HOUSE

PHILLIPS (continued)
Philomen bc1790, NC, geneal, bk rev GH 41:1:164
Sara Ida see John Jay DICKEY
Surname period, *Phillips Fam Finder*, POB 2040, Pinetop AZ 85935 – census 1850 NY, Jacob b1792 of TN, Reuben of MD, Bible rec, rec GA & KY, Theophilus of VA/PA, marr IN, fam TX & NC
Thomas H bc1790, NC, geneal, bk rev GH 41:1:164
William, w Elizabeth Iser, OH, geneal, bk rev TS 29:3:107
PHIPPS, Fam cem MO GTP 25:1:28
PIATT, Fam hist, bk rev TOP 17:4:100
PICHA, Maria Theresa see Charles MALECHA
PICKARD, James b1824, IN, WA, biog sketch WCG 3:3:20
PICKERING, Timothy f1777, w Rebecca White, MA, biog TEG 7:1:12
PICKETT, Helen Jane see James ENGLISH
PIEPENBRINK, John O b1826, w Sophie Wille, PU, IL, biog WTC 1:3:85
PIEPER, Peter bc1793, w Elizabeth Dedich Menke, GE, TX, biog GR 29:4:143
PIERCE, Benjamin bc1723, w Hannah Ames Rugg, CT, anc ch TAK 17:2:23
Lelah M b1910, WI, cem inscr WI 33:4:272
William H b1862, w Gertrude Johnson, IL, anc ch TAK 17:1:27
PIERSON, Hattie B m1895, h Weller Abrams, OH, Bible rec HJA 12:1:4
Nancy see Jesse DOLLARHIDE
Stephen b1763, NJ, lineage HL 5:3:78
William m1852, w L Jane Penson, MI, Bible rec CCM 6:4:74
PIGGOTT, Elizabeth see Mark LAMPTON

PIGGOTT (continued)
James f1776, KY, biog, bk rev
RAG 8:1:21
PILGRIMS, Hist in EN MQ
53:1:18 53:2:106
Hist in their own words, bk rev
MQ 53:1:72
PILLING, Alfred Edward b1863, w
Theresa Elliott Markwick, EN,
BC, fam rec BCG 16:3:88
PILOTE, Fam hist, bk rev LIC
13:4:223
PINSON, David Richard b1822, w
Eliza Carter, GA, AL, geneal
PT 29:1:12
PIPES, Hiram m1816, w
Elizabeth Allison Morris, NC,
geneal, bk rev CAL 6:4:90
PITCHER, Elisabeth see William
FLINT
PITTS, Jessie see J Neville
McJUNKIN
PLACE, Huldah Jane see Wil-
liam Ellsworth HUGHES
PLANK, David b1799, w Anna
Kurtzin, Bible rec MFH
6:4:136
PLATT, Richard b1603, w Mary
Wood, CT, biog ANC 22:3:107
PLOCHER, Andreas m1723, w
Anna Catharina Wegennast,
GE, geneal MFH 6:4:132
PLUMER, Caroline Fernold see
Thomas Tandy SAWYER
PLUMMER, Daniel bc1720, w
Prudence Lofton, PA, FL,
lineage FLG 10:3:102
Fam rec misc MD 1700s-1800s
MAD 27:4:140
John bc1726, MD, lineage MD
28:1:30
Philemon b1811, NC, fam rec
NCJ 13:4:226
PLUTKO, Surname period, *The
Plutko Fam Newsletter*, 16455
E Prentice Pl, Aurora CO
80015
PLYMATE, Nancy J see Thomas
McGEE
POCHE, Marie Emma see Pru-
dent BOURGEOIS Sr

POETS, Geeske see Arend
Wiards BOOMGAARDEN
POINTS, Joseph f1760, EN, PA,
children SGE 28:123:6
POIRIER, Charles m1858, w
Eulalie Proulx, QB, MA, anc
ch AGE 16:3:85
POIRIER, Edelire (Luce) see
Casimir HARVEY
Marguerite see Honore COMEAU
Marie Belzire see Zenon
BOURQUE
POLAND, Death rec translating
hints PP 3:2:6
Felician Sisters who shaped Am
Polonia, hist TE 7:2:61
Geneal letter-writing hints MCR
18:4:120 PN 9:2:25
Geneal sources for Russian PO
PN 9:2:21
Heraldry PN 9:2:33
Hist of Poles in MA & parish
direct PP 3:2:2
Hist of Poles in US, bk rev TE
7:2:92
Hist sketch of settlement in Buf-
falo NY TE 7:2:46
Hist sketch of settlement in
Wyandotte MI TE 7:3:98
Imm to Brazil & US 1890-1891
letters, bk rev MD 28:4:466
Mil & civilian decorations
1705-1985, bk rev PN 9:2:34
Natives in Bronson, Branch Co
MI mid-1800s TE 7:1:3
Natives in Buffalo NY 1880s-
1920s TE 7:2:46
Natives living in Buffalo NY who
served in the PO Army or the
Am Army in World War I
roster TE 7:2:54
Obit & deaths 1890-1899 abstr
from the *Dziennik Chicagoski*
(Chicago IL), bk rev OC
24:1:42
Ship pass list from Bremen GE
1899 to NY on board the *S S
Bonn* PP 3:2:9
Surname origins (occupational)
PN 9:2:37
Translation manual of Russian
documents, bk rev PN 9:2:39

POLAND (continued)
Ziemia Lomzynska, hist sketch PP 3:2:13
POLK, James K b1795, w Sarah Childress, NC, TN, biog sketch GD 18:1:7
POMMERN, Surname period, *Die Pommerschen Leute*, 1260 Westhaven Dr, Oshkosh WI 54904
POOLE, Amanda see Joseph Alvey CLAYTON
POOR, Edward f1851, IL, War of 1812 pension appl WTC 3:1:36
POORMAN, George W see Eliza Jane WATSON
POPE, Henderson P b1816, Bible rec OZ 8:3:113
Lucetta see Patrick M WILLIAMS
PORTER, Aimee see Henry Huntington LOMBARD
John b1759, w Sarah Clarke, VA, KY, biog KFR 13: :21
Robert f1640, CT, geneal, bk rev NYR 118:1:55
PORTEUS, Harriet Davis see Elmore PUTNEY
Moore Lee m1824, w Elizabeth Hiester Davis, PA, Bible rec SLV 5:3:6
POSTLES, Shadrach f1820, DE, OH, geneal, bk rev FRT 8:2:106
Thomas bc1700, w Sarah Nunes, DE, geneal, bk rev NGS 74:3:226
POTTENGER, John f1681, EN, MD, PA, KY, geneal, bk rev WPG 13:3:47
POTTER, Nancy see Joseph INGRAHAM
Samuel b1671, NJ, geneal, bk rev IL 19:2:111
W I f1868, PA, diary, bk rev GH 41:2:155
POTTS, Jesse b1754, w Mary Ann Sterling, VA, FL, lineage FLG 10:4:141
POULTER, John bc1595, w Mary Pope?, EN, MA, geneal NER 141:3:215

POWELL, Joseph b1734, PA, biog, bk rev GH 41:6:163
Joseph b1734, w Rachel ___, PA, biog, bk rev FRT 8:4:201
Robert Jabez b1860, w Mary C Hill, AL, anc ch PT 29:2:48
POWER, Fam cem in Owingsville KY EK 23:1:10
Walter b1654, EN, MA, geneal, bk rev KK 25:3:56
POWERS, Allen Wilburn b1849, w Mary Frances Wright, GA, geneal TCG 7:3:1
Frederick b1814, w Tresea Powers, KY, geneal, bk rev WCK 20:4:61
John d1824, w Nancy Hunter, KY, geneal, bk rev GH 41:6:163
John Lewis bc1853, w Ellen Marnetta Sanderson, TN?, IR?, AR, fam rec TRC 2:1:48
PRATHER, Eliza Mary Ann see Blassingame W HARVEY
PRATT, Angelina J see William Peck DAVIS
Henrietta see Moses LACY
Melvina see Thomas WILLSON
Olive H see Joseph Butts HIBBARD
PREDIGER, Margaret Ann b1850, Bible rec STC 10:1:32
PREDMORE, Lydia see John COVENHOVEN
Surname period, *The Journal of the Predmore/Pridemore/ Pridmore/Prigmore Assoc*, 545 Jefferson, Kimberly ID 83341
PRESBYTERIAN, geneal res hints AW 13:1:46
Hist in Warren Co OH HL 3:3:77
Persecution in IR TI 86:11:34
PRESCOTT, Surname period, *Prescotts Unlimited*, 42 Larchmont Rd, Asheville NC 28804
PRESSMILL, Rachel see Benjamin ELLIS I
PRESTON, Emilea B see Michael FRANDSEN
Medina b1741, w Anna Howard, CT, Bible rec CTN 20:2:241

PRESTON (continued)
William b1667, w Jane Deyn, PA, geneal, bk rev GH 41:6:163

PRICE, Anna Pricilla see James A ARNOLD
Fam rec misc, bk rev GH 41:1:164
Mary Ann see Adam ROYDER
Richard bc1756, w Priscilla Crabtree, PA, VA, geneal OZ 8:2:47
Surname period, *The Prices of Am*, 1661 Lauranceae Way, Riverdale GA 30296
Thomas f1779, VA, hist sketch of house QP :22:3

PRICKET, Ann see Dennis SPRING

PRINCE, Sarah see Pleasant SKAGGS

PRITCHARD, John see Mary COFFMAN

PRITCHETT, Fam hist NC, TN, IL, MO, KS 1800s-1900s, bk rev GR 29:1:20
Fam rec misc, bk rev GH 41:6:163
Surname period, *Pritchett Helping Pritchett*, 556 N 1160 E, Orem UT 84057

PRITLOE, Prissila see John SANDERS

PRITZ, Margarett see Chambers HUSTON

PROBERT, Eleanor bc1748, EN, anc ch TOP 17:4:123

PROCTOR, John f1635, geneal, bk rev NYR 118:3:177
Richard d1866, w Jane Morrow, IR, children IFL 2:9-10:14

PROPHET, James Arrington b1793, w Jemima Bingham, NC, TN, MO, geneal OZ 8:2:62

PROPPER, Frederick Chirstian b1843, w Mary Kuster, PU, IL, biog sketch WTC 4:2:43

PROUGH, Johann Casper f1748, PA, geneal, bk rev MFH 6:1:34

PROULX, Eulalie see Charles POIRIER

PROVOST, Elisabeth see Jean Francois dit FOUCAULT
Leon E, w Elizabeth Fraser/Defoy, QB, IA, NY, geneal, bk rev NYR 118:2:120

PRUDDEN, Elizabeth see Jehu BURR

PRUITT, David D bc1873, w Georgia Alice Hill, AL, anc ch NC :90:9

PRUSSIA, Casualties in the Franco-PU War 1870-1871, bk rev GH 41:4:186
Gazetteer of parish & civil jurisdictions in west PU, bk rev GGD 3:3:134
Hist of east PU in RA, bk rev WTC 13:1:32
Land & testement rec 1732-1776 abstr from *Woechentlichen Koenigsbergischen Frage- und Anzeigungsnachrichten* GGD 3:3:144
Parish & civil jurisdictions gazetteer for east PU, bk rev GGD 3:1:17
Settlement in Marquette & Green Lake Co WI 1858-1907 NGS 74:4:263

PUCKETT, Bessie f1907, h ____ Shropshire, TX, reminiscences HTR 29:4:125

PUETT, Coleman, w Ann Eliza Scott, NC, KS, geneal, bk rev KK 25:1:17

PUGH, Elmer d1932, NE, obit NA 10:1:3
William m1851, w Frances Cone, Bible rec WTC 10:2:55

PUNCH, David b1846, NS, mil rec GN 5:3:134

PURCELL, Elizabeth see James C HOXSEY

PURDY, Rebecca see James O CONKLIN
William H b1858, IL, fam hist WTC 17:4:119

PUREFOY, Anne see John DAVIS

PURINTON, Nathan b1812, VT, geneal, bk rev FRT 8:2:105

PURITAN, Hist in EN, bk rev BCG 16:1:32

PURVIANCE, D H m1872, w Emily M Williams, NC, Bible rec YTD 3:2:2

PUSHKIN, Alexander Sergeevich b1799, w Natalie Alexandrovna Pushkina, RA, biog MP 3:3:139

PUTMAN, K A see Leander COPELAND

PUTNEY, Elmore b1839, w Harriet Davis Porteus, NY, biog sketch SLV 5:3:7

PUTRAH, Mary b1852, CN, FL, anc ch TB 13:2:37

PYKE, Fam cem inscr QB GN 5:3:141

QUA, Ann see Samuel LUNDY

QUAKER, Date recording method IAN 8:3:10

Geneal misc 1905 abstr from *The Am Friend* QY 14:4:8

Geneal rec GA, Wrightsborough 1772-1793 & Friendsborough 1776-1777, bk rev VAG 31:2:152 GGS 23:3:156 NYR 118:4:244 PA 35:1:51 NC :92:2 NCJ 13:3:178 GH 41:4:188 DG 33:2:118

Geneal rec locations OC 24:3:116

Geneal res guide by Berry, bk rev GH 41:4:186 DG 33:2:120 GHS 4:2:72 NCJ 13:3:183 PM 10:4:43 KA 23:2:116 BWG 16:2:156 MN 18:4:187 ANC 22:4:158 WCK 20:3:47 WPG 14:1:46 SCM 15:4:221

Geneal res hints MGR 22:2:74

Hist of ch in Warren Co OH HL 2:2:40

Hist sketch IR 1660s TI 86:11:35

Meetings in Bucks Co PA BCN 6:4:46

Monthly meetings at Abingdon & Birmingham PA 1600s-1900s vol 1, bk rev GH 41:4:200

Queries vol 4, bk rev IL 19:2:118

QUINLEVAN, Catherine see Henry Joseph KELLY

RAAB, Rosa b1863, MI, WA, anc ch OG 13:2:40

RADCLIFF, Ann see Joseph MARRIOTT

RAE, Margt see David ALLARDICE

RAGSDALE, Surname period, *Ragsdales of Am*, POB 1654, Soquel CA 95073

RAILSBACK, Edward b1802, w Catherine Hootman, NC, IA, anc ch BHN 20:2:59

RAINES, Elizabeth see Alexander MANSFIELD

RAINEY, Surname period, *Rainey Times*, Rt 4 Box 62, Sulphur Springs TX 75482

RAINS, Fam cem Dade Co MO OZ 7:3:113

John Gilmore b1851, w Luella Russler, IA?, WA, anc ch AGS 28:2:95

RALSTON, Sarah Jane see Peter STOMBAUGH

William see Rachel Ann RUSSELL

RAMAGE, Joseph b1747, w Elizabeth ____, PA, SC, geneal, bk rev GFP 37:2:74 GH 41:4:208

RAMBIN, J A b1851, Bible rec YTD 2:2:33

James m1891, w Anna King, Bible rec YTD 2:2:32

RAMBO, Peter Gunnerson f1640, w Britta Mattsdotter, SN, DE, geneal, bk rev GFP 37:2:74 GH 41:4:208

RAMEY, Martha see Eugene TRIPLETT

RAMSAY, William Burke b1795, w Elizebeth McAnulty, KY?, geneal OZ 5:4:137

RAMSBOTTOM, Fam hist, bk rev GH 41:2:155

RAMSEY, A C f1879, MS, AL, auto 1809-1840, bk rev GH 41:2:138

Fam rec misc GA & Indian Territory, bk rev NCJ 13:3:186

Hiram bc1800, w Mary Polly Berry, VA, geneal, bk rev GH 41:2:155

RAMSEYER, Anna see Valentine BIRKY

RANDALL, David b1765, w Sarah Ann Gibson, NJ, MI, PA, fam rec AH 14:1:30

Kinnicum b1820, Bible rec MI 32:2:43

RANDLES, John b1794, w Mary Rogers, TN, MO, children OZ 8:1:26

RANDOL, David b1742, w Sarah Ann Marvin, NJ, fam hist AH 14:4:128

John Jr b1796, Bible rec WTC 9:1:17

RANDOLPH, James f1851, MO, letter OZ 6:4:147

RANKIN, David f1738, w Jennet ____, IR, VA, geneal SGE 28:122:33

RANKSTON, Lawrence b1783, w Permilia McDonald, NC, anc ch GGS 23:2:88

RANSOM, Susanna see John DERTHICK

RASMUSSEN, Nels J mc1905, w Inga Henningsen, DK, OR, biog CT 7:4:34

RATCLIFF, Richard bc1760, KY, Bible rec KA 23:2:95

RATH, Ida see John Louis ENGEL

RATHBONE, Mary Brown see Henry Wood GARDNER

RATHBUN, Surname period, *Rathbun-Rathbone-Rathburn Fam Historian*, 11308 Popes Head Rd, Fairfax VA 22030

RAUB, John f1825, w Maria Miller, fam hist LCC 4:2:54

RAULSTON, Fam hist, bk rev KA 23:1:34 SB 8:1:20

RAVENS, Bezaleel d1648, w Judith Browne, MA, geneal AG 62:3:161

Grace bc1545, h Edward Cole, MA, EN origins AG 62:3:65

RAVENSTINE, Catherine N d1909, h ____ Meyer, GE, IL, obit CRT 8:3:8

RAWSON, David bc1590, w Margaret Wilson, EN, anc ch TAK 17:2:26

RAY, Lorenzo D f1863, ME, journal DE 11:1:4

Lou Emma see J H ROBERSON

Sarah Mariah see Robert Dale CARR

RAYL, Wm m1856, w Delia S Ansley, Bible rec SLB 6:4:172

RAYMOND, Asa see Mercy NORRIS

Mary see Nathaniel STREET

RAYNSFORD, Eli m1815, w Lydia Bennett, Bible rec CTN 20:3:436

REA, Jennie see William GOODMAN

READ, Nancy b1804, anc ch OG 13:3:69

READING, John b1686, NJ, diary GMN 62:1:1 62:2:83 62:3:128

REAMS, Jasper Marion b1853, w Mary Melissa Walker, TN, anc ch WB 17:4:130

RECTOR, Fam hist, bk rev BWG 16:1:66

John Jacob f1713, GE, VA, geneal, bk rev KK 25:3:59

RED(D)INGTON, John see Sarah WITT

REDDELL, Jimmy D b1925, OK, cem inscr OPC 18:1:10

REDDY, Timothy b1776, w Isabella Scott, IR, NY, Bible rec RCP 9:1:28

REDEKER, Norman b1926, IL, CA, obit NWS 7:5:48

REDFORD, Nancy see George Washington GREER

REDING, Edna Lorena m1907, h Charles Clarke Elsbree, Bible rec MCR 18:2:38

REDMAN, Elizabeth see William Henry SHOEMAKER

Maggie see James S BLYTHE

Thomas f1777, EN, mil service MSG 7:3:155

REDMON, Polly b1781, Bible rec LAB 2:2:28

Robert m1815, w Agnes Elsbury, KY, Bible rec LAB 2:2:29

Thomas bc1790, w Mary ____, IR, IL, geneal FF 15:3:97

REED, Charles, w Chloe Roby & Margaret Phillips, OH, IN, IL, biog, bk rev IL 19:2:110

Elizabeth Almira Collins m1853, h Samuel Long, IL, children MCS 7:3:130

Elizabeth see Levi FEASTER

Isaac f1835, w Elizabeth Harper, SC, biog YTD 2:2:45

James C f1858, MI, diaries, bk rev FRT 8:3:148

Katherine see William MCCLAGHRY

Mary Jane see Jim Roe SPARKS

Orestes Seymour b1840, w Almira Helen Hickox, NY, IL, fam hist WTC 17:4:124

R S see Elizabeth A COLLINS

REEDER, Isabelle see John Thomas PADEN

REEP, Fam biblio, bk rev GH 41:3:170

REESE, Elizabeth (Pitts) see Joseph LAWRENCE

REEVES, Elijah f1853, w Martha ___, KY, IL, CA, biog sketch WCG 4:2:14

REID, Arminda see Silas SITTON

Edith see Peter E DUNCAN

Fam cem Comanche Co TX FP 30:4:179

John f1815, w Elizabeth Miller, VA, OH, fam rec NFB 19:2:29

Mary Emma see William Harding YARGER

REIHL, Barbara see John O MILLER

REIMER, Johann Friederich f1858, w Augusta Hermann, IL, geneal, bk rev GH 41:4:209

REINICKER, Mary see John THOMAS

REISINGER, Jacob b1808, w Elizabeth Keller, GE, OH, geneal, bk rev CCS 8:4:131

REITER, Mary Barbara see August HAGER

REKER, Joan Henrich m1701, w Anna Margaretha Luebbeker, GE, OH, geneal, bk rev GH 41:5:193

REMANN, Dorothy see Augustus ROSEMIRE

Frederick f1823, w Dorothy ___, IL, geneal FF 15:3:31

Sophia see George LEIDIG

RENDER, Joshua f1720, MD, VA, geneal, bk rev NGS 74:4:305

RENKIN, William f1688, w Dorothy Black, ST, IR, PA, fam rec LCC 4:1:81

RENNEKER, Garrett Henry b1830, desc, bk rev NYR 118:3:183

RENNINGER, Friedrich b1741, GE, PA, geneal, bk rev GH 41:1:164

RENTSCH, Johan b1836, w Maria Rothlisberger, SW, IA, geneal, bk rev GH 41:5:193

REPP, Michael Anton b1813, w Maria Josepha Geier, GE, KS, anc ch KK 25:4:65

REVOLUTIONARY WAR, Boston merchants: smugglers & patriots, bk rev NER 141:2:155

Courts-martial survey & index, bk rev GJ 15:2:104 MD 28:1:112 NER 141:1:65 RES 18:1:17

Defeats (4), bk rev WCG 3:7:50

Geneal rec sources at the National Archives, KS City branch PW 7:3:118

Graves located DAR 121:3:169 121:9:811

Hist of battles in NY, bk rev NYR 118:4:242

Hist sketch of the Hessian Reg Von Bose MD 28:4:400

Index to burial places of Rev patriots in & around ON Co NY, bk rev NYR 118:1:54

Lineages (artillery) of reg, bk rev GH 41:2:121

Lineages (CN) of reg, bk rev GH 41:2:121

Lineages (CT) of reg, bk rev GH 41:2:121

Lineages (DE) of reg, bk rev GH 41:2:122

Lineages (extra) of reg, bk rev GH 41:2:122

REVOLUTIONARY WAR (cont)

Lineages (GA) of reg, bk rev GH 41:2:122

Lineages (Light Dragoon) of reg, bk rev GH 41:2:122

Lineages (MA) of reg, bk rev GH 41:2:122

Lineages (misc) of reg, bk rev GH 41:2:123

Lineages (MD) of reg, bk rev GH 41:2:122

Lineages (NC) of reg, bk rev GH 41:2:123

Lineages (NH) of reg, bk rev GH 41:2:123

Lineages (NJ) of reg, bk rev GH 41:2:123

Lineages (NY) of reg, bk rev GH 41:2:123

Lineages (PA) of reg, bk rev GH 41:2:123

Lineages (Partisan Corp & Legionary Corp) of reg, bk rev GH 41:2:123

Lineages (RI) of reg, bk rev GH 41:2:123

Lineages (SC) of reg, bk rev GH 41:2:123

Lineages (VA) of reg, bk rev GH 41:2:123

Lineages of reg add, bk rev GH 41:2:121

Loyalists in Southern campaign vol 2, bk rev FRT 8:2:102

Medical men 1775-1783 roster SLB 6:1:30

Patriots index corr DAR 121:2:97 121:8:717

Pensioners living in MD, DE, DC 1840 MD 28:4:440

Pierce's Reg 1783, bk rev WCK 20:3:48 TCG 7:3:59

Pirates & patriots, bk rev CTA 30:1:53

Rec, use of PB 2:4:65

Soc of the Cincinnati, hist sketch PGB 19:4:72

Soldiers buried in IA MCN 2:4:7

Soldiers buried in Knox Co IL KIL 14:1:1

Soldiers buried in central MO SNS 3:4:2

REVOLUTIONARY WAR (cont)

Soldiers' names inscr on DAR tablet at Yorktown PA CTN 20:3:553

Vet buried in Sangamon Co IL CR 19:4:162

Women in Rev War AW 13:2:80 13:3:120 13:4:174

REXFORD, Benajah d1862, w Zeruia Squier, IL, fam hist WTC 4:4:136

REYNOLDS, Albert Nathaniel m1853, w Jane A Jack, MI, Bible rec IMP 6:1:25

Mark m1802, w Polly White, Bible rec OZ 7:4:149

Stephen b1776, NY, geneal, bk rev FRT 8:2:105

REZABEK, Dorothy f1855, h Jakob ___, CZ, IL, MO, geneal, bk rev TS 29:1:26

Fam hist BO & US 1695-1980, bk rev CSB 21:1-2:39

RHOADS, Elizabeth see Benjamin HOFFMAN

Gidney b1830, w Anna E ___ & Ruby ___, Bible rec HH 22:1:19

RHODE ISLAND, Fam hist & geneal sources, bk rev CTN 19:4:711 DM 50:3:144 NER 141:3:264

Geneal Mayflower lineage vol 2, bk rev RAG 8:3:21

Hist 1636-1986, bk rev RIR 13:2:21

Land & notarial rec tables of contents IR 13:2:27

Land & notarial rec abstr 1600s RIR 13:3:55

Mil rec, muster roll of Capt Tophams Company of Col Crarys Reg RI Forces 1775 RIR 13:1:10

North Providence, Hopkins Burial Ground hist sketch & inscr RIR 13:3:62

Pawtucket, reminiscences & new series of Reverend David Benedict, bk rev RIR 13:1:3

Providence, hist 1820-1940, bk rev NYR 118:4:241

RHODE ISLAND (continued)

Providence Plantations, lineages of Soc of Mayflower desc vol 2, bk rev CTN 19:4:707

Revolutionary War, vet with RI service or residence, listed in CT Rev pensioners RIR 13:1:14

South Kingston, tax list 1757 RIR 13:2:37 13:3:63

Whalers, crews of 1700s NGS 74:4:255

RHODES, Eva see Stephen RIFENBURG

RICE, Frank H b1862, w Nettie Jane Smith, PA, IL, anc ch KIL 15:3:35

Mary E f1859, AL, letter NTT 7:3:117

Sallie see Obediah SEAY

Surname period, *Rice Remembers*, Rt 2 Box 690, Metaline Falls WA 99153

William f1781, w Ann _____, MD, geneal, bk rev GH 41:4:209 WMG 3:4:191

RICH, Caroline see John C Breckenridge CRICE

David f1795, VT, NY, geneal, bk rev NYR 118:4:247

Surname period, *Kinfolk*, POB 142, Wellfleet MA 02667 – Herbert Thomas 1874-1943, Albert Gallatin 1829-1907, cem KS, fam NC

RICHARD, Henriette see Taddeus Nicolas LEBLANC

Marie see Alexis GAUDET

RICHARDS, Barbara see John WEAVER

Elizabeth see Christopher HART

RICHARDSON, Emma see J H SUMMERS

Joe m1883, w Lou Vina, Bible rec YTD 7:2:21

John Walter b1866, w Nora Alice Shoff, TN, OR, geneal BWG 16:1:29

Lucy Elizabeth see Augustus Edward CULBREATH

Mary b1725, MA, anc ch TEG 7:2:93

RICHARDSON (continued)

Mary see Sylvester DERBY

Mathias b1749, PA?, geneal, bk rev GH 41:1:164

Mathias b1749, w Frances Clark, NC, geneal, bk rev WPG 14:1:52

Surname period, *Richardson Fam Res & Hist News*, POB 123, Broken Bow NE 68822 – letters to editor, queries

Susannah A see Charles Caffery MARTIN

Thomas Wesley b1874, w Mary Etta McKinney, TX, anc ch VC 8:3:72

RICHMOND, Cyrus R f1864, diary abstr AH 14:3:81 14:4:122

RICHTER, John Jacob f1714, w Elisabeth Fischbach, GE, VA, geneal, bk rev GH 41:2:155

Jon Christopher, geneal, bk rev MN 18:3:140

Ruth see Anthony A DRAGUNAS

RICKARD, Isaac Newton see Ellen Virginia KAUFFMAN

Jacob dc1795, NC, anc ch TB 13:4:35

RICKELMAN, Maurice A b1917, w Catherine Pauli, IL, biog CRT 8:2:21

RICKERSON, B W m1875, w M G Barron, Bible rec HTR 30:2:43

RIDDELL, Grace b1818, ST, biog ANE 24::2

RIDDLE, William f1771, w Elizabeth Minter, NC, geneal, bk rev GH 41:6:166

RIDER, Adam f1804, MD, OH, fam hist CCG 6:3:45

Ezekiel m1811, w Susanna Seaton, Bible rec MCR 18:3:82

Sophere see Jeptha NICKERSON

RIDGLEY, Philena b1882, MN, anc ch TB 13:2:35

RIEKE, Fam hist GE & US, bk rev SCS 24:1:18

RIEMAN, Mary E see Bernard BRUMMER

RIFENBURG, Stephen bc1860, w Eva Rhodes, NY, MO, fam hist sketch OZ 6:2:45

RIGG, John f1889, w Charlotte
___, WA, fam hist sketch AB
16:1:5
RILEY, John f1840s, IR, MA,
geneal NER 141:4:359
RING, Simon Chester Ashley see
Lydia Laurentia LINDHOLM
RINGGOLD, Fam will abstr MD
MAD 27:2:54 27:3:100 27:4:138
RISDON, Harriett see Silas F
MEAD
RISING, Robert E b1875, w Julia
Locke, Bible rec CCS 9:3:79
RISSER, Peter b1713, w Elizabeth
Hershey, PA, geneal PM
10:2:21
RITCHEY, James b1816, w Eliza
Adair McKean, KY, IL, geneal,
bk rev WTC 11:1:4
RITCHIE, Susan see James
BARR
RITTEL, August f1857, w Cecilia
Kraetz, GE, OH, AL, fam rec
PT 29:3:118
RITTER, George A b1791, MD,
KY, IN, anc ch JCG 15:1:27
RIVIERE, Henry Lawson bc1775,
w Mary Weatherly, VA, FL,
lineage FLG 10:4:138
RIX, Edward F see Elizabeth A
WOODWARD
ROACH, Charles Sr b1744, w
Elizabeth Nobles & Polly
Summers, NC, biog TQR
14:1:19
ROAT, Jacob b1813, w Nancy
___, NJ, anc ch HL 6:1:29
ROBBERS, Marritje see John
SEALS
ROBBINS, Aliace A see James P
ELLINGSWORTH
Frederick b1812, w Nancy M
Woodward, IL, PA, OH, IL,
MI, biog sketch WTC 5:1:18
ROBERDS, Thomas bc1710, w
Sarah Gilbert, PA, geneal QY
14:4:1
ROBERSON, J H b1865, w Lou
Emma Ray, TX, OK, anc ch
AGS 28:2:93
ROBERTS, Fam cem Wayne Co
MO MSG 7:3:139

ROBERTS (continued)
Hattie see Stephen S OUTMAN
Isham B b1817, w Susannah
Evelyn Hyler, TN, AL, anc ch
NAS 26:1:11
Jacob Jake b1861, w Phylow
Frances Godfrey, KY, WV,
WA, biog EK 22:4:8
John Wesley b1825, w Mary C
Harbert, IL, AR, MO, children
OZ 7:3:121
Mary see Frederick SPAIN
Ramey b1832, w Mary O'Connor,
NY, IL, anc ch KIL 15:2:31
Rebecca see Jacob KELLAMS
Surname period, *Roberts Reg*,
5048 J Parkway, Sacramento
CA 95823
Susannah F see Binoni Franklin
COLDWELL
ROBERTSON, Alexander m1773,
w Margaret Robinson, KY, biog
GR 29:4:154
Fam hist TX, bk rev GR 29:2:63
Joseph W b1860, w Sarah E Pet-
tit, IN, MO, OR, anc ch KIL
15:3:34
Oscar see Anna Elizabeth FUL-
TON
Sarah Ann see William WHITE
Sarah Harriet see William Hulto
DURRANCE
William b1796, w Peggy
Alexander, VA, KY, anc ch FF
15:4:136
ROBINS, Nancy b1760, h John
White, VA, anc ch CCS 9:2:61
ROBINSON, Daniel O f1836, w
Jane Kelley, IL, fam hist
sketch WTC 4:4:143
James M m1859, w Elizabeth J
Dare, Bible rec STC 10:1:29
John Doak m1872, w Mary
ELizabeth Watson, CA, Bible
rec RT 5:1:18
Joseph f1854, IL, abstr of title
WTC 4:2:53
Margaret see Alexander
ROBERTSON
Mary see Israel BIBBINS
Ruth see Henry HUNTER
Sarah E see James WORNELL

ROBSON, James d1885, w Sabella Young, ST, cem inscr GGL 6:3:102

ROBY, Chloe see Charles REED

ROCKWELL, John b1694, w Phebe Hand, Bible rec CTN 20:1:53

RODGERS, Fam hist FR, EN, NJ TS 29:3:115

Nancy Jane see George Henry KENNEDY

RODNEY, William m1693, w Sarah Jones, DE, letter & pedigree DJ 4:1:1

ROEBUCK, Lola see William H COVINGTON

ROEH, Hans b1845, w Maria Blass, GE, IA, anc ch GWD 6:3:

ROFS, Mary Ann see Isaac MILLER

ROGERS, Benjamin d1858, WI, cem inscr WI 33:4:272

Elizabeth see Alexander EDGAR

Eunice d1870, MA, anc ch TEG 7:4:203

Fam cem Folsam LA SGE 28:123:38

Israel f1877, LA, succession THT 15:1:17

John b1611, w Ann Churchman, EN, MA, anc ch TAK 17:2:25

John f1788, w Martha Rogers, VA, will VAG 31:1:57

Mary see John RANDLES

Thomas m1828, w Lucinda Ellen Light, Bible rec STC 10:1:30

ROHM, Fam hist addenda to *Desc of John & Christiana Rohm 1804-1984* by Rohm, bk rev WPG 13:4:39

ROHRBACH, Johann Reinhart f1749, PA, VA, geneal, bk rev WTC 14:4:162

ROHWEDER, John b1839, w Eliza Wendt, PU, anc ch FIR 6:4:50

ROKEBY, Philip f1702, EN, NY, NJ, biog NYR 118:1:19

ROLAND, Fam hist EN & MD, bk rev PGB 19:4:67

ROLLER, William m1872, w Elizabeth Forgey, Bible rec OZ 7:3:97

ROLOSON, Amsey J b1834, NJ, anc ch OCG 17:3:18

ROMIG, Surname period, *Romig Reflections*, Lisa Alcala, POB 111, Green Springs OH 44836

ROMINE, Margaret C see James H CONVERSE

ROOD, Jacob f1837, OH, letter DM 50:4:173

ROOK, Mary Ann see George Henderson WEAVER

ROOSEVELT, Franklin D f1928, US, biog, bk rev REG 85:1:95

Franklin D f1933, biog of New Deal years 1933-1937, bk rev REG 85:3:275

ROOT, Samuel see Anna HURLBURT

ROPER, Amanda see Thomas M MEEK

Ephraim see Hannah BREWER

Samuel Clyde, w Tyre Lee ____, geneal, bk rev NCJ 13:2:121

ROSE, Caroline M see Philip TURPIN

Gotlieb f1779, w Maria Barbara Rose, MD, fam rec WMG 3:3:129

ROSE, John d1797, NJ, biog NGS 74:4:284

John Washington b1817, w Margaret Malinda Scott, LA, TX, anc ch DG 33:1:57

Robert bc1703, w Mary Tarent, ST, US, geneal, bk rev GH 41:5:193

Robert, CT, geneal, bk rev SCC 23:1-4:2

Surname period, *Rose Fam Bulletin*, 1474 Montelegre Dr, San Jose CA 95120 - burials OH, cem AR, taxes PA, land NC, v r CT, cem LA, news NY, Civil War TN, cem MA, census CO & MD

ROSEMIRE, Augustus m1822, w Dorothy Remann, IL, biog sketch FF 15:3:38

ROSS, Charles E d1875, IL, obit DWC 13:2:60

Edward M b1816, w Catherine T Delaney, NY, TX, anc ch VC 8:2:47

Fam coats of arms MD & DE MAD 27:3:110

Isaac S b1853, VA, Bible rec OZ 7:1:26

Susannah see James Lodwick ALFORD

William Stewart m1930, w Costa Clark, Bible rec OZ 7:1:25

ROTH, Barbara see Jacob EGLE

ROTHLISBERGER, Maria see Johan RENTSCH

ROTHROCK, Johannes b1684, PA, CO, geneal, bk rev NGS 75:1:63

ROTTINK, Fam hist NL & US 1650-1986, bk rev GFP 37:2:72

Laurens b1675, NL, geneal, bk rev GH 41:4:209

ROUND, Fam hist MA, bk rev MI 32:1:11

ROUS, Hannah see William CROWDER

ROUSH, Maude L see William CRAIG

ROUSSEAU, Marguerite see Pierre AYAULT

ROUSSEL, Christophe bc1760, w Perinne Haydel, LA, anc ch AGE 16:4:119

ROUTH, Jonathan m1827, w Katharine Barringer, Bible rec YTD 7:1:6

ROWDEN, Satterwaite b1850, w Alma Miller, MO, letter SNS 3:3:4

ROWE, Emaline Amanda see William HARKINS

ROWLAND, Agnes see James YATES

James Warren, w Katerine Elizabeth Taylor, geneal, bk rev KK 25:1:18

ROWLEY, Henry mc1630, w Sarah Palmer & Ann Blossom, EN, MA, geneal, bk rev GH 41:5:167

ROWLEY (continued)
Jireh b1777, w Elizabeth Brace, NY, fam hist WTC 17:4:114

ROY, Hannah (Proctor) see John W MORLEY

ROYCE, Robert dc1676, EN, CT, anc ch HJA 12:1:74

ROYDER, Adam b1829, w Mary Ann Price & Barbara Ellen Harrell, GE, TX, biog sketch AGS 28:2:71

RUDDICK, Isaac N m1886, w Priscilla Jane Bagley, Bible rec HH 21:4:221

RUDIN, Frederick f1751, w Elizabeth Schaublin, SW, PA, geneal, bk rev MN 18:1:39 THT 15:1:21

RUDIN, Niklaus bc1574, SW, PA, geneal, bk rev RES 18:2:79

RUDY, Frederick b1716, w Elisabeth Schaulin, GE, PA, geneal, bk rev CCS 8:4:131 CTN 19:4:710 CGS 18:1:16

RUEDI, Verena see Jakob MUR-BACH

RUEGGER, Samuel b1851, w Catherine Meyer, SW, IL, obit CRT 8:4:42

RUFFIN, Tho f1857, letter JC 13:2:31

RUGG, Hannah Ames see Benjamin PIERCE

RULAND, Acker b1856, w Susan Harris, IL, biog sketch WTC 17:4:125

RUNNINGER, Johan Jacob f1777, w Margaretha Lowenguth, GE, PA, geneal, bk rev WPG 13:4:39 GH 41:1:164

RUPERTIN, Eva see Baltas MAURER

RUSHWORTH, Agnes see Alfred CROWTHER

RUSSEL, Mary see Phineas MATTHEWS

Samantha O see John CLARK

RUSSELL, Charity see Nathaniel WILLETT

Ira, w Betsey Bickford Deering & Eunice Jerusia Lee, geneal, bk rev RAG 8:3:25

RUSSELL (continued)
John m1639, w Elizabeth ___,
MA, EN origins NEH 4:1:19
Matthew bc1735, w Jane McIntire
& Verlinda (Lamar) Jenkins,
IR, SC, geneal, bk rev NCJ
13:2:121
Rachel Ann bc1835, h William
Ralston, VA, KY, biog sketch
EK 23:1:20
Winnia C see Israel R WELCH
RUSSIA, Consular rec index &
catalog, bk rev GH 41:6:124
RUSSLER, Luella see John Gilmore RAINS
RUTHERFORD, Fam hist ST, IR,
VA, NJ, PA, bk rev TTT
11:1:27
Katherine see John WALKER
RYALS, Jesse bc1775, SC, AL,
geneal, bk rev GH 41:4:209
RYAN, Fam rec misc of several
famous Ryans IR & AA
1600s-1900s TI 86:11:8
Margaret see Henry H P KEANE
Nelley see Wm WOOD
RYDER, Adam S b1832, w Charlotte Bear, PA, mill property
LCC 4:4:72
SABEAN, Sarah Jane b1868, NS,
MA, anc ch AG 62:4:232
SABIN, Dencey see Jacob WHITING
Surname period, *Sabin/Sabine/
Sabean Geneal Newsletter*,
Apartado 10250 (1000), San
Jose, Costa Rica
SADDLER, Mary J see Thomas
McGEE
SADLER, Jane b1829, IR, anc cn
JCG 15:2:64
SAGAR, John b1831, w Catherine
Dean, EN, geneal GEN 12:2:15
Richard d1699, w Elizabeth ___,
EN, fam hist AW 13:2:77
SAGER, Caroline see Friedrich C
KRUEGER
Francis m1863, w Ellen Angell,
Bible rec IG 23:2:60
Henry f1844, w Naomi ___, MO,
OR, fam hist, bk rev WCG
3:10:95

SAGESER, Margaret see James
William GRAVES
SAHR, Margaretha see Augustus
HERBERT
SAHS, Louise see Henry J HOLM
SAINT CROIX, William d1889,
death rec NAL 3:2:19
SAINT JOHN, Marietta see John J
WALRATH
SAINT PIERRE, Edmond b1826,
w Catherine LaGarce, CN?, IL,
anc ch FF 15:4:136
SALES, James f1851, NY, MI,
account bk 1851-1880 DM
50:4:153
SALMON, Ann see Daniel
BRODHEAD
John Allen d1918, w Sarah
Clemons, OK, anc ch AGS
28:2:92
Mary see James TEMPLIN
SALOME, Margaret see Jacob
AMBROSE
SALTERIO, Giovanni Antonio
b1580, IY, geneal, bk rev GH
41:5:155
SALZMAN, Harley B b1897, IL,
obit GL 21:1:16
SAMES, Johanna see John Martin
WOERNER
SAMPLE, Jane f1847, GA, will
TCG 7:4:25
SAMPSON, Ezekiel f1767, w Lurranah ___, NY, biog sketch
OCG 17:3:19
SAMS, Orra see Thomas
FORSTER
SAMUEL, Surname period, *Samuel
Searcher*, 7805 Linda Ln,
Anchorage AK 99518
SANDEESON, Ellen Marnetta see
John Lewis POWERS
SANDERS, Fam reunion 1927 NC
JC 13:4:69
James f1881, biog, bk rev TOP
17:1:4
John m1715, w Prissila Pritloe,
VA, marr rec QY 14:4:10
Josephus b1858, Bible rec FG
29:2:56
Reuben b1764, w Keren Ann
___, NC, cem inscr JC 13:1:9

SANDERS (continued)
Sarah Ann see Jason Martin GREER Sr
SANDERSON, Electa A see Henry L DAWES
Henry Jacob b1827, w Angeline Armstrong, PA, MS, anc ch TRC 2:1:46
SANDIFER, James Dosy m1882, w Emily Elizabeth Ashby, Bible rec KFR 13: :2
SANDS, Myrtle Della see James Anderson NATION
SANDY, William b1765, w Catherine Beck, NC?, IN, geneal, bk rev WPG 13:4:48
SANFORD, William Hall m1885, w Rosa Elizabeth Weekley, Bible rec FP 30:1:12
William m1803, w Barbara Snider, Bible rec YTD 1:2:18
SAPPINGTON, Fam cem Troup Co GA TCG 7:3:45
SARGENT, Rebecca b1750, MA, anc ch AG 62:3:93
SARTIN, William A b1844, w Mary A Lambert, AL, children FTH 10:3-4:100
SARVER, Jonathan Marialie b1776, w Maria Streit, PA, geneal, bk rev WPG 13:3:46
SASSAMAN, Elizabeth see John LIPPARD
SASSMANHAUSEN, Jost Heinrich bc1721, GE, PA, geneal, bk rev GH 41:4:210
SAUL, Anna Barbara see Christian KUCH
SAVAGE, Amos b1838, IL, biog WTC 17:4:117
Surname period, *Savage Fam Depository Newsletter*, 3840 Smiths Crossing, Freeland MI 48623
SAWYER, Hosea Huston b1828, w Maria Hoyt, VT, IL, obit CRT 8:1:24
Thomas Tandy m1832, w Caroline Fernold Plumer, ME, Bible rec DM 50:4:152
SAXTON, Alva f1885, NE, biog sketch NW 9:2:19

SAYLES, John, w Mary Williams, RI, soc hist, bk rev AG 62:3:190
SCAIFE, Cordelia Jane see William Robert HICKS
SCANDINAVIAN GENEALOGY, Naturalizations 1802-1840 NY SAG 7:2:75
Res hints TEG 7:2:57
SCARF, Sarah see Samuel GRIFFIN
SCHAFFER, Ottilia see Georg MECKENDORFER
SCHALLENBERGER, Anna m1827, h Heinrich Herschy, PA, Bible rec LCH 1:2:83
SCHAPERKOTTER, Wilhelm b1859, w Minna F Kampmeier, MO, IL, Bible rec STC 10:2:88
SCHAPPLEY, Hans Georg f1748, w Magdeline Huber & Christina Speinger, SW, SC, GA, geneal, bk rev FLG 10:2:77
SCHAUBLIN, Elisabeth see Frederick RUDIN/RUDY
SCHECTER, Marinda m1859, h Henry L Miller, IL, letter IG 23:1:18
SCHEIDT, Rosa see George KLOSS
SCHELLE, Frank Joseph b1850, w Maria Anna Berning, GE, IA, anc ch SD 5:3:65
SCHERMANN, Antoni b1818, w Franciazkn ___, PO, IL, biog sketch PN 9:2:29
SCHERMERHORN, Richard see Nancy VANVECHTEN
SCHETROUPF, Catharine Elizabeth see Anthony Wayne FISHER
SCHIEBER, John f1868, MO, geneal, bk rev GH 41:2:155
SCHIEDEL, Fam rec misc ON, bk rev MI 32:2:76
SCHILLING, Christina see Heinrich MERKER
SCHINDEL, Georg Friedrich m1750, w Maria Barbara Hamm, PA, geneal, bk rev NYR 118:2:117

SCHLABACH, Moses b1859, w Lydia Yoder, geneal, bk rev MFH 6:4:131

SCHLAPPACH, Magdalena see Daniel BENDER

SCHLEGEL, Christopher f1710, PA, hist of mill LCC 4:2:39

SCHMEMTZLER, Sarah see David OWEN

SCHMITT, Erwin P b1896, IL, remembrances WTC 5:2-3:33

Peter Joseph b1818, w Anna Margaretha Wagner, GE, MN, geneal, bk rev GH 41:5:194

SCHNAKE, Christine Marie Ilsabein see Friedrich Wilhelm DONNIG

SCHNEBELE, Johann Jacob b1659, SW, PA, geneal, bk rev GH 41:1:165 FRT 8:3:153 GH 41:2:161 NYR 118:1:58 PM 10:3:40 GFP 37:2:70 CCS 9:1:24

SCHNEBELI, Maryya b1750, fam rec MFH 6:4:154

SCHNECK, Fam hist 1741-1985 US, bk rev GH 41:6:164

SCHNIEPER, Theresa see Anton BECK

SCHOENSTEDT, Christoph b1837,w Louisa Gantz, GE, IL, biog WTC 8:4:93

SCHOFFEN, Howard f1950, WA, fam hist sketch AB 15:4:92

SCHOON, Grietje f1864, h Cornelius Ton, HO, IN, IL, geneal, bk rev WTC 11:4:162

SCHORMAN, August see Johanna ENKE

SCHOTT, Elizabeth see Hugh BAIN

SCHOTTLER, Christian b1770, w Katharina Werrey & Elisabeth Sommer, GE, US, geneal MFH 6:4:141

SCHRAMM, Adam b1785, GE, anc ch JCG 15:3:101

SCHREIBER, William b1827, w Dora Oahl, GE, IL, obit CRT 8:1:25

SCHULER, Fam hist 1822-1983 GE & WI, bk rev CHG 19:1:20

SCHULZ, Henry b1911, RA, BC, auto, bk rev BCG 16:1:31

SCHUMMER, Marie Magdalena bc1795, Luxembourg, anc ch BHN 20:4:173

SCHUYLER, Fam hist NY, bk rev NYR 118:4:238

SCHWAB, Anna Maria see Andreas MEIXEL

SCHWANGAU, William f1747, US, geneal, bk rev GH 41:2:156

SCHWARTLEY, Catharine see Johannes H KOLB

SCHWARTZ, Fam hist GE & IN, bk rev SIN 8:3:83

Michael b1764, w Catharine Sheetz, PA, KY, IN, geneal, bk rev GH 41:4:210

SCHWEIZER, Johannes f1847, GE, NJ, geneal, bk rev NYR 118:3:187

SCHWIND, Alma Anna b1897, IN, Bible rec STC 10:2:96

SCOBY, Surname period, *The Scoby Scribe*, S 1013 Warren Rd, Veradale WA 99037

SCOFIELD, Mary J see John GARDNER

SCOGGINS, Hannah Ann see John Wesley DUNGEY

Nancy see Blassingame W HARVEY

SCOT, Mary see John F FRAZIER

SCOTCH-IRISH GENEALOGY, Hist in US LCH 3:2:54

Hist sketch of migration AMG 2:4:6

SCOTLAND, Aberdeen, Aberdeen Granite Yard, hist, bk rev ANE 23: :20

Aberdeen, co & burgh life 1600-1800, bk rev ANE 21: :26

Aberdeen, gazeteer, bk rev ANE 21: :27

Aberdeen, hist (pictorial), bk rev ANE 24::20

Aberdeen, hist sketch of Aberdeen Harbour ANE 24::12

Aberdeen, Lanmay, pollable persons 1696, bk rev RAG 8:5:21

SCOTLAND (continued)

Aberdeen, street names, bk rev ANE 21: :25

Aberdeenshire, Fraserburgh, residents 1861 ANE 22: :2

Aberdour Shore, hist, bk rev ANE 21: :25

Argyll, powder mill, hist sketch GWS :24:5

Clan & fam soc US SGS 36:2:72

Coalminers, bk rev CTN 20:1:145 GH 41:2:119

Emig to Am 1774-1775, bk rev WPG 13:3:48

Emig to US dictionary vol 2, bk rev RAG 8:2:24 GH 41:1:124

Extinct & dormant baronetcies, bk rev see ENGLAND, extinct & dormant baronetcies

Fam hist, bk rev GH 41:6:125

Fam hist avail in the Ferguson Lib, bk rev CTA 30:1:51

Fam hist by Ferguson, bk rev GWS :24:21 TGO 5:6:206 RAG 8:2:24

Fam hist res & source guide by Cairns-Smith-Barth, bk rev TGO 5:6:206

Geneal repositories, GGL 6:1-2:4

Geneal res guide by Fam Hist Lib, bk rev GH 41:6:125

Geneal res hints SGS 36:3:123

Geneal res hints & sources TGO 5:6:187

Geneal resources for fam hist in the Elgin (ST) Public Lib ANE 24::6

Glasgow, ship pass list 1904 to QB & Montreal on board the S S Corinthian THH :97:2

Hist of Argyle Settlement in IL, bk rev GH 41:5:170

Imm to Cape Breton, hist sketch GN 5:2:89

Imm to northwest US, bk rev SGS 36:2:100

Imm to TX 1886 (stonecutters & blacksmiths) ANE 22: :3

Kincardine Parish, census 1851 index, bk rev ANE 20: :25

Knockbain Parish, census 1851 index, bk rev ANE 21: :25

SCOTLAND (continued)

Lerwick, notes of cases of poor 1843 index ANE 20: :5

Mil rec offices with addresses ANE 23: :18

Names used syonymously AH 14:3:108

Natives banished to Am plantations 1650-1775, bk rev FAM 26:1:52

Natives buried in Beechwood Cem, Ottawa ON GWS :24:11

Oldmeldrum Chyard cem inscr, bk rev RAG 8:5:21

Prisoners of war shipped to MD 1715, bk rev EWA 24:1:52

Reg of the great seal 1306-1668, bk rev ANE 22: :29

Settlers in North Am 1625-1825 direct vol 4, bk rev FAM 26:2:114 (vol 6) NGS 74:4:315 WMG 3:2:92 DM 50:3:141 NYR 118:1:51 AG 62:3:122 SGS 36:2:102 PA 35:1:52 (vol 7) MN 18:1:38

Settlers in the Carolinas 1680-1830 direct, bk rev NGS 74:4:317

Soldier biog sketches 1800s ANE 23: :23

Tay Valley, geneal misc 1803-abstr from news, bk rev ANE 24::20

Tay Valley, source bk 1987, bk rev ANE 24::20

Wick (Landward) Caithness Parish, census 1851, bk rev ANE 22: :29

SCOTT, Adella Alcesta b1869, h Earl Reuben Fuller, auto AW 13:4:150

Francis Marion m1882, w S R Franks, Bible rec HTR 30:1:10

Isabella see Timothy REDDY

John H f1835, IR, CN, NY, geneal, bk rev GH 41:4:209

Louisa Jane b1828, MO, CA, anc ch OG 13:2:41

Margaret Malinda see John Washington ROSE

Moses d1871, w Ellen Scott, IL, will abstr IG 23:3:89

SCOTT (continued)
Nichilas b1750, VA, anc ch AA
7:4:188
Sara E see James Russell DUN-
CAN
Sarah see Jonathan ARNOLD
Thomas see Elizabeth STRUTT
William Theodore b1858, w Alta
Greene, IA, CO, biog sketch
CO 48:3:83
Zilpha see William DOCKRAY
SCOULLER, Thomas b1847, w
Anna Toy, ST, WA, biog
sketch YV 19:1:7
SCRONCE, Peter b1797, PU, IL,
anc ch THT 16:1:10
SCRUDG, Richard f1680, VA,
deed VAG 31:3:192
SEALE, Arthur A b1884, w
Ellzabeth Norwood, TX, biog
YTD 5:2:27
SEALS, John f1638, w Marritje
Robbers, EN, NY, anc ch SB
8:1:13
SEARLE, Silas Walter b1877, w
Maude Delle Hughlitt, IL, WA,
biog sketch YV 19:1:11
SEARS, Fam rec corr IL FF
15:4:144
SEATON, Francis M b1853, MO,
anc ch CR 19:2:99
Susanna see Ezekiel RIDER
SEAY, Obediah bc1790, w Sallie
Rice, AR, geneal, bk rev GH
41:1:164
SEBASTIAN, William King
b1812, AR, TN, biog sketch
TRC 2:1:25
SEE, John b1845, w Charlotte
Mary Matthews, EN, AA, biog
TGO 5:5:147
SEELEY, Surname period, *Seeley
Geneal Soc Newsletter*, 4250
Darling Rd, Rives Junction MI
49277
SELBY, David Melville f1834, w
Hannah Selby, CT, pension
appl NGS 74:3:187
SELLERS, L R b1848, w Alice
Goss, IN, KS, biog sketch KL
7:4:17

SELTZER, Frederick b1800, w
Sarah ____, PA, IL, fam hist
WTC 13:3:108
SENEY, George b1817, w Mary
Anne Fero, IR, ON, anc ch
GGL 6:4:148
SENSEL, Peter b1815, w Mag-
dalena Hoff, GE, IL, obit STC
10:2:95
SENSIBAUGH, Robert b1806, w
Elizabeth Hudson Blevins,
KY?, VA?, CA, biog sketch
SCS 24:10:201
SEON, Sarah see Daniel Wool-
ridge Outerbridge
SERGEANT, John see Margaret
WELLS
Stephen f1890, w Cynthia Grubbs,
KY, pension appl HF 3:2:68
SERGENT, Abraham bc1777, w
Elizabeth ____, NC, KY,
geneal HF 3:2:75
Margaret m1858, h James Boogs,
KY, fam rec HF 3:3:145
SESSIONS, Alexander, MA, fam
hist, microfiche rev GH
41:5:197
SETSER, Margaret b1867, h Lowe
B Wells, KY, biog sketch EK
22:4:5
SEURYNCK, Jan Baptiste m1769,
w Rozalia Theresia Boen, W
Flanders, US, geneal FAH
5:2:33
SEWARD, Fam hist NY, NJ, bk
rev NYR 118:4:239
Fam hist, bk rev,TTH 8:3:59
CTN 20:3:517
SEWELL, Alma see Henry HUS-
TON
David b1746, w Mary Elizabeth
Tullis, VA, OH, anc ch HL
5:4:100
Elizabeth d1865, h John Sewell,
GA, cem inscr CCM 6:4:77
SEYBERT, Silas Engle b1808, w
Mary Ann Jones & ____ Fin-
ley, PA, MO, children OZ
8:1:28
SEYFARTH, William b1818, w
Louise Bartling, GE, IL, fam
hist sketch WTC 4:4:139

SHACKLEFORD, Henry b1764, w Nancy ___, VA, pension HF 3:3:140

SHAFFER, Peter f1828, w Rebecca ___, IL, geneal FF 15:4:123

SHAKERS, Hist in Union Village OH & census 1850 HL 4:2:42

SHAND, John f1725, ST, MA, propinquity bk rec NGS 74:3:172

SHANDS, Thomas b1660, w Frances Harrison, ST, VA, geneal, bk rev FRT 8:1:51

SHANE, Timothy, w Hannah Blunk, geneal, bk rev GH 41:3:170

SHANNON, Fam rec misc KY, TN, VA, bk rev GH 41:6:164

Owen bc1762, w Margaret Montgomery, GA, TX, geneal MCG 10:3:112

Surname period, *Shannon Searchers*, Joyce Bridges, 11174 Springridge-Texas Line Rd, Keithville LA 71047

SHANTZ, Samuel Y m1845, w Esther Erb, Bible rec LCC 4:3:51

SHAPLEY, Surname period, *The Shapley Connection*, Brian J L Berry, POB 82-2130, Richardson TX 75083

SHARP, Jenny May b1866, IL, anc ch CR 19:4:170

Nancy b1808, TN, AR, anc ch TN 7:3:44

SHAVER, Robert Anderson b1825, w Elizabeth Johnston, AR, TN?, geneal, bk rev GH 41:6:164

SHAW, Henry f1881, TX, title deed FP 30:4:191

SHAY, Elizabeth b1819, h Abraham Kiehle Jr, geneal NYR 118:3:146

Peter b1757, w Catharine ___, NJ, geneal NYR 118:2:88

SHAYS, Daniel b1747, w Abigail Gilbert & Rhoda Havens, IR, geneal, bk rev GH 41:4:209

SHEARER, Eunice see Royal George BYRD

Frances Elizabeth see Samuel James WADDILL

SHEAROUSE, Gottlieb bc1793, w Sarah S Freyermouth, GA, FL, lineage FLG 10:4:148

SHEEHAN, Benjamin d1917, IL, obit CRT 8:4:43

Fam coat of arms MD & DE MAD 27:3:110

SHEELY, George f1862, NY, Civil War service rec BGS 19:2:68

SHEETS, John William b1858, w Mary Ann Maywalt, WA, biog sketch YV 19:1:8

SHEETZ, Catharine see Michael SCHWARTZ

SHEFFIELD, Elizabeth see William Wesley WILSON

William B f1850, pioneering WTC 12:1:6

SHELBOURNE, Samuel m1806, w Sally Pamplin & Mary Browder, VA, TN, geneal, bk rev GH 41:2:155

SHELBURNE, Thomas f1607, VA, AL, geneal, bk rev CCS 9:3:98

SHELDON, Ephraim f1776, MA, biog SCS 24:10:194

Rufus m1836, w Mary Griffin, Bible rec TFP 7: :68

SHELTON, Aubrey C see Sadie Evangeline LINSE

SHENK, Abram L b1826, w Fannie Musser, PA, biog sketch LCH 1:2:93

SHEPARD, Edmund bc1475, w Agnes/Annes ___, EN, MA, desc AG 62:4:235

John H b1817, w Allethea Daugherty, NY, CA, biog sketch SCS 24:3:61

Joseph m1850, w Mary Jane Armstrong, Bible rec WTC 9:1:25

Prudence bc1791, NY, anc ch OCG 17:2:12

William d1615, EN, MA, geneal, microfiche rev GH 41:2:163

SHEPHERD, Asa b1781, w Margaret Baker, VA, IN, geneal OCG 17:4:28

Frederick David b1810, w Elizabeth Breth, PA, Bible rec WTC 14:1:25

Neil b1923, w Alice Nelson, MT, anc BM 18:2:67

SHERIDEN, Rebekah see John LUM

SHERMAN, Mary see Theophilus CHOWNING

SHERRILL, Malinda C see John A FORD

SHERROD, Benjamin f1821, w Eliza Watkins & Tabitha (Goode) Watkins, GA, children SGE 28:124:51

SHERWOOD, Jabez b1719, w Hannah Disbrow, CT, anc ch HL 6:1:24

SHIELDS, Sylvester L d1865, TN, inventory NTT 7:4:155

SHILLING, N C see Q L ORELL

Vincent b1828, w Amanda F Gomer, Bible rec FP 30:4:175

SHILLINGTON, Thomas bapt1745, N IR, anc ch BG 8:4:90

SHIPLEY, Mary Wiley see David THOMAS

SHIPMAN, James bc1795, w Rebecca ____, NC, TN, MO, geneal OZ 7:1:29

Mary Lee m1825, h Alfred Andrews, Bible rec HH 21:4:218

SHIPP, Fam hist revised, bk rev OC 24:2:82

James Edward b1852, w May Lucinda Bingham, IN, UT, anc ch GCP 5:4:33

William dc1657, VA, geneal, bk rev NYR 118:2:119

SHIRES, Ruth see Daniel MCPHERSON

SHIRLEY, Fam hist TN, bk rev GH 41:6:164

SHOCKNEY, Patrick d1827, IR, MD, geneal, bk rev NYR 118:2:115

SHOEMAKER, Fam hist, bk rev AG 62:1:58

SHOEMAKER, William Henry b1842, w Elizabeth Redman, VA, biog HF 3:3:143

SHOFF, Daniel Brainerd b1822, NH, anc ch BWG 16:1:39

Nora Alice see John Walter RICHARDSON

SHORT, John H m1853, w Elizabeth A Parker, Bible rec MD 28:2:234

Peley (Sturgeon) b1828, w Sarah Creech, KY, fam rec HF 3:1:8

SHORTER, Reuben Clarke bc1787, w Mary Gill, AL, GA, geneal SGE 28:123:35

SHOULDERS, Rachel see Thomas BLAND

SHOVE, Edward B m1843, w Eliza M Hoxie, Bible rec BG 8:4:103

SHOWALTER, Christopher bc1774, w Ann Funkhouser, PA, IN, geneal KL 7:4:18

SHROCK, Fam hist 1807-1971 PA & OH, bk rev WTC 5:2-3:104

John C m1826, w Catherine Hochstetler, PA, OH, IN, geneal, bk rev SCS 24:12:240

SHROPSHIRE, Surname period, *International Soc of Shropshires Newsletter*, Rt 2 Box 298A, Staunton VA 24401

SHUCK, Mose bc1784, w Mary Ann Fleshman, VA, geneal, bk rev GH 41:6:164

SHULER, Margaret bc1824, PA, anc ch EK 23:1:34

SIBLEY, John f1807, journal 1807, bk rev GH 41:5:195

SIDES, Henry b1734, AL, fam hist sketch AFH 8:3:76

SIEG, Paul f1720, GE, US, geneal, bk rev GH 41:4:209

SIEPKEN, Ilse Catharine see Anton Barthold DEMTER

SIGOGNE, Abbe Jean Mande b1760, FR, NS, biog AGE 16:2:43

SIJMONS, Jannetje see Evert Everts PELS

SILAS, Howard d1857, CA, cem inscr RDQ 5:1:10

SILBY, Betsy see Levi BOWKER

SIMERSON, William f1799, NJ, agreement to keep Widow Calket GMN 62:1:8

SIMES, Anna see Julian C TUSSEY

SIMMONS, Fam hist 1746-1986, bk rev TS 29:3:108

James dc1786, w Ursula Cleveland, LA, geneal, bk rev KSL 11:3:76

Jeremiah f1781, w Lucy Sutton, NC, pension appl JC 13:3:57

Samuel Joseph b1879, w Armada (Wilson) Hoyle, IL, anc ch FF 15:4:138

Squire b1746, NA, GA, VA, geneal, bk rev VAG 31:2:151

Squire b1791, w Levicy Hunt, NC, VA, GA, geneal, bk rev GH 41:1:165 FRT 8:4:202 NCJ 13:2:122 SCM 15:2:119

William bc1793, w Sarah Hagood, TN, AL, geneal, bk rev NTT 7:3:83

William H b1838, w Millie McBride, TX, anc ch VC 8:1:22

SIMPSON, Elizabeth see John ENGLEDOW

Henry b1782, w Eunice Thompson, Bible rec CTN 20:2:241

Sarah Ellen see John E THOMPSON

Surname period, *Simpsons: A Gathering of the Clan*, POB 1654, Soquel CA 95073

Thomas b1796, w Nancy Moreland, NC, MO, biog OZ 6:2:79

SIMS, Matthew f1739, w Jamima ___, Bible rec YTD 6:1:42

SINCLAIR, Fam in Baltimore Co MD 1700s MD 28:1:2

SIPPLE, Uriah m1840, w Mariah Clark, Bible rec DJ 4:2:42

SITES, George f1775, GE, PA, VA, geneal, bk rev WPG 13:4:48

SITTON, Silas b1823, w Arminda Reid, AL, anc ch NAS 25:4:128

SITZ, Cornelia Ran see John Timothy Crenshaw DISHEROON

William b1827, w Anna Luise Klemm, PU, US, geneal, bk rev KK 25:1:17

SKAGGS, Pleasant b1851, w Sarah Prince, KY, biog EK 22:4:20

SKEEN, Fam hist US, bk rev SCS 24:10:202

SKELLS, Anna Mabel see Heil Bronson HATHAWAY

SKELTON, William bc1745, VA?, geneal, bk rev GH 41:3:172

SKENE, Isabella see George SLESSOR

SKIDMORE, Albert m1859, w Mary ___, KY, divorce HF 3:1:5

Andrew C f1861, w Louisa Forrester, KY, divorce HF 3:1:5

Henry bc1650, DE, anc ch EK 23:1:34

John, KY, biog, bk rev KA 23:2:117

SKINNER, Ann see John COLT

SLACK, Jno Stewart m1914, w Elve Moore, NY, Bible rec YTD 2:1:15

Mary Ann see Samuel OSBOURNE

SLAPPEY, Barbara S see Thomas HARGRETT

SLAPPY, Fam hist SC & GA, bk rev GGS 23:1:45

SLATER, Ira Henry m1874, w Zella E Hurlburt, IL, Bible rec WTC 14:3:116

SLAUGHTER, Della see James Calloway BUCHANAN

SLAVIN, Joseph A see Anna LaBISSONIERE

SLEDGE, Mins f1842, GA, will TCG 7:3:22

SLESSOR, George b1856, w Isabella Skene, ST?, anc ch ANE 24::17

SLIMP, Rachel see Isaac DOUGHERTY

SLOAN, Phebe see John FISK

219

SLOT, Pieter Jansen m1663, w
Mariette Jacobse Van
Winckle, HO, US, geneal,
microfiche rev GH 41:5:198
SLUSHER, William bc1797, VA,
KY, anc ch EK 22:4:36
SLUSSER, Mary Jane see Robert
BLACKWELL
SMAIL, Rhodica J see John
Phenton ABEL
SMALL, James Madison f1877, w
Sarah Elizabeth Page, OR,
WA, fam hist sketch WCG
4:1:2
John B bc1770, SC, geneal, bk
rev GH 41:4:210
Ruth see William COOK
SMALLWOOD, George D m1839,
w Mary Ann Brown, IL, obit
DWC 13:3:91
SMITH, A f1838, MD, letter BGS
19:1:11
Abraham d1806, w Molley ___,
SC, will abstr SGE 28:124:5
Alexander b1830, w Elizabeth
Phillips, OH, anc ch HL 5:3:81
Alvin L m1900, w Audra Watson,
MO, Bible rec OZ 8:1:37
Amanda see John Blair TAD-
LOCK
Anne b1785, NC, cem inscr NCJ
13:4:242
Catharine see James H YOUNG
Charles C b1847, w Louise Maria
Neilson, SW, NE, anc ch KIL
15:2:29
Clara A see Edwin D VAUGHN
Daniel d1904, w Emma ___,
lineage NAL 3:2:7
David f1866, w Protessa Smith,
Bible rec YV 19:2:52
Della Zelma see Arthur James
CHILSON
Edward m1820, w Hannah W
Townsley, Bible rec BG
8:4:100
Elias b1729, MA, biog TEG
7:2:70
Elias b1808, w Elizabeth Kistler
& Eliza Brandal, OH, geneal
TFP 7: :15

SMITH (continued)
Fam birth & death rec Highland
Co OH, bk rev GH 41:6:144
Fam hist Cape Breton CN, bk rev
GN 5:1:26
Fam hist VA, NC, SC, GA, bk
rev SCM 15:3:179 GH 41:6:164
Fam rec corr to *Adams Fam* by
Adams NEH 4:2:76
Fam rec GA, bk rev SB 8:3:103
Frederick dc1846, w Ann Phil-
lips, AL, heirs AL 3:1:12
Frederick f1879, TX, letter STK
14:4:189
George R b1804, VA, MO, obit
SNS 3:2:2
H E f18(3/5)1, MI, letter FG
29:4:115
Jacob b1839, w Sarah Jane Wol-
ford, IL, obit CRT 8:4:12
James A Sr, ST, CN, diary THH
:97:5
James H b1823, w Angeline
Phelps, NY, OH, obit TLL
12:3:53
James H f1873, OH, journal abstr
TLL 12:1:15 12:2:41 12:4:85
John, w Susannah Watson, VA,
NC, fam hist TA 22:1:12
John b1791, CT, NY, anc ch AG
62:4:231
John bapt1580, EN, VA, biog MP
3:1:49
John bc1579, w Isabelle Stanley,
EN, MA, lineage SB 8:2:56
John bc1775, NC, geneal, bk rev
GH 41:4:210
John D b1834, w Mary Gobliss,
VT, anc ch KIL 15:2:31
John H m1851, w Hannah Francis
Colvin, KY, Bible rec KA
23:2:93
Joseph Jr see Fanny ALGER
Lucy A see Thomas H THOM-
SON
Lucy Hosmer see Augustus
Rudolphus BAILEY
Margaret see Elijah WHITE
Marinus Gilbert b1819, w Anna M
Woodruff, NY, CO, biog BGS
19:4:157

SMITH (continued)
Mary see Jacob LEMMON & John PEDEN & Charles HUMPHRIES & Wyatt ALLGOOD
Nathaniel Jr b1729, w Sarah Douglass, lineage SLV 5:2:11
Nettie Jane see Frank H RICE
Rezin m1805, w Amelia Medlin, Bible rec YTD 5:1:23
Robert bc1725, ST, NY, anc ch OCG 17:2:12
Robert f1648, MA, NY, geneal, bk rev NYR 118:2:117
Robert f1772, PA, geneal, bk rev GH 41:1:165
Sally see Jeptha NICKERSON
Samuel f1755, w Sarah Hunt, BM, fam rec BBQ 4:1:10
Samuel f1786, w Mary ___, BM, fam rec BBQ 4:1:10
Samuel Phair b1852, w Mary Elizabeth Spencer, TX, Bible rec YTD 1:1:28
Sarah see William COOKE
Susanna see Samuel HAYS
Tabitha b1825, Bible rec YTD 7:1:4
Wiley b1778, w Elizabeth Hearn, GA, geneal TCG 7:4:47
SMOCK, Abraham b1790, w Catherine Gott, KY, Bible rec WTC 14:3:119
Nancy see Garrett PETERSON
SMUCKER, Silas J b1904, IN, auto MIS 19:2:26
SMYTH, Joane see John PENTICOST
Mary see Peter WATERS
SMYTHE, John b1786, ST, IR, CN, Bible rec RAG 8:2:12
SNALL, Nancy Emmaline Lunceford see Silas B CALL
SNAVELY, Irenus B b1837, w Sarah Ann Uhler, PA?, IN?, OK?, geneal GTP 25:3:55
SNEED, Emily see John Calvin PAYNE
Julia f1815, NC, letter NCJ 13:4:233
SNIDER, Barbara see William SANFORD

SNIDER (continued)
Surname period, *People Finders International*, 1312 Devanport Dr #7, Lexington KY 45504
SNODGRASS, Lucinda Jane see Daniel WILHITE
SNOW, Freelove (Dutchard?) see James FOREST
SNYDER, Emanuel f1820, w Ann Eliza ___, IL, geneal FF 15:3:39
Fam will abstr IL IG 23:1:11
Magdalena see Jacob APRILL
Susanna see Jacob LAMP
SOANE, Henry f1622, w Judith ___, EN, VA, geneal, bk rev NGS 74:3:226
SOCOLOFSKY, Gottfried f1876, GE, RA, KS, geneal, bk rev KK 25:1:17
SOLENBERGER, Solomon m1870, w Christina Stauffer, IL, Bible rec BGS 19:4:166
SOLOMON, Fam hist, bk rev NFB 19:2:22
SOMMER, Elisabeth see Christian SCHOTTLER
SONNE, Margaret see Augustus KING
SOULE, Miranda see Samuel F WIGGINS
Nella Ina see John James MORLEY
SOUTH CAROLINA, Beaufort Co, St Luke's Parish, census 1850, bk rev GH 41:3:175
Beersheba Pres Chyard inscr SCM 15:1:20 15:2:79
Calhoun Co, Sandy Run Luth Ch rec 1828-1848 SCM 15:4:183
Camden District, equity journal 1807-1809 SCM 15:1:34 15:2:103 15:3:155 15:4:202
Charleston, jail roster 1863? SCM 15:1:10
Charleston, lawyers 1859 roster SGE 28:122:36
Charlestown, residents 1782 GHS 4:2:30
Chester, Purity Pres Ch hist, bk rev GH 41:5:184

SOUTH CAROLINA (cont)

Chesterfield District, Cheraw, marr & death notices 1856 abstr from the *Pee Dee Herald* SCM 15:1:14

Clemson, Old Stone Ch Cem inscr, bk rev EWA 24:3:210

Colleton Co, deeds index 1865-1974 GHS 4:1:4 4:2:36

Edgefield Co, deed abstr 1786-1796 vol 1, bk rev NGS 75:1:65

Edgefield Co, geneal rec misc, bk rev TCG 6:4:71

Edgefield District, estate divisions 1830s SCM 15:1:43 15:2:95 15:3:148 15:4:195

Fairfield Co, marr 1775-1879, bk rev GH 41:4:200

Geneal misc 1732-1735 abstr from the *SC Gazette* SCM 15:4:222

Geneal res & rec guide by Holcomb, bk rev GHS 4:1:73

Geneal res hints SCS 24:8:162

Geneal res hints, use of the courthouse MIS 19:4:81

Georgetown District, geneal misc 1800s SCM 15:4:191

Greenville Co, Fairview Pres Ch, hist, bk rev SCM 15:1:60

Greenville Co, cem inscr, bk rev GH 41:6:146

Greenville, marr & death notices 1826-1863 abstr from the *Patriot & Mountaineer* SCM 15:2:63

Jury list 1778 suggested emendations SCM 15:1:52

Kershaw District, census 1840, bk rev GH 41:1:147

Kershaw District, tax list 1849-1849, bk rev GH 41:1:148

Laurens Co, marr performed by Rev F H Burdett 1879-1892 SCM 15:3:137

Maps index to Anderson 1897, Greenville 1882 & 1904, Greenwood 1898, Spartanburg 1887, bk rev SCM 15:3:179

Marr & death notices 1840-1853 abstr from the *Temperance Advocate* SCM 15:3:123

SOUTH CAROLINA (cont)

Marr & death notices 1853 abstr from *The Sumter Banner* SCM 15:1:16

Marr & death notices 1826-1863 abstr from Greenville news, bk rev AL 3:3:44

Mil rec, muster roll of the Columbia vol 1846 SCM 15:1:30

Mission San Francisco de Solano & Mission San Antonio de Valero bapt 1703-1783 GHS 4:1:38

Newberry Co, probate estate abstr 1787-1820, bk rev SCM 15:3:179

Ninety-six District, jury rosters 1798 SCM 15:3:164

Peedee, residents SGE 28:122:27 28:123:19 28:124:39

Revolutionary War, bounty land grants, bk rev SCM 15:1:60

Richland District, land rec 1785-1865, bk rev GH 41:1:148

Richland District, minutes of the court of ordinary 1806-1833 SCM 15:4:210

Saint Pauls Parish, commissioners of the roads minutes 1786 SCM 15:2:92 15:3:169

Soldiers & Indian traders 1726-1730, bk rev GH 41:1:147

Tax list 1733-1742, bk rev SCM 15:1:59

Tax list 1733-1742, bk rev FLG 11:1:30

Tax officials roster 1720-1721 SCM 15:3:133

Union Co, hist, bk rev SCM 15:4:221

Union Co, will abstr 1787-1849, bk rev SCM 15:1:59 GH 41:4:201 NCJ 13:3:179

Williamsburg Co, Pres 1803 SCM 15:1:9

York Co, McConnells, cem inscr SCM 15:2:113

SOUTH DAKOTA, Aberdeen, Zion Luth Ch confirmations 1912-1916 TTC 11:3:53

SPARWASSER, Catherine Maria d1917, h ___ Kern, IL, funeral notice STC 10:2:64

SPEAR, Fam members in NH with a ME connection 1800s–1900s DE 10:5:169

Fam memorial 1620–1985, bk rev RAG 8:2:26

John Edward b1816, QB, VT, IA, census rec misc, bk rev BAT 16:1:24

SPEARS, Ebenezer b1823, OH, cem inscr WC 4:1:9

Fam hist VA & KY, bk rev CHG 20:1:12

SPEER, Mathias Stephen b1818, w Almery Hudspeth, AL, MO, children OZ 7:3:122

SPEINGER, Christina see Hans Georg SCHAPPLEY

SPEIRS, Robert m1848, w Sarah A Thurston, Bible rec HJA 12:1:1

SPENCER, Fanny see John J BROWN

George Nikles b1853, w Dimpsey Applewhite, TX, Bible rec YTD 5:1:21

Jeremiah bc1751, w Tirzah Ashley, CT, PA, geneal, bk rev GH 41:6:164

Lydia see Eugene CHASE

Mary Elizabeth see Samuel Phair SMITH

Surname period, *Le Despencer*, 1600 Comfort, Lansing MI 48915 - fam IN, deaths MI, Christopher of RI, data base, cem NC, fam New Zealand, Joseph of NY

William f1885, w Sarah Ackley, CT, geneal, bk rev GH 41:2:156

SPERRY, Lauren d1857, IA, death notice AB 15:3:69

SPICER, William Washington b1834, w Elizabeth Loveall, IL, biog IG 23:2:52

SPIEGLE, Fam hist PA, NC, KY, bk rev KK 25:2:37

SPILKER, Martha d1918, IL, obit CRT 8:4:34

SPILLMAN, Halstrom M m1896, w Mabel Wilde, Bible rec MCR 18:4:112

SPINK, Clark(e) b1811, RI, anc ch TEG 7:3:159

SPIRA, Jacobus b1808, w Susan Stauffer, PA, Bible rec LCC 4:3:30

SPITLER, Martin d1838, death notice SIN 8:3:102

SPRAGG, Thomas b1729, CN, geneal, bk rev NYR 118:1:52

SPRAU, Henry bc1808, w Elizabeth M Hoffman, GE, anc ch FIR 6:3:36

SPRING, Dennis m1736, w Ann Pricket, NJ, PA, geneal, bk rev WPG 13:3:50

SPRINGER, Fam hist Biblical times to present, bk rev GH 41:6:164

SPROAT, Ebenezer b1676, w Experience Hawes, MA, geneal NER 141:3:203

SPROUL, G b1827, WA, golden wedding anniversary celebration TB 14:1:14

SPURLOCK, Alexander, w Mary Carpenter, geneal, bk rev GH 41:2:153

Surname period, *Spurlock/ Scurlock, Variants, & Allied Lines*, Pat Ford, 248 Timberhill, Bowling Green KY 42101-9069

SQUIER, Zeruia see Benajah REXFORD

STACKHOUSE, Ellen bc1635, h ___ Cowgill, EN, PA, geneal, bk rev GH 41:2:150

STAFFORD, Fam rec misc, bk rev CHG 19:4:154

Mercy bc1824, h Oscar Eddy, VT, diary abstr BAT 16:1:10

Robert b1790, GA, biog, bk rev GGS 23:1:46

STAHL, Jacob b1782, OH, anc ch CR 19:4:173

STAIGE, Laetitia Maria Anna see James MARYE & Jacques MARIE

STALLIONS, Ferebe f1792, NC, children NCJ 13:2:99

STAMBAUGH, Phillip see Mary Jane McKENZIE

STAMP, John T m1829, w Eleanor ___, MD, Bible rec MAD 27:1:28

STANDISH, Fam hist from the Norman Conquest 1066 to the Stuart period, bk rev MQ 53:4:304

STANFORD, Samuel bc1809, EN, NY, IL, geneal, bk rev NYR 118:2:118

STANLEY, Enos f1827, MO, account bk abstr 1827-1871 OZ 9:3:98

Henri b1515, EN, anc ch RT 4:4:102

Isabelle see John SMITH

STANTON, Anne see William BACKUS

Robert see Sarah E TEMPLIN

STAPP, James f1786, w Sally Burbridge, KY, IL, geneal FF 15:4:103

Melinda see Robert BLACK-WELL

STARK, Aaron d1685, w Mary Holt, ST, CT, PA, geneal LWF 6:1:36

John Franklin m1892, w Mary Ann Linton, KY, Bible rec KA 23:2:97

STARKWEATHER, Asa b1753, CT, NY, anc ch BG 8:2:38

STAUB, Henry b1808, w Mary Boxell, GE, WV, anc MD 28:4:435

STAUFFER, Christina see Solomon SOLENBERGER

Samuel b1790, w Rachel ___, PA, anc ch PM 10:1:40

Susan see Jacobus SPIRA

STEARNS, Roxanna see Nicholas GROVES

STEDDOM, Henry b1754, w Martha Pearson, SC, OH, biog sketch HL 1:5:151

STEDMAN, Judith see Benjamin WORTHINGTON

STEED, John f1738, w Martha ___, BM, will abstr BBQ 4:4:40

STEELE, Lavinia see William M DICKSON

Mary Ann b1811, KY, IN, anc ch JCG 15:3:98

STEEN, Nancy Iola b1862, Bible rec HTR 29:3:83

STEERE, Elizabeth see David MITCHELL

STEIGELMAN, Franklin m1852, w Sarah Jane Lamb, Bible rec PGB 19:3:39

STEIGER, Hendrick f1732, GE, PA, geneal, bk rev NYR 118:4:251

STEININGER, Reuben b1831, w Sophia Walters, PA, IN, anc ch MIS 19:3:70

STENDER, Mary see Philip MICHEL

STEPHENS, Edward bc1590, EN, CT, NC, geneal LOB 8:10:147

Fam cem in Martin KY EK 22:4:23

Fam index 1981-1985 to newsletters by Coppage, bk rev GH 41:4:210

STEPHENSON, Jesse b1812, w Susan Carver?, PA, geneal, bk rev WPG 13:4:39

STERLING, Margaret see David FORBES

Mary Ann see Jesse POTTS

STEVENS, Catherine see Jacob FREDERICK

Constant b1840, w Caroline Pearl Bush, FL, lineage FLG 10:4:132

Edward dc1751, NC, geneal, bk rev GH 41:4:210

John b1850, w Mary Kennedy, PA, KS, biog sketch KL 7:3:12

Joseph b1839, w Mary E McDaniel & Sarah J Beaty, KS, biog sketch KL 7:3:4

Polly see Samuel DOOLEY

Richard d1667, EN, MD, geneal LOB 8:11:165

Thomas d1658, CT, geneal, microfiche rev GH 41:5:198

STEWART, Asa A b1813, w Nancy Caroline Tucker, GA, FL, lineage FLG 10:4:153

225

STEWART (continued)
Catharine see Craven GREGG
Charles W Jr b1871, TX, funeral notice MCG 10:3:145
Fam hist VA, NC, KY, bk rev TTH 8:1:12
James b1718, IR, VA, geneal, bk rev CCS 9:2:59
James bc1725, NC, VA, geneal, bk rev GH 41:6:164
Johann Evans see Martin Baker GAY
John b1796, ST, ON, geneal, bk rev RES 18:3:136
John Protheroe m1851, w Lucinda McChesney, NY, Bible rec WTC 14:2:78
Mary A m1871, w Chuck F Kandy, IL, Bible rec WTC 14:2:79
Mehitable see Joseph Smith CRARY
Nancy Catherine see William WYATT
Surname period, *Stewart Hunting*, Shirley Hornbeck, POB 1019, Temple City CA 91780-1019
STICKEL, Adam m1842, w Elizabeth Kitch, GE, IN, fam rec MIS 19:1:2
STIEF, John M d1926, PA, obit LM 28:3:272
STIMSON, Jeptha f1836, NY, MI, biog sketch FHC 11:1:4
Roldon f1886, w Roxana Stimson, MI, will abstr FG 29:2:49
STINSON, Elizabeth see Adam Bernard HERALD
STIRES, Surname period, W Dennis Stires, RD 2 Box 3249, Livermore Falls ME 04254
STITT, Robert m1807, w Issabella McFarland, PA, Bible rec AH 14:2:61
STOCKMAN, Peter I f1804, TX, fam hist YTD 4:2:36 6:1:1
STOCKTON, Surname period, *The Stockton Fam News*, 14067 La Forge St, Whittier CA 90605
STOCKWELL, Orson m1835, w Louisa Holcomb, NY, Bible rec YTD 2:1:11

STODGILL, John b1665, VA, anc ch EK 22:4:34
STOECKLE, Joseph f1748, SW, ON, geneal, bk rev NGS 74:3:227
STOKES, Thomas b1806, w Nancy Parsons, NC, MO, biog sketch OZ 9:2:73
STOLTZE, Pauline see William DOEPP
STOLTZFUS, Nicholas b1719, GE, PA, biog, bk rev PM 10:4:44
Tennessee John f1850, PA, letters, bk rev SB 8:4:138
STOMBAUGH, Peter f1854, w Sarah Jane Ralston, IA, IL, geneal FF 15:3:94
STONE, Elizabeth see Blassingame W HARVEY
Galen Luther, w Carrie Morton Gregg, geneal, bk rev NER 141:3:262
Harley H d1918, IL, obit CRT 8:4:22
Henry b1788, w Tabitha Tuttle, MA, VT?, NY?, IN, geneal, bk rev GH 41:5:194 NCJ 13:3:186 RES 18:4:189 MSG 7:3:169 IG 23:2:64 RAG 8:4:24
John f1637, MA, geneal TEG 7:2:67
Margaret see Maths MEREDITH
STONER, David b1855, w Magdalena Beaman, IA, anc ch BHN 20:3:123
Peter C Jr b1802, w Mary Wells, NC, IN, anc ch RED 20:1:14
STONESIFER, Amos f1857, MD, diary MD 28:2:146
STOREY, William Raiford m1943, w Mary Frances Banks, NC, Bible rec CCM 6:4:76
STORIE, John Kilman b1830, w Mary Ann Patton, TN, MO, children OZ 9:2:69
STORM, Alexander Munroe b1840, ST, CN, IL, fam hist WTC 17:4:123
STORMFELTZ, Susan Elizabeth b1858, Bible rec LCH 2:1:31

STOUT, Abigail see Jonathan TREMAIN

Joseph Benjamin bc1766, w Charlotte Bonvillain, LA, geneal AGE 16:2:57

Samuel Sr b1709, NJ, anc ch TB 14:1:38

STOUTENBURGH, Pieter f1638, w Aefje Van Tienhoven, HO, NY, biog sketch KSL 11:1:26

STOW, Malinda see George Washington DEWITT

STOWE, Martha see Thomas OUTERBRIDGE

STRAW, Nicholas b1753, w Catherine Dale, PA, geneal, bk rev WPG 14:1:51

STRAYER, Mattheis f1749, w Anna Catherine ___, GE, PA, NY, geneal, bk rev GH 41:2:156

STRAYHORN, Sarah Jane see Albert A WILLIS

STREET, Nathaniel f1720, w Mary Raymond, CT, geneal NER 141:3:258

STREETER, Mason b1799, w Amelia Johnson, VT, PA, MO?, anc ch AGS 28:2:89

Surname period, *Streeter National Newsletter*, 78 Masonic St, Northampton MA 01060

Thomas S b1825, w Sarah A Miller, anc ch HL 3:3:71

STREIT, Marie see Jonathan Marialie SARVER

STRICKLAND, Alsey b1800, w Elizabeth ___, NC, GA, lineage FLG 10:3:99

Surname period, *Strickland Scene*, 1661 Lauranceae Way, Riverdale GA 30296

STRINGFIELD, Ezekiel b1762, fam rec BWG 16:2:131

STRODE, James Alexander b1842, w Mary Anne Davidson, KY, TX, anc ch YTD 7:1:14

STRONG, Matilda see Oliver McKENZIE

Peter b1774, w Rachel DeWolf, fam rec BCG 16:1:26

STROTHER, Edward Hines bc1798, w Nancy White, anc ch AGS 28:2:99

William f1673, w Dorothy ___, VA, geneal, bk rev GGS 23:2:102

STROUD, Josie see Henry GOSSMAN

Ner d1918, IL, obit CRT 8:4:45

STRUBE, Johanna Augusta see Carl Joseph BESELER

STRUCK, Henry F d1909, IL, obit CRT 8:2:29 8:4:8

STRUTT, Elizabeth m1620, h Thomas Scott, EN anc NER 141:1:34

STUART, David b1765, w Ann Allison, IR, TN, AL, children BWG 16:2:133

James f1817?, GA, land partitioning GGS 23:4:186

James E B d1864, biog, bk rev REG 85:2:183

Mary, ST, biog, bk rev MP 3:4:225

STUDEBAKER, Fam hist US 1736-1986 vol 2, bk rev GH 41:5:196

Surname period, *The Studebaker Fam*, 6555 S State Rt 202, Tipp City OH 45371

STUENKEL, Johann Heinrich b1789, w Margaretha Stuenkel, GE, IL, biog WTC 8:4:94

STULTS, Namon D b1848, w Rachel ___, MO, CO, biog sketch FI 7:3:85

STURGILL, Elizabeth see John Martin WEBB

STURGIS, Temperance (Gorham) see Thomas BAXTER

STURTEVANT, Lemuel Sargeant b1795, MA, MN, mil rec MN 18:2:76

Samuel bc1618, w Ann Lee, EN, MA, geneal, bk rev GFP 37:2:70 GH 41:1:165 41:2:161 CCS 9:3:97 FRT 8:3:152 TTT 11:4:188

STUTZ, Fam hist vol 2 1986, bk rev KK 25:1:18

STUTZMAN, Christian f1755, w Barbara Hochstedler, PA, geneal PM 10:3:25

STYLES, Mittie Jane see Daviel D BORN

SUBLETT, Mollie Garrett see Felix R TUCKER

SUGG, John Jr b1760, NC, anc ch AG 62:3:94

SUHRE, Johann bc1785, w Anna Maria Gralers, GE, IL, MO, geneal, bk rev GH 41:4:209

SUITER, George William b1826, w Eliza Fox, EN, WI, fam rec NW 9:2:10

SULLIVAN, James f1750, VA, geneal VA 25:4:3

SUMMERS, J H m1873, w Emma Richardson, TX, Bible rec YTD 6:1:36

Jefse m1823, w Mary An Mealls, Bible rec YTD 6:1:34

Polly see Charles ROACH Sr

T H b1826, w T H Summers, AL, MS, Bible rec YTD 6:1:37

SUMNER, John Buckner b1815, w Emily Howell, SC, anc ch PT 29:1:10

SURFACE, Mary see Joseph MCCARTY

SURPLUS, Catherine see John Erskine DEMAR

SUTHERLAND, Fam rec corr to *The Sutherlands of Westchester NS* by Sutherland GN 5:1:19

SUTLIFF, Barney S b1770, w Sarah Evans, CT, biog CTN 20:3:431

SUTTER, Johann August b1803, SW, CA, diary, bk rev SCS 24:12:240

SUTTON, Lucy see Jeremiah SIMMONS

Mary E see Chas Wesley HAR–RINGTON

SVENSON, Axel Fredrick see Carolina ANDERSDOTTER

SVINAAS, Beret Olsdatter see Johan HALDORSEN

SWAIM, Fam hist suppl NY, NJ, & southern US, bk rev NYR 118:4:247

SWAIN, Matilda Ann see Martin Delphos LUTHER

SWAN, Anna see Martin Van Buren BATES

Susan see Miles WEST

SWANGO, Fam hist, bk rev GH 41:6:165

SWANTNER, Fam hist Bohemia, bk rev GH 41:4:210

SWART, David see Marietta MCDOUGALL

SWARTS, Michael, geneal, IN, bk rev IL 19:2:120

SWEARINGEN, Gerret (Van) b1626, HO, DE, MD, WV, geneal, bk rev EWA 24:4:265

Rachel see David VanCLEAVE

SWEDEN, Direct for Boston MA 1881, bk rev NGS 74:3:229

Emig to US hist, bk rev CTA 30:1:51

Episcopalians in Litchfield MN 1891-1905 SAG 7:1:7

Geneal res guide by Barton, bk rev BCG 16:2:64 (by Hjelm) FRT 8:2:101 NYR 118:3:181

Geneal terms in EN WRB 10:2:15 OCN 10:1:11

Hist in Jamestown NY, bk rev GH 41:1:139 BAT 16:1:23 FRT 8:3:154

Natives in Boston MA 1881, bk rev AG 62:3:123

News holdings of Swenson Swedish Imm Res Center (IL), bk rev BCG 16:2:64

Place-names in North Am, bk rev CTA 30:1:51

Ship pass list to NY 1856 on board the *Carolina* SAG 7:1:18

SWEITZER, John d1885, w Maria ____, IL, picture of house MH 14:4:50

SWETT, Morris f1908, NY, biog TTT 11:2:71

SWITZERLAND, Canton Zurich, Affoltern Am Albis, emig 1649-1755, bk rev GH 41:4:186

Geneal res hints MP 3:1:25

Place & fam names MFH 6:2:50

SWOPE, Pearl H see Arthur Lloyd FULLBRIGHT

SYMONDS, Susanna see John AYRES

SZAL, Pauline b1887, PO, IL, PA, anc ch CR 19:4:172

SZAREK, Antoni b1819, w Regina Jarek, PO, anc ch WB 17:2:74

TACKETT, Surname period, *The American Pioneers*, 1830 Johnson Dr, Concord CA 94520 - Thomas H 1841-1910 IN, Maryland 1889-1920 KY, Alonzo Lee 1875-1939 MO

TADLOCK, Alexander Brabson b1836, w Clara Mayse, TN, biog sketch BWG 16:2:128

John Blair b1821, w Jane Walker Taylor & Amanda Smith, TN, geneal PEL 8:3:111

Lewis, w Jane Blair, TN, geneal BWG 16:4:47

TAFT, Surname period, *Talf Talk*, 71 High St, Uxbridge MA 01569

TALBOT, Edward f1807, IR, NY, geneal, bk rev CTN 20:1:137 NYR 118:4:248

Edward/William d1817, IR, NY, geneal, bk rev DM 50:4:160

TALBOTT, Joseph P see Mary Jane MILLER

Rose see Frank Dearborn BUL-LARD

TALBOYS, Mary Anne see Shubael COLLINS

TALIAFERRO, Benjamin f1784, w Martha Meriweather, VA, GA, children SGE 28:123:6

TALLMAN, Rebecca see Benjamin TURNER

TALMADGE, Mary b1776, CT, OH, anc ch BG 7:4:96

TANQUARY, James Robert b1857, Bible rec IG 23:1:9

TAPLIN, John Orange b1828, w Louisa Benjamin Hunt, VT, CA, biog sketch SCS 24:10:201

Katherine f1918, MT, letters BM 8:1:3

TAPP, Bushrod b1820, w Mary Jane Essex, VA, IL, anc ch KIL 15:2:28

TAPPERT, Dorothea see Herman KONOW

TAPSCOTT, James bc1690, w Margaret ___, NJ, geneal HL 2:3:69

TARBLE, Nathan f1820, NJ, statement GMN 62:1:26

TARBOX, Ebenizer b1678, w Mary Bream, ME, anc ch WB 17:2:75

TARBUTTON, J C m1877, w Emil J Tarbutton, Bible rec MD 28:2:235

TARENT, Mary see Robert ROSE

TARPEY, John M b1843, w Catherine Hagerty, IR, IL, anc ch KIL 15:2:28

TATMAN, Merritt H b1818, w Emma Catherine Newcomer, OH, anc ch RED 19:4:11

TATUM, Nathaniel f1711, w Elizabeth Tatum, Barbados, VA, fam rec PT 29:4:152

TAYLOE, Fam hist VA, bk rev RAG 8:1:23

TAYLOR, Ann see James GREAR/ GREER

Armstead Pride m1871, w Lidia Louisa Hegetsweiler, VA, biog sketch IAA 2:1:3

Catherine see Elijah Milton WATKINS

Charlotte b1875, h Walter P Bradstreet, autograph bk HL 2:2:37

Elizabeth M f1914, h ___ Butler, TN, bounty land claim BWG 16:1:56

Ellen see James LUTTON

Etheldred dc1793, NC, trial of murderers NCJ 13:4:229

Fam hist AL, AR, MO, TX, bk rev NTT 7:4:123

Fam hist AL NTT 7:3:95 7:4:134

Frances see Ambrose MADISON

Francis f1735, MD, land rec TNB 3:3:1

J H b1843, OK, anc ch MGR 22:3:137

Jacob b1670, w Rebekah Weeks, MA, geneal NGS 74:3:175

TAYLOR (continued)
Jane H see James Madison AL-
LEN
Jane Walker see John Blair
TADLOCK
John b1807, w Mary M ___, AL,
biog NTT 7:3:100
John m1786, w Hannah Cary, ST,
MA, geneal, bk rev CCS 9:3:97
GH 41:2:156
John m1831, w Elizabeth Nesbit,
IL, biog FF 15:3:41
Katerine Elizabeth see James
Warren ROWLAND
Margaret S see Jesse HALL
Martha Atwood b1862, h Charles
Elika Nichols, IL, obit CRT
8:4:9
Mary see Henry W CUL-
BERTSON
Rebecca Jane b1844, SC, anc ch
OPC 18:1:26
Surname period, *The Taylor
Quarterly*, 5911 Brookview Dr,
Alexandria VA 22310
Tarlton Jones b1828, w Catherine
Bodkin, KY, KS, geneal, bk rev
GFP 37:2:72
Tarlton Jones b1867, w Catherine
Bodkin, KY, geneal, bk rev GH
41:2:161
TAYLORS, Fam hist, bk rev MCG
10:2:89
TEETER, John m1868, w Mary H
Vance, Bible rec HH 21:4:213
John S b1782, w Susanna Burger,
PA, geneal NFB 19:1:3
TEMPLETON, Nehemiah Johnson
m1854, w Susan Jane Miller,
AL, Bible rec AL 4:1:21
William R see Nannie MCCOY
TEMPLIN, James f1796, w Mary
Salmon, PA, KY, geneal, bk
rev GH 41:2:156
Sara E m1868, h Robert Stanton,
Bible rec BWG 16:2:143
TENBROOK, John m1840, w Jane
Cinthelia Alexander, Bible rec
IG 23:3:79
TENEYCK, Coenradt m1645, w
Maria Boel, HO, geneal NYR
118:1:14

TENNENT, Helen Co f1818, VA,
letter VAG 31:2:132
TENNESSEE, Anderson Co, Clinton, lib hist sketch 1898 PEL
8:1:32
Anderson Co, court rec 1810-
1814 PEL 8:1:1
Anderson Co, court minutes
1810-1814 PEL 8:2:5 8:3:84
8:4:124
Anderson Co, legislative pet
1822 PEL 8:3:94
Anderson Co, Peak's School student photograph c1900 PEL
8:4:153
Anderson Co, scholastic population 1853-1861 PEL 8:1:23
8:2:13 8:3:92 8:4:132
Benton Co, marr 1837-1900, bk
rev GH 41:5:185
Blount Co, Rev War, soldiers
roster BWG 16:2:150
Blount Co, will abstr 1799-1858
PEL 8:1:5
Bradley Co, marr 1887-1901, bk
rev GH 41:2:159 BWG 16:2:157
Bradley Co, wills 1865-1883 in-
dex, bk rev GH 41:5:186
Campbell Co, court minutes
1813-1817 PEL 8:1:11 8:2:18
8:3:96 8:4:134
Campbell Co, marr 1891-1900,
bk rev BWG 16:2:157
Carter Co, hist 1865-1980, bk rev
BWG 16:1:64
Carter Co, hist reminiscences,
bk rev GH 41:6:147
Civil War, hist of the 13th Reg
TN Vol Cav, bk rev GH
41:6:147
Civil War, member roster of the
Confederate Vet SR 3:3:63
Clear Spring Academy student
roster 1894-95 BWG 16:2:118
Co rec & geneal resources guide
by Fulcher, bk rev DG 33:2:117
GHS 4:2:72 BCS 7:2:13 KA
23:2:114 VAG 31:3:234 CTN
20:2:325 SCM 15:2:120 GH
41:4:201 WCK 20:2:30 NCJ
13:2:117 OK 32:2:43

TENNESSEE (continued)

Coosa Bapt Assoc, hist 1835-1978, bk rev SR 2:1:16

Cumberland Settlements, census 1770-1790, bk rev GH 41:4:201 NCJ 13:2:117 SCM 15:2:120 WCK 20:2:30 DG 33:2:118 CRT 8:4:7 AGS 28:4:154 OC 24:2:83 OK 32:2:43

Desc of east TN pioneers, bk rev RAG 8:1:25 (2nd ed) FRT 8:3:150

Divorces 1797-1858, bk rev OK 32:1:6

Fam searchers & geneal direct, bk rev GH 41:4:201

Flat Creek, hist, bk rev GH 41:3:165

Franklin Co, cem inscr, bk rev OK 32:1:7

Franklin Co, census 1870 SR 3:3:71

Fraterville mine explosion hist sketch & roster of dead PEL 8:4:147

Geneal res aid, TN Valley Authority, use of SR 2:3:60

Geneal res aids in the Dallas Public Lib TS 29:3:83

Geneal res hints IMP 6:4:114

Geneal source materials avail PEL 8:3:116

Gibson Co, geneal misc 1824-1846, bk rev GH 41:2:146

Gibson Co, hist & geneal extracts 1869-1874 from news, bk rev GH 41:5:186

Gibson Co, marr 1870-1878, bk rev GH 41:5:186

Grainger Co, census 1830 SGE 28:122:43 28:123:7

Greene Co, Chuckey River flood 1907 BWG 16:2:122

Greene Co, hist vol 1 & 2, bk rev BWG 16:1:64

Greene Co, Rheatown, hist 1771-1977, bk rev GH 41:6:149

Greene Co, Timber Ridge Ch hist 1786-1986, bk rev GH 41:4:202

Grundy Co, cem inscr, bk rev GH 41:2:146

TENNESSEE (continued)

Grundy Co, Elk River Valley, hist, bk rev GH 41:6:147

Grundy Co, wills & estates 1844-1900, bk rev GH 41:2:146

Guntersville Reservoir cem inscr, bk rev SR 3:1:20

Hamilton Co, Anderson Cem SR 1:2:20

Hamilton Co, census 1830 SR 1:2:22 2:1:11

Hamilton Co, Fairmount Cem SR 2:1:14 2:2:36

Hardin Co, residents in 1800s, bk rev GH 41:5:186

Hawkins Co, Beech Creek Public School student roster 1904 BWG 16:1:36

Hawkins Co, census 1830-1850, bk rev GH 41:6:147 BWG 16:2:155 PEL 8:3:114

Haywood Co, marr 1859-1878, bk rev GH 41:6:148

Henry Co, hist, bk rev GH 41:5:195

Humphrey's Co, tax lists 1837-1843 & marr 1888-1900, bk rev GH 41:6:148

Humphreys Co, Bakerville, geneal misc 1897-1898 abstr from the *Bakerville Review*, bk rev GH 41:1:148

Humphreys Co, census 1880, bk rev GH 41:4:201

James Co, hist, bk rev SR 2:2:41

James Co, marr 1913-1919, bk rev SR 2:3:64

Jefferson Co, Strawberry Plains, hist 1792-1962, bk rev GH 41:4:201 SGI 4:1:22

Johnson City, WWII, honor roll BWG 16:1:58

Johnson Co, cem inscr, bk rev PEL 8:4:158

King's Mountain, battle hist, bk rev GH 41:6:147

Lawrence Co, Loretto, hist, bk rev NTT 7:1:2

Lawrence Co, Saint Joseph, hist, bk rev NTT 7:1:3

TENNESSEE (continued)

Lincoln Co, Fayetteville, marr & deaths 1823-1826 abstr from the *Village Messenger* THT 16:1:23

Macon Co, cem inscr vol 1, bk rev GH 41:6:148

Madisonville, Friendship Bapt Ch Cem PEL 8:3:103

Marion & Bledsoe Co, Sequatchie Valley, census 1830, bk rev SR 2:2:41

Marion Co, cem inscr, bk rev GH 41:5:186 PEL 8:2:33 BWG 16:2:156

Marion Co, deaths, births, & marr 1891-1910 abstr from the *Sequachee Valley News*, bk rev PEL 8:2:33

Marshall Co, court minutes 1845-1848, bk rev GH 41:6:148

Maury Co, geneal rec misc, bk rev GH 41:6:148

Memphis, lawyers 1859 roster SGE 28:121:46

Mexican War, bk rev STI 27:1:29

Monroe Co, Elazer Meth Ch Cem PEL 8:1:15 8:2:22 8:3:100

Monroe Co, Madisonville, Haven Hill Cem PEL 8:4:142

Moore Co, census 1880, bk rev SR 3:3:71

Morgan Co, cem inscr, bk rev GH 41:3:175

Nashville & Chattanooga, Civil War, hist, bk rev RAG 8:1:22

Norris Reservoir area, graves removed PEL 8:1:28 8:2:9 8:3:88 8:4:128

Ocoee Land District, hist sketch SR 2:4:82

Ocoee land grants SR 3:1:12

Polk Co, marr 1894-1907, bk rev GH 41:6:149

Polk Co, Vineland, hist sketch of Dutch settlement PEL 8:4:155

Providence Pres Ch rec 1836-1873 BWG 16:1:25 16:2:113

Rhea Co, Morgan Springs, hist, bk rev SGI 4:1:21

TENNESSEE (continued)

Roane Co, court minutes 1801-1805 PEL 8:1:19 8:2:26 8:3:104 8:4:138

Roane Co, hist 1860-1900, bk rev PEL 8:2:33

Robertson Co, chancery court loose papers abstr 1844-1872, bk rev RAG 8:1:26 FRT 8:3:149

Saint Elmo, hist, bk rev SR 3:1:20

Sequatchie, geneal, bk rev SR 1:2:24

Sequatchie Co, marr 1858-1881, bk rev SR 2:1:16

Sullivan Co, ch hist 1777-1935, bk rev BWG 16:1:66

Tipton Co, marr 1840-1860, bk rev GH 41:4:202 STI 27:1:29

Unicoi Co, Ervin, hist, bk rev GH 41:6:149

Unicoi Co, hist & geneal, bk rev GH 41:6:149

Volunteers in the war with MX vol 1 & 2, bk rev GH 41:4:201

Warren Co, census 1840, bk rev FRT 8:3:151

Washington Co, deed abstr 1780s-1814 BWG 16:1:5 16:2:93

Washington Co, estate inventories 1779-1821 BWG 16:1:13 16:2:99

Washington Co, WWII, honor roll BWG 16:1:59

Wayne Co, cem inscr & death rec, bk rev NTT 7:2:44

Wilson Co, funeral rec of Jonas Newton Carver 1902-1906, bk rev GH 41:1:149

TENNEY, Ellen b1871, h ___ Brown, WA, biog sketch TB 13:4:14

TERRIOT, Jean b1601, w Perrine Bourg, FR, anc ch MP 3:4:268

Jeanne see Pierre THIBODEAU

TERRY, Abba see Cutter DOL-BEER

James bc1768, w Mary Gooch, NC, TN, geneal, bk rev GH 41:3:170

TERRY (continued)

Jesse f1825, w Elizabeth Lindsey, TN, marr bond NTT 7:1:38

TETOIT, Marianne Joghs f1754, h David Tetoit & Anthony Altman, FR, US, geneal, bk rev WPG 13:3:47

TEVEY/TUVESON, Charles b1884, KS, MO, obit SNS 3:3:3

TEXAS, Angelina Co, cem inscr bk rev, GH 41:3:166

Angelina Co, hist YTD 4:2:10

Austin, First Southern Pres Ch member roster 1870s–1890s AGS 28:1:1 28:2:38

Austin Co, deed abstr 1837–1852, bk rev DG 33:4:242

Austin Co, Ottmer Cem STI 27:2:32

Bahia, settlers 1816 STI 27:2:26

Bexar, census 1870 STK 15:1:6

Bexar Co, census 1850, bk rev GH 41:3:166

Biog gazetteer K–M, bk rev OC 24:1:39

Bonavia, imm 1809 biog sketches YTD 3:2:32 4:1:37 4:2:38

Brazos Co, hist, bk rev STI 27:1:28

Brenham, Salem Luth Ch rec 1850–1940, bk rev STI 27:1:29

Cameron Co, Civil War, vets GTP 25:1:20

Cameron Co, marr 1866–1867 GTP 24:4:82

Castro Co, marr 1892–1916 REF 29:1:16

Cem inscr of northeast vol 2, bk rev FRT 8:3:150

Cem locations in south TX VC 8:2:39

Cert of entrance 1835 roster YTD 1:2:11 2:1:45 2:2:35 3:1:22

Cherokee Co, marr 1867 STI 27:2:9

Civil War, biog sketches of soldiers in the Old Tom Green Rifles GTP 25:3:60

TEXAS (continued)

Civil War, muster roll of Capt Mat Nolan's Company of Mounted Rangers, Rio Grande Reg, Col John S Ford GTP 25:3:71

Civil War, reminiscences 1861–65 YTD 5:1:17

Civil War, soldiers buried in Okolona MS STI 27:1:20

Coke Co, Sanco Meth Ch reg 1920s STK 15:1:25

Collin Co, anc of the Collin Co TX Geneal Soc members, bk rev GH 41:4:212 DG 33:2:118

Collingsworth Co, Quail, Quail Cem REF 29:3:57

Columbia, geneal misc 1836 abstr from the *Telegraph & TX Reg* GR 29:1:24 29:2:64 29:3:100 29:4:135

Comal Co, marr 1846–1877, bk rev MCG 10:3:143

Comanche Co, Miller Fam Cem FP 30:4:179

Concho Co, Concho Cem STK 15:2:76

Cooke Co, tax list 1851 FP 30:3:128

Coryell Co, Coffey Cem HTR 30:2:35 30:3:90

Coryell Co, Hillsdale Cem HTR 29:3:112 29:4:129 30:1:19

Dallas Co, Dallas, geneal misc 1887 abstr from the *Dallas Morning News* DG 33:3:179

Dallas Co, Dallas, hist 1860–1920 DG 33:4:226

Dallas Co, Dallas, Union Ch hist sketch DG 33:3:167

Dallas Co, deed abstr 1840–1854 DG 33:2:100 33:3:154

Dallas Co, marr 1885–1887 DG 33:1:23 33:2:80 33:3:145 33:4:206

Death rec 1903–1940 surnames Gratts through Gravette, bk rev GH 41:6:157

Deaths 1925–1934 (central TX), bk rev GH 41:5:187

Delegates to the secession convention 1861 YTD 7:2:27

TEXAS (continued)

Denton Co, tax rolls 1849-1851 FP 30:1:19

Dimmit Co, hist, bk rev GH 41:4:202

Eastland Co, marr 1874-1882 FP 30:4:180

Ellis Co, commissioners' court minutes 1851-1853 FP 30:2:76 30:3:138

Emig trails into & within state STK 15:1:14

Ennis, letters at post office 1876 FP 30:2:75

Falls Co, marr 1876-1881 HTR 29:3:109 29:4:131 30:1:21

Fam land heritage reg index AGS 28:1:12 28:2:44 28:3:115 28:4:143

Fam rec collect, bk rev RAG 8:5:13

Fam with GA ties GGS 23:2:73

Farmersville, hist 1845-1973, bk rev GH 41:4:202

Fort Worth, direct (city) 1877 FP 30:1:28 30:2:87 30:3:143

Fort Worth, Oakwood Cem FP 30:1:35 30:2:82

Galveston Co, cem inscr, bk rev GH 41:2:146

Gazetteer, microfiche rev GH 41:2:162

Geneal rec avail, bk rev GH 41:4:202 CTN 20:2:323 AMG 2:4:10

Geneal res bibl guide NGS 75:3:194 YTD 1:2:21

Geneal rec guide by Kennedy, bk rev DG 33:2:117 STI 27:2:37

Ghost towns, bk rev OPC 18:2:58

Graham, geneal misc 1882 abstr from the *Graham Leader* FP 30:2:99

Hale Co, facts & folklore vol 2, bk rev GH 41:4:202

Harlingen, founding hist sketch GTP 25:3:58

Harris Co, Houston, Christ Ch bapt 1843-1874 GR 29:3:94

Harris Co, naturalization rec 1838-1913 index GR 29:1:21 29:2:61 29:3:89 29:4:152

TEXAS (continued)

Harris, Montgomery, & Waller Co, Klein Funeral Home rec 1929-1960, bk rev GH 41:3:175

Harrison Co, residents 1880 (Caucasians only), bk rev GH 41:5:187

Henderson Co, indigent roster 1863 STI 27:2:16

Hidalgo Co, geneal rec avail GTP 25:2:50

Hill Co, census 1860 HTR 29:3:99

Hill Co, deeds 1853-1857 index FP 30:4:182

Hist of the Great Comanche Raid 1840 AGS 28:4:151

Hist of women, bk rev MCG 10:2:88

Hist vol 1 & 2 & suppl, bk rev NTT 7:1:2

Hood Co, geneal misc abstr from old ledger 1867-1868 FP 30:4:184

Hopkins Co, census 1870, bk rev MCG 10:3:145

Hopkins Co, pioneers, bk rev MCG 10:3:143

Hopkins Co, tax rolls 1846-1856, bk rev MCG 10:3:144 (1894) MCG 10:3:143

Hopkins Co, will abstr 1876-1910, bk rev GH 41:5:187

Houston, Christ Ch bapt 1847-1851 GR 29:4:162

Houston, social misc 1915 abstr from the *Houston Daily Post* VC 8:2:35

Jack Co, slave sched 1860 STI 27:1:21

Jefferson Co, probate rec bk 1 index, bk rev GH 41:4:202

Johnson Co, marr 1855-1858 FP 30:4:186

Kendall Co, probate rec 1862-1900 abstr, bk rev FRT 8:3:152 GH 41:3:166

Lavaca Co, Sweet Home, cem inscr GR 29:2:69

Limestone Co, Blair-Stubbs Funeral Home rec 1923-1928 vol 1 MCG 10:2:87

TEXAS (continued)
Limestone Co, cem inscr vol 4, bk rev MCG 10:2:87
Matagorda Co, hist, bk rev GH 41:3:166
McLennan, Civil War, Pat Cleburne Camp #222, Confederate Gray Bk 1913 HTR 30:1:11
McLennan Co, Waco, GE Meth Epis Ch hist sketch HTR 30:3:68
McLennan Co, Waco, obit 1911-1913 HTR 29:3:87 29:4:133 30:1:23 30:2:57 30:3:95
Mexican land grants 1836 map rev DG 33:2:116
Midland Co, brands 1901-1903 THT 15:1:8 15:2:26
Midland Co, hist sources list THT 15:1:14
Midland Co, marr 1909-1916 THT 15:1:5 16:1:15
Midland Co, Midland, money orders issued 1886 THT 15:1:10
Midland Co, residents 1836 THT 15:1:19
Mil rec sources avail YTD 1:2:25
Mil rec, muster roll of Capt Hayden Arnold's 1st Company in Col Sidney Sherman's 2nd Reg of TX Vol engaged in the Battle of San Jacinto YTD 4:2:16
Milam Co, census 1850-1860-1870 index, bk rev FRT 8:3:157 FRT 8:2:100
Minute men 1841-1842 STI 27:1:13
Montague Co, hist sketch FP 30:4:188
Montague Co, Montague, hist, bk rev FRT 8:2:106
Montague Co, voter reg 1874? FP 30:1:23 30:2:93 30:3:130
Montgomery Co, Civil War, soldiers biog sketches MCG 10:3:151
Montgomery Co, co rec in period MCG 10:1:11

TEXAS (continued)
Montgomery Co, deed abstr 1835-1840s MCG 10:1:37 10:3:133
Montgomery Co, Montgomery, geneal misc 1895-1897 abstr from S M Smith's scrapbk MCG 10:3:127
Montgomery Co, obit & other news items 1950s-1960s MCG 10:2:97 10:3:121
Montgomery Co, Prairie Plains, Cumberland Pres Ch, minutes of sessions 1853-1907 MCG 10:2:83
Montgomery Co, probate minutes 1835-1845 MCG 10:1:43
Montgomery Co, residents 1860 (wealthy) MCG 10:2:93
Montgomery Co, sheriffs' returns 1840-1844 MCG 10:1:27 10:2:79
Montgomery Co, slave sched 1850 MCG 10:2:73
Montgomery Co, slave sched 1860 MCG 10:2:75
Montgomery Co, teachers' cert reg 1905-1911 MCG 10:1:5
Montgomery Co, teachers' cert reg 1900-1908 MCG 10:2:58
Motley Co, hist of schools, bk rev GH 41:6:149
Nacogdoches, biog direct 1850-1880, bk rev GRI 7:1:5
Nacogdoches, births 1838-1878 YTD 4:1:21
Nacogdoches, census 1801 (foreigners) YTD 5:2:1
Nacogdoches, census 1829 YTD 4:2:17
Nacogdoches, Cross Roads Pres Ch hist sketch & communicants roll 1880s-1908 YTD 4:2:7
Nacogdoches, Nacogdoches University student roster 1858 YTD 4:2:40
Nacogdoches, obit 1891-1902 abstr from news YTD 1:1:1 2:2:41
Nacogdoches, scholastic population 1869 YTD 7:1:18

TEXAS (continued)

Nacogdoches, tax list 1865 YTD 2:1:26

Nacogdoches Co, enlistments 1836 roster YTD 1:2:8

Nacogdoches Co, McLeod, centennial address rev YTD 1:2:39

Nacogdoches Co, Melrose, names from account ledger of the firm of Hardeman Bros, General Merchandise 1848-1852 YTD 2:2:26

Nacogdoches Co, oaths of amnesty 1866 YTD 5:2:36

Nacogdoches Co, Old North Ch minutes 1830s-1850s YTD 5:1:37 5:2:7 6:1:8 6:2:20 7:1:30 7:2:33

Nacogdoches Co, Pine Knot, Old Prospect Ch member roster 1907 YTD 7:2:31

Nacogdoches Co, Sacred Heart Cath Ch deaths 1853-1934 YTD 1:2:29 2:1:35

Nacogdoches Co, school districts 1932 list YTD 1:1:23

Nacogdoches Co, student roster 1859 & 1863 YTD 5:1:27

Nacogdoches Co, tax (delinquent) list 1840 YTD 6:1:14

Nacogdoches Co, tax list 1848 YTD 1:1:19

Name changes 1839-1870 YTD 7:2:20

Name changes 1893 STI 27:1:19

Natives mentioned in AL rec 1800s AL 3:3:19 3:4:33

Natives of GE desc, roster FP 30:4:210

Navarro Co, Corsicana, letters at post office 1890 FP 30:3:126

Navarro Co, Dawson, Dawson Fam Cem FP 30:4:177

Newport, store ledger #2 1878-1881 index DG 33:2:110

Oakwood Cem FP 30:3:151

Obit & death notices 1855 abstr from *The Texas Bapt* FP 30:4:206

Oldham Co, marr 1881-1922 REF 29:2:40

TEXAS (continued)

Palo Pinto Co, tax list 1857 FP 30:2:72

Parker Co, Half Century Hist Club member roster FP 30:4:190

Pension appl abstr, bk rev GH 41:6:149 AGS 28:2:53

Praha, WWII, vet of CZ extraction ND 6:6:10

Quail Cem REF 29:4:83

Red River Co, deed abstr to 1846 vol 1, bk rev OK 32:1:8

Refugio Co, Civil War, muster rolls VC 8:1:12 8:2:31

Refugio Co, Civil War, muster roll of Capt W T Townsend VC 8:3:59

Revolution muster rolls 830s-1840s AGS 28:1:17

Robertson's Col, abstr from the introductory vol of *Papers Concerning Robertson's Col* in TX FP 30:1:4

Rusk Co, hist, bk rev GGS 23:1:44

San Antonio, Mission San Francisco de Solano & Mission San Antonio de Valero bapt 1703-1783 GHS 4:2:6

Sterling Co, soldiers & sailors discharge rec 1917-1920 STK 14:4:180

Tarrant Co, cem transcr list FP 30:4:193

Tarrant co, Civil War, Confederate soldiers roster FP 30:4:200

Tarrant Co, estate rec 1850s abstr FP 30:4:198

Tarrant Co, marr 1876 FP 30:4:194

Tarrant Co, naturalization papers FP 30:4:196

Tarrant Co, tax list 1851 FP 30:4:192

Tarrant Co, Walnut Creek Cem FP 30:4:178

Taylor Co, stories of the Jim Ned country as they were recorded, told about, & lived, bk rev GH 41:1:149

TEXAS (continued)

Three Forks of the Trinity River, memorial 1843 FP 30:2:68

Tom Green Co, road overseers appointed 1906 STK 15:1:24

Tom Green Co, San Angelo, Fairmont Cem STK 14:4:171 15:2:56

Tom Green Co, San Angelo, geneal misc 1885 abstr from the *San Angelo Standard* STK 14:4:181 15:2:74

Tom Green Co, sheriffs 1879-1954 STK 14:4:184

Tom Green Co, Wall, Wall Cem STK 15:1:27

Trinity Co, geneal misc 1907-1908 abstr from the *Trinity Co Star* THT 15:1:31

Trinity Co, marr 1876-1893 vol 1, bk rev FRT 8:1:48

Trinity Co, probate rec 1872-1986 index, bk rev GH 41:6:150

Victoria Co, Goliad, geneal misc 1885 abstr from the *Goliad Guard* VC 8:3:63

Victoria Co, Guadalupe, Shillerville Cem VC 8:1:6

Victoria Co, Nusery Cem inscr update VC 8:1:15

Victoria Co, Victoria, Bischoff Cem VC 8:3:68

Victoria Co, Victoria, Civil War, report of sick at C S Army Hospital 1862 VC 8:2:34

Victoria Co, Victoria, Evergreen Cem VC 8:1:2 8:2:26 8:3:52

Victoria Co, Victoria, geneal misc 1848 abstr from the *Texian Advocate* VC 8:1:17

Victoria Co, Victoria, letters at post office VC 8:1:5

Waco, Ch of the Assumption hist sketch HTR 29:3:86

Washington Co, deed abstr 1834-1841, bk rev GH 41:2:146 VAG 31:1:69

Webb Co, Loredo, Fort MacIntosh, mil rec from the census 1860 GTP 25:3:73

TEXAS (continued)

World War II, honor list of dead & missing for co of Bell, Bosque, Coryell, Falls, Limestone, Hill, & McLennan HTR 29:4:117

Young Co, geneal misc 1882 abstr from *The Graham Leader* FP 30:3:133

Young Co, mort sched 1860 FP 30:2:73

Young Co, tax list 1857 FP 30:4:204

THAXTON, Irene see Robert LETSON

THAYER, Charles see Sylvia ODELL

Porter Charlie b1882, VT, geneal, bk rev BAT 16:2:75

Susanna see Isaac JOHNSON

THERIAU, Jean b1601, w Perrine Bourg, FR, anc ch MP 3:4:271

THERIOT, Germain see Marguerite BOUDROT

THIBODEAU, Pierre b1631, w Jeanne Terriot, FR, children MP 3:4:269

THIRKILL, Surname period, *Thirkill-Threlkeld Newsletter*, 143 Harbord St, London SW6 6 PN, England UK

THISLER, George W b1814, w Cordelia Dimick & Eliza Warren, NY?, PA?, MI, IN, geneal KK 25:1:10

THOMAN, Susanna Bauman, anc & relatives LCC 4:1:41 4:2:27

THOMAS, Christina see William BLOODHART

David m1844, w Mary Wiley Shipley, OH, geneal, bk rev GH 41:2:156

Elias b1747, NY, fam rec AG 62:1:31

Francis Marion b1844, w Mary Livena Clifford, AR, anc ch TRC 2:1:44

Hattie d1976, MO, diaries, bk rev OZ 9:3:122

Isaiah b1848, w Cynthia Manning, PA, IN, biog sketch MIS 19:4:93

THOMAS (continued)
Jane see Miliver MARTIN
John A b1801, w Elizabeth Mathias, PA, IN, biog sketch MIS 19:4:94
John b1745, w Margaret ___, PA, OH, biog sketch MIS 19:4:96
John b1775, w Mary Reinicker, PA, IN, biog sketch MIS 19:4:95
John F m1862, w Mary A Wall, Bible rec NC :89:3
John f1818, NY, pension appl RAG 8:1:10
John Sr b1722, w Anne ___, KY, lineage VS 4:2:95
Joseph m1840, w Louise Vosburgh, Bible rec BG 8:2:31
Justie b1875, w Laura M Currie, MI, biog sketch MIS 19:4:92
Mary Ann b1836, h Van D Walling, MS, TX, obit YTD 5:2:26
THOMASON, Surname period, *The Thomason Newsletter*, 595 Idylwood Dr SE, Salem OR 97302 – fam VA, data base, Samuel D of KY, census 1754-1840 NC, fam SC & MS & AL, census 1860 AL, traditions
THOMPSON, Abraham m1796, w Elizabeth Brown, KY, IL, geneal FF 15:3:43
Adam f1736, w Elizabeth ___ & Naomi Hill, Northern IR, PA, geneal, bk rev GH 41:2:149
Ann see Robert EVANS
Christiana see William BROWN
Edgar N see Carrie BARKER
Elias f1764, RI, indenture AG 62:1:41
Eunice see Henry SIMPSON
Fam connections with Ward fam in VA, bk rev GH 41:6:150
Fam hist VA, bk rev BWG 16:1:67
George Gilmore b1818, WV, IL, IA, anc ch BG 8:3:66
James T m1884, w Polly E Heavel, Bible rec OZ 6:2:69
John E m1849, w Sarah Ellen Simpson, Bible rec IG 23:3:78

THOMPSON (continued)
John f1751, w Sarah ___, EN, bapt of twin children GM 22:7:243
Nancy M see David MOORE
Nancy Popejoy see Nicolas WILSON
Sarah Mildred see Robert HENDERSON
Surname period, *Thompson Trails Quarterly*, 10 Quiet Hills Cir, Pomona CA 91766
Thomas dc1795, w Ann Finney, PA, NC, geneal, bk rev NCJ 13:4:247
Thomas f1734, w Ann Finney, PA, geneal, bk rev GH 41:6:165
Thomas, w Ann Finney, PA, NC, geneal, bk rev PEL 8:2:33
William f1862, KY, will AG 62:3:160
THOMSON, Hugh Templeton b1871, w Emma Conger, IL, CA, biog OC 24:2:46
Samuel b1691, w ___ Glass & Mary MacDonald & Temperance ___, ST, WE, VA, geneal, bk rev GH 41:2:156
Thomas H f1888, w Elizabeth Elliott & Lucy A Smith, NY, CA, biog OC 24:2:45
THORBORN, Elizabeth b1803, NS, anc ch TEG 7:2:95
THORNTON, Andrew Hope b1903, KY, fam hist sketch SIN 8:3:78
Hannah see Daniel HARRIS
Rachel see Daniel HARRIS
THORSEN, Georgia Claypool f1906, CA, letter SS 15:1:6
THRASHER, Benton Cylvester b1855, w Elmira C Hoskins, CA, fam rec PT 29:2:47
THREET, Fam rec collect, bk rev NTT 7:3:83
THRESHER, Arthur m1684, w Mary Goodridge, MA, geneal, bk rev GH 41:1:165
THROOP, William bc1679, w Martha Coblye, CT, MA, biog AG 62:1:55

THROUP, William f1598, EN, MA, geneal MQ 53:1:70

THRUPE, John d1445, EN, MA, geneal, bk rev NYR 118:1:58

THURMAN, Surname period, *Thurman Fam Newsletter*, 1573–37th Ave, Moline IL 61265 – Wintford T b1844 & desc, Allen dc1848 & desc, John Allen obit

THURMOND, Bolton f1864, GA, letters NC :94:2 :96:7

THURSTON, Sarah A see Robert SPEIRS

TIBBETS, Love b1736, NH, anc ch CR 19:4:169

TIBBS, Samuel m1837, w Sarah Bennett, Bible rec TOP 17:1:25

TICKEL, Mary A see William BROWN

TIENHOVEN, Aefje Van see Pieter STOUTENBURGH

TILLER, Surname period, *Tiller Trails*, POB 787, Winston OR 97496

TILTON, William f1643, w Susanna ___, MA, geneal TEG 7:3:129

TIMMONS, Charles b1751, w Mary Magdalene Forney, WV, OH, children SGE 28:122:35

Surname period, *The Timmons Fam Newsletter*, POB 262, Montrose MN 55363

TINDAL, William T b1831, w Ellen Watson, ST, NY, fam rec SLV 5:3:5

TINKLER, Sarah see William MOSES

TINLEY, Samuel m1832, w Sarah Newbound, IL, fam hist WTC 12:2:49

TIPTON, Sarah see George HALLMARK

TISINGER, Sylvia Mary see Jim OLOMON

TITUS, Robert b1600, w Hanna (Carter?), EN, NY?, anc ch NAS 26:2:60

TODD, Mary f1875, h Abraham Lincoln, bk rev REG 85:2:167

TOLAR, Simeon R b1845, Bible rec JC 13:2:36

TOLBERT, Elizabeth Francis see William Dancy GREEN

Jane see John CAVE Jr

TOLE, William bc1840, w Annie McGlynn, IR, PA, geneal, bk rev WPG 13:3:50

TOLLE, Surname period, *The Tolle Fam Exchange*, 10351 16th St, Garden Grove CA 92643

TOLLEFSRUDES, Christopher b1781, NW, WI, geneal, bk rev GGS 23:2:103

TOMBAUGH, Frances see Benjamin Franklin DEARDORFF

TOMILSON, Dora Elizabeth see William Andrew LANTZ

TOMPKINS, James b1793, w Hulda Hill Jennings, NC, SC, geneal SGE 28:124:56

Stephen b1730, NC, biog SGE 28:123:25

TON, Cornelius see Grietje SCHOON

TOOHILL, Johannah see Alfred W WEBB

TOOKE, William L bc1805, w Mary ___, NC, FL, lineage FLG 10:4:131

TORBIT, Peter b1852, w Sarah Rebecca Corbin, MD, anc ch MAD 27:4:154

TOURN, Marthe Marie see Philippe CARDON

TOURTELLOTTE, Abraham d1779, CT, cem inscr CTN 19:4:618

TOWERS, Anna see William Rhadamanthus MONTGOMERY

TOWNE, Surname period, *About Towne*, 38 Sayles Rd, Asheville NC 28803

TOWNSEND, Margaret see William BRADBURY

Prudence see John FRARY

TOWNSHEND, Roger d1759, ST, cem inscr GGL 6:3:102

TOWNSLEY, Hannah W see Edward SMITH

TOY, Anna see Thomas SCOULLER

TRAFFORD, Grace see Edward Wheldon McClellan

TRAIL, Mary Hendricks, see Edwin Franklin WOODWARD

TRASK, Daniel Webster b1847, w Harriet Caroline Horne, NC, geneal, bk rev NCJ 13:3:186

TRAUX, Samuel b1789, w Drusilla Larsh, KY, MN, biog sketch MN 18:3:113

TRAVER, Martin H m1832, w Phebe Loomis, Bible rec CTN 20:2:240

TRAVIS, Sylvanus Lockey b1755, w Rhoda ____, NY, biog KK 25:3:51

TRAYLOR, Surname period, *Help!!!*, 1555 ,Candlelight Dr, Las Cruces NM 88001

Wiley f1847, GA, will TCG 7:3:21

TRAYNOR, John f1865, w Margaret Flannigan, IR, PA, geneal, bk rev GH 41:3:177

TREADWELL, Mastress b1750, w Mary Littlefield, ME, geneal DE 11:3:99

TREFFRY, John f1346, EN, geneal, bk rev NGS 75:1:63

TREMAIN, Jonathan b1742, w Abigail Stout, EN, NY, fam hist GN 5:1:16

TRENCH, Daniel Mackay b1867, Jamaica, biog, bk rev GH 41:4:210

TRIGG, Pricilla see William F CALAHAN

TRIMINGHAM, Ann see Nathaniel BUTTERFIELD

TRIPLET, Mary Matilda see Andrew Daniel MURPHY

TRIPLETT, Eugene b1852, w Martha Ramey, MS, TX, anc ch GGS 23:1:15

TRIPPET, William f1683, DE, fam hist sketch MAD 27:2:62

TROFAST, Anna Cristina see Frank Olof MOOSBERG

Anna see Frank MOOSBERG

TROWBRIDGE, Thomas f1636, EN, MA, CT, geneal, microfiche rev GH 41:4:213

TROYER, Lydia B see Daniel D MILLER

TRUDEAU, Louis b1761, w Marie Rose Chauvin, MO, anc ch AGE 16:3:89

TRUDGIAN, Fam marr in Brannel 1600s-1800s WTC 9:1:21

William f1862, IL, letter WTC 9:1:11

TRUEBLOOD, Eunice see Joseph WEEKS

TRUESDELL, Thomas b1740, w Rhoda Curtis, MA, anc ch ANC 22:3:104

TRUMBULL, James f1812, w Harriet ____, NY, MI, fam hist SHI 17:1:15

TRUYTS, Joanna see Jan PALMS Jr

TUCKER, Elizabeth P see Robert G JACKSON

Felix R b1871, w Mollie Garrett Sublett, TX, biog YTD 5:2:28

George m1748, w Elizabeth Burch, BM, fam rec BBQ 4:1:10

George m1752, w Elizabeth King, BM, fam rec BBQ 4:1:10

John b1759, w Martha Bunton?, VA, KY, geneal KFR 13: :29

Nancy Caroline see Asa A Stewart

Robert Sr bc1677, VA, geneal, bk rev FRT 8:2:103 NCJ 13:2:122

Surname period, *Tuckers of Am*, 1661 Lauranceae Way, Riverdale GA 30296

Trimingham f1757, w Jane ____, BM, fam rec BBQ 4:1:10

TUELL, Mary Ann see Richard J A CULVERWELL

TUETH, Edward f1842, IR, US, geneal, bk rev GH 41:4:210

TUFTS, Benjamin f1834, OH, letter HL 2:2:35

Surname period, *Tufts Kinsmen*, POB 571, Dedham MA 02026-0806

TULEY, Judith see John GAB-
BERT
TULLIS, Mary Elizabeth see
David SEWELL
TULLY, Cornelius Britiffe b1860,
w Emma Dawson & Minnie
Walmer, EN, geneal GGL
6:1-2:29
Jasper, IR, cousins GGL 6:3:86
6:4:130
TURBYVILLE, Elizabeth J see
William Henry PETREE
TURLEY, Wm m1853, w E A
Holland, Bible rec YV 19:1:36
TURLINGTON, Fam reunion NC
1906 JC 13:3:55
TURNER, Benjamin b1721, w
Rebecca Tallman, RI, NY,
geneal, bk rev RAG 8:5:26 GH
41:3:170 MN 18:1:41 NYR
118:3:186
Daniel dc1794, MD, goods &
chattles MD 28:4:397
Helen Hortense f1892, OH, biog
TFP 7: :21
Jane B see Randol P WILSON
Michael f1637/8, MA, rec misc
MQ 53:4:248
Sterling m1823, w Mary ___,
CN, Bible rec RT 5:2:52
Terisha dc1802, w Sarah Wim-
pey, VA, geneal TRC 1:1:28
TURPIN, Philip f1793, w Caroline
M Rose & Martha (Osborne)
McCallum, VA, notebk VAG
31:1:3
TURPLE, John William b1827,
CN, mil rec GN 5:1:29
TUSSEY, Julian C b1856, w Anna
Simes, NC, MO, biog sketch
FRT 8:1:5
TUTTLE, Hudson b1853, OH,
biog TFP 2: :97
Tabitha see Henry STONE
TWIFORD, Ann see James
CREAMER
TWOMBLEY, Lydia Jane m1887,
h John Lewis Fox, Bible rec
HH 22:1:18
TYLER, John m1844, w Julia
Gardner, OH, marr notice AH
14:2:57

TYLER (continued)
Lavina Catherine see Thomas
Haywood BROADWAY
TYNER, Martha see Samuel
VARNES
TYSON, Mary see Jan LUCKEN
Reyner b1659, w Margaret
Kunders, fam hist HL 2:3:74
UDELL, John m1816, w Emily
Merrill, OH, diary, bk rev AH
14:4:138
UHLER, Sarah Ann see Irenus B
SNAVELY
UKRAINE, Geneal res hints GEN
12:1:7
Surname origins & meanings
GEN 12:2:18
ULDERKE, Antje Oetten see Cor-
nelius Eberadus DIRKE
UMBENHAUER, John Jr b1784, w
Mary ___, PA, IL, anc ch
CCS 9:2:64
UNDERWOOD, Nathan d1802, w
Elizabeth Anderson, VA,
geneal, bk rev WCK 20:1:13
GH 41:6:165 KA 22:4:246 VAG
31:1:66
William b1759, VA, NC, geneal,
bk rev NC :94:3
UNITED KINGDOM, Geneal res
guide by Barnett, bk rev BCG
16:2:68
UNITED STATES, Alpha Delta
Pi, geneal index to the *Hist of
Alpha Delta Pi 1851-1928*, bk
rev GH 41:3:171
Am Hist Soc members who met
in Chicago IL 1904 WTC
1:1:23 1:2:52
Am of royal desc, bk rev GHS
4:2:74
Anc of members of the National
Soc Col Dames 1915-1975, bk
rev TCG 7:3:59 AL 3:3:44
Bible & fam rec index vol 2, bk
rev MCN 2:4:4
Bible rec avail at the TN Archives SGE 28:124:23 SGE
28:123:39
Biog of famous people, almanac,
bk rev APG 2:1:31

UNITED STATES (continued)

California Trail, grave inscr OC 24:2:67

Census guide by Kolb, bk rev WPG 13:3:43

Chesapeake, tobacco & slaves 1680–1800, bk rev REG 85:1:79

Co (early) list SCC 24:1:42

Co hist bibl, bk rev PA 35:1:53 BM 8:2:64

Co rec in period MCG 10:2:61 10:3:115

col land claims 1700s–1800s, map AB 15:2:45

col occupations AW 13:1:49 PCI 9:3:3

Col soldiers of the South 1732–1774, bk rev EWA 24:2:138

Constitutional development in the extended polities of the British Empire & the US 1607–1788, bk rev REG 85:3:286

Diaries & journals bibl, bk rev CTN 20:2:319

Diaries 1492–1980 bibl, bk rev NYR 118:4:245 RAG 8:2:26

Diaries 1845–1980 vol 2, bk rev VAG 31:3:229 GM 22:7:263 GN 5:3:157 APG 2:3:25

Direct (street) of the principal cities, microfiche rev GH 41:2:162

Ethnic roots in percent FTR :105:8

Fam (first) of Am compendium, bk rev PGB 19:1:11

Fam assoc, soc, & reunions 1985, bk rev MA 11:3:79

Fam hist from Blue Ridge Mountains, bk rev WTC 7:1:35

Fam rec of the southern states index, bk rev MCN 2:4:4

Founding of the US, bk rev WTC 8:3:37

Geneal encyclopedia of the first fam of Am, bk rev GH 41:3:159 NGS 75:3:234 APG 2:1:30 NYR 118:3:176

Geneal rec misc 1731–1868 abstr from *Gentleman's Magazine* (EN) BG 8:2:41

UNITED STATES (continued)

Grand Army of the Republic, hist sketch FI 7:1:8

Great Philadelphia Wagon Road, hist of migration AGA 12: :54

Hereditary reg 1986, bk rev DG 33:2:119

Hist of imm 1850s, bk rev BAT 16:4:168

Hist of imm to Am 1846–1850s, bk rev NCJ 13:3:182

Hist of twp MIS 19:4:77

Hist sketch of the Public Domain CPY 15:4:92

Hist sketch of the Apostolic Christians MH 14:2:15

Homestead Act, hist sketch SD 6:2:46

Imm going west 1830–1880 vol 1, bk rev OC 24:3:125

Imm hist sketch 1790–1921 SS 14:4:52

Indentured servitude, hist sketch MCI 5:4:109

Land dispossession & the frontier myth, bk rev REG 85:2:179

Liberty & power 1600–1760, bk rev REG 85:2:170

Life in the 1700s GL 21:4:100

Maps of southern US c100–c1700, bk rev NTT 7:4:123

Marr of some residents & guide, to documents vol 1, bk rev DG 33:2:119 GGS 23:1:46 GH 41:1:124 (vol 1 & 2) LRT 6:3:241 SGS 36:3:155 OZ 9:2:85 OK 32:1:6 FRT 8:3:154 FP 30:1:9 MD 28:1:113 STI 27:1:27 NCJ 13:1:53 (vol 2) WCK 20:1:11 GH 41:2:120 (vol 2 & 3) TS 29:1:25 (vol 3) STI 27:1:27 GH 41:3:172 SGS 36:4:206 FRT 8:3:154 NCJ 13:2:118 MD 28:4:464 WCK 20:2:30 LRT 6:4:253 (vol 3 & 4) OK 32:2:44 OZ 9:2:85 GGS 23:3:156 (vol 4) NCJ 13:3:183 TS 29:2:69 STI 27:2:37 FRT 8:3:154 (vol 4 & 5) GH 41:5:157 (vol 5) TS 29:3:107 WCK 20:3:46 GFP 37:1:23 GGS 23:4:208 LRT 6:4:253

UNITED STATES (continued)
MGR 22:3:135 MSG 7:3:171
LAB 2:4:57
Marr rec in the VA State Lib, bk
rev GQ 87:2:23
Migration trails VC 8:2:43 TB
13:2:15 PF 16:4:119 17:1:10
Mil rec (Fed) reg vol 1, 2, & 3
(1776-WWII), bk rev RD
87:1:9
Mil rec avail at the Geneal Lib &
the National Archives vol 3, bk
rev CTN 20:1:140
Missouri Valley, geneal rec
avail, bk rev CCN 87:6:
Natchez Trace, hist, bk rev RAG
8:1:23
Naturalization processes & pro-
cedures 1790-1985, bk rev CC
10:2:6
Navy, marine, & privateer personnel & widows from the pension rolls, casuality lists,
retirement & dismission rolls
of the US Navy 1847, bk rev
RAG 8:2:25 NYR 118:2:113
North Am in old Parochial reg of
ST 1700s NGS 75:1:55
Oregon Trail, deaths 1852 MGR
22:2:72 PW 7:3:127
Overland Trail, travelers 1841-
1864 bibl, bk rev RAG 8:4:22
Pardons by President Johnson for
persons who lived in AL, VA,
WV, & GA, bk rev VAG
31:2:149
Photographs out-of-town & out-
of-state (Albion MI) identified,
bk rev FRT 8:1:52
Pierce's Reg, bk rev AL 3:3:44
Plain people dress hist, bk rev
PM 10:2:43
Political parties 1789-1803,
origins, bk rev REG 85:2:176
Presidents before George
Washington, hist DAR
121:9:796
Principles of the Constitution,
signers & non-signers THH
:97:12
Public domain, hist sketch RT
4:4:96 MN 18:4:173

UNITED STATES (continued)
Railway surgeons 1880s-1890s
roster THH :97:31
Republican party & the South
1855-1877, bk rev REG 85:1:89
Retrospections of Am 1797-1811,
bk rev SB 8:1:19 GH 41:3:171
Saint George Island &
Apalachicola, hist to WWII,
bk rev RAG 8:2:23
Santa Fe Trail, hist, bk rev MGR
22:1:38
Secret & fraternal soc with ad-
dresses RES 18:2:73
Ship pass list 1835 on board the
Pilot TS 29:2:53
Ship pass list from Hamburg
1894 on board the Taormina
MP 3:3:182
Ship pass list from Havre 1894
on board the Le Bretagne MP
3:3:181
Ship pass list from Helsingborg
1894 on board the S S Venetia
MP 3:3:184
Ship pass list from Liverpool/
Queenstown 1894 on board the
Campania MN 3:3:186
Ship pass list (reconstructed)
1851 for emig from GE, AA,
BO, HG, PO, RA, SW, & Scan-
dinavia, bk rev NGS 75:3:229
Southern ch rec depositories
(partial) list SGE 28:122:11
Southern Geneal Exchange Quar-
terly contents 1957-1974 SGE
28:122:1
Southern marr before 1792 abstr
from The Am Museum SGE
28:124:1
State & co boundaries 1987, bk
rev NTT 7:4:123
Surname origins by Smith, bk rev
SGS 36:4:210 OK 32:1:5 MSG
7:1:49
Surname origins by Stein, bk rev
GN 5:2:99 NAS 26:2:68 NCJ
13:3:181 RIR 13:3:48 SHA
12:2:2 FTH 10:3-4:95 SCS
24:7:149 WPG 13:4:44 CAL
6:4:90 GFP 37:1:24 QP :22:10
NGS 74:4:316 AG 62:1:57

UNITED STATES (continued)
Surnames 1790 list of most common CCQ 4:1:21
Twp atlas, bk rev APG 2:2:28
V r 1731-1868 abstr from *The Gentleman's Magazine*, bk rev NYR 118:3:175 OC 24:2:83 KA 23:2:114 CTN 20:2:324 GHS 4:2:74 OK 32:2:43 SGS 36:4:208 WPG 14:1:45 GH 41:4:187
V r offices addresses to write for births & deaths RD 87:3-4-5:28
Wars 1675-1898 list CTN 20:1:16 AH 14:3:101 WCG 4:2:17
Wells Fargo, hist, bk rev LRT 6:1:190
West Coast, direct (business) for CA, OR, WA Territory, AK, BC, & MX 1882 OG 13:2:45
West Point, hist of school 1833-1866, bk rev REG 85:1:85
Women & Indians on the frontier 1825-1915, bk rev RAG 8:1:24
Women & the law of property in early Am, bk rev REG 85:1:81 NER 141:2:157
World War I, pictures (official) avail SLB 6:5:210
UTIE, Mary see Ruthen GARRETTSON
VALLEJO, Epifania see John Francis FRISBIE
VALLIANT, Mollie L see P R NOWLIN
VANAKEN, Surname period, *Van Aken/Van Auken Newsletter*, 5 Ellsworth Ave #1A, Danbury CT 06810
VANAMBURGH, D L b1859, Bible rec FI 7:1:21
VANBORSUM, Egbert f1638, NY, NJ, KY, geneal, bk rev WCK 20:4:61
VANBUSKIRK, Cornelius m1798, w Charlota ____, Bible rec RCP 10:1:25
Nelmay Jo see Charles Marion BROWN

VANCE, Mary H see John TEETER
VANCLEAVE, David b1787, w Rachel Swearingen, KY, geneal, bk rev GH 41:1:165
James H b1874, AR, anc ch TB 13:2:35
VANCLEVE, Fam rec misc US, bk rev STI 27:1:27
VANDEPUTTE, Walter b1889, PA, biog FAH 5:2:28
VANDERAU, Johannes b1802, w Elisabeth Margaretha Burger, GE, PA, OH, geneal, bk rev GH 41:4:211
VANDERHORST, Jacob b1836, w Mary Elizabeth Kroeger, HO, OH, anc ch FIR 6:1:10
VANDERIPE, William b1854, w Emma (Potts) Huffman, NJ, geneal NFB 19:1:11
VANDERKAR, Arent see Charlotte VANDERWERKEN
VANDERWERKEN, Charlotte b1708, h Arent Van der Kar, CN, NY, geneal NYR 118:1:1
VANGELDER, Fam hist NY, bk rev NYR 118:1:56
VANHOESEN, Jan Frnse b1608, HO?, GE?, NY, anc ch LRT 6:3:231
VANHOOK, Rachel see John LOVELESS
VANHOORN, Jan Cornellissen d1669, w Hillegonda Joris, anc ch LRT 6:2:213
VANHORNE, Eliza f1807, NJ, OH, journal of trip & geneal HL 4:1:16
Fam biog sketches IL WTC 6:4:145
VANHOUTEN, James Cross b1825, w Margaret Hill, NJ, anc ch HL 5:2:55
VANN, James d1809, GA, murder notice GGS 23:2:92
VANNATTA, Catherine see Paul COOK
Fam hist, bk rev TS 29:3:108
VANROSENVELT, Claes Martenszen f1650, NY, geneal NYR 118:4:193

244

VANSCHAICK, Fam hist, bk rev MI 32:1:12

VANSCHAIK, Cornelius Aertsen f1636, US, geneal vol 2, bk rev WPG 13:3:43

VANVECHTEN, Nancy m1777, h Richard Schermerhorn, NW, OH, biog AH 14:4:125

Teunis Dirckes f1632, NL, US, geneal, bk rev FRT 8:2:102

VANVOORHEE, Fam hist vol 1, bk rev OC 24:1:41

VANWAGENEN, Eli b1843, w Louisa Vradenburg, NY, NE, biog sketch NA 10:2:69

VANWAGONER, Jacob bc1740, NY, MI, geneal, bk rev CCS 9:3:99

VANWINCKLE, Mariette Jacobse see Pieter Jansen SLOT

VARN, Elizabeth see Readding BLOUNT

VARNES, Samuel m1841, w Martha Tyner, FL, biog sketch FLG 10:4:155

VARNEY, William bc1608, w Bridget (Knight) Parsons, EN, NH, geneal SCR 11:1:6

VARNUM, George Washington b1825, w Annie Laura Busby, DC, CA, biog sketch SCS 24:7:147

Kate see George Sylvanus IRISH

VASCOCU, Andre Jean Baptiste b1795, w Maria Faustina Chirino, LA, anc ch YTD 7:1:16

VAUGHAN, Surname period, *Vaughan, Etc. Newsletter*, POB 7435, Huntsvilel TX 77342-7435

VAUGHN, Anna see Abraham WOODY

Archillus bc1769, w Frances ____, VA, MO, children OZ 5:2:80

Edwin D m1877, w Clara A Smith, IL, Bible rec WI 34:2:83

VAWTER, Lorenzo Dow b1812, w Elizabeth Dawson, TN, AL, TX, geneal YTD 1:2:10

VEATCH, Mary see James ELLIS

VEDDER, Fam hist 1657-1985 US, bk rev MGR 22:3:134 CGS 18:4:16

Harmen Albertse f1657, HO, NY, geneal, bk rev GH 41:6:165

VEIRS, Surname period, *Viers-Veirs Quarterly Newsletter*, 1867 Robertson Dr #14, Omaha NE 68114

VERBECK, Alta see Henry ALLEN

VERMONT, Athens, births 1736-1860 BAT 16:1:7

Barnet, Barnet Center Cem BAT 16:1:18

Barnet, Stevens Cem BAT 16:1:18

Barnet, West Barnet Cem BAT 16:1:19

Brandon, deed abstr 1700s-1800s RAG 8:2:13

Burlington, St Joseph Parish, marr 1800s suppl, bk rev BAT 16:2:77

Geneal res guide by Eichholz, bk rev GH 41:1:149 CTA 29:4:131 NYR 118:1:52

Hist sketches, bk rev see NEW HAMPSHIRE, hist sketches, bk rev

Hyde Park, geneal misc 1861-1862 abstr from *The Lamoille Newsdealer* BAT 16:4:148

Index to *Some VT Anc* by the Geneal Soc of VT BAT 16:1:1

Land grantees 1749-1803, bk rev BAT 16:1:25 RAG 8:1:23 DM 50:4:160 NYR 118:3:180

Natives in MI 1876 BAT 16:1:6

Natives in Saginaw MI 1850 BAT 16:2:74

Newark, scholars roster 1842 BAT 16:2:84

Richford, hist 1795-1950, bk rev RAG 8:5:13

Stowe, hist to 1869, bk rev BAT 16:4:170

Swanton, geneal res guide, bk rev BAT 16:2:77

Towns & co, bk rev NGS 75;3:232

VERMONT (continued)
Windham Co, gazetteer 1884 index, bk rev GH 41:6:150 RAG 8:4:25 FRT 8:4:199

VERNON, Wm m1813, w Eliza D'Wolfe, RI, Bible rec RIR 13:1:4

VESIE, Nathaniel f1638, BM, fam rec BBQ 4:1:10

VETTER, Lucas f1754, w Agnes Wacker, GE, NY, geneal, bk rev GH 41:3:176 GFP 37:2:70

VIEDT, Julius Frederick b1822, w Fredericke Duhring, GE, NY, MD, DC, geneal, bk rev GH 41:4:210 GFP 37:2:72

VINA, Lou see Joe RICHARDSON

VINCENT, James A m1837, w Sarah Chacy, Bible rec THT 15:1:28

Mary Eliza see William Franklin DAVIS

VIRDEN, Alice see Josiah MARTIN

VIRGIN, Edgeenah bc1831, MO, geneal MSG 7:1:37

VIRGINIA, Accomack Co, cem inscr from lower part of co, bk rev VAG 31:1:64 GH 41:2:147

Accomack Co, personal property tax bk 1787, bk rev VAG 31:1:59

Albemarle Co, court papers 1744-1783, bk rev VAG 31:3:223

Alexandria, obit notices 1784-1915 abstr from the *Alexandria Gazette*, bk rev VAG 31:2:148 GH 41:4:203 VS 4:1:88 FCG 7:1:5 GGS 23:4:209

Alexandria, St Mary's Cath Cem inscr, bk rev GH 41:2:147

Alexandria, vignettes of hist & residents 1739-1900, bk rev VAG 31:3:227 GH 41:6:151

Alexandria (Arlington) Co, Alexandria, minister returns & marr bonds 1801-1852, bk rev VAG 31:2:149 GH 41:4:203 GRI 7:6:47 DS 24:3:164 FCG 7:1:5 CCM 6:4:80 GGS 23:4:209 QP :22:10

VIRGINIA (continued)
Alexandria City, direct 1791, bk rev GH 41:2:147 VAG 31:1:61 SB 8:2:59

Alexandria Co, Alexandria, census 1850, bk rev VAG 31:1:62 GH 41:3:175 (1860) NGS 75:3:238

Alexandria Co, Alexandria, wills, admin, & guard bonds 1800-1870, bk rev GH 41:2:147 VAG 31:1:62

Amherst Co, census 1787, bk rev LRT 6:4:254

Appomattox Co, school attendance rolls 1907-1913, bk rev VAG 31:3:227

Augusta & Bath Co, maps 1736-1800, bk rev SCS 24:5:114

Augusta Co, hist, bk rev NGS 75:3:232

Augusta Co, marr 1748-1850, bk rev NGS 75:3:238

Bedford Co, hist to 1976, bk rev GH 41:4:204

Biog dict 1607-1660, bk rev TTH 8:1:12

Botetourt Co, census 1787 & property tax list 1787, bk rev TTH 8:4:95

Boundary changes 1634-1895 atlas, bk rev FCG 7:2:23

British mercantile claims 1775-1803 VAG 31:3:205

Cabell Co, deed abstr 1814-1819, bk rev GH 41:1:152

Campbell Co, hist 1782-1926, bk rev NTT 7:3:82

Caroline Co, court rec & marr 1787-1810, bk rev GH 41:4:203 VAG 31:3:221 NCJ 13:3:180

Cem resources guide, bk rev NGS 75:1:60

Census 1787, bk rev VAG 31:2:151 TST 20:20:32

Charles City Co, geneal rec 1737-1774, bk rev VAG 31:1:61

Charlotte Co, children 1765-1789 VA 25:3:13 25:4:17

Co (burned) data 1809-1848 as found in contested election files, bk rev VAG 31:1:60

VIRGINIA (continued)

Co boundary changes 1634-1895, bk rev AW 13:4:179

Culpeper Co, marr 1780-1853, bk rev NGS 75:3:238

Cumberland Co, census 1850, bk rev GH 41:3:175 GRI 7:6:46

Cumberland Co, court order bk 1749-1756 abstr, bk rev GH 41:6:150

Eastern Shore, residents (col) whose ages were proved before court officials, bk rev MAD 27:4:146

Elizabeth City Co, Hampton, clerks 1714-1954 roster TN 7:1:8

Elizabeth City Co, deeds, wills, court orders, etc 1634, 1659, 1688-1702, bk rev VAG 31:1:60 GH 41:3:175 QP :23:9

Elizabeth City Parish, Hampton, parish reg 1800s, bk rev VAG 31:1:63 GH 41:2:147 SB 8:1:18

Fairfax Co, adm bonds 1752-1782 NGS 74:3:189

Fairfax Co, Dranesville Meth, hist, bk rev GH 41:1:150

Fayette Co, personal property tax bk 1787, bk rev VAG 31:1:59

Fincastle Co, Botetourt Parish, tithable list 1772-1773 VA 25:1:11

Frederick Co, census 1850, bk rev AW 13:1:40 GH 41:4:203 WPG 13:4:44

Frederick Co, Shenandoah Valley pioneers & their desc, bk rev WTC 4:2:49

Frederick Co, Winchester, census 1850, bk rev RD 87:6:9 FRT 8:3:149

Geneal index of surnames from publ sources, bk rev GH 41:1:150 GGS 23:1:46 (vol 2) WPG 13:3:49

Geneal res hints IMP 6:1:12 LAB 2:1:11 SGI 4:1:3

Geneal res sources & co seats MP 3:2:80

Giles Co, marr 1806-1850, bk rev NGS 75:3:238

VIRGINIA (continued)

Goochland Co, marr bonds 1781-1789 VA 25:3:3

Goochland Co, Saint James Nort,ham Parish vestry bk 1744-1850, bk rev NCJ 13:3:180 VAG 31:3:222 GH 41:4:203

Goochland Co, v r 1705- , bk rev NTT 7:3:82

Halifax Co, cem inscr vol 2, bk rev GH 41:5:195

Halifax Co, pleas 1752-1755 VA 25:1:23 25:2:24 25:3:27 25:4:25

Hanover Co, acct from the store of Thomas Partridge & Co 1734-1756 VA 25:1:33 25:2:35

Hanover Co, superior court rec 1809-1838 vol 1 & 2, bk rev VAG 31:3:222

Henrico Co, imm 1708-1710 VAG 31:2:131

Henrico Co, tax list 1800 VAG 31:2:112 31:3:178

Hist (col) by Billings, Selby, & Tate, bk rev REG 85:2:171

Hist sketch of the railroads QP :23:3

Hist theses & dissertations bibl, bk rev REG 85:1:100

Imm (children) 1618-1642, bk rev GH 41:1:150 RAG 8:2:23

Isle of Wight Co, orphans & other children 1746-1757 VA 25:2:50 25:4:45

Isle of Wight Co, processioning returns 1723 VA 25:2:18

James City Co, Bruton & Middletown Parishes, reg 1662-1797, bk rev MAD 27:2:74

Land patents 1736-1741 VA 25:1:55 25:2:55 25:3:60 25:4:47

Loudoun Co, deed abstr 1757-1762, bk rev GH 41:4:203

Loudoun Co, personal property tax lists 1787, bk rev VAG 31:1:59 (1788) VAG 31:1:59

Marr notices 1836-1887 abstr from the *VA Conference Sentinel* & the *Richmond Christian Advocate* VA 25:3:21 25:4:39

VIRGINIA (continued)
Marr of some residents 1607–1800, bk rev NTT 7:3:82
Marr rec 1624–1926 index, bk rev NYR 118:2:114
Mathews Co, cem inscr, bk rev GRI 7:8:59
Mecklenburg Co, tax lists 1782 & 1784, bk rev GH 41:4:203 GH 41:5:188 KA 23:2:115
Mil 1600s, hist, bk rev SGI 4:1:23
Mil rec, soldiers in US Army 1800–1815, bk rev WPG 13:3:49
Montgomery Co, Rev War, soldiers roster RCP 9:3:73
Natives in Carolina rec 1694–1758 VA 25:3:20
Natives living in Elkhart IN 1879 VS 4:2:92
Natives moving to OH, biog sketches SIQ 7:3:21
New Kent Co, depredations by the British 1781 VAG 31:3:163
Norfolk, French Lodge of Wisdom #16 roster TN 7:2:29
Norfolk, geneal misc 1803 abstr from the Norfolk Herald TN 7:1:14 7:2:23 7:3:45 7:4:51 7:5:70
Norfolk, geneal misc 1902 abstr from the Hist of Norfolk Co VA & Representative Citizens by Stewart TN 7:4:59
Norfolk, map 1682 & vicinity, bk rev VAG 31:1:64
Norfolk, marr lic 1853–1889 TN 7:1:15 7:2:22 7:6:83
Norfolk, Washington Lodge #2 IOOF roster 1869 TN 7:5:73
Norfolk Co, wills 1755–1772, bk rev GH 41:5:188 NCJ 13:3:180
Norfolk Co, wills 1755–1802, bk rev VAG 31:3:224
Norfolk Co, wills 1772–1788, bk rev GH 41:5:188 NCJ 13:3:180
Norfolk Co, wills 1788–1802, bk rev GH 41:5:188 NCJ 13:3:181
Northampton Co, Northampton, protest 1652 VAG 31:2:117

VIRGINIA (continued)
Northern Neck, land grants 1694–1742, bk rev NCJ 13:2:117 KA 23:1:37 VAG 31:2:147 WCK 20:2:29 SGS 36:4:209 GH 41:3:166 GHS 4:2:71 NGS 75:3:238
Northern Neck, warrants & surveys abstr 1697–1784 vol 4, bk rev GH 41:4:203 NCJ 13:3:180 VAG 31:3:225 WMG 3:4:190 NYR 118:4:240 (1730–1784 & 1747–1780 & 1710–1780) WMG 3:1:42
Obit notices 1784–1915 abstr from the Alexandria Gazette, bk rev GRI 7:6:47
Orange Co, geneal rec misc, bk rev OC 24:2:81
Orange Co, land patents, bk rev GH 41:4:203
Orange Co, pioneers, bk rev GH 41:6:150
Orange Co, wills 1734–1838, bk rev GH 41:5:189
Page Co, cem inscr, bk rev GH 41:2:147 VAG 31:1:65
Page Co, marr 1831–1864, bk rev NGS 74:4:313
Patents, interpreting headrights NGS 75:3:170
Pittsylvania Co, deed abstr 1767–1770 QP :22:6 :23:6
Pittsylvania Co, estray bk 1774 QP :22:11 :23:10
Pittsylvania Co, house hist sketches, bk rev QP :23:9
Pittsylvania Co, Oakes Fam Cem QP :22:9
Port Royal, hist, bk rev GRI 6:8:30
Portsmouth, hist, bk rev GH 41:1:151
Prince Edward Co, mil men 1776 roster VA 25:4:14
Prince Edward Co, St Patrick's Parish, processioners' returns 1760–1767 VAG 31:2:83 31:3:171
Prince George Co, court orders & return of executions 1714–1720 VA 25:1:47 25:2:11 25:3:7

VIRGINIA (continued)

Prince William Co, Civil War, claims NPW 6:6:54

Prince William Co, court order bk avail 1731-1771 NPW 6:1:7

Prince William Co, Dettingen Parish, Trinity Epis Ch plaque naming rectors 1745-1978 NPW 6:4:33 (WWI Roll of Honor) NPW 6:5:45

Prince William Co, Dumfries Store purchasers index 1758-1776 VAG 31:2:122

Prince William Co, wills 1792-1803, bk rev GH 41:4:203

Princess Anne & Southampton Co, death abstr 1870s-1880s abstr from files of Truitt Bonney TN 7:1:3

Princess Anne Co, Lynnhaven Parish reg 1838-1913, bk rev VAG 31:1:64

Residents 1607-1870, bk rev GQ 87:2:24

Richmond, Civil War, Confederate soldiers 1861-1865, bk rev GH 41:4:204

Richmond, Hollywood Cem hist, bk rev REG 85:1:100

Richmond, lawyers 1859 roster SGE 28:121:35

Richmond, local notices 1784 abstr from the VA Gazette VAG 31:1:20 31:2:135 31:3:184

Richmond, policy holders (health?, accident?) 1922 roster GRI 7:8:63

Richmond Co, voter roster 1758 VA 25:1:20

Roanoke, colonists roster TQR 14:3:136

Roanoke Co, Salem, hist, bk rev GH 41:1:151

Rockbridge Co, deeds 1778-1788 abstr, bk rev GH 41:6:151

Rockingham Co, land grant surveys 1761-1791, bk rev NTT 7:3:82

Rockingham, minute bk 1778-1792, bk rev VAG 31:3:226

Salem, hist, bk rev RAG 8:3:23

VIRGINIA (continued)

Soldiers in the US Army 1800-1815, bk rev FRT 8:1:49 GH 41:1:150

Southampton Co, deaths 1850s-1880s abstr from the files of Truitt Bonney TN 7:2:18 7:3:36

Stafford Co, geneal misc 1700s VS 4:1:85

Surry Co, co court rec 1652-1663, bk rev NCJ 13:2:117 SCM 15:1:60

Surry Co, deed abstr 1769-1778 VA 25:3:41

Tax payers 1782-1787, bk rev WCK 20:1:11 SLB 6:3:123

Timesaving aid to VA & WV anc vol 2, bk rev FRT 8:1:50

War of 1812, bounty land & pension appl, bk rev GH 41:6:150 VAG 31:3:224 DS 24:4:217 QP :22:13 NWT 8:3:15

War of 1812, prisoners held at Dartmoor 1813-1815 VA 25:2:16

Will & estate rec in the VA State Lib, bk rev WPG 13:4:44 GH 41:4:202

Williamsburg, index to the Handbk for the Exhibition Buildings of Col Williamsburg Inc 1936 VS 4:2:91

Wills from burned co 1632-1800, bk rev GH 41:4:202 VAG 31:3:221 NCJ 13:3:179

York Co, rec misc 1665-1672, bk rev VAG 31:3:223

VOELKEL, George Christoph f1848, GE, IL, fam rec STC 10:2:92

VOGT, Emma b1862, h Henry Langrehr, IL, obit NWS 7:5:49

Henry b1815, w Gertrude Burschenk, GE, IL, hist sketch of house WTC 7:1:9

Mary E b1812, h Bernard Vogt, PU, GA, OH, IL, obit CRT 8:3:41

VOLLMANN, Carl C m1877, w Marie L Wegner, MI, Bible rec PF 16:1:22

VOSBURGH, Louise see Joseph THOMAS

VOTER, Louis f1731, FR, MA, ME, geneal, bk rev NYR 118:2:120

VRADENBURG, Louisa see Eli VANWAGENEN

WACKER, Agnes see Lucas VETTER

WADDILL, Samuel James b1880, w Frances Elizabeth Shearer, VA, FL, lineage FLG 10:4:145

WADE, Rebecca b1795, MA, anc ch TEG 7:4:204

WADLINGTON, William b1736, Bible rec YTD 2:2:28

WAGGONER, Anne Maria see Alexander BLACK

WAGNER, Ana Kunegund see George Johan HOLLSTEIN

Anna Margaretha see Peter Joseph SCHMITT

John see Mary COLSON

Peter m1852, w Eva Fuchs, PU, IL, fam hist WTC 13:1:8

WAILES, Edward Lloyd d1809, GA, obit GGS 23:2:81

WAIT, Louisa see George Asa DODGE

Lucy Ann see Smith CORNELL

WAITE, Mary see Henry PETERS Jr

Susan see Andrew N DIX

WAKEFIELD, Alvin b1845, Bible rec RT 4:4:106

Harvey Sylvester b1842, w Martha Ann Leftwich, GA, anc ch GGS 23:1:16

WALDEN, William T b1859, w Sarah Telulah Moon, GA, anc ch NC :99:9

WALES, Census reg districts index, bk rev BCG 16:3:105

Censuses & census-taking 1800s GM 22:8:282

Geneal repositories GGL 6:1-2:7

Geneal res guide by Hamilton-Edwards, bk rev RAG 8:1:32 KA 23:1:34 WPG 13:3:40 TCG 6:4:72 BAT 16:1:23 MN 18:4:185 DM 50:4:161 FAM 26:3:172 IL 19:2:113

WALES (continued)

News 1750-1920 avail, bk rev ANE 23: :20

Parish ch & non-conformist chapels res guide, bk rev GH 41:6:126

Princess of, Am anc & cousins, bk rev SCS 24:7:148

Record offices guide, bk rev see ENGLAND

Surnames, bk rev NGS 74:3:233

Tithe surveys, use of, bk rev CTA 29:3:112

WALK, Martin Sr bc1707, w Catharine Clore, GE, NC, biog FC 5:2:53

WALKER, Anne see Samuel HAWES

Catherine b1795, lineage LM 28:4:292

John m1702, w Katherine Rutherford, IR, PA, geneal RED 20:1:12

Mary m1824, h Richard Cassaday, Bible rec NC :92:3

Mary Melissa see Jasper Marion REAMS

Mary see Eldridge ODOM

WALKUP, Josiah f1858, IL, abstr of Walkup's addition MCI 5:2:50

WALL, Mary A see John F THOMAS

Robert E b1777, NC, SC, Bible rec NC :91:2

WALLACE, Charles b1847, IL, anc ch MGR 22:2:89

Fam researchers direct, bk rev GH 41:4:211

Francis b1784, w Sarah Alexander, TX, fam rec STK 14:4:196

Joyce Wilkinson f1897, VA?, statement GRI 7:3:21

WALLER, David b1785, w Elizabeth Jordan, MD, OH, IN, geneal, bk rev GH 41:2:157

Richard b1755, w Sarah Ward, Bible rec VA 25:1:54

William f1784, VA, account list 1784-1799 VA 25:4:36

WALLING, Van D see Mary Ann THOMAS

WALLINGSFORD, Sarah A E see James William HARRELL

WALLIS, Jane see John K PACE

WALLS, Alva see Tabitha MILLER & Mary Louisa BROWN

WALLS, W W f1900, MO, KS, biog sketch BCS 7:1:9

WALMER, Minnie see Cornelius Britiffe TULLY

WALRATH, John J m1844, w Marietta St John, Bible rec AB 15:4:97

WALTERS, Catharine bc1760, PA, anc ch CR 19:4:171

Edward Magill b1844, w Allevenia Norris & Anna Belle Bush, VA, MD, Bible rec WMG 3:2:90

Henry M see Elizabeth Jane LOUGHRIDGE

Sophia see Reuben STEININGER

WALTHER, C F W d1887, death & burial CHI 60:2:52

WALTRIP, John b1807, w Elizabeth Downs & Jane (Wall) Faith, VA, KY, geneal KFR 13: :36

WALWORTH, John Wilson b1848, w Lenora Belle Moody, MI, geneal, bk rev OC 24:1:38

WALZ, Fam hist, bk rev TS 29:3:108

William b1846, PU, US, geneal, bk rev GH 41:4:211

WANNEMACHER, Peter bc1739, w Christina ___, PA, geneal, bk rev WPG 13:4:46

WARD, Ann see Charles FORBES

Artemas b1848, NY, obit ANC 22:2:66

James L b1833, w Emily Little, KY, IN, OK, anc ch HL 5:4:101

John Ardis Bradley b1830, w Margaret C Crawley, GA, anc ch GGS 23:2:89

Sarah see Richard WALLER

WARDEN, Eleanor see John KERR

WARDLAW, John A m1909, w Elizabeth J Amidon, CA, marr lic SCC 24:2:92

WARDLE, Jay Dumont b1885, w Clara Edith Wintermantel, MI, WA, biog sketch YV 19:1:8

WARE, David Samuel b1857, w Amanda Roselee Chesteen, MS, geneal, bk rev NGS 74:3:228

WARNELL, William f1800, GA, geneal, bk rev GGS 23:1:45

WARNER, Dora Bell see Willard Benjamin WILDER

Joe f1897, OH, NE, biog NW 9:2:24

WARNOCK, Lafayette b1824, w Lucinda Moore, IL, biog FF 15:3:21

WARREN, Archibald m1841, w Susanna ___, Bible rec LCC 4:2:35

Charles Noah see Sarah ADAMS

Eliza see George W THISLER

Martha see Mark JACKSON

Mary see Andrew McCLURE

Richard d1628, EN, MA, anc ch PGB 19:4:66

Sarah (Adams) (Bond) f1837, h Charles Noah Warren, MA, ME, MO, geneal NEH 4:2:67

William d1798, CN, biog sketch RAG 8:2:8

WASHBURN, Andrew see Emily LANGSTON

Edward Rush b1872, OH, geneal, bk rev NYR 118:3:185

WASHINGTON, Fannie H see John M COSTLEY

George b1732, VA, biog sketch OPC 19:1:25

Thos P m1836, w Elizabeth T Harris, Bible rec YTD 6:2:33

WASHINGTON, Benton Co, births 1905-1907, bk rev MCG 10:2:87

Census (territorial) rec avail EWA 24:2:137

Chelan Co, marr 1900-1930 AB 15:2:49 15:3:77 15:4:105 16:1:21

251

WASHINGTON (continued)
Chelan Co, Wenatchee Cem interment rec 1920s-1970s AB 15:2:53
Clark Co, Vancouver, Vancouver Reg 1866-1867 TB 13:2:5 13:3:9 13:4:7 14:1:5
Clark Co, Vancouver, hist to 1889 TB 13:4:2
Clark Co, WA Lodge #4 F & A M charter members 1857 & past masters 1857-1965 roster TB 13:4:23
Douglas Co, brands for horses, cattle, etc 1901-1903 AB 15:2:35
Douglas Co, real property assessment & tax rolls 1913 AB 15:2:33 15:4:89
Douglas Co, tax collect reg 1895 AB 16:1:17
Geneal res aid, eastern WA Regional Archives SGS 36:4:172
Geneal res hints RES 19:1:13
Geneal res hints, use of National Archives Seattle branch SGS 36:2:63
Geneal res hints, use of WA State Archives SGS 36:2:65
Grand Army of the Republic rec 1904-1911 RES 18:3:115
Hist of northwestern chapter #104 of Eastern Star 1900s WB 17:4:125
Index to rec publ by the Eastern WA Geneal Soc 1969-1986 EWA 24:2:82
Kittitas Co, school rec 1899 YV 19:1:37 19:2:78 19:3:117
Klickitat Co, hist, bk rev RAG 8:1:21 GH 41:2:159
Lineage bk for the National Soc US Dau of 1812, bk rev GH 41:6:152
Local items 1897 abstr from the *Franklin Recorder* TRI 26:4:52 27:1:14
Marcus, harvest festival hist sketch PB 2:3:47
Marr, bk rev GH 41:6:166

WASHINGTON (continued)
North Yakima, hist sketch YV 19:1:25
Pierce Co, geneal rec publ in *The Res* vol 1-18 (1969-1987) RES 19:1:29
Pierce Co, Sumner, residents 1889 alive in 1939 RES 18:3:145
Pierce Co, Tacoma, district court docket 1886 RES 19:1:9
Pierce Co, Tacoma, geneal misc 1886 abstr from *The Tacoma Daily Ledger* RES 18:1:9 18:2:64 18:3:106 18:4:177 19:1:7
Pierce Co, Tacoma, residents 1900 RES 18:2:74
Pierce Co, Tacoma, settlers reunion 1892 RES 18:2:62
Pierce Co, Tacoma, tax list 1886 delinquent RES 18:2:75
Pierce Co, voters reg & oath bk 1916-1919 SGS 36:4:176
Pioneers of northeast WA roster & brands PB 2:3:43 2:4:81 3:1:11
Place names, bk rev PB 3:1:8
Skamania Co, marr 1917-1920 TB 13:2:22
South King Co, surname bk 1985 of the South King Co WA Geneal Soc, bk rev WPG 13:4:38
Spanish-Am War, volunteers 1939 roster RES 18:3:117 18:4:181
Spokane, First Pres Ch bapt 1883-1912 EWA 24:3:171
Spokane, First Pres Ch communicants 1887-1924 EWA 24:4:227
Spokane, First Pres Ch marr 1884-1897 & 1902-1906 EWA 24:2:85
Spokane, geneal misc 1879 abstr from the *Spokane Times* EWA 24:1:62 24:2:119 24:3:201 24:4:245
Springdale, hist, bk rev PB 2:4:78

WASHINGTON (continued)
State legislature 1909 biog
sketches WB 17:4:127
Stevens Co, cem inscr, bk rev
PB 2:3:54
Stevens Co, Colville, pet 1889
PB 2:3:40
Stevens Co, Fort Colville, sol-
diers at fort who remained in
co 1859-1882 PB 2:3:45
Stevens Co, hist of country
schools, bk rev EWA 24:3:211
Surveyors 1800s-1980s roster TB
13:2:30 13:3:32 13:4:29 14:1:9
Thurston Co, memorials 1951 OG
13:3:74
Thurston Co, Olympia, hist
sketch of the Olympia
(building) 1889-1904 OG
13:3:70
Thurston Co, Olympia, Saint
Martin's Abbey Cem OG
13:2:42
Thurston Co, persons liable for
mil duty 1890 OG 13:1:10
Thurston Co, Rainier, Rainier
Cem OG 13:3:81
Thurston Co, wills 1876-1892 in-
dex OG 13:3:73
Union Gap, Battle of the Two
Buttes monuments YV 19:1:24
Union Gap, hist sketch YV
19:2:67
Wenas, school hist sketch 1873
YV 19:2:65
Wenatchee, cem interment rec
1900s AB 15:3:81 16:1:25
Westminster, First Cong Ch hist
1879-1929 EWA 24:1:4
Whatcom Co, Bellingham, DAR
member roster 1912-1925 WB
17:3:85
Whatcom Co, Bellingham, High
School students 1892-1909
roster WB 17:1:9 17:2:51
Whatcom Co, cem locations list
WB 17:2:42
Whatcom Co, census 1910 & in-
dex, bk rev GH 41:6:152
(microfiche rev) GH 41:6:167
Whatcom Co, direct 1904
(telephone) WB 17:1:5 17:2:47

WASHINGTON (continued)
Whatcom Co, Ebey's Prairie,
Sunnyside Cem WB 17:1:15
17:2:60
Whatcom Co, geneal holdings in
the Bellingham Public Lib WB
17:3:95
Whitman Co, Colfax, WWI, draft
reg WCG 3:5:37
Whitman Co, Farmington,
patriots & pioneers WCG
3:11:98
Whitman Co, news indices
1800s-1900s WCG 3:3:23
Whitman Co, Palouse Ch of
Christ hist sketch WCG 4:2:16
Whitman Co, Sopkane, direct
1890 WCG 3:3:22 3:4:30 4:1:6
4:2:22
Whitman Co, WWI, draft reg
WCG 3:11:100
WWI, letter & roster of the 329
Hdq Co 83rd Division Am Ex
Force 3rd Bn EWA 24:4:243
Yakima & Benton Co, deaths
1869-1907, bk rev MCG
10:2:88
Yakima & Benton Co, probate rec
1869-1907, bk rev MCG
10:2:88
Yakima Co, births 1869-1907, bk
rev MCG 10:2:87
Yakima Co, census 1900, bk rev
MCG 10:2:87
Yakima Co, geneal misc 1884-
1907 abstr from news, bk rev
MCG 10:2:88
Yakima Co, pioneers who d
1959-1960 roster YV 19:3:91
Yakima Valley, hist sketch to
1889 YV 19:3:88
Yakima Valley, settlers (early)
roster YV 19:1:15
WASHINGTON DC, Census 1820,
bk rev see MARYLAND, Cen-
sus 1820, bk rev
Geneal misc 1789-1799 abstr
from Georgetown & Federal
City news, bk rev NGS
74:4:311 WMG 3:2:91 WPG
13:4:40 MD 28:4:463

WASHINGTON TERITORY, Clallam Co, census 1889, bk rev GH 41:6:152

Clark Co, Capt Strong's Co A WA Mounted Rifles 1st Reg WA Territory Vol 1855 roster TB 13:4:24

Island Co, Camano Island, Utsalady, census 1870 WB 17:2:63 17:3:88 17:4:111

Island Co, Whidby's Island, Coveland, census 1860 WB 17:1:20

Island Co, Whidby's Island, Coupeville, census 1870 WB 17:2:67

Land (donation) claims, bk rev PB 2:3:54

Mil, hist TB 14:1:2

Property (real) statutes 1843–1889 WB 17:4:121

Snohomish Co, Stuliquamish Precinct, Utsalady, census 1870 WB 17:4:114

Thurston Co, census 1880 OG 13:1:15 13:2:49

WATERMAN, Caleb b1739, RI, biog sketch AG 62:4:245

Fam migration to Washington Co OH WC 4:2:5

Richard bc1590, w Bethia ____, EN, RI, biog RIR 13:3:47

WATERS, Ann see James HENNEN

Peter f1799, w Mary Smyth, IR, deposition SCM 15:1:31

Sarah Ann b1855, TN, fam rec, bk rev NTT 7:3:83

WATHEN, Surname period, *Wathen Fam Newsletter*, 2201 Riverside Dr, South Bend IN 46616 – War of 1812, cem KY, births 1850-1920 IN, taxes KY, census KY, marr KY, fam AA, marr CO

WATKINS, Elijah Milton b1755, w Catherine Taylor, VA, KY, biog ANC 22:3:117

George b1836, w Ann Jones, WE, EN, MO, geneal, bk rev GH 41:4:211 LRT 6:4:253 GFP 37:2:74

WATKINS (continued)
George Wycliff b1837, w Harriet May Hayden, IN, IA, NE, anc ch WTC 3:3:122

Henry, VA, geneal, bk rev NYR 118:2:118

John f1777, VA, GA, fam rec GGS 23:2:82

Tabitha (Goode) see Benjamin SHERROD

WATLINGTON, William f1696, w Ruth ____, BM, fam rec BBQ 4:1:10

William f1704,w Mary ____, BM, will abstr BBQ 4:4:40

WATSON, Audra see Alvin L SMITH

Clora Belle b1919, h ____ Simpson, FL, biog sketch FLG 10:4:134

Eliza Jane b1843, h George W Poorman, IL, obit CRT 8:4:29

Ellen see William T TINDAL

John b1694, w Hannah Goodwin, CT, geneal, bk rev BAT 16:2:76

John b1750, w Lucy Bickford, ME, biog sketch DE 10:5:171

Mary Elizabeth see John Doak ROBINSON

Susannah see John SMITH

WATTS, Tom J f1921, FL, diary abstr FLG 10:3:105

WAUGH, Charles King b1865, w Annia L Maples, TN, anc ch NAS 26:1:16

John b1687,w Margaret ____, ST, IR, CT, MA, ME, NH, geneal, bk rev GH 41:2:161 FRT 8:4:195

WEAKLEY, James d1772, w Janet Wilson, EN, PA, anc ch KIL 15:3:33

WEATHERLY, Mary see Henry Lawson RIVIERE

WEATHERS, Surname period, *Weathers-Withers Wanderings*, 1029 Cedar Crest, Atlanta TX 75551

WEAVER, George Henderson b1840, w Mary Ann Rook, TX, Bible rec YTD 2:1:23

254

WEAVER (continued)

John bc1787, w Barbara Richards, NC, TN, MO, children OZ 7:2:74

Mercy see Jonathan PADDOCK

Peter bc1766, VA, OH, geneal, bk rev GH 41:1:165

Pheobe see Chester INGERSOLL

Rachel see Joseph HARRINGTON

Sarah see Amos NEAL

WEBB, Alfred W m1860, w Johannah Toohill, Bible rec RES 18:3:135

Grandison m1863, w Eizabeth Kincheloe, KY, IN, marr rec SIN 8:3:86

John Martin b1817, w Elizabeth Sturgill, KY, fam rec EK 23:3:21

Myron Safford b1810, VT, geneal & log bk 1840, bk rev NGS 75:1:64

William Washington bc1830, w Martha A Chism, OH, IL, biog MCS 7:3:123

WEBSTER, Petrus m1753, w Mariah Mory, RI, NY, CT, marr rec RIR 13:1:2

Sarah A b1824, VT, MO?, anc ch MGR 22:2:89

WEDDING, Tabitha see Thomas Clarke HAGAN

WEED, Fam rec corr to *God's Country...* by Harris NEH 4:3:165

WEEDMAN, Christopher bc1735, w Elizabeth ___, PA, geneal, bk rev GH 41:3:170

Surname period, *Weedman Newsletter*, 21522 Sitio Verano, El Toro CA 92630

WEEKES, William d1806, CN, biog sketch & obit FAM 26:2:107

WEEKLEY, Rosa Elizabeth see William Hall SANFORD

WEEKS, Adaline see James Monroe WEST

Joseph Jr b1828, w Eunice Trueblood, IN, anc ch CCS 9:1:30

WEEKS (continued)

Rebekah see Jacob TAYLOR

WEGENNAST, Anna Catharina see Andreas PLOCHER

WEGNER, Marie L see Carl C VOLLMANN

WEIDEMANN, Johannes Heinrich f1761, GE, SC, geneal, bk rev NYR 118:2:119

WEIDMAN, Catherine see Johannes ZUG

WEIR, Adelaide see Charles L FORBES

Samuel b1791, w Mary Bowman Stephens, TN, MO, geneal OZ 9:1:28

WELBON, William b1795, w Rebecca Fisher, EN, MI, biog sketch DM 50:4:192

WELCH, Fam Bible rec corr OZ 7:4:151

Israel R m1876, w Winnia C Russell, Bible rec OZ 5:3:106

James Cornelius b1859, w Isabella Cover, Ottawa, OH, anc ch FIR 6:4:49

Mahala A b1830, h S T Patterson, IL, obit MCS 7:1:29

Nehemiah Draper b1808, w Mary Whitefield Parker, DE, geneal, bk rev GH 41:4:211

WELLINGTON, Benjamin b1743, w Martha ___, MA, fam rec NSN 12:6:53

WELLS, James f1750, w Ann ___, MD, database search, bk rev GH 41:4:211

M L K f1863, KY, journal abstr EK 22:4:22

Margaret f1890, h John Sergeant, KY, pension appl HF 3:2:66

Mary see Peter C STONER Jr

William b1605, NY, geneal, bk rev NYR 118:3:185

William Charles b1851,w Grace Bell, IL, fam hist WTC 17:4:135

WELSH, Esther see Martin BERGAN

WELTY, Abraham b1840, w Lydia Fox, OH, IN, anc ch MIS 19:2:41

255

WELTY (continued)
William E b1865, w Anna C
Welty, CO, obit FI 7:4:100
WENDT, Eliza see John ROH-
WEDER
WENGER, Joseph b1832, PA,
fam business LCC 4:2:46
WENNEKER, Frederick William
Jr b1822, desc, bk rev NYR
118:3:183
WENRICH, Thomas f1813, w Es-
ther Brand, OH, geneal NFB
19:1:13
WENTE, Louis see Johanna
ENKE
WENTWORTH, Fam rec
Limington & Porter ME DE
11:1:26
Leander d1866, CA, cem inscr
RDQ 5:1:10
WERREY, Katharina see Chris-
tian SCHOTTLER
WEST, Elizabeth see Francis
LAYTON
Frances see Manasseh Minor
James m1760, w Catrina Worin-
sen, RI, NY, marr rec RIR
13:1:2
James Monroe b1825, w Adaline
Weeks, AL, CA, obit MCA
6:2:67
James O, geneal, bk rev IL
19:2:114
Miles b1795, w Easter Adams &
Susan Swan, IN, geneal, bk rev
NCJ 13:3:186
William M bc1844, w Mariah J
____, TN, anc ch CCS 9:1:31
Zerviah f1775, RI, children NEH
4:3:130
WEST VIRGINIA, Barbour Co,
census 1910, bk rev GH
41:5:189
Births & marr 1880s–1890s TN
7:5:68
Cabell Co, deed abstr 1814–1819
see VIRGINIA, Cabell Co,
deed abstr 1814–1819
Census 1880, bk rev TST
19:47:13B
Civil War, Confederate soldiers,
bk rev GH 41:1:151

WEST VIRGINIA (continued)
Fayette Co, deaths 1880s–1890s
& births 1870s–1890s TN
7:4:53
Fayette Co, marr 1870s–1890s
TN 7:6:87
Geneal index of surnames from
publ sources see VIRGINIA,
Geneal index of surnames from
publ sources GH 41:1:150
Greenbriar Co, census 1850, bk
rev GH 41:1:153
Greenbrier Co, land entry bk
1752–1786, bk rev OC 24:1:40
Greenbrier Co, personal property
tax lists 1783, bk rev VAG
31:3:225
Harrison Co, hist, bk rev GH
41:5:189
Harrison Co, tax list 1800 VAG
31:1:35
Jackson Co, Grant District, cem
inscr, bk rev GH 41:2:147
Jackson Co, Grant District, fam
1900, bk rev GH 41:2:147
Jackson Co, Ravenswood Cem
inscr, bk rev GH 41:2:147
Jefferson Co, cem inscr, bk rev
WPG 13:4:44
Monongahela Valley, geneal &
personal hist, bk rev WPG
13:3:40
Monroe Co, marr 1799–1850, bk
rev FP 30:1:8
Nicholas Co, hist, bk rev GH
41:2:159
Nicholas Co, cem inscr, bk rev
OC 24:1:39
Randolph Co, Northern Cheat
Mountain, Elliot's Ridge, hist
of lifestyles, bk rev GH
41:2:148
Residents 1607–1870, bk rev GQ
87:2:24
Roane Co, index to *Hist of Roane
Co WV 1774–1927* by Bishop,
bk rev GH 41:2:159
Taylor Co, hist, bk rev GH
41:5:189
Wheeling, marr & death notices
1818–1865, bk rev GH 41:4:204

WESTERDALE, William b1809, w Sophia M Bampton, EN, IL, anc ch KIL 15:2:30

WESTERMAIER, Georg b1836, w Julianna Breitmeister, GE, anc ch WB 17:2:73

WESTERMANN, Agthe Alken f1857, h Heye Hindrichs Janshen Ludeman, GE, IL, geneal, bk rev GFP 37:2:69

WESTHOFF, William August b1831, w Rosa Emilie Buchel, GE, TX, anc ch VC 8:1:23

WESTMORELAND, Lewis Griffin b1827, w Ann Mosley, SC, GA, anc ch BGS 19:3:134

WESTON, Esther Amanda see James Wiser CHASE

John Sr f1766, PA, geneal, bk rev GH 41:6:165

Susanna see Sylvester MORRIS

WETMORE, Nathaniel b1661, w Dorcas (Wright) Allen, CT, IL, geneal FF 15:3:18

WETZEL, Herman Frank Christian b1898, KS, auto CHI 59:4:158

Perry S b1818, Bible rec OZ 5:2:69

WEYERSMULLER, Katherina see Heinrich HUBACH

WEYL, Anna see Michael KREHBIEL

WHALEY, David m1844, w Prudence B Corser, IL, Bible rec GFP 36:4:169

WHAREHAM, Mary see James MORREY

WHEELER, Francis M b1845, w Sarah Lemaster, KY, fam rec EK 23:3:20

John bc1618, w Ann Yeomans, EN, MA, anc ch TAK 17:2:25

John Ramey see Rachel LEMASTER

Thomas m1657, w Hannah Harrod, MA, geneal, microfiche rev GH 41:5:198

WHIPPLE, Susan see Paul Palmer KINNEY

WHITACRE, Hannah see John JARED

WHITAKER, Henry Jr f1863, w Catharine Miller, PA, letters LCH 2:2:54

John b1753, MD, KY, geneal, bk rev GH 41:2:162

William bc1814, w Rebecca Daniel, GA, FL, lineage FLG 10:4:151

WHITCOMB, Sarah b1748, MA, VT, anc ch BG 7:4:93

WHITE, Agnes d1892, IL, death notice CRT 8:2:23

Edna Lucille b1903, h ____ Byland, OH, Alberta (CN), fam hist HL 5:1:22

Elijah b1805, w Margaret Smith, NY, lineage SLV 5:1:4

Elizabeth see James JONES

Fam letters 1804-1830, VA, bk rev VAG 31:3:228

Francis Martin see William LAMPTON

Isadore E see Eugene Housel GRUBB

Jane see Samuel BYERS (Sr)

Jess Edmond b1897, w Lillian Ethel Bachelor, WA, biog sketch YV 19:1:8

John see Nancy ROBINS

Lewis mc1831, w Mary Atwood, CN, VT, fam hist BAT 16:2:79

Maria see Thomas COUPE

Mary see Benjamin INGALLS & Joseph LOOMIS

Nancy see Edward Hines STROTHER

Polly see Mark REYNOLDS

Rebecca see Timothy PICKERING

Sarah Ann see N J E HENDRIX

Thomas b1599, EN, MA, geneal, bk rev CTN 19:4:705

William b1790, w Elizabeth Hilliard & Sarah Ann Robertson, NC, geneal, bk rev NCJ 13:1:55

William m1835, w Margaret M Stewart, Bible rec RES 18:3:126

WHITEHEAD, Arthur b1685, w Mary Godwin, VA, MS, geneal, bk rev GH 41:1:165

WHITEHEAD (continued)
Daniel d1668, NY, will NYR 118:3:154
Elizabeth see George GARDNER
William W b1799, MS, geneal, bk rev CCS 9:3:97 FRT 8:4:200
WHITEHURST, Elizabeth see Henry B CAPPS
Enoch m1854, w Mary Frances Dozier, Bible rec TN 7:3:38
Willie G m1904, w Ada Caroline Whitehurst, Bible rec TN 7:4:62
WHITESIDE, Moses b1804, w Nancy Judy, IL, biog sketch MCS 7:3:102
WHITETURKEY, Simon b1826, MO, KS, OK, fam hist, bk rev GH 41:5:159
WHITFIELD, Bryan m1797, w Anne Nevill, Bible rec YTD 6:1:40
WHITGIFT, Elizabeth b1574, EN, anc ch AW 13:4:157
WHITING, Jacob m1827, w Dencey Sabin, VT, marr notice NGS 75:1:68
WHITLACH, Margaret see William GUMP
WHITLEY, Mary S see Richard DICKINSON
WHITLOCK, Esther see Moses MORDECAI
Nancy see Richard FAUCETT
WHITMAN, Caswell b1818, MO, KY, anc ch AA 8:2:93
WHITMER, Fam hist SW, VA, WV, bk rev GH 41:4:211
WHITMIRE, Christopher Columbus Sr b1774, w Betty Mouldin & ____ Lyons, SC, NC, geneal, bk rev GH 41:2:161
Columbus bc1812, w Jane Galloway & Martha Ann Driman, GE, US, geneal, bk rev GH 41:1:165
WHITNEY, James f1522, EN, lineage THH :97:26
WHITTEN, Phillip b1776, w Delilah Cain, anc ch FF 15:4:132

WHITTENBERG, Mary Malinda see Daniel Love MALLICOAT
WICKHAM, Joseph M b1856, w Mary P Hix, PA, MO, obit SNS 3:1:2
WIELANT, Maria Anna (Van) see Jacobus CLEPPE
WIES, Peter b1842, w Eva Ludwig, GE, IL, fam hist sketch WTC 17:4:137
WIESE, Hans f1853, w Anna ____, GE, US, bk rev FRT 8:4:196
WIGFIELD, Thomas b1743, VA, MD, geneal, bk rev IMP 6:1:27 FRT 8:3:152
WIGGINS, Samuel F m1876, w Miranda Soule, MI, Bible rec THT 15:2:20
WIKSTROM, John b1873, w Ruth G Wikstrom, CO, obit FI 7:4:100
WILBER, Justus P m1864, w Florene S Morgan, IL, marr rec SLB 6:5:220
Paul f1911, OH, biog TFP 2: :1
WILCONS, J C b1855, w Susana Gustin, DK, IL, KS, biog sketch BCS 7:1:10
WILCOX, Fam rec corr to *V R of Harwinton CT* NEH 4:1:32
Tyle f1762, MA, paper of denial AG 62:1:21
WILCOXON, Patty see Daniel BRUMLEY
WILCOXSON, Hannah see Peter FARNHAM
WILDE, Mabel see Halstrom M SPILLMAN
WILDER, John B m1872, w Samantha J Alward?, Bible rec IG 23:1:10
Matthew Sr bc1750, w Catherine Lee, NC, geneal JC 13:2:25
Willard Benjamin b1841, w Dora Bell Warner, ON, anc ch WB 17:2:72
WILDMAN, Frederick A f1895, OH, auto TFP 2: :45
WILES, Mary Elizabeth d1918, h Ruben Gibson, IL, obit CRT 8:4:46

WILEY, Fam hist sketch KS TOP 17:4:119

WILHITE, Daniel b1840, w Lucinda Jane Snodgrass, TN, anc ch RAG 8:2:10

Surname period, *The Wilhite-Wilhoit Connexions*, R 2 Box 43, Wellsville KS 66092

WILHOIT, Conrad bc1740, w Catherine Broyles, TN, anc ch WB 17:1:31

WILKENS, Fam cem Pierce Co WI WI 34:1:54

WILKES, Fam rec 1216-1984, bk rev DG 33:1:59

WILKIE, Olive see John CULLEN

WILKINS, Ana Josephine see Joseph Bruno MAURA

William F d1830, GA, death notice GGS 23:4:174

WILKINSON, John bc1807, w Martha Mothershed, NC, FL, lineage FLG 10:4:159

Richard m1615, w Elizabeth ___, EN, fam hist GM 22:8:284

Surname period, *Wilkinson News*, Rt 1 Box 75, Culbertson NE 69024

William f1818, BM, will abstr BBQ 4:4:40

WILL, Wilhelmina see Frederick GRASSHOFF

WILLARD, Mary (Mills) see David MELVILLE

WILLCOX, Henrietta b1814, h Oliver W Norton, NY, IL, WI, geneal, bk rev NYR 118:1:57 CCS 9:1:25

Tylee d1809, w Deborah ___, NY, cem inscr AG 62:1:23

WILLE, Friedrich b1822, w Maria Knief, GE, IL, anc ch CCS 9:2:62

Sophie see John O PIEPENBRINK

WILLENS, William d1621, NY, EN origins NYR 118:2:65

WILLETT, Nathaniel b1806, w Charity Russell, TN, MO, children OZ 6:2:77

WILLETT (continued)
Surname period, *Willett House Quarterly*, 209 Irvin Dr, Smithfield VA 23430-1411 - James of KY, v r MI, Abner of PA, Essex Co EN, Edward of VT, Robert Malcolm of LA, Edward Aaron of IA

Thomas b1611, MA, geneal, bk rev GGS 23:1:44

WILLIAMS, Ann see Richard HARDY

Ann E see Joseph R HATCH

Elizabeth see Jean Jacques FLOURNOY

Emily M see D H PURVIANCE

Harriet F see Henry FAIRBANKS

Jenette see John GRIFFITHS

John b1794, Bible rec OZ 7:3:98

Joseph see Elizabeth LEMASTER

M Malinda d1854, TX, anc ch THT 16:1:14

Martha see Thomas B NELSON

Mary see John SAYLES

Moses Allen f1849, PA, OR, diary, bk rev GH 41:4:211

Patrick M bc1817, w Lucetta Pope, KY, IL, TX, children THT 15:2:19

Surname period, *Williams Kissin Cousins*, POB 3264, Wichita Falls TX 76309

Surname period, *Williams Newsletter*, Box 3852, Granada Hills CA 91344 - fam groups, cem TN, births col, marr OH

T Franklin b1868, Bible rec FI 7:3:87

William b1588, EN, MA, geneal, bk rev CTN 20:2:323

William bc1810, w Elisabeth Hill & Margaret ___ Jackson & Hannah ___, NC, MO, geneal OZ 9:3:114

William f1827, w Cinderella Jane Bean, Bible rec YTD 7:2:22

Wyatt d1896, OK, murder OPC 19:1:30

WILLIAMSON, Catherine f1865, CA, travel note RCP 9:1:27

WILLIAMSON (continued)

Margaret Jane see James W HILL

Samuel b1688, w Mary ____ & Mary Irwin, ST, PA, geneal, bk rev GH 41:2:162 WPG 13:4:43

WILLINGHAM, Thos Henry b1825, w Cecilia Matilda Baynard, SC, GA, anc ch GGS 23:4:198

WILLIS, Albert A bc1830, w Sarah Jane Strayhorn, MO, geneal OZ 6:3:124

Eijah Chance d1851, w Rachel Wilson, OH, hist of mill HL 4:2:61

William b1775, IR, ON, anc ch PM 10:3:36

WILLS, Joseph T b1825, w Mary ____, MS, anc ch SR 3:4:87

WILLSON, Thomas b1818, w Melvina Pratt, NY, anc ch MCI 5:1:26

WILMOT, Ann see William BUNNELL

WILMUTH, Eliza b1845, TN, anc ch THT 15:2:13

WILSON, Alice Jane see Rufus Homer BONE

Billy d1901, VT, death notice BAT 16:2:51

Elizabeth Boatman see Dandridge Eliphalet KELSEY

Elizabeth see Nathan CLIFTON

George Follett b1805, MA, NC, diary, bk rev NCJ 13:2:122

James b1742, w Rachel Bird, ST, PA, biog YV 19:3:109

James bc1795, w Margaret Mesher, NC, MO, children OZ 5:2:80

Janet see James WEAKLEY

John m1747, w Susannah Gittings, MD, fam rec TNB 2:2:1

John N b1806, Bible rec IG 23:1:10

Lula see John Calhoun HURSEY

Margaret see David RAWSON

Mary see Robert G BOWEN & William Henry HARP & William Chase CROSBY & John Marion HOOPER

WILSON (continued)

Nicolas m1854, w Nancy Popejoy Thompson, IL, TX, Bible rec FP 30:3:119

Paradine Frances see John MIDDLEMAS

Rachel see Elijah Chance WILLIS

Randol P b1808, w Jane B Turner, Bible rec YTD 2:2:30

Robert b1845, ST, MO, geneal, bk rev STC 10:1:39

Sally see H C LENOX

Sarah (Sary) see Anthony HANCOCK

Surname period, *Wilson Fam Newsletter International*, POB 28215, Sacramento CA 95828

William Wesley bc1797, w Elizabeth Sheffield, VA, GA, lineage FLG 10:3:104

WILTSE, James f1853, letter FG 29:1:27

Joseph f1854, letter FG 29:1:27

Leonard b1790, w Hannah Herrington, ON, IA, anc ch GGS 23:2:84

WIMPEY, Sarah see Terisha TURNER

WINDSER, Missouri T Lavett see Alexander M GODWIN

WINEGORD, Issac Wilsey b1817, w Mary Clark, NY, FL, lineage FLG 10:3:103

WINETEERS, Fam biog NY, VA, KY, IN, IL, SD, WY, MT, ID, OH, MO, OK, NE, KS, OR, CA, TX, CO, WA, & IA, bk rev FRT 8:2:100

WINGO, Katie Ella see James McNEILL

WINKLER, Fannie Matilda see Christian Hoover MYERS

WINSLOW, Emaline f1845, IL, indenture DWC 13:3:87

Enoch M m1844, w Laura Balch, NY, Bible rec WTC 9:1:20

Fam hist, bk rev SLV 5:3:9

Hosmer Hyde b1807, w Cornelia M Winslow, EN, New EN, geneal, bk rev GH 41:3:171 CTN 20:1:136

WINSTON, Sarah bc1710, h ___
Henry, VA, biog sketch DAR
121:2:70
WINTERMANTEL, Clara Edith
see Jay Dumont WARDLE
WISBY, Joseph f1796, w Sarah
Dixon, IR, PA, VA, geneal, bk
rev GH 41:2:162
WISCHSTADT, Lillie b1904, WA,
interview YV 19:1:32
WISCONSIN, Births 1900 from the
Logan Co OK Territorial cen-
sus WI 33:4:232
Brown Co, Eaton Twp, Lily Lake
Luth Cem WI 34:2:91
Brown Co, Humboldt Twp, Hum-
boldt Cem WI 34:2:91
Brown Co, mort sched 1850 WI
34:2:70
Chippewa Co, Saapson, Twin
Lake Cem WI 34:2:95
Columbia Co, Columbus High
School alumni 1877-1893 WIW
34:2:97
Columbia Co, Marcellon Cem WI
33:4:235
Columbia Co, Scott, Pleasant
Hill Cem WI 33:4:235 34:1:19
Columbia Co, Springvale Twp
cem WI 34:1:20
Crawford Co, Soldiers Grove,
Forest Hill Cem WI 34:1:21
Dane Co, Blue Mounds Twp,
Northside GE Luth Cem WI
34:2:100
Dane Co, Christiana Twp, Utica,
7th Day Bapt Ch Cem 1850-
1901 WI 33:4:238
Dane Co, marr 1838-1839 abstr
from The WI Inquirer WI
34:2:100
Dane Co, Montrose Pioneer Cem
WI 34:1:24 34:2:99
Dane Co, Oregon Twp, Storytown
Cem WI 33:4:237
Dane Co, Windsor, Token Creek
Cem WI 33:4:238 34:1:23
Deed reg offices with addresses
WI 34:1:5 34:2:81
Dodge Co, Beaver Dam Cem WI
33:4:239 34:1:25 34:2:101

WISCONSIN (continued)
Door Co, index for the Illustrated
Atlas of Door Co WI 1899 WI
33:4:241 34:1:27 34:2:103
Door Co, marr & deaths 1862-
1864 abstr from the Door Co
Advocate WI 34:2:104
Eau Claire Co, imm from NW
WI 33:4:243 34:1:29
Eau Claire Co, marr 1860 abstr
from the Eau Claire Free Press
WI 34:1:30
Fond Du Lac Co, Empire Twp,
cem inscr, bk rev GH 41:3:166
Geneal res guide to southeast
WI, bk rev GH 41:3:175
Geneal res sources guide to the
Hist Soc of WI, bk rev MN
18:3:139 GH 41:3:166 NCJ
13:2:118
Grant Co, Fennimore, Castle
Rock Evangelical Norwegian
Ch marr 1875-1911 WI
33:4:246 34:1:31 34:2:105
Grant Co, marr 1890-1900 index,
bk rev GH 41:5:189
Green Co, Albany, Hillcrest Cem
WI 33:4:247 34:1:33 34:2:107
Green Co, Brodhead, letters at
postoffice 1861 WI 34:2:108
Green Lake Co, naturalizations
1858-1865 WI 34:2:109
Hist of early days, bk rev GH
41:6:127
Iowa Co, Linden Twp, East
Bethlehem Cem WI 33:4:250
34:1:35
Iowa Co, Linden, Salome Bapt
Cem WI 34:1:36
Iowa Co, Mifflin, Ebenezer Cem
WI 34:1:36
Iowa Co, Old non-sectarian
Mineral Point Cem WI
33:4:249
Jackson Co, hist, bk rev GH
41:5:189
Jefferson Co, deaths 1867-1868
abstr from the Jefferson Banner
WI 34:1:38
Jefferson Co, Fort Atkinson,
Lake View Cem WI 34:1:38

WISCONSIN (continued)

Jefferson Co, Sumner, Freeborn Sweet Cem WI 34:1:38

Jefferson Co, Watertown, pioneer settlers roster WI 34:1:37

Juneau Co, Camp Douglas, St James Cath Cem WI 34:2:111

LaCrosse Co, school officers & teachers roster 1900s WI 33:4:251 34:1:39 34:2:113

Lafayette Co, Elk Grove Twp, Old Elk Grove Cem WI 34:2:115

Lafayette Co, Kendall Twp, Truman, Immaculate Conception Ch Cem WI 34:2:116

Lafayette Co, Shullsburg, Evergreen Cem WI 33:4:253 34:1:41 34:2:115

Langlade Co, Summit Twp, Lakeside Cem WI 33:4:255

Lincoln Co, Corning, St Paul's Cem WI 33:4:257

Lincoln Co, Evangelical Luth Cong Cem WI 34:1:43

Lincoln Co, Somo, Somo Cem WI 33:4:258 34:1:43

Marquette Co, Buffalo Twp, United Pres Ch Cem WI 34:2:118

Marquette Co, Moundville Twp, Rood Cem WI 34:2:117

Marquette Co, Packwaukee Twp, Nott Cem WI 33:4:259 34:1:45 34:2:117

Marquette Co, Stone Luth Ch Cem WI 33:4:259

Milwaukee Co, coroner's rec 1873-1890 index WI 33:4:261 34:1:47 34:2:119

Milwaukee Co, Milwaukee, deaths 1869/73 MCR 18:1:10 18:2:30 18:3:66

Milwaukee Co, Milwaukee, v r 1869/73 MCR 18:4:103

Milwaukee Co, residents of lying-in hospitals, baby farms, boarding houses, & nurseries 1906-1918 MCR 18:2:44 18:3:73

Monroe Co, marr reg 1855-1907 index, bk rev GH 41:3:175

WISCONSIN (continued)

Monroe Co, Sparta, Mt Hope Cem WI 33:4:263 34:1:49 34:2:121

New Glarus, hist sketch GD 17:4:19

Oconto Co, Little Suamico Cem WI 34:1:123

Oneida Co, Rhinelander, Commercial Hotel Reg 1911 WI 33:4:265 34:2:125

Outagamie Co, geneal misc 1866-1869 abstr from the *Appleton Post* WI 34:2:128

Outagamie Co, mort sched 1870 WI 34:2:127

Ozaukee Co, declarations of intention & naturalizations index WI 33:4:267 34:1:51 34:2:129

Pierce Co, Ellsworth Twp, St Paul's Cem WI 33:4:269 34:1:53

Polk Co, Laketown Twp, Pleasant Valley Cem WI 34:2:131

Polk Co, Sterling Twp, Old Settlers' Cem WI 34:2:132

Portage Co, Hull Twp, DePines Cem WI 33:4:271

Portage Co, Plover Cem WI 33:4:271

Rock Co, Center Twp, Bethel Cem WI 33:4:273 34:1:55 34:2:133

Rusk Co, Dewey Twp, Tony Protestant Cem WI 34:1:57

Rusk Co, Tony Cath Cem WI 34:2:135

Saint Croix Co, Boardman Cem WI 34:1:59

Saint Croix Co, Foster Cem WI 34:2:138

Saint Croix Co, Houlton Cem WI 33:4:275

Saint Croix Co, Mann (Fam) Cem WI 34:2:138

Saint Croix Co, Richmond, Boardman Cem WI 33:4:275

Saint Croix Co, Springfield, St Bridget's Cath Cem WI 34:1:59 34:2:137

Saint Croix Co, St Joseph, Pioneer Cem WI 33:4:275

WISCONSIN (continued)

Saint Croix Co, v r 1876 abstr from the *Baldwin Bulletin* WI 34:2:138

Sauk Co, cem inscr vol 7, bk rev GH 41:1:153 (vol 8) GH 41:1:154

Sauk Co, Reedsburg, Greenwood Cem & St Peter's Luth Cem inscr, bk rev GH 41:6:152

Shawano Co, Belle Plaine, St Martin's Luth Ch Cem WI 34:1:61 34:2:139

Shawano Co, Grant, Immanuel Luth Ch Cem WI 33:4:277 34:1:61

Shawano Co, Zion United Meth Ch births 1870-1982 & deaths 1869-1982 WI 34:2:139

Sheboygan Co, mort sched 1860 WI 34:1:64

Sheboygan Co, Sheboygan, Wildwood Cem WI 33:4:279 34:1:63

Sheboygan Co, Sheboygan, direct 1868-9, bk rev GH 41:6:153

Ship pass list 1855 from Bremen on board the *Republic* WI 33:4:227

Ship pass list 1864 from Bremen on board the *Ferdinand* WI 33:4:228

Ship pass list on board the *Gerhardt* WI 33:4:227

Spanish Am War, troops deceased WI 33:4:231

Trempealeau Co, French Creek Pioneer Cem WI 34:1:65

Trempealeau Co, South Valley Cem 1862-1890 WI 34:1:66

Trempealeau Co, Town of Pigeon Cem WI 34:1:66

Trempealeau Co, Trempealeau, Greenwood Cem WI 33:4:281 34:1:65

Waukesha Co, land grants 1830s-1850s WI 33:4:283 34:1:67

Waukesha Co, Muskego, land grants 1830s-1840s WI 34:2:141

WISCONSIN (continued)

Waushara Co, Deerfield Twp, Fish Lake Cem WI 33:4:285

Waushara Co, Plainfield Cem WI 33:4:285

Wood Co, Christian Reformed Cem WI 34:1:69

WISECARVER, Frances A see Jesse HALL

WITHERSPOON, Sarah see Thomas McFADDEN

WITHINGTON, William H m1859, w Julia Chittenden Beebe, Bible rec DM 50:4:164

WITMER, John b1688, SW, PA, fam hist LCH 2:1:38

WITT, Sarah m1691, h John Witt & John Red(d)ington & Edward Bragg, MA, marr data NER 141:1:19

WITTEN, Charlotta Maria Johann see Johann Henrich HUTHMAN

WOERNER, John Martin m1854, w Johanna Sames, GE, anc ch AGS 28:2:74

WOHLTMAN, George d1918, IL, obit CRT 8:4:44

WOHLTMAN, John see Johanna ENKE

WOHLWEIDER, Anna Maria see Matthias HOFFER

WOLCOTT, Fam hist revision, bk rev NYR 118:1:59

WOLF, Theresa see Joseph KEMPF Sr

WOLFE, E Caroline see Benjamin Franklin FOSTER

WOLFENSBERGER, Jacob m1575, w Elsbeth Knecht, GE, PA, geneal, bk rev GH 41:4:211

WOLFORD, Elizabeth see David BISHOP

Sarah Jane see Jacob SMITH

WOLLETSIN, Maria see Johann BRASCH

WOMACK, Archer m1823, w Miram Kouns, Bible rec KA 23:2:89

David Jr b1785, w Sarah Ann Norris, SC, MS, children FTH 10:3-4:102

WOOD, Benson d1915, IL, obit CRT 8:1:15

Edson G f1839, IL, letter MCI 5:1:11

Isabella b1750, MA, anc ch TEG 7:1:40

Margaret see Low JACKSON

Mary see Richard PLATT

Nathanial see Lucretia LOCK-WOOD

Priscilla see Samuel Newton BOYD

Surname period, *The Wood-Woods Fam Magazine*, POB 2387, Tuscaloosa AL 35403 – imm, Samuel of VA, cem FL, fam VA & GA & Bermuda, Thomas of EN, Willie A of TX

Susan A see Osborn PENROSE

William f1887, TX, letter YTD 5:1:30

Wm m1814, w Nelley Ryan, Bible rec OZ 6:3:117

WOODALL, Perry Maxwell b1874, w Nong Emma Crayne, KY, WA, biog sketch YV 19:1:14

WOODBURY, Elizabeth see John Mercer Garnett HUNTER

WOODCOCK, Abigail see William HEWES

WOODHAM, William m1811, w Deborah Higgins, ME, geneal TEG 7:1:27

WOODHOUSE, Peter f1898, EN, WI, CA, biog, bk rev GH 41:4:212

WOODMAN, Jeannette Hussey b1818, h Richard Hooker Batchelder, ME, geneal TEG 7:2:77

Martha Jane bc1838, h Joseph Bacheller, NH, ME, geneal TEG 7:4:199

WOODRUFF, Anna M see Marinus Gilbert SMITH

Nancy see Daniel JACKSON

Nathan m1787, w Mary ____, Bible rec HL 1:5:154

William b1783, MA, NY, Bible rec NA 10:1:9

WOODSON, Emily b1864, VA, anc ch AA 7:4:188

WOODWARD, Christopher bc1594, VA, fam rec ANC 22:4:146

Edwin Franklin b1828, w Mary Hendricks Trail, TN, KY, MO, geneal OZ 8:1:27

Elizabeth A b1847, h Edward F Rix, IL, biog LC 7:2:40

Julius b1779, w Nancy Graston Johnston, VA, TN, children OZ 8:1:27

Nancy M see Frederick ROBBINS

Richard bc1708, w Elizabeth ____, VA, anc ch ANC 22:4:139

WOODWORTH, Rebekah b1799, h John Paine, MA, proof of relationship AG 62:4:202

WOODY, Abraham b1811, w Anna Vaughn & Nancy Alexander, TN, MO, children OZ 5:2:79

Fam cem Fannin Co GA SR 2:4:75

WOOLDRIDGE, Josiah, w Keziah Nichols, geneal, bk rev OC 24:1:40

WOOLEY, John N f1885, OH, letter HL 5:3:76

WOOLLEN, Elizabeth see John S LAMAR

WOOTEN, William bc1807, w Sidney Murphy, NC, FL, anc ch FLG 11:1:29

WORINSEN, Catrina see James WEST

WORLD WAR I, Anc resources by Holding, bk rev RAG 8:4:23

WORLD WAR II, Mil rec avail guide to Geneal Lib (UT) & National Archives, bk rev GH 41:2:120 TST 19:47:13B

WORLEY, Andrew Jackson b1828, w Sarah Ann McCain, VA, anc ch HL 5:2:54

WORNELL, James Maston b1844, w Sarah E Robinson, MO, obit SNS 3:5:3

WORNICK, Isabella Catherine see Rial BRYANT

WORTHINGTON, Benjamin b1768, w Judith Stedman, VA, AL, children PT 29:2:42

Daniel b1698, CT, anc ch BG 7:4:95

Surname period, *Worthington Desc*, 6619 Pheasant Rd Rt 16, Baltimore MD 21220

WREATH, Benjamin f1839, w Mary ___, IR, KS, geneal, bk rev KK 25:1:18

Benjamin, w Mary Hamilton, IR, PA, geneal, bk rev TOP 17:1:3 OK 32:1:7

WRIGHT, James, w Mary ___, fam source data, bk rev GH 41:6:165

James J d1922, WA, anc ch TB 13:3:38

John A see Lucy A COWDEN

John d1784, PA, VA, geneal, bk rev GH 41:4:212

Luther f1900, w Elizabeth ___, IL, fam hist sketch WTC 17:4:128

Martha Jane see J H H BURKE

Mary Frances see Allen Wilburn POWERS

WUHRMAN, Hans bc1340, SW, US, geneal, bk rev GH 41:4:212 GH 41:5:194

WYATT, Mary see Bailey ANDERSON

William bc1787, w Nancy Catherine Stewart, MD, lineage FLG 10:4:136

WYLAND, William Wesley b1707, w Louisa L Landis, SW, HO, US, fam hist MIS 19:3:63

WYLIE, William see Sarah Caroline McFADDEN

WYNN, Christena b1845, IN, OK, anc ch OPC 18:1:27

WYNNE, John bc1705, VA, geneal, bk rev NYR 118:2:117 NGS 75:3:236

WYOMING, Fremont Co, hist vol 3, bk rev SLB 6:5:221

Natrona Co, cem inscr 1889-1950 vol 1, bk rev GH 41:2:148

WYOMING (continued)

Natrona Co, geneal res guide by Natrona Co Geneal Soc, bk rev GH 41:2:148

Riverton, Davis Funeral Home rec 1918-1951 index, bk rev GH 41:3:166

WYOTT, Margaret see Richard ALLEN

WYRICK, Martin m1846, w Elizabeth Loy, NC, geneal, bk rev NCJ 13:1:55

Sophia see Elijah GUM

YALES, Fam hist US & WE, bk rev CTN 20:3:516

YARD, Mary see Henry MERSHON

YARGER, William Harding b1843, w Mary Emma Reid, PA, WI, KS, biog sketch SNS 3:6:5

YATES, James bc1776, w Agnes Rowland, SC, FL, lineage FLG 10:4:140

James f1684, PA, geneal, bk rev OZ 7:1:8

YEAKLEY, John b1807, w Matilda Grills & Eliza Allen & Louise McCray & Margaret Cochron, MO, obit OZ 5:3:121 (children) OZ 5:3:123

YELKIN, Anna Catherine see Joseph MARRIOTT Jr

Joseph b1839, w Catherine Dierks, GE, CA, biog sketch SCS 24:4:89

YELM, Ander Jansson b1804, w Anna Nilsdotter, SN, IL, anc ch KIL 15:2:29

YEOMANS, Ann see John WHEELER

YODER, Christian bc1758, w Magdalena ___, PA, fam rec LM 28:1:256

Christine see Joseph BACHMAN

Jacob bc1726, w Anna Beiler(?), anc ch MFH 6:1:35

YORK, Hannah b1783, CT, anc ch TEG 7:2:94

YOUEL, Surname period, *The Youel Log*, POB C, Earlyville VA 22936

265

YOUNG, George B b1808, w Margaret Leeper, TN, MO, children OZ 5:3:123

George F bc1812, w Ruth Ann Benson, RI, MI, biog sketch DM 50:3:106

James H m1821, w Catharine Smith, Bible rec HL 2:3:84

Jessie b1830, w Emmelie Buller, LA, anc ch KSL 11:2:60

John dc1781, w Sarah Norfleet, NC, children BWG 16:1:54

Morgan bc1713, w Elizabeth Mills, ST, NJ, IL, fam hist WTC 5:1:15

Moses f1863, ME, letters DE 11:1:27 11:2:67 11:3:107

Sabella see James ROBSON

Samuel f1790, SC, deed SCM 15:1:42

Sarah Emmaline f1877, IL, OR, rec of trip YV 19:1:22

Surname period, *Born Young*, 347-12th Ave N, S St Paul MN 55075

Thomas b1811, w Abigail Ogden, PA, OH, fam rec STK 14:4:188

William Sr f1684, w Mary? ___, VA, geneal NGS 74:4:244

YOUNGBLOOD, Edith see James Eldridge OGBURN

YUGOSLAVIA, Hist sketch MP 3:4:207

YUNKER, Richard S b1839, OH, IL, obit CRT 8:4:38

ZACHARY, Catherine see Andrew Jackson DAVIS

ZAKHEIM, Fam hist PO, GE, US, bk rev NYR 118:3:185

ZANE, Catherine see Alexr LONG

Robert b1642, NJ, geneal, bk rev NGS 75:2:156

ZARSKY, Josef b1835, Moravia, TX, biog ND 6:2:2

ZEITLER, Fam hist vol 1, bk rev GH 41:1:166

ZELLERS, Heinrich b1704, GE, VA, geneal, bk rev GH 41:1:166 FRT 8:4:197

ZELLNER, Surname period, *Zellner Anc*, 1839 Crestwood Cir, Stockton CA 95210

ZETTER, Elizabeth see Nicholas M C BROWER

ZIEGLER, Andreas b1744, w Henrietta Sophia Neidig, PA, geneal, bk rev WPG 13:4:43

ZIMMER, Mary see William BACHMANN

ZIMMERMAN, Edward David b1822, Bible rec WMG 3:4:171

Henry bc1764, PA, OH, desc, bk rev NYR 118:2:121

Israel f1828, w Catharine Bartsher, OH, PA, geneal AG 62:4:215

Jannes Janssen b1792, w Hille Harms Beyen, GE, geneal, bk rev GH 41:4:212

Wilhelmina Emma see Hermann MOOG

ZINGSHEIM, Ambrose b1868, w Julia ___, WI, anc, bk rev GH 41:3:177

ZIVNEY, Frank see Anna APT

ZOOK, John b1817, w Barbara Ambrose, PA, OH, geneal PM 10:4:25

ZUG, Christian d1787, w Anna Kanabell, GE, PA, anc ch MFH 6:4:146

Johannes b1770, w Catherine Weidman, PA, OH, anc ch PM 10:2:34

ZWANZIGER, John George b1810, BA, MD, geneal, bk rev WMG 3:2:91

ZWIRNMANN, Martha b1874, GE, IL, obit NWS 7:5:47

ZYSK, Wiktoria see Feliks Faustyn MACIORA